PIONEERS OF CALIFORNIA

True Stories of Early Settlers in the Golden State

BY DONOVAN LEWIS

WITHDRAWN

Donovan Lewis

november, 1993

3 1901 02530 2177

SCOTTWALL ASSOCIATES
San Francisco
1993

CONTRA COSTA COUNTY LIBRARY

Cover design: Lawrence R. Peterson
Book design: James L. Heig, Scottwall Associates

First Edition: 9 8 7 6 5 4 3 2 1
Copyright © 1993, Donovan Lewis

Published October 1993
Scottwall Associates, Publishers
95 Scott Street
San Francisco, CA 94117
Telephone (415)861-1956

No part of this book may be reproduced in any form
or by any electronic or mechanical means, including
information storage and retrieval systems, without
permission in writing from the publisher, except
by a reviewer, who may quote brief passages.

Printed in the United States of America

ISBN 0-942087-06-2

This book is dedicated to Maryella Lewis,
who fifty years ago pledged to share my life

ACKNOWLEDGMENTS

A BOOK IS NOT MERELY a creation of its author. It may begin that way, but by the time it sees fruition, many others have had a hand in it. This book really began with the pioneers who had the courage, motivation and foresight to overcome unbelievable obstacles, to settle and develop what was to become the golden State of California. This book was made possible by their diaries, letters, memoirs, autobiographies, and the biographies written by others. To them, and to those who preserved their written records, the author is eternally thankful.

I am deeply grateful to the highly efficient and helpful staff members of the El Dorado County Library, the Bancroft Library at the University of California in Berkeley, the California State Library in Sacramento, the History Room at the San Francisco Public Library, and the California Department of Parks and Recreation, who provided vital historical references and photographs.

I also thank Maryella Lewis, who helped edit the manuscript by reading it aloud several times; Charles L. Hill, of Lotus, who provided endless photocopies and a guided tour of the Oregon-California Trail, and others who read portions of the manuscript and offered valuable constructive criticism.

Finally, I thank James Heig, editor and publisher, whose efforts improved the book substantially.

TABLE OF CONTENTS

FOREWORD

IT HAS BEEN SAID there is no history, only biography. The goal of this book is to present in a single volume the most pertinent biographical information available on many of the more important California pioneers. Other than the time-consuming research this required, the most difficult task was choosing the pioneers to be included. Time constraints and the sheer mass of material forced certain criteria:

First came the particular pioneer's lasting achievements; second was the availability of accurate historical data; third was the author's subjective judgment. Research was often limited to secondary sources and previously published biographical information. To research only primary documents scattered throughout the land on so many pioneers would have been prohibitively time consuming and unwarranted for our purpose. Among hundreds of unsung pioneers, those included in this volume stand out because of their connection with meaningful events that contributed to the early settlement and eventual statehood of our thirty-first state.

Because so many pioneers were involved in overland travel, the hide and tallow trade, Mexican politics, the overthrow of Governor Manuel Micheltorena, the Bear Flag Rebellion, the Mexican War and the Gold Rush, there is a good deal of unavoidable duplication. One cannot explain each pioneer's role in these dynamic events without some redundancy. Since many readers will want to read about a single pioneer, his story must be as complete as possible within the scope of the book. Each chapter is intended to stand on its own, but chapters offering more detail on identical subjects are cross-referenced.

The author, a confirmed California history buff, aimed to include, in one volume, biographical data on the more prominent California pioneers; an enlarged encyclopedia so to speak. While a number of publications offer abbreviated biographical sketches of pioneers, they usually contain only a paragraph or two—at most, a page or so. For example, noted historian Hubert H. Bancroft's *Pioneer Register and Index, 1542-1848*; also Dan Thrapp's three-volume set, *The Encyclopedia of Frontier Biography*, which includes some California pioneers. Our hope is to bridge the gap between those and full-length biographies, containing a glut of material.

In lieu of a lengthy bibliography at the end of the book, a shorter reading list is included at the end of each chapter, so that the reader seeking information about only one historic figure will have a list of sources immediately at hand. Bracketed reference numbers in the chapters refer to the sources listed. The "Historical Calendar, 1542—1850" lists important historical events, including the confusing Mexican governorships. The pioneers' names on the opening page of each chapter include the Spanish version only if they became Mexican citizens.

The men and wo;men included here are, of course, not all of those who came to California before the Gold Rush. Others underwent equally harrowing adventures, and survived to make vital contributions to the state. It is fascinating to see how these lives intersected, how many of these people knew each other, and how the huge upheaval of the Gold Rush affected their lives. The stories of these pioneers, taken together, form a history of early California in a humanistic mode.

Donovan Lewis
Placerville, California, 1993

HISTORICAL CALENDAR: 1542 – 1850

A s a prelude to the biographical studies that follow, a chronological listing of the more important events leading up to California's statehood in 1850 seems appropriate. Early California history predates the arrival of Pilgrims at Plymouth Rock; it began a mere fifty years after Christopher Columbus discovered the Western Hemisphere.

1542-43: Spanish mariner Juan R. Cabrillo explores the coast of Alta California. Discovers San Diego Bay but misses San Francisco Bay. He dies on this voyage and is allegedly buried on San Miguel Island.

1579: Fleeing north with stolen Spanish loot, English privateer Francis Drake sails along California coast toward Oregon. Returns to land his leaking ship above San Francisco Bay to make repairs. Leaves marker claiming "New Albion" for England.

1602-03: Spanish mariner Sebastián Vizcaíno explores California coast, names ports such as San Diego, Santa Barbara, Monterey and Punta de los Reyes, now Point Reyes. Reclaims land for Spain but misses San Francisco Bay.

1769-70: Spanish King Carlos III sends about 225 men, divided into two overland parties and two ships, north from Mexico to explore Alta California. First land division led by Gov. Gaspar de Portolá, with Fr. Junipero Serra. Second land division led by Capt. Fernando Rivera, with Fr. Juan Crespi. After establishingSan Diego de Alcala, first Franciscan mission in Alta California, the Portolá expedition moves north to finally discover San Francisco Bay by land. Later Portola finds Monterey.

1769-1823: Mission era begins with the building of San Diego de Alcala, first of 21 missions built during this 54-year period.

1775-76: Juan B. de Anza leads first overland emigration party from Mexico to Los Angeles, Monterey and San Francisco Bay.

1792-94: British sea captain George Vancouver makes thorough survey of coastline for Great Britain.

1809-12: Russians establish settlements at Bodega Bay and Fort Ross to exploit sea animals for fur trade.

1821-22: Mexico overthrows Spain to become independent. Alta California taken over by Mexico; most Franciscan padres leave and are replaced by Mexican priests.

The Mexican Era

BECAUSE ALTA CALIFORNIA was sparsely populated and so remote from Mexico City, the Mexican government tended to treat it like a wayward stepchild. Between 1825 and 1830 it was considered a penal colony; upwards of 150 convicts were transported there. An even larger number of artisans, professionals and farmers emigrated there in 1834. Even the tiny army consisted largely of ex-convicts, who were often unpaid and sometimes larcenous. As a result they were hated and feared by the populace. Mexico kept sending governors, some of whom were so incompetent and unacceptable they were recalled after short tenures. In all there were twelve Mexican governors (two of them serving twice) and fifteen administrations between 1822 and 1846, when the U. S. took over. The following list of governors may help clarify this era:

ARGÜELLO, LUIS: Nov. 1822-Nov. 1825 (temporary and provisional)
ECHEANDIA, JOSÉ: Nov. 1825-Jan. 1831 (capital moved to Monterey)
VICTORIA, MANUEL: Jan. 1831-Dec. 1831 (deposed)
ZAMORANO, AUGUSTIN: Dec. 1831-Jan. 1833 (unofficial—Northern California only)
ECHEANDIA, JOSÉ: Dec. 1831-Jan. 1833 (Southern California only)
FIGUEROA, JOSÉ: Jan. 1833-Sept. 1835 (died in office)
CASTRO, JOSÉ: Sept. 1835-Jan. 1836 (temporary appointment)
GUTIÉRREZ, NICOLAS: Jan. 1836-May 1836 (a Spaniard who came with Figueroa)
CHICO, MARIANO: May 1836-Aug. 1836 (deposed after three months)
GUTIÉRREZ, NICOLAS: Sept. 1836-Nov. 1837 (deposed by Castro and JUAN B. ALVARADO, who assumes office Dec. '36)
CARRILLO, CARLOS A.: Dec. 1836-July 1837 (opposed by Alvarado, he resigns)
ALVARADO, JUAN B.: July 1837-Dec. 1841 (replaced by M. Micheltorena)
MICHELTORENA, MANUEL: Jan. 1842-Feb. 1845 (deposed by Alvarado & Castro)
PICO, PIO: Feb. 1845-Aug. 1846 (capital moved to Los Angeles; Pico deposed after the U.S. takes over.

DURING THE 1820s and 30s Alta California became a virtual cattle empire. Old Spanish-Mexican families with huge land grants dominated the economy. They lived lives of comparative ease and luxury, while the peon classes (mostly Indians) did the work. Fiestas and fandangos were the order of the day, and hospitality was extended to all visitors. It was said a stranger could travel from San Diego to San Francisco Bay without spending a *peso*. The *rancheros* furnished room, board and fresh horses all along the way. Some even left spending money in their guest rooms.

1823: Last Franciscan mission established in present Sonoma.

1826: Yankee Jedediah Smith leads fur trapping party overland from Santa Fe into California–the first to do so.

1830-40: More and more foreigners, including American trappers and traders, begin arriving. Though rather primitive, the comparatively easy *ranchero* lifestyle appealed to many. Most visitors were seafarers who traveled along the coast trading goods needed by the *rancheros* for cattle products such as hides, horns and tallow. Some stayed to marry into *ranchero* families and obtain land grants to become hacendados (landowners) themselves.

1834-37: Mexican Government secularizes missions and sells or leases mission lands to private citizens. Indian converts released; many return to former tribal ways; others work for landowners as field workers, servants or *vaqueros* (cowhands). A few acquire land.

1835: Richard H. Dana Jr. stops in California ports on trading vessel Pilgrim. Later writes *Two Years Before the Mast.*

1839: John A. Sutter arrives to establish his New Helvetia settlement at confluence of the Sacramento and American rivers.

1840: Alarmed by real or imagined threats of a Yankee takeover, Mexican authorities arrest many foreign settlers (including Americans) in the Isaac Graham affair. After being shipped off to Mexico for trial, they are returned and freed.

1841: U.S. Navy Commander John Wilkes charts coastal and inland navigable waters.

1841: John Sutter gets land grant and buys out Russians at Ft. Ross.

1841: Bartleson-Bidwell emigration Party arrives overland from Missouri, the first to cross the Sierras into the San Joaquin Valley

1841: Rowland-Workman Party enters Southern California from Santa Fe.

1842: Under the impression that war has been declared with Mexico, U.S. Navy Commodore Thomas ap Catesby Jones invades Monterey. Convinced by Thomas O. Larkin that no war exists, he apologizes and leaves. Small gold strike made in Southern California.

1844: U.S. Army Capt. John C. Fremont arrives overland March 8 with "topographical engineers" to map area. Leaves in late March.

1844-45: Now a Mexican citizen, John A. Sutter recruits volunteers to fight Mexican rebels threatening to overthrow Gov. Manuel Micheltorena. Despite Sutter's efforts, Micheltorena is deposed and replaced by Pío Pico in Los Angeles. Sutter is captured but finally released with his rights and privileges restored.

1845 (Dec.): Capt. John C. Fremont returns to Sutter's Fort on second "topographical" expedition.

1846: Many important historical events took place during 1846, including the Mexican War. The following monthly calendar will help clarify this turbulent period:

January 24: Fremont and his men go to Monterey to see Gen. José Castro.

March 5-8: After a confrontation with Castro, Fremont's men fortify the ridge atop Gavilan Peak. Three days later Fremont evacuates the area and heads north toward Oregon.

May 9: Marine Lt. A. Gillespie reaches Fremont near Oregon with secret message and letters from Washington D.C.

May 13: President James Polk signs declaration of war against Mexico. Though the U. S. Army is fighting along the Mexican border, no one in California knows about the war.

May 24: Heading south from Oregon, Fremont and his men reach PeterLassen's ranch on their way to Sutter's Fort. They do not know war had been declared.

June 10: American settlers, fearing Castro will force them out of California, band together to fight back. Hoping to enlist Fremont's help, they capture Mexican Army horses and drive them to Fremont's camp near present Sutter Buttes (Sutter County).

June 12: Congress accepts 49th parallel as official boundary with Great Britain to the north.

June 14: After recruiting additional volunteers and consulting with Fremont, 33 American settlers ride to Sonoma and capture General Mariano Vallejo and three of his aides. The next day a crude Bear Flag is raised, and California is declared independent from Mexico.

June 16: Gen. Stephen Kearny leaves Ft. Leavenworth with a small army for Santa Fe and California. Mormon Battalion follows later.

June 25: Fremont decides to enter the fray and rides to take charge of volunteers at Sonoma. He also takes command of Sutter's Fort, where Vallejo and his men are incarcerated. Sutter is allowed to stay but has little authority. Fremont and volunteers invade Yerba Buena to disable big guns at presidio; kills three civilians near Mission San Rafael before returning to Sutter's fort.

July 2: U.S. Navy Commodore John Sloat sails into Monterey.

July 7: Assuming that war has been declared, Sloat invades Monterey and raises U.S. flag without opposition.

July 9: U.S. Flag raised over the rest of Northern California.

July 15: U.S. navy Commodore Robert Stockton arrives in Monterey to replace Sloat.

July 19: Fremont goes to Monterey with his regulars and volunteers.

July 26: Fremont and his men enter Navy as mounted troops and sail south to San Diego.

July 29: Fremont and his men invade San Diego without opposition.

July 30: Sam Brannan sails into San Francisco Bay with over 200 Mormon immigrants, thus doubling the population of Yerba Buena.

August 8: Fremont marches north to San Pedro to join Stockton.

August 14: Stockton's forces invade Los Angeles without opposition.

August 18: Gen. Stephen Kearny occupies Santa Fe on way to California.

Throughout September and October hundreds of overland emigrants arrive at Sutter's Fort, having left Missouri without knowing about the war. When they learn of it on the trail, they are too far along to turn back.

September 3: Stockton promotes Fremont, names him commandant of the territory and sails north to Yerba Buena.

September 5: Kit Carson heads east with news that California has been taken.

September 15: Fremont departs overland for the north, leaving Capt. A. Gillespie in charge of Southern California.

September 16: Mexicans in So. Calif. revolt against Gillespie's harsh military rule. Capt. José Flores's men confront Gillespie.

October 4: Gillespie and his small garrison, forced from Los Angeles to San Pedro and take refuge aboard a merchant vessel to await reinforcements.

October 6: U.S. Ship Savannah arrives at San Pedro. Capt. Mervine's attempt to retake Los Angeles fails at Battle of Rancho Domingo. General Kearny meets Kit Carson on his way to Santa Fe, sends his dispatches on with another courier; insists that Carson guide him to San Diego.

October 25: Stockton reaches San Pedro with reinforcements. Decides not to attack; instead, he sails for San Diego.

November 1: Donner emigrant party trapped at Truckee Lake by heavy snow.

November 15: Mexicans in the north battle against American forces at La Natividad (near Salinas) with casualties on both sides.

November 29: Fremont, who has been gathering horses, departs overland for Los Angeles with additional volunteers.

December 2: Gen. Kearny reaches Warner Ranch in Southern California. Capt. Gillespie takes reinforcements from San Diego to join him.

December 6: Kearny and Gillespie engage Gen. Andres Pico and his lancers at Battle of San Pasqual. U.S. forces suffer heavy casualties; Mexicans virtually none.

December 12: Kearny's battered forces escorted to San Diego by military relief party.

December 29: Stockton and Kearny combine forces, and march toward Los Angeles.

January 1847: "Battle of Santa Clara" takes place at Mission Santa Clara with no casualties. Mexicans engage U.S. forces at the San Gabriel River crossing, and are finally driven off. Mexicans engage U.S. forces at Battle of La Mesa, actually a skirmish that forces Mexican retreat. Los Angeles retaken by the U.S. without further casualties. Fremont's forces meet retreating Mexicans at Cahuenga Pass. Gen. Andre Pico capitulates to Fremont and signs "Treaty of Cahuenga", ending the fighting in California.

As senior military officer in charge of American land forces, Gen. Kearny is furious that Fremont accepted Pico's surrender. He declares the treaty invalid; nevertheless, it is approved. After appointing Fremont military governor, Stockton leaves with his fleet. Fremont refuses to accept orders from Kearny, believing he remains under Stockton's command. Upon Stockton's departure, Kearny and Fremont clash over who will govern.

Mormon Battalion finally arrives in San Diego from Santa Fe.

February 1847: Relief party leaves Johnson's Ranch to assist Donner Party. Kearny sails north to Yerba Buena to set up a government. Donner relief party starts back with some survivors.

March 1847: Second relief party reaches Donner camp. Col. Jonathon Stevenson's New York Volunteers reach San Francisco. Third Donner relief party leaves to bring out survivors. Fremont makes long, fast ride to see Kearny in the north. Returns to Los Angeles in an incredible eight days with no results. Fourth Donner relief party leaves Sutter's Fort.

April 1847: Col. Richard Mason arrives in Los Angeles to order Fremont's volunteers disbanded. Fremont refuses, but later relents. Final Donner relief party leaves. Last survivor brought out this month. Fremont placed under arrest by Kearny for insubordination, rides overland to join Kearny at Yerba Buena. By now many of Sutter's men, including James Marshall and John Bidwell, have returned from fighting in theMexican War.

June 1847: Kearny leaves for the East with Fremont in tow.

August 1847: James Marshall leaves Sutter's Fort with small crew to construct a sawmill in Cullomah (Coloma) Valley.

January 1848: James Marshall discovers gold at Sutter's uncompleted sawmill.

February 1848: Treaty of Guadalupe Hidalgo signed to end Mexican War.

March 1848: Sutter's sawmill completed; word about gold discovery begins to leak, and the curious begin to arrive in Cullomah. Second gold strike made by Mormon mill-workers at confluence of North and South Fork of the American River (Mormon Island).

May 1848: Sam Brannan announces gold discoveries in Yerba Buena, starting a gold rush that virtually empties coastal communities. As the Treaty of Guadalupe Hidalgo is ratified by the U.S. & Mexico, word of the gold discovery spreads to the East Coast and around the world, and the greatest migration in history begins.

September 1849: Military Governor Richard Mason calls together a Constitutional Convention at Colton Hall in Monterey. Delegates from all over California come to participate in forming a new state government.

September 9, 1850: Congress finally approves statehood, and California becomes the 31st state in the Union.

The intrepid men and women who came before the gold discovery came for land, not gold, and it is these pioneers we honor in this publication. California state parks and monuments honoring these people are located statewide. See state park publications for details.

nal goal had been California, or possibly they became discouraged by the wet climate in Oregon. Most came to California by ship around treacherous Cape Horn. With the exception of a few intrepid explorers like Jedediah Smith and Joseph R. Walker, no one had crossed the lofty Sierra Nevada in either direction. Of course many Spanish soldiers and missionaries had traveled north from Mexico into Alta California, but few others came overland.

In effect, travel from the United States to the West Coast was tantamount to a journey to any foreign land. It was much faster and easier to reach Europe. In addition, the Mexican Government did not encourage

John Bidwell as a young man
Courtesy California State Library

Sierra Nevada range. After Robidoux returned to Missouri from his California trip, he gave lectures extolling the virtues of that vast Mexican domain. Two years after his arrival in California, "Doctor" John Marsh bought a huge cattle ranch on the eastern slope of Mt. Diablo, not far from San Francisco Bay.

An avid letter-writer, Marsh wrote to friends in Missouri telling of the unlimited opportunities in his newly adopted home. Some of these reports were published in Missouri newspapers. He even described a route across the Sierras—which he had never traveled—and offered assistance to any who reached his ranch.

OVERLAND TO CALIFORNIA

The 1841 Bartleson-Bidwell Party

THE BARTLESON-BIDWELL PARTY was the first organized group of emigrants to attempt an overland journey from Missouri by crossing the formidable Sierra Nevada directly into California. The fact that they were unsuccessful in bringing their wagons all the way does not diminish the importance of this epic journey. They proved that such an endeavor was indeed feasible, and subsequent writings by some of the members encouraged others to try it in succeeding years.

So begins the saga of this first courageous step into the unknown. Because of their extraordinary achievements, five members are covered in separate chapters; however, to make this account complete, all 34 are included herein with some biographical information. One has to wonder what it was that motivated this party to attempt such a dangerous overland journey in 1841. There was no known route once they left the comparative security of the Oregon Trail south or west of Fort Hall. Wagons had never been taken into California; in fact, few men had made it across the Sierra Nevada barrier even without wagons. First some general background:

Two who had previously made the difficult journey overland to California were French trapper Antoine Robidoux in the early 1830s, and John Marsh, a guileful pseudo-physician, in 1836 (see Marsh). Both travel...... .he Old Spanish Trail from Santa Fe, thus avoiding the

Independence, Missouri, was the jumping off place for most emigrants heading for Oregon. By early April 1841 they were beginning to gather there. Some, lured by optimistic tales of men like Robidoux and Marsh, were opting for California instead of Oregon. Among them was a group known as the "Western Emigration Society," which set down basic rules and regulations to be followed by those who joined.

Fur trappers and missionaries had established a trail of sorts to Oregon by the end of the 1830's. It followed the North Fork of the Platte River to the Sweetwater River, crossed South Pass to the Bear River and turned north to Fort Hall on the Snake River. Despite the treacherous terrain, unpredictable Indians and foul weather, wagons were making it as far as Fort Hall. Carts might make it to Walla Walla.

From there the emigrants made their way on foot or horseback to The Dalles on the Columbia River. Rather than cross the rugged Cascade Range, many risked drowning by floating through dangerous rapids of the great river to Fort Vancouver in log canoes or rafts. A few made their way south around Mt. Hood and directly into the Willamette Valley.

What was it that drove them to gamble everything– even their lives– on such a risky venture? An obvious answer is land– land they had heard was rich, free and plentiful. Another less tangible reason for going west involved man's ancient quest for adventure and freedom. Besides, if Americans didn't settle this land someone else would. Already the British surrogate– the Hudson's Bay Company– controlled vast areas north and east of the Columbia River.

The fact that possession of Oregon territory was in dispute didn't seem to matter. It was claimed by Mexico, but except for missions at San Rafael and Sonoma, virtually no Mexicans inhabited the area north of San Francisco Bay; in fact, the Russian Government had established a settlement at Fort Ross, about eighty miles north of there. This was the only non-Indian settlement between San Francisco Bay and Oregon.

A smattering of settlers traveled south from Oregon to Alta California by ship or overland, via the Siskiyou Trail. Perha immigration by foreigners; they were supposed to apply for Mexican passports before entering the country. Sale of land to foreigners was discouraged, and they could not obtain land grants unless they converted to Catholicism and became naturalized citizens of Mexico.

Naturally this was repugnant to devout Protestant Yankees like John Marsh, who found ways to purchase land. Others married into Mexican families. They could then apply for generous land grants from the government. As harsh as these regulations seemed, they failed to discourage determined foreign entrepreneurs who recognized that business opportunities in California outweighed the risk.

Californians were often viewed as ignorant peons or indolent ranchers. Actually many *Californios* were Castilian Spanish, not to be confused with *mestizos* (those of mixed Indian blood). While many were illiterate, some, like Mariano Vallejo, managed to acquire considerable education. Cowhides and tallow were the main sources of income; cured hides brought about two dollars each from foreign traders. Because *rancheros* had thousands of acres of grazing land and virtually free labor, cattle cost practically nothing to raise. These wealthy *hacendados* (landowners) could afford to be generous with their hospitality. As immigration increased, the Mexicans became more and more ambivalent. Some foreigners were welcomed with traditional warm hospitality, while others were not. But still they came. Thus one can understand what led to Missouri's "Western Emigration Society" in 1841.

A MONTH AFTER NOTICES about the society were published in Missouri newspapers, hundreds of would-be emigrants signed up from far and wide. Then came adverse publicity in the papers from disillusioned men who had been to California. The most outspoken of these was a lawyer, Thomas Farnham, who wrote about how foreign settlers had been arrested and treated cruelly by the Mexicans the year before (see Graham). They had been accused of fomenting revolution against the Mexican government; over forty had been arrested and shipped off to San Blas, Mexico, for trial. This unsettling news apparently scared off all but the boldest members of the shrinking emigration society.

They had agreed to meet at Sapling Grove outside Independence around May 1; however, only a young schoolteacher named John Bidwell, his companion George Henshaw, and one other wagon with several people were there. Fortunately others drifted in over the next few days until there were around 55 men, women and children. Some were bound for Oregon and others for California (see Bidwell).

A fortunate incident was the surprise arrival of Father Pierre-Jean De Smet with two other Catholic missionaries. They led a party of fourteen, including a support group and some foreign adventurers. Fortunately they had engaged experienced frontiersman Thomas

Fitzpatrick to pilot them to Fort Hall near present Pocatello, Idaho. From there they intended to make their way to Oregon as best they could. A short time after the combined party left in early May, they were joined by another small party, including Joseph Chiles, John Bartleson and some German immigrants (see Chiles). Another addition was Joseph Williams, an elderly Protestant preacher who was traveling alone. John Bartleson was elected captain and John Bidwell secretary. Later, Bidwell wrote, "[Bartleson] was not the best man for the position, but we were given to understand that if he was not elected captain, he would not go; and he had seven or eight men with him, and we did not want the party diminished."

By then there were approximately 77 in the party, of which about half were bound for Oregon. The large Kelsey family from Kentucky split into two groups. Two brothers, Andrew and Benjamin– with Ben's teen-aged wife, Nancy, and their infant daughter–chose California. The rest were going to Oregon. When other members of the Kelsey family asked Nancy Kelsey why she would risk her life and that of her baby by accompanying her husband on such a perilous journey, she reportedly said: "Where my husband goes, I go. I can better endure the hardships of the journey, than the anxieties for an absent husband." [1]

The rest of the Bartleson Party was made up of young men seeking adventure or a new start in life. Most were unmarried. Often they formed "messes" that shared wagons and cooking chores. One thing many had in common was ignorance of frontier skills and Indian lore. About half had knowledge of firearms, but few were experienced hunters. What knowledge they had about wagons and livestock came from farming. None possessed accurate information about California or how to get there. They knew only that they needed to head west and slightly south once they split off from the others near Fort Hall.

Later they admitted that if it hadn't been for Thomas Fitzpatrick– especially his skill in dealing with Indians– they would never have made it. But even he could not help them once they left the Oregon Trail. They weren't certain how much food to carry or what kinds. Space, weight and budget constraints were always determining factors. Vehicles ranged from two-wheeled carts to various sized farm wagons. Most chose oxen to pull the wagons, but a few used mules and even horses. Horses needed ample water and grass, while oxen and mules could survive on less. Children made do without milk, for milk cows were a luxury and were left behind. They had cured meat, such as ham and bacon, but it was assumed that hunters in the party would provide fresh meat along the way.

Fitzpatrick had his work cut out for him from the start. First he had to show Bartleson and others how to pick suitable campsites and how to corral and protect vital livestock from thieving Indians, who were sure to plague them. Campsites had to have good water, a source of fuel and enough grass or fodder for the animals to feed on. Protection from the elements was also desirable but not as vital as good grass and water. Without strong, healthy livestock they would be stopped in their tracks.

In 1841 emigration was so light that good campsites were not difficult to find. The route followed a virtual highway of rivers as a source of water and grass. The first river they followed after crossing the Missouri was the Kansas. This led to the Little Blue, which flowed north to the Big Blue in present day Kansas.

By the time they reached the Platte River on June 1, they had endured enough drenching rains, hub-deep mud-holes and dangerous river crossings to become seasoned travelers. June 4 brought their first serious encounter with Indians, when young Nicholas Dawson– who had wandered off while hunting– was accosted by a band of Cheyenne braves. Robbing him of his mule, his guns and most of his clothing, he was set free to walk back to the wagon train. After he returned later in the day to tell his frightening tale, Fitzpatrick hurried the train to a defensible position, where they formed a square with their wagons to defend themselves.

Sure enough, a well-armed band of Cheyennes thundered up and reined in their blowing horses to stare at the travelers. Fitzpatrick and another experienced frontiersman, John Gray, used the pause to parlay with them. While a peace-pipe was being passed around, Fitzpatrick convinced the Indians to return Dawson's mule and rifle. From that day on, Nicholas Dawson was known as "Cheyenne Dawson."

A few days later the Indian scare was forgotten when the men managed to kill several buffalo. On June 9 the travelers crossed the treacherous South Fork of the Platte River so they could reach the North Fork. This was to be their highway for hundreds of miles and weeks of relatively easy travel. They camped at Ash Hollow, minus several head of livestock lost in the river but thankful for no human casualties.

An ironic tragedy struck them on June 13, when George Shotwell accidentally shot and killed himself with his own gun. He was buried beside the trail. After passing the distinctive pinnacle of Chimney Rock and the colorfully eroded cliffs around Scott's Bluff, they reached Fort William (Laramie) on June 22. They had traveled 625 miles in 42 days, an average of 15 miles per day. Not bad for a party of greenhorns. Not far from the fort they experienced a violent storm on a hot day as described by John Bidwell:

> First came a terrific shower, followed by a fall of hail to the depth of four inches, some of the stones being as large as turkey eggs; and the next day a waterspout– an angry, huge, whirling cloud column,

which seemed to draw its water from the Platte River– passed within a quarter of a mile behind us....Had it struck us it doubtless would have demolished us.

Most of July 1 was spent crossing the North Fork of the Platte River, which curved away to the left (south) of their route. This crossing cost them an overturned wagon and loss of a mule, a cheap price to pay. Ten days later they were in the valley of the Sweetwater River at Wyoming's Independence Rock. They stopped there a few days to hunt buffalo and "make meat" by slicing it into thin strips to dry in the hot sun and wind. It seems likely that at least some of them climbed the rock as well.

Their food supplies were dwindling fast, and a substantial meat supply was vital. They crossed the Continental Divide over South Pass in mid-July and soon were camped on the Green River, sharing a campsite with a large band of trappers led by Henry Fraeb. (Fraeb and some of his men were killed by hostile Sioux warriors a few days later.) After reaching the Bear River in early August, they followed it north to Soda Springs, where the Bartleson Party was to split off for California.

Fitzpatrick pleaded with them to give up their foolhardy quest and continue with the others to Oregon. A few were so inclined, while some decided to return east. From 33 to 36 emigrants, including Father De Smet and his missionary party, pressed on for Oregon. Six of De Smet's party had already left to return east, one man (Shotwell) was dead and four others left for the East at Soda Springs.

Thus 32 men, plus Nancy Kelsey and her baby, were still determined to head for California; however, several of them accompanied the Oregon travelers about 40 miles to Fort Hall to get supplies and information on the route. They were to join their companions later near the Great Salt Lake. After an emotional separation, the Bartleson-Bidwell Party followed the Bear River as it turned south toward the Salt Lake.

Here Bidwell describes another adventure. It was a stifling hot day, and sighting a snow-capped mountain nearby, adventurous James John, better known as Jimmy John, challenged Bidwell to climb it and get some snow. Distances were deceptive, and it took the two young men much longer than they planned to get near the snow. Darkness overtook them before they reached it. Spotting the flickering fires of Indians below, they decided to stay where they were. By dawn they were close to freezing and the snow-capped peak was tantalizingly close.

Neither of the stubborn young men would give in to the other and they finally reached the snow by mid-morning. Filling a neckerchief with snow, they hurried down the mountain by a different route. Somehow they made their way around the Indians and were fortunate to locate the wagon train. By then their worried companions had given them up for lost, assuming they had been killed by Indians.

To their anxious question, "Where have you been?" they could only say sheepishly, "we have been up on the snow." With that they proudly displayed their snow, which had melted to a small iceball. [4] Nevertheless it proved they had reached the top of the mountain and added to their prestige as "fearless explorers." We can be sure that Bartleson had another name for them, and probably told it to them in no uncertain terms.

I N LATE AUGUST the relieved party left the Bear River before it drained into the vast salt lake. Here they were joined by the men who made the detour to Fort Hall. All they had to show for it were vague instructions to head westerly and look for Mary's River (the Humboldt). This they were to follow until it disappeared into a sink near the Sierra Nevada range. The men had been unsuccessful in buying any food supplies at Fort Hall.

The information about Mary's River was not new to them. The question was, in what direction was the river and how far? And where amidst the seemingly endless salt flats and scraggly sage brush would they find water and grass? Finally their prayers were answered when they came across moist ground, some small springs and blessed green grass. There they rested for several days, while Bartleson and Charles Hopper went ahead to scout out a feasible route.

By the time the scouts returned many days later, the distressed emigrants had given them up for lost and begun following their tracks. Bartleson's statement that they had found a small stream believed to be a tributary of Mary's River offered badly needed hope. But when he added a warning that wagons couldn't make it, their hopes were promptly dashed. Nevertheless, they followed the scouts toward the promised stream. As predicted, there was little water or fodder along the route; soon some of the animals were floundering and unable to continue.

Benjamin and Andrew Kelsey apparently had more foresight than the others, for they abandoned their two wagons on the spot and strapped their meager belongings on pack animals. It took three more days of torturous travel before the drastic decision was made to abandon the other six wagons. Everything except absolute necessities was jettisoned, and the remainder strapped to any animals fit for travel. Bidwell describes their first day as follows:

> It was but a few minutes before the packs began to turn; horses became scared, mules kicked, oxen jumped and bellowed, and articles were scattered in all directions. We took more pains, fixed things, made a new start, and did better, though packs continued occasionally to fall off and delay us.

Many were walking by now, even Nancy Kelsey carrying her baby.

Her bitter tears must have been overflowing. Although John Bartleson was their official captain, Benjamin Kelsey sometimes assumed the leadership role because of his frontier experience and instinct in finding the way when others were lost. He and his brother, Andrew, were described as "rough men, often in trouble with the authorities." Others from Kentucky were Joseph Chiles, James Springer and Grove Cook. Such men had few social graces, but they were invaluable in the wilderness.

Once the wagons were left behind, the struggling group was growing desperate and was no longer a viable emigrant party trying to pioneer a road. Instead, they were a hopelessly lost and frightened band of individuals fighting for survival. By staying near the base of the Ruby Mountains, they found water to sustain themselves. By the third week of September they apparently crossed over Harrison Pass and stumbled on to the river they had been seeking for so long (now the Humboldt).

By then they were out of food and began slaughtering their oxen one by one. But at least they were heading in the right direction toward the infamous sink. Then came a vast scorching desert before they crossed the Carson River and made their way to the Walker River. Somehow they missed the river that was later named the Truckee. Now it was a matter of following the Walker River south, while they sought a pass through and over the huge granite barrier looming to the west.

They ate their last ox before they crossed near present-day Sonora Pass and followed the Stanislaus River west. At the crest they must have been praying that the San Joaquin Valley would be in sight. Instead they saw nothing but seemingly endless rows of peaks and gorges. Scouts searched ahead for a likely route, and by strenuous trial and error they made some progress before the daring Jimmy John found a way through and disappeared. Andrew Kelsey and Thomas Jones went ahead to seek help from John Marsh (see Marsh).

Days later the bedraggled and starving group reached the valley floor and camped along the Stanislaus River with no sign of those who had gone ahead. Food was the immediate problem, and the hunters managed to kill enough deer to meet their needs. They knew only that John Marsh's ranch lay somewhere to the north, along the San Joaquin River .

According to Josiah Belden's memoirs, Andrew Kelsey and Jones returned shortly with food sent by Marsh (see Belden). Others in the party say Jones returned with one of Marsh's Indian ^, bringing food on pack animals. Meanwhile, Jimmy John had made his way half-starved to John Sutter's New Helvetia settlement, near the confluence of the Sacramento and American rivers (see Sutter).

When John gasped out his tale about the plight of the broken Bartleson Party, Sutter immediately dispatched two of his domesticated

John Bidwell as a young man
Courtesy California State Library

January 1848: James Marshall discovers gold at Sutter's uncompleted sawmill.

February 1848: Treaty of Guadalupe Hidalgo signed to end Mexican War.

March 1848: Sutter's sawmill completed; word about gold discovery begins to leak, and the curious begin to arrive in Cullomah. Second gold strike made by Mormon mill-workers at confluence of North and South Fork of the American River (Mormon Island).

May 1848: Sam Brannan announces gold discoveries in Yerba Buena, starting a gold rush that virtually empties coastal communities. As the Treaty of Guadalupe Hidalgo is ratified by the U.S. & Mexico, word of the gold discovery spreads to the East Coast and around the world, and the greatest migration in history begins.

September 1849: Military Governor Richard Mason calls together a Constitutional Convention at Colton Hall in Monterey. Delegates from all over California come to participate in forming a new state government.

September 9, 1850: Congress finally approves statehood, and California becomes the 31st state in the Union.

The intrepid men and women who came before the gold discovery came for land, not gold, and it is these pioneers we honor in this publication. California state parks and monuments honoring these people are located statewide. See state park publications for details.

OVERLAND TO CALIFORNIA

The 1841 Bartleson-Bidwell Party

THE BARTLESON-BIDWELL PARTY was the first organized group of emigrants to attempt an overland journey from Missouri by crossing the formidable Sierra Nevada directly into California. The fact that they were unsuccessful in bringing their wagons all the way does not diminish the importance of this epic journey. They proved that such an endeavor was indeed feasible, and subsequent writings by some of the members encouraged others to try it in succeeding years.

So begins the saga of this first courageous step into the unknown. Because of their extraordinary achievements, five members are covered in separate chapters; however, to make this account complete, all 34 are included herein with some biographical information. One has to wonder what it was that motivated this party to attempt such a dangerous overland journey in 1841. There was no known route once they left the comparative security of the Oregon Trail south or west of Fort Hall. Wagons had never been taken into California; in fact, few men had made it across the Sierra Nevada barrier even without wagons. First some general background:

Two who had previously made the difficult journey overland to California were French trapper Antoine Robidoux in the early 1830s, and John Marsh, a guileful pseudo-physician, in 1836 (see Marsh). Both traveled there via the Old Spanish Trail from Santa Fe, thus avoiding the Sierra Nevada range. After Robidoux returned to Missouri from his California trip, he gave lectures extolling the virtues of that vast Mexican domain. Two years after his arrival in California, "Doctor" John Marsh bought a huge cattle ranch on the eastern slope of Mt. Diablo, not far from San Francisco Bay.

An avid letter-writer, Marsh wrote to friends in Missouri telling of the unlimited opportunities in his newly adopted home. Some of these reports were published in Missouri newspapers. He even described a route across the Sierras—which he had never traveled——and offered assistance to any who reached his ranch.

Independence, Missouri, was the jumping off place for most emigrants heading for Oregon. By early April 1841 they were beginning to gather there. Some, lured by optimistic tales of men like Robidoux and Marsh, were opting for California instead of Oregon. Among them was a group known as the "Western Emigration Society," which set down basic rules and regulations to be followed by those who joined.

Fur trappers and missionaries had established a trail of sorts to Oregon by the end of the 1830's. It followed the North Fork of the Platte River to the Sweetwater River, crossed South Pass to the Bear River and turned north to Fort Hall on the Snake River. Despite the treacherous terrain, unpredictable Indians and foul weather, wagons were making it as far as Fort Hall. Carts might make it to Walla Walla.

From there the emigrants made their way on foot or horseback to The Dalles on the Columbia River. Rather than cross the rugged Cascade Range, many risked drowning by floating through dangerous rapids of the great river to Fort Vancouver in log canoes or rafts. A few made their way south around Mt. Hood and directly into the Willamette Valley.

What was it that drove them to gamble everything– even their lives– on such a risky venture? An obvious answer is land– land they had heard was rich, free and plentiful. Another less tangible reason for going west involved man's ancient quest for adventure and freedom. Besides, if Americans didn't settle this land someone else would. Already the British surrogate– the Hudson's Bay Company– controlled vast areas north and east of the Columbia River.

The fact that possession of Oregon territory was in dispute didn't seem to matter. It was claimed by Mexico, but except for missions at San Rafael and Sonoma, virtually no Mexicans inhabited the area north of San Francisco Bay; in fact, the Russian Government had established a settlement at Fort Ross, about eighty miles north of there. This was the only non-Indian settlement between San Francisco Bay and Oregon.

A smattering of settlers traveled south from Oregon to Alta California by ship or overland, via the Siskiyou Trail. Perhaps their original goal had been California, or possibly they became discouraged by the wet climate in Oregon. Most came to California by ship around treacherous Cape Horn. With the exception of a few intrepid explorers like Jedediah Smith and Joseph R. Walker, no one had crossed the lofty Sierra Nevada in either direction. Of course many Spanish soldiers and missionaries had traveled north from Mexico into Alta California, but few others came overland.

In effect, travel from the United States to the West Coast was tantamount to a journey to any foreign land. It was much faster and easier to reach Europe. In addition, the Mexican Government did not encourage immigration by foreigners; they were supposed to apply for Mexican passports before entering the country. Sale of land to foreigners was discouraged, and they could not obtain land grants unless they converted to Catholicism and became naturalized citizens of Mexico.

Naturally this was repugnant to devout Protestant Yankees like John Marsh, who found ways to purchase land. Others married into Mexican families. They could then apply for generous land grants from the government. As harsh as these regulations seemed, they failed to discourage determined foreign entrepreneurs who recognized that business opportunities in California outweighed the risk.

Californians were often viewed as ignorant peons or indolent ranchers. Actually many *Californios* were Castilian Spanish, not to be confused with *mestizos* (those of mixed Indian blood). While many were illiterate, some, like Mariano Vallejo, managed to acquire considerable education. Cowhides and tallow were the main sources of income; cured hides brought about two dollars each from foreign traders. Because *rancheros* had thousands of acres of grazing land and virtually free labor, cattle cost practically nothing to raise. These wealthy *hacendados* (landowners) could afford to be generous with their hospitality. As immigration increased, the Mexicans became more and more ambivalent. Some foreigners were welcomed with traditional warm hospitality, while others were not. But still they came. Thus one can understand what led to Missouri's "Western Emigration Society" in 1841.

A MONTH AFTER NOTICES about the society were published in Missouri newspapers, hundreds of would-be emigrants signed up from far and wide. Then came adverse publicity in the papers from disillusioned men who had been to California. The most outspoken of these was a lawyer, Thomas Farnham, who wrote about how foreign settlers had been arrested and treated cruelly by the Mexicans the year before (see Graham). They had been accused of fomenting revolution against the Mexican government; over forty had been arrested and shipped off to San Blas, Mexico, for trial. This unsettling news apparently scared off all but the boldest members of the shrinking emigration society.

They had agreed to meet at Sapling Grove outside Independence around May 1; however, only a young schoolteacher named John Bidwell, his companion George Henshaw, and one other wagon with several people were there. Fortunately others drifted in over the next few days until there were around 55 men, women and children. Some were bound for Oregon and others for California (see Bidwell).

A fortunate incident was the surprise arrival of Father Pierre-Jean De Smet with two other Catholic missionaries. They led a party of fourteen, including a support group and some foreign adventurers. Fortunately they had engaged experienced frontiersman Thomas

Fitzpatrick to pilot them to Fort Hall near present Pocatello, Idaho. From there they intended to make their way to Oregon as best they could. A short time after the combined party left in early May, they were joined by another small party, including Joseph Chiles, John Bartleson and some German immigrants (see Chiles). Another addition was Joseph Williams, an elderly Protestant preacher who was traveling alone. John Bartleson was elected captain and John Bidwell secretary. Later, Bidwell wrote, "[Bartleson] was not the best man for the position, but we were given to understand that if he was not elected captain, he would not go; and he had seven or eight men with him, and we did not want the party diminished."

By then there were approximately 77 in the party, of which about half were bound for Oregon. The large Kelsey family from Kentucky split into two groups. Two brothers, Andrew and Benjamin– with Ben's teen-aged wife, Nancy, and their infant daughter–chose California. The rest were going to Oregon. When other members of the Kelsey family asked Nancy Kelsey why she would risk her life and that of her baby by accompanying her husband on such a perilous journey, she reportedly said: "Where my husband goes, I go. I can better endure the hardships of the journey, than the anxieties for an absent husband." [1]

The rest of the Bartleson Party was made up of young men seeking adventure or a new start in life. Most were unmarried. Often they formed "messes" that shared wagons and cooking chores. One thing many had in common was ignorance of frontier skills and Indian lore. About half had knowledge of firearms, but few were experienced hunters. What knowledge they had about wagons and livestock came from farming. None possessed accurate information about California or how to get there. They knew only that they needed to head west and slightly south once they split off from the others near Fort Hall.

Later they admitted that if it hadn't been for Thomas Fitzpatrick– especially his skill in dealing with Indians– they would never have made it. But even he could not help them once they left the Oregon Trail. They weren't certain how much food to carry or what kinds. Space, weight and budget constraints were always determining factors. Vehicles ranged from two-wheeled carts to various sized farm wagons. Most chose oxen to pull the wagons, but a few used mules and even horses. Horses needed ample water and grass, while oxen and mules could survive on less. Children made do without milk, for milk cows were a luxury and were left behind. They had cured meat, such as ham and bacon, but it was assumed that hunters in the party would provide fresh meat along the way.

Fitzpatrick had his work cut out for him from the start. First he had to show Bartleson and others how to pick suitable campsites and how to corral and protect vital livestock from thieving Indians, who were sure to plague them. Campsites had to have good water, a source of fuel and enough grass or fodder for the animals to feed on. Protection from the elements was also desirable but not as vital as good grass and water. Without strong, healthy livestock they would be stopped in their tracks.

In 1841 emigration was so light that good campsites were not difficult to find. The route followed a virtual highway of rivers as a source of water and grass. The first river they followed after crossing the Missouri was the Kansas. This led to the Little Blue, which flowed north to the Big Blue in present day Kansas.

By the time they reached the Platte River on June 1, they had endured enough drenching rains, hub-deep mud-holes and dangerous river crossings to become seasoned travelers. June 4 brought their first serious encounter with Indians, when young Nicholas Dawson– who had wandered off while hunting– was accosted by a band of Cheyenne braves. Robbing him of his mule, his guns and most of his clothing, he was set free to walk back to the wagon train. After he returned later in the day to tell his frightening tale, Fitzpatrick hurried the train to a defensible position, where they formed a square with their wagons to defend themselves.

Sure enough, a well-armed band of Cheyennes thundered up and reined in their blowing horses to stare at the travelers. Fitzpatrick and another experienced frontiersman, John Gray, used the pause to parlay with them. While a peace-pipe was being passed around, Fitzpatrick convinced the Indians to return Dawson's mule and rifle. From that day on, Nicholas Dawson was known as "Cheyenne Dawson."

A few days later the Indian scare was forgotten when the men managed to kill several buffalo. On June 9 the travelers crossed the treacherous South Fork of the Platte River so they could reach the North Fork. This was to be their highway for hundreds of miles and weeks of relatively easy travel. They camped at Ash Hollow, minus several head of livestock lost in the river but thankful for no human casualties.

An ironic tragedy struck them on June 13, when George Shotwell accidentally shot and killed himself with his own gun. He was buried beside the trail. After passing the distinctive pinnacle of Chimney Rock and the colorfully eroded cliffs around Scott's Bluff, they reached Fort William (Laramie) on June 22. They had traveled 625 miles in 42 days, an average of 15 miles per day. Not bad for a party of greenhorns. Not far from the fort they experienced a violent storm on a hot day as described by John Bidwell:

> First came a terrific shower, followed by a fall of hail to the depth of four inches, some of the stones being as large as turkey eggs; and the next day a waterspout– an angry, huge, whirling cloud column,

which seemed to draw its water from the Platte River– passed within a quarter of a mile behind us....Had it struck us it doubtless would have demolished us.

Most of July 1 was spent crossing the North Fork of the Platte River, which curved away to the left (south) of their route. This crossing cost them an overturned wagon and loss of a mule, a cheap price to pay. Ten days later they were in the valley of the Sweetwater River at Wyoming's Independence Rock. They stopped there a few days to hunt buffalo and "make meat" by slicing it into thin strips to dry in the hot sun and wind. It seems likely that at least some of them climbed the rock as well.

Their food supplies were dwindling fast, and a substantial meat supply was vital. They crossed the Continental Divide over South Pass in mid-July and soon were camped on the Green River, sharing a campsite with a large band of trappers led by Henry Fraeb. (Fraeb and some of his men were killed by hostile Sioux warriors a few days later.) After reaching the Bear River in early August, they followed it north to Soda Springs, where the Bartleson Party was to split off for California.

Fitzpatrick pleaded with them to give up their foolhardy quest and continue with the others to Oregon. A few were so inclined, while some decided to return east. From 33 to 36 emigrants, including Father De Smet and his missionary party, pressed on for Oregon. Six of De Smet's party had already left to return east, one man (Shotwell) was dead and four others left for the East at Soda Springs.

Thus 32 men, plus Nancy Kelsey and her baby, were still determined to head for California; however, several of them accompanied the Oregon travelers about 40 miles to Fort Hall to get supplies and information on the route. They were to join their companions later near the Great Salt Lake. After an emotional separation, the Bartleson-Bidwell Party followed the Bear River as it turned south toward the Salt Lake.

Here Bidwell describes another adventure. It was a stifling hot day, and sighting a snow-capped mountain nearby, adventurous James John, better known as Jimmy John, challenged Bidwell to climb it and get some snow. Distances were deceptive, and it took the two young men much longer than they planned to get near the snow. Darkness overtook them before they reached it. Spotting the flickering fires of Indians below, they decided to stay where they were. By dawn they were close to freezing and the snow-capped peak was tantalizingly close.

Neither of the stubborn young men would give in to the other and they finally reached the snow by mid-morning. Filling a neckerchief with snow, they hurried down the mountain by a different route. Somehow they made their way around the Indians and were fortunate to locate the wagon train. By then their worried companions had given them up for lost, assuming they had been killed by Indians.

To their anxious question, "Where have you been?" they could only say sheepishly, "we have been up on the snow." With that they proudly displayed their snow, which had melted to a small iceball. [4] Nevertheless it proved they had reached the top of the mountain and added to their prestige as "fearless explorers." We can be sure that Bartleson had another name for them, and probably told it to them in no uncertain terms.

IN LATE AUGUST the relieved party left the Bear River before it drained into the vast salt lake. Here they were joined by the men who made the detour to Fort Hall. All they had to show for it were vague instructions to head westerly and look for Mary's River (the Humboldt). This they were to follow until it disappeared into a sink near the Sierra Nevada range. The men had been unsuccessful in buying any food supplies at Fort Hall.

The information about Mary's River was not new to them. The question was, in what direction was the river and how far? And where amidst the seemingly endless salt flats and scraggly sage brush would they find water and grass? Finally their prayers were answered when they came across moist ground, some small springs and blessed green grass. There they rested for several days, while Bartleson and Charles Hopper went ahead to scout out a feasible route.

By the time the scouts returned many days later, the distressed emigrants had given them up for lost and begun following their tracks. Bartleson's statement that they had found a small stream believed to be a tributary of Mary's River offered badly needed hope. But when he added a warning that wagons couldn't make it, their hopes were promptly dashed. Nevertheless, they followed the scouts toward the promised stream. As predicted, there was little water or fodder along the route; soon some of the animals were floundering and unable to continue.

Benjamin and Andrew Kelsey apparently had more foresight than the others, for they abandoned their two wagons on the spot and strapped their meager belongings on pack animals. It took three more days of torturous travel before the drastic decision was made to abandon the other six wagons. Everything except absolute necessities was jettisoned, and the remainder strapped to any animals fit for travel. Bidwell describes their first day as follows:

> It was but a few minutes before the packs began to turn; horses became scared, mules kicked, oxen jumped and bellowed, and articles were scattered in all directions. We took more pains, fixed things, made a new start, and did better, though packs continued occasionally to fall off and delay us.

Many were walking by now, even Nancy Kelsey carrying her baby.

Her bitter tears must have been overflowing. Although John Bartleson was their official captain, Benjamin Kelsey sometimes assumed the leadership role because of his frontier experience and instinct in finding the way when others were lost. He and his brother, Andrew, were described as "rough men, often in trouble with the authorities." Others from Kentucky were Joseph Chiles, James Springer and Grove Cook. Such men had few social graces, but they were invaluable in the wilderness.

Once the wagons were left behind, the struggling group was growing desperate and was no longer a viable emigrant party trying to pioneer a road. Instead, they were a hopelessly lost and frightened band of individuals fighting for survival. By staying near the base of the Ruby Mountains, they found water to sustain themselves. By the third week of September they apparently crossed over Harrison Pass and stumbled on to the river they had been seeking for so long (now the Humboldt).

By then they were out of food and began slaughtering their oxen one by one. But at least they were heading in the right direction toward the infamous sink. Then came a vast scorching desert before they crossed the Carson River and made their way to the Walker River. Somehow they missed the river that was later named the Truckee. Now it was a matter of following the Walker River south, while they sought a pass through and over the huge granite barrier looming to the west.

They ate their last ox before they crossed near present-day Sonora Pass and followed the Stanislaus River west. At the crest they must have been praying that the San Joaquin Valley would be in sight. Instead they saw nothing but seemingly endless rows of peaks and gorges. Scouts searched ahead for a likely route, and by strenuous trial and error they made some progress before the daring Jimmy John found a way through and disappeared. Andrew Kelsey and Thomas Jones went ahead to seek help from John Marsh (see Marsh).

Days later the bedraggled and starving group reached the valley floor and camped along the Stanislaus River with no sign of those who had gone ahead. Food was the immediate problem, and the hunters managed to kill enough deer to meet their needs. They knew only that John Marsh's ranch lay somewhere to the north, along the San Joaquin River .

According to Josiah Belden's memoirs, Andrew Kelsey and Jones returned shortly with food sent by Marsh (see Belden). Others in the party say Jones returned with one of Marsh's Indian ^, bringing food on pack animals. Meanwhile, Jimmy John had made his way half-starved to John Sutter's New Helvetia settlement, near the confluence of the Sacramento and American rivers (see Sutter).

When John gasped out his tale about the plight of the broken Bartleson Party, Sutter immediately dispatched two of his domesticated

Indians with pack animals laden with jerked meat and flour to search them out. Meanwhile, the Bartleson Party was making its way north along the San Joaquin River. Apparently Sutter's Indians never found them. At any rate they were led to John Marsh's ranch on the eastern slope of Mt. Diablo, where they arrived in early November.

M ARSH MUST HAVE BEEN taken aback by the sight of a young woman with a baby and 31 emaciated men walking or riding what was left of their broken-down horses and mules. He had been on the ranch only a few years, and the place was far from impressive, consisting of a small adobe house, a corral and a few outbuildings. Summer had been very warm, and all vegetation except for a few trees was brown, dry and ugly.

Once Marsh had gathered his wits and learned who these pathetic people were, he ordered his Indian workers to slaughter one fat hog and possibly a steer for a feast. He even used some of his precious wheat seed to make tortillas. When he had mailed those letters east the year before, he hoped for some response but nothing like this! What was he to do with all these people? They didn't look like they had a dollar among them, and their livestock was virtually worthless.

Marsh had some training as a doctor and passed himself off as a full-fledged physician with a degree from Harvard. But his main focus was cattle ranching; in fact, he took most of his medical fees in breeding stock. He was an unmarried, parsimonious man who carried on relationships with Indian women and had little to do with his Mexican neighbors. Except for his domesticated Indians, it appears he had become a recluse.

Faced with feeding these helpless people, he soon became morose and moody. Some of the men began taking beaver and otter along the river. But before they began drifting away, Marsh told them he had to provide Mexican authorities with a complete list, and they would have to go to San Jose and request passports from Mexican officials there. When most of them complied, they were immediately arrested and jailed. Then all the tales they had heard about Mexican cruelty came home to roost.

Finally Marsh was required to appear in San Jose to guarantee their good behavior by posting bond. Only then did Gen. Mariano G. Vallejo reluctantly release the prisoners and issue them passports. Though the passports had cost him nothing, Marsh charged each emigrant $5.00 for them. Such high-handed treatment offended and disillusioned them, and they couldn't wait to be shed of the niggardly Doctor Marsh.

By then it was mid-December 1841, and John Bidwell and some companions headed up the Sacramento River toward John Sutter's more hospitable settlement. Later the Kelseys joined them, and we can be sure they all celebrated a thankful and joyous Christmas together. Considering the unbelievable hardships they endured, it seems miraculous that the 34 plucky emigrants all reached California safely.

Another overland party entered California that same year: the Rowland-Workman Party came via the southern route, apparently following the Old Spanish trail from Santa Fe into Southern California. According to *The Recollection of Robert H. Thomes,* this party included: William Workman, John Rowland (not to be confused with Roland in the Bartleson-Bidwell party), and Benjamin D. Wilson, all of whom settled in the Los Angeles area (see Wilson). Among others, three who migrated to Northern California and became well known ranchers are Albert G. Toomes, William Knight and William Gordon. [2]

An alphabetical list of those arriving in California with the Bartleson-Bidwell Party follows: [3]

1. Bartleson, John †*
2. Barnett, Elias
3. Belden, Josiah
4. Belty, William*?
5. Bidwell, John*
6. Brolaski, Henry L.*
7. Chandler, David W. †
8. Chiles, Joseph B.*
9. Cook, Grove C. †*
10. Dawson, V. W. †*
11. Dawson, Nicholas "Cheyenne"
12. Green, Talbot (Paul Geddes)
13. Henshaw, George †*
14. Hopper, Charles*
15. Huber, Henry*
16. John, James "Jimmy" *
17. Jones, Thomas
18. Kelsey, Andrew †
19. Kelsey, Benjamin
20. Kelsey, Nancy
21. Kelsey, Martha Ann
22. McDowell, John †
23. McMahan, Sam. "Green"
24. McMahan, Nelson
25. Nye, Michael C.
26. Patton, A. Gwinn †
27. Rickman, Robert
28. Roland, John †
29. Schwartz, John L. †
30. Springer, James P.
31. Thomes, Robert H.
32. Walton, Ambrose
33. Walton, Major †
34. Weber, Charles M.

* Those returning to Missouri in 1842. † Deceased prior to 1856

SOME OF THE PARTY did not like what they saw in California, especially after their unpleasant experience with John Marsh and the Mexican officials in San Jose. Soon they were making plans for a return journey to Missouri. Others liked what they saw and were returning east to escort friends or family members back to California in later years. Those returning to Missouri in 1842 chose Joseph Chiles as their leader. Names followed by double asterisks were reported deceased on a list published in 1856 by James P. Springer. [4]

Following is an alphabetical list, combined with biographical information, of those who remained in California or returned shortly thereafter (the list also includes some who migrated to Oregon):

BARNETT, ELIAS. A native of Kentucky, Barnett was born in 1805. By 1831 he was living in Missouri. After arriving in California a decade later, he seems to have divided his time for the next two years working for John A. Sutter and for George Yount on his Napa Valley ranch (see Yount). In 1843 he apparently settled in or near Pope Valley, where the following year he married Maria Salazar Pope, widow of William Pope and mother of five. He served with John Sutter's rag-tag "army" in 1844-45 in support of Mexican Governor. Manuel Micheltorena.

Barnett returned to his family during the following spring. That fall his wife gave birth to twins and finally obtained legal ownership of her deceased husband's land holdings in Pope Valley. Barnett appears to have taken part in the Bear Flag Revolt in its later stages in July 1846, and in October he joined Colonel John C. Fremont's California Volunteers to fight in the Mexican War (see Fremont).

Barnett rode south with Fremont to Cahuenga Pass, on the outskirts of Los Angeles, where Mexican General Andres Pico surrendered in January 1847. Barnett returned home that spring and apparently became a farmer. He and his wife had several more children over the years and adopted others as well. Barnett died in Pope Valley in 1880 at the age of 75.

BELDEN, JOSIAH. See separate chapter.

BELTY, WILLIAM. He was a German immigrant from Missouri. According to historian Hubert H. Bancroft, he may have returned to Missouri, where he died. But Bancroft goes on to say that a man with the same name served in Fremont's volunteers during the Mexican War and is named in Thomas O. Larkin's records at Monterey in 1847-48 (see Larkin). According to a man who claimed to have helped bury him, Belty "was killed by a fall from his horse in the mines in 1848."

BIDWELL, JOHN. Probably the most famous of all this esteemed group, his life is covered in a separate chapter.

BROLASKI, HENRY L. (sometimes Brolasky). After leaving Marsh's ranch, he went with Josiah Belden to San Jose and then to visit Isaac Graham's ranch near Santa Cruz. From there they traveled to Monterey, where Belden went to work for Thomas O. Larkin. In 1842 Brolaski sailed for Callao, Peru, where he succeeded his brother in a trading enterprise. By 1848 he was reported in St. Louis. Upon learning of the gold discovery, he apparently went back to California to try his luck. He was reported living in St. Louis in 1870.

CHANDLER, DAVID. Employed by Jean J. Vioget for several years, he was in Benicia in 1847 before sailing to Honolulu. He returned within a year– probably because of Marshall's gold discovery– and died a short time later.

CHILES, JOSEPH. See separate chapter.

COOK, GROVE. A divorced native of Kentucky, he was described as a "likable but wild young man" by Josiah Belden. His ex-wife, sister of the famed Sublette brothers, charged that he was a drunkard who often abused her. She died two years after her divorce, leaving her daughter, Theresa. The girl died in an 1849 cholera epidemic in St. Louis. Cook became a Mexican citizen in 1844 and a year later settled at Sutter's Fort to run a distillery. While there, Cook killed the son of a Walla Walla Indian chief in a gun fight over a mule. When Sutter exonerated him, it almost led to war with the Walla Wallas. In December 1845 Cook married Rebecca Kelsey Fowler, divorced daughter of David Kelsey, who had immigrated from Oregon and died shortly after.

In 1846 Cook moved to Yerba Buena, then bought the Rancho de los Capitancillos outside San Jose. After discovering a quicksilver mine on his ranch, Cook and Josiah Belden exploited it until Belden dropped out. Later Cook amassed a fortune but lost it all in a gold mining venture. He died in Santa Cruz in February 1853.

DAWSON, V. W. Little is known about this man, who apparently was not related to Nicholas "Cheyenne" Dawson. He apparently migrated to Oregon with the Kelsey family in an 1843 cattle drive. Historian H.H. Bancroft states he may have drowned there in the Columbia River.

DAWSON, NICHOLAS "CHEYENNE." A native of Pennsylvania, Dawson was born in 1819. After getting a good education, he emigrated to Missouri. Like John Bidwell, he acquired land in the "Platte Purchase" area, where he did some farming and school teaching. Nicknamed "Cheyenne," after his traumatic experience with Cheyenne Indians on the way out, he operated a small store in Monterey for a short time before moving to Santa Cruz.

In Monterey he worked for Job Dye, who was in the lumber business— as was Thomas O. Larkin. Both Dye and Larkin, who was represented by Josiah Belden, had stacks of lumber on the beach awaiting transport. Upset because Larkin had cut back on orders for lumber, irate lumbermen apparently set fire to the lumber on the beach with the hope that lumber orders would increase.

Dawson did what he could to save the burning lumber, but it was too late. While Dye lost some lumber, Larkin lost all of his and was forced to close his operation there. In 1844 Dawson went east to Arkansas, where he settled down and got married four years later. He returned to California during the 1849 gold rush and made some money freighting. He returned home to his family in 1851 and moved the following year to Austin, Texas. He died there in 1903, the second oldest surviving member of the Bartleson-Bidwell party. His extensive memoirs were published in 1901.

GREEN, TALBOT (real name Paul Geddes). A native of Pennsylvania, he was born in 1810. By 1832 he was working for a bank and married Henrietta Frederick. He deserted her and his four children in 1841 to emigrate to California. After arriving there with a heavy and mysterious bundle or bag he claimed was lead for ammunition, he joined Josiah Belden to obtain employment from Monterey trader Thomas O. Larkin. He did well enough to become a partner in early 1846. By the following year he was collector of the port and had bought land in Yerba Buena (San Francisco), where eventually Green Street was named for him.

He was already a partner in the successful trading firm, Mellus, Howard & Co. of Yerba Buena– later called Howard and Green– when he moved there. Within a few years Green became a wealthy business- man and a City Councilman. In October 1849 he married Sarah Montgomery, widow of Allen Montgomery of the 1844 Stevens- Murphy Party (see Sarah Wallis for more details).

HOPPER, CHARLES. A native of North Carolina, he went east with Chiles in 1842 but returned with his family in 1847. Because of his pre- vious trail experience and proven leadership ability, he was elected cap- tain of the emigrant party with whom he and his family traveled. Later he took up farming in Napa Valley near his old friends, Chiles and George Yount. Part of his written narrative of the famous 1841 emigra- tion was published in Napa Valley newspapers in the 1870s. Considered one of the area's leading citizens, Hopper died in 1880 at the age of 81, leaving five children.

HUBER, HENRY. An immigrant from Germany, he was a grantee of Honcut Rancho in 1845 but lost his title in an 1853 land dispute. He was at Sutter's Fort in 1841 and 1846, where he operated a distillery. Later he owned property in San Francisco, where he had a liquor store.

JOHN, JAMES "JIMMY." A native of Ohio, John was born in 1809. At age four his mother died, and he was raised by his maternal grandpar- ents. He tried various occupations over the years, apparently with little success. He married in 1838, but his wife died seven months later.

After coming to California, John emigrated to Oregon in 1842 with F. Ermatinger's Hudson's Bay Company trapping party. He first settled on the Tualitin Plains, but moved to Linnton a year later. In 1846 he moved across the Willamette River, where, in 1852, he founded the town of St. Johns. He never remarried, and died in 1886 at age 77.

JONES, THOMAS. He was living in San Jose in 1845, where he applied for a land grant a year later. He apparently died in 1879 in Yuba County.

KELSEY, ANDREW. After arriving in California, Andrew accompanied Benjamin and Nancy Kelsey to Oregon in 1843, where they joined their brothers, David and Samuel. They journeyed together to California the following year. In 1846 they took part in the Bear Flag Rebellion, and in 1847 Andrew and a partner named Stone established a ranch near Clear Lake (now Kelseyville).

After learning of Marshall's gold discovery in the spring of 1848, Andrew joined Benjamin to look for gold in the vicinity of Coloma (see Marshall). They struck it rich a few miles east at a place named in their honor (Kelsey). Andrew then returned to join Stone at their Clear Lake ranch. Both men were killed in an Indian attack in the fall of 1849. In 1850 a small army sent to punish the Indians killed hundreds of them.

KELSEY, BENJAMIN AND NANCY. See Nancy Kelsey.

McMahan, Nelson (sometimes McMahon). Apparently a first cousin of Samuel Green McMahan, he may have traveled to Oregon with his cousin in an 1843 cattle drive. He probably returned to California with him in 1845, but nothing else is known.

MCMAHAN, SAMUEL GREEN (sometimes McMahon). A native of Missouri, he was born in 1819. After his arrival in California he wintered at Sutter's Fort, and in 1842-43 he went to work for John Wolfskill on his Putah Creek ranch. He traveled to Oregon in 1843 with a cattle drive and returned to California in 1845 with Joseph Clyman (see Clyman). After serving briefly in the Mexican war, he acquired a ranch from Wolfskill in Yolo County (see Wolfskill). He married Lavenia Yount, widow of John Yount (nephew of George Yount), in 1860. McMahan died in Dixon in 1884 at the age of 65 and is buried in the Sacramento City Cemetery.

NYE, MICHAEL C. Nye became a naturalized Mexican citizen in 1844 and acquired the Willy Rancho on the Yuba River near present-day Marysville. This was apparently for his services in the Micheltorena campaign. In 1847 he married Mrs. Harriet Pike of the ill-fated Donner Party. He was at his Marysville ranch in 1858, but later went to Oregon, possibly because his Marysville land grant claim was invalidated by the Land commission. Nye's wife died in Oregon in 1870, after which he remarried. He died in Prineville (Cook Co.), Oregon, in 1906 at the age of 85, the last remaining member of the Bartleson-Bidwell Party.

SCHWARTZ, JOHN L. A native of Germany, Schwartz was born in 1797. He obtained a land grant on the Sacramento River in Yolo County, where he established a fishing station, raised produce for sale and built a boat. The boat was used to trade throughout the delta, but his land grant was eventually invalidated. He died in 1852 at age 55.

SPRINGER, JAMES P. A native of Kentucky, Springer was born in 1812. A college graduate, Springer apparently did not find himself until he made the journey to California in 1841. After returning to Missouri with Chiles in 1842, he published numerous pamphlets and articles extolling California and became a guide for subsequent emigrant parties.

Nearly a decade passed before Springer brought his family to California in 1852. The family settled in or near present-day Saratoga in Santa Clara County. By 1859 he was a member of the California State Legislature. He died in McCartysville in 1861, leaving a wife and daughter.

THOMES, ROBERT H. Born in 1817, Thomes was a native of Maine. He worked as a carpenter at San Francisco in the early 1840's until moving to Monterey a few years later. There he became a partner of Albert G. Toomes in the building business (Thomes & Toomes). After becoming naturalized in 1844 he was granted Tehama Rancho by Gov. Manuel Micheltorena. This ranch became the center of present-day Tehama County. He remained there the rest of his life, becoming one of the area's leading citizens. His old friend, Toomes, also acquired a ranch nearby. Thomes died in 1878 at the age of 61, leaving nine children.

WALTON, MAJOR. Though Major returned to Missouri with Chiles in 1842, he apparently returned to California with Chiles and Joseph R. Walker in 1843. Nothing more is known except his death prior to 1856.

WEBER, CHARLES M. See separate chapter.

These notable pioneers left their marks in many places, and some attained positions of great importance. Bidwell Mansion State park in Chico and other state monuments throughout Northern California honor these remarkable pioneers. See California State historical publications for details.

BIBLIOGRAPHY

–Bancroft, Hubert H. *California Pioneer Register and Index.* Regional Publishing Co., Baltimore, MD, 1964.

–Barnett, William A., descendant of Elias Barnett, provided author with information on Barnett and other members of the Bartleson-Bidwell party.

–Bidwell, John. "Echoes of the Past," *The Century Illustrated Monthly,* 1890. Reprinted by State of California, 1974. Except for [1, 2, 3 & 4], all quotations were taken from this source.

–Callizo, Joe. "The Barnett Family," *Pope Valley News,* 1985.

–Nunis, Doyce B., Jr., editor, *Josiah Belden, 1841: Overland Pioneer.* The Talisman Press, Georgetown, CA, 1962. [3]

–Nunis, Doyce B., Jr., editor, *The Bidwell-Bartleson Party.* Western Tanager Press, Santa Cruz, CA, 1991. [2 & 4]

–Stewart, George R. *The California Trail.* University of Nebraska Press, Lincoln, 1962. [1]

Juan Bandini and one of his daughters
Courtesy California State Library

– 2 –

JUAN BANDINI (DON JUAN)

1800-1859

ORN IN LIMA, PERU, in 1800, of Italian parentage, Juan Bandini
lived most of his life in Alta California. He received a good education in Lima before migrating to San Diego around 1820, probably with his father, José Bandini, who built a large house there. Don
Juan apparently completed his education in Mexico before marrying
Dolores Estudillo, daughter of prominent California landowners. By
1828 Bandini had four children and had entered public life as a member
of the *diputacion* (deputy or legislator). His father died in 1841.

Don Juan Bandini was named Commissioner of Revenue in San
Diego from 1828 to 1832, collecting customs duties. He also played an
important role with José Carillo, Pío Pico and Yankee trader Abel
Stearns in deposing the hated Governor Manuel Victoria (see Stearns).
In 1832 he opposed Agustín Zamorano's counter revolt. Two years later
he journeyed to Mexico City as a member of Congress and returned
later as Vice President of a California colonization program, headed by
José M. Hijar and José M. Padres. During that period, Bandini also
served as supercargo of the trading vessel *Natalia* and Inspector of
Customs for California under acting Governor Carlos Carillo.

Unfortunately for Bandini, the program to tempt or coerce colonists
from Mexico to relocate in California was doomed to failure. When
powerful *Californios,* such as Gov. José Figueroa and Mariano Vallejo,
refused to recognize the authority of either Padres or Hijar, Bandini saw
it as the most significant failure of his career (see Vallejo). At about this
time he was accused of smuggling, which didn't help his cause.

During 1836-37 Bandini was a leader in an abortive attempt to oust
Gov. Juan Alvarado, who had taken over from Nicolas Gutiérrez. He
was lucky to escape imprisonment and lost a great deal of credibility for
his efforts. Apparently he had nothing against Alvarado, but had a
vendetta against Angel Ramirez, one of his close advisors.

According to Richard Dana's book *Two Years Before the Mast,*
Bandini sailed from Monterey to Santa Barbara in January 1836 aboard

the vessel Alert to attend a wedding of a prominent family. Dana described Bandini:

> ..accomplished, poor, and proud, and without any office or occupation...He had a slight and elegant figure, moved gracefully, danced and waltzed beautifully, spoke the best of Castilian, with a pleasant and refined voice and accent, and had, throughout, the bearing of a man of high birth and figure. Yet here he was, with his passage given him, (as I afterwards learned,) for he had not the means of paying for it, and living on the charity of our agent. He was polite to every one, spoke to the sailors, and gave four reals—I dare say the last he had in his pocket—to the steward who waited upon him.

Dana's comments about Bandini's poverty seem grossly exaggerated, for Bandini was a business associate of successful Los Angeles trader Abel Stearns. He had also acquired the Rancho Tecate, where he was raising livestock. In 1837 Bandini attended the wedding of his good friend Hugo Reid in San Gabriel (see Reid). That same year Indian hostilities broke out along the San Diego-Baja California frontier. When natives attacked Rancho San Ysidro, killing members of the Ybarra family, the news spread quickly throughout the San Diego area. Many local *rancheros*, including the Bandinis, made their way to safety in San Diego. Before long the Indians raided, sacked and burned Bandini's vacated Rancho Tecate.

Without a place to shelter his family in 1838, Bandini moved to San Gabriel, where the benevolent Governor Alvarado appointed him administrator of Mission San Gabriel. The missions had recently been secularized by the Mexican government, and administrators were appointed to properly dispose of vast mission assets, including land, livestock, buildings and furnishings. Shortly after Bandini moved to San Gabriel, his bachelor friend and partner, Abel Stearns, came to live with him and his family.

Then Alvarado granted Bandini the Rancho Jurupa, a large holding in what became part of Riverside and San Bernardino Counties. In 1839 Bandini gave tentative possession of mission property known as Rancho Santa Anita (present Arcadia) to Hugo Reid and his Indian wife, Victoria. Reid later acquired legal title from Governor Alvarado.

By 1840 Bandini had lost his wife, leaving him with three girls: Arcadia, Isadora and Josefa, and two boys: José Maria and Juanito. Shortly after, he married Refugio Argüello, daughter of Santiago Argüello, owner of Rancho Tia Juana near San Diego. During the next decade, he had five more children by Refugio, who became a close friend and confidant of Victoria Reid. Both Hugo Reid and Stearns were Godfathers to Bandini's children; they were all very close.

APPARENTLY BANDINI'S fortunes were turning; a year or two later he acquired more land, including Ranchos Rincon, Cajon de Muscupiabe and San Juan Capistrano. In 1841 Abel Stearns, then in his mid-forties, married Bandini's fourteen-year-old-daughter, Arcadia. They then moved to a mansion Stearns built in Los Angeles. Soon Arcadia's younger sister, Ysidora, moved in with them.

In March 1843 the Bandinis visited the Reids at Santa Anita and later witnessed the marriage of Victoria Reid's son, Felipe (from a former marriage) in San Gabriel. That same year Bandini sold Jurupa Rancho to Don Benito Wilson (see Wilson). In December 1844 he witnessed the sale of Rancho Azusa to his new friend, Henry Dalton; Dalton later bought Rancho Santa Anita from Hugo Reid (see Dalton).

Though Bandini had always leaned toward revolutions that took place on a regular basis in early California, he apparently played no active role in the ousting of Governor Manuel Micheltorena in 1844-45, when Pío Pico took over. Nevertheless, Bandini was named Secretary of State under newly appointed Governor Pico and played an important role in deciding the fate of John A. Sutter, who had actively supported Micheltorena with volunteer troops. Sutter had been captured by rebel forces led by José Castro, and was incarcerated in Los Angeles awaiting a hearing (see Pico & Sutter).

Thanks to Bandini's influence and benevolence, Sutter was paroled, restored to his former status and allowed to keep his large Sacramento land grant. During 1845-46, while serving as Pico's Secretary of State, Bandini was also a member of the Assembly. The Capital had been moved from Monterey to Los Angeles, and he and Pico became outspoken foes of General José Castro, who controlled Mexican troops in the North. They apparently viewed him as a threat to their regime.

By early 1846 Bandini had acquired the huge Guadalupe Rancho in Baja California, where he established another cattle ranch. He now owned three ranches, two of them stocked with thousands of livestock. Rumors of possible war with the United States were raging and the *Californios* faced a dilemma. Some preferred occupation by a foreign government, such as the United States or England, to that of the current and seemingly indifferent government in far away Mexico City. Others sought independence for Alta California under the protection of a foreign power such as England.

Among those who favored independence and British protection were Pío Pico, Juan Bandini and Henry Dalton. When word came that 10,000 Mormons from the United States were allegedly on their way to settle in California, plans were made to thwart the effort (actually fewer than 300 Mormon settlers sailed into San Francisco Bay at the end of July with Samuel Brannan). (See Brannan.)

A convention was scheduled in Santa Barbara, where it was hoped Pico could sway the representatives in the direction of a British protectorate. The British Pacific fleet commodore, who had been appraised of the situation, agreed to cooperate in the event Pico was successful. Another scheme, promoted by a Catholic Priest, was to transplant 10,000 Irish Catholics into California to offset the feared Mormon takeover.

The Santa Barbara convention was delayed because of a conflict between Pico and General José Castro. Before it could take place, U.S. Navy Commodore John Sloat invaded Monterey in early July without a shot being fired in anger. Within a matter of days the Stars and Stripes were raised over all of Northern California, and plans were under way to invade Southern California. One can imagine the surprise and disappointment the British commodore must have experienced when he sailed into Monterey a few days after the invasion to see U.S. Navy ships at anchor and the American flag fluttering from atop the Custom House.

U.S. Navy Commodore Robert Stockton replaced Sloat within a week, enlisting the help of U.S. Army Captain John C. Fremont and his battalion of army topographers and volunteers (see Fremont). When they invaded Southern California by sea, it fell into their hands without opposition when Governor Pico and General Castro fled to Mexico seeking help. Always the pragmatist, Bandini joined his father-in-law, Santiago Argüello in welcoming Stockton and Fremont as old friends in San Diego.

Later Bandini and Argüello presented Fremont with a fine, well-trained horse. He and Argüello then explained their acceptance of the occupation to local citizens, urging them to do the same. It seems that U.S. occupation had become more palatable than other alternatives. Though there was a short-lived uprising in Southern California that saw American occupation forces driven back to San Pedro, they were soon back in San Diego, planning a march north with reinforcements brought from Santa Fe by General Stephen Kearny.

EVEN BEFORE THE FIGHTING WAS OVER in early 1847, Bandini helped provide Stockton with badly needed supplies and livestock. According to William Heath Davis in his book, *Seventy-five Years in California,* Bandini invited Commodore Stockton to take over a good portion of his San Diego "mansion" as his headquarters (see Davis). A quotation from Davis states:

> The commodore was accustomed to have the [navy] band play during the dinner hour and to invite the Bandini family and ladies of San Diego to dine with him and listen to the excellent music...Bandini had in his dwelling a very large hall where he gave

dancing parties during the commodore's stay in San Diego, at which he and his officers and the best families of the town participated...

In 1847 Stockton named Bandini a member of the newly formed Legislative Council, with Juan B. Alvarado, Mariano Vallejo, Thomas O. Larkin, Santiago Argüello and others. Bandini was appointed alcalde of San Diego in 1848, when he built a large and costly store-building that nearly broke him. Disillusioned with life in California, he returned to his Rancho Gualalupe in Baja California and reactivated his abandoned Mexican citizenship.

By 1852 Bandini had become a Mexican judge but couldn't seem to control his maverick ways. In 1855 he became involved in a failed revolution and returned to California. He died in Los Angeles in 1859, leaving his wife and many children. Bandini's San Diego house (Casa de Bandini) is located in historical Old Town; in 1869 a second story was added and it became a hotel and stage stop. A state historical marker identifies the site of Agua Mansa, once part of Bandini's Jurupa Rancho (present Colton), which he donated for the town before selling the ranch to Benjamin Wilson.

BIBLIOGRAPHY
–Bancroft, Hubert H. *Register of Pioneer Inhabitants of California 1542 to 1848.* Dawson's Book Shop, Los Angeles, CA, 1964.
–Dakin, Susanna Bryant. *A Scotch Paisano In Old Los Angeles: A Biography of Hugo Reid.* University of California. Press, Berkeley, 1939.
–Dana, Richard H. Jr. *Two Years before the Mast.* Rainbow Classics, World Publishing Co., Cleveland, OH, 1946.
–Davis, William Heath. *Seventy-Five Years in California.* John Howell Books, San Francisco, 1967.
–Dillon, Richard. *Fool's Gold.* Coward-McCann, Inc., NY, 1967.
–Ferris, Robert G. *Explorers And Settlers.* U.S. Dept. of Interior, Washington D.C., 1968. Photo and description of Casa de Bandini.
–Harlow, Neal. *California Conquered.* University of California Press, Berkeley, 1982.
–Jackson, Sheldon G. *A British Ranchero In Old California: Henry Dalton and the Rancho Azusa.* Arthur H. Clark Co., Glendale, CA, 1987.
–Wright, Doris Marion. *A Yankee In Mexican California: Abel Stearns, 1798-1848.* Wallace Hebberd, Santa Barbara, CA, 1977.

Midshipman Edward Fitzgerald Beale, 1839
Courtesy California State Library

– 3 –

EDWARD F. "NED" BEALE

1822-1893

LTHOUGH EDWARD FITZGERALD BEALE is relatively unknown, he played one of the most important roles in helping California achieve its "Manifest Destiny." His experiences in California began when he took part in the Mexican War as an officer in the U.S. Navy under Commodore Robert Stockton. As a member of John C. Fremont's "Naval Battalion of Mounted California Riflemen" in San Diego, he took part in assisting Gen. Stephen Kearny and dragoons when they reached Warner's Ranch, about 50 miles northeast of San Diego, in poor condition.

Under Captain Archibald Gillespie, Beale fought in the ill-fated "Battle of San Pasqual" against Gen. Andres Pico's Mexican lancers. After Kearny's forces suffered many casualties, Beale and Kit Carson underwent horrific hardships making their way through Mexican lines to seek help from Commodore Stockton at San Diego.

Following the gold discovery in January 1848, Beale went on his own to take gold samples to the East Coast. His descriptions of California helped trigger the subsequent gold rush. Through his friendship with Fremont, Beale became a close friend of Thomas Hart Benton, and in 1852 he was appointed Superintendent of Indian Affairs in California (See Fremont).

He was also friendly with President James Buchanan, who in 1857 appointed him superintendent of a transcontinental wagon road project in the Southwest. While engaged in this difficult work, he experimented with camels for use in packing supplies and equipment through the desert. Later he acquired the giant Rancho Tejon south of present-day Bakersfield, where he became a successful livestock rancher and friend of local Indians.

Beale was born with a silver "bosun's pipe" in his mouth, so to speak. His maternal grandfather was U.S. Naval hero, Commodore Thomas Truxtun, and his own father, George M. Beale Jr., served in the navy during the War of 1812 and for many years thereafter. Other family members also served in the navy, and it seemed he was destined to do the same from the time of his birth on February 4, 1822.

His parents, George and Emily Truxtun Beale, had married in 1819 and were residents of Bloomingdale Farm in Washington, D.C. at the time. There they constantly entertained young naval officers, who filled little Ned's head with fascinating tales of the sea. Ned Beale spent his youth at his mother's family home in Chester, Pennsylvania. In 1832 he and his older brother, Truxtun, attended Georgetown University until their father's death in 1835. He left his wife and five children.

Through political connections with President Andrew Jackson in 1836, Ned Beale received an acting midshipman's warrant in the U.S. Navy. He reported for duty in Philadelphia on his 15th birthday, where he was assigned to the U.S.S. *Independence* for training. His strict regime included seamanship, navigation and learning to be a future "officer and gentleman." Though he was known to be quick tempered, and at times an intemperate drinker, he did well enough to make full midshipman by 1839.

A FTER STUDYING at the Philadelphia "Naval Asylum" and passing his final exams in 1842, Beale was appointed a Passed Midshipman, equivalent to a present-day ensign. Within three years he became acting sailmaster aboard the U.S.S. *Congress* under Commodore Robert Stockton. When war with Mexico appeared imminent, Stockton received orders to sail the *Congress* around Cape Horn to join the Pacific squadron. There he was to replace Commodore John Sloat, who was ill and sought retirement.

When the *Congress* reached the West Indies, Stockton learned that a British squadron was heading for the Pacific. Fearing that the British might strike a deal with Mexico to take over Oregon and California, Stockton needed to send dispatches to Washington. He could not turn back and did the next best thing by placing Beale aboard a Danish vessel heading for Europe. It was hoped that Beale could then find another ship going to America and make his way to Washington with the vital dispatches and information regarding British intentions toward California and Oregon.

But as fate would have it, Beale could not find another ship until he landed in Dover, England. He reached New England—probably Boston—in early 1846 and made his way to Washington as ordered. After delivering the dispatches and passing along what information he had garnered to President Polk and the Navy Department, he was told to stand by for further orders. Meanwhile, the *Congress* had reached Peru, and U.S. Army Capt. John C. Fremont had arrived in California with a brigade of "topographers" to survey the country and test the

Mexican defenses in case war was declared. In March 1846 Beale received the following orders:

> You are permitted to take passage on the U.S. Frigate *Potomac* about to sail from Norfolk for Vera Cruz, thence to make your way in the best manner you can to Mazatlan and report to Commodore Sloat for the purpose of rejoining the Frigate *Congress*. Should you take advantage of this permission, you will take in charge and convey the accompanying packages to Commodores Sloat and Stockton...

The *Potomac* landed Beale at the Isthmus of Panama. He then crossed to Panama City, where he received a message from Stockton to sail south to Callao, Peru, to rejoin the *Congress*. Three weeks later he was back aboard the *Congress* and had delivered his dispatches to Stockton. Early the next morning the frigate hauled anchor and made her way to Honolulu in the Sandwich Islands.

Though they didn't know it, President Polk had declared war against Mexico in mid-May and General Taylor had moved his men across the border into Matamoros. Gen. Stephen Kearny was preparing to lead his troops overland to Santa Fe, and by June American settlers in California had stolen a herd of horses from the Mexican Army. These were delivered to Captain Fremont, who had moved his men to Sutter Buttes from Oregon for possible use against the Mexicans.

COMMODORE SLOAT in Mazatlan received word that hostilities between the U.S. and Mexico had commenced; he did not know that the president had declared war. Even so, he sent the U.S.S. *Portsmouth* north to San Francisco Bay and the *Cyane* and *Levant* to Monterey. He then tried to slip out of Mazatlan on the *Savannah* without alarming the British, who also had a warship there.

By July 2 Stockton and Beale were half-way to Monterey aboard the *Congress*, and Commodore Sloat was anchored off Monterey, the capital of Mexican Alta California. Unaware of President Polk's declaration of war, Sloat and U.S. Consul Thomas O. Larkin were planning their strategy (see Larkin). Word of the Bear Flag Rebellion, and knowledge about the fighting in Mexico, finally motivated Sloat to act. On July 6 he sent the following message to Captain John Montgomery aboard the *Portsmouth* in San Francisco Bay:

> I have determined to hoist the flag of the United States at this place tomorrow, as I would prefer being sacrificed for doing too much than too little. If you consider you have sufficient force, or if Fremont will join you, you will hoist the flag at Yerba Buena, or at any other proper place, and take possession of the fort and that portion of the country.

On the morning of July 7th, Comm. Sloat issued the following general order to his other two ships at anchor in Monterey Bay:

> We are about to land on the territory of Mexico, with whom the United States is at war; to strike their flag and hoist our own...It is not only our duty to take California, but to preserve it afterwards as part of the United States, at all hazards.

With that 140 armed sailors and 85 marines were landed, and the Stars and Stripes were raised over the custom house. There were no casualties and no shots fired, except for a booming twenty-one gun salute from the American ships. Sloat then issued orders to locate Captain Fremont and have him report to him in Monterey; further, the U.S. Flag was to be raised over Yerba Buena, Bodega, Sonoma and Sutter's fort. Fortunately, those objectives were accomplished without bloodshed. Fremont was reported to be on his way and General José Castro and his men were said to be retreating south toward Los Angeles.

The morning of July 15th saw the surprise arrival of the British warship *Collingwood*, under Admiral Seymour. When the admiral spied the Stars and Stripes fluttering over the customs house, any hopes he had of gaining control for Great Britain were surely dashed. By coincidence, the *Congress* with Commodore Robert Stockton and Ned Beale arrived about the same time. They had expected to find Commodore Sloat there, but the sight of the U.S. Flag flying over the customs house caught them by surprise.

A few days later a stir of excitement in the eastern hills announced the arrival of Captain Fremont's motley band of soldiers and volunteers. Behind Fremont rode his five Delaware Indian bodyguards, and behind them rode Marine Lt. Archibald Gillespie and scouts Kit Carson and Alex Godey. The exotic meld of well-armed soldiers, Indian warriors and buckskinned frontier settlers must have been a sight to behold.

Sloat was critical of Fremont's previous unauthorized actions and ordered him to keep his undisciplined men in check to avoid further impetuous acts. He felt fortunate in taking northern California without casualties and did not wish to engage the enemy without provocation. Eight days later, Stockton relieved Sloat from duty. Grateful to be relieved, Sloat transferred to a smaller ship and sailed for the East Coast.

Beale first met Fremont at his camp outside Monterey, and the two hit it off right away. Fremont later described their first meeting in his memoirs:

> I first met Edward Beale in Monterey in July of 1846. At our meeting commenced intervals of agreeable companionship on interesting occasions that resulted in a family relationship which has continued for forty years.

Stockton's aggressiveness was the opposite of Sloat's caution, and he wasted little time in enlisting Fremont and his men into the unique "Naval Battalion of Mounted California Volunteer Riflemen." This entitled Fremont and his men to military pay and benefits. At the same time, Stockton promoted Fremont to Major and Gillespie to Captain. It seems that they, too, hit it off very well together. Beale, a good horseman, was put in command of a troop of mounted riflemen—a kind of naval or marine cavalry.

Because their activities would require many hours in the saddle, Beale had his men sew cowhide patches on the seats of their pants. It wasn't long before they were known as the "leather-ass dragoons." Preparations were then made to take Fremont and his California Volunteers aboard the U.S.S. *Cyane,* which would land them at San Diego. There they were to acquire horses and make ready to move overland at a moment's notice. Their mission was to "take, or get between the Colorado and General Castro." Stockton and his men were to land at San Pedro to secure the port and Los Angeles.

Meanwhile, the merchant ship *Brooklyn* reached Yerba Buena at the end of July with Samuel Brannan and more than 200 Mormons. They had been hoping the Mexicans would be more receptive than hostile Americans in the Midwest. To Brannan's dismay he saw the U.S. Flag atop the custom house there and knew they were too late (see Brannan).

When the *Cyane* reached San Diego and disembarked most of Fremont's men, Beale and his riflemen were transported to San Pedro on the *Congress.* The march to Los Angeles went unopposed, and Stockton took possession of the nearly deserted pueblo without bloodshed. He then sent Kit Carson and some men with dispatches about the easy victory to be delivered in Washington. After naming Fremont commandant of Southern California with around 50 occupation troops, Stockton took Beale and his riflemen back to Monterey and then to Yerba Buena for supplies. Their plan was to sail down the coast to invade mainland Mexico.

Fremont was then ordered to ride north with some of his men, leaving Major Gillespie in charge of Los Angeles. Fremont ended up in Sonoma as commander of the Northern District with the promise of becoming military governor. Stockton, thinking everything was under control, made ready to turn over his command and leave for Mexico.

Then an exhausted messenger named "Lean" John Flaco arrived from Los Angeles. He had made the four hundred-plus-mile ride in an incredible four days, bringing word that the Mexicans in Los Angeles had revolted against Major Gillespie's harsh military rule. Paroled Mexican Captain José Flores had galvanized other parolees and volunteers into a formidable force, which had driven Gillespie and his outnumbered troops to seek sanctuary aboard a ship off San Pedro.

Stockton ordered Captain Mervine to take the *Savannah* south to assist Gillespie and told Beale to find Fremont and have him take his battalion to San Francisco. After Beale brought Fremont there, Stockton ordered Fremont to move his battalion overland to Los Angeles and to recruit more men and horses along the way. Stockton, with Beale and his riflemen, were to head for Southern California aboard the *Congress.*

ARRIVING AT SAN PEDRO, Stockton found Captains Mervine and Gillespie there on the Savannah. There he learned that Mervine had mounted a attack to retake Los Angeles. Upon suffering a serious defeat from Mexican volunteers under Captains José Carrillo and José Flores at Rancho Dominguez (near present Compton), he had retreated back to San Pedro. To his credit, Mervine had also sent a ship to San Diego and was successful in taking it back from Mexican forces. Soon all the ships sailed south to San Diego, and Stockton made his headquarters at the Bandini "mansion" (see Bandini).

Major Gillespie resumed command of the marines there and ordered Beale and Capt. Gibson to take some men and round up as many horses and beef cattle as possible. Despite harassment by Mexican lancers in the area, during which one of their men was badly wounded and later died, Beale and Gibson were successful in bringing back badly needed livestock.

A short time later a messenger arrived with the startling news that Gen. Stephen Kearny was camped at Warner's Ranch—about 50 miles northeast of San Diego—with a force of over a hundred dragoons. Furthermore, Kit Carson was with him, having been intercepted on the trail to Santa Fe. Kearny was asking Stockton to send men and escort him to San Diego.

Gillespie and his marines were chosen. They left December 3, taking Alex Godey, Ned Beale and some of his riflemen with them. Despite cold, rainy weather, Gillespie and his men reached Kearny in two day's time. Very likely, old friends Godey and Kit Carson were glad to be reunited. Beale couldn't help noticing how trail-worn Kearny's men and horses were. He suggested that they take the left fork in the trail back to San Diego to avoid Gen. Andres Pico's lancers, who were in the area.

But despite the poor condition of his men and animals, Kearny craved a victory over the Mexicans, whom he had heard would not fight unless they had overwhelming odds in their favor. Hoping to avenge his defeat in Los Angeles, Gillespie urged Kearny to seek out the Mexicans and attack. Kearny then ordered a small group ahead to scout out the exact location of Pico's men and to estimate their strength.

The scouts located Pico's men in San Pasqual Valley but were spotted by sentries, thus jeopardizing the hoped-for element of surprise. It was a dark, drizzly and miserably cold night, so General Kearny apparently thought a surprise attack was still feasible. With orders to proceed carefully, Kearny's men moved out just before dawn on December 6. Captain Abraham Johnston led off with a force of 12 men, closely followed by Kearny with another small group. The main force was behind them.

Ned Beale followed with three pieces of artillery. Soon they spotted Pico's camp with some of his men stirring about a sputtering fire. Captain Johnston either jumped the gun or was ordered to launch an immediate attack with his 12 poorly mounted men. Having been forewarned by Kearny's scouts earlier that night, some of the Mexican lancers had kept their horses close by them. When they saw the Americans charging, they quickly mounted and met the charge head on with their deadly lances. Others began firing rifles from the ground.

Captain Johnston fell almost immediately with a ball through his head. His death halted the charge, allowing the horseless Mexicans time to sprint for their mounts. Kearny led his dragoons in a charge against the Mexicans, who retreated and split their forces into two groups. One group circled to the rear of the charging *Americanos*, catching them in a classic pincer maneuver. As the Mexicans charged from the rear, the Americans turned to meet them. Only then did the other group of Mexicans wheel their horses and charge from their rear until the Americans were surrounded.

Many were unhorsed and jabbed repeatedly with long lances, unable to bring their sabers into play. Carnage amongst the Americans was devastating. Captain Moore died in a hand-to-hand duel with Andres Pico, when his saber broke off at the hilt. Gillespie was unhorsed, lanced repeatedly and had his front teeth knocked out. He survived by feigning death. Kit Carson did the same when he was unhorsed. Even General Kearny was wounded, receiving lance stabs in the buttocks.

Beale and his men were attacked while setting up a field piece. One man was killed by a lancer, but Beale stood his ground and shot the lancer in the leg. Despite the fierce fighting, Beale managed to get an artillery piece into action and the Mexicans withdrew, leaving him with a superficial lance wound. Kearny and his shaken and wounded men then took refuge on a hill. It could be defended, but they had no water and little food. It became known as Mule Hill after they began eating their pack animals.

Kearny had lost 19 dead and 18 wounded, while Mexican casualties were light, and still they held the upper hand. Beale suggested that they send to San Diego for assistance, and Kearny agreed. Alex Godey and an Indian guide slipped through the Mexican lines and made their way to San Diego. Though Stockton wanted to help, he had neither horses nor *carretas* to send to carry the wounded.

Meanwhile, the beleaguered Americans had improvised Indian travois, which were strapped to the few remaining horses to move the wounded. In this way they managed to hold off the Mexicans and make their way to Rancho San Bernardo. When Alex Godey and a companion tried to return to Kearny with Stockton's regrets, they were captured by the Mexicans. In a last ditch effort to seek help, Ned Beale, Kit Carson and an unidentified Indian crawled through the Mexican lines that night and made their way 30 miles to San Diego on foot.

They were near collapse when they arrived there on their bleeding, lacerated feet. By a stroke of luck, the *Portsmouth* had arrived in San Diego that day, allowing Stockton to mount a company of 180 sailors and marines to assist Kearny. Stockton's forces reached the hapless soldiers two days later, and they were escorted into San Diego.

THE TRAUMATIC EXPERIENCE left Beale physically and mentally drained, and he was forced to remain in San Diego to be cared for by a Mexican family. In an attempt to whitewash his San Pasqual fiasco, Kearny wrote reports that suggested an American victory. He implied that the Mexicans had broken off the engagement after suffering many casualties, and his badly outnumbered troops had made a successful withdrawal to San Diego. Actually the numbers were nearly even, with about 150 combatants on each side, and the Mexicans suffered few casualties.

Kearny conveniently forgot to mention the heroic roles played by Beale, Kit Carson, Alex Godey and the Indian guides in seeking help, without which Kearny's men might have been annihilated by Andres Pico and his lancers. To show their appreciation, 20 of Beale's shipmates took up a collection and ordered a lieutenant's dress sword and epaulets. They presented the gifts to Beale with a certificate of appreciation, hoping he would be promoted to full lieutenant. Instead, he was made "Acting" Lieutenant.

In mid-December the combined forces of Kearny and Stockton marched north toward Los Angeles. The march went unopposed until they reached the San Gabriel River. There the Mexicans made a valiant attempt to stop them with combined artillery fire and inspired charges by mounted lancers. When the Americans breached their defense, the Mexicans retreated but continued harassing them until they neared Los Angeles. This time the pueblo was occupied for good. The Mexicans ceased all resistance at Cahuenga Pass in early January 1847 when they were confronted by John C. Fremont and his volunteers who had moved down from the north.

Once the occupation was secure, Stockton and some of his men— including Kit Carson—traveled overland back to San Diego. Beale was with them when they boarded the *Congress* and once again he became a sailor. But not for long, because in February Stockton ordered Beale and Carson to deliver dispatches to Washington. They were told to go "by the most expeditious route overland," and again Beale became a "leather-assed" rider.

They left San Diego in late February 1847 with a ten-man escort, fortunate to miss most of the lengthy and heated controversy between the three commanders, especially the bitter feud between Kearny and Fremont that ultimately resulted in Fremont's arrest. Beale and Carson followed the same trail east to Santa Fe that Kearny had used on his westward trek a short time before. After resting a few days in Taos, while Carson visited his family, they continued on to Fort Leavenworth, where they switched from horses to a steamboat for the voyage to St. Louis.

They then went to the home of Senator Thomas Hart Benton to deliver letters from John C. Fremont to his wife, Jessie Benton Fremont, who was staying with her parents. After a pleasant visit there, the two couriers reached Washington in May 1847, having covered over 3,000 miles in less than three months. Upon delivering their dispatches, they found themselves sought-after celebrities. Everyone wanted to hear their war stories—especially those about the Battle of San Pasqual.

Later they were entertained at the Washington home of Senator Benton, where they met many of the important people of that era. Fremont arrived at Washington in August, where he was slated to undergo a court martial to answer charges of insubordination and treason made by General Kearny. Senator Benton swore to humble Kearny for making what he considered grossly unfair charges against his son-in-law, whom he considered a hero.

The full extent of Benton's vindictiveness is displayed in a letter to Fremont dated October 7, 1847: "We shall demolish him [Kearny] with all ease & overwhelm him with disgrace." [1] Both Jessie and the Senator made personal calls on President Polk to present Fremont's side of the thorny issue.

NED BEALE and Kit Carson appeared at Fortress Monroe as defense witnesses for Fremont in a preliminary hearing. They both admired Fremont and had little use for Kearny after his slanted reports about San Pasqual. Although Beale still suffered spells of illness from his ordeal there, he requested Senator Benton's help in returning to active duty. Finally, in early October, Beale received orders to return to California with Naval dispatches.

Kit Carson received orders about the same time to escort a brigade of troopers to California, and they left together. Jessie Benton accompanied them by river-boat as far as St. Louis and saw them off to Fort Leavenworth. Somewhere along the way Beale suffered another bout of illness and was forced to turn back. Carson continued on without him. Two weeks of rest seemed to cure Beale, but in September Jessie Fremont requested that he remain in Washington to testify in her husband's behalf at his court martial. He did so with no results.

In early January 1848 Beale received orders to rejoin the Pacific squadron. After a detour to Jamaica, he reached Panama and made his way to the U.S.S. *Ohio* commanded by Commodore Thomas ap Catesby Jones in Callao, Peru. Meanwhile, Fremont's court martial found him guilty of all charges, and he resigned his commission.

In May Beale's ship, the *Ohio*, was in Mexican waters when word came about the discovery of gold at Sutter's Sawmill in present Coloma several months earlier (see Sutter). Eager to return east, Beale volunteered to take the news and some official dispatches to Washington. Commodore Jones agreed and Beale left in late July to cross Mexico overland from San Blas, via Mexico City, to Vera Cruz. From there he would go by ship to the East Coast. He had purchased some gold samples, which he took with him, and one of the dispatches he was to carry—written by Commodore Thomas ap Catesby Jones to the Secretary of Navy—explained the problems caused by the Gold Rush:

> Nothing, sir, can exceed the deplorable state of things in all upper California at this time, and the maddening effect of the gold mania. Even men having a balance due them of over $1000 have deserted. For years to come it will be impossible for the United States to maintain any naval or military establishments in California, as no hope of reward or punishment is sufficient. To send troops out here would be needless as they would immediately desert.

Though Beale was pursued and nearly killed by bands of determined *bandidos* on his journey across Mexico, he reached Mexico City in August. After resting for a few days, he left for Vera Cruz which he reached after 60 hours of hard riding. He rested there only a few days before boarding a ship heading for Mobile, Alabama. There he caught riverboats up the Mississippi and Ohio rivers to Pittsburgh. He went from there to Washington by stage, arriving in mid-September 1848. Beale's dispatches and gold samples were the first real evidence delivered there, and he again found himself the center of attention.

Before long other dispatches and gold samples were delivered from Colonel Richard Mason by Lt. Lucian Loeser. Most of Beale's gold was displayed at the U.S. Patent office, while the remainder was fashioned into an engagement ring for his patient fiancee, Mary Engle Edwards. After being feted in New York by Senator Benton and others, Beale was given yet another assignment to deliver dispatches in Santa Fe, California and Oregon.

This time he would go overland, and he left for Fort Leavenworth in mid-November with some raw recruits heading for Oregon. After passing Bent's Fort, they encountered terrible freezing weather, endured Indian attacks—during which Beale was nearly killed—and finally made their way to safety at Santa Fe on Christmas day. Beale described his condition as "on foot and nearly naked." The journey was turning into a disaster, and he discharged seven unfit men and recruited eight others.

LEAVING SANTA FE in January 1849, they were caught in a blizzard crossing the Sierra de los Mimbres. Seven men deserted him there and were never heard from again. Following the trail he had taken two years before with Kit Carson, Beale crossed the Mojave desert into the San Joaquin Valley, via Tejon Pass; by April had delivered his dispatches to Colonel Richard Mason in San Francisco.

After only two days, he was ordered to carry more dispatches to Washington. Reaching Panama City by ship, he was surprised to meet Jessie Fremont, who was seeking a ship to San Francisco along with thousands of frantic gold seekers. With the help of friends, she had journeyed to Panama with her daughter, Lily. Fremont was traveling overland to meet them in San Francisco. The Isthmus crossing had become fairly routine for Beale, and he reached Washington in May 1849.

With him he had carried an eight-pound chunk of consigned gold, which went on display at Barnum's Museum in Philadelphia. Beale then went to Chester, Pennsylvania to wed Mary Edwards in her father's home. Unbelievable as it sounds, he left the next day with more dispatches for California. Though his wife wished to accompany him, he refused, assuming it would be too hard on her. Again he traveled the Panama route and by coincidence met his boyhood friend, Bayard Taylor, a journalist for Horace Greeley's *New York Tribune,* who was on his way to California to write about the Gold Rush. He knew Beale would be of great assistance, and he convinced the Naval courier to take to time off to travel with him.

After delivering his dispatches in San Francisco, Beale and Taylor visited with John and Jessie Fremont in San Jose, where they learned of Fremont's successful gold mining on his Mariposas ranch. Moving on to Stockton, they traveled upriver to the Southern mines. There they ran into Andres Pico, who was mining with a group of Mexicans. They spent some interesting hours reminiscing over the war before moving on. When Beale's leave ran out they returned to San Francisco.

In September he and Taylor traveled to Monterey to cover the Constitutional Convention, after which Beale spent time with the Fremonts in their new San Francisco home. He left for the East that fall with dispatches, including a draft of the new California Constitution. After delivering them in Washington, he joined his lonely bride in Chester, Pennsylvania, arriving there before the end of the year.

In March 1850 Beale became the father of a new daughter, named Mary, after her mother. He also was the proud recipient of Taylor's new book *El Dorado*, which the author dedicated to him. By then Robert Stockton had retired from the navy and became associated with William H. Aspinwall in a company to install gold mining machinery on property leased from J. C. Fremont at his Mariposas ranch. In April Beale left for California to carry naval dispatches and to oversee delivery of Stockton's mining machinery, which was aboard the same vessel in which he traveled. Upon completion of these heavy responsibilities, Beale returned home that fall to find that his long awaited promotion to full lieutenant had been received. He was also granted a one year liberty or leave of absence.

Meanwhile, returns from the Stockton-Aspinwall mining investment had proved disappointing, and Stockton turned to Ned Beale for help. When offered the position of Superintendent of California operations, Beale accepted the job and left for California in mid-January 1851. It wasn't long before Beale realized the mining venture would not pay off without another substantial investment.

He knew the company would not approve it, so he sold off the machinery for what it would bring and looked for other investment opportunities. Having observed that freighting supplies to the mines paid handsomely, he bought a string of pack mules, hired capable mule skinners and began a freighting venture. Within a year he earned the company about $100,000 and had pocketed $13,000 in commissions for himself. Finding that he enjoyed the challenge of self-employment, he submitted his resignation to the Navy.

For years Beale had been disturbed by shoddy treatment meted out to the Indians, especially those in California, who were suffering greatly from cruel treatment by argonauts during the Gold Rush. With help and blessings from Senator Benton and other political friends, Beale was appointed Superintendent of Indian affairs for California.

After receiving an adequate congressional appropriation during the spring of 1852, he moved his family to San Francisco. His mission was to investigate conditions and submit recommendations to control and protect California Indians. In San Francisco he was befriended by Governor Bigler and Lt. Ulysses S. Grant, then called Sam Grant.

Soon the sympathetic governor appointed Beale a General in the State Militia to provide more leverage in dealing with the army over Indian affairs. After confirming that conditions for Indians were even worse than he thought, Beale took his family east again to submit his reports to President Fillmore. His reports were apparently well received, for one of President Fillmore's last acts was adding the Nevada Indians to Beale's jurisdiction.

Beale's appointment was approved by incoming President Pierce, who also appointed Kit Carson Indian Agent for New Mexico and Thomas Fitzpatrick, another Fremont guide, as agent for tribes of the upper Platte and Arkansas rivers. Finally congress passed another appropriation bill to provide five Indian reservations in California, half of what Beale had requested.

While Beale was trying to save the Indians from what amounted to mass extermination, congress authorized explorations in the west to open more dependable routes. With the help of Senator Benton, Beale was to lead one of these parties on his way back to California. Besides opening a viable road, he was to look for possible sites for Indian reservations. This time Mary would stay at her family home in Chester.

Beale hired as his assistant, Gwynne Harris Heap, a friend eager to see the West. He left Westport Landing in mid-May 1853 with Heap and eleven others, all riding horseback and leading pack-mules. The Beale-Heap party was successful in finding a new central route over the Rockies, and they entered California the end of July, via Cajon Pass into San Bernardino Valley.

Beale acquired valuable experience dealing with Indians from varied tribes along the way, but he apparently located no reservation sites and built no roads. Perhaps the expedition provided mostly a convenient, expense paid journey back to California. Senator Benton's interest was in establishing a route for a railroad; his priorities did not include potential Indian reservations. Heap's journal tells of his relief at arriving safely in California:

> We obtained fresh horses, and a gallop of thirty-five miles...brought us to the city of Los Angeles, where every kindness and attention was shown us by Mr. Wilson [Don Benito], Indian Agent, and his accomplished lady...The remainder of our party arrived two days later, and thus, without serious accident to any of the men, and with the loss of only three of the mules, we accomplished the distance from Westport to Los Angeles in exactly 100 days.

UPON HIS ARRIVAL in Los Angeles, Beale resumed his duties as Commissioner of Indian Affairs and began scouting out possible reservation sites. In this formidable task he used Benjamin Wilson—also known as Don Benito Wilson—who was a well-to-do settler and Indian Agent in Los Angeles (see Wilson). Accompanied by Wilson and others, Beale explored the vast San Joaquin Valley for likely sites. They selected a southeastern corner of an area called Tejon Valley—south of present-day Bakersfield—as the best choice for a full scale reservation.

Alex Godey, Beal's old friend from San Pasqual, had been managing Fremont's Mariposa cattle ranch and operating a ferry on the San

Joaquin River. When he learned that Beale had returned to California, he joined him as a sub-Indian Agent. He knew the Tejon country better than most and was well liked by Indians there. Beale's aim was to find good land with adequate water and to teach the Indians to be self sufficient through agriculture, without moving them great distances from their homelands. It was similar to the old Franciscan mission objectives.

Unfortunately he found himself in a constant conflict with government bureaucrats who disagreed with his concepts, whether for philosophical or for selfish reasons. Even those who agreed, including Senator Benton, were unable to gain enough Congressional support for the funding to carry out his somewhat grandiose plans. Beale used what funds he did have to move 500 Indians from the Feather River to the Tejon reserve, which was called the Sebastian Reservation. Beale's wife and daughter joined him there in June 1854.

Shortly after, he submitted a report stating that 2,500 Indians there had planted 2,000 acres in wheat, 500 in barley and 150 in corn. Twelve white men were also employed, including Gwynne Heap. In his zeal to get things done, Beale over-spent his budget, his record-keeping was not the best and his reports were tardy. As a result, Special Treasury Agent J. Ross Browne was sent to audit his books.

Though he found no evidence of fraud or gross negligence, Browne could not defend Beale's cost over-runs. Finally Beale took Mary with him to Washington to defend himself in person. He was replaced as superintendent by Thomas Henley. In 1855, J. Ross Browne went to Washington to testify for Beale, who was eventually vindicated but not reinstated to his former position.

He and Mary sailed from New York to California later in the year, accompanied by J. Ross Browne and his family. During his absence, the U.S. Army had authorized construction of Fort Tejon on the upper elevations of reservation property. It was to protect Indians living on the upper reservation and in the lower stretches of the San Joaquin Valley below. By the time of Beale's arrival, construction of adobe buildings for the fort was just getting underway.

To his dismay, Beale found conditions under Superintendent Henley were deteriorating rapidly. When he attempted to assist Henley in correcting obvious problems, he was ignored, and watched helplessly as disillusioned Indians left the reservation. An article in the *Sacramento Union* summed it up succinctly:

> The Tejon reservation, for which so much was hoped, is nothing but a byword. It is a year since Henley stepped into the shoes of Lieutenant Beale, who had carried out to the fullest extent the designs of the government. Henley's mismanagement of Indian affairs has resulted in the thorough and complete wreck of this once flourishing establishment.

Apparently the army agreed. Construction of Fort Tejon was halted at the half way point because there were not enough Indians left in the area to warrant it.

Though Beale was out of work, he purchased (in his wife's name) the 49,000 acre Rancho la Liebre, which adjoined the Tejon reservation, for three cents an acre. Indians who lived on his property were urged to stay; in effect, the Beales were establishing their own private reservation, where they built a large adobe ranch-house—the first home they had ever owned.

Alex Godey had been employed as Henley's assistant, but left to join Beale and another partner to raise cattle on the ranch. When Mary was ready to give birth to her second child, the Beales left the ranch in the capable hands of Godey and moved to San Francisco. While there, Beale was asked by the governor to assert his commission as a general in the militia to quell a serious Indian uprising in the Tule River region.

Beale was given no funds to carry out his mission, but he convinced the Indians to return to their reservations, where they would be fed by the government. Henley, still Superintendent of Indian Affairs, took exception to what he considered Beale's interference in his duties. He refused to honor the peace agreement, but Beale's mission had been accomplished to the satisfaction of the army and he returned to San Francisco in July. He found the city controlled by the vigilantes and in need of a sheriff. Beale was appointed sheriff, but he was opposed by some because he was a non-resident, and the incumbent refused to step down. He may not have served at all; if so, he did not seek a "second term" because by 1856 he had other fish to fry. The "fish" turned out to be camels.

FOR YEARS certain army officers had entertained the idea of using camels rather than mules to transport supplies across the desert. The idea had been revived by Major Wayne in 1853, and he finally persuaded Secretary of War Jefferson Davis to approve a trial run a year later. Though he knew nothing about camels, Beale thought the idea had merit. Eventually 78 camels were procured and brought to Texas. There they languished while politicians wrangled. Finally in 1856 an expedition was authorized to survey a wagon road from New Mexico to the Colorado River. Some of the camels were to be used on a trial basis, and President Buchanan named Ned Beale to lead this unusual expedition.

He was allowed 25 soldiers as an escort and was to "start construction of the road which he would make passable for loaded wagons throughout." After reaching the Colorado, he would "proceed to Fort Tejon along the route best adapted to the passage of troops." Beale's estimated budget of nearly $50,000 was approved in April 1857. He hired his old companion Gwynne Heap as his first assistant, and they recruited others who they thought could do the job. The entire party was then transported by ship to Texas, where they would pick up the camels.

Teamsters, packers and mules were added, and Jesse Chisholm, who later blazed the "Chisholm trail" from Texas to Kansas, was hired as a guide. Their first destination was Howard's Ranch near Camp Verde, Texas, where Beale acquired eight dromedaries and 17 bactrians and their foals. Only two knowledgeable Arab "cameleers" agreed to go along, so it was imperative that others learn to control the difficult beasts. They were known for their odor and habit of spitting on handlers. A few days were required before the horses and mules would accept the camels. Their journey to destiny began in June.

IT TOOK A MONTH to cover the 500 miles to El Paso, and by then Beale's appreciation of camels had increased dramatically. He wrote, "I would rather undertake the management of twenty camels than five mules." They knelt to be loaded—albeit with much moaning and groaning. They ate brush rather than grass, often went without water and did not need shoes. And they carried 500 to 700 pounds each, compared to 200 per mule. The camels even carried kegs of water and bags of grain for the mules.

The expedition reached Albuquerque by August 5th without serious incident. There the party bought a flock of sheep and drove them along to provide fresh mutton. Arab camel drivers did not like beef. Beale found the Zuni pueblo, about 12 miles from the present-day Arizona border, of much interest. Following the 35th parallel west, they mapped as they went and established a road still used today.

Soon Beale's party passed "Beale's Spring," near present-day Kingman, and entered the Black Mountains. When they reached the Colorado River, they found the formerly treacherous Mojave Indians "fat, merry, barefoot and semi-naked." One greeted them with fractured English: "God damn my soul eyes. How do do!" [2] They traded old clothes and trinkets for fresh vegetables and fruit, and ferried their supplies across the river in India-rubber rafts brought for that purpose.

Despite warnings that camels couldn't swim, they finally crossed at a place promptly named "Beale's Crossing." They then followed the U.S. Surveyor's trail from the Colorado River toward Los Angeles. Beale sent a few men with two camels to Los Angeles, while he continued on to Fort Tejon with the main party. Construction had resumed there, and new buildings had been completed. Beale judged it one of the finest forts on the Pacific Coast.

In January 1858 Beale led his camel caravan to Los Angeles and left-the on the 10th for the return journey east. Reaching Beale's Crossing on the Colorado River January 23rd, they were amazed to find the steamboat *General Jesup* there, just returned from an exploratory voyage upstream. The picture is described in a letter Beale wrote:

I had brought the camels with me, and as they stood on the bank, surrounded by hundreds of wild, unclad savages, mixed with these the dragoons of my escort, and the steamer slowly revolving her wheels preparatory to start, it was a curious and interesting picture.

Beale decided to send the camels and some of the soldiers back to Fort Tejon, while he continued on by horse and mule. Retracing the trail he had taken westward, he found it being used by Indians and other travelers, making it a recognized "road." When they reached the Zuni pueblo in mid-February, Beale sent more of the soldier escorts back to Fort Defiance. Beale's party reached Albuquerque on the 21st, where he disbanded his expedition.

He traveled to Missouri by stagecoach, stopping overnight in St. Louis, where he ran into his old friend, U.S. "Sam" Grant, who had fallen on hard times since leaving the army four years earlier and was farming a place he called "Hardscrabble." When Beale reached Washington, his expedition was highly praised for its work, and he was requested to lead another "Camel caravan" to return and finish what he had started.

In August 1858 Beale received orders to acquire camels, recruit workers and pick up an army escort to "connect the road with the work you were engaged on last year." Again Jessie Chisholm was hired as a guide. The road was to connect Fort Smith, Arkansas, with Albuquerque and continue on to Southern California. Camp Verde, Texas, was to supply 25 camels, while other camels were to bring supplies from Fort Tejon and meet Beale's work party at the Colorado River crossing.

The expedition, including Beale's brother, George, left November 1, 1858 and spent two miserable months in bad weather completing the section from Fort Smith to Albuquerque. It was spring the following year before they approached the Colorado River, by which time Beale's supplies were running low. The supply train from Fort Tejon was late, having been delayed because of Indian attacks. The Mojaves were again on the war path and had raided a cache to steal most of the supplies brought from Fort Tejon.

As a result, Beale took some men and traveled to Los Angeles to acquire more badly needed supplies. Though this group also suffered Indian attacks on the return trip, they got through and mid-summer had completed most of the difficult road work, including grading and tree and rock removal. By August 1859 Beale had returned to his family in Chester, and by the following year he had another child. The pesky road across present-day Arizona was finally completed.

Beale then moved his family back to the California ranch near Fort Tejon, which was slated to be abandoned. But before anything was done the Civil War broke out, and the entire garrison left for the East in June

1861. The fort remained vacant except for a year in 1863-64, when it was occupied by California volunteers. It was then abandoned for good but has since been restored as a state historical park.

Shortly after President Abraham Lincoln's inauguration, Beale was appointed United States Surveyor General for California. This required a move to San Francisco, where he and Mary leased the recently vacated Fremont house on Black Point (today's Fort Mason). John C. Fremont had been recalled to the Army and made a Major General. Jessie and the children moved east with him, leaving writer Bret Harte, whom Beale hired as a clerk.

While the new Surveyor General was learning his job, he and Mary were devastated by the death of their two-year-old son. Beale worked out his grief by trying to induce former foes, such as the Pico brothers in Los Angeles, to be loyal to President Lincoln (see Pico). A large group of Confederate sympathizers in California threatened to rebel if the conscription laws were applied to them. As a result, Beale urged Lincoln to repeal the draft in California. He did so, and the fledgling state was the only one granted this costly concession.

Theodore Judah was leading a survey team in the Sierra Nevada to lay out a site for the Central Pacific Railroad, and Beale was required to keep a team of his own surveyors with them to protect government interests. Construction of the railroad commenced on the Sacramento side of the Sierra Nevada in 1863. Meanwhile, Beale's farming and cattle raising enterprises were doing well with help from the Indian population who lived on his property. With money to invest, he bought into silver and gold mines.

By 1863 Fremont's house was taken over by the army for Fort Mason, and Beale moved his family to Nob Hill. By the following year, Beale, still only 42 years old, had had enough of his vexing government job. He was terminated in April and moved his family back to the ranch. While this was going on, France invaded Mexico and deposed President Pablo Juarez. Napoleon III replaced him with Ferdinand Maximilian Josef of Austria as emperor. Juarez retaliated by forming an army and crusading to oust the French. Beale took great interest in these events, to the extent of urging President Lincoln to purchase Baja California. But the president, deep in his own Civil War worries, was not able to concern himself with Mexico.

An ardent Juarez supporter was wealthy Samuel Brannan, the "Jack Mormon" who had brought a ship-load of Mormons to San Francisco in 1846 to establish his new "Zion". He agreed to finance and equip 100 volunteers to fight under Juarez, and Beale agreed to act as agent in shipping Juarez a large consignment of Austrian arms from Canada. Brannan's mercenaries sailed for Mexico during the spring of 1864.

When Beale's 5,000 rifles were confiscated in San Francisco by the port collector, he took his family to Washington, D.C. to appeal his case. He must have known President Lincoln was enduring extreme stress over the dreadful Civil War, yet he obviously felt the situation in Mexico could not be ignored. The President's reply follows:

> Napoleon has taken advantage of our weakness in our time of trouble in utter disregard of the Monroe Doctrine, but my policy must be to attend to one trouble at a time. If we get well out of our present difficulties and restore the Union, I propose to notify Napoleon that it is about time to take his army out of Mexico.

Beale returned to the ranch alone, a disappointed man. With the end of the Civil War in 1865, General U.S. Grant ordered Gen. Philip Sheridan to place himself in a position to assist Juarez against Maximilian in Mexico. Beale's 5,000 rifles, along with several thousand of the army's new repeating rifles, were then sent to Juarez. In 1867 Maximilian surrendered to Juarez and was promptly shot.

MEANWHILE, Beale was adding to his properties. In 1865 he bought the 97,000-acre Rancho El Tejon for $21,000, after which he bought the 35,000-acre Rancho Agua Caliente for $1,700. Both adjoined his Rancho la Liebre. In October 1866 he bought Rancho Castaic from Robert S. Baker for $65,000. This purchase included the abandoned Fort Tejon. He and Baker then entered into a cooperative stock-raising enterprise. Buildings at the fort were used by Beale as an outpost ranch for some of his workers. His four ranches—comprising some 203,000 acres—were then combined under the name Ranchos Tejon.

The ranch was known nationally as one of the largest sheep ranches in the country and remained in the Beale family for over 50 years. It spread forty miles from newly formed Kern County over the Tehachapi Mountains into Los Angeles County. During the mid-1860's, Beale graded a road from Fort Tejon into the San Fernando Valley, via "Beale's Cut" north of Mission San Fernando. When his road was completed, he negotiated a twenty-year contract with Los Angeles County to operate it as a toll road.

In 1872 Beale, Baker & Co. marketed 175,000 pounds of wool, grazed 125,000 sheep and 25,000 head of cattle. Beale also invested in other land, including 48,000 acres of Mission San Buena Ventura and a four-story hotel and office building in Chester, Pa. He had been a heavy supporter of his friend, Gen. U.S. Grant, who was elected president in 1868. Before Grant's re-election in 1872, Beale bought (in his wife's name) the historic family home, Decatur House, near the capitol in Washington, D.C. It was completely remodeled, and Mary Beale decorated and furnished it.

This and the family home in Chester became their homes for the rest of their lives, and Beale spent only two months a year at Rancho Tejon. Senator John Blain's youngest daughter, Harriet, married Beale's son, Truxtun, there. Beale's daughter, Emily, married John Roll McLean, publisher of the *Washington Post*. In 1875 Beale bought a 427 acre horse ranch and mansion near Hyattsville, Md. It was widely known as Hitching Post Hill, and the name was retained by the Beale family. Used as a summer home it was well known for raising quality horses.

IN 1876 President Grant named Beale United States Minister to Vienna, Austria, where he moved with his family that same year. During their exciting year in Vienna, Beale's last daughter, Mary, fell in love with George Bahkmeteff, Secretary for the Russian Embassy. When the Russian asked for her hand in marriage, Beale was violently opposed. But with his own family approving the marriage, Beale finally gave in.

When Grant's second term as president expired, the Beales joined the ex-president and his family in Paris for a joyful reunion. The Beales returned to the U.S. in 1878 and spent the following year at Ranchos Tejon. A terrible drought ravaged the land that year, during which Beale lost thousands of sheep and other livestock. He did manage to save 7,000 head of cattle by driving them to the Los Angeles area.

Beale was in Washington, D.C. in 1885, when his mother died. This was followed a short time later by the death of his best friend, Sam Grant. These tragedies took a toll on Beale, but he recovered to resume his busy schedule and annual commuting to California. He had invested in the Star Oil Company with his friend and partner, Robert Baker. The Star Oil Company eventually became Standard Oil of California, and Beale became a millionaire.

In March 1893 Beale returned home exhausted after helping on the reception committee for President Grover Cleveland's second-term inaugural ball. He went to bed with jaundice and died April 22 at the age of 71. After an elaborate memorial service, his cremated remains were buried at Chester Rural Cemetery.

Beale's career is surely one of the most amazing in California history. He had a special talent for being at the epicenter of the historic events of his lifetime. He counted among his friends the major figures in the nation, and he made countless contributions to California, Arizona, the Chester area in Pennsylvania, Washington, D.C., and the nation as a whole. El Morro National Monument in New Mexico was inscribed by men in Beale's camel caravan in 1857. Streets in Bakersfield, California, and San Francisco are named for him, as is a U. S. Air Force base.

See also Fort Tejon State Historical Park and a state historical landmark at the site of Bealville at Rancho le Libre in Kern County. There is also a state historical marker showing the site of the Sebastian Indian

Reservation on I5, about 7 mi. south of Mettler at Grapevine. In San Diego County is the San Pasqual Battlefield State Historic Park and plaques near there at Mule Hill and at Warner's Ranch. A pyramidal monument of stones honors Beale in Kingman, Arizona. It contains a plaque that sums up his life very well:

Edward Fitzgerald Beale
1822—1893
Pioneer In The Path of Empire
Hero In The War With Mexico
Lieutenant In The United States Navy
Appointed General By the Governor of California
Commanded Exploration of Wagon Route to the
Colorado River With the Only Camel Train
in American History, 1857-1858

BIBLIOGRAPHY

–Bancroft, Hubert H. *California Pioneer Register and Index.* Regional Publishing Co., Baltimore, MD, 1964.

–Benton, Thomas Hart. "Letter to John C. Fremont dated 7 October 1847." Southwestern Museum, Los Angeles, courtesy Charles Hill, Lotus, CA. [1]

–Briggs, Carl and Clyde Francis Trudell. *Quarterdeck & Saddlehorn, The Story of Edward F. Beale.* Arthur H. Clark Co., Glendale, CA, 1983. All quotations except [1] & [2] taken from this volume.

–Davis, William Heath. *Seventy-Five Years In California.* John Howell Books, San Francisco, 1967.

–Egan, Ferol. *Fremont, Explorer for a Restless Nation.* University of Nevada Press, Reno, 1985.

–Gay, Teressa. *James W. Marshall, A Biography.* Talisman Press, Georgetown, CA, 1967.

–Harlow, Neal. *California Conquered.* University of California Press, Berkeley, l982.

–Taylor, Bayard. *El Dorado.* University of Nebraska Press, Lincoln, 1949.

–Thompson, Gerald. *Edward F. Beale & The American West.* University of New Mexico Press, Albuquerque, 1983. [2]

James P. Beckwourth, Mountain Man
Courtesy California Department of Parks & Recreation

– 4 –

JAMES P. BECKWOURTH

1798–1866

WHILE JAMES PIERSON BECKWOURTH had visited California several times in the 1830s and early 40s as a large-scale horse thief, he did not reside there until after James Marshall's gold discovery in 1848. And though he remained in California only a decade, he left a rich legacy. His many years as a mountain man, during which he lived with, fought and loved Indians, trained him well for later life in the Far West. His father, Sir Jennings Beckwith (an inherited title), served as an officer during the Revolutionary War, after which he settled on a farm in Fredericksburg, Virginia. He was a slave owner or overseer and apparently had an enduring relationship with a slave named "Miss Kill."

Born April 26, 1798, James Beckwith (later changed to Beckwourth) was the third of thirteen children sired by his father. When he was around eight, the family pulled up stakes and moved west to land nestled between the confluence of the Missouri and Mississippi rivers east of St. Charles, Missouri. Virtually raised as a slave himself, young Beckwourth toiled in the fields with the other slaves and became as tough and sinewy as rawhide.

Indians in the area were hostile, forcing neighbors to band together in blockhouses during their frequent attacks. At age nine, Beckwourth was sent on a mule to deliver a sack of husked corn to a nearby gristmill to be ground into meal. As he passed a neighboring house about a mile from home, he was scared witless by the sight of the entire family lying dead and scalped from a recent Indian attack. The boy carried the gory sight in his memory forever.

At age fourteen, Beckwourth was sent to St. Louis and apprenticed to a blacksmith. After learning his trade and sprouting into a husky lad of nineteen, he got into a brawl with his employer over an affair with a girl. It ended with young Beckwourth leaving the area in search of a job. Instead of following his trade as a blacksmith, he traveled in a keelboat with some other men up the Mississippi River toward Galena, in northwestern Illinois, where they were to work in a lead mine.

But first they had to contend with large groups of Sauk and Fox Indians, who controlled the area. Several weeks of intense negotiations taught Beckwourth the Indians' ways and how to get along with them. As they grew to trust him, they showed him their prime hunting grounds. Soon he found himself working as a professional hunter for the mine workers; his stalking and skills with a rifle improved rapidly.

After 18 months at Galena, Beckwourth left for New Orleans, finding that he enjoyed traveling. His wanderlust afflicted him for the rest of his life. He was in his prime by 1824, when fur trapping was coming into its own. That fall he left St. Louis as a horse buyer and hunter with General Ashley's Rocky Mountain Fur Company. There he found himself with the likes of Jedediah Smith, Jim Bridger and James Clyman (see Smith & Clyman).

Thomas Fitzpatrick joined them at Fort Atkinson, and Ashley's party of 25 men rode off leading many pack mules loaded with trade goods and food. They had one wagon, the first to be used north of the Santa Fe Trail. After traveling up the Platte River Valley in late fall, where they hoped to trade with Pawnee Indians, they were devastated to find their villages deserted. Winter was upon them and food was running low by the time they reached the confluence of the North and South Forks of the Platte River. There they finally found some Pawnees who were willing to trade. Continuing up the South Platte, their wagon had to be abandoned in deep snow drifts. In late January 1825 Beckwourth caught his first sight of the Rocky Mountains, and they made camp at present-day Greeley, Colorado. It was there that he learned the tricky trade of beaver trapping.

TWO WEEKS LATER they were on their way again, this time across the Continental Divide, via the Great Divide Basin. Upon reaching the Green River near its confluence with the Big Sandy, Ashley split the party into four groups to trap in opposite directions. Beckwourth was assigned to James Clyman's group, and they were to meet the others later. Before long they were joined by a band of seemingly friendly Indians, who attacked them at night without warning. One trapper was killed, but Beckwourth and the others fought valiantly and escaped.

After reuniting with the main party farther down the Green River, they made their way to a trapper's rendezvous on Henry's Fork in early July 1825. Beckwourth was enthralled with the sight of trappers and Indians meeting to exchange furs for trade goods and thoroughly debauching themselves. Here, racial differences were forgotten; a black man was as welcome as anyone.

Beckwourth decided to return the following year, but first he would help deliver 9,000 pelts to St. Louis. He found the journey east much easier than his trip west, when they crossed South Pass and followed the

Wind River toward the Big Horn. Along the way they were visited by a large band of Crow Indians, who were looking for two of their missing warriors. Unbeknownst to the Indians, the two Crows had been killed by the trappers when they were caught rifling their furs the day before.

Upon receiving gifts, the Indians calmed a bit and finally left. There were more skirmishes with hostiles before the trappers reached the Big Horn River. Buffalo were plentiful, and enough were killed and skinned to provide hides to make bullboats. These were used to float the men and furs down to the Yellowstone River and finally to Fort Union on the Missouri River. There Beckwourth met Edward "Cut nose" Rose, another black trapper. Their rarity alone guaranteed comradery.

Fortunately the trappers met an expedition with keelboats at the fort, and they agreed to transport them downriver to St. Louis. It was September when Beckwourth left the party at Council Bluffs, where he had family, including his father. Later he moved on down to St. Louis. Ashley made a fortune from his furs and gave his men a $300 bonus. For the first time Beckwourth had real money, and he used some of it for a rip-roaring spree.

By the end of October 1825 he was again on his way from St. Louis as a free trapper under Jedediah Smith. This time they traveled up the south bank of the Missouri River to the Kansas, which was followed to the Republican River. Because of severe weather and food shortages, they remained there. By then many of their horses and pack mules had died, and Moses "Black" Harris was selected to journey 300 miles on foot into Pawnee Indian country to replace them. If he was unsuccessful, he was to make his way back to St. Louis to seek help from General Ashley. When Smith asked for volunteers to accompany Harris, Beckwourth was the only one. They would be carrying 25-pound backpacks of food and trade goods, plus their guns and ammunition, and no one else felt capable of keeping up with the fleet-footed Harris.

Beckwourth was able to keep the pace, however, and he learned a great deal from the mountain man about Indian lore and living off the land. The weather was freezing, and their provisions were gone by the time they reached the Pawnee village. To their dismay the Pawnees had already left for their winter quarters, which was too far distant. This meant a nine to ten day-trek back to the Missouri River, living off the land along the way.

To lighten their loads, they discarded everything except their guns and ammunition—even their blankets. With the help of friendly Indians, they finally reached the river. Harris went back to St. Louis, while Beckwourth wintered at F. G. Chouteau's trading post. General Ashley's party picked him up in March 1826, and they returned to join Smith and his men near the Grand Island of the Platte River.

Now that they were reunited with fresh livestock, the party moved up the North Fork of the Platte River, over South Pass, and once again reached the Green River. In June they joined the second trapper's rendezvous at Cache Valley (present Utah), which was even larger than the year before; it became an annual affair at different locations.

This was to be General Ashley's last year in the mountains, as he sold out to Jed Smith, William Sublette and David Jackson. In his autobiography, Beckwourth wrote about Ashley's dramatic departure from the business. They had had their differences, some of them serious; nevertheless, Ashley had been a mentor to Beckwourth, and the parting was bitter-sweet. Following is Beckwourth's version of Ashley's farewell words to him:

> I like brave men, but I fear you are reckless in your bravery...Caution is always commendable, and especially is it necessary in encounters with Indians. I wish you to be careful of yourself, and pay attention to your health, for, with the powerful constitution you possess, you have many valuable years before you...Whenever you return home, come and see me, James; you will be a thousand times welcome; and should you ever be in need of assistance, call on me first. Goodbye. [Beckwourth continues]: He left the camp amid deafening cheers from the whole crowd. I did not see him again until the year 1836.

WHEN THE rendezvous ended, Beckwourth joined William Sublette's group, which moved north toward the Teton range, via the Snake River into Blackfoot country. Trapping along the upper Columbia and Missouri rivers, they were among the first white trappers to enter the area that eventually became Yellowstone National Park. They did well there before returning to Cache Valley for the long winter.

While there, they were attacked by a large party of vengeful Blackfoot Indians, who stole some of their horses. During the fierce fighting, Beckwourth allegedly slipped away to seek help from another party of trappers in the area. According to Beckwourth, who was known for telling tall tales, they rode back just in time to save the others from certain disaster; however, Beckwourth reportedly took an arrow in his right arm. When the Indians finally rode off, they left many dead. Four trappers were killed and seven wounded.

By now Beckwourth was a well-seasoned, well-respected mountain man who seemed capable of nearly any challenge. During the spring of 1827 he joined Thomas Fitzpatrick to trap the Portneuf and Bear rivers, before they joined the trapper's rendezvous at Bear Lake. Beckwourth's Indian fighting skills were needed there when the encampment was attacked by Blackfoot Indians seeking revenge against the trappers and their friends, the Snakes. When it was over, the Indians broke off the fighting with heavy casualties. Finally they were beginning to believe that their arrows and clubs were no match for the trapper's rifles and canny fighting ability.

With the rendezvous at an and, Beckwourth reportedly joined a party led by William Sublette and traveled into Blackfoot country. He and another daring trapper apparently separated from Sublette to trade with the treacherous Blackfeet along the Beaverhead River, a tributary of the Upper Missouri. Several weeks later Beckwourth and his partner rejoined Sublette to winter in an area of the Snake River protected from the worst of the weather.

When the spring thaw permitted, Sublette's party moved to the Salmon River in present-day Idaho, where one of the party was killed by Blackfeet. Several more skirmishes with the determined hostiles drove them back to the Snake River and south to Bear Lake for the 1828 rendezvous. Shortly after, Beckwourth and two companions made contact with another party led by Robert Campbell. When they were attacked by Blackfeet, they made a stand for a few hours before their ammunition ran dangerously low. Beckwourth and another man then rode through the furious tribesmen to seek help from Sublette's party at Bear Lake. When they returned with reinforcements, they found the Indians gone and Campbell's party safe.

B ECKWOURTH, Campbell and a small party journeyed into Powder River country that fall, where they were joined by a band of friendly Crow Indians. A trapper named Caleb Greenwood, who loved tall tales, told the Crows that Beckwourth was really a Crow Indian like themselves (see Greenwood). Greenwood was "married" to a Crow woman himself; he liked them and thought they would accept Beckwourth if they thought he was one of them. When pressed for details, he explained that Beckwourth had been stolen by Cheyennes as a young child. Later he had been sold to the trappers and had become the greatest brave among them.

This story served Beckwourth well as he moved farther into Crow country. He was trapping alone with James Bridger, when they separated to check out adjoining creeks for beaver. Suddenly Beckwourth found himself surrounded by Crow Indians, who took him prisoner and forced him to their village. Some of them had heard Greenwood's story, and they examined him thoroughly, especially one old squaw. With an excited look, she sprang up and pronounced him her long lost son!

Beckwourth dared not deny it, and for the first time in this hostile land he began to feel secure and decided to join them. Later he wrote:

> ...I said to myself, "I can trap in their streams unmolested and derive more profit under their protection than if among my own men, exposed incessantly to assassination and alarm." I therefore

resolved to abide with them, to guard my secret, to do my best in their company, and in assisting them to subdue their enemies. [1]

After resigning from Smith, Jackson and Sublette in 1829, Beckwourth was befriended by an Indian named Big Bowl and soon found himself engaged to marry one of Big Bowl's daughters, a comely young lass named Still Water. To seal the bargain, one of Still Water's brothers presented Beckwourth with 20 good horses. Still Water turned out an excellent choice; she proved a good wife for the exuberant bridegroom, sewing him a handsome new outfit of clothes from the finest buckskin. His new Indian name was Morning Star. He may have had another wife called Pine leaf and probably had children by them both.

A FEW YEARS LATER in 1833 he was employed by the American Fur Company, originally organized by John Jacob Astor. He continued trapping and encouraged the Crows to do the same and trade with his company. Though Beckwourth did not share the Crow's joy in raiding other tribes for horses or slaves, he was forced to take part on occasion and proved himself time and again as a mighty warrior. He also discouraged them from drinking firewater, which had brought ruin to many.

Bad luck and bad decisions during almost constant inter-tribal warfare had proven costly to the Crows, especially when their main chief, A-ra-poo-ash was killed on the battlefield. Before he died, he proclaimed Morning Star, or Red Arm, as Beckwourth was now being called, as the new Crow Chief. One of his first acts as chief was to move his people to the banks of the Rosebud River (Montana), where he gave them a rousing speech. He then led them on a full-scale attack against the Blackfeet, which resulted in a decisive victory for his howling Crow warriors. As a result, Beckwourth's Indian name was changed to Medicine Calf.

Beckwourth adapted well to life with the Crows and devoted a good portion of his life to them. The name "Crow" was coined by white men from the French word Corbeaux. The Indians of that name called themselves Absaroka, meaning sparrow hawk. Their territory included much of what we now call Yellowstone Park, and they were surrounded by the Blackfoot to the north; the Flathead, west; the Snakes (Shoshone), south; the Sioux and Assiniboine to the east.

The Crows were among the world's finest horsemen and counted their wealth by the number and quality of horses they owned. This was the prime motivation behind their almost constant raids on neighboring tribes and white men alike. As did other plains tribes, they depended on buffalo for their sustenance. Other than hunting these shaggy beasts, their main activities consisted of waging war, horse theft, robbery and kidnapping, all considered legitimate Indian practices at the time.

For Beckwourth to maintain his tribal status as chief, he had to lead his warriors in these pursuits without regard to the white man's different moral code. There is little doubt that he enjoyed the calculated risks, thrills and prestige these depredations offered an adventurous young man like himself. But as he matured, these activities began to pale, and he drew the line at attacking whites; in fact, he often went out of his way to protect them. Nevertheless, there were those who said—with some justification—that he was as savage as any Indian.

During the summer of 1835, Beckwourth joined his old friend, Thomas "Peg-Leg" Smith and a renegade Ute Indian named Walkara to trade furs for horses in California. The horses would be herded back to the Rocky Mountain area to be sold at a large profit. With around sixty Ute warriors, they and a few other white men left Sanpete Valley (Utah) and traveled the Old Spanish Trail to the pueblo of Los Angeles.

When they found horses expensive and not easily obtained there, Walkara grew impatient and turned his warriors loose to raid ranchos of around 600 horses, which were quickly driven out of the country toward their homeland. Beckwourth and Smith were tarred by the same brush, so to speak, and saw no alternative but to run off with them. To have stayed behind would brand them as consorts of the ruthless Ute raiders, and they would risk severe punishment at the hands of the furious *rancheros*.

After wintering near the Great Salt Lake, Beckwourth and Smith drove their share of the horses to Bent's Fort to sell. Beckwourth returned to the Crows, but after having spent a decade with them, he found himself longing to see St. Louis and his family again. His feelings at the time are expressed in his autobiography as follows:

> In good truth, I was tired of savage life under any aspect. I knew that, if I remained with them [the Crows], it would be war and carnage to the end of this chapter, and my mind sickened at the repetition of such scenes....I felt I was not doing justice to myself to relapse irretrievably into barbarism.

He left his people in 1836 under the care of Samuel Tulloch, chief trader for the American Fur Company at Fort Cass, located north of the Big Horn River. Beckwourth had helped establish this trading post four years earlier. In St. Louis Beckwourth located one his sisters, who told him of his father's death many years before. He found a few old friends, but they failed to recognize him at first because he dressed like an Indian and looked the part. While he was there that fall he joined a small company of volunteers as a captain in the U. S. Army to fight in the Seminole Indian campaign in Florida.

When their ship sailed for Tampa, via New Orleans, it ran aground near its destination and most of the men were taken off by a rescue vessel. Captain Beckwourth and twelve others stayed aboard until their valuable horses and fodder could be saved. Although Beckwourth served primarily as a courier, he did take part in the bloody battle of Okeechobee. As might be expected, he didn't take well to military life and did not re-enlist after his term ran out in the spring of 1837.

BACK IN ST. LOUIS Beckwourth returned to fur trading with William Sublette and Louis Vasquez in Cheyenne Indian country. He helped establish trading posts on the South Platte River well above Bent's Fort on the Arkansas River. Two years later he again joined with "Peg-leg" Smith and Walkara to plan another horse raid in Southern California.

Because Beckwourth wasn't known there, he was chosen to travel around the area to scout out the best horses vulnerable to theft. Walkara and the others would follow during the spring of 1840 with around 150 Ute warriors to perform the actual thefts. The well-planned raids took only three days to accumulate nearly 5,000 horses, which were quickly driven over Cajon Pass and east across the Mojave Desert. This was the largest theft yet.

The horses were sold or traded off at Fort Bridger and Bent's Fort, after which Beckwourth worked for William Bent. Later he started a trading venture of his own in the south Platte country of present-day Colorado. He also married a young Mexican girl named Louisa Sandoval. With some other trappers, he helped build a small fort and settlement called Fort Pueblo, which later became Pueblo, Colorado. John C. Fremont and Kit Carson visited Beckwourth there in 1843 heading west and again in 1844 going east.

Apparently Beckwourth didn't do well at the fort, because later that same year he joined fifteen other men in a pack train loaded with trade goods and whiskey, again heading for Los Angeles. While trading there, Beckwourth got caught up in the overthrow of Governor Micheltorena on the side of the rebels led by former Governor Juan Alvarado and General José Castro.

After Micheltorena was deposed in early 1845, Beckwourth may have been forgiven for his prior crimes because of his service to the rebels. He continued his trading ventures but also spied out good horses that were vulnerable to theft. When war between the United States and Mexico appeared inevitable the following spring, he and his companions executed another well-planned raid to steal over a thousand horses, which were again driven safely over Cajon Pass into Utah territory.

When Beckwourth returned for his wife, he found she had remarried and left with his daughter, Matilda. Leaving the area with his profits from the stolen horses, he and a horse-stealing partner bought a small hotel and bar in Santa Fe. By then war had broken out between the U.S. and Mexico, and General Stephen Kearny was in Santa Fe with a small army preparing to leave for California. General Kearny, who apparently made Beckwourth's hotel his headquarters, then used Beckwourth as a courier between Santa Fe and Fort Leavenworth.

A few months after Kearny and his men left during the fall of 1846, Beckwourth joined a band of volunteers under Col. Sterling Price to drive Mexican forces out of Taos. About a year after the Mexican War was over, and U. S. occupation forces controlled California, news about the James Marshall's gold discovery in January 1848 began circulating. Upon hearing the news early that summer, Beckwourth wasted little time in selling out his business to join the gold rush (See Marshall).

While he did not do well at mining, he did better peddling goods and miner's supplies throughout the Southern mines. In 1850 Beckwourth engaged a friend to take down his life's story as he could not write. But before it was completed, the two of them parted and Beckwourth did some prospecting in the Northern mines. In 1851 he discovered an easier route across the northern Sierra Nevada range and convinced some Marysville investors to finance a wagon road there to enhance their businesses. The route is now called Beckwourth Pass.

Beckwourth then traveled to Truckee Meadows (now Reno, Nevada) to persuade emigrants and argonauts to try his new route. Successful in his quest, Beckwourth led a wagon train across his pass into the newly established town of Marysville that autumn. Unfortunately, the town burned to the ground that very night, and he was forced to curtail any more travel there until the following year.

WHILE WAITING OUT the winter at Indian Bar, near Marysville, Beckwourth met a journalist named Thomas D. Bonner and offered to let him finish his memoirs and autobiography. This the former newspaperman agreed to do in 1852, and it was subsequently completed and published in 1856 (see bibliography under Shepard). Unfortunately it is so loaded with exaggerations and outright fabrications that it is considered unreliable as an objective historical source.

That spring Beckwourth claimed land on the west side of his newly discovered pass, where he constructed a small hotel and store. He hoped the place would attract many travelers who would use this route in lieu of the more difficult Truckee Pass (now Donner Pass) to reach the northern mines. The tiny settlement and the pass were both named for the aging mountain man.

When the gold rush began slowing and business fell off at Beckwourth's tiny settlement, he left and returned to St. Louis in the late 1850s. Some say a vigilance committee ran him out for horse theft. From there he went to Denver in 1859 to run a store for his old friend, Louis Vasquez and Louis's nephew, A. Pike Vasquez. He did well there, and a year later—at age 62—he married Elizabeth Ledbetter and bought land in the Denver area, where he built a store and began farming.

Four years later his wife left him, taking their only son with her (an infant daughter had died earlier). Shortly after, Beckwourth took an Indian wife named Sue. By November 1864 Beckwourth was working as a guide for Col. J. M. Chivington, who led his troops to Sand Creek (Colorado) and virtually wiped out an entire tribe of Cheyenne Indians in the notorious Sand Creek Massacre. Though many white settlers applauded the action, Beckwourth later expressed his revulsion at the infamous affair.

He returned to Denver to resume farming but also did a good deal of trapping. In 1866 he gave up the farm to join some other trappers in his old haunts on the Green River. Bad luck plagued them; one drowned and the rest, except for Beckwourth, were killed by Blackfoot Indians.

FOLLOWING THE CIVIL WAR in 1866, Plains Indians were growing more hostile as they fought for existence against increasing numbers of white emigrants. Beckwourth was persuaded by the U. S. Army to return to the Crow nation in an attempt to convince them that it would be to their advantage to make peace with the white men. Though he had not been in Crow Country for thirty years, Beckwourth agreed to try it. Perhaps he sought the good times of his youth when he left to rejoin the Crows.

By then they had moved far north to the headwaters of the Missouri River, a difficult journey for a 68-year old man suffering from painful rheumatism. Beckwourth chose a soldier named James W. Thompson to accompany him. They completed the journey in 1866 and were greeted warmly by older Crows who remembered their ex-chief. According to Beckwourth's memoirs, they were overjoyed and wanted him to stay to help regain their lost power and lead them to victory, as in the old days.

Beckwourth knew he could not stay and tried hard to explain his position. Finally they seemed to accept it, and he and his companion were honored with a great farewell feast. As Beckwourth ate the meat that had been carefully prepared for him, he allegedly became deathly ill. Within moments he was dead, apparently from poisoning. According to W. N. Byers, a noted Colorado newspaper publisher at the time, the Crows justified the alleged poisoning by stating: "...He [Beckwourth] has been our good medicine. We have been more successful under him than under any other chief." Their excuse, it was alleged, was that if they could not have him living it would be good medicine to have him dead.

Some say this story is a myth. We will never know for certain; however, his companion, James Thompson, was quoted as saying,

> Jim complained of being sick...and soon after commenced bleeding at the nose. On his arrival at the village he [Beckwourth] and Thompson were taken into the lodge of "The Iron Bull" and were his guests while they remained. There Beckwourth died and was buried by his host." [2]

As an early black argonaut, Beckwourth was one of an estimated thousand or so who had emigrated to California during the early part of the gold rush. By 1851 there were an estimated 700 at Negro Bar and Negro Hill, an area of rich diggings on the upper American River, just outside of present Folsom. The Negro Bar settlement took its name from "the several hundred negroes" who mined there in 1849. It boasted a store and a hotel; it was probably the largest black community in California at that time. A flood in 1852 washed away the settlement, and the people moved to higher ground at Granite city, now the City of Folsom. [3] The original Negro Bar now lies under the waters of Lake Natomas, part of the Folsom Lake State Recreational Area.

Coincidentally, another black pioneer, William Leidesdorff, once owned the land where Negro Bar and the city of Folsom are located (see Leidesdorff). When Leidesdorff died in 1848, Capt. Joseph Folsom acquired the property from Leidesdorff's heir, his West Indian mother.

When we consider James Beckwourth's disadvantages as an illiterate former slave, his achievements are truly remarkable. Perhaps we can forgive his early forays into California as a horse thief; after all, he was only doing what many Indians did naturally. In California an important mountain pass marked by a state monument (State Highway. 70), a mountain peak and a town are all named in his honor.

BIBLIOGRAPHY

–Bancroft, Hubert H. *Register of Pioneer Inhabitants of California, 1542 to 1848.* Dawson's Book Shop, Los Angeles, 1964.

–Clyman, James. *Journal Of A Mountain Man.* Mt. Press Publishing Company, Missoula, MT, 1984.

–Dillon, Richard. *Fool's Gold.* Coward McCann, Inc. New York, 1967.

–Dillon, Richard. *Humbugs and Heros.* Yosemite-DiMaggio, Oakland, 1983.

–Egan, Ferol. *Fremont, Explorer for a Restless Nation.* University of Nevada Press, Reno, 1977. Reprinted 1985.

–Felton, Harold W. *Jim Beckwourth, Negro Mountain Man.* Dodd, Mead & Co., New York, 1966. All quotations except [1, 2 & 3] are from this publication.

–Shepard, Betty, ed. *Mountain Man, Indian Chief.* Taken from Beckwourth's 1856 autobiography, *The Life and Adventures of Jim Beckwourth.* Harcourt, Brace & World, Inc. New York, 1968.

–Oswald, Delmont R. "James P. Beckwourth," as published in *Trappers of the Far West.* University of Nebraska Press, Lincoln, 1983. Republished from *The Mountain Men and the Fur Trade of the Far West.* A. H. Clark Co. Glendale, CA, 1965. Quotes [1] & [2] taken from this publication.

–Utley, Robert M. *The Indian Frontier of the American West, 1846-1890.* University of New Mexico Press, Albuquerque.

–Yost, Walt. "History strikes it rich at Negro Bar." *Sacramento Bee*, Feb. 14, 1993. [3]

Josiah Belden
Courtesy California State Library

– 5 –

JOSIAH BELDEN (DON JOSE)
1815 – 1892

JOSIAH BELDEN is one of the intrepid pioneers who came west to California with the Bartleson-Bidwell Party in 1841. Born May 4, 1815, in Upper Middletown, Connecticut, Josiah Belden came on his father's side from old English stock by the name of Bayldon. His mother, Abigail McKee Belden, died when he was four. Eleven years later he was forced to leave school when his father died, and he moved to Albany, New York, to live with an uncle.

He learned the jewelry trade there, but at age twenty-one he gave in to his itchy feet and traveled throughout New England, down the Mississippi to New Orleans and overseas to Liverpool, England. A year later he returned to establish a mercantile and cotton trading business in Mississippi. By age 26 Belden found himself bored with his humdrum life as a merchant. This led to his decision to board a steamship heading for the colorful fur-trading center at St. Louis and then to Independence. In 1841 he caught a virulent case of "California fever."

Before long he met other footloose young men like himself who sought adventure in the untamed West. Oregon territory sounded interesting, but when they heard about the wonders of California from frontiersman Antoine Robidoux, they were immediately intrigued. Then, after reading Dr. John Marsh's letters extolling the virtues of California in local newspapers, they were sold. Most so-called experts said an overland trek directly to California was impossible, especially with wagons. Nevertheless, Belden joined George Shotwell, Henry Brolaski and David Chandler to buy a wagon, form a "mess" and join with others who dared try the "impossible."

Once Belden's party was organized and outfitted, they joined John Bidwell and others at Sapling Grove. The emigrant train left there with around 70 men, women and children, including a party of Catholic missionaries led by Father De Smet and piloted by Thomas Fitzpatrick. Later they were joined on the Kansas River by John Bartleson and a small party, including Joseph Chiles and Charles Weber.

John Bartleson was elected captain, and John Bidwell secretary. Their first real tragedy occurred in mid-June, when Belden's companion, George Shotwell, accidentally shot and killed himself by pulling his loaded rifle out of a wagon barrel-first. As Belden solemnly helped dig a grave for his friend along the trail, he must have wondered if he had done the right thing in joining such a hazardous venture. Excerpts from Belden's memoirs describe the journey west:

> We left about the 10th of May. We had made some rules for our protection against the Indians, setting guard, patrols &c. The company divided into watches for guard, each taking it in turn. There was one woman in our party Mrs. Kelsey; the missionaries had none. We moved along very gradually; a part of the wagons were drawn by oxen, and part by mules. We had riding animals besides. We took as much provision as we could haul and carry, to last us until we should get into the buffalo country, when we expected to supply ourselves by hunting...We reached Fort Laramie [June 22— a few days after Shotwell's death], and passed on into the Black Hills, and near the Wind River Mountain, and came to Independence Rock on the Sweetwater Creek [early July], and when we got into buffalo country, we stopped two or three days and killed buffalo, and jerked the meat, and made packs of that to carry us through. Meantime we were travelling through a country pretty badly infested by the Crow and Blackfeet Indians.

Upon reaching the Bear River, the emigrants followed it north to Soda Springs, where the Bartleson-Bidwell Party—with Belden's "mess"—was to split off from the missionaries and others bound for Oregon. Belden describes it in his memoirs:

> After separating from the missionaries, we followed Bear River down nearly to where it enters Salt Lake. There we found a great difficulty in getting water...traveling several days, passing over a very desert country where there was scarcely any food for our animals, and very rough getting along with our wagons, we finally came to a spot where there was moist ground, some springs, and a little patch of green grass. While there we did not know which direction to take...but we had heard...that there was a river somewhere, which was then called Mary's River, which ran...westward... Before we struck this river [the Humboldt] we were so delayed by our wagons that we concluded to abandon them, and we took what things we could and packed them on to our horses and oxen, and what we could not carry, we left with our wagons standing in the plains. We were then within sight of the Sierra Nevada mountains, which we knew we had to cross. But we could see no appearance of any opening or depression which we might avail to get across. Then we struck south, until we finally came to what is known as Walker's River.[The rest of the journey to Marsh's Ranch is covered in Chapter 1]

AFTER LEAVING Marsh, Belden and Brolaski stayed on a ranch near San Jose for a few days, resting from their ordeal. Obtaining the loan of fresh horses, they left for Santa Cruz, stopping off at Isaac Graham's Rancho Sayante (see Graham). Belden found himself fascinated by the people and their generous, easy going lifestyle. A few days later Belden and Brolaski rode on to Monterey. Belden describes his experiences there in his memoirs:

> I stayed there a little while, and there I became acquainted with Mr. Larkin, who was afterwards American Consul, and made arrangements with him to go over to Santa Cruz and take charge of a store there, which he wished to establish as a branch, and I went over to manage the business there for him—a store of general merchandise. We carried on the usual business there, selling goods and taking pay in hides and tallow, and buying lumber...This was mostly the redwood lumber, and was worth about forty or forty-five dollars a thousand then...I continued there about two and a half years in that kind of trade & selling goods. Finally, after having accumulated a large quantity of lumber that I had no sale for, at the beach, some 150 thousand feet more than I could dispose of, I stopped buying, and the sawyers, as I supposed, in order to make a new market for lumber, when I was gone into Monterey on one occasion, set fire to the lumber and burned it up, and this disgusted Mr. Larkin so much that he closed the business up, and I went into Monterey.

Belden was on hand when U.S. Navy Commodore Thomas ap Catesby Jones sailed into Monterey Bay, dropped anchor and immediately invaded the town, thinking war had been declared by the U.S. against Mexico. Belden reportedly helped hoist the Stars and Stripes over the Customs House before Thomas O. Larkin was able to convince Jones that war had not been declared.

By the spring of 1844 Belden was in partnership with William G. Chard, operating a small store and boarding house for American seamen who had requested aid from U.S. Consul Larkin (see Larkin). Later that same year, Mexican rebels—led by former Gov. Juan B. Alvarado and Gen. José Castro—fomented a revolution against Mexican Governor Manuel Micheltorena.

When the governor left Monterey with troops to put down the revolution in Southern California, he left a small force of soldiers to guard the town and his own house, where his wife had been left in charge. Señora Micheltorena had little faith in the men who guarded her; in fact, she feared them as the ex-convicts and hard cases many of them were. As a result, she appealed to her husband's friend, Consul Larkin, for help. Incredibly, she asked that a few Americans be assigned to guard her against her own countrymen. Larkin immediately turned to Belden for assistance in recruiting some American volunteers to assist her. Belden described it himself:

> I got some five or six Americans, and we armed ourselves well with American rifles, and went there. Mrs. Micheltoren[a] had a room fitted up for us, a kind of armory, and we went and stayed there every night, for four or five weeks, I think, and kept guard to protect the house, and the public property in the offices there.

Meanwhile, a company of rebels had surrounded the town and demanded its surrender. Some of the frightened inhabitants advised Señora Micheltorena to capitulate and avoid bloodshed, but she refused to give in. Instead, a deal was struck to allow the rebels occupation of the fort if they would leave the town in the hands of the loyalists.

When word came in early 1845 that Micheltorena was defeated, he was placed on a ship to be taken back to Mexico. But first the ship sailed north to Monterey to pick up Señora Micheltorena and her servants. This allowed the ex-governor time to wind up his affairs and turn over the reins of government to Governor. Pío Pico in good order (see Pico).

By then Belden had become a Mexican citizen and was awarded a 21,000-acre land grant on the upper Sacramento River by Micheltorena for services rendered to his grateful wife. After dissolving his partnership, Don Jose Belden left with Robert Thomes to occupy his Rancho Barranca Colorado (Red Bluff). Apparently short of funds, Belden made a deal with William Ide, a newly arrived emigrant, to run the ranch for him (see Ide). Leaving his ranch in Ide's hands during the spring of 1846, Belden went to Yerba Buena (San Francisco) and took employment with trader John Paty.

WHEN PATY closed his business that fall, Belden was employed by trader William Heath Davis (see Davis). His business trips to Southern California led to a business venture with Mellus & Howard in San Jose. There Belden became a partner in the firm known as J. Belden & Co. But even before then the Bear Flag Rebellion took place in Sonoma. California was declared an independent republic by the aggressive "Bears" and William Ide was elected "president."

Three weeks later word was received that the United States had declared war against Mexico, and the short-lived Bear Flag was replaced by the Stars and Stripes. As a citizen of Mexico, Belden was caught on the horns of a dilemma. He could not bring himself to fight against Americans and sought to remain neutral, as many other American settlers tried to do. He continued with his trading activities, and by the end of 1847 had become part owner of a quicksilver mine near San Jose.

In the spring of 1848 Belden got word of James W. Marshall's gold discovery at Sutter's sawmill (See Marshall). Belden headed for the gold country and tried his hand at mining with marginal results. He then fell back on his merchandising skills in San Jose and made a rich "strike" supplying goods and services needed by gold-crazed argonauts.

By 1849 Belden had sold his interest in Rancho Barranca Colorado to William Ide. This and other astute real estate investments made him wealthy enough to retire from merchandising. In February he married Sarah Margaret Jones, who had come to California in 1846. After the Constitutional Convention was held in the fall of 1849, San Jose was declared California's capital and the first legislative body met there.

By 1850 San Jose was a city, and Belden was elected its first mayor. This honor gave him great satisfaction, considering that he had been imprisoned upon his arrival there in 1841. In succeeding years the Belden family traveled extensively, living the high life of the wealthy. A geological surveyor, William Brewer, later wrote of a visit to Belden's home in 1861:

> I went out of town [San Jose] a mile and visited the residence of a wealthy citizen, Mr. Belden. He and his wife had come early (1841), poor, had got rich, visited Europe, brought back many works of art, etc. He lives here very comfortably on his money, has a fine house, pretty grounds, etc. We spent two or more hours most pleasantly in looking over pictures, photographs, etc., which he had brought from Europe.

Belden had built a fine two-story house on ten prime acres in the mid-1850s. A solid Republican, he served as a delegate to the Republican National Convention in 1876. Apparently yearning for the East, he moved his family to New York City in 1881. There he became a member of the Union League Club and a director of the Erie Railroad. He died there April 23, 1892 just short of his 77th birthday.

BIBLIOGRAPHY
—Bancroft, Hubert H. *Register of Pioneer Inhabitants of California 1542 to 1848.* Dawson's Book Shop, Los Angeles, CA, 1964.
—Ide, Simeon. *Conquest of California By the Bear Flag Party. A Biography of William Ide.* Rio Grande Press, Glorieta, NM, 1967.
—Nunis, Doyce B. Jr. *Josiah Belden, 1841 California Overland Pioneer: His Memoir and Early Letters.* Talisman Press, Georgetown, CA,1962. All quotations came from this publication.

John Bidwell
Courtesy California Department of Parks & Recreation

– 6 –

JOHN BIDWELL (DON JUAN)

1819 – 1900

THOUGH HE WAS DESCENDED FROM ANGLO-SAXONS, Abram Bidwell was a deserter from the British Army in Canada, when he married Clarissa Griggs in 1816. Their second child, John, was born in New York August 5, 1819. Four more children followed before the Bidwell family moved to Pennsylvania and then Western Ohio, always chasing the elusive rainbow of the expanding western frontier. Despite the moves, John Bidwell got a better than average education for that era; he attended Kingsville Academy in Ashtabula County, where he eventually taught school.

By age twenty Bidwell was on his own, walking to Cincinnati with $75 in his pocket. From there he went by river-boat to Burlington, the tiny capital of Iowa Territory. Learning that land was available for the taking along the Iowa River, Bidwell homesteaded 160 acres of farmland. Within a matter of months he found some of his neighbors suffering from the chills and fever of the dreaded ague, a form of malaria. Heeding their warnings, Bidwell left on foot and headed south to the Missouri River. He probably went by boat to Platte County, Missouri, where land was becoming available from the "Platte Purchase." This rich, former Indian land was being opened for homesteading. Young Bidwell described it as follows:

> The imagination could not conceive a finer country—lovely rolling, fertile, wonderfully productive, beautifully arranged for settlement, part prairie and part timber. Every settler had aimed to locate a half-mile from his neighbor, and there was as yet no conflict. Peace and contentment reigned. Nearly every place seemed to have a beautiful spring of clear cold water. The hills and prairies and the level places were alike covered with a black and fertile soil. I cannot recall seeing an acre of poor land in Platte County.

It's easy to see why Bidwell decided to settle there, as James W. Marshall had done before him. His plan was to obtain land and bring his father there from Ohio. Meanwhile, needing money, he accepted a teaching position in a country school near Weston on the north side of the river. He began teaching there in June 1839. Government surveyors came that fall to "lay out the country," allowing Bidwell to file his claim for a quarter section of land he coveted.

The following year he journeyed down the river to St. Louis to buy badly needed supplies and clothing. He was gone about a month, and when he returned he was shocked to find an intimidating bully occupying his claim. Although Bidwell had done considerable work on the place, he had not lived on it as required. As a result, he found he had no legal rights, and lost out to the aggressive "jumper." Bidwell had invested nearly everything in his land; he was too upset and disillusioned to seek more. The ague was bad there, too. James W. Marshall also suffered from it, but whether they knew each other then is uncertain.

A T ABOUT THIS TIME Bidwell heard frontiersman Antoine Robidoux extolling the virtues of California. Though it was Mexican territory, foreign settlers were welcome there, said Robidoux, who made it sound like paradise. After his disappointing experience in Missouri, Bidwell was in the mood for something new and daring. He found other men who agreed to accompany him to California, and they organized the "Western Emigration Society."(The story of how this organization evolved into the Bartleson-Bidwell Party is covered in chapter one; this chapter will cover it from Bidwell's perspective only.)

When it came time to separate from the Oregon-bound party at Soda Springs south of Fort Hall, 32 emigrants headed southwest toward the Great Salt Lake. Among them was the only woman, eighteen-year-old Nancy Kelsey, her husband, Benjamin, and their infant daughter (see Kelsey). The only directions the Bartleson-Bidwell Party had were described by Bidwell as follows:

> We must strike out west of Salt Lake...being careful not to go too far south, lest we should get into a waterless country without grass. They also said we must be careful not to go canons, and wander about, as trapping parties had been known to do, and become bewildered and perish.

Not very specific for the vast, virtually unexplored country they would be traveling. It was nearly September before they sighted the north shore of the Great Salt Lake. This was salt-desert country with little good water or fodder. Getting wagons through hilly terrain required much back-breaking pick and shovel work. Time and food was running out, and it was time for drastic action. Wagons and everything except basic necessities had to be abandoned. Vital supplies were then strapped to the backs of remaining livestock, even the oxen. Endless days of hardship brought them to Mary's River (present-day eastern Nevada), later to be named the Humboldt by John C. Fremont (see Fremont).

The horrific journey across the Sierra Nevada to John Marsh's San Joaquin Valley ranch is covered in chapter one. After resting at Marsh's ranch a few days, most members of the party journeyed to San Jose to obtain passports to remain in the country. Once they overcame problems with the Mexican government, when they were arrested and temporarily thrown into jail, most of them get their coveted passports by paying Marsh a $5.00 fee. Bidwell was shocked to learn that no passport had been issued for him—apparently Marsh was hoping that he could keep him on as a hired hand in a form of bondage (see Marsh).

Bidwell wanted none of that. He borrowed a horse from a sympathetic friend and rode to San Jose to get his own passport. Instead, he found himself arrested and thrown in the same calaboose where his friends had been jailed. Fortunately a Yankee resident there talked Gen. Mariano G. Vallejo into issuing Bidwell a passport after he'd spent three miserable days in jail (see Vallejo). After a short return visit at Marsh's ranch, Bidwell, Chiles, Charles Weber and Huber headed up the Sacramento River to visit John Sutter's New Helvetia (see Weber & Sutter). Bidwell wanted nothing more to do with Marsh and thought Sutter offered the best opportunity for employment. It was now mid-December, raining and flooding. The short journey took eight days instead of the two Marsh had estimated. Arriving at Sutter's Fort just before Christmas, Bidwell describes the scene in his memoirs:

> Sutter received us with open arms and in a princely fashion, for he was a man of the most polite address and the most courteous manners, a man who could shine in any society. Moreover, our coming was not unexpected by him. It will be remembered that in the Sierra Nevada one of our men named Jimmy John became separated fromthe main party. It seems he...found his way down to Sutter's establishment...Through this man Sutter heard that our company of thirty men [and one woman] were already somewhere in California....

Shortly after their arrival, they were joined by the Kelsey family, who had come upriver by boat. It seems a certainty that they enjoyed a hearty Christmas celebration after the terrible hardships they had endured on the way out. It hadn't been much better during their stay with the niggardly John Marsh.

In early 1842 Bidwell was hired by Sutter to go to Bodega Bay and Fort Ross to oversee the dismantling and shipment of buildings and property Sutter had bought from the Russians there. He was employed at this task for about fourteen months before being transferred to Sutter's new "Hock Farm" on the Feather River, where he became foreman. But before then he and Peter Lassen had made a fast trip into the northern Sacramento Valley to recover some stolen horses (see Lassen). It was on this trip that Lassen became enamored with land along Deer Creek, and Bidwell with land where present Chico lies.

Then came exciting news. Pablo Gutiérrez, one of the Hock Farm employees, told Bidwell he had seen signs of gold on the nearby Bear River. Bidwell accompanied him to the site, but they found no gold. Gutiérrez insisted it was because they needed a *batea,* a wooden bowl Mexican miners used to wash gold out of sand and gravel. Because none were available, and they had more pressing things to attend to, the matter was dropped.

IN OCTOBER 1844 Bidwell became a naturalized Mexican citizen; as Don Juan Bidwell he applied for and received a two-league land grant, Rancho Ulpinos, encompassing present Rio Vista. Finding it too swampy and mosquito infested for a desirable settlement, he later traded it to Pierson Reading for a lot in Yerba Buena.

Next came news about an insurrection against Mexican Governor Manuel Micheltorena. He had come to California from Mexico, bringing with him several hundred ex-convict troops. Though he was proving to be a fairly effective governor, his *cholo* troops were feared and hated by the *Californios* because of their depredations against them. As a result, former Governor Juan Alvarado had joined with General José Castro and other dissidents in Southern California to overthrow the governor and rid themselves of his troops. In fairness, it should be pointed out that Micheltorena's men were seldom paid and only fed sporadically.

John Sutter had befriended Micheltorena and liked him, especially after the governor offered him another huge land grant if he helped put down the insurrection. Among other things, Sutter was a soldier at heart, and he quickly raised a small army of employees, trappers, Indians and settlers to join Micheltorena's troops and deal with the rebels. John Bidwell was one of Sutter's early recruits and became his aide-de-camp.

Then came an incident that cemented Sutter and Bidwell's resolve in the matter. Pablo Gutiérrez, an old companion of Sutter's from his Santa Fe trading days, the man who had brought Bidwell news about gold on the Bear River—where Gutiérrez now had a land grant—was brutally killed by Castro's men. He had been apprehended and hanged as a spy, while carrying in his boot a secret message between Sutter and the governor.

In January 1845 Sutter led Bidwell and his band of volunteer soldiers toward San Jose to join the governor. This show of force was enough for Castro, who led his rebel troops south toward Los Angeles. There he expected reinforcements, who would surely defeat

Micheltorena's band of renegade savages for good. Though Dr. John Marsh wanted no part of the dispute, Sutter had the power to conscript and drafted him into his "army" as a lowly recruit.

This private war of personalities was partly responsible for Micheltorena's defeat later in the year. Marsh was a skillful orator, and he was able to turn Sutter's volunteers against the entire campaign. By the time they reached Southern California some were deserting, while others switched sides to help the rebels. Some historians say the entire conflict was a sham—a show of force to allow the governor to save face while taking his hated troops back to Mexico.

After a one-day artillery duel between the two forces near Cahuenga Pass—where not a single human casualty took place—Sutter and Bidwell were captured by General Castro, and imprisoned near Mission San Fernando. Micheltorena capitulated shortly thereafter, and he and his men were escorted to San Pedro, placed aboard a ship and sent back to Mexico. Pío Pico was named acting governor, and a tribunal was formed to try Sutter.

There were those who would have hanged him for treason, but cooler thinking prevailed, and he was set free after swearing allegiance to the new administration. It was probably during this period that Bidwell had a chance to follow up on his hunch about gold in California. After being freed, he rode to a spot near Mission San Fernando, where a French Canadian named Baptiste Ruelle had found gold in 1841. Another gold discovery had been made a year later by a *vaquero* named Francisco Lopez in nearby Placerita Canyon. After observing the small-scale, rather primitive mining methods used by the Mexicans, Bidwell was determined to look for gold when he returned north.

He and Sutter then made their way back to Sutter's Fort–which was now completed–chastened and better informed in the foibles of Mexican politics. After an absence of only a few months, Sutter found things at the fort a shambles, and it took him the rest of the year to recover financially. He was ably assisted in his recovery by Bidwell, whom he hired as his bookkeeper and secretary.

MEANWHILE Bidwell had received another two-league land grant on the Sacramento River, encompassing present Colusa. He had coveted land farther north in the vicinity of present Chico, but it had been claimed by a friend. Later he did manage to acquire a portion of the Farwell grant near there, which he began to stock with cattle.

Two more important events took place in 1845; one occurred in July, when erstwhile millwright James Marshall appeared from Oregon and was hired by Sutter as a handyman (see Marshall). The other came late in the year with a second surprise visit from Captain John C. Fremont, Kit Carson and a contingency of soldier-explorers. Fremont and his army "topographers" had been in California the year before on an exploratory mission, arriving at the fort in a starving condition (see Fremont). Sutter had re-outfitted them so they could return East. Now Fremont had returned, again requesting livestock and supplies as before.

Sutter was away at the time, and Bidwell was in charge. When he was unable to supply all the mules and blacksmithing services Fremont demanded, the captain became miffed and felt he had been slighted. Sutter, returning a few days later, reported Fremont's arrival to General Vallejo as required. He was sorry the haughty captain had left the fort with hard feelings but agreed that Bidwell had done his best to accommodate him. There had been talk about possible war with Mexico for some time. Many, including Sutter and Mexican nationals, thought Fremont's arrival was no coincidence.

When Fremont went to Monterey to pay a visit to General Castro, he was received warmly enough and given permission to explore the area surrounding Monterey. But within days, Castro issued orders for Fremont to leave the country or be forced out. This ultimatum angered Fremont, who retired to Gavilan Peak near Mission San Juan Bautista. After a few days of bluffing and counter-bluffing by Castro, Fremont took his men and left for Oregon. The story of the Bear Flag Revolt and the Mexican War has been described in other sections of this book. Except for Bidwell's role in these vital events, they will not be repeated.

AFTER THE Bear Flaggers successfully stormed Sonoma, they took General Vallejo and three of his advisors prisoners, and incarcerated them at Sutter's Fort. Bidwell was placed in charge of the prisoners before Fremont replaced him with Lieutenant Edward Kern. Bidwell had little use for Fremont's high-handed methods, but was sympathetic toward the cause and went to Sonoma to join the "Bears."

Almost immediately he was placed on a committee consisting of Commander William Ide and Pierson Reading, another of Sutter's trusted clerks (see Ide). They were charged with drawing up a pledge or statement of purpose for the Bears. Bidwell submitted the following simple statement, which was finally adopted. "The undersigned hereby agree to organize for the purpose of gaining and maintaining the independence of California."

Despite the fact that the Bears had taken Sonoma on June 14, they dated the statement July 5, 1846, to accommodate Fremont, who was taking over as commander. Bidwell was appointed a lieutenant, even though he had not sought it, and he and the other volunteers began training. Within a few days they received word of Commodore Sloat's invasion at Monterey, and the American flag replaced the Bear flag at

Sonoma on July 9th. Bidwell's attitude toward the short-lived Bear Flag was rather negative, as stated in his own words:

> So much has been said and written about the "Bear Flag" that some may conclude it was something of importance. It was not so regarded at the time: it was never adopted at any meeting or by any agreement; it was, I think, never even noticed, perhaps never seen by Fremont when it was flying. The naked old Mexican flagstaff at Sonoma suggested that something should be put on it. [William] Todd had painted it, and some others had helped to put it up, for mere pastime....

While the original Bear Flag was a symbol, it is an historic relic and was used as the basis for the design of the California State Flag. Upon being sworn in to serve in the U.S. Armed Forces under Commodore Robert Stockton, Bidwell was shipped south with the rest of Fremont's volunteers. Things had gone well for the Yankees to that point. As Bidwell stated,

> We simply marched all over California from Sonoma to San Diego and raised the American flag without opposition or protest. We tried to find an enemy, but could not. So Kit Carson and Ned Beale were sent East, bearing dispatches...announcing the...conquest of California..."

Shortly after Stockton appointed Fremont Commandant of military forces, Fremont promoted Bidwell to Captain and Magistrate of the San Luis Rey District, which took in most of Southern California. His headquarters were located at Mission San Luis Rey near present Oceanside. Shortly after Fremont left Los Angeles for the North, leaving Captain A. Gillespie in charge of the Los Angeles garrison, the previously placid Mexicans decided to make a fight of it. Led by a paroled Mexican officer, José Flores, they confronted the badly outnumbered Gillespie and forced him and his troops to leave. After Flores' men drove Captain Gillespie and his men to a ship anchored off San Pedro, they occupied Santa Barbara and headed for San Diego.

When Bidwell learned of it at Mission San Luis Rey, he fled to San Diego. Finally he other token defenders were forced to seek refuge aboard a whaleship anchored in San Diego Bay. Unaware that the same thing had happened in Los Angeles, Bidwell undertook the hazardous assignment of sailing a ship's boat north to San Pedro to get word to Stockton. By the time he located Gillespie in San Pedro, a courier had already left for the North with the bad news.

When Stockton returned with reinforcements, San Diego was retaken and became the staging area for a victorious counter-attack on Los Angeles by the combined forces of Stockton and General Stephen Kearny in the south and Fremont advancing from the north. By then

Bidwell had been named quartermaster and promoted to major. When the fighting was over in January 1847, Bidwell was discharged with the other volunteers and returned "home" to Sutter's Fort. There he became Sutter's agent and helped survey the new settlement of Sutterville, about three miles downriver from Sutter's embarcadero.

WHEN SUTTER decided to build a water-powered gristmill and sawmill, he called on James Marshall, who had also returned from the Mexican War during the spring of 1847. A site for the gristmill was chosen a few miles upstream from the fort on the American River. The sawmill required a good stand of timber; Bidwell, Sam Kyburz and others were sent to find such a site in the surrounding mountains.

Finally they chose tiny Cullomah Valley (now Coloma), on the South Fork of the American River, about forty miles east of Sutter's Fort. Marshall took a crew of workers there that autumn and construction began. The sawmill was not yet finished when Marshall found gold on January 24, 1848. By the time the mill was completed in March, word of the discovery had leaked. By May, the Gold Rush had begun.

Bidwell and some companions were the first to find gold on the North Fork of the Feather River, not far from the site Pablo Gutiérrez had shown him several years earlier. Bidwell made a rich strike there in mid-1848, which started a gold rush in its own right. The place became known as "Bidwell's Bar," and a town sprang up; a few years later it became the county seat of Butte County. In 1849 Bidwell was selected to serve as a delegate to the Constitutional Convention, but he was in the mountains and did not receive the message in time. At about this time he sold his Rancho Colusa grant to Robert Semple for $2,000. Semple went on to establish the town of Colusa there (see Semple).

Bidwell spent two summers working his mines, using mostly Indian labor. With this newly found gold wealth, he was eventually able to purchase 28,000 acres of land known as Rancho Del Arroyo Chico, about a hundred miles north of Sutter's Fort, not far from Bidwell's Bar. In 1849 he was elected to the State Senate and served for one year. By then Bidwell had switched from mining to ranching and was living on his new ranch in a log cabin.

He spent the next few years building up the ranch with a variety of livestock, vineyards, fruit trees and vast grain fields. In 1851 came a most difficult decision, when his old friend and mentor, John Sutter, offered Bidwell his most prized possession, his only daughter, Eliza, in matrimony. Bidwell did not love Eliza and certainly didn't want to marry her. But how could he refuse his old friend's generous offer without alienating the entire Sutter family? But refuse her he must; though he did it tactfully, there is little doubt that their relationship was never the same again.

By 1853 Bidwell was growing so much wheat he decided to build a water-powered gristmill, and began selling good-quality flour throughout the area. Within a few years he had built a two-story adobe house and became one of the premier agriculturists in the country, employing hundreds of workers—mostly Indians. In 1860 he dedicated land to establish the town of Chico, contributing not only land but many thousands of dollars for churches, schools and parks.

Innovation and diversity were the keystones of his success; for example, he pioneered production of casaba melons, olive oil, dried fruits and nuts. Another innovation was a huge grain harvester drawn by forty mules. In addition to his farming activities, Bidwell became immersed in Democratic politics. After serving as a state senator, he was sent to Washington, D.C., to lobby for statehood and to deliver a 125-pound block of gold-bearing quartz as a contribution to the Washington Monument. In the early 1860s he built a steam-powered sawmill and acquired partial ownership of a river boat. He later sold his interest in the river boat to Pierson Reading.

After helping to organize Union forces during the Civil War, Bidwell was appointed a brigadier general in the state militia; thereafter he was known as "General Bidwell." Soon the new general had a mini-war of his own to fight. Thousands of Chinese immigrants had arrived to work on the Central Pacific Railroad and other projects, and Bidwell and other ranchers were hiring some of them as farm laborers. Strong anti-Chinese groups in the area castigated Bidwell for hiring these "Celestials," but Bidwell fought back until they burned his barn with $10,000 worth of hay and began boycotting his farm products. Finally he was forced to lay off most of them.

IN 1864, at the age of 45, Bidwell was elected to the Congress of the United States. While serving in Washington, he met J.C.G. Kennedy, a high-level Washington official, and his lovely daughters, Sallie and Annie. Before long he found himself helplessly in love with Annie, who was twenty-one years his junior. Pretty and petite, Annie was a rather serious, religious girl, who had no interest in marrying anyone, let alone a middle-aged Congressman from the western wilderness.

Still she enjoyed Bidwell's company, and he pursued her relentlessly. When his term of office expired in 1866, he left to tour Europe, finding that his thoughts remained on Annie. After returning to Washington, he refused to leave until Annie promised to correspond on a regular basis. Upon his return to California, having been influenced by Annie's staunch temperance beliefs, he tore out his acres of wine grapes, replanting with vines to produce raisins.

He also decided to run for governor on the Union Party ticket. Because of his anti-monopoly platform, powerful railroad interests effectively destroyed the Union Party, and Bidwell went down to defeat.

Annie Kennedy Bidwell
Courtesy California Department of Parks & Recreation

Disgusted and disillusioned by politics, Bidwell threw himself into his neglected farm duties and continued building the opulent mansion he had started before going to Washington. He hoped it would prove an incentive to help Annie change her mind about marrying him. Perhaps it did, for a year later he finally won her hand. He returned to Washington in the spring of 1868 for the wedding. It proved to be the highlight of the social season and was attended by President Andrew Johnson, General U.S. Grant and many other political leaders.

When Bidwell brought his wife home to Chico, the mansion was still incomplete. This allowed Annie the rather pleasant task of furnishing and decorating it. Her good taste became evident when the mansion became the most prominent showplace north of San Francisco. The Bidwells loved to entertain, which they did lavishly, despite the fact that liquor was never served. Annie was a militant prohibitionist. Many family members on both sides came to visit during this period, some staying to settle nearby.

A devout Christian, Annie immediately took an interest in the Indians who lived and worked on the ranch. She taught Sunday school classes for them, gave sermons and eventually acquired authorization from the Presbyterian Church to perform baptisms, marriages and funerals. The grand upstairs ballroom of her home was never used for dances; instead, Annie converted it to a huge sewing room and taught Indian women how to sew there in grand style.

A new independent political party had been formed by 1875, consisting of Democrats, Republicans and others who opposed railroad and other powerful monopolies. Bidwell was again talked into running for governor but ran into the same kind of vicious campaigning that had undone him before. Among other things, he was accused of being an overly-moralistic, anti-alcohol fanatic, a slaver and a land monopolist. Because of his early-day decision to take Mexican citizenship, he was even accused of being ineligible to run. This, of course, was nonsense; the 1848 Treaty of Guadalupe Hidalgo offered U.S. citizenship to any California resident who wished to have it, and virtually all residents took advantage of this offer, including Bidwell. Nevertheless, he was unable to rise above these bitter accusations and was again defeated.

With Annie at his side, Bidwell continued to fight against the financial stranglehold held by the monopolists, and he and Annie added women's rights to their cause. They also traveled extensively and spent many hot summers camping out in the mountains surrounding Chico. Higher education became another of their causes, and they donated land, money and other gifts to many schools. The land for California State University at Chico was donated by the Bidwells, and they served as trustees for the school there.

FINALLY, IN 1890, Bidwell became the nominee of the Prohibitionist Party for governor. Though he knew there was little chance of his being elected, he gave his all and became the National Prohibitionist Party nominee for President of the United States in 1892. Though he did not actively campaign for the office, his nomination acceptance speech received wide publicity for the party, and he received more votes than any prohibitionist candidate before then.

Bidwell remained in good health and actively worked on the ranch until he was felled by a heart attack or stroke while cutting firewood on the morning of April 4, 1900. After receiving medical treatment, the eighty- year-old pioneer rallied a bit before being dealt the final blow that same afternoon. He had fathered no children. Annie lived alone in the mansion another eighteen years, continuing with her charitable work and donating to worthwhile causes. In 1905, she gave 1,900 acres to the City of Chico to be used as a public park. A few years later, she added another 301 acres.

TODAY BIDWELL PARK stretches along both sides of Chico Creek for ten miles. When she died in 1918, the mansion and remaining land was given to the Presbyterian Church with the stipulation that it be used as a co-educational school. Later it was sold to Chico State College for use as a women's dormitory. Finally it was transferred to the California State Park system for preservation and use as a state historical park, which it remains to this day. A state marker identifies the location of Bidwell's Bar at Lake Oroville State Recreation Area. There is a Bidwell Street in the city of Folsom and a site called Bidwell Point on Hwy. 162 near Elk Creek, west of Willows. A full-length portrait of Bidwell, painted by Alice M. Reading, daughter of Pierson Reading—the "father" of Shasta County—hangs in the State Capitol.

BIBLIOGRAPHY

–Bancroft, Hubert H. *History of California,* Vol. I-VI. History Co. San Francisco, CA, 1886. Repub., Wallace Hebberd, Santa Barbara, CA, 1966.

–Bidwell, General John. "Echoes of the Past," *Century Illustrated Monthly.,* 1890. All quotations taken from this publication.

–Dillon, Richard. *Fool's Gold,* Coward McCann, Inc. NewYork, 1967.

–Dillon, Richard. *Humbugs and Heros.* Yosemite-DiMaggio Press, Oakland, CA, 1983.

–Harlow, Neal. *California Conquered.* University of Calif. Press, Berkeley, 1982.

–Hunt, Rockwell D. *John Bidwell, Prince of California Pioneers.* Caxton Printers, Ltd., Caldwell, Idaho, 1942.

–Nunis, Doyce B. Jr., Ed. *The Bidwell-Bartleson Party.* Western Tanager Press, Santa Cruz, 1991.

–State of Calif. Div. of Parks and Recreation. *Bidwell Mansion State Historic Park.* An undated brochure.

–Stewart, George R. *The California Trail,* University of Nebraska Press, Lincoln, 1962.

–Wilcox, Del. *Voyagers To California.* Sea Rock Press, Elk, CA, 1991.

Notes

Samuel Brannan
Courtesy California State Library

SAMUEL BRANNAN

1819 - 1889

WHEN SAMUEL BRANNAN WAS BORN in 1819, his father, Thomas Brannan, was getting long in the tooth. A hard-drinking Irish farmer from Saco, Maine, Thomas was raising a new family with his second wife, Sarah, who was much younger than he. Samuel was the youngest of five born since 1805, and there were older offspring from Thomas' first marriage. When Samuel was still a youngster, his mother was ailing and he was raised primarily by his older sister, Mary Ann.

"Old Tom" as he was called, had become a cantankerous tyrant, especially when he drank, often beating his wife and children over trivialities. Over the years Mary Ann Brannan assumed the role of mother and protector over her younger siblings, especially after Samuel's older brother, Johnny, left home in disgust. When Mary Ann finally broke away to marry at the age of twenty-seven, her father was so resentful she feared he would take it out on fourteen-year-old Samuel, so she and her new husband, Alexander Badlam, took Samuel with them to their new home in Ohio.

They arrived in Painesville, Ohio, in 1833, and Samuel helped Badlam build a house and general store. Soon young Brannan was apprenticed to a local printer to learn the trade, and Mary Ann began a family of her own. At age eighteen, Samuel quit his job and went to visit his mother in Maine. His father had died shortly before, leaving a small estate in which Samuel shared. From Maine, Brannan made his way to New Orleans in 1838 to join his older brother, Thomas Jr.

The two pooled their resources to open a publishing firm. The business was just beginning to bloom when New Orleans was struck by a devastating epidemic of cholera. When his brother died from the dread disease, Samuel placed his printing press in storage and fled north to Indianapolis, where he worked as a printer before sending for his press to begin another publishing business. This must have been a troubling period in Brannan's life. First he learned of the death of his mother, and then the business failed. Distraught, he returned to the home of his foster parents in Painesville, Ohio.

It was there in 1842 that Brannan was introduced to Mormonism. The Badlams were recent converts and would not be satisfied until their "adopted" son joined their new faith. Brannan also met Harriet Hatch, a buxom, blonde Mormon girl, and they were married soon after Brannan's baptism. Life went fairly well for the newlyweds until Hattie became pregnant. As she gained weight, she grew slovenly and neglectful of herself and her amorous husband. When he turned to others for solace, she quite naturally berated him and threatened divorce.

Perhaps to escape his unhappy marriage, Brannan became ordained as a Morman missionary and traveled the area seeking converts. He was absent during the birth of his daughter and did not see Hattie or his child until 1844, when he returned home a sick man. After regaining his health, Brannan resumed his missionary duties, this time heading for Connecticut. He stayed there in a boarding house operated by Frances Corwin, a widow and recent Mormon convert, and her attractive daughter, Ann Eliza.

BEFORE LONG BRANNAN found himself falling in love with Ann Eliza, whom he called "Lizzie" or "Liza." She was everything Hattie was not, and he made up his mind to have her. Torn between his need for Liza and his failed marriage to Hattie, he wrote Mormon leader Joseph Smith for guidance. He thought Hattie might have divorced him but did not know for certain. At any rate, Hattie had told him she never wanted to see him again. Finally he decided not to tell Liza about his former marriage.

Apparently Brannan gained permission to take a second wife, and Samuel and Ann Eliza were married in the parlor of widow Corwin's house. A short time later, Brannan broke the news to his new mother-in-law that he and Liza were moving to New York. The church was paying to move Brannan's printing press there so he could start publishing a Mormon newspaper called *The Prophet*. Mrs. Corwin, unable to bear the thought of losing her only daughter, decided to sell out and move to New York with the newlyweds.

Shortly after arriving in New York in 1844, Brannan met William Smith, younger brother of Mormon Prophet Joseph Smith. William Smith was to write editorials for *The Prophet*, but agreed to share that task with Brannan. A short time later came the disturbing news of Joseph Smith's murder by a band of lawless gentiles. When it appeared that Brigham Young would take over the church, William Smith set out to discredit him.

Brannan then found himself torn between the Smiths and the rising power of Brigham Young in the church hierarchy. Because of his close relationship with the Smiths, he sided in with William Smith against Young. The conflict came to a head in early 1845, when church officials replaced William Smith as president of the Atlantic States Mission.

Not only that, but Smith was to appear in Nauvoo, Illinois, to be tried for treason against the church. Brannan was also suspect and faced excommunication. When Brannan appeared in Nauvoo to explain his side of the affair to Brigham Young, he was pardoned and extended the "hand of friendship." By mid-1845 Brannan found himself the father of a new son, whom he and Liza christened Samuel Jr.

Then came news the Mormons had been fearing: Illinois Governor Ford issued a proclamation ordering the Mormons to leave the state by February 1, 1846. Discrimination by gentiles against the Mormons had resulted in bloodshed and threatened to break into outright warfare. In a letter to Brigham Young, the governor suggested that the colony should head west, possibly to California, for their own safety.

Once the reluctant Mormons agreed that California seemed to offer their best hope, they decided to send a shipload of emigrants to San Francisco Bay under the leadership of Samuel Brannan. He was to acquire land there and make preparations for others to follow. After chartering the ship *Brooklyn* in New York, Brannan had it remodeled to carry 250 people, all the supplies needed to sustain them, plus general cargo destined for Honolulu to help defray expenses. Though he wasn't a Mormon, his young printing devil, Edward Kemble, agreed to accompany Brannan.

When they had overcome obstacles from crooked politicians seeking to delay the voyage, Brannan loaded his family and followers aboard, and the *Brooklyn* sailed in February 1846. A few sickened and died from various causes along the way, and by the time they rounded treacherous Cape Horn they were running out of food and water. A fortunate stop at Juan Fernandez Island off the Chilean coast allowed a welcome respite while they gathered what they needed.

Resuming their journey, they reached Honolulu in late June, 136 days after leaving New York. The tropical scenery must have seemed like paradise to the weary travelers. But the sight of U.S. warships and news of the Mexican War caught them by surprise. Brannan saw it as a God-given chance for them to seize land in California with few worries about troublesome nationalistic laws. He even advocated purchase of arms and ammunition to "drive the Mexicans into the sea," if necessary.

They bought a hundred rifles to augment six small cannon already aboard the *Brooklyn*. When they set sail for San Francisco Bay two weeks later, they left seeds of Mormonism that lay dormant but eventually flourished in the islands. The last stage of the voyage took about a month, during which Brannan had to excommunicate a few errant followers for practicing polygamy during the voyage. They anchored off Yerba Buena Cove in late July, where they spotted the American Flag fluttering in the breeze. It had been raised by U. S. Navy Captain John Montgomery nine days earlier.

Their feelings were terribly ambivalent; Brannan saw it as a symbol of further religious oppression. "Damn that flag!" he was quoted as saying. Others saw it as a positive sign, hoping the people there would prove more tolerant. At first, Captain Montgomery gave them a cool reception. But after meeting some of them, he warmed up and invited the ladies aboard his ship, the *Portsmouth,* for an afternoon reception. With American women as scarce as diamonds, they were welcome even if they were Mormons.

Once issued landing permits, the new immigrants quickly went to work setting up a temporary camp near the village of Yerba Buena, the only settlement there and a dreary one at that. An independent lot, some of the party left the immediate area to establish themselves in more desirable locations. Brannan picked a site near the waterfront, where he built a house for his family. Though he did his best to hold his flock together, they were losing their unity by mid-summer. Fortunately Brannan had brought along his printing press and enough type to start a job printing business with the help of Edward Kemble. Kemble didn't stay long, though; he soon left to join John C. Fremont's California Volunteers (see Fremont).

B RANNAN STILL SOUGHT a permanent location for the contingent of Mormons he knew were leaving Nauvoo. Finally he located just the place on the Stanislaus River near its confluence with the San Joaquin River. He convinced some of the Mormons to move there, and they began construction of a settlement named New Hope. Once it was under way, Brannan left it in the hands of an assistant and returned to San Francisco.

As the end of the Mexican War neared in early January 1847, Brannan began publishing a newspaper, the *California Star.* The only other newspaper in the territory was the *Californian*, published in Monterey by Robert Semple and Walter Colton (see Semple). From the very beginning, Brannan saw great potential in the Bay Area and used his newspaper to extol it. Robert Semple must have seen it too, for he moved he moved his newspaper to Yerba Buena a short time later.

On January 28th acting alcalde, Washington Bartlett, issue a proclamation changing the name of the former pueblo to San Francisco. Then came word that another large group of Mormons were serving in General Stephen Kearny's Mormon Battalion in Southern California. Now that fighting in the Mexican War had ended, the men would soon be discharged from the army; Brannan knew many of them would head north to join him at New Hope or Yerba Buena.

In early April, when Liza Brannan was expecting their second child, Samuel announced his alarming decision to visit New Hope, then go east to intercept Brigham Young, who was heading west. He was aware that Young might favor settlement on the Great Salt Lake, because of its isolation, and hoped to talk him out of it. He was convinced that California offered the best opportunity for success as the new Mormon Zion.

By then Sam's life with Liza was growing stormy. She and her mother were tired of living in the "wilderness," as they put it, and were eager to taste the delights of big city living once again. By contemporary standards, Brannan was apparently a workaholic who neglected his wife. Her complaints were many, so Brannan was probably glad to get away for awhile. Leaving her in tears, he headed for New Hope and found it a shambles. The man chosen to head the project there had taken over the only dwelling as his own, leading to virtual mutiny by the others. Though he did his best to smooth things over, Brannan left New Hope fearing the entire settlement was doomed to failure. He turned out to be right.

Traveling to Sutter's Fort, he chose Charles C. Smith and one other young man to accompany him and left for the mountains. They crossed via Truckee Pass in early April, passing the hideous specter of the Donner Party death camp. There they found Lewis Keseberg, the sole remaining member, who was awaiting evacuation. After sharing their food with him, they went on their way.

IN EARLY JULY, Brannan's party found Brigham Young and his followers on the Green River, northeast of the Great Salt Lake. Though Brannan tried his best to sell Young on the virtues of California, the wary president made no promises, stating he would recognize the right spot when he saw it. A few days later an advance party of the "sick detachment" of the Mormon Battalion arrived with word that the main group under Captain James Brown would soon be joining them.

Young asked Brannan to go and intercept Brown's group, while Young continued on to the Great Salt Lake. Brannan was to bring Brown and his men there as soon as possible. Brannan found them a week or so later, and by the end of July they spotted the smoke of Young's camp on the eastern shore, near the south end of the lake. When Brannan saw the wooded land sloping gently toward the vast, blue lake, he knew he had lost the argument. Later he heard about Young's simple statement upon first viewing the isolated grandeur: "This is the place," he said, and that was that.

At first Brannan saw the decision as a disastrous defeat. He and

Brigham Young had bitter words, and Brannan alienated others as well. He and Charles Smith left for home with James Brown and William Squires, but along the way they had a serious falling out. Brannan and Smith then left the other two behind to make their own way, which gave Brannan a chance to think things over. He knew a good portion of the Mormons in California were satisfied with their lives; they would not make the long move to Salt Lake. Others would settle in California, especially young men from the Mormon Battalion. Brannan saw himself as leader of the church in San Francisco and would collect tithes as he saw fit. Potential wealth was within his grasp with his newspaper and a new gristmill.

They had reached the Truckee River when they spotted a group of mounted men approaching. When they stopped to talk, Brannan was amazed to learn they were from the Mormon Battalion in Southern California. Their spokesman was an intelligent young man named Henry Bigler. Brannan quickly explained about the men following and why he wasn't traveling with them."They bring mail and instructions from President Young," he told them. "Young asks that only married men should join him at the Great Salt Lake; there isn't food enough for all. He asks that single men stay in California to earn money until he sends for them next year; then they should join their brethren at Salt Lake." With that, Brannan and Smith continued on their way.

IT WAS SEPTEMBER when they reached Sutter's Fort. Henry Bigler had told Brannan that his party had passed through there in August; a few Mormons had stayed behind to work for Sutter (see Sutter). He was building some mills and needed craftsmen badly. One of the mills was a water-powered sawmill being built by James W. Marshall in Cullomah (now Coloma), about forty-five miles east of the fort on the South Fork of the American River (See Marshall).

The other was a gristmill under construction a few miles upstream from the fort. When Brannan told Sutter that Henry Bigler and other members of the Mormon Battalion would be coming within a few days, Sutter was elated. The Mormons had proven to be industrious, capable workers, and he was prepared to hire more of them. Before leaving, Brannan and Smith made arrangements with Sutter to open a mercantile store there. Though Smith and Brannan were to be equal partners, the store would be called "C. C. Smith & Co."

When Edward Kemble returned after serving in the Mexican War, Brannan hired him to run his *California Star*, finding that it had deteriorated during his long absence. With New Hope a failure and Brigham Young entrenched at Salt Lake, Brannan liquidated the assets of the California expedition company and distributed the proceeds to its members. About then Liza Brannan gave birth to a girl they named Adelaida, with the nickname Addie.

C. C. Smith & Co. did well from the start, and Brannan made a round trip to Sutter's Fort every two weeks on Sutter's launch, which had become a virtual ferry up and down the Sacramento River. He was there in late January 1848, shortly after James Marshall arrived during a rainstorm. Marshall left the next morning, and Brannan thought Sutter had seemed rather preoccupied and nervous since Marshall's unexpected visit.

Some say Sutter confided in Brannan about Marshall's accidental discovery of gold, swearing him to secrecy. It is doubtful that this really happened, as Sutter and Marshall had sworn to keep it quiet until the mills were finished. They feared that once word got out they would be unable to keep anyone on the job. As it subsequently turned out, they were right. Brannan knew it for sure in February, when some Mormon gristmill workers told him about a gold strike they had made on the upper American River. In early March it came out in Semple's *Californian* as follows:

GOLD MINE FOUND: In the newly made raceway of the sawmill recently erected by Captain Sutter on the American fork, gold has been found in considerable quantities. One person brought $30.00 worth to New Helvetia, gathered there in a short time. California no doubt is rich in mineral wealth. Great chances here for scientific capitalists. Gold has been found in almost every part of the country.

A few days later the *Star* confirmed that "valuable minerals" had been found. Brannan's editor, Edward Kemble, refused to take the news seriously. But rumors were flying; surely Brannan would have told his own man if he had intended him to know. Instead, he told Kemble he would "look into it" during his next trip to Sutter's Fort. It's likely that Brannan was keeping it quiet until he cornered the market on miner's equipment. In April he sent a special edition of 2,000 newspapers to the East, confirming the gold discovery. He then opened another store at Mormon Island, where his friends had made the gold strike in late February.

As late as May, Brannan's beleaguered editor was still editorializing that the whole thing was a sham concocted by the rival newspaper to outsell the *Star*. Brannan must have been chuckling to himself the whole time. Finally Kemble went to Cullomah Valley to see for himself. Spring flooding had slowed mining in the area, and the young, naive editor saw little evidence of the wild tales he had heard. He returned to San Francisco convinced the story was exaggerated at best.

Ironically it was his own employer who finally changed his opinion in May by bringing a glass bottle partially filled with gold into town.

Brannan quickly made the rumors official as he paraded around showing off his gleaming metal, shouting, "Gold! Gold from the American River!" Whether by design or coincidence, the publicity worked and everyone began making plans to leave for the gold fields. Some didn't bother making plans; they simply locked their doors and ran for the first boat heading upriver. Within a week the town was semi-deserted. Shortly after, both newspapers ceased to exist, along with many other business enterprises.

QUICK TO seize any opportunity to capitalize, Brannan opened another store near Sutter's Mill at Cullomah, whose name had been shortened to Coloma. He had cornered the market on many things the miners needed and waxed fat on his sudden wealth. Thirty ounces of placer gold were sent to President Polk by acting Governor Richard Mason, along with a letter and map confirming the richness of strikes being made every day. When this news was publicized in the East, it quickly spread throughout the world.

By the following year, thousands of eager gold-seekers were risking life and limb to reach the gold fields before they played out. One of the greatest migrations the world has ever seen was under way and would not stop for many years. Who benefited the most? Sam Brannan and other entrepreneurs like him who provided the transportation, supplies and equipment men needed to reach the gold fields and sustain themselves, while they dug out the precious metal that was supposed to make them rich. Unfortunately, only a small percentage of them got rich; most barely eked out a precarious living—or died in the attempt.

Once Edward Kemble became a believer, he did well enough in the mines to buy out both newspapers, which he merged into the *Alta California*. Brannan was glad to get out from under the pesky newspaper so he could devote his time to more lucrative affairs. In addition to his other enterprises, he had been collecting tithes from the Mormon miners. Instead of turning them over to the church, he kept them in his personal safe. Finally Brigham Young sent emissaries to collect the tithes. In a noisy showdown, Brannan refused to turn over the money, saying he didn't trust the emissaries. When they claimed the money belonged to the Lord, Brannan was said to have replied, "Then it's His receipt I want, not yours!"

As a result of this altercation, Brannan was immediately excommunicated from the church forever. He seemed relieved to be shed of the burdens, along with whatever restraints the church had imposed. Material wealth became his guiding light and he pursued it with vigor. He bought land in Sacramento, which was beginning to boom. He became a partner in a hotel and tavern in San Francisco and opened another store there. Brannan even got into the China trade, dealing in silk, tea, and other oriental goods.

Now that Brannan was beginning to make real money, his frustrated wife began nagging him about visiting New York, or even better, a voyage to Europe, as his partner C. C. Smith was planning. The following quotes from a letter Liza wrote to Mary Brannan, wife of Brannan's brother, John, reveal her feelings at the time. (This copy incorporates mistakes as they occurred.)

> September 2, 1848: We are living in one of the most healthy places in the world and I am quite contented and happy for the time being, that is untill we make our fortunes, but we would never think of setling here for life, and I rather think that too or three years will find us in New York or somewheres there abouts where we can enjoy life. that is if we have good luck as at present: but now is the time for making money. Mary if you and John had come out here when we did you would now of been independent for John could of made five dollars a day the year around ... I send by Mr Mellus three rings which we got made of the gold from the mines, one for your self, and one for Jane, Daniels wife, and one for Mary A. Badlam [Brannan's half-sister]. You must deliver them with my love and best wishes for their welfair and hapiness...I think of you often and of N.Y. also for that is the place of my child hood and I look forward with joyous heart to the time when I shall return. There is many things I would like to write of if I had time. I will send a little of Samuels hair for you all And I hope this will find you in the enjoyment of good health
>
> Yours with love and respect
> A. L. Brannan [1]

With so many immigrants streaming in, crime was running rampant and there was more talk about forming a vigilance committee. Then Brannan got a letter from his brother, Captain John, who told him he was bringing the first steamship around the horn and would be coming for a visit. If he liked the area, he might give up the sea and stay. Perhaps it was Liza's letter that helped him make the decision. At any rate, Brannan decided to hire him to help manage his many business affairs.

Liza was still after her husband to travel and enjoy life more; he owed it to his neglected family, she said. Brannan put her off, stating that he needed time to train a new manager. Besides, he was running for the town council; a gang of "hounds," made up mostly of ex-convicts from Australia, were the scourge of the town, and by mid-1849 Brannan was out to get them.

A force of 230 men volunteered for "The Light Guard," and they went after the gang, arresting over twenty of them. They were brought to trial, but most escaped conviction on technicalities of the law. Brannan was disgusted, but he was elected to the council largely because of his efforts to bring down the hated "Hounds." One of his first acts was to provide a badly needed jail by remodeling the idle brigantine, *Ephemia*, for that purpose. Not satisfied, Brannan got an ordinance passed requiring the convicts to work on public projects for their keep.

BRANNAN'S FRIEND, Captain Sutter, had been reduced to near poverty by then. Squatters were living all over his land, and thieves had killed or stolen most of his livestock. Without a labor force to do the work, he was unable to get his crops in and his industries had shut down for lack of help. His son, August, had come from Europe to help his befuddled father straighten out his tangled financial affairs. Their only remaining asset was land in Sacramento, and this was being sold to pay off Sutter's horrendous debts. Brannan offered to help, but first he had business to attend to in San Francisco.

The business involved financial problems San Francisco faced, plus a devastating fire that destroyed a good portion of the city. That and other problems caused Brannan to resign his position on the city council. It didn't seem to bother him much, as he began spending more time in Sacramento. August Sutter was selling off lots for his father and Brannan wanted some for himself. Through a series of manipulations some thought conniving and deceitful, Brannan managed to acquire numerous valuable lots from the beleaguered Sutters at little or no cost. Friendship apparently meant nothing when it came to business. What land he couldn't get through conniving, he bought with a huge note and little cash as a down payment. He ended up owning or controlling about one-fourth of Sacramento.

By 1851 crime involving the "Sydney Ducks" in San Francisco had gotten out of hand, and Brannan helped organize the Committee of Vigilance. After they hanged a man, the city district attorney charged Brannan and several others with murder. As a defense, the other committee members signed a statement that they were equally guilty. They included many of the influential businessmen in town, so the charges were dropped. After the Committee of Vigilance hung a few others, Brannan dropped out and turned over the reins to William Coleman. Brannan had other fish to fry. Together with Senator William Gwinn, he helped push through a congressional bill to form a land commission to study the tangled web of land titles in the fledgling state. By now he and Liza had four children; their youngest, Don Francisco, had died in infancy.

It was about then that Brannan sailed to the Hawaiian Islands to invest (and lose heavily) in real estate; nevertheless, it is said that he almost talked King Kamehameha into ceding the islands to him. By the time he returned to San Francisco with a thinner wallet, Brannan had heavy family responsibilities; he was beginning to drink heavily and was becoming known as a womanizer. Running short of cash, he left for the East, where he borrowed heavily from New York financiers. While there he ordered a new $10,000 fire engine for the city from his own funds.

Brannan's older brother, Captain John, had long been his manager; soon his duties included looking after Sam's neglected family. After a torrid romance with the notorious Lola Montez, Brannan began construction of a four-story office building. Among his other interests, he owned a lumber mill on Yerba Buena Island, a biscuit factory near Mission Dolores and a bookstore. In addition, he bought and stocked a large ranch on the Feather River near Marysville.

In the prime of his career, Brannan was like a dynamo; he owned land all over California and in Hawaii, but still was not satisfied. He became a man about town, buying expensive champagne for everyone of consequence. Finally Captain John took over his messy finances and placed his errant younger brother on an allowance. By 1856, Brannan had become widely known as the wealthiest, most influential man in California. He had bestowed on his frustrated wife a generous property settlement, whereupon she took the children and moved to a chateau in Geneva, Switzerland, in what appeared to be a trial separation.

Captain John Brannan had grown to hate Liza'a ambitious social climbing and constantly fretted over Samuel's shenanigans. Surprisingly, Samuel obtained Liza's financial backing in 1857 to open the Brannan Bank in San Francisco, said to be the first commercial bank in the state. It later became the Pacific Bank. Next, Brannan became enamored with the Napa Valley; nothing would do except to build an opulent resort hotel complex there. He named it Calistoga after a drunken attempt to say "Saratoga of California" got twisted around. It was known for its spouting geysers and health-giving hot springs, and Brannan lavished much of his wealth in its development.

Captain John cautioned that he was putting too many eggs in one basket by liquidating most of his other properties and borrowing too heavily. Brannan seemed unperturbed, seeing the resort as a new challenge. Besides, he liked it there. But the work took a physical toll on his abused body, and he soon developed a chronic cough, even spitting blood at times.

Besides the resort, he planted acres of vineyards and built a brandy distillery, placing Donner Party survivor Lewis Keseberg in charge. Before long the Napa Valley became world renowned for quality wines and brandy. Transportation to Calistoga was poor, so Brannan helped extend the Napa Valley Railroad—which ran between Vallejo and Napa—to his resort.

Meanwhile he had suffered belated pangs of conscience over his ill treatment of his first wife, Hattie, and their daughter, Elmira. They were brought to San Francisco, where Hattie soon remarried. Later, Captain John developed physical symptoms similar to his brother's (probably tuberculosis), and in 1862 he took a sea voyage for his health. Instead, he died at sea, and his remains were preserved in a brandy cask until the ship returned to San Francisco.

Devastated by the loss of his brother, Brannan failed to heed the warning about his own physical condition. Captain John was replaced by Brannan's nephew, Alexander Badlam Jr., who came to manage his business affairs. Against advice from Alexander and others, Brannan invested heavily in bonds to assist the Mexican leader, Benito Juarez, who was attempting to oust the hated French Emperor Maximilian from Mexico. Not only that, but Brannan organized a group of volunteer mercenaries, armed them, and smuggled them into Mexico to fight on the side of the revolutionaries to oust Maximilian.

MEANWHILE, Liza Brannan had returned with the children. Sammy was a graduate engineer, but had trouble finding a job. The girls were still at home, and Brannan put them all up in an opulent house at 930 Clay Street in San Francisco, complete with servants. He then watched the bills come in with some apprehension. Though he was worth millions on paper, he was always strapped for ready cash. In 1868 Brannan got in an altercation over a sawmill he was trying to repossess and was shot and seriously wounded in the ensuing fracas.

Brannan recovered from his wounds fairly fast, but his relationship with his wife was deteriorating faster than his health. When he cut her allowance, she accused him of adultery with a friend's wife. Finally she threatened to divorce him and drag his relationship with the "other woman" through the courts. Brannan wouldn't stand for that, and offered her half his assets for an amicable divorce. They were divorced in 1870, with Liza taking much of the property and all of the cash Brannan could raise by liquidating most of his assets. Thus a relationship that had endured many tribulations ended with vindictiveness on both sides.

The costly settlement ended with the collapse of Brannan's shaky house of cards, which had been built largely on credit. Given more time, he probably could have survived. But his wife was adamant and demanded $500,000 cash immediately. One can scarcely blame her, as she had put up with Brannan's drinking and womanizing for years. Finally it had been his downfall. After saying goodbye to Calistoga in 1877, he headed for Mexico for a new start. Maybe there he could exchange his Juarez bonds for land. It was always land he believed in, and he thought of starting a new American colony.

But first Brannan stopped in Monterey and convinced old Manuel

Castro to use his influence to help him acquire land in Mexico. Juarez was dead and could offer no help; whatever land he got would have to be through Castro. By 1882 it looked as if Brannan had pulled off another coup. Somehow he had acquired 1,500 leagues of land in Sonora. He then returned to New York and San Francisco, trying to induce settlers to come there once the surveying was completed.

Later, snags developed with the Mexican government, and the deal fell through. Meanwhile, Liza had lost her money in risky silver-mining stocks and was taking in boarders to make ends meet. Alexander Badlam, known as Alec, finally learned that Brannan was living in Mexico with a girl named Carmen. In 1882 he heard they had married, and that Brannan now owned valuable acreage near Guaymas, where he was still trying to get his colony started. But it seemed that old age and ill health had taken a heavy toll. Though he had quit drinking, Brannan wasn't able to finalize his grandiose plans.

After things went sour in Mexico, Brannan moved to Arizona in 1885, where he was selling pencils. Two years later was back in San Francisco. He sailed south to San Diego two weeks later, where he attempted to sell real estate. Apparently financed by Alec Badlam in 1888, he acquired a few acres of land in Escondido, where he lived in a boarding house and planted fig trees. When Alec learned of his uncle's ill health, he went for a visit and was shocked at what he found. Brannan had apparently suffered a stroke in Mexico; one arm was limp, and he was lame from the old gunshot wound. He told Alec that Carmen had left him.

Then came an unexpected letter from Brannan's Odd Fellow's lodge in San Francisco. It brought him good news and a check. It seemed that land he had given them for a cemetery had proven profitable to the lodge. They had set aside part of the profits in a trust for Brannan, and he would be getting regular checks. The amount was modest, but at least he was able to hire a kindly Mexican woman to care for him.

Brannan was also pressing the Mexican government for a cash settlement for his land there. He reportedly received a cash settlement of $49,000 and allegedly returned to San Francisco, where he had Alec Badlam pay off all his debts. When he was through, he had $500 left, which he took in gold double eagles. After visiting with old friends in the area, he sailed back down the coast to San Diego and returned to Escondido. Some accounts state that this simply isn't true; Brannan received no settlement and made no trip north.

Whatever the facts, Brannan suffered another stroke, after which his kindly Mexican woman continued to care for him. A truly remarkable man, though a bit of a scoundrel, Brannan died in Escondido May 5, 1889 (some accounts say May 14), at the age of seventy. After his body lay in an undertaker's vault for over a year, Alec Badlam paid the over-due account and had Brannan's remains interred at Mt. Hope Cemetery in San Diego. His gravestone reads:

"SAM" BRANNAN
1819 – 1889
California Pioneer of '46
– Dreamer – Leader –
And
Empire Builder

AFTER a long period of impoverishment, Liza died in San Francisco at age 93. Two state plaques in San Joaquin County mark the site of New Hope and the landing place of the ship *Comet* that brought the Mormons there. Two more at Calistoga (Napa Co.) identify the Brannan's store and cottage; a street in San Francisco is named after him, as is the office of the *Star* Newspaper at the corner of Washington Street and Brenham. Also the "Brannan House" building is located in Old Sacramento State Park. Many were Brannan's flaws, but greater were his achievements. Surely, few lived a fuller life.

BIBLIOGRAPHY

–Bailey, Paul. *Sam Brannan and the California Mormons.* Westernlore Press, Los Angeles, 1943
–Bancoft, Hubert H. *History of California,* Vol. I-VI. History Co. San Francisco, 1886. Reprinted, Wallace Hebberd, Santa Barbara, 1966.
–DeVoto, Bernard. *The Year of Decision: 1846.* Houghton Mifflin Co., Boston, 1942.
–Brannan, Ann Eliza. Copy of original letter to Mary Brannan (Capt. John's wife) dated Sept. 2, 1848. Charles Hill collection, Lotus, CA. [1]
–Davis, William Heath. *Seventy-five Years in California.* John Howell Books. San Francisco, 1967.
–Dillon, Richard. *Fool's Gold.* Coward McCann, Inc. New York, 1967.
_Dillon, Richard. *Humbugs and Heros,* Yosemite-DiMaggio, Oakland, CA, 1983.
–Gay, Theressa. *James Marshall, A Biography.* Talisman Press, Georgetown, CA, 1967.
–Scott, Reva. *Samuel Brannan and the Golden Fleece.* Macmillan Co., New York, 1944.
–Stellman, Louis J. *Sam Brannan, Builder of San Francisco.* Exposition Press, New York, 1953.
–Wainscott, Karen. "California's First Millionaire–The Saint's Sinner." *Sacramento Bee,* Sept. 11, 1988.
–Wilcox, Del. *Voyagers To California.* Sea Rock Press, Elk, CA, 1991.

Notes

Peter H. Burnett
Courtesy California Department of Parks & Recreation

– 8 –

PETER H. BURNETT

1807 – 1895

A NATIVE OF NASHVILLE, TENNESSEE, Peter H. Burnett was born into a long line of native Southerners November 15, 1807. His parents, George and Dorothy Hardeman Burnet, owned a few slaves but were far from wealthy. When Peter added a second "t" to his surname at age 20, he apparently thought it added class to the name. Little did he know that he was to become the first elected governor of the new State of California 23 years later.

Peter was the first son born to his parents, but altogether there were four more sons and three daughters. His mother's family, the Thomas Hardemans, were well-to-do and probably had misgivings about their daughter's marriage to a poor farmer-carpenter like George Burnet. When Peter was around four the family moved to a farm in Williamson County; in 1817 they followed their in-laws—the Hardemans—to Howard County, Missouri. Conditions there couldn't have been much better, according to Peter Burnett's vivid description in his memoirs:

> We spent the first winter in a large camp with a dirt floor, boarded up on the sides with clapboards, and covered with the same, leaving a hole in the center of the roof for the escape of smoke. All the family lived together in the same room, the whites on one side and the blacks on the other. [1]

Later they took up a 160-acre homestead on newly opened land in Clay County, Missouri. Peter Burnet's sporadic education consisted of the basic "three R's," with emphasis on English grammar. He later told how the family existed mostly on parched corn and wild game. When he left home at age 20, his father presented him with a good horse and saddle, a "new camlet coat, $20 in cash and a good suit of jeans." By the time he reached Nashville, his horse was badly worn, and he felt like a poverty-stricken outcast among his "rich kin," the Hardemans.

This was about the time that Peter added the other "t" to his last name, making the spelling Burnett. At loose ends at the time, Peter decided to accompany his uncle Blackstone Hardeman to Bolivar in Hardeman County. Almost immediately he landed a job as a hotel clerk at the munificent salary of $100 per year. A few months later he was offered $200 a year to work as a clerk-bookkeeper in a log-cabin store near Bolivar.

Shortly before his 21st birthday, Burnett fell in love with a pretty, petite seventeen-year-old girl, Harriet Rogers. Though Burnet feared he had too little to offer in the way of material goods, they were married in August 1828. Harriet was much more religious than Peter, and she proved a good choice. Besides her beauty, she had strong convictions and excellent common sense. About a year after the wedding, Burnett was able to buy his employer's business—on credit, of course.

Unfortunately the business did poorly until Burnett bought some whisky, which he sold at a good profit. When he found he was developing a taste for it, he quit drinking entirely. He did the same with tobacco, which he never used after getting sick from strong cigars. After becoming involved in killing a burglar, he also developed a lifetime aversion to shedding human life. His rather pious wife probably influenced his decisions in these matters.

In 1830 Burnett's older brother, Glen O., came to Hardeman County and ended up marrying Harriet's sister, Sarah. It was about then that Burnett decided to close the largely unprofitable store and study law. His brother was planning to take his new bride to a farm in Clay County, Missouri; Burnett sent his wife and infant son with them while he stayed to sell off the merchandise and collect debts owed him.

Later he went together with one of his wife's brothers to buy a law library, which they studied diligently until both were felled by "fever" (probably ague or cholera). Burnett recovered, but his promising young brother-in-law died from it. Crushed by the loss, Burnett wound up his business affairs and headed for Clay County to rejoin his wife and young son. The joyous reunion took place in April 1832.

After taking a job in a mercantile store for $400 per year, Burnett continued his law studies. Fifteen months later he qualified to practice law. By 1839 he had gained a reputation as a good speaker and writer. Later he joined two other lawyers to represent John Smith Jr. and several other Mormon leaders who had been jailed in Liberty, Missouri, for treason, arson and robbery, alleged to have taken place in Davis County.

When "Burnett and Associates" were successful in getting the Mormons released on a writ of habeas corpus, Mormon-haters in the area were incensed to the point where the lawyers feared for their own safety. As a precaution, they armed themselves and were surrounded by armed friends. Fortunately they were not attacked, and it wasn't long before most of the Mormons left for Illinois.

In 1840 several Missouri counties were merged into a new judicial district, and Burnett was appointed District Attorney. He served a total of three years, after which he felt utterly drained from so many serious litigations. He moved his growing family to Platte City, Missouri, where a daughter was born in 1841. Burnett was probably acquainted with James W. Marshall at that time. The following year Burnett bought an interest in the town of Weston in Platte County and moved there. It was then he began taking an interest in Oregon—especially when he learned that generous portions of good fertile land were available for home-steading. He was deeply in debt because of business losses and saw Oregon as a way of making a comeback.

Harriet Burnett had been ailing for some time (possibly from ague), and Peter thought a change in climate might be good for her; in fact, her doctor told them the trip west "would kill her or cure her." Burnett wasted little time organizing a wagon train of like-minded people. By then his family numbered seven, and he packed plenty of supplies in three wagons. He had five men along and joined with other emigrants about twelve miles west of Independence. Most of the estimated 875 people bound for Oregon left there in mid-May.

Burnett's party included Pierson Reading, Dr. Marcus Whitman and Jessie and Lindsay Applegate. John Gant (or Gantt) was hired to pilot them to Fort Hall, and on June 1st Burnett was elected captain. His captaincy lasted about a week, when he resigned in disgust over irre-sponsible actions by some of the emigrants. He was replaced by William Martin.

TRAVELING ON the Oregon Trail, they crossed South Pass in early August. By then things were turning grim; two deceased men had been buried along the trail and food was running low. Upon reaching Ft. Hall, John Gantt and Pierson Reading left them to join Joseph Chiles' California-bound party (see Chiles). Dr. Whitman agreed to pilot Burnett's group part way to Oregon and provide an Indian guide for the final leg to Ft. Vancouver.

Burnett may have known that James Marshall and others would be following the next year, for he left them a letter at Ft. Hall: It warned that if they were short of food, they should send men ahead to obtain supplies at Ft. Vancouver. The men could then return and meet them along the trail. This valuable advice was followed by Marshall's party in 1844 (see Marshall).

Whitman had taken two-wheeled carts to his mission at Waiilaptu, near Ft. Walla Walla, but he had never taken wagons. Nevertheless, Burnett's party managed to get their wagons through to Walla Walla by the end of October. Burnett left his wagons and weary livestock there, while he took his family to The Dalles by boat, where there was a

Methodist mission. Burnett then continued to Ft. Vancouver, pre-sumedly in the same boat.

When Burnett's group reached Fort. Vancouver, they found John C. Fremont there purchasing supplies for his U. S. Army exploration party, which had been left at The Dalles (see Fremont). Burnett made housing arrangements at the fort for his family with Chief Factor (manager) John McLaughlin, who loaned him and Fremont a boat and pilot so they could return to The Dalles. Once Burnett had his family settled at Ft. Vancouver, he accompanied some others to establish the town of Linnton, a few miles up the Willamette River.

In May 1844 Burnett moved his family to land he acquired near Oregon City. He then returned to Walla Walla for his livestock and wag-ons. Although the area was in contention between Great Britain and the U. S., the American settlers established a provisional government in 1843. Later Burnett became a member of "The Legislative Committee of Oregon."

In 1845 Jesse Applegate opened a new trail into the south portion of the Willamette Valley from Fort Hall, and Samuel Barlow opened a toll road around the south side of Mt. Hood from The Dalles. Crude as they were, these trails offered emigrants a chance to get wagons through to Oregon without facing the deep gorges and terrifying rapids of the Columbia River. The migration to Oregon increased even faster in 1846 after a treaty establishing permanent boundaries was approved between the U. S. and Great Britain. By then Burnett was a judge of the Oregon Supreme Court and had joined the Catholic Church in Oregon City. As the only Catholic in his family—and one of the few in Oregon—he learned what it was like to suffer verbal abuse from religious bigots.

IN 1847 came the dreadful news of the massacre of Dr. Marcus Whitman, his wife, Narcissa, and others at Whitman's Mission at Waiilaptu. Trusted Cayuse Indians in the area had become disillusioned with the missionaries and made a sneak attack on mission personnel. News about it did not reach Oregon City for over a week, at which time a volunteer army of 500 men was recruited to punish the renegade Cayuse Indians.

A year later Burnett was dumbfounded by the news that his old Platte County neighbor, James W. Marshall, had discovered gold in California. Within days most of the able-bodied men in Oregon had left for California or were preparing to do so. Peter Burnett was more cau-tious than most, but even he began making plans to leave. Though he was well established in Oregon, his finances had not improved and he was still deeply in debt. Rather than hurry down the Siskiyou Trail on horseback as many did, he organized a full-scale wagon train, to be piloted by Thomas McKay.

McKay, a Hudson's Bay Co. trapper, had made the journey several times but never with wagons; in fact, no one had tried taking wagons south from Oregon before. McKay knew the Siskiyou Trail was too risky; instead, he headed for the Applegate Trail. In September, Captain Burnett with 150 men and 50 wagons followed him to the Klamath lakes. There they turned south, while McKay, Burnett and others scouted ahead for a viable wagon route.

After passing Goose Lake, they found a new road heading southwest. Later they learned it had been blazed by a small wagon train led by Danish emigrant, Peter Lassen (see Lassen). The road followed the Pit River until it looped to the north, where Lassen's party left the river to travel around the east side of a lofty volcano that today bears his name. Burnett's party soon caught up with the slower-moving Lassen Party, which they found in pitiful condition. Some wagons had been abandoned or cut into two-wheeled carts and people were starving. They blamed Lassen, who feared for his life from angry members of the party.

Thanks to Burnett's careful preparations, his party had plenty of provisions and were able to feed the unfortunates. Once their strength returned, the entire group attacked the rough terrain with renewed vigor. Soon they had blazed a crude wagon road along Deer Creek to the Sacramento River and Lassen's ranch (see Lassen). After resting there a short time, they continued down the great valley to John A. Sutter's "Hock Farm" on the Feather River (see Sutter).

Having established New Helvetia (Sutter's Fort), John Sutter expanded his farming and ranching activities to his Hock Farm and financed the sawmill in Cullomah (present Coloma), where James Marshall had discovered gold (see Marshall). After leaving the Hock Farm, Burnett and a few others headed for the Yuba River, where they had heard rich gold deposits could be found. In early November they stopped at a place called Long's Bar, where about 80 people were busily engaged in placer mining.

Burnett liked what he saw, whereupon he and two partners—a nephew, Horace Burnett, and a brother-in-law, John Rogers—bought a 20-foot claim on credit. Using a homemade rocker, the partners were able to average over three ounces of gold per day, which allowed them to pay off the mining claim within a short time. By mid-December the weather was turning cold and Burnett had accumulated a modest "stake in his poke." He left the mines on the 19th and headed for Sutter's Fort to rest and survey the possibilities of resuming his law practice.

There he found Dr. William Carpenter, an old friend from Missouri. Dr. Carpenter had rented small quarters at the fort, where he was practicing medicine. The two friends agreed to share the quarters so Burnett could practice law there. They also shared a homemade bed Dr.

Carpenter had been using—cozy indeed. They took their meals in the "hotel," which was probably being operated by Samuel Kyburz and his wife in the old barracks.

Captain Sutter had run up heavy debts during the years when he was building his agricultural empire. He had left his wife and five children in Germany when he emigrated to the U. S. in 1834, but had recently sent for his oldest son, John A. Sutter Jr. When Sutter's son (called August) arrived late in 1848, he was placed in charge of selling off his father's land to pay off his back-breaking debts—especially the huge amount owed the Russians for the impulsive purchase of Fort Ross in 1841.

August hired Peter Burnett to handle legal matters. Burnett was to receive a twenty-five-percent commission for each lot sold. His job involved paper-work required to ensure proper title transfers and see that creditors were paid off in an orderly manner. Meanwhile, John Sutter Sr. had moved to his beloved Hock Farm. He had instructed his son to sell lots in Sutterville, a subdivision located on higher ground, three miles downriver from the *embarcadero* (at present South Land Park). Instead, Sutter Jr. and Burnett found the market near the embarcadero in Sacramento City far more lucrative.

B Y THE TIME John Sutter's debts had been paid off in mid-1849, he had learned about his son's decision to sell lots in Sacramento City. Furious and feeling betrayed, he fired both Burnett and his son, August. August later left the country in disgrace, but Burnett sued Sutter for breach of contract and settled for more than a hundred Sacramento City lots.

At about this time settlers in the area decided they needed some kind of formal government until California could be admitted to the Union. Delegates were selected to attend provisional government meetings at San Jose, Sacramento and San Francisco. After Peter Burnett was elected president, he appointed a committee of five to draw up a "preamble and resolutions expressive of the sense of the meetings." The committee consisted of Samuel Brannan, John S. Fowler, John Sinclair, Pierson Reading and Barton Lee. On his first visit to San Francisco in 1849, Burnett fell in love with the Bay Area (see Brannan).

Burnett returned to Sacramento in April. When his wife and children arrived in San Francisco from Oregon on a coastal sailing vessel, Burnett found housing for his family in San Francisco and moved there June 1st. Almost immediately he became a member of the Legislative Assembly of San Francisco, made up of a group of concerned citizens pressing for statehood. Crime was an ever-increasing problem; vigilante groups had been dealing with it but were becoming a problem themselves. In early June General Bennet Riley, the military governor, issued a proclamation denying the Legislative Assembly the right to establish a formal government. Apparently he was concerned that they might declare the territory independent from the U. S. and felt obligated to squelch it.

Burnett then left for Sacramento to settle his dispute with Captain John Sutter over the sale of Sutter's land. During his absence from San Francisco, he was elected judge of the "Superior Tribunal of California." The reader will recall how Sutter had fired both Burnett and his son, August, for selling Sutter's land in Sacramento City. It is interesting to read a subsequent statement written by August Sutter about the outcome:

> I have the firm belief that if Judge Burnett could have been retained for the management of our affairs up to the present date [1855], my father would be, now, one of the richest men in California. [2]

Upon his return to the Bay Area, Burnett bought a house in San Jose for the sake of a daughter who was dying from consumption. He thought the damp climate in San Francisco was bad for her and hoped the dryer climate in San Jose would be of some benefit. Between that and Burnett's policy of virtually force-feeding the girl, she eventually recovered her health.

During this period he sold about half of his Sacramento property for $50,000, considered a fortune then. In September 1849 Burnett was elected Chief Justice by the other justices. He was living in Monterey when General Riley called for a Constitutional Convention to establish a formal government for California. Forty-eight delegates, elected from throughout the state, were to attend the convention at Colton Hall in Monterey.

Seizing the opportunity, Burnett declared himself a candidate for governor. Then, while convention business was taking place, Burnett stumped the gold country giving campaign speeches. On November 13, 1849 the new constitution was ratified, and Burnett was elected governor. He had defeated runner-ups William Sherwood and John Sutter by a wide margin; thus Peter Burnett had the distinction of becoming the first civilian to serve as governor of California.

CALIFORNIA was admitted to the Union September 9, 1850, and Burnett resigned his office in January 1851. He returned to the practice of law in a partnership with two other prominent lawyers in San Francisco. By then he had built a spacious new home in Alviso, where he had other business interests. Four years later he had the house dismantled and moved nine miles to San Jose, where it was reconstructed. He had retired from his law practice by then, devoting his time and considerable abilities to other interests. During the summer of 1856 he was stricken by chronic neuralgia, which plagued him for many years.

Despite Burnett's painful ailment, he and his wife took their first ocean voyage around the horn to New York in early 1857. After arriving in New York, they traveled to Missouri, where they visited with friends and relatives. By December Burnett was back in Sacramento, where he was appointed a justice of the Supreme Court of California. He resigned in October 1858, possibly due to his wife's death that year.

Casting around for new business opportunities in the early 1860s, Burnett invested in banking. In June 1863 he was chosen president of the "Pacific Accumulation Loan Co.", replacing Samuel Brannan, who had resigned. This required a move back to San Francisco. Later, when the bank began to fail from under capitalization, Brannan stepped in to save it with another hefty investment.

The bank eventually recouped its losses and grew to become the Pacific Bank, making Burnett and Brannan wealthy and prominent men. After retiring in 1880, Burnett continued to reside in San Francisco until his death in May 1895 at the age of 87. Two children preceded him in death, and he left two sons and two married daughters. He was buried in the Catholic cemetery in Santa Clara, and a street in San Francisco was named in his honor.

Historian Hubert Bancroft had mixed feelings about Burnett, as the following extract shows:

> Burnett has never been credited with any brilliant abilities, nor charged with any great weakness; lacking force and decision in official positions; an honest, industrious, kind-hearted, diplomatic, lucky man; of many but harmless whims in private life...[3]

Most of us would settle for an objective obituary like that. Though he spent only half of his life in California, Gov. Peter H. Burnett deserves a place on the honor roll of early California pioneers. His portrait hangs in the State Capitol.

BIBLIOGRAPHY

–Bancroft, Hubert H. *California Pioneer Register and Index*. Regional Pub. Co., Baltimore, MD, 1964. [3]

–Burnett, Peter H. *An Old California Pioneer*. Biobooks, Oakland, CA, 1946. [1] Most quotes taken from this publication.

–Corning, Howard McKinley, Ed. *Dictionary of Oregon History*. Binsford & Mort, Portland, OR, 1956.

–Davis, William Heath. *Seventy-five Years in California*. John Howell Books. San Francisco, 1967.

–Dillon, Richard. *Fools Gold, A Biography of John Sutter*. Coward-McCann, Inc. New York, 1967. [2]

–Egan, Ferol. *Fremont, Explorer for a Restlass Nation.* University of Nevada Press, Reno, 1985.

–Faragher, John Mack. *Women And Men On The Overland Trail.* Yale University Press, New Haven, 1979.

–Harlow, Neal. *California Conquered.* University of California Press, Berkeley, 1982.

–Jackson, Donald Dale. *Gold Dust.* Alfred A. Knopf, New York, 1980.

–Lewis, Oscar. *Sutter's Fort: Gateway to the Gold Fields.* Prentice-Hall, Inc., Englewood Cliffs, NJ, 1966.

NOTES

Joseph Ballinger Chiles
Courtesy California Department of Parks & Reccreation

– 9 –

JOSEPH BALLINGER CHILES (DON JOSE)

1810 – 1885

O
NE OF TEN CHILDREN parented by Jack and Sarah Ballinger
Chiles, Joseph B. Chiles was virtually born a frontiersman July
16, 1810 in Clark County, Kentucky. Not much has been
recorded about his early life, but he got some education between planting and harvesting times on the marginal family farm. By the time
Joseph had sprouted into a tall, gangly young man with eager blue eyes
and fiery red hair, most of his older siblings had migrated to Missouri.

At age 20 Joseph Chiles married Polly Ann Stevenson, and a year
later they moved to Missouri to be near Joseph's older brothers. Polly
Ann died six years later, leaving her distraught husband with four small
children to raise. Fortunately his relatives were able to care for them.

The following year found 28-year-old Joseph Chiles serving in the
U.S. Army during the Florida Indian Wars. After his Commanding
Officer was killed during the Battle of Lake Okeechobee, Chiles was
breveted a Lieutenant. In later years he was given the honorary title of
Colonel. By February 1841 he was out of the army and living in
Westport, Missouri. There he listened to a first-hand account of the
wonders of California from trapper-explorer, Antoine Robidoux.

After the meeting with Robidoux, Chiles and other members of the
enthusiastic audience began signing up for a membership in the Western
Emigration Society. This group was to begin outfitting themselves with
the necessary livestock, vehicles and supplies required for the long overland journey to California. They were to meet in early May about twenty miles west of the Missouri River at a place called Sapling Grove.

A few days later Chiles and Bartleson, with some German immigrants, met the main party at the Kansas River as promised. Also joining
them was Reverend Joseph Williams, a Protestant preacher traveling
alone. The newly established but uncharted Oregon Trail would be used
by all of them as far as Soda Springs, where the California group would
split off and head southwest.

Bidwell was secretary, and when Bartleson was elected captain it became known as the Bartleson-Bidwell Party (see Chapter 1) After an incredibly difficult journey west across the Sierra to John Marsh's ranch on the eastern base of Mt. Diablo, Joseph Chiles found he had something in common with powerful *Californio* Mariano Vallejo—a mutual friendship with George Yount (see Vallejo & Yount)).

When Vallejo learned that Chiles intended to visit Yount in Napa Valley, he insisted that Chiles stop along the way and pay him a visit in Sonoma. But first Chiles wanted to visit Captain John Sutter at his New Helvetia settlement (see Sutter). Having settled at the confluence of the Sacramento and American rivers two years before, Sutter was gaining a reputation as a hospitable host. Once Chiles and the others overcame worrisome problems with Mexican authorities over their illegal entry into the country, they were issued passports and were free to travel.

While some of the party stayed along the San Joaquin River to trap beaver and otter, Chiles, Bidwell, Rickman, Henry Huber and Charles Weber headed northeast to visit Sutter at New Helvetia. After a long drought the weather turned rainy during their 80 mile trip, delaying their arrival until just before Christmas. The Kelsey clan joined the weary group for a holiday celebration, and Sutter made good his reputation as a generous host (see Kelsey & Bidwell).

Before Chiles and Rickman left, Sutter convinced them to visit Monterey to get acquainted with Thomas O. Larkin and other American settlers in the area. Sutter wrote to Larkin January 26, 1842:

> I took the liberty to introduce to your acquaintance Capt. Joseph Chiles and Cornell [Colonel] Rickman lately of Missouri, two gentlemen of my acquaintance when I was in Missouri; both of them was very highly respected there and have a good deal of property....
> I am all time happy to do everything for American citizen when it lays in my power and so I think you will do the same....
> Very respectfully, Your Most Obt.. Servt., J.A.. Sutter

Sutter was not above exaggerating military titles, or anything else for that matter, to make a good impression. On the other hand, his letter demonstrates a conscientious attempt to aid his fellow man. After leaving New Helvetia, Chiles and Rickman returned to the San Joaquin River, where they met Charles Hopper and headed for Monterey.

They were warmly received there by Thomas O. Larkin and his American wife, Rachel (see Larkin). Chiles learned that if he intended to request a land grant from the Mexican Government, he would have to become a naturalized citizen of Mexico. Apparently this didn't bother Chiles; he had become captivated by the country and recognized its unlimited possibilities. He and Hopper then traveled north to Santa Cruz to visit Isaac Graham and study his sawmill there. (see Graham).

Like Chiles, Graham was a roughshod, Kentucky-born frontiers-man. He offered hospitality and provided valuable information about life in California and the instability of Mexican politics. When Chiles and Hopper left, heading for San Jose, Chiles intended to look for a good site for a water powered sawmill or gristmill. His millwright friend, William Baldridge, would be just the man to help him if he could get him out to California. Baldridge had wanted to accompany Chiles on this trip, but had been unable to leave. Chiles decided to return to Missouri in the spring and bring Baldridge with him the following year.

After a short visit in San Jose, Chiles and Hopper continued north to Yerba Buena (San Francisco). There were only a few residents there at the time, including pioneer traders, Jacob Leese and William Richardson (see Richardson). Hopper described it as a "miserable place, nothing but a lot of sandhills. There was one hut, a sort of tavern." After spending the night there, they hired Kanaka Bill Davis to take them across the bay to Sonoma Creek in his trading vessel (see Davis). Then they walked to Sonoma to visit Mariano Vallejo.

THE GENIAL Vallejo treated them with typical California hospitality and freely discussed Chiles' plans to build a gristmill. Vallejo took a liking to the earnest, ambitious red-head, and offered to help him locate a suitable site for the mill whenever Chiles was ready. Encouraged by their reception, Chiles and Hopper borrowed horses from the general and headed into Napa Valley to visit George Yount at his Rancho Caymus.

While staying with Yount, Chiles and Hopper explored the sur-rounding area thoroughly and discovered a lovely little valley hidden among the rolling hills near Yount's ranch. Chiles was smitten with it and decided to make application for a land grant as soon as possible. It was a perfect site for a ranch and the water-powered mill he planned. First he and Hopper would return to New Helvetia, via Wolfskill's ranch on Putah Creek, and then journey down the Sacramento River to the San Joaquin River (see Wolfskill). There Rickman and other members of the emigration party waited for them.

When Chiles and Hopper reached New Helvetia, they found Sutter building a spacious, high-walled, adobe fort. From then on, New Helvetia was known simply as "Sutter's Fort." After leaving there, they stopped by John Marsh's ranch at the base of Mt. Diablo and picked up a packet of letters from him to be delivered in Missouri.

After reuniting with their companions on the San Joaquin River, they made preparations for the long journey east. This time their route was to take them south through the San Joaquin Valley, exiting east through Walker Pass. Unable to locate it, they crossed over Tejon Pass instead and then headed northeast to the Humboldt River and on to

Fort Hall. Going southeast to the Green River, they heeded warnings about hostile Indians and detoured farther south over rough, uncharted land toward Santa Fe. They finally ended up on the Santa Fe Trail, which took them to Independence. It was early September when they arrived, after an incredible, zig-zag journey of over 4,000 miles.

Chiles enjoyed visiting with his children, but realized they were still too young for the trip to California. They would have to wait until they were older; if it took another trip, so be it. He then paid a visit to George Yount's wife. He found she had divorced Yount, assuming he had deserted her, and remarried. Yount's oldest daughter, Frances, had married Bartlett Vines and had two children. Her husband had a yen to go to California, so they agreed to accompany Chiles on his return trip. Yount's youngest daughter, 18-year-old Elizabeth, agreed to go along with the Vines family. Yount's son wanted nothing to do with his father.

Chiles' next chore was to recruit his friend, Billy Baldridge, and gather the supplies needed for the return trip to California, including machinery to build a water-powered mill. By the time they left in May 1843, there were thirty well mounted men, six women and three wagons in the Chiles party, including Pierson Reading, whose phonetically spelled name was used for the city of Redding. When they camped about thirty miles from Westport, they were visited by John C. Fremont, who was also on his way west with a party of U.S. Army Engineers on a surveying trip (see Fremont) . With him was Thomas Fitzpatrick, who was glad to see his old traveling companion, Joseph Chiles. At the Kaw River crossing, the Chiles party met another larger party traveling to Oregon. Later some of them joined Chile's group until there were around fifty people in the party.

A FEW DAYS LATER they met Joseph R. Walker, an old friend of Chiles' from Missouri, on his way east with a load of beaver pelts (see Walker). Walker suggested that Chiles try the route into California he had discovered years before—one that provided an easier crossing of the Sierra Nevada. This route went south along the eastern base of the mountains into present-day Owens Valley, before a crossing was made at present-day Walker Pass into the San Joaquin Valley—the elusive pass that Chiles had missed on his way east.

Chiles offered Walker $300 if he would guide them, which Walker agreed to do once he delivered his furs to Fort Laramie. He was to meet Chiles later along the trail. After catching up with Chiles somewhere west of Fort Laramie, he guided the party to the Vasquez and Bridger Trading Post, where they rested a few days. When they reached Fort Hall, Walker refused to leave until Chiles bought a few badly needed but terribly expensive beef cattle.

The party was still critically short of food, so Chiles left most of the food, the wagons and the women and children under Walker's care. Chiles then took all the men but two on horseback toward Fort Boise in an attempt to buy more supplies. They were to meet Walker, Baldridge and the others in the San Joaquin Valley after the wagons had been brought across Walker's Pass. Imagine Chiles' despair when they finally reached Fort Boise only to find no supplies available at any price. Rather than see them perish from starvation, the manager at Fort Boise let them have enough food to last about three weeks if they ate only one meal a day. The Chiles Party now had no choice except to reach Sutter's Fort by the fastest route possible.

While the Chiles Party was blazing a trail from Fort Boise (following the Malheur River (Oregon) and what later became Lassen's Trail), to Sutter's Fort on their restrictive diet, Walker was having problems of his own. He had never taken wagons across his new route; to his chagrin he found it impossible, especially with a group of inexperienced men, women and children tagging along. He was forced to abandon the wagons with most of their personal goods, including Chiles's vital mill machinery. Billy Baldridge must have spit bitter gall when he buried it all in the hot sands of Owens Valley.

Three weeks later, Walker's group of bedraggled emigrants crossed over Walker Pass into the San Joaquin Valley near present day Visalia. By then Chiles's party had reached Sutter's Fort, and were accumulating supplies to resume the journey south to Walker Pass. But when Walker found no sign of Chiles in the great valley, he led the miserable migrants westerly to the Salinas River, where game could be found in some abundance. There they camped while awaiting word from Chiles.

By mid-December Walker had heard nothing and led his party north to a rancho near Mission Soledad. After spending Christmas there, they broke into small groups and went their separate ways. Billy Baldridge and the family of Bartlett Vines went north to San Jose to get the necessary permits from Mexican authorities. Apparently they had better luck than did the members of the Bartleson-Bidwell Party in 1841, including Chiles himself. Somehow they got their permits and went to Sutter's Fort, while Walker went to Monterey to buy horses.

Meanwhile, Chiles had traveled to Walker Pass without learning of Walker's whereabouts. After spending a good deal of time looking for them, he and his discouraged men returned to Sutter's Fort, where they were reunited with Baldridge, Elizabeth Yount and the Vines family. It was then that Chiles learned about the loss of his mill machinery. Apparently feeling sorry for them, Sutter provided transportation for all on his launch to San Pablo Bay and on up the Napa River.

In early spring 1844 Chiles delivered George Yount's family safely to Yount's Rancho Caymus in the Napa Valley. The tearful and joyous reunion must have made the hardships of getting there seem well worthwhile. Almost immediately Chiles and Baldridge made their way to the lovely hidden valley Chiles had described so often. Within hours after arriving they were sketching a gristmill and choosing a site on the creek that ran through the property.

By early fall Chiles had his Mexican citizenship papers and immediately filed a petition for a land grant within the valley he claimed. In November Governor Manuel Micheltorena approved it, subject to final approval by the Departmental Assembly which was to meet in Monterey later in the year. But so far as Chiles was concerned, the land he coveted was legally his. He named it Rancho Catacula after an Indian name for the valley. Later he would rue the day he did not follow up to ensure final approval by the Mexican Assembly, as it nearly cost him his land.

Later Chiles was approached by John Sutter to join his small army of volunteers to put down a rebellion against Governor Micheltorena. Somehow Chiles was able to avoid joining Sutter and continued to work with Baldridge in building up his ranch. Perhaps Sutter empathized with him and decided not to enforce his right to conscript Mexican citizens. The short-lived fiasco saw Micheltorena deposed as governor in early 1845. Chiles wrote to Thomas O. Larkin, who was now the U.S. Consul in Monterey, "We are all well and living in peace here, so much so that we have almost forgotten there is a war in the country."

Instead fighting for a lost cause as Sutter did, Chiles and Baldridge went to work building a cabin, tilling the soil for wheat and acquiring breeding livestock. By the following year they were working on the gristmill Chiles had dreamed about for so long. After tremendous effort by both men, it was finally finished and predated a larger mill constructed in 1846 by Dr. Edward T. Bale just north of present-day St. Helena.

IN MID-1845 Chiles attended a meeting in Sonoma to discuss the possibility of California obtaining independence from Mexican rule. But before anything was done, the Bear Flag Revolt took place in mid-June 1846. A group of American dissidents had captured Sonoma and taken General Vallejo and three of his aides to be incarcerated at Sutter's Fort. California was declared an Independent Republic and remained so for about three weeks, until U.S. Navy Commodore Sloat invaded Monterey and raised the Stars and Stripes.

Soon all of Northern California was under American jurisdiction, and Capt. John C. Fremont was recruiting volunteers to fight the Mexican War in Southern California. A few days after the Bear Flaggers had taken Sonoma, Chiles and Baldridge rode there to see what was happening. There they met old friends, including the Benjamin Kelsey family and Bartlett Vines. They stayed on to see John C. Fremont's arrival and enjoyed a momentous July 4th celebration. Neither Chiles nor Baldridge wished to be involved in the rebellion and returned to the ranch right after the fourth. They also stayed clear of the resulting Mexican War.

Emigrants were pouring into California during the fall of the year, and Chiles went to Sutter's Fort to recruit some of them to work on his ranch and operate the gristmill. In this he was successful, and by November he had recruited and bonded the Jones, Brown and Allen families. It was almost like having a large family of his own, and Chiles enjoyed the confusion and noise of children once again. He was known as a good fiddler and often played for group singing and dancing.

THINGS WERE GOING WELL for Chiles by mid-1847, when he and George Yount had a serious falling out over some cowhides. Chiles had accused Yount of stealing cows, and Yount sued Chiles for slander. The charges were finally dropped, but the friendship ended on a bitter note. Later that summer Chiles decided it was time for him to return to Missouri for his children, who he thought would be old enough to stand the journey the following spring. He was nearing forty now, and was beginning to think about taking another wife.

First he went to Sutter's Fort with the hope of finding someone to accompany him east. There he found a large party led by none other than Commodore Robert Stockton, who was traveling overland to the East. When Chiles asked to join Stockton's party, Stockton placed him on the military payroll to assist Caleb Greenwood as a professional guide (see Greenwood). The journey was to be made by heading south through the Mojave desert and east along the Santa Fe Trail, which Chiles had traveled in 1842. Other than enduring harassment by hostile Indians, the party safely reached Independence by the first of November.

Chiles enjoyed another visit with his children, explaining his plan to take them west the following spring. Then he traveled to Washington D.C. to observe Fremont's court-martial. The trial ended in late January 1848; Fremont was found guilty of most charges. Chiles then returned to Missouri and began his preparations to leave for California in May.

Among his fellow travelers were Caleb Greenwood, with several of his children, and a former schoolteacher named Alden S. Bayley and his four sons. Bayley was carrying mail to Oregon. By then they probably knew that James Clyman's "Mosquito Creek" train was ahead of them (see Clyman). By the time they reached the north fork of the Platte River, Chiles noted a new trade when he saw piles of stinking buffalo hides and tongues being hauled from the prairie by the wagon-load. Upon reaching Fort Hall, Chiles and his party learned that Snake Indians along the Oregon Trail were on the warpath. This resulted in the Bayley family astutely changing their minds about going to Oregon; instead, they would travel to California with Chiles.

That meant that the mail they were carrying would be the first regular mail to cross into California directly and would have to be forwarded to Oregon. Later, when Chiles and his party were camped on the Humboldt River, they were joined by a party of Mormons on their way east, via Sutter's Fort to the Great Salt Lake. From them they learned that Clyman was still ahead, and heard the fantastic news about James Marshall's gold discovery at Sutter's Mill in California (see Marshall). They also learned of a new route the Mormons had blazed across the Sierras over Carson Pass.

With that in mind Chiles led his party directly to the Carson River, via a new route that became known as the Forty-Mile Desert. This new route was used by nearly everyone after that. With a crude map supplied by the Mormons, Chiles located and crossed Carson Pass—probably the second to do so after Clyman. By October 31 Chiles' party was camped safely on Weber Creek east of present day Placerville.

B ECAUSE OF the gold craze, Chiles found California a different place from what he remembered. As luck would have it, many Oregonians were there after gold, and they picked up their mail directly from the Bayleys. Rather than get caught in the almost irresistible quest for gold, Chiles headed for his ranch, which he reached a week or so later.

He was pleased to find everything running smoothly under the capable guidance of Billy Baldridge. Once again the adobe ranch house was filled with the laughter and arguments of children. But there was a difference— this time they were his own. His arrival was saddened by Billy Baldridge's decision to leave for the gold country. Chiles managed to resist the temptation, and profited instead from the huge demand for flour and beef. In 1849 he was doing so well he sent for two of his brothers and a nephew to assist him. Billy Baldridge had never returned and he needed help.

His three girls had settled well on the ranch. Only his son, James, seemed dissatisfied; Chiles sent him east to school in Missouri. Soon Chiles entered into a partnership to operate a ferry across the Sacramento River near the present-day "I" Street Bridge. He also bought land not far from William and John Wolfskill's ranch along Putah Creek and some other land bordering the American River above Sutter's Fort.

By 1853 Chiles was a grandfather, but he was still restless and addicted to travel. It was time for another trip to Missouri. This trip was uneventful until he reached Independence in late September. It was there he met Margaret Jane Garnhart [or Garnett], a comely lass of 26 from Harper's Ferry. At age 53, Chiles fell in love for the first time since losing his wife. He and Margaret Jane were married in Independence on Christmas Day that same year. By the time they left for California in May of the following year, Mrs. Chiles was five months pregnant.

Chiles found the trail much easier, since so many had traversed it during the Gold Rush. It was a good thing, for he was bringing a thousand head of sheep with him. Unfortunately, he lost most of them while crossing the South Fork of the Platte River. Undaunted, he bought two thousand head of mixed livestock in Salt Lake City. He lost more stock crossing the desert, but the miserable trip was made joyous when his wife bore a healthy baby boy near present-day Winnemucca, Nevada.

In a tongue-in-cheek note written to his brother, Joel, Chiles wrote: "We have a fine boy and call him William, we found him on the Humboldt on our way out, not bad luck." Despite heavy losses of livestock on the trip west, Chiles remained in good financial condition. Upon his return home he began planning a new house for his family. The following year he had a baby daughter and had bought additional acreage at Rutherford. It was there the new house was built. Within a few more years he had several more children.

Unfortunately Chiles suffered severe financial losses in succeeding years and ended up losing his land and home in Rutherford. The family then moved back to Rancho Catacula. By 1872 his finances had improved enough to allow construction of a new house in St. Helena, and once again he moved his family. He also bought property in Lake County near beautiful Clear Lake. By early 1885 Chiles' health was deteriorating. He died June 6, 1885 at age 75, leaving many descendants; his funeral was one of the largest ever held in Napa County.

Chiles Road in Yolo County is named after the family, and a state marker in Chiles Valley, Napa County, commemorates his early gristmill, said to be the first "American-built" mill in Northern California; it may have been predated by one built by George Yount (see Yount).

BIBLIOGRAPHY

–Bancroft, Hubert H. *History of California*, Vol. I-VI. The History Co., San Francisco, CA, 1886. Republished, Wallace Hebbard, Santa Barbara, CA, 1966.

–Bryant, Edwin. *What I Saw in California*. University of Nebraska Press, Lincoln, 1985.

–Giffen, Helen S. *Trail-Blazing Pioneer; Colonel Joseph Ballinger Chiles*. John Howell Books, San Francisco, 1964. All excerpts and quotations are taken from this publication.

–Gilbert, Bil. *Westering Man, The Life of Joseph Walker*. University of Oklahoma Press, Norman, 1989.

–Nunis, Jr., Dr. Doyce B. (Ed.) *The Bartleson-Bidwell Party*. Western Tanager Press, Santa Cruz, CA, 1991.

–Stewart, George R. *The California Trail*. University of Nebraska Press, Lincoln, 1962.

NOTES

JAMES CLYMAN

1792 – 1881

JAMES CLYMAN was born February 1, 1792 on a farm in Fauquier County, Virginia. His father held a life-lease on the land, which was owned by none other than George Washington. Located in the foothills of the Blue Ridge Mountains, the farm was a good place for young Clyman to learn hunting skills. When James—who had a basic grade-school education—was fifteen, his family moved to Stark County, Ohio, where they settled on land of their own.

There were many hostile Indians in the area, and young James joined a group of volunteer rangers to fight them. During the War of 1812 Clyman joined the army, where he learned elements of surveying. In 1818 he left the family farm and acquired one of his own in Indiana. He moved often after that, working on farms, until he began hauling supplies for a surveying party and assisting the surveyor.

By 1822 he was a full-fledged surveyor, and by the following year he was in St. Louis, where he was hired as a clerk by William Ashley to join a fur trapping expedition. The large party was transported up the Missouri River in keelboats, which could sail but had to be towed from shore when the wind failed. It was back-breaking work, and by the time they reached Council Bluffs some of the men quit. Clyman stuck it out, and as they continued upriver they met Jedediah Smith, who also worked for Ashley and was heading for St. Louis by boat to replace horses stolen by Indians. This rendezvous probably took place near today's Pierre, So. Dakota, in Arikara Indian country (see Smith).

Desperate for horses, Ashley decided—against the advice of Smith and others—to trade gun-powder and rifle-balls for horses at a nearby Ree (Arikara) village. He did get some badly needed horses, but while some of the men, including Smith and Clyman, were ashore for the night, the Indians staged a sneak attack. After killing some of the white men, the Indians drove Smith, Clyman and other survivors into the river. Their only chance was to swim for the keelboats anchored offshore.

After drifting helplessly past the boats, Clyman was drowning when a man named Gibson dragged him into a skiff. Within moments Gibson was shot in the abdomen by an Indian, but they managed to land the skiff on the far shore. Gibson, who assumed he was dying, insisted that Clyman leave him behind and make his escape. Clyman managed to get away from the Indians, finally making his way to one of the keelboats, which had drifted downstream. There he found someone else had picked up Gibson, who lay dying. Clyman watched, horrified, as the man who had saved his life died before his eyes. Meanwhile, Ashley had sent Jedediah Smith to the Yellowstone trading station to seek help. He then sent one of the boats downriver to request help from the army in St. Louis.

The resulting conflict involved hundreds of U.S. troops, Sioux Indians and Ashley's men, who attacked the Ree fortress without a clear-cut victory on either side. But at least the Rees were driven off, and Ashley's keelboats were able to resume their journey upstream.

IN THE FALL of the year, Clyman joined a trapping party led by Jedediah Smith. Among them were William Sublette, "Black" Harris, "Cut-Nose" Rose and Thomas Fitzpatrick. As they worked their way northwest into prime beaver country, Smith was grievously wounded by a maddened grizzly, and Clyman had to sew his torn scalp and nearly severed ear back in place.

When Smith was well enough to travel, they worked their way to a Crow Indian encampment and spent the winter of 1823-24 in the Wind River Mountains. In early spring they made their way to the Sweetwater River and trapped their way west, living off the land. It was then they rediscovered South Pass. They wouldn't have known it except they noticed the springs flowing west instead of east.

In March they reached the Green River, where the party split; Smith took one group south while Clyman led another one north. They were to meet later at the Big Sandy River. When Smith failed to show up by mid-June, Fitzpatrick, Clyman and some others crossed South Pass from west to east and made their way to the North Platte River. Somewhere near present-day Casper, Wyoming, they were attacked by hostile Indians, where Clyman lost his horse and most of his supplies. Somehow the group got separated, and Clyman was forced to continue on foot. He was out of food and ammunition when he reached the Missouri River and virtually crawled into Fort Atkinson (later Ft. Leavenworth) in the autumn of 1824.

There he met Captain Bennet Riley, who later became military governor of California. Riley introduced the destitute, starving Clyman to Colonel Leavenworth, who assigned him to an army company for ten days so he could replace his tattered shoes and clothing and eat regularly at the mess. Later, Fitzpatrick and the other trappers arrived in equally poor condition. This remarkable journey of 600 miles, which Clyman made on foot, eventually became the main route to the west—the famed Oregon Trail.

CLYMAN took part in other trapping expeditions over the next two years, one of which led to circumnavigating the Great Salt Lake in skin canoes. This was followed by the 1826 exploration of Yellowstone Lake by a party believed to have included Clyman. The virginal streams and rivers of western Montana were rich with beaver, but it was Blackfoot country and not many dared to enter it. Among those who did in 1825 was 33-year-old James Clyman with one companion. Clyman thought they had the answer to the Indian threat. Cunningly they tended their traps only at dawn and late evening. During the day they would hide out in isolated camps and cure their pelts.

As the trapping season drew to a close, their success may have dulled their reflexes. Crossing a stream with their heavily-laden pack animals, they passed through a grove of bottom-land timber and emerged directly into a large Blackfoot encampment. Any sign of weakness would have meant almost certain death. Instead of running, Clyman led his frightened companion directly to the chief's lodge. There he confronted the amazed chief and used sign language to convey a message that he and his friend sought food and lodging for the night.

Surprisingly, the perplexed chief ordered squaws to bring food. During the meal Clyman listened to the Indian's conversation; he understood enough to realize they planned to torture and kill him and his friend. Speaking softly to his companion, Clyman told him to watch closely and do exactly as he did. At dusk, when Clyman thought the time was right, he leaped to his feet, dashed out of the lodge and ran hard for the nearby creek. His friend followed, pursued by whizzing arrows and rifle-balls.

When Clyman reached the water, he dove deep and swam swiftly to the opposite shore. There he found an overhanging bank and thrust himself under it. Seeing no sign of his friend, he assumed he had been taken. Finally Clyman made his getaway on foot, thankful to be alive but cursing the loss of his friend, the valuable livestock, supplies and pelts. His friend was never heard from again.

In 1827 Clyman came out of the mountains with 278 pounds of beaver pelts and began looking for a less hazardous way of making a living. After selling the furs in St. Louis for $1,251, he bought farmland near Danville, Illinois, where he entered into a partnership and opened a general store. Two of his brothers were recruited to help on the farm. By then Clyman was 35 years old, described as about six feet tall, rawboned, slender and a little stooped.

In 1832 Clyman left the store to join a company of mounted volunteers to fight during the Black Hawk "War" in northwest Illinois. Two of his fellow volunteers were Abraham Lincoln and James F. Reed (see Reed). After being discharged as a lieutenant in 1834, Clyman returned to Danville and his neglected business. Declining business led him to close the store in 1839 and to sell his land.

Even before then Clyman had other interests. One was a partnership formed to build and operate the Ross Mill, a sawmill near Milwaukee, Wisconsin. During that period he was appointed Colonel of Militia in Milwaukee. Later, in a fracas with local Indians over a canoe, Clyman was shot in the arm and leg, which took several months to heal properly. Upon his recovery, he used his surveying experience to place milestones along the state road between Indiana and Chicago.

BY 1844 word about opportunities for rich, free land in Oregon and California had spread far and wide, and Clyman became inflamed with the idea of emigrating. Suffering from a chronic cough, he traveled from Wisconsin into Arkansas and on to Independence, Missouri, where most emigrant parties organized. By April Clyman's health was better, and an estimated 1,500 people were ready to leave for the West. This was more than the combined total of all previous overland emigrations.

Clyman, at age 52, joined a party of around 500, captained by Col. Nathaniel Ford. In addition to the three parties bound for Oregon, there was one, led by Elisha Stevens and Martin Murphy, bound for California (see Murphy). One of the Oregon-bound groups, organized by Cornelius Gilliam, went together with Ford's party and hired Clyman's old friend, Moses "Black" Harris to pilot them. James W. Marshall, who later discovered gold in California, traveled in Gilliam's party (see Marshall).

Following the Oregon Trail with its usual dangers and hardships, Clyman's party reached The Dalles on the Columbia River in early October. They then made a difficult crossing over the Cascade range around the south side of Mt. Hood, reaching the Willamette River and the site of present-day Oregon City on the 13th.

Clyman described that part of the long journey, which he appears to have made without wagons, as the worst of the entire trip (Samuel Barlow opened the trail to wagons as a toll road in 1846). A few days after arriving at Oregon City, Clyman and two others rowed a skiff down the Willamette river to its confluence with the mighty Columbia, where they visited Fort Vancouver.

Clyman spent the winter of 1844-45 exploring the Willamette Valley, and by spring he had joined a party heading south toward California. Included in this party of 39 was a widow, listed as "Mrs. Payne," and her three children. Also with the group was Samuel "Green"

McMahon, listed as captain, and James W. Marshall. The following directions for using the Siskiyou Trail were written by Joel P. Walker, who had traveled the trail several times:

> Be careful to never camp in the timber if it can be avoided.
> Be careful to never Let any Indians come amongst you.
> Never Lit [sic] the Indian have any ammunition on any account.
> Keep close watch both day and night.
> Never neglect camp guard on any account.
> Never fire a gun after crossing the Umqua mountain untill [sic] you cross the siskiew [sic] mountain perhaps Five days travel
> Keep yourselves close as possible in traveling through the Brush.
> Never scatter after game or [make] any other division.
> Keep your guns in the best firing condition.

PERHAPS THESE INSTRUCTIONS were responsible for the party getting safely through to California. They reached the head of the Sacramento River by June 28th, and continued down the Sacramento Valley until July 1st, when Franklin Sears killed two Indians for no apparent reason. Later several men fired across the river and killed another Indian as if for target practice. To them, the only good Indian was a dead Indian. Finally they reached a good campsite on Cache Creek, near a ranch belonging to William Gordon. Later they were visited by William Knight, John Wolfskill and other settlers who brought them food and told about the vagaries of Mexican politics, including the recent overthrow of Governor Micheltorena.

After resting their worn horses a few days, James Marshall and some others headed for Sutter's Fort to seek employment, while Clyman and the remainder decided to head toward the Napa Valley. After passing by Berryessa's Ranch, they stopped at George Yount's ranch at present-day Yountville. They then headed north and visited Andrew Kelsey's camp near Clear Lake. By July 20th they had turned south to visit Sutter's Fort (see Sutter). Clyman wasn't very impressed:

"The captain keeps six or eight hundred Indians in a complete state of slavery. As I had the mortification of seeing them dine, I may give a short description." He went on to say how they were slopped like hogs, when a form of grain gruel was poured into wooden troughs, where the Indians scooped it out with their hands.

Clyman left Sutter's Fort after a few days, heading west to explore the area around Monterey and Santa Cruz. There he visited with Isaac Graham, who operated a distillery and sawmill near Santa Cruz (see Graham). He also met U.S. Consul Thomas O. Larkin in Monterey, before heading back north to George Yount's ranch. He had spent nearly a month seeing the country before going back to the Clear Lake area, where he stayed at Kelsey's camp and spent several weeks hunting deer and elk. While there he met Old Caleb Greenwood and his two sons, John and Britton (see Greenwood).

By now it was early 1846. John Fremont was in the area with his U.S. Army Topographical Corps, and Clyman wrote him a letter offering to bring some men and assist Fremont in his surveying activities (see Fremont). By then Clyman was ready to return home to Wisconsin, via Missouri, and apparently hoped to return with Fremont. A partial extract of Fremont's reply follows:

> To James Clyman, Esq. at Yount's Mills, California
> Dear Sir,
> I am placed in a peculiar position. Having carried out to the best of my ability, my instructions to explore the far west, I see myself on the eve of my departure for home, confronted by the most perplexing complications. I have received information to the effect that a declaration of war between our government and Mexico is probable, but so far this news has not been confirmed...Under these circumstances I must make my way back home alone and gratefully decline your offer of a company of hardy warriors...
> —Yours respectfully, John C. Fremont

Clyman then drifted south to Gordon's ranch in present-day Yolo County. Some of his former companions were there preparing to leave for Oregon. They had become disillusioned with California, especially the Mexican population, whom they thought "barbarous." By early May, Clyman and some friends had dried a good deal of meat for the return trip east.

After passing through Sutter's Fort, where they probably bought more supplies, they headed up the Feather River to Johnson's Ranch on the Bear River. There they met Lansford Hastings and bought more meat before joining his party to make their way over the lofty Sierra Nevada, via Truckee Pass (see Hastings & Johnson). With them were several families, including Caleb Greenwood and sons. When they reached Brady's Hot Springs, near the Humboldt sink, Clyman suffered the loss of his pet water spaniel, "Lucky", when the dog dashed into the spring for a drink and was instantly parboiled. "I felt more from his loss than for any other animal I ever lost in my life," said Clyman. "He had been my constant companion in all my wanderings since I left Milwaukee."

Lansford Hastings had recently published a book describing the Oregon-California Trail, in which he told about a new shortcut to Fort Bridger. It would bypass Fort Hall, which was far to the north, by heading almost directly east around the south end of the Great Salt Lake. It was mostly dry, arid land, but Hastings said there were ample springs along the route. Fremont had made the crossing going west the year before, and Hastings—who had never traveled it himself—was eager to explore it (see Hastings).

Both Clyman and the Greenwoods were against trying it. When they reached the turn-off on the Humboldt River in mid-May, the Greenwoods and those with families chose the Fort Hall route. Clyman and a few others then agreed to accompany Hastings with pack-horses on the new shortcut. After a two-week trek across forbidding terrain, they were within sight of the Salt Lake by the first of June.

After crossing the Wasatch Mountains through Weber Canyon, they reached Fort Bridger on June 11. Within a week they were joined by other members of the party, who had taken the Fort Hall route. Travel on the new route—now called "Hastings Cutoff"—had been shortened, but the time difference was minimal. Nevertheless, Hastings was enthusiastic about it, and praised it to anyone who would listen.

Meanwhile, Clyman and a few other prudent men such as Joseph R. Walker warned emigrants not to try the Hastings route with wagons. No one had taken wagons across, and Clyman thought it extremely difficult if not impossible. Nevertheless, two large parties agreed to meet Hastings at Fort Bridger to attempt the new shortcut.

The Harlan-Young party arrived there first, and the Donner-Reed party was expected to arrive soon. Clyman had specifically warned James F. Reed—his old friend from the Black Hawk War—against trying the so-called shortcut. Nevertheless, Reed talked the Donners into it "to save time"–a decision that ultimately proved disastrous (see Reed).

By the end of June, 1846, Clyman and some companions—including the Greenwoods—had reached Fort Laramie. They followed the Platte River route east and arrived at Independence, Missouri, where they disbanded July 23rd. Clyman spent the next eighteen months visiting friends and relatives in Wisconsin. By the spring of 1848, he had gathered a party of emigrants heading for California. The Lambert McComb family was a large part of it. They left Missouri the first of May. Another group—led by Joseph Chiles and his children—left a short time later. Caleb Greenwood, who was also bringing his children west, joined Chiles for at least part of the trip (see Chiles).

In August 1848, near the Humboldt Sink, Clyman's group—known as "The Mosquito Creek Train"—met a party of Mormons heading east from Sutter's Fort. Brigham Young had started a large Mormon settlement at the Great Salt Lake, and the party of Mormons, who had served in the Mexican War, were on their way to join him there. It was then that Clyman's group learned about James W. Marshall's discovery of gold at Sutter's sawmill in California (see Marshall).

Some of the Mormons had helped Marshall build the sawmill in Cullomah (Coloma) and found quantities of gold for themselves. They had also blazed a new trail from California over Carson Pass on their way east. It was south of Truckee Pass but offered a better route, they said. Clyman's party decided to try it, and became one of the first—probably the first—to take wagons over Carson Pass heading west. Chiles's party followed close behind, and it soon became a main route. Some members of the party caught "gold fever" and headed for the mines. Clyman and the McCombs took time to do some gold prospecting in the area around present Placerville and Coloma, but continued on to the Napa Valley, arriving there in early September.

BOTH CLYMAN and the McCombs settled in Napa, where McComb acquired land. Clyman lived with them, helping to build a house and "laying out the place." He also began courting Lambert McComb's daughter, Hannah. Lambert died in December 1848, only three months after arriving in California. Miss Hannah McComb was 30 years younger than 67-year-old Clyman when they married in August 1849. The wedding was apparently the first to take place in Napa. George Yount probably attended, along with the Chiles family, who had settled near there.

In March 1850, Clyman bought part of Salvador Vallejo's old ranch near Napa and began farming. He added to it in 1855 by acquiring property from his mother-in-law. By 1866 the Clymans had five children, of which four died from scarlet fever; the lone survivor was a twin daughter named Lydia. After the loss of their other children, Clyman and his wife adopted three daughters. At the age of eighty, Clyman was still actively engaged in operating a successful dairy farm and fruit orchard. He also had time to write poetry:

> And now the mists arise
> With slow and graceful motion
> And shews like pillow in the skies
> Or island in the ocean

Clyman took little part in public affairs, but he often entertained his friends and children with tales of his past. He is remembered as "a bent, weather-beaten figure, often taking his rifle to the mountains in search of a deer or perhaps a grizzly—like himself the last of his race." He spent many contented hours sitting in the sun writing his memoirs. Among the visitors in his old age were famed midget performers Tom Thumb and his wife, who were relatives of the family. James Clyman died on his farm December 27, 1881, at the age of 90;. He was buried at the cemetery of Tulocay. His wife, Hannah, followed him in 1908 at age 86.

BIBLIOGRAPHY

–Bancroft, Hubert H. *History of California,* Vol. 1-VII. History Co., San Francisco, CA, 1886. Republished, Wallace Hebberd, Santa Barbara, CA, 1966.

–Cleland, Robert Glass. *This Reckless Breed of Men.* Alfred A. Knopf, New York, 1950.

–Camp, Charles L. *James Clyman, Frontiersman.* Champoeg Press, Portland, OR, 1960. All quotations taken from this publication.

–Clyman, James, ed. by Linda M. Hasselstrom. *Journal Of A Mountain Man.* Mountain Press Publishing Co., Missoula, 1984.

–Crosby, Alexander L. *Old Greenwood, Pathfinder of the West* (based on the book by Chas. Kellky & Dale L. Morgan). Talisman Press, Georgetown, CA, 1967.

–DeVoto, Bernard. *The Year of Decision-1846.* Houghton Mifflin Co., Boston, 1942.

–Gay, Theressa. *James Marshall, a Biography.* Talisman Press, Georgetown, CA, 1967.

–Hafen, LeRoy R., Edito., *Mountain Men and Fur Traders of the Far West.* University of Nebraska Press, Lincoln, 1982.

–Stewart, George R. *The California Trail.* University of Nebraska Press, Lincoln, 1962.

NOTES

– II –

HENRY DALTON

1803 – 1884

BORN TO A LARGE FAMILY in the Limehouse section of London—the largest city in Europe at the time—Henry Dalton first saw the light of day October 3, 1803. His middle-class parents, Winnell T. and Anne Wolfe Dalton, supported their family in the tailoring and merchandising business, providing well for their five sons and three daughters. Henry's schooling ended when he was seventeen. He was learning the tailoring trade a few months later, when he signed aboard a ship heading for South America as a lowly cabin boy. When the ship reached Callao, the seaport for Lima, Peru, young Dalton had seen enough of the sea and left the ship to seek a new career.

Peru had recently been freed from Spanish rule. Callao and its sister city, Lima, were bustling trade centers, welcoming commerce from all over the world. Dalton found sanctuary in Lima with the English trading company Gibbs Crawley and Co. He was taken in as one of the family by the Crawleys, while Mr. Crawley taught him the competitive trading business.

While in Lima, Dalton befriended fellow Englishman William Hartnell (see Hartnell). After Hartnell left Lima for California in 1822, they carried on a lively correspondence. A sample from Dalton to Hartnell reflects his youthful zest for life:

> On Xmas day, we had rather a grand dinner when 104 Britons sat down to beef and pudding. After taking a small portion of wine (say six bottles each) we retired to the race ground where hunting and racing became the sport...

Dalton did well at his new occupation to become a skilled accountant. A rather brash and over-confident young man, he overstepped his bounds after two years with Crawley by contracting for an entire shipload of goods on his own. Dalton had done other impetuous things, but this was too much for Crawley. To his credit, he allowed Dalton to collect profits from his indiscreet trading venture before firing him.

With what seemed a fortune of $3,200 at his disposal, Dalton decided to go into business for himself in Callao. "Enrique Dalton & Co." did well from the start, and after tiring of heavy freight bills he bought the trading vessel *Manly* in 1827. Later he added the *Rose,* the *Julia* and others to his growing fleet. Besides a store, he also owned two large warehouses on the waterfront in which he kept his trade goods.

Since Callao had no bank, Dalton's store became an informal bank, and he soon gained recognition as the British Consul's agent there. His financial interests spread into mining, and within a few years Dalton had become a wealthy and prominent member of the community. By then he had developed a relationship with a local beauty; over the years he had several children by her.

Dalton also developed a close friendship with Hugo Reid, a likable young Scotsman who arrived in Callao in the late 1820's and was employed by Dalton as a clerk in his store (see Reid). Two years later Reid sailed to Hermosillo, Mexico, where he entered into a trading venture partially financed by Dalton. When gold mines in the area played out after a few years, Reid closed the business and went to California to seek new opportunities.

A SERIES OF PROBLEMS and political instability in Peru during the 1830's was followed by a bitter dispute between Dalton and another partner, which dragged on for many years. Another blow came in 1840, when Dalton began suffering from an undisclosed illness. Meanwhile, his business affairs deteriorated, largely because of cheating by some of his ship captains.

Finally Dalton had to liquidate many of his assets, including his ships. He managed to keep his favorite ship, *Rose,* which he intended to use to regain his lost fortune. In the fall of 1841, Dalton re-outfitted the *Rose* (later renamed the *Sun*) and filled her hold with trade goods bound for Mexico. Much of the cargo was bought on credit with a one-year deadline before crushing interest would be added.

Contrary winds slowed the vessel, and when they finally arrived in San Blas, Mexico in January 1842, Dalton found trading conditions poor because of political upheavals and exorbitant duties. To avoid these high duties, he managed to smuggle $7,000 worth of goods ashore before moving north to Mazatlan, where he smuggled another $38,000 worth of goods ashore. Before long a series of unforeseen problems dogged Dalton's trading ventures until he owed more than he could repay. But at least he recovered his health.

Finally he was forced to sell the Sun and other personal property to pay impatient creditors in Peru something on account. By then he was acquiring even more trade goods and leased a ship to transport them to California. He hoped to make a comeback there by trading his goods for hides and tallow. England had her eye on California, and Dalton saw not only financial possibilities for himself, but political possibilities for Great Britain as well.

In addition, Dalton had learned of a gold strike near Los Angeles, which he intended to exploit if possible. In October 1843 Dalton's chartered ship anchored off dreary-looking San Pedro. No sign of civilization could be seen except two small buildings on a nearby hill. Dalton made his way to Los Angeles, where he learned that his old friend Hugo Reid was away. Fortunately, Reid's good friends, Abel Stearns and Juan Bandini, were willing to help him (see separate chapters).

Stearns offered to rent him storage space in San Pedro and a room in his Los Angeles building for use as a small store. This would suffice temporarily, and Dalton rode north to visit the gold mines at Francisquito Canyon. He found forty or fifty Mexicans and Indians there panning gold with some success. After acquiring several bags of "paydirt" for assay, Dalton returned to his ship and sailed north to Monterey.

IN MONTEREY he established a business relationship with Thomas O. Larkin before going on to Yerba Buena (San Francisco), where he sold some goods to the Hudson's Bay Company representative (see Larkin). When he returned to Mazatlan in 1844, he had done well and decided to settle in California. He knew he would need a trading vessel, so he bought the *Julia Ann*, captained by a Danish mulatto, William A. Leidesdorff (see separate chapter).

Leidesdorff quit the sea two years later and went into his own trading business in Yerba Buena. While there he acted as a salaried agent for Dalton. Under a new captain, the *Julia Ann* was kept busy running up and down the coast between Mazatlan and Monterey, and Dalton became a well known and respected California trader. Gold trade from the Los Angeles area mines proved disappointing, as did fur trading with China. Despite these setbacks, Dalton bought property in "downtown" Los Angeles where he built a new store. Meanwhile, Gov. Manuel Micheltorena was fighting for his political life and was short of funds. Alcalde Luis Arenas, who owned the five-square-league Rancho Azusa east of Los Angeles, owed the Mexican Government $1,000.

Arenas was willing to sell the ranch to pay this indebtedness if a buyer could be found. After learning of this, Dalton offered to buy it. *Rancheros* were forbidden by law to sell land to foreigners; however, because Micheltorena was strapped for funds, the rules were bent and the purchase was quickly approved. Dalton acquired a fine parcel of land on the Azusa (San Gabriel) River, nestled against the Sierra Madre mountains. He also got livestock, a vineyard, an irrigation system and several adobe buildings. Dalton occupied his property in March 1845, and immediately reorganized the work force, as outlined in his journal:

Tuesday, March 18, called all the people on the rancho servants and not servants for the purpose of knowing them. Gave warning to all that did not work to leave the place. Divided the working hands. Gave six to Sr. Benabe for work of the timbre [sic], the rest to other occupations on the rancho cleaning the vineyard on the ditch, cutting firewood.

A sawmill was built to provide lumber to construct a newer, larger house for Dalton. The hard-pressed workers went on to construct a winery, stables, granaries and tannery pits. The ranch soon became known as Dalton Hill, and for thirty-six years it was the Dalton homestead. Dalton proved an able farmer, experimenting with tobacco and cotton, and growing wheat. Both the winery and tannery were expanded to produce good wine and quality leather.

Before long he added additional land to the thriving ranch, finally coming to control the San Gabriel Canyon and what became known as Dalton Canyon. In addition there were two leagues of vacant land stretching west from his ranch toward Mission San Gabriel. It was mission land, but since secularization in 1834, it had lain dormant. Dalton petitioned Pío Pico for this land with payment of $400. It was approved after Dalton gained favor with the mission padre by virtually showering the few remaining mission Indians with food and gifts.

Dalton named his new 9,000 acre acquisition "San Francisquito." Though he was called "Don Enrique," he avoided the required Mexican citizenship by "purchasing" his land, keeping his British citizenship intact throughout his life. By then he had apparently grown greedy for even more land; he bought Rancho Santa Anita from his old friend, Hugo Reid for $2,700. Reid had developed it into a place of true beauty, but was tired of ranching and hard-pressed for money. Dalton now controlled 45,000 acres of prime land stretching from Mud Springs (San Dimas) on the east to the edge of San Pascual (Pasadena) in the west. In less than three years since arriving in California, he had become one of its largest *hacendados* (landholders). He also owned prime property in Los Angeles, where he operated his thriving trading enterprises.

On the liability side of the ledger, he lost his business in San Francisco after a dispute with William Leidesdorff, who died a short time later in 1848. Hostile Indians were causing problems in and around Rancho Azusa. One can scarcely blame them. After being enticed (or coerced) into the missions, most of them had been cast out after secularization and then saw mission lands, livestock and other property gobbled up by greedy administrators and their friends and relatives.

Finally Pío Pico and Hugo Reid, who was *juez de paz* (Justice of the Peace) in San Gabriel, requested American settler Don Benito Wilson to organize and lead a band of fighting men to punish the troublesome thieving Indians (see Wilson & Pico). Though his expedition resulted in the death and capture of a good many hostiles in the Mojave Desert, it did little to settle problems with local Indians. As a result, Reid persuaded Pico to appoint Dalton as *majordomo* of the mission in early 1846.

DALTON WORKED to prevent further deterioration of mission property and attempted to pacify the remaining Indians. Six months later he saw little progress from his efforts and resigned. Even before then, the country was rife with rumors about possible war between Mexico and the United States. It was said that 10,000 Mormons were on their way to settle in California to escape religious persecution in the United States.

This talk alarmed English settlers such as Dalton and other separatists like Pio Pico and Juan Bandini who favored independence from Mexico under British protection (see Bandini). There was even a plot to import 10,000 Irish Catholics into California to offset the alleged takeover by Protestant emigrants. A conference was scheduled in Santa Barbara to discuss these problems, but before it could take place U.S. Navy Commodore John Sloat settled it by occupying Northern California in early July 1846.

As expected, this was shortly followed by an invasion of Southern California by Commodore Robert Stockton and Major John C. Fremont and his "California Battalion." There was little or no resistance by the Mexicans after Governor Pico and General José Castro fled to Mexico. Unfortunately this short peace was interrupted when two young firebrands, Sebulo Varela and José Flores, recruited a sizable force of Mexican patriots and forced Stockton's meager occupation forces out of Southern California.

An abortive attempt by some of Stockton's men to re-take Los Angeles in early October ended in defeat for the Americans during the Battle of Rancho Dominguez. And though Dalton exulted in these Mexican victories, he kept a low profile until he was approached by José Flores for badly needed food, clothing, gun-powder and other supplies for his destitute volunteers. Possibly Flores threatened to confiscate these things from Dalton's Los Angeles store if he didn't sell them for a draft on Mexican Government funds. Possibly Dalton saw a chance for a quick profit, or perhaps he wanted to do his part to help Flores defeat the Americans. Whatever the reason, Dalton sold him $30,000 worth of supplies, and gave him $1,200 cash. This allowed Flores and his men to continue the fight. Dalton spent many years trying to live it down.

Another reason for his support of Flores may have been personal; he had begun courting young Maria Guadalupe Zamorano, sister of Flores' wife. Dalton then prepared to leave for Mexico City to collect his draft

in the amount of $60,000, double the value of the supplies he had sold
to Flores. This was the agreement made by Flores at the time of the sale.
Benito Wilson was furious with Dalton for making the sale in the first
place and penned an angry and untrue account as follows:

> In a few days we heard of the hellish plot concocted by Flores and
> Henry Dalton (whose wives were sisters) to send us as prisoners
> and trophies to Mexico, having its conception in Dalton selling the
> remains of an old store to Flores as Commander in Chief, for the
> pretended purpose of clothing the soldiers, and Flores giving to
> Dalton drafts for large amounts against the Mexican treasury.

Dalton did not marry fourteen-year-old Maria Guadalupe until
nearly a year later, and there was never any evidence of the plot Wilson
describes. Before Dalton could leave for Mexico, the entire picture
began to change. Stockton again took San Diego, and General Stephen
Kearny had arrived there from Santa Fe with a small army. (Before his
arrival, he had been badly mauled by Andres Pico and his mounted
lancers at San Pasqual).

Now that Kearny and Stockton had combined their forces, they
began a march toward Los Angeles in December. When Andres Pico
and the remaining Mexican troops retreated north, they encountered
Fremont's forces at Cahuenga Pass and were stopped cold. Pico capitulated to Fremont on January 13, 1847; finally the fighting was over for
good. Stockton's men immediately took over Dalton's Los Angeles
house, using it as barracks.

Dalton stayed out of sight on his ranch during this period for the
most part, while Abel Stearns kept him informed. Meanwhile, Fremont's
men confiscated more than fifty horses from Dalton's herd. Later when
he tried to collect $8,050 in damages for these losses, including those
suffered at San Pedro and Los Angeles, he was unable to collect anything. As he had feared, the American victory cost him dearly. By spring
he had lost everything except his ranches and considered himself "poor
as a rat."

Despite his losses, Dalton decided it was time to marry. He was
approaching his mid-forties and had fallen deeply in love with pretty
Maria Guadalupe Zamorano. Though she was still in her mid-teens,
Californio girls seemed to mature early, and she was ready for marriage.
The marriage of young girls to older men was certainly not unprece-
dented. Abel Stearns had previously married fourteen-year-old Arcadia
Bandini, and that marriage seemed successful.

After being baptized into the Catholic faith as Perfecto Hugo
Dalton (named after his friend, Hugo Reid), Dalton married Maria
Guadalupe at the San Gabriel Mission on July 14th, with Reid standing
up for him. This marriage proved a fruitful one, and over the years they

had eleven children; seven survived childhood. Dalton spared no expense making his young wife happy and contented.

HE DEVOTED the next decade going from one business venture to another to make ends meet. He still had ideas about traveling to Mexico to collect on the Flores drafts, realizing it was his best hope of regaining wealth. He still owed about $38,000 to creditors in South America. Along with everyone else, Dalton was startled by the news of James Marshall's gold discovery at Sutter's mill in January 1848. But instead of joining in the gold rush, he devised another trading expedition to Mexico. He knew there would be a huge demand for goods of all kinds in California and hoped to acquire them in Mexico. After chartering a trading vessel, Dalton went along as supercargo with 3,000 ounces of gold dust to buy cargo.

Once he had purchased cargo at Guadalajara, he rode horse-back to Mexico City to plead his case for the $60,000 owed him by the government. He spent two months there presenting his case to every official who would listen, but left with empty pockets and empty promises. On his return voyage to California, he vowed never to go to sea as supercargo again. But at least the voyage proved profitable, and he returned home to Rancho Azusa with something to show for his efforts.

Much of this was lost to an 1849 mining venture, where he "grub-staked" a group of eager argonauts in the northern gold-fields, only to see them desert him to go out on their own. Next he came upon the idea of driving a herd of beef cattle to the southern mines near Stockton. Cattle that sold for their hides in Los Angeles could be worth up to $75 a head delivered to the mines. After contracting with a crew of *vaqueros* to drive them, Dalton rounded up virtually all of his cattle and sent the *vaqueros* on their way with a thousand head.

The drive went well until the cattle were deep into the San Joaquin Valley, where hostile Tulare Indians attacked the hapless *vaqueros*. The cattle were lost, and once again Dalton felt "poor as a rat." Over the next few years it seemed that everyone profited from the gold rush except Dalton. Cattle drives to the north had become commonplace, but most followed the safer route paralleling El Camino Real along the coast.

Dalton's young wife enjoyed living in Los Angeles because of its active social life with almost constant *bailes* (balls), fandangos and fiestas. As a result Dalton spent more and more time there in various business enterprises such as taverns and blanket making. This was made possible by the arrival of Dalton's brother in the early 1850's. George Dalton and his family settled at Rancho Azusa and managed ranching activities, while Henry managed his Los Angeles interests. Slowly his fortunes began improving.

This halcyon period was interrupted by the death of Hugo Reid in December 1852. The Daltons saw to it that he had a fine funeral, and took Reid's nearly destitute Indian wife under their wing. When statehood for California was being debated in 1849 and 1850, the Dalton's opposed it, fearing huge increases in property taxes would wipe them out. After losing that battle when California was admitted to the Union September 9, 1850, they then fought against the "land law" passed by Congress in 1851, which required land grant holders to prove their ownership to a land commission.

The law affected not only foreign grantees such as Dalton, but native Californians from old families as well. The next decade proved a bonanza for lawyers, as hundreds of landholders were forced into legal hearings and court actions to prove their grants. Many of them were unable to do so and saw their cherished lands severely reduced or forfeited entirely. Meanwhile, Dalton had acquired many properties in the Los Angeles area.

Hard-pressed for money as he often was, he decided to subdivide his Rancho San Francisquito east of Mission San Gabriel. It was divided into forty-and fifty-acre parcels and included a townsite known first as Lexington, then Lickskillit and finally El Monte, the first English-speaking town in Southern California. He also built a sizable gristmill called Azusa Mills on the San Gabriel River, north of his Rancho Azusa home. He used it to help promote his real estate sales.

Although Dalton's *majordomo*, Martin Duarte, did his best to operate Rancho Santa Anita efficiently, it had become a liability and Dalton sold it in 1854 to circus owner Joseph Rowe for $40,000. Despite his best efforts, other land sales were lagging, and Dalton devised a lottery scheme to move it. He offered 434 prizes of prime real estate at $1.00 a chance in 1855, assuming he would sell at least 84,000 chances.

Instead, he sold a total of 166 tickets and dropped the entire promotion three weeks before the drawing was scheduled. Amazingly, only one ticket holder sued him, but it went through the appeals court system before it was finally dropped. This and other financial losses drove him in 1857 to make another journey to Mexico City in an attempt to collect on his old Flores debt. By then interest charges brought the amount due him to over $186,000! Finally the Mexican Government approved it at $103,840 and issued bonds for that amount. The bonds were to be paid off in one year, but Dalton received only $1,500, enough to pay his way home in 1858.

Dalton then concentrated his efforts on Rancho Azusa by expanding his lucrative winery activities. He also produced wheat and barley to keep his gristmill running. A small gold rush occurred in 1859 on the east fork of the San Gabriel River. It resulted in the short-lived town of

Eldoradoville, which was washed away during the flood of 1862. Again Dalton was thwarted in his attempts to cash in on gold mining.

After another trip to Mexico in 1861 in an abortive attempt to collect his mounting Mexican debt, Dalton returned home and liquidated his holdings in Los Angeles. He was left with Rancho Azusa, but even this was jeopardized by an alleged crooked or inept and hasty land survey made in 1861 by Henry Hancock. If affirmed it would have resulted in the loss of much of Dalton's best ranch property. Of course Dalton fought it, and by the early 1870's it had been re-surveyed twice. Even then the surveys proved inconclusive, and Dalton stood to lose over 18,000 acres, leaving him with 16,000.

MEANWHILE swarms of squatters had moved in on the disputed land until he was virtually surrounded by them. Though he tried every legal means to evict them he was unsuccessful. If these problems weren't enough, the squatters began taking Dalton's irrigation water from the river above him. During wet years he could stand it, but during droughts it became a life and death matter which nearly led to bloodshed. Dalton's seventeen-year-old son, Winnell, armed himself with a virtual arsenal in case it came to that. Finally in 1876 the numerous squatters used their political clout to gain control. In addition to Dalton's land, they now controlled even his precious water rights. Dalton is quoted on the subject from an 1879 letter:

> Since then [1867] their [the squatter's] numbers have increased so much that they have done just as they pleased and ruined me completely. Having many votes they control everything...They proceeded to condemn my land to take my water...and even made me pay for my own water, and have had my son frequently arrested for using my own water.

By then his daughter Louisa had married Lewis Wolfskill, son of the wealthy and prominent William Wolfskill of Los Angeles (see Wolfskill). The ranch was left in Lewis's hands when Dalton again headed south for Mexico city in another attempt to collect on his overdue bonds. During his prolonged absence things went from bad to worse on the ranch, and young Wolfskill was required to borrow a large sum to hold off creditors who wanted to foreclose on the ranch property.

When Dalton finally returned in 1875, he found California a different place. Citrus groves were dotting the landscape and a mini land rush had begun. New towns had sprung up from Pasadena in the west to Pomona in the east. Dalton's children were growing fast, and he had previously adopted three more. They needed schooling, so Dalton opened a school on his ranch and hired a teacher.

But events were culminating within Dalton's web of tangled financial affairs. By 1881 he had lost everything to creditors and was forced to move his large family out of the house they had lived in for thirty-five years. In effect he was a pauper; at age 78 he was too old to begin again. In desperation, he received permission to move into a tiny adobe he had previously built for his miller. In tears, the dejected family shoehorned themselves and their meager possessions into the cramped adobe.

Two unexpected windfalls from Mexico in 1883 kept the family going, until Dalton was hired as foreman by the new owner of the neglected Rancho Azusa to get it productive again. Hiring some Chinese laborers, Dalton did such a good job that the grateful new owner deeded him forty acres and the house in which he and his family were living. Though his spirit was still willing to make a comeback, Dalton's body could not stand the pace, and he died January 21, 1884 at the age of eighty.

Dalton fought statehood and the notorious "land act," realizing that it could cost him his land. In retrospect, he was proven right. Rancho Santa Anita changed hands several times before becoming the heart of the city of Arcadia. Rancho Azusa became the thriving city of Azusa, and Lexington evolved into the city of El Monte. Dalton undoubtedly brought some problems on himself, but the price he eventually paid seems excessive.

BIBLIOGRAPHY

–Bancroft, Hubert H. *History of California,* Vol I-VI. History Co., San Francisco, 1886. Republished, Wallace Hebberd, Santa Barbara, CA, 1966.

–Dakin, Susanna Bryant. *A Scotch Paisano in Old Los Angeles.* University of California Press, Berkeley, 1939.

–Jackson, Sheldon G. *A British Ranchero In Old California: The Life and Times of Henry Dalton and the Rancho Azusa.* Aurthur H. Clark Co., Glendale, CA, 1987. Quotations were taken from this publication.

–Wright, Doris Marion. *A Yankee In Mexican California: Abel Stearns, 1798-1848.* Wallace Hebberd, Santa Barbara, CA, 1977.

NOTES

William Heath Davis
Courtesy California Department of Parks & Recreation

– 12 –

WILLIAM HEATH DAVIS

1822 – 1909

IN 1791, NEW ENGLAND TRADER Oliver Holmes set sail from Boston, destination China, via Honolulu in the Sandwich Islands (now Hawaii). Holmes never made it to China; instead, he fell in love with the islands and settled in Honolulu. Shortly after marrying a Polynesian princess, he was appointed Governor of Honolulu by King Kamehameha I and soon became a wealthy and powerful man.

Later, Sea-Captain William H. Davis settled there and married Holmes's eldest daughter, Hannah. Two sons followed the union: Robert G. in 1819 and William Heath Davis, Jr. in 1822. Captain William H. Davis, Sr. died a few months later, probably of excessive drinking. Apparently there was bitterness between Captain Davis and his wife, Hannah, for she changed her name back to Holmes soon after his death. Only William, Jr., made any effort to keep his father's memory alive.

Hannah Holmes re-married a few years later. Her new husband was John Coffin Jones, probably the most prominent American trader in Honolulu. As the official U.S. Commercial agent, he also acted as U.S. Consul. When William Davis's older brother, Robert, was sent to New England for formal education, Captain Jones took nine-year-old William to Sitka, Alaska, and then to California aboard his trading ship.

California made a lasting impression on young Davis. Upon his return to Honolulu, he was enrolled in the Oahu Charity School, run by strict Protestant missionaries. The name alone created a negative image, and William detested it. In 1833 his step-father interrupted his education and took him on another trading voyage to California. While anchored off Santa Barbara, Jones officiated in the marriage of Thomas O. Larkin to Rachel Holmes aboard the ship. Later, Larkin became U.S. Consul at Monterey (see Larkin).

After this exciting second voyage, life at the Oahu Charity School paled by comparison. But Davis stuck it out until age sixteen, when he abruptly left Honolulu and sailed to California to join Nathan Spear, his uncle (by marriage), who was a prominent trader in Yerba Buena (now

San Francisco). Perhaps Davis' move from the islands was hastened by an unhappy marriage in January 1838. Davis never mentioned it in later years and no further information about his first wife has come to light.

Nathan Spear operated stores in Monterey and Yerba Buena in partnership with Jacob Leese and William Hinckley. Davis settled in Yerba Buena and began working for his uncle. A year after his arrival, Spear established a wind-powered gristmill, the first in Northern California. By then Davis had proved himself and was placed in charge of Spear's ship, the *Isobel*, which plied the waters in and around San Francisco Bay to transport grain to the gristmill and coarse flour to nearby ranches.

IN JULY 1839, Swiss emigrant John A. Sutter arrived in Yerba Buena with a party of native Hawaiians and Germans. He needed his people and supplies transported up the Sacramento River to establish a settlement to be called New Helvetia (see Sutter). Necessary arrangements were made with Nathan Spear. Seventeen-year old "Kanaka Bill" Davis, as he became known, was assigned to lead a tiny flotilla of two ships and a four-oared pinnace up the river. Davis was to command the *Isobel*, while Captain Jack Rainsford captained the smaller *Nicholas*.

Camping ashore at night, Sutter explored surrounding terrain to find a suitable site for New Helvetia. This went on for well over a week, until they passed the confluence of the Sacramento and American rivers and reached the Feather and Bear rivers. Finally Davis and his men had had enough of the heat, the pesky mosquitos and wilderness living. They then returned to the American River, where Sutter directed the ships about two miles upstream. They anchored off a gravel-bar below a tree-covered knoll to the west and began unloading cargo. That knoll was soon to contain the most important settlement in the interior of Northern California.

Amidst the roar of salutes fired from Sutter's three brass cannon the next day, Davis set sail and the two ships headed back downstream. By the time they reached Carquinez Straits, Davis and his men were out of food and virtually living on brown sugar. Fortunately, ranchero Ygnacio Martinez ran cattle in the area, and Davis's men managed to kill a one of his steers for food. Told of it later by Davis, the hospitable Martinez apologized for not being able to offer bread and wine to go along with his beef.

After returning to Yerba Buena, Davis went back to his regular chores in and around the great bay. Soon he learned that his step-father, John C. Jones, had left his wife (Davis's mother, Hannah) in Honolulu and moved to Santa Barbara. It seemed he had become fed up with domineering missionaries in the islands, and had grown tired of his marriage. Hannah Jones stayed in Honolulu, where she owned property, and was in constant litigation with the "infernal missionaries," as she called them.

Before long Jones became enamored with Manuela Carrillo, daughter of prominent *Californio* Don José Carrillo. Jones married her before his divorce from Hannah was finalized. In 1840 Governor Juan B. Alvarado instigated a purge of "foreigners" who were suspected of plotting to overthrow the Mexican Government. The leader was said to be Isaac Graham, who ran a liquor still near Santa Cruz (see Graham).

Both Davis and Nathan Spear were arrested, along with many others, but they were not jailed as others were; instead, they were confined to Mission Dolores for twenty-four hours and then released. A dance was given in their honor that night. Others were not so fortunate. Graham and many of his companions were roughly treated and sent by ship to San Blas, Mexico, for trial and punishment.

Finally they were released and returned to Monterey, with all rights restored. Despite this fiasco, Davis loved California and was determined to stay. Later he was thwarted in his attempt to become a Mexican citizen. His arrest during the Graham affair made this impossible, but he was allowed to stay on a semi-permanent basis with a renewable passport.

WHEN DAVIS CAME OF AGE he began thinking about taking a wife, and he fell in love with Maria Jesus Estudillo, lovely young daughter of José Joaquin Estudillo of San Leandro. As a prominent, well-to-do family, the Estudillos' opposed their daughter's marriage to a part-Kanaka, Protestant trader, and did not encourage the relationship. Never one to take no for an answer, Davis pursued her from afar.

Meanwhile, Davis was traversing the waterways in the *Isobel*, sailing northeast on the Sacramento river to trade with John Sutter and his neighbor, John Sinclair. In 1841 Davis and Spear also had a close relationship with U.S. Naval Commodore Charles Wilkes, who was leading a party of naval officers on a charting expedition.

Not only Americans, but also the French, were interested in the area. Explorer Eugene Duflot de Mofras came to observe the area for the French Government, and there were visits from British interests, including the ever present Hudson's Bay Company. The Russians already occupied an area north of Bodega Bay, including their settlement at Fort Ross; however, it was rumored they were trying to sell it.

Davis learned much about world affairs from these educated men, including the fact that California was vulnerable to almost any determined foreign effort to occupy the country. He also learned about unfair customs duties levied by the Mexican Government against the importation of foreign goods. As a result, ship captains had devised clever ways of smuggling trade goods into the country. Davis was quick to grasp both the necessity and the crafty methods used in the smuggling trade.

The vast majority of trade involved acquisition of cowhides, tallow and cow horns, which the *Californios* traded for processed food and manufactured goods from New England. Finally the day came for Davis to leave Spear and strike out on his own. In 1842, at the age of twenty, he became supercargo for Captain James Pattie on the ship *Don Quixote,* supervising all mercantile operations on the ship between the West Coast and the Sandwich Islands (Hawaii).

By the following year Davis was an associate of Paty, McKinley and Fitch. His frequent voyages to Honolulu allowed him to renew his relationship with his mischievous, flirtatious mother and his older brother, Robert. They and other friends in the islands were helpful in Davis' efforts to develop trade for the *Don Quixote.* Eventually this trade involved ports from Alaska to Old Mexico.

Finally Davis had saved enough money to buy a small parcel of real estate in Yerba Buena. He also had acquired many influential and prominent friends throughout California, including Hugo Reid, Abel Stearns and Juan Bandini in Southern California (see separate chapters). He was in Los Angeles in early 1845, when John A. Sutter and Governor Manuel Micheltorena led a motley force of Mexican troops, Indians and American settlers against rebel forces led by former Governor Juan Alvarado, José Castro and the Pico Brothers.

ALVARADO and his allies were attempting to overthrow Micheltorena, who had sought help from Sutter to fight the rebels. Davis feared Alvarado because of his former arrest, but managed to stay out of the resulting conflict. Following Micheltorena's defeat and forced departure to Mexico, Pío Pico was named governor and the capital was once again moved from Monterey to Los Angeles (see Pico).

Glad to escape from the confusing hot-bed of Mexican politics, Davis returned to Yerba Buena. There he learned that Nathan Spear intended to sell his business interests. Spear wanted to form a partnership with one Edward T. Bale, a former English ship's surgeon, to construct a large gristmill in the Napa Valley. Davis could not afford to buy Spear out and continued to work with Captain Paty.

In 1845, Davis was offered a partnership with Honolulu merchants, Eliab Grimes and his younger nephew, Hiram. He knew the elder Grimes well and trusted him to be honest and fair. The bargain was struck, with the understanding that Davis would command their trading vessel, *Euphemia.* Eliab Grimes owned a large cattle ranch near Sutter's Fort, and he would divide his time between the ranch and running the firm's store in Yerba Buena. The younger Grimes would operate their store in Honolulu. To all outward appearances, Davis was the owner and master of the *Euphemia.* Under his astute management the firm prospered from the start. Shortly after the election of President James K. Polk (see Polk), Davis received the following note from U.S. Consul, Thomas O. Larkin in Monterey:

> Should there be a war you may find a good chance for employ for your vessel being under a neutral flag. . You may depend on my giving your Brig something to do.

Davis knew war with Mexico was probable, and Larkin's note seemed to confirm it. As a citizen of the Sandwich Islands, Davis owed allegiance to neither country, especially Mexico, whose government had earlier rejected his application for citizenship. His suspicions about war were confirmed when the *Euphemia* entered Monterey Bay in July 1846, and Davis sighted the Stars and Stripes fluttering above the Customs House. His ship was probably the first merchant vessel to arrive after the occupation.

He found himself warmly welcomed by American Commodore Sloat, who explained how Northern California had been taken with little or no fighting. It could be different in the South, where an invasion was in the making. After Commodore Robert Stockton had relieved Sloat, Davis sent the *Euphemia* to Honolulu to obtain supplies badly needed by the Navy. He and Monterey trader Thomas O. Larkin soon became major military suppliers.

Before long Commodore Stockton authorized Davis to purchase arms for his growing army of volunteers under command of John C. Fremont. Davis bought arms from Samuel Brannan, who had brought a shipload of Mormons from New York in mid-July (see Brannan). There were times when Davis and Larkin found themselves hard-pressed to meet the insatiable demands of goods from both the military and civilian populations.

Fremont had no means to pay his California Battalion volunteers; the men were in dire need of supplies, which Davis delivered to Fremont in Santa Barbara. Davis then sailed to San Diego to renew his acquaintance with Commodore Stockton. He was there in January 1847 when word was received that Mexican forces had surrendered to Fremont. The war appeared over, so Davis sent the *Euphemia* and another chartered ship to San Pedro, while he rode overland on horseback to Los Angeles.

Lt. Colonel Fremont had been appointed Military Governor by Stockton and had never settled his debt to Davis. When Davis tried to see him about it, he was rebuffed by Fremont's subordinates. Davis left Los Angeles with bitter feelings toward Fremont's apparent lack of concern and with unpaid bills totaling over $5,000. Davis ordered the *Euphemia* north, while he traveled overland via El Camino Real.

Upon his return to Yerba Buena, Davis found his business in disarray and was forced to spend weeks getting it straightened out. Learning that his mother was ill in Honolulu, and that Eliab Grimes was there also, Davis was again forced to leave the business in the hands of subordinates. A few days after his arrival in Honolulu, his mother died. As Davis put it, her loss was "the first real sorrow I ever experienced."

Shortly after his return to Yerba Buena, it became clear that the American conquest would change the economy of the area drastically. Commerce was shifting from Monterey to Yerba Buena, and trade in cowhides and tallow was being replaced by beef and other commodities. By then Davis was ready for bigger and better investments and helped form a corporation to build badly needed wharves in the harbor. Unfortunately, the military government refused permission for the wharves and the project was thwarted. Disappointed and disgusted, Davis dropped out of the corporation, which later went on to build wharves at a tremendous profit.

Despite his temporary setback, Davis's store in Yerba Buena grew into one of its busiest centers, and he profited greatly. He and his partners also invested heavily in importing lumber from Oregon. Though they were making money, relations between Davis and Hiram Grimes had grown strained over the years. Eliab was growing old and Davis began looking for a way out of the partnership.

But before then, another more important decision was at hand. For years Davis had kept in touch with Maria Estudillo; now it was time to court her seriously. Family traditions had kept their courtship at a distance, and Davis asked mutual friends to intercede with Maria's stubborn father. Upon Davis' promise to convert to Catholicism, permission was finally granted to announce the engagement.

WILLIAM HEATH DAVIS was married to Maria Jesus Estudillo at Mission Dolores in November 1847. U.S. Alcalde, Washington Bartlett—who renamed Yerba Buena San Francisco—approved the marriage by signing the necessary documents. Davis spent the next few months adjusting to married life and building up his trading ventures. One of them involved his attempt to re-kindle the declining tallow trade. It came to disaster when the elderly *Euphemia* struck a rocky crag near Monterey. Fortunately the ship did not sink; it was salvaged and repaired at Davis's personal expense. Feeling he had been wronged by his partners, Davis was more determined than ever to break away from them. A short time later, he was in Honolulu when he received word of James Marshall's gold discovery at Sutter's Sawmill in Cullomah (now Coloma). See Marshall.

Quick to capitalize on the Gold Rush, Davis sent quantities of hardware and supplies to the gold fields and sold them at astronomical prices. Soon gold replaced silver coins as a medium of exchange, and Davis had difficulty in disposing the large amounts of gold he collected. But it did allow him to acquire enough wealth to buy the *Euphemia* and finally terminate his partnership with the Grimeses.

He immediately formed another partnership with a young Bostonian named David Carter. By the end of 1848, they had doubled their original investment and were well on their way toward real wealth. Carter then left for the East to purchase a new trading vessel, while Davis continued with their lucrative trade on the West Coast. Though he was still in his mid-twenties, he was elected a school trustee and helped establish the first public school in San Francisco.

Davis also was appointed treasurer of an association formed to build the first American Catholic Church there. The following year, he was elected to the City Council. While serving as a councilman, he and Sam Brannan had the city purchase the leaky old *Euphemia* for use as a city jail. Not only that, but Davis's store furnished the balls, chains and handcuffs for the improvised prison. He and William Leidesdorff also sold large quantities of lumber to the city to build wooden sidewalks (see Leidesdorff).

Crime in the city had become rampant, so Davis joined with Samuel Brannan in a vigilance group sworn to rid the city of criminals from Australia called "The Hounds" (see Brannan). After hanging a few, wrongdoers the vigilantes were partially successful in bringing the crime rate down. Housing for the thousands of gold seekers arriving in town was so scarce that Davis and others began renting out camp sites on their vacant property. During David Carter's long absence, Davis entered into several other brief partnerships in various trading ventures.

While demand for nearly everything remained high, it was becoming increasingly difficult for retailers to obtain merchandise. Davis had to send vessels farther and farther away to obtain goods to sell in California. Meanwhile, he was growing impatient for his partner's expected arrival with a new ship crammed with valuable merchandise. That alone could make them both wealthy. But unbeknownst to him, Carter had become ill on his way East and had died shortly after reaching Boston. This tragedy was only one that struck Davis within a short time. The first of his many offspring suddenly died. He also lost Jane Holmes Spear, his favorite aunt, and wife of Nathan Spear. Spear died about a year later.

To ease his grief, Davis immersed himself in various business activities, including the building of streets and roads, housing, and transportation. This led to a large investment in a steam-powered riverboat, which failed to materialize. Despite the loss of several similar opportunities, which would have made him one of the richest men in California, Davis had become a wealthy, influential citizen.

IN SEPTEMBER 1849 he constructed San Francisco's first multi-level brick building. Four stories high, it stood at the corner of Montgomery and California Streets. Upon its completion, he leased it to the U.S. Government as a customs house. But it did not stand for long; in 1851, a series of fires destroyed much of the city, including Davis's new building. He later estimated his losses from the fires at around $750,000.

This heavy loss, plus huge, long-range investments in other areas, caused his financial health to falter. Even before the disastrous fires occurred, Davis had become interested in developing a new town in San Diego. The old town, clustered around the presidio, was too far removed from the anchorage for easy transport of cargo unloaded from ships. In March 1850, he formed a partnership with several other investors to lay out a new townsite closer to the waterfront.

There he personally built a huge $60,000 wharf by importing lumber and supplies from all over the nation. A new Army barracks was built on land donated by the partners, and several hundred men were stationed there. "New Town" was starting off well, but from the very start it was plagued by a shortage of water. Wells were dug at great expense, with few results; finally, cisterns were installed to catch what rainfall there was. A hotel, saloons, billiard rooms and stores were built.

Davis was devoting most of his time, energy and capital to San Diego, and was forced to travel north to draw on his remaining investments there. His long and frequent trips to San Francisco distressed his pregnant wife, who had moved to San Diego to be with him. To please her, Davis began selling various assets and business interests in San Francisco. Unfortunately, he was reducing his income accordingly.

By the time New Town was almost built, Davis began pulling back from it to enjoy himself. While he was never a spendthrift, he did enjoy a full life and began neglecting his financial interests and his family with pleasure trips throughout the area. New Town attracted neither the population nor the trade Davis had envisioned; the new wharf was seldom used. A letter he wrote in 1850 tells of his plight at that time:

> All the funds I have drawn from the store and other sources have been eaten up in the expenses of the town...We meet with much opposition from the inhabitants of the old town and beach—they make every effort in the world to crush us...I am on my back and unwell.

Finally he returned to San Francisco to salvage what he could from his store there. He found it mis-managed and stocked with obsolete merchandise. In desperation he sold his holdings there for one tenth of their book value. To add to his problems, the businesses in San Diego were also failing due to a combination of bad management and dishonesty on the part of employees.

Davis's substantial real estate investments in San Diego turned sour, and he was forced to liquidate most of it with heavy losses. Much of it was eventually acquired by Alonzo E. Horton, who has received credit for founding modern San Diego. Perhaps Horton deserves this credit; however, Davis also deserves credit for being the early pioneer. It appears he was ahead of his time in developing American San Diego. Chagrined and devastated by his losses, Davis and his family returned to San Francisco. The Civil War period drove coffin nails into what assets were left in San Diego, as shown in the following letter to Davis from one of his remaining agents in 1867:

> ...you are indebted to the California Volunteers for appropriating it [Davis' store] to their own use for various purposes and lastly for firewood... Pantoja House [billiard parlor, etc.] shared the same fate at the hands of these miserable specimens of humanity in Uncle Sam's uniform who enlisted because they were too lazy to work.

By the early seventies, Davis had decided to file legal claims against the U.S. Government for losses he incurred from members of the armed forces in San Diego. He devoted the next decade and what savings were left in pursuing his claim for $60,000. Finally, in 1885, he was awarded $6,000, barely enough to pay his expenses and legal fees.

Long before then, Davis's father-in-law, José Joaquin Estudillo had offered Davis the job of managing his vast Rancho San Leandro. A short time later, Don José died, leaving Davis to oversee the entire operation. Davis had little ranch experience and had to learn from his subordinates. It didn't take long for him to realize that many improvements were needed to become competitive with other ranchers in the area. He also recognized the need to diversify and began planting fruit orchards.

The years following the Gold Rush saw the transition from archaic farming methods to a more aggressive expansionism. This change was complicated by swarms of displaced argonauts looking for land. Cattle theft was rampant and brazen squatters challenged large landholders' rights and titles. For years Davis had tried to buy land bordering the east side of San Francisco Bay from Vicente Peralta. He knew the area was ripe for development, but Peralta always refused to sell. Finally a group of aggressive squatters virtually took over portions of Peralta's land and systematically stripped him of his cattle. Soon he was forced to sell to speculators the land which eventually became the city of Oakland.

DAVIS ALSO faced serious squatter problems, to the point where he began wearing a pistol on his belt. He and the Estudillo family spent a fortune in legal fees trying to stem the flow of squatters and preserve their property. Finally a compromise was struck, which allowed the squatters to purchase land on which they had been living. Once these onerous problems were behind him, Davis entered into a partnership with his brother-in-law, John R. Ward, to found the city of San Leandro.

Two hundred acres of waterfront property were obtained from their mother-in-law, Doña Juano Estudillo. A hotel and stores were constructed and a plank road built that led to a new wharf. By now, Davis's wife had borne him thirteen children, some of whom had died. In 1857, a dispute with Doña Juana Estudillo and one of her sons caused Davis to resign as ranch manager. This left him and Maria with only 200 acres of their own to farm. Davis leased additional acreage from nearby Rancho Felipe, near the present day Oakland Airport. Davis Road was named after him there.

The Davis family made a decent living from farming operations for a number of years; however, a series of disasters caused them to sell their land. There were droughts, a grasshopper plague and finally the earthquake of 1868 that destroyed their house. Davis moved his large family to Oakland, where they faced the transition from a ranch lifestyle to life in the city. To complicate it, the country was in an economic depression and Davis had trouble finding work. Then his youngest child, Willie, was killed by a fall from a horse.

The older children did what they could to help support the family; Davis tried selling real estate; then he and two of his sons sold insurance. As he aged, Davis seemed to have lost his purpose in life. Perhaps his early successes had spoiled him for such a humdrum existence; he drifted from one occupation to another. Like his Mexican family, he enjoyed music, wine and festivities of any kind.

Because of his discontent, Davis joined the "Workingman's Party," which was trying to rid the country of Chinese immigrants. It was their contention that these "Celestials" were taking away their jobs. By the late eighties he was spending much of his time in his beloved San Francisco, where he began looking for financial backing so he could write his memoirs. It took several years, but he finally succeeded in getting the publishers of the *San Francisco Call* and *Bulletin* to provide enough backing so he could support his family and devote all his time to writing.

AFTER RENTING SPACE in San Francisco's Montgomery Block, Davis moved there alone to concentrate on his writing; thus a new occupation opened for him. Like other writers who do not pursue the profession seriously until later in life, Davis had dabbled in it much earlier. Lack of formal education hindered him at first, but the more he wrote the better it was. Even critics had to admit that his colorful descriptions and knowledge of early California history were above reproach.

Some of Davis's poems had been published earlier in James Hutchings' *Illustrated Monthly Magazine* over the initials W.H.D. A few of his historical articles were published in various newspapers, and he wrote *Glimpses of the Past* expressly for historian Hubert H. Bancroft. He then wrote *Sixty Years in California,* which drew good reviews from newspaper critics, and is today a standard reference.

Unfortunately, Davis became so obsessed with his project that he could not bring it to a conclusion. Eventually it became what was described as a "literary monster," containing two volumes of 1,200 pages each. He continued pushing up the completion date until, in 1905, he was calling it *Seventy-Four Years in California*. Finally his backers had had enough and canceled their financial support.

By then Davis saw his family infrequently and was at his wits' end. To raise money, he began selling portrait space in his alleged volumes at $350 a page and later at much reduced rates. On the night of April 17, 1906, Davis locked his door and took the ferry across the Bay to visit his neglected family in Oakland. The next morning saw the devastating earthquake and fire that reduced most of San Francisco to a fiery ruin.

LATER, Davis returned to the city and picked his way through the rubble to the Montgomery Block, where he had toiled for so many long years. Though the condemned building still stood, there was no sign of his huge manuscript. Whether it was stolen or destroyed by vandals was never known. His eleven-year old grandson said of his grandfather's return to Oakland, "I can see him coming up the street, and sinking down on the front steps in tears."

Having lost his wife earlier, Davis moved to Hayward to live with a married daughter. He spent his remaining years strolling around Hayward, reminiscing with anyone who would listen. Eventually he suffered a stroke that left him paralyzed but mentally alert. He died in 1909 at the age of eighty-seven.

In 1929 fragments of Davis' many writings were put together, condensed and published by John Howell under the title, *Seventy-Five Years in California*, a "must" for early California historical research and plain good reading. Davis Road in Alameda County is named after him, as is Davis Street in San Francisco.

BIBLIOGRAPHY

CarilloBancroft, Hubert H. *History of California*. Vol. I-VI. History Co., San Francisco, 1886. Reprint, Wallace Hebberd, Santa Barbara, CA, 1966.

–Davis, William Heath. *Seventy-Five Years in California*. John Howell Books, San Francisco, 1967.

–Hague, Harlan, and Langum, David J. *Thomas O. Larkin*. University of Oklahoma Press, Norman, 1990.

–Dillon, Richard. *Fool's Gold*. Coward McCann, Inc. New York, 1967.

–Phelps, William Dane. *Alta California, 1840-1842* (Phelp's Journal). Arthur H. Clark Co., Glendale, CA, 1983.

–Rolle, Andrew F. *An American in California*. Huntington Library, San Marino, CA, 1956. All quotations taken from this publication.

Dr. Nicholas August Den
Courtesy California State Library

– 13 –

NICHOLAS A. H. DEN (DON NICOLAS)

1812 – 1862

A NATIVE OF IRELAND, 24-year old Nicholas Den was a stocky, rather homely young man with steely-blue eyes and curly blonde hair. He had been studying medicine in his final year at Trinity College, Dublin, when he received news that his father could no longer pay for his education, forcing him to drop out in early 1836.

Within a matter of days, Den was aboard a ship heading across the Atlantic. After spending some time in Newfoundland and Nova Scotia, Den sailed for Boston. His ship docked near the trading vessel *Pilgrim,* which had just returned from California with a load of cowhides and tallow. Intrigued, Den spoke to some of the *Pilgrim's* seamen, who filled his eager head with exotic tales about the warm weather, easy living and willing, buxom girls on the West Coast. Within a short time he had signed aboard the trading vessel *Kent* and was on his way to see California for himself.

Like the *Pilgrim,* the *Kent* was a hide drogher; because of his superior education, Den was made supercargo in charge of trading manufactured goods for cowhides and tallow. From his first sighting of Monterey, Alta California, Den recognized his feelings as a classic case of love at first sight. While there Den was befriended by American trader, Thomas O. Larkin (see Larkin). When Den spoke of settling in Monterey, Larkin convinced him that Santa Barbara offered better opportunities for an ambitious young man like himself. Though Den found it hard to believe that Santa Barbara could compare favorably with Monterey's natural beauty and climate, he decided to visit the tiny Southern California pueblo before making a final decision.

It was December 1836 when the ship made its way down the coast. The voyage south was rough, cold and uncomfortable until the ship passed into the relative calm on the lee side of Point Conception and the Channel Islands. Though the foothills of Santa Barbara were not as lush and verdant as Monterey, the looming backdrop of mountains stretching toward azure skies gave it a distinctive beauty of its own. With fewer than 1,000 inhabitants, the pueblo consisted of small adobe buildings built around the crumbling presidio constructed fifty years earlier. A white twin-towered building with a red-tiled roof dominated the scene from a hillside above. Den learned later that this lovely structure was considered the queen of the Franciscan missions.

The ship's arrival triggered a burst of activity, as traders and local *hacendados* began hauling hides and tallow to the wide beach in squealing wooden-wheeled *carretas*. Since there was no wharf, the ship's boats made their way ashore through the tumbling surf, drenching Den and the others with chilling sea-water. Once ashore, Den was hard put to tally all the hide and tallow purchases. He did find time to befriend an American settler, Daniel Hill, who assisted him as a translator. Hill then invited Den to spend the night at his home.

Hill, a New England seaman, had left his ship in 1822 to settle in Santa Barbara, where he became a naturalized Mexican citizen and married a lovely Mexican girl from the prestigious Ortega family. Den, enticed by the warmth of Daniel Hill and his family, decided to settle in Santa Barbara. Hill even mentioned the possibility that Den might acquire a valuable land grant just up the coast. But first he would have to become a citizen of Mexico.

Den's mind was whirling when he told the *Kent's* captain that he was leaving the ship. How would he ever explain to his family a decision to give up his Irish citizenship to become a naturalized Mexican? He had been born in 1812 to Emanuel and Katherine O'Shea Den of Kilkenny County, an upper middle-class family with a long list of impressive pedigrees.

When Daniel Hill learned that his new friend, Nicholas Den, had studied medicine, he was elated. Santa Barbara was in need of a doctor, and Hill did his best to convince Den to open a medical practice. This Den refused to do, stating that he was not licensed and not interested. He did agree, however, to help people in need if no doctor was available. What he really wanted was to become a cattle rancher. He had heard how well other California *rancheros* were doing with seemingly little effort, and he dreamed about the same kind of life.

But first he had to get adequate land. Hill took him on horseback the next day to see a property called Rancho Dos Pueblos, named after two deserted Indian villages. The property line began near the Goleta Estuary, extended north to the foothills and stretched westerly along the coast for about ten miles. Totaling 15,000 to 16,000 acres, it was considered a fairly small ranch by Mexican standards. Several streams of clear water crossed the property on their way to the sea. Den was mesmerized by the thought of owning beautiful Dos Pueblos. His first step would be to learn ranch work and the local language. If it took a year or two, so be it; he would then file for his citizenship. Once that was approved, he would apply for his land grant. Then, if someone didn't beat him to it, Dos Pueblos would be his.

The next day Hill took Den to visit his in-laws, the Ortegas, at their ranch a mile and a half up Refugio Canyon. This huge ranch was nearly self sustaining with many workers. Den spent the next year of his life learning the language and the cattle business from Don José Vincente Ortega and his hardy *vaqueros*. Meanwhile, Hill had sold his Santa Barbara home and built another on his own ranch northwest of Dos Pueblos.

Hill and Den visited back and forth, and before long the young Irishman became known as "Doctor" Den or *el medico* because of his medical abilities. He often received wine or brandy for his services, which he sold to raise cash. He also began small-scale farming on Dos Pueblos land, raising fruits and vegetables which he sold to ships that called at Refugio Bay.

IN 1838 an American settler offered Den 500 cattle at a bargain price. Den did not have enough money and knew of no way to get it. But just before the final date for acceptance, he received a rare visit from Fr. Narcisso Durán. The Franciscan padre handed the flabbergasted Nicholas Den a heavy wicker basket containing enough silver coins to make the purchase. He then turned and left. Den could scarcely wait to drive his cattle to Dos Pueblos, determined to repay the kind padre some day.

Soon Den was being called *Don Nicolas*, a title used to honor respected men of property. Within a short time his cattle were increasing to the point where he sold enough to buy a lot in Santa Barbara. When he applied for permission to build a house there, he was told he would have to wait for his Mexican citizenship. He decided to go through with his application, and in 1841 he took the oath of allegiance to the Republic of Mexico. A year later he applied for his long awaited land grant. He also applied for a smaller grant nearby called *San Antonio y Cienegita*. Both grants were approved that same year; however, Fr. Durán filed an objection to the Dos Pueblos grant, stating that the land belonged to the mission. Den refused to take the protest seriously and staked out his boundaries with deep pride in his coveted acquisition.

When Den had first met Daniel Hill in 1836, Hill's oldest daughter, Rosa Antonia, was a girl of eight. By the time Den's land grant was approved, she was a lovely girl of fifteen and deeply in love with him. As the area's most eligible bachelor, Den had his choice of many pretty girls, but none matched Rosa's beauty in his adoring eyes. Before news of their betrothal was made public, Den had been busy building not one, but two houses for his new bride. The best, one with a wooden floor and wood shingles on the roof, was being built on his Santa Barbara lot as their main residence. The other at Dos Pueblos was not quite as large or opulent, per the standards of the day.

THE WEDDING was scheduled for the spring of 1843, but before then the land grant protest filed by Fr. Durán came to light in a most alarming way. Governor Alvarado had been replaced by Manuel Micheltorena from Mexico. Apparently Micheltorena was under orders from Mexico City to reaffirm and re-establish mission properties wherever possible. Because he was a zealous missionary, Fr. Durán grasped the opportunity to seize mission lands that had been sold or granted during secularization.

This placed Den in an awkward position. He hated to confront the padre who had provided money to get his first cattle herd started. But the land meant everything, and he was determined to fight for it. Fortunately the matter was compromised at a hearing in Los Angeles, when the padre agreed to claim only one-third of Dos Pueblos. Den agreed, realizing that he might get it back once another governor came to power.

Now that the unpleasant matter had been settled, Den devoted his time and energy to finishing his houses while Rosa planned their wedding. The wedding was held at Hill's ranch, in the parish of Mission Santa Ines, June 1, 1843. By then Den's fortunes had increased greatly, and he installed his 16-year-old bride in the Santa Barbara house with plenty of servants to maintain it.

In early September, Den and his wife were on the beach watching anxiously as a load of their new furniture was being brought through the treacherous surf in small open boats. Den's jaw must have dropped with surprise when he met the young man coming ashore with the furniture. It was none other than his 22-year-old brother, Richard Somerset Den, from Ireland. They had not seen each other for a decade, and Den was glad to hear that his father's finances had improved enough to allow his brother to finish medical school at Trinity College, Den's alma mater in Dublin.

Although Dr. Richard Den had not planned to remain in California, he was stung by the same "bug" that had bitten his older brother. After spending a week in Santa Barbara, he decided to stay and set up a medical practice. A short time later he became involved in some unfortunate incidents with tainted smallpox vaccinations. His practice suffered accordingly, and he moved to Los Angeles for a new start.

In July 1844 Rosa presented her beaming husband with a healthy baby daughter. When the baby was only a few weeks old, Den was elected *alcalde* of Santa Barbara and its environs. This made him the presiding officer over the *ayuntamiento* (council), which governed local affairs.

He soon became the most influential citizen in the area; his duties were prescribed as follows:

> Encouraging industry, restraining vice, punishing crime, distributing public land, drawing up contracts, safeguarding the rights of orphans, and summoning citizens by beat of drum to the public plaza, there to promulgate new regulations by word of mouth [because so few could read].

During his tenure in early 1845, a rebel band—led by ex-Governor Alvarado and General José Castro—deposed Governor Micheltorena, allegedly to rid themselves of his hated *cholo* troops. Pío Pico, former administrator at Mission San Luis Rey, was named governor and the capital was moved from Monterey to Los Angeles. Pico was greatly feared by the mission padres, who grimly predicted the end of the mission era. They were not far wrong; within a matter of weeks Pico sent emissaries to Santa Barbara, where they demanded that Fr. Durán surrender the mission to them. The haughty Durán defied them, and they left seeking further orders.

Other missions were not so fortunate. Pico began dismantling their power and influence by selling or leasing their properties to anyone who had the price. Mission Santa Ines was sold for $7,000. Finally Fr. Durán turned to Alcalde Den for assistance. Seeking a solution to avoid outright sale of the Santa Barbara Mission, Den met with Daniel Hill. After a brief consultation, the two agreed to offer Pico $100 per month to lease the property for one year. Fr. Durán went along with the idea and wrote Governor Pico:

> It seems that Don Nicholas A. Den of Dos Pueblos Rancho, with his father-in-law Don Daniel Hill, have made an offer to rent the Mission of Santa Barbara for $1,200 annually. They are worthy and honorable persons.

Surprisingly, Pico accepted the offer in November 1845, and the two elated partners took "possession", realizing they had probably saved the mission from destruction. A lot could happen in a year, and they would worry about it when the time came. They had no idea how prophetic their thinking was, as the Santa Barbara Mission building was one of the few to remain intact with Franciscan padres in charge. By January 1846, more than a thousand head of cattle from mission property at Rancho San Marcos had been re-branded by Den. Either the livestock went with the deal or he bought them separately.

By then rumors of possible war between Mexico and the United States were rampant. Rather than submit to the *Americanos*, some Californians would have preferred protection from Great Britain. A surprise visit from an Irish countryman brought Den a pleasant respite from talk of war. Thomas Meehan was supercargo on an English vessel that had anchored in Refugio Bay. Learning that Den was an Irishman, he borrowed a horse and came for a visit. The two of them hit it off so well that Meehan quit his ship and was employed by Den as his *major-domo* (foreman).

When Den needed more grazing land to support his growing herds, he struck a deal with Pío Pico to purchase the 35,000-plus acre Rancho San Marcos (see Pío Pico). His brother, Richard, had done well with his Los Angeles medical practice and agreed to buy an interest in the San Marcos property. But before this could take place, Den's friend, Fr. Narciso Durán died, and Rosa Den gave birth to a second boy.

On June 9 the deal for Rancho San Marcos was closed, and the Den brothers became the proud owners. Richard Den also bought Hill's interest in the mission lease. Meanwhile, Hill had applied for a one-league land grant at La Goleta. This was approved by Pico about the same time as Den's acquisition at San Marcos. Though the Den brothers didn't know it, the Bear Flag Rebellion took place at Sonoma in mid-June, and California was declared an Independent Republic.

Three weeks later U.S. Navy Commodore Sloat landed troops at Monterey, and the picturesque pueblo fell without a shot being fired. Within a matter of days the "Bear Flag" at Sonoma had been replaced by the Stars and Stripes, which was also raised over Yerba Buena (San Francisco) and Sutter's Fort. In effect, Northern California had been occupied by U.S. forces without any real battle, with few if any casualties.

The first contact Santa Barbarans had with U.S. forces was when Commodore Robert Stockton's ship *Congress* anchored offshore. Nicolas Den and others watched anxiously when a smallboat was rowed ashore with ten marines in full battle dress. There was no Mexican flag flying ashore, so an American flag was hoisted on an empty flagstaff.

Though Den was not an American and was no longer the alcalde, Commodore Stockton appointed him the *commandante* with responsibility to enforce martial law. Stockton left Den no alternative as he turned abruptly and left. Obviously Den had been recommended by someone of authority—probably Thomas O. Larkin. Ten marines were left under a Midshipman as an occupying force. They were to assist Den in enforcing the ten o'clock curfew and any other regulations he deemed necessary to keep the peace.

By September, Stockton thought the war was all over. He returned on the U.S.S. *Congress* to withdraw some of his marines for duties elsewhere. In an attempt to pacify the Californians, he held a grand ball aboard the *Congress,* to which all the leading citizens were invited. Of course, Nicolas Den and his wife were honored guests. Thus ended the first occupation. But things were not as peaceful as they seemed.

A week after Stockton's departure, Den was back at Dos Pueblos when he was told that armed, mounted *Americanos* were camping on his ranch property. Riding out to investigate, he found Col. John C. Fremont with some of his "California Volunteers "(see Fremont). Fremont told him that he had been appointed Military Governor and was heading north to set up a government. Fremont left the next morning and later wrote rather poetically of his experience with Den in September 1846:

> Near the sea on the journey I came across some very attractive spots. The garden of Dr. Nicholas A. Den near Santa Barbara was one of these. It extended to the verge of a low sea-bluff on the level lowland between the mountains and the sea; and in the midst of many fruits which were clustered together in a luxuriance almost wild, and the home comforts around, the sheltered security was made felt by the sullen waves as they were thrown back, disappointed from the shore....

After such a description, is it any wonder Fremont returned to settle in California after the war?

STOCKTON'S HOPE for a quick, easy victory against the Mexicans came to a rude end in Los Angeles. Disheartened by the harsh military rule enforced by Captain A. Gillespie, Mexican firebrands Serbula Verela and José Flores rallied a band of fighters and ran Gillespie and his men out of Los Angeles to San Pedro, where they took refuge aboard a ship. Flores then led about 200 men north to Santa Barbara to "liberate" the pueblo from new U.S. occupying forces. Because of Den's appointment by Stockton as *commandante*, Flores considered him a traitor and threatened to execute him and take all the American settlers as prisoners. Fortunately for them, the handful of U. S. occupation troops got word of Flores' invasion in time to flee into the mountains.

When Den heard of Flores' intentions, he rode to Santa Barbara to confront him. He was then arrested and thrown into the calaboose with other prisoners. But when Flores learned that he was the brother of Richard Den—his own volunteer medical surgeon—Nicolas Den was released and allowed to resume his duties as *commandante* and *alcalde*.

Knowing that his presence would be required there for the duration of the war, Den moved his family from the ranch to Santa Barbara. He knew Tom Meehan would run the ranch as though it were his own. Toward the end of November, Den was confronted by Mexican soldiers and asked to provide quarters for them and an important American prisoner. To Den's surprise the prisoner turned out to be U.S. Consul Thomas O. Larkin, who was ill and badly shaken by the experience. He had been taken prisoner while attempting to reach Yerba Buena, where his wife and critically ill daughter had been evacuated. His daughter died shortly after his capture.

Den talked the soldiers into allowing Larkin to stay with him and Rosa, at least until he recovered from his illness. Larkin was later taken to Los Angeles. The fighting ended when Lt. Col. John C. Fremont's forces, heading south toward Los Angeles, confronted Gen. Andres Pico and his Mexican army being driven north by the combined forces of Commodore Stockton and General Stephen Kearny. After the Mexicans capitulated and signed the Treaty of Rancho Cahuenga, Larkin returned to Monterey, where he gave the Dens credit for saving his life. Den's tenure as commandante and alcalde came to an end when he was replaced by a U.S. military appointee. He and Rosa were glad to return to Rancho Dos Pueblos and their thriving cattle ranching operation. As Den had expected, Tom Meehan had performed well as *majordomo*.

IN THE SPRING OF 1848 came the news about James W. Marshall's startling gold discovery at Sutter's mill (see Marshall). A few weeks later Den was surprised by a visit from his brother, Richard, who was on his way to the gold fields. Though Den was sorely tempted to join him, he stayed behind. Rosa was expecting another child, and he had his ranch responsibilities. Instead, he told his brother to size up the situation and he might join him the following year.

By the fall of 1848 Colonel Richard Mason had been named Military Governor and revoked certain land grants made by Pío Pico, including the Den brother's purchase of Rancho San Marcos. Den appealed the decision and finally won out in a subsequent decision by the U.S. Land Commission. Meanwhile, in March 1849, Den decided to leave both ranchos in Meehan's capable hands while he visited his brother in the gold fields.

Den had been forewarned about what to expect in the chaotic gold country, but the sheer masses of gold-maddened argonauts fighting to make a quick fortune—or scratch out a meager living—shook him to the core. He found his brother on the Calaveras River, treating a sick miner. Don Ricardo Den, as he was known, had found it much more lucrative to treat the sick than to pan for gold.

While there, Nicolas Den came close to losing his life when he attempted to interfere during a lynching. Den was certain the man to be hanged was innocent and threatened to stop the proceedings. Only quick interference by his brother saved him from joining the hapless victim on the same tree. But the awful experience never left Den, and he developed a lifelong hatred for vigilante activities of any kind.

Another experience in the gold country brought a different kind of revelation, when Den had to pay an ounce of gold for a small, leathery piece of beef. It seemed ludicrous! He had ten thousand head of cattle at home which brought a mere two dollars a head for their hides. Here they would be worth a fortune—perhaps forty or fifty dollars a head. The more he and his brother discussed it, the more feasible it seemed to drive a herd north. They could start out with a thousand or so and see how it went. Once the decision was made, Den could hardly wait to get back to his ranch and get a herd started north. A week later he was home, and making preparations for a drive which Tom Meehan would lead. Meehan was scarcely out of sight when Den began gathering another herd.

Den's herd was one of the first to arrive in the north, and the jubilant Tom Meehan brought back leather bags crammed with gold. He had sold the herd for $50 a head in exchange for $41,000 in gold ingots. The next herd was driven north within a matter of days. This time there were nearly 2,000 head, and they brought close to $100,000. By then other ranchers had joined the beef bonanza and prices began to drop. In 1850 Den drove three more herds north, where they sold for $35 a head.

While in San Francisco on business, Den and his brother became charter members of the Society of California Pioneers. In a year's time, they had become two of the wealthiest and most prominent men in California. Though Nicolas Den was pressured to run for governor or the U.S. senate, he refused to enter politics. He did, however, consent to serve as chairman of Santa Barbara's first grand jury, and he also became County Assessor.

ABOUT THE TIME CALIFORNIA became the 31st state on September 9, 1850, an ex-sergeant of Colonel. Jonathon Stevenson's New York Regiment returned to Santa Barbara from Los Angeles. This unsavory character was Jack Powers, a professional gambler and suspected outlaw. He brought with him a band of hard cases who had served with him in the army during the late war. Upon their arrival in Santa Barbara, Powers called on Den to rent a small parcel of land on his San Antonio grant to be used as his headquarters. Unaware of Power's intentions to use the property as an outlaw hangout, Den leased him the land for one year. The smooth-talking, sophisticated Powers soon gained a reputation in the pueblo as a wealthy philanthropist and all-around good fellow. Although Den was no longer *alcalde,* he recognized Power's potential for evil. It wasn't long before his suspicions came to fruition.

Den had rounded up 1,000 head of cattle for a drive to market. Powers and his gang learned of it and decided to steal the entire herd. When their scheme was made known to Meehan and Den, Meehan wanted to form a vigilante group and attack the gang by force. But because of Den's aversion to vigilante groups, he insisted on allowing the sheriff to handle it. The sheriff was a known consort of Powers; though he tried to avoid taking action, Den coerced him into it and the outlaw's plan was thwarted.

Rather than try to convict Powers of attempted cattle theft, Den ordered him and his gang to leave his San Antonio property. They left temporarily, but not before Powers threatened to "get even" with Den. Three weeks later, Tom Meehan was riding alone up the Rufugio Trail when he was ambushed and killed by Powers' right hand man, Pat Dunn, and two henchmen. Den was at his ranch when a rider came in leading a pack-mule bearing Meehan's bullet-torn body. Den listened in shocked silence as the rider explained how he had found Meehan's body just off the Refugio Trail.

Though Den suspected Powers and his men, he had no proof. As it turned out, he didn't need proof. Pat Dunn and two others confessed the killing to the sheriff, claiming it was done in self defense. Despite the fact that Meehan had been shot in the back, they claimed he had attacked them and they had fired back merely to protect themselves. There were some who agreed with Den that it had been a cold-blooded killing, but the three killers were never tried.

Again Den wrestled with his conscience about forming a vigilante group. He knew he was marked for death himself, but again decided against using vigilantes. But after several attempts were made to ambush him he began surrounding himself with armed men. Powers and his gang seemed to be running the town, and Den feared for his life and that of his wife and family. To add contempt to injury, Power's gang had returned to Den's San Antonio grant and were living there as squatters.

When Den ordered them off, they threatened to kill not only him, but his family as well. In desperation, Den obtained a court order to evict Powers and demanded that the sheriff enforce it. The reluctant sheriff was obliged to form a posse to carry out the eviction. A large force of volunteers was mobilized with a small cannon to fight in the expected mini-war. But before they left town, three of Power's men rode in, brazenly lassoed the cannon, and yanked it from its carriage.

In the ensuing gun battle the sheriff shot two of the attackers; the third fled to Power's hangout with the posse in pursuit. The affair ended in a stalemate, but Powers was finally persuaded to give up and leave. Two of Meehan's killers were now dead, and at last Powers had been evicted from Den's property. But Pat Dunn was still at large, more troublesome than ever. He had escaped punishment for at least two murders, and he continued to threaten and harass the Nicolas Den family.

Realizing it was foolhardy to keep his family in town, Den sold his house to the Catholic Church at a bargain price for use as an Apostolic college. He then moved Rosa and the children back to Dos Pueblos. In the mid-1850's, Dunn finally went too far and was imprisoned for attempted murder. After serving six years, he was released and reportedly died later in Arizona.

The era of *Americano bandidos* culminated with the brutal killing of two cattle buyers during a robbery near Mission San Juan Bautista. At least one of the robbers had been shot during the robbery; a black stallion with a brand from a Santa Barbara ranch had been killed. Jack Powers was known to ride such a horse; furthermore, the saddle was identified as his. A posse then headed for Santa Barbara to arrest the wily outlaw. Meanwhile Powers had returned there to obtain medical care to remove a large-caliber bullet from his leg. Somehow he escaped arrest and apparently fled the country; he was never seen there again.

FINALLY EVENTS CALMED enough so Den felt free to escort his two oldest sons east to board a ship bound for England. The boys were going there for a formal education, but after reaching New York the younger refused to go and returned home. Den continued on to England with his older boy and enjoyed the experience greatly. He returned home bearing many gifts, including a stunning silver tea set and a shiny new surrey for Rosa. A colorful coachman named Greenleaf C. Welch was hired to drive it.

Then came a breach between Nicolas and Richard Den: Richard brought suit against his brother to gain outright ownership of Rancho San Marcos, which had been held in both names. Richard lost the suit; though he vowed never to speak to Nicolas again, they remained business partners. The dynamic decade of the 1850's ended with news that the notorious Jack Powers had gone to Mexico, where he was stabbed to death in a fight over a girl. Den must have breathed a deep sigh of relief over his arch-enemy's demise.

During the next decade the Den brothers acquired more grazing land and increased their herds accordingly. Because Den's Dos Pueblos property was located on *El Camino Real,* the main road along the coast, Den's home became renowned for its generous hospitality, fine meals and beautiful gardens. In 1860, Don Nicolas and Rosa took an extended trip abroad. After visiting their son in England, they spent over a year journeying throughout Europe.

Christmas week of 1861 saw one of the worst rainstorms and floods of that century in the Santa Barbara area. Within a short time Dos Pueblos Creek had become a raging river. Den watched helplessly as a virtual wall of water destroyed crops and bore off irreplaceable top-soil. But at least the house, which stood on high ground, was spared. The former estuary adjacent to the sea became a silt-filled swamp, but the ranch itself was not devastated.

Soon the Dens were again enjoying prosperity. By early 1862 they were planning a trip around the world, but on the chilly, rainy night of

March 2nd, Den was in bed nursing a chest cold. Suddenly a desperate local Indian appeared at the door seeking medical help for his wife. She was suffering a difficult childbirth and the midwife could not cope. Against the advice of Rosa, "Doctor" Den quickly dressed and accompanied the man to his distant *casa*. The baby died, but Den managed to save the man's wife before he returned home to his warm bed in the early morning hours .

Rosa was anxious when she saw how drawn and exhausted he looked. The dreadful rattle of congestion in his lungs worried her more than anything. She sent one of her sons to Santa Barbara to get the doctor and did what she could to make her feverish husband comfortable. The doctor and a priest arrived about 5:00 p.m., and Den's illness was diagnosed as double pneumonia. Don Nicolas died the night of March 3, 1862 at the age of 50, with the shaken priest giving him his last rites.

A large, elaborate funeral was held in the old mission, and friends came for miles around to pay their respects. Doña Rosa was 35 at the time of her husband's death, and had ten children to raise. The oldest was 16 and the youngest was an infant of ten months. Fortunately Den left her a wealthy woman, and she never lacked for hired help.

The following year Southern California suffered one of the worst droughts in history. Even dependable Dos Pueblos Creek ran the lowest anyone could remember. Livestock died by the thousands; their rotting carcasses could be smelled for miles. By mid-1864, the number of cattle on Rancho Dos Pueblos dropped from 25,000 head to 40.

A year later Rosa lost her father, Daniel Hill, and was at her wits' end trying to keep things together. Finally she turned to her coachman and English tutor, Greenleaf C. Welch, for solace. She ended up marrying him a short time later. It was good that Don Nicolas did not live to see the disintegration of his massive cattle empire.

The boundaries of Den's Dos Pueblos Rancho are described as beginning near the Goleta estuary, extending north to the foothills and stretching westerly along the coast for about ten miles. This appears to include the city of Goleta, west to Naples.

The Carillo Adobe at 11 E. Carillo Street, Santa Barbara, is a state historical site. This home, built by Daniel Hill in 1825, was the home of Den's wife, the former Rosa Ortega. She was the grand-daughter of Lt. José Francisco Ortega, founder and first *commandante* of the Royal Presidio of Santa Barbara. There is a state historical marker at this site.

BIBLIOGRAPHY

–Bancroft, Hubert H. *California Pioneer Register and Index.* Regional
   Publishing Co., Baltimore, MD, 1964.
–Davis, William Heath. *Seventy-Five Years In California.* John Howell
   Books, San Francisco, 1967.
–Hague, Harlan & Langum, David J. *Thomas O. Larkin.* University of
   Oklahoma Press, Norman, 1990.
–Tompkins, Walker A. *Santa Barbara's Royal Rancho.* Howell-North
   Books, Berkeley, 1960. All quotations are from this publication.

– 14 –

TAMSEN DONNER

1801 – 1847

S ELDOM HAS ANYONE been so severely tested as Tamsen Donner, tragic victim of the ill-fated Donner Party in 1846-47. Seven years after her marriage to George Donner, a 62-year-old, well-to-do farmer, they had joined an emigrant party heading west on the Overland Trail for California.

Born in Massachusetts in 1801, Tamsen was a widowed, 38-year-old school teacher when she married George Donner around 1839. He had been widowed twice before and had many children. Most were grown by then, leaving him with two young daughters to raise. Tamsen was childless at the time of her marriage to Donner; what better choice could he make than this tiny but mighty woman, who had proven her mettle with a successful career in the demanding teaching profession?

D espite their large age difference, their marriage proved fruitful, and they quickly produced three daughters of their own. When they pulled their roots in Springfield, Illinois—heading west to an uncertain future– they had five girls with them ranging in age from three to fourteen. They were accompanied by George Donner's older brother, Jacob, his wife, Elizabeth and their seven children. The James F. Reed family of seven went along; there were also seven young hired men and a hired girl in the party (see Reed).

Three heavy, overloaded wagons were taken by each family, each pulled by four yoke of oxen (two to a yoke). They also had saddle horses, milk cows, beef cattle and extra oxen. In addition, Tamsen Donner had insisted on bringing along enough books and supplies to start a seminary in California. She intended her girls to have proper educations. No group started out better prepared; however, poor judgment caused their eventual downfall. They had been warned that their wagons were too heavy and bulky; they had been warned to stay on the proven trail from Fort Bridger to Fort Hall before heading southwest to the Humboldt River and California.

Apparently they had little trouble on the journey to Independence, Missouri, and were feeling overconfident by the time they joined a large company of emigrants there. Most were heading for Oregon, but a good number wanted to go to California. By the time the Donners and Reeds reached Fort Bridger at the end of July, they had lost so much time they were seduced into trying a new "short cut" advocated by a young opportunist, Lansford Hastings (see Hastings). Against advice from experts, most agreed to try it.

Instead of saving time, this new route– which ran south of the Great Salt Lake– proved almost impossible for wagons. When they reached the eastern base of the formidable Sierra Nevada mountains in late October, they prayed for good weather. But it was not to be; the first and largest element of the party reached the lower slopes of Truckee Pass (present Donner Lake) at the end of the month in a driving snow storm. Even before it abated, a few hardy men attempted to cross the summit without success.

B Y THE FIRST WEEK in November they all knew crossing with the wagons was impossible. After several unsuccessful attempts to climb out on foot, some moved into the Schallenberger cabin, as it became known, while others made permanent campsites at the eastern end of the lake. Though the Reeds had left their wagons far behind, Mrs. Reed and her four young children had made it to the Lake Camp; her husband, James, had left for Sutter's Fort earlier. All told there were 56 frightened people there.

An axle had broken on one of the Donner wagons, and the Donner Party—25 in all—were forced to make camp at Alder Creek, about six miles northeast of the lake camp. While shaping a new axle with his axe, George Donner slashed his hand, leaving him disabled and the party stranded. While the Donners knew their plight was serious, they did not consider it a disaster at that point. They had food enough to last a month, or so, and plenty of livestock. Surely the weather would ease before long, and they could be on their way again. But fate dealt them a losing hand. George Donner's wound did not heal; instead, it got worse. When the starving livestock wandered off in search of fodder, they couldn't dig through the snow to get at it. Soon they began to die, most of them buried deep in snow until even their frozen, life-sustaining carcasses could not be found.

Staples grew scarce, and hunting for game proved unproductive. They knew more than fifty others were trapped at the lake camp, but they faced the same crisis and could offer no help. By Christmas they were all going hungry. They knew they were doomed unless help reached them very soon. And despite Tamsen Donner's loving care, her husband's poor condition grew even worse. She often went without food to ensure that he and the girls shared what little there was.

By the time a relief party led by A. Glover arrived in mid-February, the Donners were existing on boiled ox-hides and faced starvation. Both George Donner and his brother, Jacob, were too ill and weak to travel. Glover's party did manage to evacuate six of the party, including the two oldest Donner girls. Although Tamsen Donner was strong enough to travel, she flatly refused to leave her husband, as did Jacob's wife, Elizabeth.

A rescue party led by James Reed arrived in early March to find the horror of cannibalism in stark evidence. Jacob Donner had died and his body went to feed others. His wife had refused to eat him and was near death. George Donner still lived, and again Tamsen refused to leave him. Instead, she stayed while the those who were still living were evacuated.

Tamsen made a deal with two of the rescuers, Charles Cady and Charles Stone, to take her three young daughters to Sutter's Fort. Instead, they took them only as far as the lake camp, where they were left with "the half-crazed Mrs. Murphy." [1] The oldest was six; the last thing Tamsen Donner taught them to say was, "We are the children of George Donner."

Elizabeth Donner died shortly thereafter; now only Tamsen and her husband remained alive at the lonely deathcamp. Despite their desperate plight, they probably gave thanks that all the girls had been evacuated. Then came the disturbing news that the three younger girls were still at the lake camp. Feeling betrayed, Tamsen made the exhausting hike there to see for herself and to make sure they were finally evacuated. William Eddy, who was there with a small rescue party, promised to take them out. Again Tamsen refused to leave; instead, she returned to her dying husband at Alder Creek.

B Y THEN everyone had been evacuated from the lake camp except Lewis Keseberg, who could not travel because of an injured foot. When George Donner finally died a short time later, his loyal wife cleansed his wasted body and wrapped it in a sheet. Only then did she leave the desolate, horror-stricken camp. A final rescue party led by Captain Fallon reached the lake camp in mid-April to find no one there except Keseberg, who had been surviving on the flesh of the dead. At the Alder Creek camp, they found George Donner's body, but there was no sign of his wife. After salvaging what they could, they returned to the lake where they pressed Keseberg for an explanation.

Finally the distraught German told them that Tamsen Donner had made her way to the lake after her husband's death about a week earlier. He claimed she was incoherent and wanted to leave immediately to find her girls. Keseberg stated that he had dissuaded her from such a foolish act, and that she had died that very night. Yes, some of the flesh found in his cook-pot was hers, he reportedly admitted. But no, he had not killed her, as some members of the party accused him of doing for fresh meat. Under duress, he finally admitted that he had gone to the Alder Creek camp to recover some money Tamsen allegedly told him about. He had hidden it, and it was to be given only to the surviving Donner girls. Finally he was forced to divulge the hiding place, and Fallon recovered over $500.

L EWIS KESEBERG was brought to Sutter's Fort in April 1847. There Edward Coffeemire, one of the rescue-team members, accused him of killing Tamsen and probably killing another member of the party named Wolfinger earlier. At the urging of John Sutter, Keseberg brought suit against Coffeemire for defamation of character. A hearing was held before Alcalde John Sinclair, and though Keseberg won his case, he was awarded a token one dollar in damages.

Despite the fact that Keseberg won his case, many believed him guilty, and he spent the rest of his life trying to live it down. Whether Tamsen Donner died a natural death or was murdered, her children survived and were later adopted. If George Donner had died a few weeks earlier, Tamsen would have been saved along with her girls. Was her decision to stay by the side of her dying husband the act of a selfless heroine, a martyr or both? One thing is certain– she was a tower of strength. Donner Memorial State Historical Park, a few miles west of Truckee off I-80, includes the lake camp site. The Alder Creek campsite, a few miles north of Truckee off Highway 89, includes a short self-guided hiking trail.

BIBLIOGRAPHY
–Bancroft, Hubert H. *History of California,* Vol. I-VI. History Co., San Francisco, 1886. Republished, Wallace Hebberd, Santa Barbara, 1966.

–Bryant, Edwin. *What I Saw in California.* University of Nebraska Press. Lincoln, 1985.

–Crosby, Alexander L. *Old Greenwood, Pathfinder of the West.* Talisman Press, Georgetown, CA, 1967.

–DeVoto, Bernard. *The Year of Decision: 1846.* Houghton Mifflin Co., Boston, 1942.

–King, Joseph A. *Winter of Entrapment.* P. D. Meany Publ., Toronto, 1992. [1]

–Lewis, Oscar. *Sutter's Fort.* Prentice-Hall, Inc., Englewood Cliffs, NJ, 1966.

–McGlashan, C.F. *History of the Donner Party.* A.L. Bancroft & Co., San
    Francisco, 1881 (Several subsequent editions).
–Wilcox, Del. *Voyagers to California.* Sea Rock Press, Elk, CA, 1991.
–Stewart, George R. *Ordeal by Hunger.* Houghton Mifflin Co., Boston,
    1936.
–Stewart, George R. *The California Trail.* University of Nebraska Press,
    Lincoln, 1962.

John Charles Fremont
Courtesy California Department of Parks & Recreation

– 15 –

JOHN CHARLES FREMONT

1813 – 1890

T HE OLD ADAGE, "Like father, like son," could have been coined
for John Charles Fremont. Not only did he carry his French emigrant father's name, he inherited many of his characteristics,
including an adventurous spirit, daring courage and keen intelligence.
His father's scandalous relationship with Anne Whiting Pryor demon-
strated his spirit of adventure.

An attractive southern belle, Anne was the daughter of Colonel
Thomas Whiting. After his death, Anne endured an unhappy marriage
to a much older man named Major Pryor. Then she met John C.
Fremon (the T was added later), who was teaching French in
Richmond. An amorous affair began, and after a showdown with Pryor
Anne left him and ran off with Fremon to Savannah, Georgia.

John Charles Fremon, Jr. was born January 21, 1813, after which
the family moved to Nashville, where Anne gave birth to a daughter.
Next they moved to Norfolk, Virginia, and during that period another
son was born and Major Pryor died, enabling Fremon Sr. and Anne to
marry. John Charles Jr., usually called Charlie, was five years old when
his insolvent father's life was cut short, leaving Anne with three young
children to raise.

Shortly after her husband's death, Anne moved to Charleston, South
Carolina. From the very start, young Fremont seemed to attract influential mentors. He proved an alert student in school, learning subjects
such as Greek ahead of his age. As a youngster he was chosen to become
a law clerk by prominent attorney, J.W. Mitchell, who sent him to prep
school at the age of fourteen.

His studies at prep school allowed his admittance to Charleston
College as a junior. He did well there and developed an interest in
astronomy as well as mathematics–that is, until he met a fiery, black-
haired Creole girl. His school attendance and grades plummeted, and he
was expelled a few months short of graduation. It was about then that
his younger sister died.

Fremont was teaching mathematics at the age of twenty in a private school when he met his next mentor—a well-known botanist, Joel R. Poinsett, who got him posted as a mathematics instructor aboard a navy ship heading for South America. When that voyage ended, Fremont landed a position as assistant surveyor for the U. S. Topographical Corps. Under leadership of Army officers, this party was to survey a railroad route from Charleston to Cincinnati. Then came a surprise: Possibly thanks to Joel Poinsett's influence, Fremont received his bachelor's degree from Charleston College five years after being expelled.

WITH THE railroad survey concluded, Fremont found a surveying job with the government, which planned to evict Cherokee Indians from their land and relocate them farther west. Thus, Fremont gained experience dealing with Indians and living off the land. Despite the privations he endured, he later wrote, "Here I found the path which I was destined to walk..."

In 1838 Fremont was hired by the U. S. Army Topographical Corps and ordered to Washington, D.C., again thanks to Poinsett's influence as Secretary of War. At first, Fremont was disappointed and frustrated by his boring new post in Washington. Then came news that explained it all—he was to take part in exploring and mapping the huge "Louisiana Purchase," covering much of what is now the northern Midwest. It had been relatively unexplored; boundaries were vague, and no accurate maps existed.

Led by renowned French scientist, Joseph N. Nicollet, the party traveled by boat to St. Louis in 1838 to be outfitted, and then traveled up the Mississippi to Fort Snelling, near what is now St. Paul. The two-year expedition—made in two stages with a break in between—concentrated mostly on territory along the Mississippi, Missouri and Minnesota rivers as far north as Devil's Lake on the Cheyenne River. The expedition made a triumphant return to Washington in 1839, when Fremont received word of his only brother's death.

Fremont was not the same man who had left Washington earlier. He was now an army lieutenant and a seasoned, resourceful leader who had learned celestial navigation and was helpful in assisting Nicollet complete meticulous maps of their expedition. During that period they were visited by many prominent Washingtonians who were interested in their work, among them Senator Thomas Hart Benton from Missouri. Benton often invited them to his Washington home to discuss the possibility of American settlements in the Far West, especially the Pacific Northwest, which was still dominated by Great Britain. Nicollet was now in poor health, and Benton turned to Fremont as a possible successor.

Senator Benton had five children, a boy named Randolph, and four girls. The two oldest girls were attending boarding school, so Fremont didn't meet them until later. When he did, he was immediately attracted to sixteen-year old Jessie, and she to him. It was a classic case of love at first sight, which the stern senator and his wife were determined to squelch. They felt Jessie was much too young, and Fremont's background and status as an underpaid junior army officer left much to be desired.

Benton used his considerable influence to have Fremont lead an expedition to explore the Des Moines River in Iowa Territory. The task was to take a year, but Fremont worked fast and was back in Washington within six months. Jessie Benton was still determined to marry Fremont, and her stubborn parents were just as determined to thwart them.

When a clergyman was found to perform the ceremony on the sly, Charles and Jessie were married in October 1841. The marriage was kept secret until Fremont finally confronted the enraged senator with the news. After threatening to throw them out, Benton gave in and Charles moved into the family home. Lieutenant Fremont had now acquired another powerful mentor.

Seven months later, and with his wife expecting their first child, Fremont found himself leading an expeditionary force into the Far West. He was instructed to survey the newly established Oregon Trail to South Pass and prepare accurate maps. With him was 12-year-old Randolph Benton and an older friend. After boarding a riverboat heading up the Missouri River, Fremont met a rather short frontiersman named Christopher "Kit" Carson. What Carson lacked in stature, he more than made up in courage and ability to survive in the wilderness. He and Fremont struck up a lasting friendship that began when Carson hired on as a guide for $100 per month.

They left Chouteau's Landing at the mouth of the Kansas River June 10, 1842, with more than twenty men and eight two-wheeled carts. There were also extra horses, mules and oxen. While most of the men were French Creoles, two others were Charles Preuss, a German artist and topographer, and Lucien Maxwell, Carson's brother-in-law. Shortly before they reached Fort Laramie, mountain man Jim Bridger warned that Sioux Indians were threatening to kill any white men who trespassed on their territory. Despite the warning, Fremont was determined to press on.

Reaching Fort Laramie in mid-July, they were again warned not to continue. Leaving Randolph Benton and his friend behind, Fremont and the others left later in the month. Though they met Indians along the way, they were not attacked, and they reached South Pass in early August. Fremont was intrigued by the Wind Mountain Range and decided to explore it before returning. After planting the U. S. Flag on present-day Woodrow Wilson Peak, they started back. Part of the journey was made by floating some of the men and equipment down the Platte River in an innovative rubber raft. This nearly proved disastrous when the raft capsized and many supplies were lost. At Bellvue (confluence of the Platte & Missouri rivers), a wooden boat was built to float the company down the Missouri to St. Louis.

Fremont reached Washington and Jessie in late October. Two weeks later he was the proud father of a baby daughter, Elizabeth Benton Fremont, called "Lily" all her life. Fremont spent the next few months writing a 120-page book about the trip, which became a great help to increasing numbers of emigrants along the Oregon Trail. It was given the ungainly but descriptive title: *Report of an Exploration of the Country Lying Between the Missouri River and the Rocky Mountains on the line of the Kansas and Great Platte Rivers.*

FREMONT and Senator Benton then began promoting another expedition to the Pacific Northwest. In March 1843, Fremont escorted baby Lily, Jessie and her mother to St. Louis to join the senator. A young family servant and Charles Preuss were to join the expedition later. Time passed quickly as they outfitted themselves for the long journey ahead. Fremont insisted on taking along a twelve pound mountain howitzer, mounted on wheels, for protection against hostile Indians. There were also wagons and carts to haul supplies.

Kit Carson was to join them before they reached South Pass, but Fremont had also hired a mountain man, Thomas Fitzpatrick, as a guide. Several others from his previous expedition also joined them. Finally they were ready to leave, and Fremont kissed his tearful wife a tender adieu at the end of May. Besides considerable livestock, the party consisted of nearly forty men, a dozen carts, one covered wagon and the howitzer.

They left Westport, Missouri, in early June; by mid-month Fremont and a small group had split off from Fitzpatrick and the wagons to make better time following the Republican River toward St. Vrain's Fort on the South Fork of the Platte River (present Colorado). Near there they were joined by Kit Carson and his partner, Alexis Godey. Later Fitzpatrick's party rendezvoused with the others at St. Vrain's.

Again Fitzpatrick's wagon party was split off, to meet Fremont later at Fort Hall. Fremont and the faster-moving party then left the main trail to make their way along the Laramie River, before heading northwest to cross the Rockies at South Pass. They then turned south, passing by Ft. Bridger, to the Bear River. Kit Carson was sent to Ft. Hall to bring back badly needed food, while Fremont explored the Great Salt Lake with a few of the group in a leaky 18-foot inflatable boat. They were virtually starving when Carson and Fitzpatrick arrived with food.

Fremont's subsequent report, stating that the area was suitable for agriculture, proved decisive in the later settlement by Brigham Young and the Mormons.

Fremont's party was again running short of food when they reached Fort Hall in mid-September. It snowed the next day, and eleven of the party were sent home while the rest pushed on. The reduced party again split into two groups, and Fremont's group reached an Indian encampment on the Snake River, where they were able to trade for dried salmon-trout. Next came a stop at Fort Boise, a Hudson's Bay Company outpost, followed by a visit to Dr. Marcus Whitman's mission and nearby Fort Walla Walla, where Fitzpatrick left the wagons. At last they had reached the mighty Columbia River.

Continuing on to The Dalles, Fremont left most of the men at Reverend Lee's mission with Kit Carson. He then went by canoe to buy food at Fort Vancouver, the only major settlement in that part of the country. When he returned in mid-November, the united party headed south along the Deschutes River at the eastern base of the Cascades. Though the wagon and carts had been left behind at Ft. Walla Walla, the cumbersome howitzer remained a burden. It was winter by then, and the cold heavy snow made the journey much more difficult.

UPON REACHING the Upper Klamath Lake in December, they turned east to one of the Warner lakes and headed south through the Great Basin. By mid-January 1844, they were losing livestock and had passed a huge body of water they named Pyramid Lake. Finally they reached Truckee Meadows (now Reno). Despite the fact that Mexico had forbidden Americans from entering their territory, Fremont led his men into the towering Sierra Nevada Range, intending to find a crossing. They were desperate for food and knew Sutter's Fort on the American River was the closest place to find it. No one had crossed the Sierra Nevada in winter—it was too cold and the snow much too deep.

They had climbed only part way by the end of the month, when the troublesome howitzer was finally abandoned. Local Indians guided them for awhile, but they left with a warning that the struggling party would never make it across the elusive summit. Temperatures were in the sub-zeros and men had to pack down loose snow by foot to get the remaining livestock through.

They had eaten most of their stock, even their dog. Their meal on February 3rd was described as pea soup, mule and dog. On the 27th it was mule-head soup. They were literally starving when Fremont and Carson struggled over the summit with a small advance party to an Indian village. One of the Indians said he was a *vaquero* (cowboy) for Captain Sutter, and agreed to guide them to Sutter's Fort. Fremont and his advance party straggled into the welcoming walls of the fort in early

March. Their route over the summit is now known as Carson Pass.

Sutter immediately mounted a relief party to bring in Thomas Fitzpatrick and the rest of the starving men. They were found on the South fork of the American River, where they were fed and brought to the fort a few days later. Rest and good food revived Fremont and his men, after which Captain Sutter re-outfitted them with livestock and supplies.

Leaving Sutter's Fort in late March, Fremont headed south through the great San Joaquin Valley. After an easterly crossing over the mountains, via Walker's Pass into the Mojave Desert, they reached a river they named the Mojave and joined the old Spanish Trail. This led them northeast until they left it below Sevier Lake. Near there they were overtaken by Joseph R. Walker, who was also returning east from California (see Walker).

Continuing on past Utah Lake and the Wasatch Range, they reached Fort Uintah before Walker led them south, following the west side of the Rocky Mountains to Bent's Fort on the Arkansas River. Walker and Carson left Fremont there to finish his journey to the Santa Fe Trail, and on to his starting point at Kansas Landing fourteen months after leaving.

The expedition disbanded there in late August, and Fremont went by riverboat to St. Louis, where his wife and daughter were living in Senator Benton's home. Though some had given him up for dead, his wife knew better. After a joyous reunion, and a few days spent greeting friends and well-wishers, the family returned to Washington. There they learned that Fremont's old friend and mentor, Joseph Nicollet, had died.

THE NEXT MONTHS were devoted to writing a detailed report and drafting accurate maps. Fremont's report was completed in March 1845, and 10,000 copies were printed by order of the Congress. Meanwhile, Washington was rife with rumors about possible war with Mexico. President Polk had been elected with an expressed expansion policy in mind, involving both Texas and California. Also, the question of boundaries between the U.S. and England in the Pacific Northwest demanded attention, and Fremont's report confirmed the possibility of further migration.

A visit with General Scott and President Tyler resulted in simultaneous promotions for Fremont to brevet captain as a fitting reward for his successful journeys. After President Polk took office March 1st, Fremont visited him as well. Soon another expedition was being planned with vague written instructions to explore the Arkansas and Red River country. Apparently unwritten orders called for much more than this, including exploration west of the Rockies and even into California—a formidable task indeed. Fremont also received instructions in the event of war with Mexico. He was also told to expect a message from a courier, Marine Lt. Archibald Gillespie, if war seemed inevitable.

Many of Fremont's former comrades joined him, and he arrived at Bent's Fort (present-day Colorado) in early August 1845. By then Edward Kern had replaced Charles Preuss as artist. Kit Carson joined Fremont there, and by August the well-equipped brigade prepared to leave Bent's Fort. One group, guided by Thomas Fitzpatrick, was to explore the Arkansas and Red rivers as directed, while the main party of about sixty men led by Fremont and Carson headed farther west.

Joseph R. Walker and Old Bill Williams met them at different places along the trail to the Great Salt Lake, which Fremont again explored. Bill Williams left them there, after which Fremont's party blazed a trail directly west across the gleaming salt desert. During this phase, the party was split into two groups. Theodore Talbot, Ned Kern and Joseph Walker led the main party southwest along the river Fremont named the Humboldt, while Fremont and Carson led the a smaller group farther south. They were to meet later at a large lake Fremont named after Walker (now Walker Lake, Nevada).

Fremont's group arrived at the lake in late November; the main party arrived four days later. Fremont decided to split the party as before: he and Carson would take the smaller group to Sutter's Fort, via Truckee Pass, while Walker led the main party south to the pass he had discovered on a previous journey. After crossing into the San Joaquin Valley, they would meet Fremont at Tulare Lake.

Fremont reached Sutter's Fort on December 10, 1845; though in his memoirs he stated that Sutter was there to greet him, John Bidwell's statement contradicts this (see Bidwell). Bidwell states that Sutter was absent, and that he, as Sutter's chief clerk, tried to fill Fremont's many needs. When he was unable to satisfy all of these needs, Fremont allegedly left with hard feelings. To add to Fremont's discomfort, his splinter group became involved in an Indian fight in the San Joaquin Valley and was unable to locate the main party.

Fremont returned to Sutter's Fort in mid-January, 1846, with no word from the main party. He then took Sutter's launch into San Francisco Bay to visit William Leidesdorff, after which he went on to Monterey to seek permission from General José Castro to survey a route to the Pacific Coast (see Leidesdorff). Castro granted his request, and Fremont set out to explore the area. Meanwhile, his main party had reached Tulare Lake in the great valley. Finding no sign of Fremont, they headed north toward Sutter's Fort. Somewhere near the Calaveras River they received news that Fremont was at San Jose and immediately headed there. They rendezvoused with Fremont about eight miles south of San Jose at William Fisher's Rancho Laguna Seca.

Apparently because of difficulties between Fremont's men and local rancheros, Castro changed his mind about Fremont's stay in California, and in late February ordered him out of the territory. This infuriated Fremont; instead, of leaving, he led his men to the peak of a nearby mountain, fortified it, and made camp there. Today it is called Gavilan Peak, or Fremont Peak. Castro sent troops to dislodge Fremont, but after some blustering gestures they left without a fight. When three days passed without a direct challenge, Fremont decided to evacuate and leave the area. Joseph Walker left him there, while Fremont led his party north to explore the Feather and Bear rivers.

SOMETIME in May Fremont established a camp on the south shore of Upper Klamath Lake. Settler Samuel Neal, an ex-member of Fremont's earlier expedition, found Fremont there to report that Marine Lieutenant Archibald Gillespie was on his way with letters from Washington. Though Peter Lassen and a comrade were escorting the marine, Neal feared that Gillespie wouldn't make it through hostile Indian country. Instead, he suggested that Fremont send an armed escort after him (see Lassen).

The next morning, Fremont and Kit Carson led eight others south to find Gillespie. They found the exhausted lieutenant and his escorts camped on the Klamath River. Gillespie carried letters from home along with instructions. No one knows to this day what they contained, but they probably relieved Fremont from his surveying duties and warned him that war with Mexico appeared likely. Fremont's memoirs state,

> I sat by the fire...going over and over the home letters. These threw their own light upon the communication from Mr. Gillespie and made the expected signal. In substance their effect was: The time has come. England must not get a foothold. We must be the first. Act; discreetly, but positively. [1]

On orders from President Polk, U.S. Consul Thomas O. Larkin had been negotiating the purchase of Alta California by the United States. Unknown to Larkin or anyone else in California, hostile events in Texas made this unlikely, if not impossible. In late April Mexican forces attacked General Zachary Taylor's Dragoons on the Rio Grande River, and on May 13 a declaration of war against Mexico was approved by Congress.

If Gillespie's visit didn't cause enough excitement, the next event certainly did when the Lassen-Fremont camp was attacked by Klamath Indians. Three men were killed before a hurried defense routed the hostiles. Saddened by the tragedy, Fremont had the bodies of his men carried back toward the main camp at Upper Klamath Lake. Another skirmish there proved that the Indians were still on the war-path, so Fremont led a retaliatory raid against them. Fourteen Indians were killed without any losses to Fremont's men. After the remaining hostiles fled, the village was burned to the ground. One Indian loosened an arrow at Lucien Maxwell, but the wily hunter threw himself off his horse and shot the Indian dead.

Fremont was mystified by the savage hostility of the Indians until he remembered there was a Hudson's Bay Company outpost west of there on the Umpqua River. He suspected the British wanted him out of the territory and may even have incited the Indians to attack him. To complicate matters, he received a message from Captain Sutter that General José Castro was inciting Indians to attack foreign settlers to drive them out. Furthermore, Castro allegedly warned that his army would help. When settlers sought Fremont's assistance, events began building to a climax.

FREMONT MOVED his camp south to Sutter Buttes in early June and initiated a reign of terror against local Indians he suspected were planning to attack the settlers. A short time later a band of settlers led by Ezekial Merritt seized a herd of Mexican Army horses and drove them north to Fremont's new camp. By then Merritt had recruited more men, and after riding throughout the night of June 14, they made a successful dawn attack on General Mariano Vallejo's stronghold in Sonoma.

Merritt and others then took Vallejo and several of his men to Sutter's Fort to be imprisoned, while William Ide and others replaced the Mexican flag with a crudely made one containing a star, a bear and the words, "California Republic." The frustrated settlers had seized the initiative and given birth to a new Independent Republic. This campaign became known as the Bear Flag Revolt or Rebellion, and the volunteers were called "Bears" or "Bear Flaggers" (see Ide and Vallejo).

Fremont encouraged and advised the rebels, but he and his men remained behind the scenes. He then brought his men back to Sutter's Fort and virtually took it over. Sutter was allowed to stay, but Fremont was clearly in charge. Their strained relationship came to a head when Sutter insisted on treating Vallejo and his companions more like guests than prisoners. Fremont apparently regarded Sutter–who was a naturalized Mexican citizen–as a disloyal American. He ignored the fact that both Sutter and Vallejo were sympathetic to the U.S. cause, as were many *Californios*. Most preferred U.S. occupation to that of England or France, both of whom posed possible threats.

When Castro learned of the takeover in Sonoma he sent troops to recover the town. When the "Bears" asked Fremont for help, he decided the time had come to take direct action. He hurried to Sonoma with his men to join the Bear Flag volunteers and quickly replaced William Ide as commander. He then named Ezekiel Merritt as his adjutant. By then

Fremont had nearly a hundred men divided into four companies called "The California Battalion."

Hoping to engage Castro's forces, they hurried to Mission San Rafael and crossed San Francisco Bay, where they spiked the Mexican guns that supposedly protected the entrance to the great bay. On the way, Fremont coined the famous name, "Golden Gate" for the entrance. Later, at Mission San Rafael, Fremont made a decision that could have cost his career.

Three Mexican civilians, Francisco and Ramon de Haro (twins, aged about 20) and José Berryessa, their uncle, were apprehended by Kit Carson and a few companions. Apparently Carson thought they were spies, and when he asked Fremont what he wanted done with them, Fremont was said to have replied, "I have no room for prisoners." Carson and his companions then shot all three dead. Because no one there was aware that war with Mexico had been declared, this seemingly wanton killing was perceived by some as cold-blooded murder.

AFTER A FEW skirmishes with Mexican troops in the area, Fremont appropriated supplies and horses from local rancheros and led most of his men back to Sutter's Fort. On July 2nd, U.S. Commodore John Sloat sailed into Monterey, and raised the American flag on the 7th. Sloat had been waiting for word that war had been declared before taking Monterey, and had done so only a few days before the arrival of a British warship.

The Bear Flag and Mexican flags were quickly replaced by the Stars and Stripes throughout Northern California, and Fremont was finally free to go on the offensive. Commodore Sloat then sent word to Fremont to bring his men to Monterey and report to him. After placing Lieutenant Edward Kern in charge of Sutter's Fort, Fremont led his motley band of volunteers to the former Mexican Capital at Monterey.

Commodore Sloat had been ill and was almost immediately replaced by Commodore Robert Stockton. There was no senior army commander in California, so Stockton swore Fremont and his volunteers into the U.S. Navy so they could be paid and draw government supplies. Fremont was then promoted to Major. The northern end of the territory seemed secure from Mexican interference; however, General Castro was taking his troops south to join Governor Pío Pico in Los Angeles to make a fight of it.

Fremont and his men were loaded aboard navy ships and transported to Southern California to join forces with Stockton's men. They occupied San Diego, while Stockton's men landed at San Pedro without resistance. Fremont and his men joined Stockton in time for the bloodless invasion of Los Angeles; by then Gov. Pío Pico and Gen. José Castro had fled the area. The invasion is described by Fremont:

In the afternoon the combined force entered Los Angeles without opposition...having more the effect of a parade of home guards than an enemy taking possession of a conquered town.

Incredibly, the invasion force was accompanied by a navy brass band, which later played concerts in the plaza. A short time later Commodore Stockton returned to sea, leaving Fremont in charge as military governor and Captain Gillespie acting as secretary and commandant of the Southern District. On September 1st, Fremont left on an overland journey to the north to recruit more men and horses for possible use by Stockton when and if he decided to invade Baja California.

All went well in Los Angeles until the population began to chafe under Gillespie's harsh military rule and rebelled. Paroled Mexican Army officer, José Flores then joined forces with José Carillo and others to lead a company of volunteers against Gillespie's 50-man occupation troops. Badly outnumbered, Gillespie capitulated at the end of September and was "escorted" out of Los Angeles to seek refuge aboard a ship anchored off San Pedro. A messenger had already ridden north to inform Stockton, who made preparations to send help by sea.

Before sailing south, Stockton ordered Fremont and his men to ride south and assist in defeating the revitalized Mexican army. Meanwhile, Gen. Stephen Kearny had arrived in Southern California with a small force of dragoons to join Stockton's forces. Though the Mexicans won the subsequent battles of Rancho Dominguez and San Pasqual, they were finally caught between the combined forces of Stockton and Kearny in Southern California, and Fremont's small army coming from the north. In mid-January 1848 the Mexicans capitulated to Fremont at Mission San Fernando and signed the Treaty of Cahuenga. Finally peace reigned again.

By then Fremont had been promoted to Lt. Colonel; as Commodore Stockton's military governor, he soon found himself caught in a power struggle between Stockton and General Kearny. Both insisted they had legal jurisdiction over the military and civilian population. Feuding between them continued into the spring of 1847, while they awaited clarification from the president. Fremont described his untenable situation beautifully:

My path of life led out from among the grand and lovely features of nature, and its pure and wholesome air, into the poisoned atmosphere and jarring circumstances of conflict among men, made subtle and malignant by clashing interests.

Unfortunately for Fremont, official word finally came from Washington relieving Stockton of command. Fremont requested a transfer, but was denied. He was now at the mercy of the vindictive general,

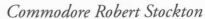
Commodore Robert Stockton

General José Castro
Both pictures courtesy
California Department
of Parks & Recreation

who did all he could to humiliate him. Leaving Fremont to stew in the boiling caldron at Los Angeles, Kearny moved to Monterey to take over as Military Governor.

Lt. Philip St. George Cooke had arrived in Los Angeles with the Mormon Battalion in early spring, threatening a renewal of the rebellion among *Californios*, who feared and hated the Mormons. There were rumors that a large Mexican army was heading north from Mexico City to retake Alta California, and while Fremont had been acting as governor he had signed notes for some $600,000 to cover military expenses. These and other problems led him to the conclusion that he must travel north to confront Kearny face to face.

Taking his black servant Jacob Dodson and Don Jesus Pico with him, Fremont gathered a string of strong horses and began his historic ride to Monterey. Leaving the morning of March 22, 1847, and trading for fresh horses along the way, they rode the 420 miles to Monterey in three days and ten hours. Incredibly, the grueling ride did not impress Kearny. He reluctantly granted Fremont an audience at Thomas O. Larkin's house, where he was staying, but took no action to help settle the vexing problems that Fremont laid before him. Disgusted, Fremont offered to resign his commission, which was refused by Kearny. Furthermore, Fremont was ordered back to Los Angeles to disband his California Volunteers, after which he was to return to Monterey with his original group army topographers.

Colonel Richard Mason, who had taken part in these frustrating conversations, had become as vindictive as Kearny in humiliating Fremont. Two days later Fremont and his two aides rode back to Los Angeles in about the same record time it had taken them to reach Monterey.

IN MID-APRIL, Colonel Mason arrived in Los Angeles with orders from Kearny to oversee the dismantlement of Fremont's forces. Finally relations between the two military leaders became so strained that Fremont challenged Mason to a duel. Fortunately, nothing came of it. In May General Kearny arrived in Los Angeles by ship with Colonel Jonathon D. Stevenson and a regiment of New York volunteers to replace the Mormon Battalion, whose men were due for discharge. Shortly after, Fremont led his remaining topographer unit overland back to Monterey. Kearny also returned there by ship.

In early June Kearny left Richard Mason in charge as Military Governor and moved most of his troops to Sutter's Fort on their way east. In disgrace—and forced to eat their dust—were the disgruntled Col. Fremont and the remainder of his men. They left Sutter's in mid-June 1847; by the time they reached Fort Leavenworth in late August, Fremont was stunned to learn that charges had been filed against him by

General Kearny for three violations: mutiny, disobedience and unlawful conduct. He was then ordered to Washington to answer the charges.

When he reached Kansas Landing, he was met by his wife, who had learned of the charges and rushed there to greet him. Soon they were back in St. Louis, where Fremont was given a hero's welcome. After he and his wife reached Washington, a formal court martial was quickly organized. After a lengthy and widely publicized trial, Fremont was shocked by a verdict of "guilty" on all charges. He was to be dismissed from the service, pending review by the president.

President Polk dismissed the more serious charge of mutiny but affirmed the other two. He did, however, order Fremont reinstated to the Army with full privileges. Fremont refused to accept the clemency and promptly resigned his commission. The pain of this ordeal was partly softened in mid-July 1848, when Jessie gave birth to a boy whom they named Benton. Tragically, little Benton died three months later.

Before Fremont left California, he had authorized Thomas O. Larkin to negotiate purchase of a ranch for him. But now he decided to lead another expedition, privately financed, to survey a practical all-weather railroad route across the Rocky Mountains. Meanwhile, his wife and daughter were to make their way to San Francisco via the Isthmus of Panama.

The new expedition consisted of more than thirty men, including Preuss, Alex Godey, Ned Kern and two of Kern's brothers. Kit Carson was not going this time; instead, "Old Bill" Williams was hired to guide them from Pueblo. It was late November 1848, and the snowpack threatened to be heavy when they began climbing into the higher elevations.

B Y EARLY December they were high in the mountains, where Fremont and Bill Williams had a dispute over the best route. This may have been an omen, for after following Williams' route they found themselves in a precarious position. Snow and ice covered what fodder there was for the horses and mules, and one by one they began dying. Icy gales and sub-freezing temperatures took a terrible toll, with some of the men suffering from frozen feet, hands and faces.

It became impossible to proceed or retreat until a drenching rain melted the snow enough to allow a slow, painful withdrawal. Christmas dinner consisted of roast mule meat. This expedition proved an unmitigated disaster, and Fremont was lucky to get out alive. Before it ended in February 1849, ten of his men were dead, all his livestock and supplies were gone, and he nearly lost a leg from frostbite. Incredibly, he managed to put together yet another outfit in Albuquerque, New Mexico, with the help of Lucian Maxwell and Kit Carson, who had settled in Taos.

This time Fremont was interested only in the fastest route to San Francisco, where he was to join his family, who had gone ahead. By then he had heard about the California gold rush from some Mexicans he met on the trail, and he was eager to check out the ranch Thomas O. Larkin had purchased for him. After arriving in California in late spring, 1849, he found Larkin had bought him a huge tract of wilderness in the Sierra foothills at a place called the Mariposas.

At first Fremont was upset because he had wanted a ranch near San Jose. But when he learned that gold had been discovered in the area of his new ranch, he suddenly felt much better. Fremont lost no time in grubstaking a party of Mexicans to mine his property for gold on shares. When the deal was settled, he resumed his trip to San Francisco.

Jessie had suffered terribly during the difficult journey across the Isthmus of Panama. In Panama City she became temporarily trapped with thousands of eager gold seekers trying to get passage on a ship to San Francisco. Living conditions there and in San Francisco were deplorable, as argonauts swarmed into the hastily-built towns like ants to sugar. Luckily Jessie managed to find accommodations in San Francisco, where she and Lily anxiously awaited Fremont's arrival.

Fremont arrived there ten days later, and after a passionate reunion they moved to Monterey. They spent the next few months commuting to the Mariposa ranch, where Fremont built a small house. Gold mining was beginning to pay off handsomely, and as usually happens during a gold rush, argonauts were quick to respond to any rumors of a successful gold strike. Soon they were converging on Fremont's property, and he found himself helpless to stop them. Besides, he had other things on his mind.

IN LATE 1849 a Constitutional Convention was called in Monterey to draft a State Constitution and to petition Congress for statehood. William Gwinn and Fremont were elected U.S. Senators to represent the proposed state after Fremont ran on a pro-railroad, anti-slavery platform. The Fremonts left for the East Coast on New Year's Day 1850, via the Panama Isthmus, where both John Charles and his wife fell ill with malaria.

When California was admitted to the Union on September 9, 1850, Fremont and Gwinn were seated in the Senate and submitted a batch of bills to benefit the new 31st state. When Fremont's short term of office ended in March 1851, he and Jessie returned to California to catch up on neglected chores at their Mariposa ranch. Fremont ran for re-election to the Senate on his same pro-railroad, anti-slavery platform, but this time he lost. Apparently too many of the new argonauts were pro-slavery.

It was just as well, because Fremont had other problems to deal with on the ranch. It had never been properly surveyed, the title was clouded by differences between Mexican and U.S. laws, and Fremont did not have written proof of ownership. Meanwhile, his wife had been living in a house they bought in San Francisco, where she gave birth to another son, John Charles Fremont, Jr. A few weeks later the house burned to the ground, and Jessie and the children were forced into temporary housing.

A short time later the Fremonts left on a voyage to Europe to rest and recuperate. They were living in Paris in February 1853, when their fourth child—another daughter—was born. She died six months after they returned to the United States. Frustrated by this tragedy and the failure of his last expedition into the Rocky Mountains, Fremont decided to finance yet another expedition there. He was still determined to prove the feasibility of an all-weather railroad route.

BY MID-SEPTEMBER 1853, he was again ready to leave from Westport Landing (now Kansas City). With him were more than twenty men, including ten Delaware Indians and a photographer named Carvallo. Though they suffered severe hardships, and one of the men actually died sitting on his horse, this expedition was successful in proving a railroad was possible. At last Fremont felt vindicated for his previous failure.

Before he returned to Washington, where Jessie Fremont was spending the winter of '53-'54, she had given birth to a fifth child, a boy they named Frank Preston Fremont. Fremont then spent time in the New York studio of famous photographer Mathew Brady, helping to process Carvallos' daguerreotypes.

In the spring of 1855, the Fremonts moved to New York where two important events took place: They acquired legal title to their Mariposas ranch, and Fremont accepted the first ever Republican nomination for President of the United States. Billed as the "Pathfinder," he ran an anti-slavery campaign against Democrat, William Buchanan, and whig, Millard Fillmore. After a bitter campaign, during which his father-in-law—always a loyal Democrat—deserted him, Fremont finished second to Buchanan.

The Fremonts then returned to California to resume their lives as ranchers and gold miners. At the time of Thomas Hart Benton's death in 1857, Fremont and his family were settled at Las Mariposas in Bear Valley. Following a bitter battle with claim jumpers and squatters, the mines were further developed and small villages sprang up in Bear Valley and the new county seat at Mariposa. Meanwhile, Fremont had been constructing a lovely new house for Jessie on Black Point (now Fort Mason), overlooking their beloved Golden Gate.

When Jessie first saw it in 1859, she was so smitten she wanted nothing more than to spend the rest of her life there with her family. But storm clouds were looming on the horizon: Although Fremont had been pouring money into his gold mines, the pay-off was declining. War between the North and South seemed imminent after Abraham Lincoln was elected in 1860, and Fremont knew he would become involved when it happened.

H E WAS IN Paris in 1861 seeking financing, when war was declared. Seizing the initiative, as was his custom, he immediately began purchasing arms there for the Union without official approval. Fortunately, the government backed him, and by the end of June he was back in Washington. President Lincoln appointed him a Major General and placed him in command of the Western Department of the Army, headquartered in St. Louis. Though Missouri was in turmoil, split by supporters of both the North and the South, Jessie and the children joined him there.

Because of a shortage of trained men and supplies, Fremont faced insurmountable odds when the fighting began, and his forces suffered many casualties when they tried to suppress guerrilla tactics used by the rebels. In desperation, he jumped the gun by issuing a proclamation to free slaves of all "persons in the State of Missouri directly proven to have taken an active part with their enemies in the field." He also placed the state under martial law.

While many praised those courageous acts, others—including President Lincoln—were displeased to say the least. Thus began a rift between the two that was never bridged. The end of Fremont's military career came after a bitter feud with the powerful Francis Blair family. A letter from Lincoln to newspaper editor Montgomery Blair in September reflects the president's feelings toward Fremont at the time:

> General Fremont...is losing the confidence of men near him, whose support any man in his position must have to be successful. His cardinal mistake is that he isolates himself and allows nobody to see him; and by which he does not know what is going on in the very matter he is dealing with. [2]

A series of regrettable events led to Fremont's being relieved of command. He resigned his commission in June 1864. Prior to the presidential 'election that year, his many friends and supporters urged him to accept nomination by a third party to run against Lincoln. He did accept it, but finally declined to run for the sake of unity; besides, he was much too busy helping to build a railroad across Kansas, and he and his wife were living the high life, with two mansions in New York. The San Francisco house they loved had been taken over by the army.

Income from the gold mine had declined dramatically, and tremendous debts had accumulated. Most of the ranch property was sold off, including all the stock held by the Fremonts in the mine venture. After paying debts, Fremont invested what was left in railroad stocks, which eventually proved worthless. The New York mansions and all the expensive art work and furnishings went next. By 1870 the Fremonts were left with virtually nothing.

Jessie Fremont came to the rescue by writing and selling a series of magazine articles. Finally friends influenced President Rutherford Hayes to appoint Fremont the Territorial Governor of Arizona. The Fremonts packed what goods they had left and moved to Prescott. Before long Jessie was taken ill and had to return to New York, while Fremont moved to Tucson.

IN 1881 Fremont resigned as governor to join Jessie in New York, where he immersed himself in the business world in an attempt to recoup his lost fortune. Jessie continued with her writing, much of which was devoted to transcribing her husband's lengthy memoirs. Fremont's attempts to interest financiers in western projects proved unsuccessful; in 1887, he became so ill with chronic bronchitis that his doctor ordered him to a drier climate. There were no funds for the move, so his concerned wife prevailed on Collis Huntington to provide railroad tickets and expense money so they could travel to Los Angeles. They lived there in virtual poverty in a small cottage on Oak Street. A one verse quotation from a poem allegedly written by Fremont tells of his plight at that desperate point of his life:

> The buoyant hopes and busy life
> Have ended all in hateful strife
> And thwarted aim.
> The world's rude contact killed the rose,
> No more its radiant color shows
> False roads to fame. [3]

After regaining his health in 1889, Fremont left alone for Washington and New York, still determined to recoup his financial losses; again he was unsuccessful. Finally in 1890, Congress restored his military rank as Major General (retired) and granted him a pension of $6,000 per year, of which he collected very little. On July 13, 1890, he became ill during the night and slipped quietly away at the age of 77. He was buried at Piermont, New York.

Jessie Fremont was granted a widow's pension and given a house at the corner of Hoover and 28th Street in Los Angeles, where she lived modestly until her death there twelve years later. Her ashes were taken east and buried beside her husband. So ends the saga of two of California's greatest pioneers.

A city near San Jose is named after Fremont, as are many streets and schools throughout California. Historical markers identify the sites of Gaviota Pass, Rancho Las Mariposas and the townsite in Bear Valley; however, nothing remains but a few ruins. Fremont Peak State Historic Park atop Gavilan Peak commemorates Fremont's short stand there in 1846.

BIBLIOGRAPHY

–Bancroft, Hubert H., *History of California,* Vol. I-VI, History Co., San Francisco, 1886. Repub. Wallace Hebberd, Santa Barbara, 1966.

–Bryant, Edwin. *What I Saw in California.* University of Nebraska Press, Lincoln, 1985.

–Davis, William Heath. *Seventy-Five Years in California.* John Howell Books, San Francisco, CA, 1967.

–DeVoto, Bernard. *The Year of Decision-1846.* Houghton Mifflin Co., Boston, 1942

–Dillon, Richard. *Fool's Gold.* Coward-McCann, Inc. New York, 1967.

–Dillon, Richard. *Humbugs and Heros.* Yosemite-DiMaggio, Oakland, CA, 1983.

–Egan, Ferol. *Fremont, Explorer for a Restless Nation.* Doubleday & Company, Inc. Garden City, New York, 1977.

–Fremont, John C. *Memoirs of My Life.* Belford, Clarke & Co., NY, 1887.

–Gay, Theressa. *James Marshall.* Talisman Press, Georgetown, CA, 1967.

–Grivas, Theodore. *Military Governments in California, 1846-1850.* Arthur H.Clark Co., Glendale, CA, 1963.

–Harlow, Neal. *California Conquered.* University of California, Berkeley, 1982.

–Hawgood, John A. (editor). *First and Last Consul, Thomas O.Larkin and the Americanization of California.* Huntington Library, San Marino, CA, 1962. Quotation[2] came from this publication.

–Hefferman, William Joseph *Edward M. Kern, Artist-Explorer.* Kern County. Historical Society, 1976.

–Ide, Simeon. *Conquest of California by the Bear Flag Party, a biographical sketch of William Ide.* Rio Grande Press, Glorieta, NM, 1967.

–Nevin, David. *Dream West.* A factual novel. G.P. Putnam's Sons, New York, 1983.

–Smith, Fredrika Shumway. *Fremont Soldier, Explorer, Statesman.* Rand McNally & Co., New York, 1966. Quotations [1] and [3] from this publication.

–Stegmaier, Mark J. & Miller, David H. *James F. Milligan, His Journal of Fremont's Fifth Expedition-1853-54).* Arthur H. Clark Co., Glendale, CA, 1988

–Taylor, Bayard. *El Dorado.* University of Nebraska Press, Lincoln, 1949.

Isaac Graham
Courtesy California State Library

– 16 –

ISAAC GRAHAM

1800 – 1863

AT THREE O'CLOCK in the morning on April 7, 1840, Isaac Graham was awakened in his Salinas Valley ranch-house by a deafening blast from a pistol. The explosion was accompanied by a sharp burning sensation on his neck, followed by several more shots, at such close range that the blinding flashes burned his shirt. A single buckshot wounded his left arm, and he was nearly smothered by the thick, acrid smoke from black powder. The smoke may have saved him, making it difficult for the assassins to take accurate aim. When the assassins ceased fire to reload their weapons, Graham and his shaken companion, Henry Naile, made a dash for freedom.

This dramatic scene, and the conclusion to follow, should be accepted for what it is—a very subjective account, paraphrased from Graham's own testimony made during a subsequent journey to Mexico City.

During their desperate escape attempt, Naile was speared by a Mexican lance that pierced his thigh, and he suffered another wound that nearly severed his Achilles tendon. Other shots were fired at Graham before he was wrestled to the ground by four Mexican soldiers. One of them tried to stab him in the chest with a knife, but the blade passed between his arm and body. Finally they forced him to his feet and marched him up a small hill, where General José Castro allegedly waited. Though Castro had ordered the attack, it may have been another Mexican officer who carried it out.

Angered by the failure of his men to kill Graham, the officer is said to have struck him on the head with the flat of his sabre, knocking him down nearly senseless. The soldiers then passed the loop of a lasso over one arm, while a mounted cavalryman took a few wraps of the lasso around his saddle horn. Then, while several of Castro's men yanked at Graham's free arm, the cavalryman spurred his horse in the opposite direction in a vicious attempt to dislocate Graham's arms.

Fortunately for the harried ex-trapper, the lasso broke before serious damage was done. The infuriated officer then ordered Graham shot, but he was saved by an Indian servant who shielded Graham with his own body. The accomplice who had lanced Naile then turned against the brutal officer. "This is not what you promised me," he allegedly spat, whereupon the officer cursed him and knocked him off his horse. He then ordered him trussed with rope.

Graham had gained a nefarious reputation with the Mexican government as a heavy drinker and trouble maker and was accused of plotting a revolution against them. Though the officer had lost patience with him, it appears that calmer heads prevailed. Finally Graham was placed in irons, while the Mexicans plundered his house of everything of value, including $3,700 in cash.

Graham was then taken to Monterey as a prisoner, while his seriously wounded friend, Naile, was left to suffer alone. After being imprisoned in Monterey, Graham was given a token "hearing" before a Mexican tribunal and quickly found guilty of treason toward the Mexican Government. On April 23rd, he and around forty other American and English settlers—all accused of the same crime—were placed aboard a ship that set sail for Mexico.

Certainly this had to be the low point in this remarkable settler's life, at least since his arrival in California sometime around 1833. In his Mexico City testimony he stated it was 1835 when he arrived in Upper California; however, other evidence points to his arrival a year or two earlier. Being illiterate, he kept no diary.

There is a lot we don't know about Graham, and what we do know isn't always pleasant. Like many others of that era, he was a rough-and-tumble mountain man who had honed his frontier skills while stalking elusive beaver along the Rocky Mountain chain. Isaac was born on September 1, 1800, to Jesse Graham and his wife, the former Jane Cock, in Botetourt County, Virginia. One of twelve children, Isaac was three when the family moved to Lincoln County, Kentucky.

Within a few years Jesse Graham died, leaving his widow with all those children to raise. Since the children went to work at an early age, they received little formal education. Isaac never learned to read or write. While seven of his older brothers fought during the War of 1812, Isaac served an apprenticeship as a jockey. He apparently had a small wiry stature.

By age 18 he may have grown too large to be a jockey, for he joined a group of other young men and struck out for the Missouri frontier seeking adventure. He apparently ended up in Marthasville, where he spent several years near his mother's cousin, Daniel Boone. He was near the old man's side when he died in 1820. He then drifted to Jonesville, Tennessee, where he married one of the Jones girls. They had four children during the next few years.

Either he couldn't cope with family responsibilities or became involved in some kind of criminal act. In any event, by 1830 he had fled Tennessee and traveled to Fort Smith, Arkansas, where he launched a new career as a free trapper. Under the leadership of elderly Col. Robert Bean, Graham and a group of inexperienced trappers headed for the Arkansas River. Among them were young Henry Naile, Job Dye, George Nidever and Jacob Leese. After a brief skirmish with fierce Comanche Indians, half of them returned to Fort Smith.

As winter neared, they headed south into the warmer climate of New Mexico, where they wintered at Arroyo Seco, twelve miles from Taos near the Rio Grande River. After a disappointing season, the party split up. Some of them accompanied Ewing Young to California during the fall of 1831, while Graham and the rest decided to stay and continue trapping under the leadership of Alexander Sinclair.

THAT SPRING they moved north to the Platte River and did well for the first time. They returned to Arroyo Grande with a good catch of furs and enjoyed their new-found prosperity immensely. The following summer found them at the annual trapper's rendezvous at Pierre's Hole (now Wyoming). There they met noted trappers from all over the territory, including the Sublette brothers, James Bridger, Thomas Fitzpatrick, Capt. Bonneville and Joseph R. Walker (see Walker). Later, a large band of Blackfoot Indians staged an all-out attack against Sinclair's party, including Graham and others who had left Pierre's Hole and were camped a few miles away. Knowing they were badly outnumbered, they sent a rider back to Pierre's Hole to seek help.

Many trappers responded, resulting in a fierce engagement with the determined Blackfeet before the Indians were driven off. Alexander Sinclair was killed in this battle, leaving Graham and his companions leaderless. After returning to Pierre's Hole to regroup, they chose George Nidever as captain and headed for Mary's River (the Humboldt) to finish out the season. Spring found them trapping along the North Fork of the Platte River, after which they joined the 1833 fur trapper's rendezvous on the Green River.

As expected, many well-known trappers and adventurers were there, including Joseph R. Walker, Capt. Benjamin L. E. de Bonneville and many free trappers. Nidever and some of his men joined Joseph R. Walker's company—a unit of Bonneville's brigade—which was heading for California. Though it is possible that Graham and Naile accompanied them, it is doubtful.

The period from 1833 to 1836 is devoid of factual information regarding Graham's activities. We do know that he and Naile showed up in an 1836 census taken in Los Angeles. It seems likely that they journeyed into Southern California on the Old Spanish Trail in 1834 or 1835. Shortly thereafter, he, Naile and another partner leased property in Pajaro Valley, about 25 miles east of Monterey. They built a crude liquor distillery at La Natividad that reportedly became a hangout for "runaway drunken sailors and ruffians." Thus began a period of notoriety that Graham never lived down.

With the untimely death of Governor José Figueroa in September 1835, Alta California endured a period of political unrest, during which four governors held sway. During this period Graham got interested in politics, no doubt seeking powerful friends. This era culminated with Graham recruiting a band of about fifty frontier riflemen to assist Juan B. Alvarado in overthrowing Governor Nicolas Gutiérrez. For this action, which took place in November 1836, Graham and his men were to receive generous land grants.

Later, when Governor Alvarado was threatened by opposition in Southern California, Graham and his riflemen again came to his aid and helped put down the rebellion. Once Alvarado had consolidated his power, he apparently saw no need to curry favor with these crude *Americanos* any longer. Gradually they became estranged, especially when the promised land grants failed to materialize.

Naturally Graham and his followers felt betrayed; they began making threats against the government. As a result, Alvarado assigned men to keep a close eye on Graham's sometimes questionable activities. After Graham was arrested and jailed for stealing cattle, he tried recruiting a party to leave the country. When that failed, he apparently resigned himself to government harassment.

This continued until that fateful night of April 7, 1840, when the assassination attempt was made as described in the opening paragraphs. This action, which has come to be known as "The Graham Affair," resulted in the arrest of nearly all foreign settlers, especially those who had not become naturalized citizens of Mexico.

After what many historians refer to as a "sham trial," a few settlers, including Dr. John Marsh, were released. Forty-seven of them, including Graham, were crammed aboard a ship and sent to San Blas. After landing there, they were marched fifty miles to Tepic. The long march under miserable conditions took a toll on Graham and the others; however, upon their arrival they were given reasonably good care. This was largely due to the interest and influence of the British Consul, Eustace Barron, at San Blas. Apparently there was no U.S. Consul there.

Graham was imprisoned one year, during which he was interrogated and sent to Mexico City to dictate his statement about the affair. Finally he and the other political prisoners were declared innocent of the charges and released. Furthermore, it was ruled that they were entitled to just compensation for financial losses incurred from their arrest. Eustace Barron then arranged for the settlers return to California at the expense of the Mexican Government. They landed in Monterey July 20, 1841; their return was described by historian H. H. Bancroft:

> They came on shore, dressed neatly, armed with rifles and swords and looking in infinitely better condition than when they had departed..."

Francis Mellus later described the scene in his journal:

> . . the return of some of the foreigners who were sent from here in April of last year to Mexico. They returned in a Mexican vessel (schooner) at the expense of the Mexican Government. Mr. Graham, who before was a raw Kentucky man, has returned quite polished; he was the principal sufferer.

GRAHAM'S rather triumphant return made him a folk hero to foreign settlers, which must have embarrassed Governor Alvarado accordingly. During Graham's long absence, his partner, Henry Naile, had recovered from the lance-wound incurred during the assassination attempt. He had then been ordered to dispose of the partnership assets and leave the country, but was saved from deportation by the arrival of a U.S. warship commanded by Captain French Forrest. Apparently Forrest had been sent to investigate reports of abuse toward Americans some by Mexican officials.

When Forrest's interest in the "Graham Affair" stayed Naile's deportation, he was probably on hand to greet Graham when he arrived in Monterey from Mexico. Then began a lengthy legal battle to recover the heavy losses Graham and his partners had incurred during the affair. To the chagrin of Governor Alvarado, he was ordered to assist Graham and the others in obtaining necessary evidence of their losses. In the meantime, Graham and Naile had acquired property called Rancho Zayante, located in rich redwood country on the San Lorenzo River about eight miles north of Santa Cruz (near present Felton).

Because neither of them was a Mexican citizen, they acquired it in the name of Joseph L. Majors, who was a citizen. This transaction resulted in another partnership consisting of Graham, Naile, William Ware, Frederick Hoegel and Peter Lassen (see Lassen). After Majors got title to the property in April 1841, Hoegel and Lassen began construction of a water-powered sawmill. Upon Graham's return to Monterey, he and Naile bought out Hoegel's and Lassen's interest in the mill. When completed, it became the first water-powered mill in the territory. In addition to the lumber business, Graham and Naile stocked cattle on the ranch and added another distillery. They were doing well financially but had not improved their reputations as men of little principle, who harbored thieves and drunks. After Governor Alvarado was replaced by Manuel Micheltorena in 1842, Graham petitioned the new governor to gain possession of his land in his own name; nevertheless, the property remained in the name of Joseph Majors.

Throughout this period, Graham continued to press his case for damages incurred during his arrest by complaining to various U.S. Naval officers who visited Monterey. One of these was Commodore Thomas ap Catesby Jones, who had landed an invasion party at Monterey in 1842, believing war had been declared against Mexico. After Monterey trader Thomas O. Larkin convinced him war had not been declared, the chagrined Jones apologized to Mexican officials and withdrew his forces (see Larkin).

Graham took advantage of Jones' visit by filing a deposition with him listing losses incurred of over $36,000. After Thomas O. Larkin was appointed U.S. Consul in 1844, Graham did the same with him. Larkin forwarded the appeal to Washington D.C. with a recommendation that the U.S. State Department should press the Mexican Government for payment. Still nothing happened.

WHILE Governor Manuel Micheltorena was well liked personally, he had brought with him from Mexico over 300 so-called soldiers, who were mostly ex-convicts and derelicts recruited off the streets. Furthermore, they were poorly paid or not paid at all, leading to many petty thefts and other depradations against the native Californians. Hatred of these *Cholos* led to a rebellion against Micheltorena by ex-Governor Alvarado, General José Castro and others in Southern California.

John A. Sutter—a powerful settler from New Helvetia on the Sacramento River—pledged to raise a small army and come to the aid of Micheltorena (see Sutter). Graham and his gang of sharp-shooting frontiersmen apparently saw this as an opportunity to get back at Alvarado, while gaining favor with the governor. Though repudiated by many other foreigners in Santa Cruz, they joined Sutter's little army.

Sutter's "army" marched off to join Micheltorena's men in early January 1845. The mock war ended with the "Battle of Cahuenga" on the outskirts of Los Angeles the following spring. Strangely enough, no human casualties resulted. Some historians believe that the entire affair was a charade to allow Micheltorena a face-saving way out of his predicament; Sutter became the goat. After being held prisoner for about a month and threatened with death, he was released. Many of his men had become disillusioned along the way and had deserted before the last "battle."

Graham stuck it out to the end and returned home, vowing never to be involved in politics again. Fortunately for him, Alvarado did not succeed Micheltorena as governor; instead, Pío Pico was named governor and the capital was moved from Monterey to Los Angeles. Apparently

Graham sought solace with 21-year-old Tillatha C. Bennett. Shortly thereafter, his old friend and partner, Henry Naile, was shot to death by a business associate named James Williams. The affair was described by Thomas O. Larkin as follows:

> For some weeks the Williams and Graham & Naile have had a dispute respecting the mill. On Saturday the 11, Williams & Naile met at St. Cruz with Arbitrators binding themselfs under a Bond of 2000$ each to abide by the decision. During the day (so said) Naile often drew his pistol on James W. and was prevented from firing. On the Ws. leaving the place on Horse back, Naile followed, stopt him, pulled off his coat & drew on W. a six Barreled pistol. Mr. Martin prevented his using it....Yesterday all the parties again met at the mission. Williams was there before Naile. When the latter rode up he jump'd off his horse, and under the horse's neck presented his gun, or rifle. Jas. Williams at the moment presented his rifle and fired. His ball wint thro' Naile breast who immediately fell.

Williams was jailed a short time for the killing but later released. Apparently Naile had willed his interest in Rancho Zayante to Graham before the shooting—at least that's what Graham claimed. This was not fully accepted at the time, and a public administrator was later appointed to resolve the issue. Although Graham viewed Naile's killing as cold blooded murder, he apparently never sought revenge against Williams; in fact, he settled the financial dispute that had resulted in Naile's death by buying out Williams' interest in the mill.

Graham seemed to blame U.S. Government authorities for not seeking justice against Williams, for he refused to take part in the 1846 Bear Flag Rebellion or the resulting war against Mexico. Some of his bitterness may have resulted from a petition filed by Joseph Majors and others against him. Once a close friend, Majors accused Graham of:

> .. perpetually corrupting the peace of our vicinity and for the last six years has not ceased to invite or attempt revolutions, challenges for duels, assassinations, and disobedience of the laws even to the extent of arming himself when summoned...

THINGS SEEMED to go wrong for Graham after that, and he became involved in several lengthy and costly lawsuits. If that weren't enough, a 24-year-old-son, Jesse, appeared on his doorstep in September 1849. Graham had deserted his family nineteen years earlier when he left to join a trapping party. Graham had never communicated with his family; he didn't even know whether they were alive or dead. After coming to California during the Gold Rush, Jesse Graham had located his father through a friend.

By then Graham was nearly fifty and had "married" young Tillatha Catherine Bennett. Known as Catherine, she was the daughter of Mary Bennett, widow of Vardamon Bennett. Graham's "marriage" not been a formal ceremony; instead, they had merely signed a document witnessed by Graham's friend, William Ware, and Catherine's brother, Winston Bennett. At the time of the "wedding", Mary Bennett had complained to Thomas O. Larkin and asked that he force Graham into a legal marriage ceremony. Graham flatly refused to abide by Larkin's request and the matter was dropped.

The subsequent birth of two daughters in 1846 and 1849 seemed to have healed the breach between Catherine and her mother. But the arrival of Jesse Graham played havoc, especially when Catherine and her family learned that Graham's first wife was still alive and there were several other Graham children. Apparently time eased some of the tensions, because Jesse and another of Graham's sons became reconciled with their errant father, and Catherine was expecting another child. This was a big year for Graham, as his claim for damages during his arrest by the Mexicans was finally approved for payment in the amount of $38,125. This may have been the only such claim approved.

A T THE END of March 1850, Graham and Jesse left for San Jose on a business trip. During their absence, Graham's wife allegedly broke into his strong box and took several thousand dollars worth of gold. She then packed up her two girls and sailed for Honolulu in an attempt to escape a deteriorating relationship with Graham. Before she left, it was said that she had a box containing a dead infant sent to her sister, Mary Ann. Her baby had either been stillborn or died after a premature birth; she left word that it had died because of her husband's abuse.

"I say he murdered it," she later wrote, "because it was abuse that I received from him. His hands was its death." What she failed to mention was that she had fled to Honolulu with a male companion. When Graham returned home a few days later, he was naturally enraged and shocked by his wife's sudden departure. He accused his wife's sister of complicity in the theft of his gold and had her arrested. She was later acquitted and released. He also offered a reward for information regarding his wife's whereabouts and swore he would not rest until he found her.

Ironically, after Catherine Graham reached Honolulu with her male friend, the man died. Shortly after, she sailed for Oregon Territory and moved to Oregon City. Meanwhile, Graham and his sons became firmly allied against the Bennetts, which resulted in vicious accusations and dire threats on both sides. At the urging of Mary Bennett, Alcalde Adna Hecox ordered Jesse to post bond of $1,000 to ensure his good behavior (see Hecox). Instead, Jesse retaliated by shooting to death Catherine's brother, Dennis Bennett, and wounding her mother. Jesse then fled the area with a price on his head.

A year later Graham located his wife in Oregon and went to get his two girls. After recovering them and the rest of his stolen gold, he returned to Santa Cruz, leaving his wife destitute in Oregon. Somehow she made her way back to Santa Cruz and filed suit against Graham for custody of the girls. She won her suit, but Graham was granted visitation rights and Catherine was required to stay in the area. She then filed another suit against Graham for personal damages and assault. This case went to a jury trial, the first of its kind to be tried in the fledging State of California (by then Graham's first wife had divorced him).

The complicated case dragged through the courts for two years before being ruled on by the State Supreme Court. The judge ruled in Graham's favor and established legality of common law marriages in California. It seems that Graham may have been right about his wife being an unfit mother, because he finally gained possession of his girls. In 1852, Catherine gave birth to an illegitimate child. This did not seem to hinder her, as she married again the following year and had six more children.

GRAHAM, meanwhile, had settled down with his girls and led an apparent exemplary life. He was even elected to the Santa Cruz County Board of Supervisors in 1855. But his problems were far from over. He still was having trouble gaining clear title to his Rancho Zayante and paid his adversary, Joseph Majors, $1,000 for his interest in the property. Finally the title was cleared, but the exact amount of land involved was still unclear.

Despite these problems, Graham had prospered handsomely from the Gold Rush and built a fine new house in Santa Cruz. He also owned Rancho del Ano Nueva to the north. But over the years, other law suits and land speculations depleted Graham's resources. His legal fees were enormous, resulting in his attorney filing a lien against Graham's property for non-payment. His financial problems were exacerbated by the death of his fourteen-year-old daughter, Annie, in 1863.

In late October of the same year, Graham was in San Francisco to hear the court decision regarding the legal acreage allotment for Rancho Zayante. It was established at 2,658 acres, a figure Graham was satisfied with. Apparently enjoying his stay in San Francisco, Graham remained there until November 8, when he suddenly died. The body of the controversial old frontiersman was shipped back to Santa Cruz and laid to rest next to his daughter in Evergreen Cemetery. In his will Graham left all his property to his surviving daughter, Matilda Jane, then married to David Rice. Rice was named his executor, but Graham's lawyer got title to Rancho Zayante because of his previous lien. Graham was no longer alive to protect his beloved ranch.

Another irony after his death involved his son, Jesse, who had fled after killing Dennis Bennett. After an absence of 38 years, 63-year-old Jesse Graham was arrested in Fresno, where he had been living for many years. He was held in jail while his trial took place. By his own testimony, he had served as a ranger during the Mariposa County Indian wars. He had then returned to the South, where he served in the Confederacy during the Civil War. He returned to California after the war and settled in Fresno County as a farmer. Jesse Graham's defense rested on the basis of self defense. The long trial ended with a hung jury; however, Graham was enjoying increasing public support by then. In September 1888 the indictment against him was dismissed and he was released.

There is no doubt that Isaac Graham lacked refinement and ethics; he may have been guilty of downright crimes. He's certainly not the type one would wish a daughter to bring home for dinner. So why include him in a book that venerates worthy pioneers who made important contributions to California? There's no easy answer, except that he became involved in most of the important historical events of that dynamic era. Despite Graham's many character flaws, he was known as being generous to a fault. He was one of the earliest of Americans to settle in California, having arrived around 1834 or 1835. He operated the first water-powered sawmill in the area, providing badly needed redwood lumber for early settlers.

Once he had weathered his earlier reputation as a nefarious rounder, he seems to have settled down to become a devoted father and successful businessman during his later years. His many legal battles certainly tested and contributed to the honing of California's legal system; in fact, the decision making Graham's common-law marriage legal determined existing law. As stated in *The Trials of Isaac Graham* by Doyce B. Nunis, Jr., "No historical treatment of the state can fail to take due notice of Isaac Graham—trapper, hunter, rifleman, ranchero, litigant." Nothing remains of Rancho Zayante except Graham Hill Road at today's town of Felton.

BIBLIOGRAPHY

—Bancroft, Hubert H. *History of California*, Vol. I-VI. History Co., San Francisco, CA, 1886. Repub., Wallace Hebbard, Santa Barbara, 1966.

—Davis, Wm. H. *Seventy-five Years in California.* John Howell-Books, San Francisco, CA, 1967.

—Dillon, Richard. *Fool's Gold.* Coward-McCann, Inc., NY, 1967.

—Ellison, William Henry, Ed. *The Life and Adventures of George Nidever [1802—1883].* McNally & Loftin, Publishers, Santa Barbara, CA, 1984.

—Hafen, LeRoy R. (editor). *Mountain Men and Fur Traders of the Far West.* University of Nebraska Press, Lincoln, NE, 1965.

—Hawgood, John A. *First and Last Consul; Thos. O. Larkin and the Americanization of California* Huntington Library, San Marino, CA, 1962.

—Lyman, George D. *John Marsh, Pioneer.* Chas. Scribner's Sons, NY, 1933.

—Nunis, Doyce B., Jr. *The Trials of Isaac Graham.* Dawson's Book Shop, Los Angeles, CA, 1967. Quotations taken from this publication.

—Nunis, Doyce B., Jr. *The Bidwell-Bartleson Party,* Western Tanager Press, Santa Cruz, CA, 1991.

—Phelps, William Dane. *Alta California, 1840-1842* (his journal). Arthur H. Clark Co., Glendale, CA, 1983.

—Rolle, Andrew F. *An American in California, the Biography of William Heath Davis.* Henry Huntington Library, San Marino, CA, 1956.

—Rowland, Leon. *Santa Cruz, The Early Years.* Paper Vision Press, Santa Cruz, CA, 1980.

*This portrait, identified as Caleb Greenwood, is probably
one of Old Caleb's sons, since photography had not yet evolved
when Caleb, born in 1763, was the age
of the man in this photograph.
Courtesy Bancroft Library*

– 17 –

CALEB GREENWOOD

1763 – 1850

CALEB GREENWOOD: The colorful name alone helps describe this remarkable frontiersman. Unfortunately he was illiterate, so all information comes from outside sources; diaries, memoirs and quotations written by others who knew him. As a result, little is known about his youth, and there are missing links throughout his long, adventurous life. He spent only his last few years in California, but they were dynamic ones. Like a crusty old grizzly, he left his family tree with deep marks.

Greenwood was apparently born in Virginia around 1763. It is said that he left home at age eighteen after shooting and killing a sheriff, who was helping a creditor to collect a bad debt owed by his father. As the story goes, the creditor was willing to accept his father's black cook (possibly a slave) in payment of the debt. When the creditor and the sheriff tried to drag the protesting woman away with them, Caleb ran out of the house with a rifle and blazed away. The frightened creditor escaped injury, but the sheriff died on the spot.

As a result Caleb's father sent the boy away, telling him to leave the country for good. He apparently headed for Tennessee or Kentucky and farther west into Indian country. Shortly after Lewis and Clark returned from their momentous expedition in 1806, hundreds of adventurous men had gone into the mountains to trap beaver, whose cured skins— called plews— were worth from $4 to $12 each, depending on size and quality.

Greenwood was one of those trappers who became known as "mountain men." During 1810-11, he worked as a meat hunter for John Jacob Astor's trapping party located on the Missouri River north of present-day St. Joseph. A year later he was working for a rival firm named the Missouri Fur Company at Fort Osage, Missouri. It was owned by a wily Spanish trader named Manuel Lisa. Greenwood was 49 years old by then and still unmarried.

When Lisa's party headed up the Missouri River that spring, Greenwood was with them. After reaching good beaver country, Lisa made peace with the Arikara Indians and received permission to build Fort Manuel near the boundary of North and South Dakota. There Greenwood became a fur trapper, but did poorly and ended the season owing Lisa for supplies he'd bought on credit. He signed a note for it and returned to St. Louis in May 1813.

By November 1815 he was working on the Arkansas River for traders A. P. Chouteau and Jules de Mun, and they worked their way toward the Rocky Mountains near the present-day Kansas-Colorado border. Continuing on to Pueblo, Colorado, they completed their season of trading and headed for St. Louis. Greenwood and a few companions went on ahead, only to be attacked by Pawnee Indians who stole everything they had of value, including their rifles. When de Mun's group reached them later, they were starving. They arrived in St. Louis during the spring of 1816.

Six years passed before Greenwood was heard of again. This was when he led a group of trappers near the headwaters of the Missouri River. He was 59 at the time and probably working as a free trapper for William Ashley and Andrew Henry. By 1825 Greenwood was camped with a party near the mouth of Weber Canyon a short distance south of present-day Ogden, Utah. Then came a trapper named Zacharias Ham, who told of a rendezvous planned that summer by William Ashley on Henry's Fork of the Green River.

This rendezvous was the first of many annual get-togethers, where traders packed in supplies the trappers needed and traded them for furs. It attracted trappers from hundreds of miles around and allowed them to stay in the mountains instead of making the long, dangerous trek to St. Louis to sell their furs. It also attracted many Indians, who brought their families and camped nearby to join in the ribald festivities.

"Old Greenwood", as he was being called by then, arrived at the first rendezvous with 200 pounds of beaver plews, for which he was credited with around $600. Instead of staying in the mountains, he first elected to head toward St. Louis with General Ashley's party of 25 men. But rather than float down raging rivers in fragile bullboats with the others, Greenwood left on horseback to follow the Platte River.

In late November he reached Fort Atkinson as evidenced by a storekeeper's record: "Greenwood came from the mountains." He bought a horse there for $95 and left shortly before Christmas with a French trapper, heading west for Crow Indian country. There he finally took a wife, a Crow woman named Batchicka Youngcault. She was reportedly half French and was undoubtedly a good deal younger then her 63-year-old mate. He also met James Beckwourth, a trapper whom Greenwood passed off as a long lost Crow warrior (see Beckwourth).

Greenwood was living with the Crows in 1834, but he was not one to settle very long in one place. One story relates how devoted his wife was to him. It seems he had developed eye disease somewhere along the way. When his wife insisted that he go to see a doctor, she reportedly paddled him more than 2,000 miles down the Yellowstone and Missouri Rivers to St. Louis. Later the old mountain man's eyesight improved enough for them to try farming in the Missouri Valley.

By then they had several children, some with unique names. The oldest was John, born around 1827. Then came Britton (or Britain) Bailey, Governor Boggs, William Sublette and James Case. Obviously the boys were named after men Greenwood admired. There was a daughter named Angeline and another, born in 1843, named Sarah Mojave. Greenwood was 80 years young by then.

His wife died shortly after the birth of Sarah Mojave and was buried somewhere in St. Louis. By 1844 Greenwood had apparently placed his younger children with friends or relatives because he and his two eldest sons, John and Britt, were guiding an emigrant party west to Fort Hall. Some were going on to California; no one had taken wagons into California, and Greenwood had never been there himself. He had been to Fort Hall, though, and saw no reason why he couldn't go on to California if he chose.

The Bartleson-Bidwell Party had made it there three years before, but had abandoned their wagons northwest of the Great Salt Lake and endured terrible privations before arriving safely in the San Joaquin Valley (see separate chapter). Another party led by Joseph Chiles and Joseph R. Walker had nearly made it in 1843. Walker got their wagons as far as present-day Owens Valley, California, before abandoning them. He then led the party on horseback across a pass (later named in his honor) into the lower San Joaquin Valley (see chapters on Chiles & Walker).

G REENWOOD'S PARTY was made up of Missourians leaving from Council Bluffs, Iowa. About half were heading for Oregon. None had heard about Walker's failure to get wagons through to California, but that knowledge probably wouldn't have stopped the California-bound group anyway. Captained by a middle-aged blacksmith and former Indian Agent named Elisha Stevens, they called themselves the Stevens-Townsend-Murphy Party. Dr. John Townsend was a physician, and Martin Murphy Sr. was a 58 year-old immigrant from Ireland, via Canada (see Murphy). All of them except Elisha Stevens had extended families with them.

Also with the party was Dr. Townsend's young brother-in-law, Moses Schallenberger, a gunsmith named Allen Montgomery with his wife, Sarah (see Sarah M. Wallis), and 64 year-old Isaac Hitchcock and family. Altogether there were 40 wagons with nearly 70 men, women and children. They left Council Bluffs in mid-May, traveling along the north side of the Platte River, which later became the Mormon Trail. Making made good time, reached Fort John (later Ft. William; finally Ft. Laramie) by the end of June. This historic journey to California is covered in the Martin Murphy chapter and need not be repeated here.

Most of them reached Sutter's Fort in December 1844, split into two groups and without their wagons. Some of the party had been left behind in the mountains with the wagons. Regardless of their rather desperate circumstances, Sutter was elated to see so many able-bodied men on hand. He was busy recruiting a small army to assist in his efforts to keep Mexican Governor Manuel Micheltorena in power. Mexican rebels, led by ex-Governor Alvarado and Gen. José Castro, were threatening to oust the governor; as a loyal Mexican citizen—more likely because he had been promised more land by Micheltorena—Sutter was committed to saving his regime.

DESPITE OLD GREENWOOD'S AGE, Sutter recruited him and his sons, along with many others in the Stevens-Townsend-Murphy Party. Even these three leaders joined the bizarre campaign. Apparently Sutter had convinced them that they couldn't reach the two parties stranded in the mountains until spring and that the food they had would sustain them until help could be sent later. Whatever the reason, the new recruits joined Sutter's motley brigade, made up mostly of disgruntled settlers and Indian warriors.

The so-called Micheltorena War ended in Southern California with an abortive artillery duel that somehow resulted in no human casualties. Governor Micheltorna was overthrown in February, 1845, and replaced by Pío Pico in Los Angeles. Sutter was held prisoner for about a month before being released. Meanwhile his defeated volunteers were making their way back to Sutter's Fort any way they could.

After the collapse of Sutter's army, Old Greenwood and his sons returned to Sutters' Fort, where they learned that the stranded members of the Stevens-Murphy Party had been evacuated and were all right. They then traveled north to explore the area north of Napa Valley. Now that a trail for wagons had been blazed across the Sierras, others decided to try it by heading east. On May 12, 1845, Greenwood and sons were leading a party of twelve to Fort Hall. One of them was William Winter, who kept a good written account of the journey.

It was a bit early to make such a trip; the snow was still deep in the higher elevations and spring runoff had swollen the rivers and creeks to dangerous levels. The travelers had much difficulty in mounting the summit, but when they looked down on the sparkling waters of Truckee Lake, they found the eastern slopes nearly free of snow. While resting at the lake, John Greenwood located a detour around Truckee River

Canyon that saved them from retracing the punishing trip along the rocky riverbottom.

The new route wound northeast of the river to Alder Creek and on through a place called Dog Valley until it rejoined their old trail near present-day Verdi, Nevada. Later this cutoff was used by nearly all emigrants; it remained in use into the early 1900's. After losing a few horses to hostile Indians along the Humboldt River, the party made it safely to Fort Hall in 39 days. The California Trail was now firmly established, and Old Greenwood wasted little time exploiting it.

Though John Sutter was a naturalized Mexican citizen and an alcalde, he did not share the hostility of many native Californians toward foreign emigrants. Actually, he hoped to attract them to the area surrounding his settlement so he could sell them livestock, supplies and possibly land. Old Greenwood was well aware of this, and agreed to guide as many emigrants to Sutter's domain as possible.

As a result, he and his sons stayed at Fort Hall waiting for the first of the 1845 emigration to arrive in mid-July and early August. When they did, he and his sons paid them visits to praise California and demean Oregon. His reasons were twofold: He probably had some kind of deal with Sutter, and he would be charging a pilot's fee of $2.50 per wagon to guide them. One can imagine how persuasive and colorful the bearded, buckskinned-clad mountain man must have appeared with his two part-Indian sons beside him. In effect the Greenwood team became early and effective real estate boosters for Sutter's Fort. One of those who was swayed by Greenwood was Benjamin Bonney, who later wrote:

> After Greenwood had spoken the men of our party held a pow-wow which lasted nearly all night. Some wanted to go to California, while others were against it. Barlow, who was in charge of our train [probably Samuel K. Barlow], said that he would forbid any man leaving the train and going to California.
> The meeting broke up in a mutiny. Barlow finally appealed to the men to go to Oregon and make Oregon an American territory and not waste their time going to California to help promote Sutter's land schemes. Next morning old Caleb Greenwood with his boys stepped out to one side and said: "All you who want to go to California drive out from the main train and follow me...."

Bonney was the first to follow, and seven other wagons joined him amidst cat-calls and words of doom hurled at them by Barlow's followers. Words like, "Goodbye, we will never see you again. Your bones will whiten in the desert or be gnawed by wild animals in the mountains." Ten wagons, including the William Ide family, left Fort Hall with the Greenwoods (see Ide). By mid-August other wagons had joined them until there were 50, including James and Eliza Gregson (see Gregson).

Somewhere along the Humboldt River, John Greenwood's hatred for "Digger" Indians got the best of him and he shot one dead for no valid reason.

This infuriated the emigrants, who demanded action from Old Greenwood. To save face, he agreed that the Indian killer "should be shot on sight." Of course, by then, John had conveniently left the wagon train, not to return until later when things had cooled down. Another incident involving Indians was caused by a powerful, intimidating bully who wanted a slave. He was successful in capturing a young Indian and, much to the disgust of the others, tried to break his spirit with a whip. When the Indian escaped one night, taking some of the Texan's valuables—including a fine rifle—everyone rejoiced. By the time they reached the Truckee River, after crossing the Forty-Mile Desert, they were low on food and patience. This time they followed the Dog Valley trail, as Greenwood had done going east, and they made better time reaching Truckee Lake.

Under guidance from William Ide and Greenwood, raising the wagons over the pass went fairly well, and they reached Bear Valley before the end of September. Three days later, one of the emigrants named Snyder wrote: "Men in bad humor. Expected to reach the plains ere this." They did sight the Sacramento valley that afternoon, but were delayed in arriving at Johnson's Ranch and Sutter's Fort because some of them were suffering from poison oak. Snyder wrote that his face was "swelled so bad that I could not see."

Though some of them had become separated, most reached Sutter's Fort by October 1st, after which the Ide family and a few others arrived. In all, about 50 wagons with 250 to 300 emigrants finally rolled in, the first to make it without abandoning any wagons. Greenwood's purse was fattened accordingly. Along with a number of others, Old Greenwood and sons then headed northwest through the picturesque Napa Valley. James Clyman, a settler who had arrived in Napa Valley earlier that year, wrote:

> a young Mr [Britton or John] came in haveing been out some weeks hunting and Trapping in the mountains north he brought in a beautifull specemin of pure Sulpher and he informs me he saw greate Quantities of this mineral...

The following spring Greenwood, age 83, met Clyman and Lansford Hastings at Johnson's Ranch on their way east, and they all traveled together (See Hastings & Clyman). They began the climb toward the summit in April 1846, and had to fight heavy snow and swollen streams, making the ascent terribly difficult. Once over the summit, travel was easier, and they had few problems until Clyman's pet dog was accidentally parboiled at Brady's Hot Springs when it fell in trying to get a drink.

An entry in Clyman's diary dated May 13th stated that the company included "19 men and boys, 3 women, 2 children and about 150 horses and mules..." Apparently there were no wagons or carts. It is interesting to note that this was the date the U.S. declared war on Mexico; however, they knew nothing about it. Because of the large numbers of livestock and a shortage of grass, the party split into groups. One of them was led by Lansford Hastings, who had gone overland to Oregon in 1842 and published a book entitled, *The Emigrant's Guide to Oregon and California*.

In that book he described a proposed shortcut from Fort Bridger to California. Rather than making the long loop north to Fort Hall before dropping back south to the Humboldt River, he recommended going around the south end of the Great Salt Lake as John C. Fremont had done the year before. One could then strike northwest, he suggested, and join the newly established California Trail along the Humboldt River closer to the sink. The irony was, he had never tried it himself.

Finally the opportunity had come, and he persuaded Clyman and some of the others to try it. The Greenwoods, however, took the proven route to Fort Hall, and escorted the family groups there. They hoped to entice emigrants who reached Fort Hall that summer to head for California with themselves as pilots. Besides, Greenwood wanted to bring some of his children back to his newly adopted California home near Clear Lake. The Greenwoods must have settled fairly close to the Kelseys, who had moved there earlier (see Nancy Kelsey).

GREENWOOD BROUGHT some of his children to Fort Hall that summer. Along the way he had agreed to pilot a small wagon train led by Charles Imus and Joséph Arams to California. With them was the Hecox family (see Hecox). After guiding them safely to the Humboldt Sink, Greenwood and family left them there. He apparently wanted to make faster time over the pass to avoid winter storms. He did make good time, for he had his family settled in upper Napa Valley about the time that the Imus-Aram Party reached Sutter's Fort in early October. By November, some of Fremont's volunteer army recruiters came across Greenwood's hunting camp near Clear Lake. This event is well described by Edwin Bryant:

> The hunting party consisted of Mr. Greenwood...and three sons of Mr. G., one grown, and the other two boys 10 or 12 years of age, half-breed Indians, the mother being a Crow. One of these boys is named "Governor Boggs" after ex-governor Boggs of Missouri, an old friend of the father. Mr. Greenwood, or "Old Greenwood," as he is familiarly called,...is about six feet in height, raw-boned and

spare in flesh, but muscular, and not withstanding his old age, walks with erectness and elasticity of youth. His dress was of tanned buckskin, and from its appearance one would suppose its antiquity to be nearly equal to the age of its wearer. It had probably never been off his body since he first put it on....

Shortly after this meeting came the Donner Party tragedy (see Donner & Reed). When Caleb Greenwood learned of it in early February 1847, he traveled to Yerba Buena (San Francisco) to volunteer his services. He joined James Reed's party, which left by boat February 7, 1847. After arriving on Sonoma Creek, Greenwood hurried north to get his sons, Britton and William Sublette (age nine), along with some horses. It was the 23rd by the time Reed's rescue party left Johnson's Ranch on the Bear River. With them rode Old Greenwood and sons, as they made their way into the mountains with pack animals loaded with precious food.

It was soon apparent that pack animals could not contend with the deep snow, and they had to be left behind with most of the food supplies. To his chagrin, Old Greenwood was delegated to stay behind with his young son, while Britt Greenwood, Reed and the others continued on foot with what food they could carry. They had traveled only a few miles when they were surprised to meet another rescue party bringing out some Donner Party survivors, including Reed's wife and two of his four children.

After greeting his weeping wife and passing out food, Reed led off with Britton Greenwood and the others until they struggled over the summit to the Truckee Lake camp. Reed found his two younger children barely alive, along with others who had been existing on human flesh. Some of the party then went on to the Alder Creek camp, where the Donners and others were trapped about eight miles northeast of the lake. Those who could travel were brought out, and food was left for those remaining behind. Britton apparently rejoined his father and younger brother, who had been left below. Years later, William Sublette Greenwood's wife, Sarah, described the experience:

> There was a lady among them who had become insane...but they managed to get to Emigrant Gap with her. There my husband's father Caleb Greenwood strapped her on a horse and my husband [then] the 9-year-old boy led the horse by a halter into Sacramento (Sutter's Fort)....

By now Old Greenwood was 84 and, incredibly enough, he decided to pilot Commodore Robert Stockton and his 49-man party to Missouri. He was assisted by Joseph Chiles. One story of Greenwood's relationship with Stockton had to do with an Indian attack that resulted in Stockton's receiving an arrow wound in his posterior. When asked whether the arrow could have been poisoned, Old Greenwood replied, "Yes, by God! And you have not half an hour to live!" Stockton's supposed reply was,

> You old liar! Do you suppose you can frighten me? If you had said I might die within a few days or a week, I might have thought you believed what you said. Begone out of my sight before I blow out your brains!

AFTER REACHING ST. JOSEPH, Stockton's party disbanded and Greenwood was on his own. It was 1848 before he made the return trip to California, this time guiding a party led by M.M. Wambough, who had traveled east with the Stockton party a year earlier. Accounts of the 1848 California trip indicate that Old Greenwood was accompanied by most of his children. Apparently four of his sons had gone east before then, as they had all been in California at one time. Now that he had the two girls with him, Greenwood's family was intact for the first time. Apparently they were accompanied part of the way west by Joseph Chiles and his children.

While they were crossing the dreaded Forty-mile Desert, they met a group of Mormons heading east toward Salt Lake City. From them they learned of James Marshall's discovery of gold in Coloma Valley and the rush that followed (see Marshall). After reaching California, Old Greenwood and his sons wasted little time heading for Coloma with everyone else.

By then Coloma was a bustling boom town, and the Greenwoods built themselves a small cabin near Sutter's mill. The two girls probably helped with cooking and other chores while the men mined for gold. There is no evidence that Old Greenwood did much mining, but he did spend time telling tall tales to the greenhorns. One tale repeated for years was about an alleged lost lake, where gold nuggets lined the shore like glittering pebbles. Hundreds cursed Greenwood as they searched in vain for "Gold Lake." Later, Greenwood cursed his son, John, after he took part in an Indian massacre in the area, during which he scalped one of the Indians.

During the summer of 1849, Old Greenwood moved his family a few miles northeast to "Greenwood Valley", where they settled for a while. There was gold there, and soon a small settlement was established. To no one's surprise, it was named Greenwood. Later, part of the family moved to a camp near Nevada City. There Old Greenwood reached the end of his final trail. He died somewhere between the winter of 1849 and the summer of 1850; no one knows exactly where or when.

It's said he was accompanied only by his youngest son, James, who was about nine at the time. James had to hike out to find help to bury his father, who had died during the night outdoors under the stars. Unable to obtain finished lumber for a coffin, the burial party stripped two huge pieces of rounded bark off a large and probably downed pine tree. Greenwood's body was then encased in the bark like a cocoon, and he was laid to rest wrapped in an old buffalo robe. What could be more fitting for an old mountain man?

Though old Greenwood spent only the last few years of his life in California, his contributions were substantial; he bridged the gap between the 18th and 19th centuries. While the tiny town of Greenwood in El Dorado County was actually named after his son, John, in 1849, (identified with a historical marker), John would certainly share the remembrance with his colorful father.

BIBLIOGRAPHY

–Bancroft, Hubert H. *History of California,* Vol. I-VII. History Co., San Francisco, 1886. Republished, Wallace Hebbard, Santa Barbara, 1966.

–Bryant, Edwin. *What I Saw In California.* University Nebraska Press, Lincoln, 1985.

–Camp, Charles L. *James Clyman, Frontiersman.* Champoeg Press, Portland, OR, 1960.

–Crosby, Alexander L. *Old Greenwood, Pathfinder of the West* (based on the book by Charles Kelly & Dale L. Morgan). Talisman Press, Georgetown, CA, 1967. Quotations cited in the text were taken from this publication.

–DeVoto, Bernard. *The Year of Decision, 1846.* Houghton Mifflin Co., Boston, 1942

–Dillon, Richard. *Fool's Gold.* Coward McCann, Inc. New York, 1967.

–Gay, Theressa. *James Marshall.* Talisman Press, Georgetown, CA, 1967.

–Hecox, Margaret (Memoirs of, edited by Richard H. Dillon). *California Caravan.* Harlan-Young Press, San Jose, CA, 1966.

–Kelly, Charles and Dale L. Morgan. *Old Greenwood.* Talisman Press, Georgetown, CA, 1965.

–Stewart, George R. *The California Trail.* University of Nebraska Press, Lincoln, 1962.

–Unruh, John D. Jr. *The Plains Across.* University of Illinois Press, Chicago, 1979.

NOTES

Eliza Gregson
Courtesy California Department of Parks & Recreation

– 18 –

ELIZA GREGSON

1824 – 1889

ELIZABETH MARSHALL, known as Eliza, was born March 15, 1824 in Manchester, England. Her parents were John and Anna Marshall, natives of Northern England, and their story reads like a Charles Dickens novel. John, a machinist, made good wages but lost much of it to gambling. When Eliza was four the family moved to Stockport and then to Derbyshire, where they were living in 1836. After John Marshall lost everything in a cotton yarn business, he scraped up enough money to leave the country.

Leaving his wife and five children behind, he sailed to the United States for a new start. Eliza and the children then moved to Hayfield, where 13-year-old Eliza and her older brother found work in a cotton yarn factory. They worked long hours for low pay, subsisting mostly on "treakle and oatmeal mush." Somehow they managed and were soon joined by Eliza's recently widowed aunt and her two girls.

There was a good deal of joyous excitement in 1839 when John Marshall sent money enough so the whole family could leave for America. They settled in Pawtucket, Rhode Island until 1843, when 19-year-old Eliza married a young blacksmith, James Gregson, 21, who hailed from Lancashire, England. Shortly after the wedding, the newly-weds moved to Gregson's family home in Philadelphia.

A year later, with eighteen dollars in dimes, they moved to Illinois. Eliza wanted to escape from the cotton mills and feared her husband was not brawny enough for heavy blacksmith's work. "Not very stout" was her description of him. A son was born in the fall of 1844 but died three months later. By then Eliza's parents had separated, and her mother, Anna Marshall, and three of Eliza's siblings moved to Illinois to join the Gregsons in their cramped, leaky cabin.

By the spring of 1845 the destitute family decided to head for Oregon to obtain good, free land they heard was available. They put together an outfit of one wagon and three yoke of oxen for the journey. There were six in the family, and they picked up one passenger along the way in Iowa (apparently to help with the expenses). The passenger was not identified, but family members included James and Eliza Gregson, Eliza's mother, Ann Marshall, and her children John, Henry and Mary Ann Marshall.

They probably joined the Oregon Trail outside of Independence, as most emigrants did then, and apparently traveled alone much of the time. They reached the Snake River outside of Fort Hall before running out of supplies and money. There the Gregsons joined Elija Bristow's party as hired hands. According to Eliza's memoirs, she did the washing and cooking, while James drove Bristow's team. Eliza's teen-aged brothers, Henry and John, probably drove the oxen pulling the Gregson wagon.Though they were heading for Oregon, they learned that some emigrants were going to California. Since the Stevens-Murphy Party had proven a year earlier that it was possible to get wagons across the Sierra Nevada, the numbers of emigrants were increasing. California sounded good to the Gregsons, so they took the turnoff west of Fort Hall to head southwest.

OLD CALEB GREENWOOD and his grown sons were guiding a party of about 50 wagons to California, and the Gregsons joined them along the way (see Greenwood). Also with Greenwood were John Grigsby and William Ide; this wagon train is sometimes referred to as the Grigsby-Ide Party (see Ide). The trip went fairly well until they reached a spot Truckee Meadows (now Reno, Nevada), where hostile Paiute Indians began shooting arrows into the grazing livestock, killing a good number of them, which the Indians later butchered and ate. Seeking revenge, one of the emigrants laced a dead heifer with strychnine and left it for them.The Gregsons lost all their oxen except one yoke (two oxen). Realizing that one yoke was incapable of pulling their wagon, they were faced with a terrible decision. Possibly they had heard about a similar dilemma that forced the 1841 Bartleson-Bidwell Party to abandon their wagons. (See Chapter 1).

Rather than abandon their wagon, they cut it down into a two-wheeled cart, loaded it with essential supplies, and went on their way. All but the sick had to travel on foot; Eliza Gregson and her mother walked the rest of the way to California. To get wagons over the summit of the Sierra Nevada near Truckee Lake (now Donner Lake), some had to be dismantled and hauled up piecemeal. They finally limped into Johnson's Ranch (now near Wheatland) on October 20, 1845 (see Johnson).

After reaching Sutter's Fort a few days later, James Gregson was hired by John A. Sutter, who was always on the lookout for skilled craftsmen. The Gregsons were then sent to Sutter's "Pine Woods" sawpits on the Cosumnes River to work (before the advent of powered sawmills, boards had to be sawed off logs by hand. Usually the logs were dragged over a pit, and a man went into the pit to handle one end of a long saw, while another man climbed up on the log to handle the other end). Gregson undoubtedly worked there with Allen Montgomery (see Sarah Wallis). They worked at the sawpits until Christmas Eve, when they returned to Sutter's Fort.

During the first part of 1846 the Gregsons worked on a ranch owned by Thomas Hardy near the confluence of the Sacramento and Feather rivers. There they lived in a crude tule "wigwam", as Eliza called it. Following a dispute with Hardy, they returned to Sutter's Fort, where James did some blacksmithing and helped dig ditches around pastures as a substitute for fences. There was little paid work for Eliza, and they barely existed.

Along with Montgomery, Gregson took part in the 1846 Bear Flag Rebellion when they helped seize a herd of horses from the Mexican Army. After General Vallejo and his aides were captured at Sonoma and incarcerated at Sutter's Fort, both James Gregson and Allen Montgomery joined John C. Fremont's California Volunteers to fight in the Mexican War.

Eliza gave birth to their daughter, Anna, a few weeks before James left. She is said to be the first white child born in the entire region, and Indians came from miles around to see her. During the absence of James and Allen Montgomery, both wives stayed at Sutter's Fort. Among those living at the fort was Lt. Edward Kern, who was left in charge during John Fremont's absence.

Eliza Gregson and Sarah Montgomery shared quarters with a Mrs. Leahy and her two children. Very probably they all attended Sarah Montgomery's famous quilting bee early in 1846. Eliza states in her memoirs that while there she taught reading and writing to Mrs. Leahy's children and to Sarah Montgomery as well. In early 1847 the occupants of the fort received word about the awful plight of the Donner Party, who were trapped by snow at Truckee Lake (now Donner Lake). When rescue parties brought out some survivors, Eliza and the others did what they could for them. At last, by April 1847, all the survivors were out, the Mexican war was over, and men in Fremont's California Volunteers began coming home, including James Gregson, who arrived that summer.

Sutter then sent him to the Bear River to help get out some heavy granite millstones for a grist mill, to be constructed a few miles up the American River from the fort. Later James became deathly ill with "Sacramento fever." Devoted care by Eliza—during which she fed him "herbal" tea made from cow manure—apparently pulled him through.

After his recovery, Eliza took her sick baby, Anna, to Yerba Buena

James Gregson
Courtesy California Department of Parks & Recreation

(San Francisco) for medical care. When little Anna was well, they traveled back upriver on the short-lived steamboat *Sitka*. The Gregson memoirs state that John Sutter asked them to go to Coloma in late December 1847 to assist James Marshall on a sawmill he was building. James Gregson later wrote:

> My wife was to cook for one or two men. I was to work three years and be paid in cattle. The morning we were to start for [Coloma] from Sutter's Fort, Marshall came into the fort with a little vial of about an ounce, greenish glass, which was over half full of scale gold. I looked at it and this was the first gold seen in the country.

This contradicts statements claiming that the Gregsons were in Coloma during the gold discovery, documented as January 24, 1848. There are other discrepancies with well known facts about the gold discovery, leading to the conclusion that some dates and facts in the Gregson memoirs may be in error. They were written from memory many years after these events took place, and confusion is certainly understandable.

THE GOLD DISCOVERY is well documented by others who were on the scene, and there is no mention of the Gregsons being there at the time. Jennie Wimmer, wife of Peter Wimmer, was the camp cook, and they lived there with several of their children. Marshall took some gold samples to Sutter's Fort a few days after his discovery, arriving after dark in a rain storm. He left the next morning and reached Coloma that evening. (see chapter on James Marshall). If the Gregson's were in Coloma in late December and January as they say, they must have left prior to the gold discovery.

James Gregson's story of Marshall's bringing gold samples to Sutter's Fort in a green vial makes them sound more like the samples Sam Brannan displayed at Yerba Buena in May. (See Samuel Brannan). Historian H.H. Bancroft agrees the that Gregsons were in Coloma during the gold discovery; however, it seems logical that other workers who were definitely there would have confirmed it, including Marshall himself.

An entry in Sutter's diary, dated January 25, 1848 (the day after Marshall's gold discovery), states: "...Lennox, Gregson & Jones arrived from Sonoma." If Gregson was in Sonoma on the 24th, he could not have been in Coloma on the same day—or is Sonoma being confused with Coloma?. Another entry in Sutter's diary dated January 28th, simply states: "Mr. Marshall arrived from the mountains on very important business." This is supposedly the first news Sutter received about Marshall's gold discovery.

The Gregsons must have been in Coloma later, as evidenced by an entry in John A. Sutter's diary on May 4,1848. "James Gregson arrived from the sawmill to get some work done, and he left again in the afternoon." The sawmill was completed by then, and it appears that the Gregsons did go to Coloma sometime after the gold discovery.

Eliza may have gone to Coloma to relieve Jennie Wimmer from demanding cooking chores during her pregnancy; she gave birth to a son, Benjamin, in early August 1848. Eliza says she visited Jennie in Diamond Springs and later assisted during Benjamin's birth. The Gregson role in the gold discovery is indeed confusing, and one must rely on the diaries of those who were documented as being there, e.g., Henry Bigler, Azariah Smith and James Brown.

THE GREGSON FAMILY had been mining for gold in the Coloma area with some success, when James became very ill toward the end of 1848. At about this time Eliza gave birth to another daughter they named Mary Ellen. Both the girls were sick as well, and a doctor told them they should leave the goldfields. They then moved to the Sonoma area, where Eliza apparently supported them by taking in washing, ironing and sewing.

By the spring of 1849 James was feeling well enough to make another attempt at mining, but again returned home feeling ill. That fall Eliza was joined by her mother, her two sisters and her brother, Henry. James and Henry then went to Sacramento, where they allegedly bought some lots in Sutterville. After building some adobe houses there, they were washed out by floods. By 1850, the Gregsons and Henry Marshall obtained a 160-acre ranch from John B. R. Cooper, a well known trader from San Francisco. Located in Green Valley, Sonoma County, it was well suited for farming and seemed capable of supporting the entire family.

A short time later Eliza was accidentally shot in the shoulder; it took her months to recover. In 1852 the Gregsons had another boy, John, followed by a sister in 1854. Several more followed until there were eight in all. The Gregsons were among the first to grow wheat successfully in the Sonoma area and remained there the rest of their lives. Eliza died February 1, 1889, and James followed her a decade later on August 1, 1899. They both are buried in nearby Green Valley Cemetery.

The Gregsons were among the first to establish a successful agricultural community in Green Valley, Sonoma County. Most important of all, perhaps, they exemplified the pioneer spirit that brought people like them from the depths of poverty and despair to success in an untamed land. Eliza Gregson is often portrayed in living history programs at Sutter's Fort Historical State Park, Sacramento.

Brentwood Library
Contra Costa County Library
104 Oak St.
Brentwood, Ca. 94513
925-516-5290

Customer ID: 21901020283291

Title: Pioneers of California : true stories of
early settlers in the Golden State /
ID: 31901025302177
Due: 30 Nov 2015
Circulation system messages:
Item checked out.

Total items: 1
11/9/2015 3:13 PM

Renew online or by phone
ccclib.org
1-800-984-4636

Have a nice day!

BIBLIOGRAPHY

–Bancroft, Hubert H. *History of California,* Vol. I-VI. History Co., San Francisco, CA, 1886. Reprinted, Wallace Hebberd, Santa Barbara, CA, 1966.

–Gay, Theressa. *James W. Marshall.* Talisman Press, Georgetown, CA, 1967.

–Gregson, Eliza and James. "The Gregson Memoirs," from *California Historical Quarterly,* 1940. Quotations were taken from this publication with the courtesy of Mrs. Clara Neilson of Pollock Pines, California, a direct descendant of the Gregsons.

–Paul, Rodman. *The California Gold Discovery.* Talisman Press, Georgetown, CA, 1967.

–Stewart, George S. *The California Trail.* University of Nebraska Press, Lincoln, 1962.

–Sutter, John A., et al. *New Helvetia Diary: Sacramento, CA-1845-48.* Grabhorn Press, San Francisco, 1932.

NOTES

– 19 –

WILLIAM E.P. HARTNELL

(Don Guillermo)   1798 – 1854

THE SECOND SON of Squire Hartnell, William Hartnell was a native of Lancashire, England, where he was born in 1798. After being baptized in the Church of England, he enjoyed the affluent lifestyle of a young country squire. By age sixteen he had completed a basic education in Lancashire and was sent off to the well-respected College of Commerce in Bremen, Germany.

His studies there were interrupted a year later when he received news of his father's sudden death. Surprisingly, Squire Hartnell left no estate; he had co-signed a note for a friend who had defaulted, leaving the hapless squire holding an empty purse. Young Hartnell was forced to leave school and return home to help his older brother support his mother and younger siblings.

After moving in with his Uncle Edward Petty in London, Hartnell searched in vain for work. At age 18 he was a tall, good-looking lad with knowledge in languages, accounting and shorthand. Despite these assets, work was hard to find in England at the time. Finally Hartnell found work as a bookkeeper with John Begg & Company, worldwide traders headquartered in Chile.

Hartnell used his time on the long voyage to learn Spanish. Because he knew Latin and German, he found Spanish fairly easy. After landing at Buenos Aires in early March 1819, he was required to make a thousand-mile overland journey across South America to Santiago, Chile; apparently the ship was not prepared to make the treacherous voyage around Cape Horn. He reached Santiago on his twenty-first birthday, finding it an exciting city indeed.

He found John Begg an exacting taskmaster, but did well in learning the competitive trading business. Within a year he was entrusted with more responsibility and was taking business trips to the nearby port city of Valparaiso. Being a naturally gregarious, fun-loving young man, he nearly broke his health from over-work and too many long nights with fast girls and hard drink.

When he was diagnosed as having contracted consumption, his employer transferred him to Valparaiso. When his health improved, he was made supercargo on a cocoa trading voyage up the coast to present-day Ecuador. This was a period when the Spanish were attempting to hang onto their shaky power in the Americas and were suspicious of English traders. As a result, Hartnell's attempts to obtain cargo were only marginally successful, and he returned to Valparaiso in 1821. His health was restored, but he had little else to show for his efforts.

When General San Martin entered the port of Callao in 1821 as "protector of the citizens," the beleagered Spanish Viceroy fled. Soon the "patriot flag" flew over the port city, and the Spanish were ousted, first from South America and then North America. Almost immediately, slaves were freed and trade restrictions lifted. John Begg wasted little time taking advantage of this and expanded his activities accordingly. Before long he had procured a virtual fleet of merchant ships and placed them into service between South America and England.

JOHN BEGG & COMPANY was accumulating vast profits, but Hartnell and other salaried employees were frustrated because they did not enjoy a share. This resulted in a risky business venture between Hartnell, Begg and Hugh McCulloch to trade in hides and tallow along the California coast. Hartnell would become resident manager in Monterey, while McCulloch acted as supercargo on their trading vessel, John Begg. Begg was the financier and demanded five-eighths of the profits. Though Begg had driven a hard bargain, the agreement was signed in March 1822.

The John Begg reached San Diego in early June, the first vessel to be greeted by new port authorities appointed after Mexican independence had been declared from Spain. One of these may have been Juan Bandini (see Bandini). The generous authorities granted the new trading company land where they could build a store and warehouse. Heading on up the coast in good spirits, Hartnell and McCulloch arrived at Monterey Harbor in late June.

A courtesy visit with Governor Pablo Sola and Fr. Mariano Payeras—head of the California mission system—resulted in their granting Hartnell and McCulloch rights to contract with the missions for trading manufactured goods for cowhides, tallow and horns—the only viable export the vast ranches had to offer. The two elated partners then set out to visit all the missions to contract with the padres in charge. They enjoyed some success but met with fierce competition from other traders, especially in Southern California.

By the following year, Governor Sola had been replaced by Luis Arguello, who was persuaded to grant "Macula y Arguello" (the Spanish version of McCulloch and Hartnell) the "right to trade in all ports of

California and also in all the landfalls and bays nearest the missions." Furthermore, he granted them permission to establish stores and warehouses in San Pedro and Monterey. This gave them a real advantage over their competitors, who were restricted to anchoring only in San Diego and Monterey.

By this time they had befriended influential *Californios* such as Juan Bandini in the San Diego area. They were riding high, as expressed in a tongue-in-cheek letter written by Hartnell in July 1823:

> I make myself as comfortable as I can here; the only thing that is wanting to make life agreeable are a few damsels to play with on a winter's evening. But providence has so ordained, that I am to do penance in this place for the many sins I have committed elsewhere; and it is my duty to submit without repining to its wise decree.

By 1824 Hartnell was not riding so high. He had become morose over personal problems and was again drinking heavily. He was saved from oblivion by Father Luis Martinez, a young priest who had become a personal friend and converted him to Catholicism that very year. This helped his trading career in a land where non-Catholics were prevented from marrying or owning land. But it did nothing to endear him to his friends and relatives; gradually some of them cut him off from their lives. He was convinced he had made the right choice, and changed his name by adding the middle initials "E. P." in honor of his uncle, Edward Petty.

At about this time he fell in love with the fifteen-year-old daughter of Don José de la Guerra y Noriega, one of the wealthiest and most prominent rancheros in California. The family lived near Santa Barbara, and Hartnell had known them since his early trading days in 1822. Maria Teresa de la Guerra had been thirteen then, and now that she had blossomed into a lovely young lady, Hartnell found himself hopelessly in love with her.

During this courting period Hugh McCulloch left California, leaving Hartnell in full charge of trading operations there. With his "new lease on life," Hartnell applied himself and found that he enjoyed the challenge. In San Pedro, he had an adobe store and warehouse constructed—the first building in the area. Hoping to expand his trading operations to the Russians in Sitka, Alaska, Hartnell learned some Russian to complement his knowledge of other languages.

His wedding to Teresa de la Guerra took place in April 1825 at the Santa Barbara Mission, when Teresa was sixteen and Hartnell was twenty-seven. Meanwhile he had started construction of a house in Monterey, where they would reside after their marriage. This project was being supervised by Scotsman David Spence, an old friend and business associate there. The festive wedding was the social event of the season, with celebrations continuing for many days. It was a proud and happy day for Hartnell when he brought his lovely young bride to her new home in Monterey. His future had never seemed brighter.

Unfortunately, such bliss seldom endures. Hartnell watched helplessly as trading fell off from ever increasing competition from other traders. Company profits began to sag, and some of Hartnell's employees began running similar businesses on the side. A change of governors added another punishing blow. When Governor Argüello was replaced by José Echeandia, he increased import duties and restricted all trading vessels to San Diego and Monterey to better control them.

An extensive written appeal from Hartnell to Governor Echeandia in 1826 resulted in some ports being opened to company ships to pick up mission products. Hartnell's good fortune was given added emphasis by the birth of his first son. Good was again followed by bad, when a project to pack salt beef in locally-made oaken barrels met with only marginal success. Economic news from Europe was bad; a depression with world-wide consequences brought Begg, Hartnell and McCulloch to the point of bankruptcy.

To add to their problems, two trading vessels were lost, one off San Diego, the other off Ireland. News of his mother's death added to Hartnell's depression. One bit of hope was a close friendship with Capt. John B. R. Cooper, another English trader who appeared in Monterey in the early 1820's and married one of Mariano Vallejo's sisters. Vallejo and his nephew, Juan B. Alvarado, had been tutored by Hartnell in their younger years and remained on good terms with him (see Vallejo).

COOPER SETTLED in Monterey as a friendly competitor with Hartnell. In 1826-27, the English frigate Blossom visited Monterey, captained by Commander Frederick Beechey. It wasn't long before Beechey and Hartnell had become fast friends, to the point where Commander Beechey recommended that the Mexican Government should approve Hartnell as England's Vice Consul. Though his title was never made official by Mexico City, Hartnell acted in that capacity for several years.

Finally the time had come to dissolve the partnership between Begg, Hartnell and McCulloch, which had been steadily been losing money. The matter was too complicated to settle through correspondence, so Hartnell made preparations for a voyage to Lima, Peru, where Begg was living. This was at the time when Mexico had decreed that all Spanish citizens should leave Mexican territory, including California. Franciscan padres and others were virtually fleeing the country in fear for their lives.

When Hartnell's father-in-law, José de la Guerra, was threatened with expulsion, he made ready to leave for Mexico City to plead his case. Though he had been born in Spain, he had come to the country as a young boy and felt like a native. Hartnell joined him and two of his sons at their Santa Barbara rancho, and they sailed south with two destinations in mind—the de la Guerras for San Blas and Hartnell for Lima. The de le Guerras were turned back at San Blas, but Hartnell went on.

He found conditions in South America much different from when he had left there four years earlier. Once an accounting of company assets and liabilities was made, Hartnell was dismayed to find that the partners' debts amounted to around $30,000. His share was a shocking $19,000. Despite this set-back, Hartnell was determined to carry on the trading business in California by himself. He sailed for home with a cargo consigned by various traders, including Scotsman Hugo Reid.

After enjoying a warm welcome at home, Hartnell was surprised to find that Teresa had enlarged the house to accommodate their growing family and ever-increasing numbers of house-guests. By then his business associate, David Spence, had become a Catholic convert and married a *Californio* woman. Not only that, but he was leaving Hartnell to start a trading venture of his own in Monterey—another friendly competitor with whom Hartnell would have to contend. It seemed a cadre of British traders was settling the area, including Hartnell, Cooper and Spence.

For years Hartnell had wanted to acquire land of his own to start a cattle ranching and farming operation. He knew this would require him to renounce his English citizenship and become a citizen of Mexico. This he did in 1830, at which time he arranged with the Soberanes family to share-crop some of their land at Rancho Alisal, near Salinas. An excerpt from a letter he wrote during the early 1830s is self explanatory:

> At last I have become a ranchero although not entirely in the way I would have chosen. The Soberanes have granted me an equal right with them in the Aliso property, giving me permission to pasture as many cattle as I consider advisable, to build a house and to plant as many [grape] vines and orchard trees as we need and in return I must help them at seed times...I have about 500 head of cattle which I plan to pasture there this month; so we shall soon see if as a Rancher I have the same ability, or better say lack of ability, that I showed as a Trader.

For years Hartnell had been hoping to cultivate trade with Russian fur hunters; however, the Mexican governors had thwarted him. But when Governor Victoria was replaced by José Figueroa in 1833, the picture began to change. Encouraged by Figueroa's more receptive attitude, Hartnell made a trip to the Russian settlement at Fort Ross to look into trade possibilities. He was impressed not only by the picturesque setting and efficient operations there, but by the stalwart settlers themselves.

Russian Governor F. P. von Wrangell offered Hartnell warm hospitality and ended up by promising to make him the exclusive trading agent for the Russian-American Fur Company with a rather handsome salary. The offer was put into writing, and Hartnell hurried it to Governor Figueroa for final approval. When the governor approved it in early 1835, Hartnell thought he was finally on the elusive road to prosperity. Unfortunately the salary he was to receive never materialized, and when Figueroa died unexpectedly a few months later, the deal collapsed.

MEANWHILE, Hartnell had begun construction of an adobe house on his ranch property. He was traveling back and forth between there and Monterey, where he continued his hide-trading activities, primarily with the missions. Meanwhile his former partners were pressing him for payment of the $19,000 indebtedness he had incurred. He was growing desperate when an old friend came to his aid indirectly. Hugh McCulloch had endorsed over Hartnell's note to Dr. Stephen Anderson, who was returning to California after a long absence.

Among changes Anderson noted were ominous rumblings of mission secularization, which had been ordered by the Mexican Government in 1826 and was only now being carried out. Nevertheless, he decided to renew his former trading activities and began canvassing the missions for business. To his surprise, he found that most of the padres remained loyal to Hartnell and that some kind of accommodation would be necessary if he were to conduct business with the faithful padres. To Hartnell's delight, Dr. Anderson offered to discharge his debt if he would notify the padres that his trading rights were being transferred to Anderson. Thus, Hartnell satisfied his long-standing debt and was free to pursue his ranching activities.

Meanwhile, Hartnell had not found his "crop sharing" arrangement with the Soberanes entirely satisfactory, and was trying to obtain land of his own. With the help of his father-in-law, Don José de la Guerra, Hartnell managed to acquire 3,000 acres of Rancho Alisal in his own name. Still, his income was not sufficient for his growing family, and he again sought help from his father-in-law. A school for boys was needed in the area to avoid having to send them abroad. Hartnell had the background for it, and had tutored boys from good families such as the Alvarados and Vallejos. "Why not open a boarding school for boys?" Don José suggested. He even offered to help finance it.

This idea appealed to Hartnell. He enlisted the aid of Father Patrick Short, an experienced well-respected teacher from Honolulu. Father Short had endured much discrimination from the predominantly Protestant missionaries there and was glad for the opportunity to come to California. Hartnell's Monterey home was used as the school's headquarters, for which Governor Figueroa had granted additional land.

The school got off to a slow start, with only a few students. They included two Indian boys, one the son of trader Hugo Reid and his Indian wife, Victoria, who lived in San Gabriel (see Reid). But once word spread that a good education was available at *El Seminario de San Jose,* it soon outgrew the facilities in Monterey. Hartnell and Short then decided to construct a new two-story adobe building on Hartnell's Alisal ranch property.

They were settled there by mid-1835, and within a year there were about forty people connected with "Hartnell's School," as it was being called. The sudden death of Governor Figueroa, who had been an ardent supporter of the school, dealt it a blow from which it never recovered. It closed its doors in mid-1836, a year after moving to its new location. Thus the death of Figueroa not only killed Hartnell's deal with the Russian-American Fur Company, but his school as well.

One can imagine his despair. It seemed as though everything he touched turned sour except his family, which kept growing. By the time Father Short returned to Honolulu, political turmoil in California was rampant. The turnover of governors became a joke as Nicholas Gutierrez succeeded José Castro and was replaced by Mariano Chico. Chico was then ousted by Gutiérrez, who became governor again. By then, Hartnell's ex-pupil, Juan B. Alvarado, saw his chance to seize power.

Alvarado enlisted the help of American settler, Isaac Graham, who recruited a band of 25 hard-bitten frontier sharp-shooters (see Graham). Together they marched on Gutiérrez's Monterey headquarters and forced him to leave the country in fear for his life. Alvarado lived to regret becoming beholden to Graham and his cronies; nevertheless, he was installed as governor.

Recognizing Hartnell's financial plight, Alvarado named him official Tax Collector and Administrator of Customs. His compensation was set at five-percent of all taxes collected. Quickly he established an improved system of tax collections, which increased his income accordingly. By then secularization of the missions had become a scandal; certain unscrupulous mission administrators were fattening their purses by siphoning off mission livestock and other assets for their own benefit.

Alvarado needed a trustworthy official to visit all the missions to inventory the assets and get an accounting of their disposal. What better person was there than William Hartnell for this difficult task? He had dealt with the missions for many years and knew their business operations better than most. A salary of $2,000 per year was established, which would mean an actual cut in his income.

Most of Hartnell's friends advised him to turn down the job; it was a "no win" situation, they said. He would be locking horns with the powerful *Californios*, who would certainly take offense at any critical remarks Hartnell might submit to the governor. Hartnell apparently felt obliged to assist Alvarado, so he finally agreed to take the job. The visits to the missions would take place during 1839 and 1840, requiring Hartnell's absence from home for many months. This upset Teresa Hartnell; she later said her husband accepted the position "chiefly to oblige his friend, Alvarado," and it caused him "much annoyance and little profit."

Before he left, Hartnell insisted that his written instructions be approved by Father Narciso Durán, long-time president of the missions. This astute move gained him blessings from the clergy, along with civil authority granted by the governor. Whether by chance or design, deterioration of the missions had reached the point of no return. Mission Indians had dropped from 23,000 to around 6,000; cattle from 140,000 to about 50,000 and other livestock had dropped accordingly.

Spanish padres who had been allowed to stay were stripped of all but rudimentary power; mission lands had been broken up and granted to laymen, with the exception of a few small grants to neophyte Indians. Many mission buildings had been destroyed or were virtually melting into the clay from which they had originated.

HARTNELL began his tour at the original mission located in San Diego, before working his way north. With the blessing of Father Durán, he confronted a renegade padre at Santa Barbara and notified him of his discharge. Upon reaching Mission Santa Inez, he stated how he had "found failure in responsibility on the part of civil administrators" everywhere except San Gabriel and San Juan Capistrano, which had been administered by Don Juan Bandini (see Bandini). This, of course, cast an unfavorable light on powerful men such as Pío Pico, the administrator at Mission San Luis Rey. Pico lost little time joining with others to castigate Hartnell's credentials and abilities.

It wasn't until he reached Sonoma and visited the newest mission, San Francisco Solano, that he ran into real opposition. General Mariano G. Vallejo, the mission administrator, refused to open his books to Hartnell and would not allow him entry into mission precincts. Though Vallejo had once been a student of Hartnell's, he stone-walled his ex-tutor to the point where Hartnell was forced to accept a prepared report on the mission's condition.

With his first tour completed, Hartnell returned home to prepare a complete report for Governor Alvarado. Though the governor was upset by the negative aspects of the report, he was pleased with Hartnell's work and collaborated with him to publish new regulations meant to improve conditions. He also granted Hartnell a salary increase and more authority. The new rules reduced authority of mission administrators and increased authority of padres over spiritual matters. Before the new regulations were finalized, they were submitted to Father Durán for approval. His comments are worthy of repeating:

The reglamento closes the door to fraud and robbery, but also in improvement. The doctor is prevented from killing the patient, but has no power to cure him.

In January 1840 Hartnell began his second tour at Mission San Jose. But by March his hopes of doing an even better job were dashed by two messages: General Vallejo refused to relinquish authority over Mission San Rafael, and Father Durán refused to cooperate in placing the new regulations in effect. The discouraged mission presidente simply didn't think they would do any good.

When Hartnell tried to visit Mission San Rafael, General Vallejo placed him under arrest and had him carried across the bay "for having ventured to interfere in matters concerning the northern frontier." Hartnell remained a prisoner until he conceded in writing that "Vallejo's views in this particular case were correct." He was then allowed to continue his mission tour. Seizing on Vallejo's success in the North, Pío Pico tried the same tactics at Mission San Luis Rey in the South (see Pico).

This time Hartnell fought back. He obtained a summons that required armed soldiers to escort Pico to a Los Angeles court to explain himself. Hartnell probably regretted this action, for he was placed on the defensive and forced to answer counter-charges made by Pico. Nevertheless, he had the satisfaction of seeing Pico discharged as Mission Administrator. Warned of a death threat by his friend, Don Nicolas Den—and with his tour in disarray—Hartnell returned home and submitted his resignation to Governor Alvarado (see Den). Another healthy baby boy helped dispel his gloom over the failed second tour, and he was glad to see it end.

No attempt was made to find a successor. Apparently Alvarado knew it was too late to save the missions. To make matters worse for Hartnell, the promised salary was never paid. Again his father-in-law came to his aid. He sent his son, Pablo de la Guerra, on a grand tour of Europe, which created an opening for Chief of Customs. Hartnell, now age 42, fell heir to it and was responsible for collecting duties from traders like Cooper, Spence and Thomas O. Larkin in Monterey, and Abel Stearns in Los Angeles (see chapters on Larkin & Stearns).

Larkin, an American step-brother of John Cooper, had become a Monterey trader since his arrival in 1832. He had become very successful and played an important role in assisting American settlers, much as Cooper, Spence and Hartnell had been doing for settlers from the British Isles. It's fair to say that their help to others was never limited solely to members of their own ethnic backgrounds. Larkin later became United States Consul.

Other countries besides England and the U.S., who recognized California's rich potential were France and Russia. All recognized the weakness of Mexican rule, and probably entertained the idea of annexation at one time or another. Because of his position as Chief of Customs, Hartnell came in contact with many foreigners. He kept his multi-lingual expertise in practice by entertaining many of them at his home.

In 1840 came the notorious so-called Isaac Graham affair. It began when an influential padre warned Governor Alvarado that foreign settlers—primarily Americans—were plotting to overthrow the government. Alvarado took the warning seriously enough to order General Vallejo into action. He was to arrest Graham and other suspicious foreigners, who would then be deported to Mexico to stand trail for treason. Acting on orders from Vallejo, General José Castro did most of the arresting.

Thomas Larkin and a few other foreigners were spared this humiliation, and Larkin did all he could to help the prisoners before and after their arrest. Finally the prisoners were found innocent and released in Mexico. Most were returned to California, including Graham himself. Later, Graham was awarded damages from the Mexican Government.

ALSO IN 1840 the Hudson's Bay Company sought permission to establish a trading store at Yerba Buena (San Francisco). They wished to trade and trap otter and beaver skins in California waters. After Alvarado gave his permission, William G. Rae was named local manager, with James Forbes as his assistant. Both were natives of the British Isles and became good friends of the Hartnells. One settler who came into conflict with the Hudson's Bay Company was John A. Sutter.

Sutter depended on fur trapping income, and resented competition by the British-held Hudson's Bay Company. After Sutter purchased the settlement at Fort Ross from the Russians in 1841, he forbade the "Honorable Company" to trap in any adjacent waters. Though he tried to get Governor Alvarado and General Vallejo to back him up, they preferred to take a neutral stand on the vexing matter.

In 1842 came the abortive invasion of Monterey by U.S. Navy Commodore Thomas ap Catesby Jones, who thought war had been declared against Mexico. He feared a takeover by England's navy in support of Mexico and impulsively landed troops to replace the Mexican Flag with the Stars and Stripes.

It took the combined efforts of Hartnell and Thomas O. Larkin to convince him of his embarrassing error. After apologizing to local government officials, Jones withdrew his men and hired Hartnell to help draft a written apology to the new Governor, Manuel Micheltorena. Juan Alvarado had been replaced as governor by order of Mexico City, when Micheltorena landed with a small army made up of ex-convicts from Mexico.

The new governor was still in Southern California at the time, so Commodore Jones sailed there to pay his respects in person. Replacement of Alvarado came as a blow to Hartnell, who lost his lucrative position as Chief of Customs. But with the help of influential friends, he received an appointment to organize a new treasury department in Yerba Buena. This meant another move, but Hartnell needed the income desperately.

By early 1845 Governor Micheltorena had been deposed, and Pío Pico was named governor in Los Angeles. Upon returning to his Alisal ranch in March, 1846 Hartnell was surprised by a visit from Captain John C. Fremont and his company of U.S. Army "engineers," who camped there (see Fremont). Fremont had been exploring the area with permission from General José Castro. Before long Castro changed his mind and ordered Fremont and his men to leave the country. Infuriated, Fremont led his men atop Gavilan Peak, near Mission San Juan Bautista. There he raised the U.S. Flag and defied Castro for several days before retreating north to Oregon. In early July Northern California was occupied by U.S. Naval forces under Commodore Sloat and Captain Fremont.

THOUGH Hartnell had affirmed loyalty to Mexico, he refused to flee south as did some loyalists. Instead, he became editor of the *Californian*, California's first newspaper, published in Monterey by Robert Semple and Walter Colton (see Semple). Later Hartnell sailed to Honolulu to "tend to business matters." He probably did this to avoid taking sides during the war. When he returned to Monterey, California was a possession of the United States.

After being appointed Military Governor, Fremont was quick to find good use for Hartnell by hiring him as a customs official and interpreter. Upon Fremont's forced departure, Hartnell stayed on with Governor Richard Mason, operating his own ranch on the side. He also applied for U.S. Citizenship and became embroiled—as so many *Californios* did—in lengthy litigation to prove ownership of his lands.

When news of James Marshall's gold discovery in Coloma was received in Monterey in the spring of 1848, most able-bodied men rushed off to make their fortune in the gold fields. Hartnell's health had deteriorated over the years, and at age 50 he simply wasn't up to making such an arduous journey or performing the physical labor of mining gold. Instead, he completed his difficult assignment of preparing copies of current Mexican and English laws for use throughout the territory.

By then General Bennet Riley, the new Military Governor, ordered Hartnell to San Francisco. There Hartnell was to print several hundred copies of the laws for wide distribution. He found the former sleepy village of Yerba Buena a booming gold town of hastily built wood and canvas shacks. Later, he was named a delegate and translator at the Constitutional Convention called by General Riley in the fall of 1849.

After donating his Monterey house as a dormitory for Dominican nuns, Hartnell retired to his ranch. The nuns were starting a girl's school on his old property, and he immediately enrolled some of his daughters there. Shortly after, his health began to fail, and he died February 2, 1854 at the age of 56. He left his wife, Teresa, with most of the eighteen children he had fathered, the youngest a three-year-old boy.

If one were to use material wealth as a measure of success, William Hartnell would fail. He finally did acquire land, but money eluded him. The fact that he managed to support a large family for many years proves he had some earning power, but it never seemed enough. If sheer numbers of children is a criterion, Hartnell was successful indeed. One fine legacy left in his name, reflecting his pioneering work in education, is Hartnell Community College in Salinas.

BIBLIOGRAPHY

–Bancroft, Hubert H. *California Pioneer Register and Index*. Regional Publishing Co., Baltimore, MD, 1964.

–Dakin, Susanna Bryant. *The Lives of William Hartnell*. Stanford University Press, Stanford, 1949. All quotations are from this publication.

–Dakin, Susanna Bryant. *A Scotch Paisano in Los Angeles: Hugo Reid's Life in California, 1832-1852*. University of California Press, Berkeley, 1939.

–Davis, William Heath. *Seventy-Five Years in California*. John Howell Books, San Francisco, 1967.

–Harlow, Neal. *California Conquered*. University of California Press, Berkeley, 1982.

–Hague, Harlan & David J. Langum. *Thomas O. Larkin, A Life of Patriotism and Profit in Old California*. University of Oklahoma Press, Norman, 1990.

–Jackson, Sheldon G. *A British Ranchero In Old California, The Life and Times of Henry Dalton and the Rancho Azusa*. Arthur H. Clark Co., Glendale, CA, 1987.

–Phelps, William Dane. *Alta California* (Phelp's journal). Arthur H. Clark Co., Glendale, CA, 1983.

–Unruh, John D. Jr. *The Plains Across*. University of Illinois Press, Chicago, 1979.

Notes

Lansford Warren Hastings
Courtesy California Department of Parks & Recreation

LANSFORD WARREN HASTINGS

1819 – 1870

L ANSFORD HASTING'S BOOK, *The Emigrant's Guide to Oregon and California*, was first published in 1845. It sold well to those heading for Oregon, but because only nine of its 150 pages were devoted to the California Trail, few California-bound emigrants used it. And with good reason—Hastings had never traveled the trail himself.

In his book Hastings touted his infamous cutoff, or shortcut, around the south end of the Great Salt Lake. He described California as "a land of milk and honey, populated by barbarians, but soon to be displaced by a new democratic republic controlled by industrious Yankees." [1] These facts alone reflect the man's character and enormous ego, reinforced by his later unsuccessful attempts to establish "independent republics" in the Pacific Northwest, Alta California, the American Southwest and Brazil. It seems that he always coveted control of the people and the environments he chose for himself.

Details of Hastings' parentage and early life are scant. Reports indicate that his parents were New England Yankees with a Protestant English-Irish ancestry. They later emigrated to Mt. Vernon, Ohio, and had several sons. Even Lansford's birthdate is suspect; various census records show him born earlier, but 1819 seems appriopriate. At least we know he graduated from law school, for he did practice law off and on and was twice appointed a judge.

He ostensibly married Catherine McCord in the late 1830s and may have had at least one child. When Hastings decided to emigrate to Oregon in 1842, apparently two of his adolescent brothers, Daniel E. and James H., accompanied him on this overland journey. Another brother, Lyman H., joined them later in California during the gold rush. Hastings apparently left his family in Ohio. [2]

The 1842 Oregon emigration party was captained by Dr. Elijah White and piloted by famed frontiersman, Thomas Fitzpatrick, who had returned to Fort Laramie after guiding the Bartleson-Bidwell Party to Soda Springs in 1841. [3] Also along was James M. Hudspeth. Early in the journey Dr. White was overthrown as captain after an altercation, possibly involving the killing of annoying dogs. Despite his youth and obvious inexperience, Hastings was chosen to take over as captain. This may have been "the first immigrant party to Oregon," which apparently means the first to bring women and children along.

An interesting tale that allegedly took place before they crossed South Pass is worthy of note. Upon reaching Independence Rock, they stopped—as most parties did—to leave their names inscribed for posterity. Apparently Hastings and one other were doing such an inspired job that the wagon train went off and left them.

Before they realized what had happened, a band of howling hostile Indians captured them and stripped them of their clothes and other personal effects. Some of the Indians were for scalping them, but mercenary members of the tribe convinced the others that they should ransom their captives for more valuables. When they caught up with the wagon train to make their demands, crafty Tom Fitzpatrick out-talked them, managing to gain freedom for the frightened young men with some food and a few trinkets.

THE ARDUOUS JOURNEY, which ended at Oregon City in early October, opened Hasting's eyes to many possibilities existing in the Far West. While in Oregon he acted as an attorney for Dr. John McLaughlin, Chief Factor (manager) of Ft. Vancouver. After announcing in favor of an independent Pacific Coast government, Hastings organized an emigrant party to California the following spring. With him, very likely, were his brothers and James Hudspeth. This was a classic case of the far-sighted leading the myopic, because Hastings had never been to California himself. Though they fought off hostile Indians and endured the usual hardships of such travel, Hasting's self-confidence and natural abilities saw them through.

Upon reaching John A. Sutter's uncompleted fort that summer, the ebullient Hastings soon became a fast friend of Sutters'. As history proved later, they were two of a kind; both were solid entrepreneurs who saw vast opportunities in California and could scarcely wait to capitalize on them. After exploring the lower Sacramento River, Hastings admired a place outside of present Collinsville, near the confluence of the San Joaquin and Sacramento rivers. There he dreamed of establishing a town he would call Montezuma. A true visionary, he saw a chance to profit from trade that was sure to occur along that strategic stretch of the river. Though he was never successful in this venture, his vision was later verified by the eventual successful founding of other towns in the area.

Along with many others, Hastings believed that California should shed Mexican rule and become an independent republic. Once this was accomplished, the American settlers hoped to persuade the native

Californians to embrace protection from the United States. This would secure it from the real threat of British or French domination, which some *Californios* and a few settlers from Great Britain or France would have preferred.

Of course Hastings saw himself as a great leader in the new republic. He even discussed the possibility of becoming its first president. In 1844 he sailed to Mexico on his way back to the East Coast. He then undertook a hazardous overland trek across Mexico to board a ship on the Gulf of Mexico, probably at Tampico or Veracruz. It is unclear where Hastings landed in the U.S.; he could have sailed to New York or Boston. A logical alternative is New Orleans, where he might well have taken a riverboat upstream to his previous home in Ohio.

Upon his arrival, he took time to write his *Emigrant's Guide.* Unable to find a publisher, he went on a lecture tour throughout the Midwest to raise money to publish it himself. It was published at Cincinnati in early 1845 and sold better then expected. As events later unfolded, Hastings probably met Samuel Brannan in New York, where the Mormon leader was planning to sail to California with a ship-load of Mormon emigrants. Perhaps Brannan had read Hasting's book and looked him up. However it happened, Hastings was influenced to lay the groundwork for a Mormon settlement Brannan wanted in California. It seemed a natural for Hasting's dream of Montezuma.

As stated previously, Hasting's new publication described a shortcut to California. Known as the Hastings Cutoff, it eliminated a long detour to Fort Hall; by coincidence, it roughly followed a route John C. Fremont was to take during the fall of 1845, leading around the southern end of the Great Salt Lake before heading west across the salt desert. Some said the book was "optimistic to the point of being irresponsible." Historian Hubert H. Bancroft described it as "worthless."

Though Hastings had never traveled the California Trail himself, he was anxious to try it. He traveled part of it during the summer of 1845, when he led a ten-man party, including Robert Semple, from Missouri to Sutter's Fort (see Semple). They rode horseback, leading pack mules, and took no wagons. Fort Bridger (Wyoming) was the jumping off place for his proposed new shortcut.

IT WAS LATE in the season, and though Hastings had detoured there—ostensibly to avoid hostile Indians—he failed to convince his less adventurous followers to try his new shorter route. Instead, they chose the safer Fort Hall route. The northerly trek had delayed them, but Hastings hurried them along to the Humboldt River. They barely made it across the lofty Sierra Nevada before snow closed Truckee Pass, reaching Sutter's Fort on Christmas Day. To his chagrin, Hastings had brought with him only ten settlers after promising Sutter he would be bringing nearly a thousand.

Finally Hastings got a chance to travel his new shortcut, when he and frontiersmen James Clyman, James Hudspeth and Caleb Greenwood led a pack-train of eastern-bound emigrants from Johnson's Ranch (near present-day Wheatland, CA) in the spring of 1846 (see Clyman & Greenwood). After splitting up on the Humboldt River, Greenwood led most of the travelers—including the women and children—northerly to Fort Hall, while Clyman, Hastings and Hudspeth took the new route east to Fort Bridger. They arrived there in early July, confirming that the new route could save horsemen weeks of travel time. But could travelers make it with wagons?

JOHN C. FREMONT had told U.S. Consul Thomas O. Larkin about this shortcut when he arrived in Monterey earlier in the year (see Fremont). Word of Fremont's comments probably reached Hastings before he left California, adding to his credibility. He made the most of it by spreading the word everywhere he could. Good money could be made by guiding wagon trains; Hastings wanted his share. More importantly, perhaps, he wanted the fame and admiration it might gain him.

While it was true that no one had traveled his route with wagons, Hastings was sure it could be done. James Clyman and well-known mountain man Joseph R. Walker were skeptical, and cautioned the emigrants against trying it (see Walker). Nevertheless, Hastings sent messages east along the trail that he would meet wagon trains at Fort Bridger and guide them on the new shorter route. This sounded good to some of them, and by mid-July 1846 he had recruited several parties. At the same time, Caleb Greenwood was at Fort Hall promoting the California Trail to emigrants bound for Oregon. He had worked out some kind of deal with John A. Sutter to steer emigrants to his settlement and hoped to collect hefty piloting fees for doing so.

Among Hasting's recruits was the Harlan-Young Party with around 200 people and 40 wagons. Their departure from Fort Bridger was delayed while they waited for another group, the Donner-Reed Party. James Bridger and his partner, Louis Vasquez, promoted the new route because it brought them business. Even so, they wondered whether wagons could make it. Every day counted, but still the Donner Party had not arrived. On July 20 Hastings gave in to pleas from the Harlans to get started, and they headed southwest on the new route. To his credit, Hastings did leave instructions at Fort Bridger regarding the route to be followed.

Imagine how the Donner party felt when they reached the fort a few days later and found Hastings gone. The enraged Donners sent James Reed on ahead to overtake Hastings, demanding that he wait and guide them as promised (see Reed). Reed did catch up, but rather than delay the Harlans and others he was piloting, Hastings gave Reed rather vague instructions for a better wagon route and continued on his way. When Reed returned with the bad news, most of the discouraged emigrants decided to head north on the "tried and true" Fort Hall trail. But Reed and the Donners were made of sterner stuff, choosing to follow the new route. They were already behind, but hadn't Hastings assured them the new route would save time? They left the fort at the end of July.

Though Hasting's followers endured terrible hardships crossing the rugged Wasatch Mountains through steep, narrow Weber Canyon, they finally got all but one of their wagons safely onto the salt plain east of the Great Salt Lake by August 6th. On the same day the Donners found a note left on the trail by Hastings to send a rider ahead for instructions. Again Reed rode off to catch up with the elusive trail blazer.

Overtaking him south of the lake, all Reed got were instructions to avoid taking the wagons down Weber Canyon. Instead, they were to try a different route that Hastings merely pointed out to the perplexed young man. With that Hastings rode off, leaving Reed on his own. It seemed that Hastings had abandoned the Donner Party to their fate. Perhaps he felt more loyalty to his earlier followers, knowing that their safety would be jeopardized by delay. In retrospect, his decision proved a good one for them.

The frustrated Donner Party spent days scouting a route. Even then it had to be hacked out by hand, sapping precious time and energy from the discouraged emigrants. By the time they reached the salt flats at the end of August, they were far behind. Now that the terrain was flatter, they should make better time. But would they? Lack of water and unexpected mountain barriers made for slow going indeed. When they finally reached the well-traveled Humboldt Trail in present Nevada, they were the last emigrant party of the season. Hasting's "shortcut" had proven a fiasco.

THE DONNER PARTY tragedy is a story in itself and will not be repeated here (see Tamsen Donner). About half of the party perished from starvation after becoming trapped by snow at Truckee Lake (now Donner Lake). Most of the survivors didn't get out until rescuers reached them during the spring of 1847. As for Hastings and the Harlan Party, they made it across Truckee Pass before snow blocked it, arriving at Sutter's Fort in late fall 1846.

Part of the blame lies with the Donners and others, who were determined to travel in large heavily-laden wagons against the advice of experts. They also took a foolhardy risk on a new untried trail despite many warnings. Hastings, of course, had to accept some of the blame, and it tarnished his reputation forever. Incidentally, the wagon trail blazed by the Donners over the Wasatch Mountains to the Great Salt Lake was used by the Mormons when they emigrated there a year later.

HASTINGS was disappointed that he had been away during the Bear Flag Revolt in mid-June 1846; he felt confident that he would have been one of its leaders. But now that war had been declared with Mexico, the short-lived Bear Flag had been replaced by the Stars and Stripes all over California. Nevertheless, Major John C. Fremont was recruiting volunteers to fight rebellious Mexicans in Southern California.

When Hastings offered his services, he was appointed a captain in Fremont's forces. Before reporting for duty, Hastings and John Bidwell helped John Sutter lay out a new settlement about two miles down from Sutter's Sacramento River embarcadero. It was on higher ground, not as vulnerable to flooding as the embarcadero area. Sutter wanted to name it Montezuma; however, because Hastings had reserved that name for his location on the lower Sacramento river, it was named Sutterville. By the fall of 1846 Hastings had acquired land at Montezuma, where he built an adobe house. The old adobe still stands today under sponsorship of the Solano County Historical Society.

Hastings also acquired land at Sutterville, which was apparently shared with at least one of his brothers. It was said that Hastings promoted Montezuma and (or) Sutterville as possible havens for large numbers of Mormons he expected to arrive. Morman newspaper publisher Samuel Brannan must have convinced him this was so, for Brannan was attempting to entice more Mormons to California (see Brannan). He had already brought a shipload of over 200 Mormons to Yerba Buena (San Francisco) in late July. But as things turned out, the only Mormon settlement attempted was New Hope, located near the confluence of the Stanislaus and San Joaquin rivers (present Ripon). It was abandoned a year later after being flooded out.

In mid-October the U.S. warship *Congress* was loaded with 160 volunteers to reinforce Captain A. Gillespie's beleaguered troops at San Pedro. A few others, including Major Fremont and Hastings, boarded the chartered ship *Sterling* to gather horses at Santa Barbara. Along the way the two ships were separated, and Fremont got a message that U.S. forces in the Los Angeles area had suffered a serious setback with loss of all their livestock.

Rather than continuing south, Fremont ordered the *Sterling* to Monterey. He then sent Captain Hastings to San Jose with a few men to assist Charles Weber in acquiring badly needed horses and tack (see Weber). Weber proved rather ruthless in obtaining these vital things, virtually stripping local ranchers of horses and drawing their wrath. This and other grievances set off the "Battle of La Natividad," shortly before

Fremont's overland departure for Los Angeles in late November. The fighting stopped just outside Los Angeles in early January 1847, when the Mexicans capitulated to Fremont and Gen. Andres Pico signed the Treaty of Cahuenga.

The following spring Sutter sent Hastings and others to scout the countryside for a suitable site for a sawmill he intended to build. Ultimately, a site in Cullomah Valley (now Coloma) was chosen and James Marshall began construction of the sawmill in early autumn 1847 (see Marshall). By then Hastings had gone to San Francisco, where he bought some real estate and began practicing law. In May 1847 he was elected to the School Board, and in September he became a judge of the Northern District. After James W. Marshall's epic gold discovery at Sutter's sawmill in late January 1848, Hastings went to the gold fields. He must have done fairly well, for in July he married 19-year-old Charlotte Catherine Toler at Sutter's Fort. The daughter of Hopeful Toler, who opposed the marriage, Charlotte's mother was a native of Venezuela and probably a Catholic. Apparently Hasting's first wife, Catherine, had died or divorced him by then.

Later Hastings formed a partnership with John Sutter to open a miner's supply store in present Coloma. They called it "Sutter, Hastings & Co., Developers of Mining Properties and Dealers in Mining Supplies." It was housed in the double cabin that formerly sheltered the Peter Wimmer family and the sawmill workers during construction of Sutter's Sawmill. An ad in the Sacramento *Placer Times* dated May 12, 1849, read as follows:

> L.W. Hastings & Co. have on hand at their store in Coloma about half a mile this side of the saw-mill, and fifteen miles this side of the Middle Fork [American River], an extensive assortment of everything used by the gold washers, which they will sell so low that the miners may well save themselves the trouble of packing from the low country. Coloma is distant from Sutter's Fort forty-one miles.

Sutter was no longer a partner in the business when that ad ran. Toward the end of 1848 he had fallen on hard times and had sold out his interests in the sawmill and the store, during which he had bitter words for Hastings: "The store made money," he said, "but I lost. Hastings was a bad man." Sutter then left the fort and moved to his ranch on the Feather River—a retreat he called the Hock Farm. Hastings later sold his store to a lucky "49'er" who had struck it rich near Coloma.

As Sutter's fortunes continued to decline, he brought his son, John Junior (called August), from Europe to assist him in dealing with his onerous financial difficulties. Sutter Sr. and Hastings were still promoting land sales at Sutterville, where Hastings had a personal interest with land of his own. His brothers, Daniel and James, who eventually ran the American Union Hotel and a stockyard there, also had personal stakes. [4] But other factions, including Samuel Brannan, convinced August Sutter that a town named Sacramento should be laid out adjacent to the embarcadero.

Opportunist Samuel Brannan began promoting it, along with many others who thought Sutterville was too far removed from the trade center surrounding the embarcadero. Meanwhile, John Sutter had turned over control of his shaky business affairs to his son, August, and brought his long-suffering wife and the rest of his family from Europe to live with him at the Hock Farm.

ATTORNEY Peter Burnett was hired to assist August Sutter in selling his father's land (see Burnett). Later, John Sutter claimed that his son had allowed himself to be influenced by Samuel Brannan and others, who had conspired to steal his land. Sutter Sr. was especially upset by his son's abandonment of Sutterville and the subdividing of land surrounding the oft flooded *embarcadero*. Because Hastings had a substantial financial stake in Sutterville, he joined in the fight to save it.

August Sutter had little use for Hastings, thinking he was taking advantage of his father. Hastings thought August was doing the same; in fact, at one point, Hastings got in a heated argument with August Sutter and threatened to kill him. [5] But at least he and John Sutter agreed about Sutterville. Finally Sutter Sr. got so exasperated he fired both August and Peter Burnett. He then hired General Albert J. Winn to handle his property sales. August Sutter moved to Mexico a short time later. A strange twist to the story is quoted from a curious statement made by John Sutter to historian H. H. Bancroft in 1876: "Had I not been snowed in at Coloma [doubtful but possible], Sacramento never, never would have been built!"

After being hired by Sutter, General Winn allegedly borrowed between five and ten thousand dollars from Hastings and Samuel Hensley (in Sutter's name), with interest at 10% per month. When the amount due reached $35,000, Hastings and Hensley attempted to collect by attaching Sutter's precious Hock Farm. They finally accepted Sutter's note for the amount due and settled it by obtaining Sacramento land from him. In July 1849 Charlotte Hastings gave birth to William W. in Sutterville. After returning to his Montezuma adobe with his family, Hastings operated a ferryboat from about present Collinsville, across the river to the present Contra Costa County. Combined with his real estate ventures, this put him well on his way toward accumulating the wealth and power he had envisioned from the very beginning.

During the fall of 1849, U.S. Military Governor Bennet Riley called for a Constitutional Convention to be held in Monterey. Lansford Hastings and John Sutter Sr. were selected to represent Sutterville and Sacramento; after Sutter's legal difficulties with Hastings, this must have been a bitter pill for Sutter to swallow. But all was forgiven after a long dissertation about state boundaries was endured, after which thirty-year-old Hastings introduced Sutter as follows:

"I understand that my friend, Captain Sutter, desires to speak on this question. The house, I have no doubt, will be much pleased to hear him." [6]

Afterward, when Sutter ran for governor, he was defeated by Peter Burnett. As a delegate, Hastings worked hard to ensure that capital punishment would not be permitted under the state constitution; however, his efforts ended in failure.

Hastings returned to Sacramento following the convention to practice law, joined by his wife and son. In 1850 his brother, Lyman, arrived from the East; in September Lansford must have suffered financial reverses, for at least some of his Sutterville property was sold at a sheriff's sale. Another child, Isobel, was born to Hastings in early 1851 or late 1852, followed by Henry Clay a year later. Little Henry died in 1854, to be replaced by Irving B. the following year. Another daughter, Amelia, was born at Sutterville in June 1857. Most family information comes from census rolls, courtesy Julie Hastings-Barnes (see bibliography).

By 1858 Hastings had traded his abandoned Montezuma adobe for four mules and other personal property worth $1,000, and the family had emigrated to Fort Yuma, Arizona territory. A notice dated March 1, 1858 in the *Sacramento Union* follows:

Fort Yuma correspondence, Feb. 9, 1858: Judge L. W. Hastings, and his interesting family, late of Sutterville, arrived here some time since, and intend making this his permanent residence.

After settling in Arizona City (present Yuma), Hastings became postmaster, practiced law, and in 1860 was appointed Judge of the 3rd Judicial District. This may not have been as important as it sounds, for Arizona City was thus described in the *Los Angeles Star,* May 21, 1859:

Arizona City consists of one store and a boarding house with a population of 10 or 15 persons, exclusive of Indians.

Another son, Henry T., was born there in 1860. Even before then Hastings was working hard to have his little corner of the country declared an independant territory, claiming that the U. S. was collecting taxes without allowing them adequate representation. And though he was a Northerner, Hastings began working for the Confederacy after the

Civil War began in April 1861, plotting to annex Southern California and Arizona Territory.

On August 10, 1861, Charlotte Hastings gave birth to another daughter, probably Elizabeth, in San Pedro, California. This event apparently took place while the family was enroute to San Francisco. Tragically, Charlotte died in Alameda County per the following notice in the *Daily Evening Bulletin*, San Francisco:

> Alameda County, died 27 August 1861 Charlotte Catherine, wife of Judge L. W. Hastings, 33 years old, leaves a brother, her husband, and 5 young children.

Records indicate that Charlotte had seven children; one (Henry Clay) died in 1854; another child must also have died before 1861. Following his wife's death, Hastings apparently placed his daughter, Isobel, in a Catholic convent in Benicia; his other children were either placed under care of friends or stayed with their father. [8]

In 1863 he journeyed to Mazatlan, where he apparently made another cross-country journey to the Gulf of Mexico, and on to Texas and Louisiana. In December Hastings met with Confederate leaders in Richmond to present his grandiose plans to recruit troops in California—ostensibly as gold prospectors—to take over Arizona Territory. President Jefferson Davis then nominated him as a major in the Confederate Army; his commission was approved by the Confederate Senate in February 1864.

Ironically, his brothers Daniel and James fought on the Union side, with James becoming a prisoner at the dreaded Andersonville prison camp. In 1867 James was living in Latrobe, California; he was living in Ohio when he died in 1878. Daniel returned to Sutterville after the war, where he was accidentally killed in 1867 with a shotgun blast to the head. He left a wife and seven children. [9]

LANSFORD HASTINGS apparently remarried in the late 1860s, for he reportedly had another daughter, Mrs. Anna McPherson, who died in Yuma in 1907. After the South lost the war in 1865, Hastings journeyed to Brazil to obtain permission from the government to establish a colony for "high-toned conquered people" who could not accept Union rule. In 1866 he chose a large parcel in the province of Para, near the junction of the Tapojos River and the mighty Amazon (present Santarem). He returned to Alabama in the U.S. the following year, where he published *Emigrants Guide to Brazil*. In Montgomery he gathered 115 ex-patriots, who sailed with him to Brazil in 1867.

By 1876 the colony consisted of 22 families, with more than a hundred active workers. Perhaps Hastings was still pursuing his dream of Montezuma, where he could rule unopposed. Unfortunately Hastings never lived to see his fanciful dream come true; he reportedly died at sea on another voyage from the U. S. to Brazil in 1870 at age 51. His daughter, Isobel, died later that same year in San Francisco. Whether Hastings was a charlatan or an enlightened visionary is open to question. Historian H. H. Bancroft said of him.

> He was an intelligent, active man, never without some grand scheme on hand, not overburdened with conscientious scruples, but never getting caught in anything very disreputable.

This quotation sums up his life fairly and succinctly.

BIBLIOGRAPHY

–Bancroft, Hubert H. *History of California.* History Co., San Francisco, 1886. Republished, Wallace Hebberd, Santa Barbara, CA, 1966.

–Biographical files re L. W. Hastings, State Library, Sacramento, Ca.

–Bryant, Edwin. *What I Saw in California.* University of Nebraska Press, Lincoln, 1985.

–Clyman, James. *Journal Of A Mountain Man.* Mt. Press Pub. Co., Missoula, 1984.

–Corning, Howard McKinley, ed. *Dictionary of Oregon History.* Binfords & Mort, Portland, OR, 1956.

–DeVoto, Bernard. *The Year of Decision-1846.* Houghton Mifflin Co., Boston, 1942

–Dillon, Richard. *Fool's Gold.* Coward McCann, Inc., New York, 1967. [5-6]

–Gay, Theressa. *James Marshall, The Discoverer of Gold in California.* Talisman Press, Georgetown, CA, 1967.

–Gilbert, Bil. *Westering Man, The Life of Joseph Walker.* University of Oklahoma Press, Norman, 1990.

–Hague, Harlan & Langum, David J. *Thomas O. Larkin.* University of Oklahoma Press, Norman, 1990. [1]

–Harlow, Neal. *California Conquered.* University of California Press, Berkeley, 1982.

–Hastings-Barnes, Julie (great-grand-daughter of L. W. Hasting's brother, Daniel E.). Personal interview and family records, April 1993. [2,4,7-9]

–Lewis, Oscar. *Sutter's Fort: Gateway to the Gold Fields,* Prentice-Hall, Inc., Englewood Cliffs, NJ, 1966.

–Stewart, George R. *The California Trail.* McGraw-Hill, New York, 1962. Reprinted by Bison Books, University of Nebraska Press, 1983. [3]

–Stewart, George R. *Ordeal By Hunger.* Houghton Mifflin Co., Boston, 1936.

–Unruh, John D. Jr. *The Plains Across.* University of Illinois Press, Chicago, 1982.

Margaret Hecox
Courtesy Special Collections, University of California, Santa Cruz

— 21—

MARGARET M. HECOX

1816 – 1908

L IFE REALLY BEGAN for 20-year-old Margaret Hamer in July 1836
when she married Rev. Adna Hecox, a 30-year-old widower and
temperance leader from Michigan. Raised and educated in
Pennsylvania, Margaret went with her new husband to Apple River,
Illinois. There Hecox found work as a lead miner and carpenter to augment his scant income as a licensed preacher.

Facing a bleak future in 1846 with four children to raise, they
agreed to make a new start in the golden land called California. By early
spring they had joined a small emigrant party led by Charles A. Imus,
and were heading west with their meager worldly goods packed in a
farm wagon pulled by plodding oxen. The overland trek from Illinois to
St. Joseph, Missouri, offered a chance to trail-break themselves and their
oxen before crossing the Missouri River by ferry into Indian country.
Incessant rain made overland travel miserable, when large companies of
Mormons traveling ahead left the trail a muddy quagmire. Once the
faster-moving Imus Party passed the Mormons, they made better time
to their destination in St. Louis. By mid-May there were 23 wagons in
the party and Joseph Aram had replaced Charles Imus as captain.

Margaret Hecox's memoirs show her flair for writing as she describes
a war dance put on by young Indian warriors for the wide-eyed emigrants:

> When the warriors had ceased congratulating themselves upon
> their great doings they were cheered by their companions with sav-
> age grunts and yells. And I, a poor weak woman, sitting in the
> shelter of the darkened wagon, hugging my baby to my bosom,
> with three badly scared little girls crouched at my feet, shed bitter
> tears at the thought of the old home. I wondered what had pos-
> sessed my husband, anyway, that he should have thought of bring-
> ing us away out through this God-forsaken country. I feared that
> we were to be scalped or taken prisoners before morning....

After reaching Independence Rock on July 3rd, they stayed to celebrate Independence Day and climbed the monolith to add their names to those on top. Near that famous landmark Margaret encountered a stampeding herd of buffalo:

> In a moment they were upon us. It was not a large band, perhaps a hundred or more. They usually traveled by the thousands. The oxen were terribly excited and reared and plunged in an effort to break away...Fearing for the safety of my children, I attempted to reach our wagon, near the head of the train. A large cow buffalo made directly for me. I crawled under our wagon and the cow tried to follow me. I commenced kicking her in the head. But somebody's rifle dispatched her before she had a chance to injure me....

After crossing the Continental Divide, they caught up with the larger Donner-Reed Party on the Green River. Traveling toward Fort Bridger together, they were met by Lansford Hastings, who tried to talk them into using his new shortcut around the south end of the Great Salt Lake. Instead, Captain Charles Imus heeded advice from frontiersman James Clyman, who had just returned from California with Hastings on this shortcut and didn't think wagons could make it (see Hastings, Reed & Clyman chapters).

Caleb Greenwood, who also left California with Hastings and Clyman, had stayed on the well-traveled trail to Fort Hall. After the Imus Party refused Hastings' offer to guide them, they hired Greenwood to pilot them on the California Trail from Fort Hall. The old whitebearded mountain man was returning to California with several of his grown children (see Greenwood). The Donner-Reed party had fallen behind schedule and chose the "Hastings Cutoff" with the hope of making up time. They were to meet Hastings later at Fort Bridger in present-day southwest Wyoming.

WHEN THE Imus Party reached the infamous Humboldt Sink and learned they were ahead of Hastings and the Donners, they knew they had made the right decision. Here Greenwood and his children left them; apparently the wagons were traveling too slowly for Greenwood. He intended to travel hard and cross over Truckee Pass well before winter snows built up. Greenwood left instructions about the trail, and apparently Chief Truckee himself offered to guide the Imus group across.

Upon reaching the intimidating granite precipices looming over Truckee Lake (Donner Lake), the group scouted out an easier trail over the difficult pass, via Coldstream and Emigrant Canyons. When it became better known it displaced the old trail. Later, when they camped on the Bear River, some thought they had discovered gold when shiny, golden particles stuck to clothes they were washing in the river. It was probably mica, but some swore they had found gold.

They reached Johnson's Ranch October 1, 1846, ahead of the Harlan-Young Party, which was being guided by Lansford Hastings. Hastings had left the Donner-Reed Party to its own devices when they were late arriving at Fort Bridger. When the Donners met with disaster after becoming trapped by snow at Truckee Lake, Hastings never lived it down. In retrospect, his decision to leave on time with the Harlan-Young Party probably saved them from sharing the awful fate of the Donners. Another passage from Margaret Hecox's memoirs is worthy of repeating:

> It was on the first day of October, 1846, that our eyes rested upon the Sacramento Valley. It was four o'clock in the afternoon when our train halted on an elevation, while our wondering eyes looked down upon the new land, our future home. We were silent a moment in thanksgiving. Then from the throats of those weary emigrants burst forth a loud and long "hooray" which echoed through the hills. We dropped to our knees and gave thanks to God, who had watched over us and brought us safely through the perils and privations of the long journey.

A short time later they were approached by some men from John C. Fremont's California Volunteers, who were recruiting men to fight the Mexicans. The Imus Party had arrived just in time to become embroiled in the latter part of the Mexican War, and most of the young men agreed to join Fremont's Volunteers.

When they arrived at Sutter's Fort a few days later, John A. Sutter greeted them personally. Because of the Mexican War, the fort had been taken over by Captain Fremont for use as his headquarters. The place was crammed with war refugees, so Fremont suggested that the new arrivals should head for Mission Santa Clara to seek sanctuary there.

Since the missions had been secularized by the Mexicans in the late 1830's, they had fallen into disrepair. Fremont said they should hurry there to fortify the old buildings in case the Mexicans decided to attack. Fifty-seven of them, including the Hecoxes, took their wagons and made their way through San Jose to the broken-down mission in mid-October.

Faced with a leaky roof and filthy conditions generally, they threw up hasty barricades and tried to make themselves comfortable. Many of the men had joined Fremont by then, enticed by pay and rations; however, a 35-man military unit was formed with Joseph Aram as captain. Eventually about 140 emigrants were living at Santa Clara under hardship conditions.

While hostile Mexicans never actually attacked, they allegedly tried to starve the emigrants. If not for the kindness of *rancheros* Ignacio Alviso and Maria Bernal, the Mexican wife of George Bellomy, they probably would have starved. Alviso provided wheat, which they ground into coarse flour with a coffee grinder. Maria smuggled in whatever foodstuffs she could, and another benevolent *ranchero* drove in beef cattle when he could.

IN LATE November George Harlan with other members of the Harlan-Young Party arrived at Santa Clara seeking refuge. With them was the Peter Wimmer family. Apparently this group brought typhoid fever, for within a short time Harlan's wife and Samuel Young's infant son died from the dreaded malady. Others, including Samuel Young and Adna Hecox, also suffered from it. While they managed to recover, others were not so fortunate and the death-toll mounted.

Francisco Sanchez, acting Commandant of Mexican forces in Yerba Buena (San Francisco), had willingly surrendered to American forces early in the occupation with the understanding that Mexican citizens would remain unmolested. But Fremont's California Volunteers were in desperate need of horses, saddles and other supplies, which could only be found on local ranches.

Though German immigrant Charles Weber had taken Mexican citizenship earlier, he became a sergeant in Fremont's Volunteers and was charged with the onerous task of obtaining the necessary horses and supplies (see Weber). With help from Lansford Hastings and other zealous followers, Weber and his men virtually raided Mexican ranches throughout the area, stripping them of the needed livestock and supplies. For payment Weber's men issued vouchers to be honored by the U.S. Government. Few were so honored.

Naturally Weber's high-handed methods infuriated the Mexicans, who united behind Francisco and Antonio Sanchez to form a militant band of hostile volunteers. Later, after Fremont and most of his men headed for Southern California, the so-called Sanchez militia of about 100 men became increasingly belligerent. When they threatened the refugees at Mission Santa Clara, Captain Aram's men had to stand around-the-clock watches. But because of the typhoid fever epidemic, many of the men were too ill to stand watch. Margaret Hecox and a few other women had to fill in, as she relates:

> I was always timid; a bug could frighten me into a spasm. I couldn't stand idly by, however, when danger threatened and my services were needed. I knew that if I couldn't shoot straight I could at least sound the alarm. The soldiers who were not sick were almost dead from lack of sleep. I put on my husband's hat and overcoat, then grasping our old flintlock between my shaking hands I went forth in the darkness to the corner of the wall assigned to me....A terrible feeling of loneliness and desolation held me in its grip....

By the time the Sanchez militia decided to attack the mission on January 2, 1847, the emigrants had been reinforced by elements of the U.S. Navy with one piece of field artillery and Charles Weber's Rangers. After a few shots from the field-piece, the Mexicans retreated with only a horse and two or three men wounded on either side. Later this was referred to as the "Battle of Santa Clara." Compared to other battles, it pales to insignificance.

After hostilities in Southern California ceased, Sanchez surrendered his forces to the Americans and the fighting was over. The typhoid epidemic took a much larger toll of Americans than the war in Northern California, leaving fourteen dead at Santa Clara alone. Though he was ill himself, Adna Hecox was kept busy reading scriptures over their pitiful remains.

The Hecoxes left the dreary mission in the spring of 1847 with their "patched up old covered wagon" and headed for Santa Cruz, where they had decided to settle. Eight days later they reached the tiny village of Soquel—just to the south of Santa Cruz—where they camped near the sea in a tiny unused cabin. After their depressing winter at Santa Clara, springtime in Soquel must have seemed like paradise.

Before long Adna Hecox had a carpentry job with Michael Lodge, building a sawmill there. Next they leased a building, which Margaret Hecox turned into a boarding house for the sawmill workers. When word of James Marshall's gold discovery reached them during the spring of 1848, Hecox moved his wife and family to Santa Cruz and set off for the gold country with nearly everyone else. This event is well described in Margaret Hecox's memoirs:

> Mr. Hecox was one of a group who first discovered the rich mines of Hangtown, now Placerville. He and his two partners picked up six pounds of gold in one day. Later he and Captain Aram took a load of goods to the mines and cleared $2,200 on the transaction. . . [Adna] came home shortly afterwards and suffered a long illness.

AFTER RECOVERING his health, Hecox again returned to the mines. By then there were seven Hecox children, and the family was prospering. Before California was admitted to the Union in September 1850, Hecox served as the last alcalde (mayor & justice of the peace) in Santa Cruz and was active in many civic affairs there. Later he became County Treasurer. Hecox was always active in temperance activities, which must have put him at odds with Isaac Graham, a notorious liquor distiller (see Graham). Graham also operated a sawmill in the Santa Cruz area for several years and was often in trouble with government officials. While serving as Santa Cruz's last alcalde, Adna Hecox tangled with Graham's son, Jesse, ordering him to post a $1,000 bond to guarantee good behavior after Jesse made threats against his father's in-laws. After carrying out these threats in a shooting spree, during which one man was killed and a woman wounded, Jesse Graham fled the country.

WHEN A LIGHTHOUSE was constructed at Santa Cruz in 1869, Adna Hecox was named the light-keeper. Ten years later the lighthouse had to be moved inland 300 feet because of erosion. After Adna's death in 1883, he was succeeded by his daughter, Laura, who operated the beacon until her retirement at age 62. One writer in 1904 described Laura:

> A most pleasant little woman, standing guard at the front door, armed with a big feather duster. Everywhere inside the lighthouse, everything was spotless and speckless. To keep it that way, Miss Hecox often gave visitors' apparel a deft whisking before admitting them inside [2].

Not once during her 33-year tenure did Laura allow the lamp to fail. The Hecox family lived in the lighthouse for 46 years, during which three members died and three others were married there. Margaret Hecox lived there until her death in 1908, just short of her 93rd birthday.

The following eulogy, written by T.H. d'Estrella, was printed in the *California News* in February 1908:

> On Saturday afternoon, January 18th, 1908, Mrs. M.M. Hecox, the grandmother of Douglas Tilden, California's widely famed deaf-mute sculptor, breathed her last peacefully at the Santa Cruz lighthouse where she had resided for nearly forty years, her husband being the first keeper and her youngest daughter holding that position ever since.
>
> Mrs. Hecox was one of the noblest women that ever breathed under the glorious skies of California. Her many deeds of kindness have been recounted not only in her home circle, but also by the rich and the poor, the strong and the weak, regardless of race...visits to her home by deaf people have always been of particular interest to her, so that we can almost claim her as "Grandma," as her famous grandson, Douglas Tilden, does...She leaves five daughters and two sons, eleven grandchildren and ten great-grandchildren.

A tribute like that is hard to follow. What can be said is that the Hecox's certainly earned a prominent place in our pioneer hierarchy. The old lighthouse was torn down in 1948 to be replaced by an automated, unmanned tower. In 1867 the Mark Abbott Memorial Lighthouse was constructed by the Abbott family. One of the few privately built lighthouses in the country, it now contains a surfing museum.

BIBLIOGRAPHY

—Bancroft, Hubert H. *Register of Pioneer Inhabitants of California, 1542 to 1848.* Dawson's Book Shop, Los Angeles, 1964.

—Faragher, John Mack. *Women And Men On the Overland Trail.* Yale University Press, New Haven and London, 1979.

—Gay, Theressa. *James Marshall, A Biography.* Talisman Press, Georgetown, CA, 1967.

—Hecox, Margaret M. (Her memoirs, edited & intro. by Richard H. Dillon). *California Caravan.* Harlan-Young Press, San Jose, CA, 1966. Quotations taken from this publication.

—Levy, JoAnn. "Under Siege at Mission Santa Clara." *The Californians,* Volume 7, Number 4, 1990. [1-2] Michael Sherrell, publisher, Sebastopol, CA,

—Perry, Frank. *Lighthouse Point..* GBH Publishing, Soquel, CA, 1982.

—Regnery, Dorothy F. *The Battle of Santa Clara.* Smith and McKay Printing Co., San Jose, CA, 1978.

—Rowland, Leon. *Santa Cruz, The Early Years.* Paper Vision Press, Santa Cruz, 1980.

—Stewart, George R. *The California Trail.* University of Nebraska Press, Lincoln, 1962.

The William Ide Adobe:Courtesy California Department of Parks & Recreation

— 22 —

WILLIAM BROWN IDE

1796 – 1852

O THER THAN HISTORIANS and picnickers who may have visited the State Park named in his honor, few people know about William Ide's contributions to early California. His parents, Lemuel Ide and the former Sarah Stone, were of English ancestry and natives of New England. They married in 1793, and William was born three years later in Rutland, Massachusetts. An older brother, Simeon, had been born two years earlier.

Later the Ides moved to Vermont, where twin daughters, Sarah and Mary were born in 1798. Though Lemuel Ide was a good carpenter, his finances plummeted and he was forced to leave his family under the care of his wife's brother. Even before then little William Ide had been temporarily "adopted" by Rev. Isaac Beals. He lived with the reverend and his wife until age nine.

Meanwhile, Lemuel Ide had been moving around to find work. Finally his finances improved enough to allow purchase of a small farm. In 1805 he was able to re-unite his family there, and four years later he was elected to the Vermont State Legislature. William learned his father's carpentry trade as a youngster, getting a better-than-average education along the way. By age twenty-three he was skilled enough to build a house for his brother, Simeon. He was also a surveyor and good with the English language.

In 1820 William Ide married Susan G. Haskell, settling in Massachusetts. Six children later he gave in to his itchy feet and began moving west, first to Kentucky, then Ohio and finally Illinois, where he bought a farm just outside Springfield. By 1845, Ide was pushing fifty and dissatisfied with his lot in life. He made a meager living teaching school but wanted something better for himself and his family.

Ide had heard that good free land was available in Oregon; maybe this was the opportunity he had been seeking. He sold the farm early that spring and used the proceeds to buy two custom-made wagons to go with one he had. He bought livestock and supplies, and by early

April 1845 the family set off in their three wagons for Independence, Missouri. There were thirteen of them by then, including several hired men who worked for their meals and an expense-paid trip west.

Arriving in Independence a month later, they joined a large wagon train piloted by Joe Meek and captained by John Grigsby. Because of his farm experience, Ide found himself appointed chief herdsman over hundreds of oxen and beef cattle—a taxing job indeed. By the time the wagon train reached Fort Hall it was called the Grigsby-Ide Party; Ide considered himself and his entourage able to carry on alone if necessary.

At Fort Hall they met the colorful old mountain man, Caleb Greenwood (see Greenwood). He appeared to be an agent for John A. Sutter, who was encouraging settlers to come to Sutter's Fort. "Old Greenwood" had been sent to guide anyone wishing to take the chance of getting wagons through to California. He was assisted by two of his half-Crow Indian sons. After absorbing Greenwood's fascinating sales talk like dry sponges, Ide and others, including the Jarvis Bonney family and Jacob Snyder, chose to follow the fledgling California Trail. Ide's daughter, Sarah Ide Healy, who was eighteen at the time, wrote a vivid description of the Greenwoods:

> Our pilot's name was 'Old Greenwood', and his son John, (whose mother was a Crow Indian). They were mountain men, and dressed the same as Indians...None of our company were killed by the Indians; but John Greenwood, son of the pilot, shot down an Indian by the road-side, and afterwards boasted of it...I was more afraid of these two men than of the wild Indians.

Sarah Healy goes on to describe the most difficult part of the journey when the party hauled their wagons over the granite walls above Truckee Lake (now Donner Lake):

> At night we camped at the foot of the rocky mountain—the Sierra Nevada; and were told by the pilot that we would have to take our wagons to pieces, and haul them up with ropes. Father [Wm. Ide] proposed to build a bridge, or a sort of inclined railroad up the steep ascent, and over the rocks; but few of his companions would listen to any such scheme. So he went to work with the men and fixed the road.

What Ide did was to identify several fairly level steps on the cliff that were deep enough for oxen to gain footing and pull a wagon from the step below. This way a wagon could be hauled up the cliff, step by step. Of course everyone had to climb on foot, carrying whatever they could to lighten the wagons. In this manner, the wagons were hauled up, one at a time. It's hard to imagine the difficulties and patience this required, but after two days of Herculean effort they were all on top.

To add to their worries, they met a pack train heading east and were told the Mexicans would probably take them all prisoners as soon as they arrived in the valley below. Some were for staying in the mountains until the following year, but cooler heads prevailed, and they continued on their way. They were lucky. A year later the Donner Party became trapped at Truckee Lake. About 40 of the Donner group died from starvation, while others resorted to cannibalism (see T. Donner).

By November 1, 1845, the Grigsby-Ide party were resting at Sutter's Fort and counting their blessings for having arrived safely. Ide had brought with him a circular saw and some mill-irons. When settler Peter Lassen learned of this, he urged Ide to head 125 miles north to his ranch to build a sawmill. He told Ide to move his family into a vacant house on his ranch, and said he would join them in a week (see Lassen).

Unfortunately, things didn't work out that way. When Lassen arrived, he had brought another family with him and demanded possession of the house. The disgusted Ide family gathered their livestock, repacked their wagons and left with bad feelings all around. After traveling about seven miles, they came across another family camped on the Sacramento River on a ranch owned by R. H. Thomes. The rainy season had started, so Ide built a small log cabin to shelter his family for the winter.

After spending a wet, miserable and hungry winter, Ide met a settler, Josiah Belden, who owned a nearby cattle ranch and needed someone to run it for him (see Belden). He offered Ide a half interest if he and his family would live on it and care for Belden's cattle for three years. This generous offer sounded good to the Ide family, and they moved into their partially completed cabin on Belden's ranch in April 1846. At last things seemed to be going their way.

THEN CAME NEWS that shook the entire territory. It seemed the Mexican Government was fed up with so many foreigners moving into the territory without passports. General José Castro was reportedly under orders to drive them out of the country—by force if necessary. The alarmed settlers immediately got together and paid a visit to the Sutter Buttes camp of Captain John C. Fremont to seek his help. Fremont had recently brought his company of U.S. Army "Topographers" there from Oregon after moving them out of California at the insistence of General Castro (see Fremont).

Fremont apparently fanned flames of hatred against Castro but told the men he could only act in self defense. The angry settlers then took matters into their own hands; they were not about to let the Mexicans push them out. Quickly they formed a volunteer militia of sorts and elected a fiery frontiersman, Ezekiel Merritt, as their captain. Early in June Merritt led a small band of volunteers on a daring raid that resulted in the capture of about 250 horses from the Mexican Army. By then they knew war between the U.S. and Mexico was probably inevitable.

This raid was followed by a successful surprise raid on General Mariano Vallejo's stronghold at Sonoma (see Vallejo). Under Merritt's astute leadership, around thirty men—including Ide and Grigsby—surrounded Vallejo's house in the early hours of June 14 and took him and others in his household prisoners without a shot being fired. Captured were the general and his family; his brother, Captain Salvador Vallejo; their brother-in-law, Jacob Leese, and the general's secretary, Victor Prudon. Also taken was the alcalde, José Berryessa, who was later reinstated.

Once Vallejo saw he was helpless he treated his captors as guests, serving them food, wine and brandy. Long talks, generously lubricated by drinks, took place while the exuberant volunteers decided what they should do next. It was agreed that the prisoners would be taken to Sutter's Fort and jailed; however, some wanted tangible rewards for their efforts. They advocated looting Sonoma and then fleeing to escape probable retaliation by General José Castro. When Ide and Robert Semple heard this talk, they were furious, and both made speeches denouncing the idea. Ide was quoted as saying:

> I will lay my bones here, before I will take upon myself the ignominy of commencing an honorable work, and then flee like cowards, like thieves, when no enemy is in sight. In vain will you say you had honorable motives. Flee this day, and the longest life cannot wear off your disgrace! Choose ye! Choose ye this day, what you will be! We are robbers, or we must be conquerors! [1]

This fiery speech, with Semple's backing, turned the tide, bringing uniformity to the group (See Semple). Ide was elected commander and governor of the new republic; John Nash was elected Chief Justice, similar to alcalde. Vallejo's family and Berryessa were freed; however, the four top officials previously named were escorted to Sutter's Fort by Merritt, Semple and Grigsby to be incarcerated as planned. Meanwhile, Fremont had moved his men just outside Sutter's Fort and had virtually taken it over.

HAVING SECURED Sonoma, the triumphant volunteers moved into Vallejo's vacated barracks and set to work organizing a temporary government to administer the independent republic they intended to establish. A flag was needed by the new republic to replace the hated Mexican flag, so William Todd—a relative of Mrs. Abraham Lincoln—took on the task. A piece of unbleached muslin, apparently furnished by Nancy Kelsey and other women present there, was crudely painted with a grizzly bear, a red star and the words "California Republic". This flag was proudly raised on June 14, 1846 as a symbol of defiance against General Castro's alleged threats to oust them.

Commander Ide and the "Bear Flaggers" then organized defenses to protect Sonoma against possible retaliation by Castro. Meanwhile, Ide's son, William, Jr., had been employed by John A. Sutter before leaving for the Santa Cruz Mountains to make redwood shingles. When he learned that General Castro was looking for him, he fled into the wilderness to escape capture. Later he gave himself up. After interrogating him for several days about his father's activities, Castro finally freed him.

THE DAY AFTER the Bear Flag was raised, Ide and the others drew up a formal proclamation, declaring the territory independent from Mexican rule and setting out rules and regulations for its administration as follows:

> ALL PERSONS, INHABITANTS OF THE COUNTY OF SONOMA AND COUNTRY AROUND. REQUESTING THEM TO REMAIN AT PEACE; TO PERSUE THEIR RIGHTFUL OCCUPATIONS,—WITHOUT FEAR OF MOLESTATION   The Commander-in-chief at Sonoma gives his inviolable pledge to all persons in California, not found bearing arms, or instigating others to take up arms against him, that they shall not be disturbed in their persons, property, religion, or social relations to each other, by men under my command....And he further premises that a Government, to be prosperous and ameliorating in its tendency, must originate among its people: its officers should be its servants, and its glory its COMMON REWARD!
> (Signed) WILLIAM B. IDE, Commander

After designing the flag, William Todd volunteered to take a message about the successful rebellion to U.S. Naval forces anchored in San Francisco Bay. After he left, the volunteers spent the next few days translating the treaty and proclamation into Spanish. Todd returned on the 16th or 17th with Lieutenant John S. Misroon from the U.S. warship, *Portsmouth*. Lieutenant Misroon brought with him a letter from his commanding officer, Captain John Montgomery.

The letter stated that, while the captain was disturbed by the unauthorized action taken by the bear flaggers, he was thankful they appeared to be acting responsibly. Furthermore, he said he was unable to assist them in any way unless and until war was declared with the United States. Despite this, a small party of bear flaggers managed to get a keg or two of gunpowder from the *Portsmouth* at a later date.

On June 19th Thomas Cowry and George Fowler were sent to obtain a keg of badly needed gunpowder from a settler on the Russian River. Somewhere along the way they were attacked and captured by a band of General Castro's cavalry. Unfortunately, blind hatred and possible revenge against the surprise attack on Sonoma and the jailing of General Vallejo, prompted the Mexicans to kill their helpless prisoners. They not only killed them but allegedly mutilated their bodies. This atrocity did more to galvanize the Bear Flaggers than anything the Mexicans could have done.

When William Todd turned up missing on another mission, they assumed that he had been captured by Castro's men. Determined to get him back before he was executed in the same manner, around twenty volunteers rode with Henry L. Ford to find him. After a triumphant skirmish at the Indian rancho of Olompali between Santa Rosa and San Rafael, resulting in some Mexican casualties, they returned with Todd unharmed. On June 25 they received threats that Castro was preparing to attack Sonoma that very day. Defenses were strengthened and the bear flaggers anxiously awaited his arrival. Just before dawn they heard the ominous sound of horses approaching in the distance.

The men tensed for battle, only to be confronted by John C. Fremont and Kit Carson with about 70 men, who had come from Sutter's Fort as reinforcements. Either Fremont had secret orders to go on the offensive or he took it on himself to do so. Everyone knew that war between the United States and Mexico was only a matter of time; Fremont apparently intended to hurry it up a bit.

FROM THE BEGINNING Fremont was clearly disturbed by Ide's proclamation, thinking it too conciliatory toward the enemy—especially Castro, whom he hated with a vengeance. He had little use for Ide as well, thinking him a bit eccentric—possibly even a Mormon. The fact that Ide had gained power over the "bears flaggers" may have bothered Fremont as well. But after studying Ide's written proclamation more thoroughly, he seemed to change his negative attitude and appeared more tolerant.

Fremont spent several days scouting Castro's troops, managing to get some men across San Francisco Bay to spike the old bronze cannons at the presidio. A short time later, near Mission San Rafael, three unarmed Mexicans were captured by Kit Carson and shot to death with Fremont's tacit approval. Later he had Ide draw up conditions for annexation to the United States and assumed command from him retroactive to June 14.

On July 9, shortly after Fremont's volunteers were reorganized, a courier arrived from Captain Montgomery with an American flag and news that war had officially been declared in May; furthermore, Monterey had been taken without bloodshed by U.S. Naval forces under Commodore John Sloat. There was great cheering and rejoicing when the short-lived bear flag was replaced by the Stars and Stripes. Ironically, Will Ide suddenly found himself a private in Fremont's

California Volunteer Battalion. He had gone from governor and commander of the new republic to a private under Fremont in less than a day. He later wrote scathing narratives about how Fremont had done him grievous wrongs when he first arrived in Sonoma and found Ide in charge. Fremont apparently claimed that Ide was a Mormon, which was considered an insult at the time; there is no evidence to support such a claim.

Along with the other volunteers, Ide was marched to Monterey in late July and sworn into the U.S. Armed Forces by Commodore Stockton, who had taken over from Sloat. The men were then loaded aboard U.S. warships to be transported south to San Diego and Los Angeles. Castro had retreated south and joined Mexican forces there to fight off the expected invasion by the United States.

Descriptions of the Mexican War are fully covered in other chapters of this book and will not be repeated here. It's safe to say that William Ide served out his enlistment with honor, if not distinction. After being discharged that fall, he found himself stranded in Southern California with no money and few clothes. Rather than try to obtain a horse for the long journey home, he prevailed on a sea captain to work off his passage on a ship heading for San Francisco.

As the story goes, he was working as a ship's carpenter, sawing wood, when Commodore Stockton said to the captain:

> 'Captain, do you know who that old man...is?'... (pointing to Mr. Ide). 'No; I didn't ask his name,' replied the captain. 'Well, that is Governor Ide, of the Bear Flag party.' 'Can that be so? Do you know him?' asked the captain. 'Yes, I know him,' was the reply. Whereupon the Captain called his Steward and said to him: 'Here, Steward, go tell that man sawing wood, yonder, that the Captain wants to see him in his office.'....'and on his said introduction, he [Ide] was made welcome, not only to his passage, but to as good fare and accommodations as the ship afforded.'

Ide arrived home at Belden's ranch (now Tehama Co.) in November, but was back in Sonoma in April 1847, taking part in a public meeting in behalf of Alcalde John H. Nash. In early Ide was appointed a government surveyor by Military Governor Richard Mason. By then he had bought part of Josiah Belden's *Rancho de la Barranca Colorada*—Red Bluff Ranch—so-called because of a high red cliff on the west bank of the Sacramento River. He was in Monterey during the spring of 1848 when he learned of James W. Marshall's eventful gold discovery. He immediately joined others in the mad rush to the gold fields.

Ide acquired enough gold to make a voyage east and purchased additional land north of his ranch, where he apparently built an adobe house. Located at the head of navigation, where the California-Oregon

Trail crossed the Sacramento River, it linked Sacramento and the Mother Lode with Shasta and the Northern Mines. A ferry established there during the 1850's was known for three decades as the Adobe Ferry; however, recent study indicates that Ide may not have lived there.

Ide's wife, Susan, died in the late 1840s. Despite this tragedy, Ide went on to hold several offices in Colusa County, including that of judge at the county seat. He was living in Monroeville, about thirty miles south of his ranch, when he apparently caught smallpox. He died alone in December 1852 at the age of 56. Neither he nor his wife lived long enough to enjoy the fruits of their labors. Historian Hubert Bancroft wrote that Ide was "rather eccentric and fond of lengthy reports and political theorizing; nevertheless, he was a most worthy and honest man with remarkable tact and executive ability....Some said he was a Mormon, but there is no evidence. "[2]

Ide's contributions to California mostly involve the Bear Flag Rebellion, and his many services to Colusa County. A marker honoring Ide identifies the site of Monroeville on Hwy. 45 near Hamilton City. His name is also carried by a state historical park on the Sacramento River, about two miles northeast of the city of Red Bluff.

BIBLIOGRAPHY

–Bancroft, Hubert H. *History of California*, Vol. I-VI. History Co., San Francisco, CA, 1886. Republished, Wallace Hebberd, Santa Barbara, 1966. [2]

–Bryant, Edwin. *What I Saw In California.* University of Nebraska Press, Lincoln, 1985.

–California Div. of Parks and Recreation; a pamphlet, "William B. Ide Adobe State Historic Park" (undated).

–DeVoto, Bernard. *The Year of Decision-1846.* Houghton Mifflin Co., Boston, 1942

–Egan, Ferol. *Fremont, Explorer for a Restless Nation.* University of Nevada Press, Reno, 1977, 1985. [1]

–Hague, Harlan & Langum, David J. *Thomas O. Larkin..* University of Oklahoma Press, Norman, 1990.

–Harlow, Neal. *California Conquered.* University of California, Berkeley, 1982.

–Ide, Simeon. *Conquest of California by the Bear Flag Party: A biographical sketch of William Ide.* Rio Grande Press, Inc., Glorieta, NM, 1967. All quotes except [1 & 2] are taken from this publication.

–Lee, Hector. *Tales Of California.* Letter Shop Press, Santa Rosa, Ca, 1974.

–Stewart, George R. *The California Trail.* University of Nebraska Press, Lincoln, 1962

NOTES

Ishi, the last Yahi Indian
Courtesy California State Library

– 23 –

INDIANS OF CALIFORNIA

RATHER THAN attempting to single out an individual Native American, this chapter covers California Indians in general, naming a few with exceptional stories. Because the subject matter is complex and space limited, only a general treatment is possible.

There were more than a hundred tribes or "tribelets," totaling an estimated 250,000 to 300,000 Native Americans, in pre-Spanish Alta California. As the 1800s progressed the count plummeted. Indians died mostly from white men's contagious diseases: syphilis, smallpox, bullets and bad whiskey. In recent years the decimation appears to have stopped; the U.S. census shows that the American Indian population in California increased from about 16,000 in 1900 to an estimated 39,000 by 1960. Those identified as "Indians" had at least one-fourth Native American blood, and a good portion of them had immigrated to California from other states. Descendants of the original tribes of Alta California are only a fraction of the total.

The term "tribe" is used loosely, because the name denotes linguistic groups, *rancherias* (villages) and collections of villages, containing several hundred persons within a designated area. After 1769 the Franciscan missions became demographic units in their own right, although at any one mission the *neophytes*, as the Indian converts were called, may have come from a dozen or more different tribes. During the height of their success in the early 1820s, the missions held an estimated 20,000 Indians under subjugation.

The controversial mission era had a profound effect on California Indians, good or bad, depending on sources quoted. The original purpose of the missions in the 1700s was to strengthen the Spanish hold on California by establishing missions, pueblos (towns) and presidios (forts) at strategic locations along the coast. These ambitious enterprises required thousands of workers, recruited from native Indian tribes for the most part. In turn, these "aborigines" would be converted to Christianity and taught trades and agricultural methods. Theoretically this would prepare them to make their own way in a civilized society.

Methods used to subjugate the Indians varied from mission to mission, depending on the padre in charge. As in any human endeavor, some of these dedicated Franciscans were skilled and benevolent administrators, while others were not. Ethnohistorian Florence Shipek states that the Kumeyaay people of early San Diego thought the Spanish padres were "the most powerful, dangerous and thieving witches they had ever encountered" [1].

THERE IS little doubt that many abuses of Indians took place, such as flogging and incarceration for minor infractions of rules laid down by the padres. These rules included attending mass, learning Spanish and working as directed. Indians who ran off were pursued by soldiers and brought back to face stiff punishment. In short, the missions practiced a form of involuntary servitude—a polite name for slavery. That it was all done in the name of God does not alter the fact that the missions could never have survived, let alone flourished, without the soldiers to enforce the rules.

When harsh measures were used against the Indians, they were easily justified by "being for their own good." Pagan souls surely bound for hell were being saved through Christianity. Trades and agricultural methods were being taught, along with the civilized Spanish language. Eventually the more promising "neophytes" would be granted a few acres of land (originally their own) and a few head of livestock (to replace wildlife driven off or killed), so they could become self sufficient.

Unfortunately this seldom happened, largely because of the overthrow of the Spanish by the Mexicans in 1821-22, and the subsequent secularization of the missions by the Mexicans, beginning in 1834. This event left large numbers of mission Indians adrift. Some were "hired" by Mexican rancheros, often in a form of virtual serfdom, while the rest returned to their tribal lifestyle.

California Indians had more linguistic groups than any other area of similar size. This is why the mission padres tried to enforce use of the Spanish language. The Indians ranged in size from the tallest, the Mojave with an average of nearly 5'7", to the shortest, the Yuki at around 5'2". There appear to be five groups with distinct physical differences such as head, face and nose shapes, among other characteristics.

Archaeological studies indicate that Indians settled in California at different times in various locations, ranging from about 4,000 BC to 1,000 AD, although they may have been present as migratory hunters much earlier. Those migrating from the Pacific Northwest brought their forest culture with them, while those from the Southwest brought desert culture. Perhaps some of their physical differences evolved over the centuries because of California's diverse climates, elevations and food sources.

Except for a few tribes along the Colorado River—and mission Indians in later years—they did not grow food for sustenance, relying instead on hunting, fishing and gathering. White men lumped them into the derisive category of "Diggers" because they dug roots and gathered acorns off the ground as a mainstay of their diet. Game was plentiful in many areas prior to the gold rush, and they did well hunting and fishing. Desert Indians sometimes relied on rodents, reptiles and insects as a source of protein.

Emigrants and argonauts in the 1800s thought them rather primitive in comparison with Plains Indians, who rode horses and lived by hunting buffalo. The Plains tribes were skilled horse thieves, had better weapons and were far more war-like. Hostile encounters with these Indians often reflected unfavorably on California Indians, who were usually more docile. Yet many California Indians had a rich cultural and ceremonial life. When they did resort to stealing livestock, it was usually for food. Later, many became expert horsemen (*vaqueros*).

California *rancheros* and a few early white settlers, such as John A. Sutter and John Marsh, prized Indians as ranch hands and *vaqueros*; however, many early explorers and landless settlers, especially argonauts during the gold rush, hated all Indians. They considered them vermin and drove them off or killed them with legal impunity. When pushed too far, the Indians would fight back with disastrous results for all. Modocs in the north and Mojaves in the south are good examples.

During warm weather native men wore little or nothing, while women usually wore a short split skirt or apron made from animal skins, tules or shredded bark. In cold weather both sexes wore wraps made from fur or bird-skins sewn together. Some wore hats with unique shapes or styles. Animal-skin moccasins were worn in the north, while crude sandals were worn in the south.

Strings of sea-shells were used as money by many, even those who lived inland from the sea. Often worn as necklaces, their value varied; the smaller the shell the more valuable they were. Examples of Yokut money values are: Fine for killing a man of importance: 15 strings; an ordinary man: 10 strings; purchasing a slave: 1 or 2 strings; a house: 3 strings [2]. Smoking tobacco and pipes were common among most tribes. Musical instruments included rattles, flutes, whistles, clapsticks and footdrums. Dancers at religious ceremonies were beautifully dressed and decorated. [3]

Some tribes had head men or chiefs, who were elected or inherited their positions. Some chiefs could take more than one wife, while ordinary men could not. Girls usually "married" shortly after their menstrual cycle began. Adultery by women was punished in various ways, including cutting (or biting) off their noses, or being killed by their husbands. Divorce was by simple abandonment, or by the woman placing the man's goods outside the dwelling. Children were sometimes kidnapped and sold into slavery, especially after the gold rush began.

Housing varied, depending on climate and available materials. Northern tribes used drift-wood planking. In forested areas large strips of bark were stood on end in a conical shape like tipis. Some houses were built partially underground, as were sweat houses the men enjoyed as part of ritual preparations for the hunt or religious ceremonies. Some tribes allowed use of sweat houses by women and children. In the great San Joaquin Valley, houses were thatched with tules and brush fastened to bent willow frames. They were sometimes covered with earth, in both rectangular and conical shapes. Many were communal.

Shaman or medicine men and women carried out religious rites and tended the sick. Good shaman did good deeds, like bringing rain, while evil shaman could be hired to harm or kill an enemy. They were greatly feared. About half the tribes buried their dead, while others cremated theirs, along with prized possessions. When they were buried, all of themselves (including their spirit in their "things") were buried or burned with them. This is one reason today's Indian descendants resent grave plundering by amateur archaeologists or souvenir hunters. It's unlikely that many of us would tolerate having the graves of our ancestors opened and plundered without permission. Wailing, crying, breast beating and self-inflicted wounds were common death rites. Widows were often required to shave or burn off their hair and cover their scalps and faces with pitch for a year or more.

PERHAPS a logical way to break down the different tribes within California is geographically. There are far too many to list separately, so in this general list only the larger groups are shown. Some of them have disappeared over the years. Moving north from the Mexican border, coastal Indians included:

    Yuman, including Diegueño (San Diego)
    Serrano, including Luiseño, Juaneño, Gabrielano & Fernandeño
        (Los Angeles)
    Chumash (Oxnard-Santa Barbara)
    Salinan (North of Morro Bay)
    Esselen (South of Monterey)
    Costanoan (Monterey to San Francisco.)
    Coastal Miwok (North of San Francisco)
    Pomo (North of Santa Rosa)
    Yukian (North of Ft. Bragg
    Mattole (Upper Mattole)
    Bear River (South of Eureka)
    Wiyot (Eureka)
    Yurok (North of Eureka)
    Tolowa (Crescent City)

Ocean fish and shellfish were mainstays in their diets; however, they also went inland to kill game and gather acorns. In protected waters they used boats made from woven tules, bark sewn together and sealed with asphaltum, and redwood or pine "dugout" canoes capable of travel 30 miles out to sea. Both poles and paddles were used. Fish were caught by harpooning, hooking, netting or poisoning. Most California Indians wove baskets, and the feather Pomo baskets are thought to be the best made anywhere. Many were watertight and were used as cooking pots by inserting hot rocks to heat liquids. A few tribes used clay pots.

RIVER PEOPLE lived mostly along the main tributaries of the Sacramento, Klamath and Eel Rivers. They augmented their acorn diet with fish (especially salmon) and game. Over 500 plants were used as food, medicine or basketry. Again going south to north, they included:

Yokuts	Central & northern Wintun
Miwok	Yana
Southern Maidu (Nisenan)	Karok
Central & Northern Maidu	Shastan
Southern Wintun (Patwin)	Hupa (Hoopa)

Tribes in the northeast, who lived in the mountainous terrain of Northern California or in arid lands bordering Nevada, included the Mono Paiute, Washo (Lake Tahoe & surrounds), Northern Paiute, Shastan, and Modoc. Indians bordering the Colorado River were Yumans, including Yuma, Chemehuevi and Mojave. These tribes made clay pots and grew wheat, corn, melons and beans. The central and eastern part of Southern California were inhabited by the Yuman and various Paiute and Serrano groups.

A chief of the Northern Yokut in the present-day Stockton area became an important historical figure. Chief Estanislao had once been a passive and obedient Indian at Mission San Jose, but in 1829 he broke away and formed a band of hostiles that made life miserable for rancheros in the area called the Tulares (Tules) [4].

Mariano Vallejo, a nineteen-year old Mexican Army officer at the time, was placed in charge of a sizable expedition to deal with Estanislao's depredations (see Vallejo chapter). When attacked by Vallejos' troops, the Indians drove them off after a lengthy engagement, during which several old Indian women were killed. Though Vallejo was charged with undue brutality because of this action, he was eventually cleared. One of Vallejo's men, not so fortunate, was sentenced to five years in jail for killing a woman.

Shortly after this action, Chief Estanislao returned to the mission, where all was forgiven. The Stanislaus River, and later Stanislaus County, were named after his misspelled name. He died of smallpox in 1839.

A TRUE STORY, comparable to *Robinson Crusoe,* involves an Indian woman who lived alone for eighteen years on San Nicolas Island, a distant link in the Santa Barbara Island chain. Most of the offshore islands were occupied by Indians at one time, but when the Russians and their Aleutian hunters began killing off the fur-bearing animals— otter, seals and sea lions—in the early 1800s, the Indians were removed or killed off.

As the story goes, a ship was evacuating Indians from San Nicolas Island in 1835 during heavy winds. Somehow a young woman had over-looked bringing her baby along. When the captain was unable to return to the island because of the weather, she allegedly jumped overboard and swam back. The ship then sailed off without her. Though the captain intended to return for her later, the ship was in demand at other locations and was soon wrecked off San Francisco Bay.

Though hunters continued to visit the island, the woman was afraid to show herself and was successful in avoiding them. After her child died in infancy, she continued to live there alone. In 1853 George Nidever and another party of seal hunters appeared; Nidever had come to California with Joseph R. Walker in 1833. After spotting what appeared to be the print of a rather small, naked foot in the sand, they began a thorough search of the island; after finding no one, they left.

A few weeks later Nidever returned for another search. This time his party was successful in finally capturing the frightened, middle-aged woman. She spoke a tongue none of them recognized; she could never communicate except by sign language (she was probably from the Aleutian Islands). Nidever and his Mexican wife then took her into their home in Santa Barbara. Though they did their best to care for her, she withered away and died within a few months. Today we would probably diagnose her strange ailment as severe depression. She was christened Juana Maria by the local priest at the time of her death and was buried next to the Santa Barbara Mission [5].

A WELL DOCUMENTED STORY involves a mature Yahi Indian man named Ishi from the Yana group, a tribe inhabiting a wild and iso-lated area on the upper reaches of the Sacramento River. Apparently there was no gold there and no reason for white men to bother these Indians, who remained virtually isolated and "wild." Unfortunately all thefts of food, supplies or livestock anywhere in the area were blamed on these so-called wild Indians.

Of course this brought the wrath of the white man to their doorstep, and they were hunted down and ruthlessly killed in the late 1860s. By 1870 only a handful had managed to escape. Somehow they survived and continued their native lifestyle until 1910, when a lone sur-vivor was found. Hunger and loneliness had finally driven the desperate man to a slaughterhouse on the outskirts of Oroville, where he was captured and housed in the local jail.

Fortunately someone had the presence of mind to notify the anthropology department at the University of California, and T. T. Waterman went to investigate. What he and his associates, A. L. Kroeber and Saxton Pope, learned later astounded the scientific community. The middle-aged man they named Ishi (Man) was the last living Indian in the state from what they termed the "stone age." Ishi was taken to the Museum of Anthropology at the university in San Francisco, where he was given living quarters (the museum was later moved to Berkeley). He also lived at Waterman's nearby home. He remained in the area for the rest of his rather short life, learning a form of pidgin English so he could tell his story. Later he was put on the staff as an assistant janitor.

While he did adopt some of the white man's ways during this period, there were some he could not tolerate. He would drink nothing unless it was transparent, like water or tea. He ate no boiled food or any sauces or gravies. He would not shake hands with anyone and seldom wore shoes. He had never seen crowds of people before, and during a trip to San Francisco it was not the lofty buildings, smoky automobiles or noisy trains that fascinated or frightened him—it was crowds of people and trolley cars with their clanging bells.

Ishi was a fine craftsman when it came to making bows, arrows and arrowheads. He made beautiful arrowheads out of almost anything that was hard enough to be chipped, even thick glass bottles. Anthropologists and other interested parties had unequalled opportunities to study Ishi's unique lifestyle and culture until his death in 1916. He died from tuberculosis, which he apparently contracted after his "capture." He was cremated with some of his treasures, his ashes stored in a pottery jar of Pueblo design at Mt. Olivet Cemetery. Ishi had lived the life of a white man about six years, and it was estimated that he was in his mid-fifties at the time of his death. Waterman once wrote about Ishi:

> He looked upon us as sophisticated children; smart but not wise. We knew many things, and much that was false. He knew nature, which is always true. His were the qualities of character that last forever. He was kind, he had courage and self restraint. His soul was that of a child; his mind, that of a philosopher. Ishi saw Western civilization as having only two useful products—glue and matches.[6]

THE AUTHOR, a long-term resident of El Dorado County, has some knowledge and access to local Indian culture. One local Indian, Sam Kessler, born June 4, 1860, was a Southern Maidu, or Nishinan, and lived all his life in the Camino-Placerville area. Nishinan is the

Indian name for Indian or people. Sam's grandfather's Indian name was *Pitchak*, which meant Lizard in the native tongue, but he was called "Captain Tom." Indian head men (*Houk* or *Huk*) were often called captain, hence the title. It's said that Captain Tom lived for 150 years, but no dates are available. His *rancheria* (village) was called Saskian, and stood on the present site of Camino, a few miles east of Placerville. During this period he built a large "round house" (*Kum*), where religious and social gatherings were held. These meetings, which often involved dances, were called *Lumai* ("Big Times"), and one was held when Captain Tom bestowed the title of captain on his grandson, Sam Kessler.

Kessler's Americanized name was taken from a man who had killed an Indian many years before. This was done to punish the killer by bringing trouble to his soul. Sometime in the late 1800s Sam married Susie Jones Kessler, who was half white, and they subsequently had ten children. The Nishinan (Southern Maidu) did not settle much farther south than Pleasant Valley or Nashville, on the North Fork of the Cosumnes River. South of there lived the Korni (Miwok), and despite language barriers, there was considerable intermarriage. There was also some fighting over hunting grounds, as there was with the Washo to the east.

Sam Kessler was known as a great story teller; as the following example shows:

> When a medicine man [shaman] wanted to kill his enemy he would cause a scorpion to bite a piece of liver, after which he would rub the liver on his big toe nail. When everyone was gathered together for a Big Time, the medicine man would single out his enemy and casually stumble over the latter's foot as if he had not seen it. As the medicine man tripped over the foot, he was careful to scratch it with his toe nail that had been rubbed with the poisoned liver, and so his enemy would die.

Sam passed down the beliefs of his tribe to his descendants:

> No one must threaten a bear or tell another Indian what he would do to a bear, because bears understand the speech of men.
> The dead were first burned (according to the bargain which Coyote made with the other animals...) and what was left of the body was decked with beads, put into a basket and buried.

Sam was very indignant at the white people who came to dig in Indian grave yards "to look for beads". He said that no Indian would ever disturb the dead, and that people were afraid to visit a graveyard at night because the dead were about at that time. When an Indian died, his clothes and his house were burned, because it was considered to be bad luck for any living person to use anything which had belonged to a dead person [5]. The foregoing quotations from Sam Kessler came from his descendants, Frances Kessler Arnold and her children, who live in El Dorado County [7]. Sam Kessler died in 1941 at the age of 81, and his wife followed in 1962 at the age of 91. They are buried in Camino.

NATIVE AMERICANS took from the land only what they needed for survival, but look what has happened to California since the arrival of white settlers a mere two hundred years ago. The vast environmental problems we face today are well documented. It is clear who set the best example.

Numerous museums in California are dedicated to Indian culture:

California State Indian Museum, adjacent to Sutter's Fort State Historical Park, Sacramento

Indian Grinding Rocks State Historic Park, featuring Miwok culture, Amador County

Kule Loklo, Marin County., featuring the Coastal Miwoks

Lowie Museum, University of California, Berkeley

Southwest Museum, Los Angeles

San Diego History of Man

Bowers Museum, Los Angeles

Jesse Peter Museum, Santa Rosa Community College

Antelope Valley Indian Museum, Palmdale

Morongo Valley Museum, Ridgecrest

BIBLIOGRAPHY

– *The American Heritage Book of Indians*. American Heritage/Bonanza Books, New York, 1982.

–Arnold, Frances Kessler and Arnold, M. W. Sr. Personal files on the Southern Maidu and the Kessler-Arnold family. El Dorado County, CA. 1928. [7]

–Bancroft, Hubert H. *Register of Pioneer Inhabitants of California, 1542 to 1848*. Dawson's Book Shop, Los Angeles, 1964.

–Castillo, Edward. "The other Side of the Christian Curtain:" *Californians* Magazine, Vol.10, no. 2, 1992. [1]

–Dillon, Richard. *Humbugs and Heroes*. Yosemite-DiMaggio, Oakland, CA, 1983.

–Hammond, George P. *The Weber Era in Stockton History*. Friends of the Bancroft Library, University of California, Berkeley, 1982. [4]

–Heizer, R. F. & Whipple, M. A., Editors. *The California Indians*. University of California Press, Berkeley, 1951, 1971. [5 & 6]

–McKittrick, Myrtle M. *Vallejo, Son of California*. Binfords & Mort, Portland, OR, 1944.

–*National Geographic,* "Indians of North America," December 1972.
–*National Geographic,* "Native American Heritage," October 1991.
–National Geographic Society. *The World of the American Indian.* Washington, DC., 1974 [2].
–*Richards, Jim.* "'Big Time' At Miwok Village, Chaw-Se." *Mt. Democrat,* October 2, 1987.
–Tanner, Thomas. Lead Ranger, State Indian Museum, Sacramento, CA. Notations written on sample manuscript, 1992. [3 & 6]
–Wainscott, Karen. "The First Sacramentans." *Sacramento Bee,* August 19, 1984.

— 24 —

WILLIAM JOHNSON
And Johnson's Ranch

NORMALLY each of these chapters features the life of a specific pioneer. In this case, however, a place and a person will be featured. William Johnson is the person, but precious little is documented about his life. Until recently very little was known about Johnson's Ranch, either, but thanks to Jack and Richard Steed of Sacramento, we now have reliable information.

In 1845 this obscure place with its crude facilities became a virtual Mecca on the California Trail. It was the first settlement on the Truckee Route where civilized comforts—such as they were—could be found west of the formidable granite summit of the Sierra Nevada range. There, worn livestock could be traded for fresh, and lost livestock could be replaced. Some food was also available.

The ultimate goal of most emigrants—at least until the 1849 Gold Rush began—was Sutter's Fort, at the confluence of the Sacramento and American rivers. But it lay about 40 miles southwest of Johnson's, and by the time emigrants reached Johnson's Ranch they were so trail-worn and destitute that some needed help to make that last 40 miles.

The first Bear River settler was Pablo Gutiérrez, an employee of John Sutter. Gutiérrez had been working under Sutter's majordomo, John Bidwell, at the Feather River Hock Farm (see Sutter & Bidwell). Near there, Gutiérrez claimed to have found gold in 1844. He then applied for and received a 22,000-acre land grant along the Bear River, built some kind of a crude shelter, and began exploring in earnest.

Gutiérrez told Bidwell about the gold, but before anything was done about it they were caught up in the rebellion against Mexican Governor Manuel Micheltorena. A naturalized Mexican citizen, Sutter was obliged to raise a small army of volunteers to help the governor keep his office. Another inducement was Micheltorena's promise to grant them land.

Sutter already possessed a grant of nearly 50,000 acres along the Sacramento River, but more was always welcome. It may have been a promise to assist the governor that allowed Gutiérrez get his land grant.

But it was this very assistance that did him in. Sutter found the courageous Gutiérrez a reliable courier to carry messages to the governor in Monterey. During his second trip he was captured by rebels, commanded by Gen. José Castro. When a message was found in the heel of his boot, Gutiérrez was executed as a spy.

Though Micheltorena was overthrown and expelled from California, Sutter managed to retain his land and powers as an alcalde. The ex-governor kept his promise to grant land to Sutter and others before he was deposed; however, many of these grants were later declared invalid. Under his powers as alcalde, Sutter handled the estate of his compadre, Pablo Gutiérrez, and sold his land at auction to William Johnson and Sebastian Keyser.

A native of Boston, Johnson was a mate on the ship *Alciope*, which sailed to California from the Sandwich Islands (Hawaii) in 1840. Like so many sailors before him, he apparently liked what he saw in California and jumped ship. By 1842 he had formed a partnership with Jacob Leese–a successful trader in Yerba Buena (San Francisco)–to operate a small trading vessel on the Sacramento River. In 1845 he and Sebastian Keyser bought Pablo Gutiérrez's land for $150.

Keyser, a young German trapper, had met John Sutter and Pablo Gutiérrez at the 1838 trapper's rendezvous in the Wind River Mountains. They traveled together to Fort Vancouver, where Sutter left them to continue his journey to California by ship. After making their way by ship to California with Peter Lassen in 1840, Keyser and Gutiérrez joined Sutter at New Helvetia. It may have been there that Johnson met Keyser. Upon occupying their land in 1845, Johnson and Keyser constructed adobe buildings near old campsites used by early frontiersmen such as John Work and the 1844 Stevens-Murphy Party with Old Caleb Greenwood and sons, the first to bring wagons across the Sierra Nevada (see Greenwood & Murphy).

Pierre T. Sicard, a French ex-sailor and carpenter, acquired a land grant across the river from Johnson's in 1844, probably from Micheltorena. He occupied it about the same time Johnson and Keyser moved onto their land. Old Greenwood and his went east in early 1845 as agents for John Sutter, hoping to persuade some of the Oregon-bound emigrants to follow them to California instead. Among those who followed the Greenwoods were the William Ide and Jarvis Bonney parties. Another party led by Lansford Hastings was the last to make it that year.

By the time these parties reached Johnson's Ranch in the fall of 1845, it was hoped the place would be ready for business. It would definitely be ready when the ever-increasing emigrant parties began arriving during the autumn of 1846. All would be hungry for fresh beef by then and business should be good. And it was. During the spring of 1846, the Greenwoods met Lansford Hastings and James Clyman at Johnson's Ranch on their way east again. Hastings hoped to entice more emigrants to follow him back to California on his so-called shortcut, which went south of the Great Salt Lake (see Hastings & Clyman).

Swiss emigrant Heinrich Lienhard, who visited Johnson's Ranch in 1846, described it in his book From St. Louis to Sutter's Fort, 1846:

> Finally a couple of small houses came into view on the elevation to the right along Bear Creek. A new adobe house was in the process of being built, with the work being done by stark-naked Indians. Mr. Johnson, the owner, was an English sailor...Sicard [a neighbor], as well as the short fellow, Johnson, had Indians as wives. Johnson even had two. [1]

Lansford Hastings' efforts in recruiting emigrants to California eventually resulted in a tragedy that really put Johnson's Ranch on the map. It began at Fort Bridger in July 1846 when a fateful decision was reached by James Reed and George and Jacob Donner. Instead of traveling the longer but tried-and-true route to California via Fort Hall, they opted for the shortcut being promoted by Lansford Hastings. The Donner Party story has been told in chapters on Tamsen Donner, James Reed and Lansford Hastings, and will not be repeated here.

THE FIRST WORD anyone received about the disaster was at Johnson's Ranch, when two local Indians escorted a living scarecrow named William Eddy into the settlement in mid-January 1847. When he gasped out the news that six other starving emigrants were stranded a few miles away, food was collected and several volunteers followed the Indians back to get them. Once they were safe at the settlement, the gruesome story came out.

The timing couldn't have been worse to mount rescue attempts, because most able-bodied men were still away serving in the Mexican War. Nevertheless, at Sutter's Fort, John Sutter, Alcalde John Sinclair and Captain Edward Kern, who was in charge of the Fort, collected food and livestock and recruited a seven-man rescue team led by Acquilla Glover. Sutter's launch was sent downriver to notify people at Yerba Buena (San Francisco), including James Reed, who had formerly been banished from the Donner Party and was in Yerba Buena. His wife and four children were still with them in the mountains.

Acquilla Glover's seven-man party reached Johnson's Ranch on February 2, 1847. There they gathered more food and recruited additional volunteers, including the indomitable William Eddy. Fourteen men and a string of pack animals loaded with food left Johnson's, headed into the snow-clad slopes above. Finally the rescue party escorted their weakening charges over the summit and back toward safety at

Johnson's Ranch. By the spring of 1847, all the living (about half of the original party) had been rescued by subsequent rescue parties.

One of the survivors was a teen-aged girl, Mary M. Murphy. She had been orphaned by the tragedy, and her older sister left her at Johnson's Ranch when she went to live in San Francisco. Later Mary Murphy wrote a letter which sums up her fate:

> Mr. [William] Johnson asked me to go riding with him one after-noon while he rounded up some horses. Knowing I was uncertain of my future, and having fallen in love with me, Mr. Johnson pro-posed marriage. In June 1847, at the age of 18 [probably closer to fifteen], I became Mrs. Johnson. For several months I was busy serving to all of Mr. Johnson's wishes—doing his cooking and washing and trying to make a home out of a cattle ranch. I knew he was a crude man and I sometimes overlooked many of his faults; but I could not love a man who abused me with the rest of the ranch hands. He proved to be a drunken sot. Because of that I got in touch with the rest of the family and secured an annulment of my marriage from the church...

Apparently the ex-Mrs. Johnson went to live with her sister, Sarah and her husband, at Cordua's Ranch at the confluence of the Feather and Yuba rivers. Cordua's ranch foreman was Charles Covillaud, an emi-grant who had arrived there a few months earlier. He and Mary Johnson Murphy fell in love and were married at Sutter's Fort on Christmas Day 1847. Covillaud made a fortune during the subsequent Gold Rush and went on to found the City of Marysville in 1850, which he named after his attractive young wife.

THE NEXT EVENT that established Johnson's Ranch was the Gold Rush, when thousands of argonauts came through on their way to the gold fields. Soon land prices were escalating, and the two partners decided to sell out. Johnson was the first to sell in the spring of 1849, and Keyser sold the following fall. Ironically, rich gold deposits were found all around them. Apparently there was a problem with Johnson's original Mexican title, because in 1852 he tried to re-claim his land.

Johnson's claim was denied in 1856, after which he apparently sailed to Honolulu. He was there the following year when he signed a "Quit Claim" deed for Henry Robinson, the new owner of the land. Johnson apparently never left Honolulu, although there is no proof of this. At any rate he dropped out of sight while there.

Sebastian Keyser also married a girl connected indirectly with the Donner Party. She was Elizabeth Rhoads, sister of John Rhoads, one of the seven volunteers who first reached the stranded Donner Party. After selling out his interest in the ranch, Keyser and his wife moved to the Cosumnes River, where Keyser operated a ferry for William Daylor. In

January 1850 he was swept away by the flooding, raging river and drowned.

Camp Far West, a U.S. Army camp, was established in 1849 near Johnson's Ranch to prevent war between the miners and Indians. A square acre was surveyed for building sites and tents erected for a temporary camp. Finally the camp was built and staffed by two companies of the 2nd Infantry. Indians in the area were not hostile, and the fort only lasted about three years. The site now lies near the waters of a reservoir appropriately named Camp Far West Reservoir just outside the town of Wheatland. Hydraulic mining and natural flooding changed the course of the Bear River until the place was unrecognizable. Later, levees built to protect the area from flooding changed it even more.

L ATE IN 1849 Henry Robinson and his partner, Eugene Gillespie, subdivided property on the ranch and named it Kearney after the General of the same name (actually spelled Kearny). Two sawmills were also being constructed. Subsequently the land was divided and sold several times, but the town of Kearney failed to materialize. During mid-1850's a hotel was built on the property by J. L. Burtis.

That same year a bridge was built across the Bear River by Claude Chana, who is credited as the first to find gold in Auburn Ravine. A post office was established at or near Johnson's Ranch in 1853, possibly at Kempton. At any rate, it was moved to the nearby farm town of Wheatland in 1866. During the 1850s the settlement at Johnson's Ranch began to die. Annual floods tore out bridges, and shorter, better routes were discovered to the gold fields. It was reported that the devastating flood of 1862 wiped out whatever buildings remained at the original site. This is open to question, but hard evidence indicates that by the 1870s nothing remained.

Despite the great historical significance of Johnson's Ranch, its exact location remained a mystery until it was recently uncovered by the stubborn dedication of local historian Jack Steed and his son, Richard. Unfortunately it lies on private property, thus preventing public access. But finally it has been charted, and historical plaques in Wheatland and on Highway 49 tell something of its past. Another plaque and small monument identify the trail at Johnson's Crossing.

BIBLIOGRAPHY

–Bancroft, Hubert H. *Pioneer Register and Index.* Dawson's Book Shop, Los Angeles, CA, 1964.

–Bidwell, John. "Echoes of the Past." *The Century Illustrated Monthly Magazine*, 1890. Reprint by State of California, 1974.

–Bryant, Edwin. *What I Saw In California.* University of Nebraska Press, Lincoln, 1945.

–Crosby, Alexander L. *Old Greenwood, Pathfinder of the West* (based on book by C. Kelly & D. Morgan). Talisman Press, Georgetown, CA, 1967.

–Davis, William Heath. *Seventy-Five Years in California.* John Howell Books. San Francisco, CA, 1967. (Ships arriving in California-1840)

–DeVoto, Bernard. T*he Year of Decision-1846.* Houghton Mifflin Co., Boston, 1942

–Lienhard, Heinrich (Gudde, ed.) *From St. Louis to Sutter's Fort, 1846.* University of Oklahoma Press, Norman, 1961.

–King, Joseph A. *Winter of Entrapment.* P.D. Meany Pub., Toronto, 1992.

–Steed, Jack. *The Donner Party Rescue Site.* Sacramento, 1988 & 1991. [1]

–Stewart, George R. *The California Trail.* University of Nebraska Press, Lincoln, 1962.

–Stewart, George R. *Ordeal by Hunger* Pocket Books, New York, 1936 & 1960.

NOTES

Nancy Kelsey
Courtesy Phyllis Gernes and California State Library

– 25 –

NANCY KELSEY

1823 –1896

A NATIVE OF Barren County, Kentucky, where she was born August 1, 1823, Nancy Roberts was three when her family moved to Jackson County, Missouri. Raised on the frontier near Independence, she was fifteen when she married 25-year-old Benjamin Kelsey in October 1838. He was a rough-shod Kentuckian, whom she described as a "man of adventurous disposition." Neither had much education; apparently they lived from hard-scrabble farming and hunting. Nancy had her first child, a daughter named Martha Ann, when she was sixteen. She lost another baby in early 1841, shortly before she and Ben decided to join other members of the Kelsey clan in the Bartleson-Bidwell wagon party to head for new opportunities in the Far West.

Though some were going to Oregon, others–including the Ben Kelsey family–were heading directly for California. When asked why she decided to make such a hazardous journey with an infant, Nancy Kelsey made her now famous statement: "Where my husband goes, I go. I can better endure the hardships of the journey, than the anxieties for an absent husband." [1] Perhaps she was wiser than her years and informal education indicated.

The dramatic journey of the 34-person Bartleson-Bidwell Party to Marsh's ranch in California is covered elsewhere and will not be repeated here (see Bartleson-Bidwell). Though these emigrants endured extreme hardships, during which they were forced to abandon their wagons near the border of present-day Utah and Nevada, they all made it safely. Several of them left reminiscences of this epic journey.

"Cheyenne" Dawson remembered this image, after the wagons were abandoned: "I looked back and saw Mrs. Kelsey [Nancy] a little behind me, with her child in her arms, barefoot and leading her horse–a sight I shall never forget" [2]. The spectre of this courageous girl carrying her baby across the endless desert is unforgettable.

As the weary, starving party crossed the Sierra Nevada near Sonora Pass, they raided an Indian cache of acorns, which they ate quickly without adequate preparation. "My husband came very near dying of cramps," Nancy remembered. "We killed a horse and stayed over until the next day, when we were able to go on." [3]

When they finally straggled down the Stanislaus rivershed into the San Joaquin Valley, Nancy Kelsey finally collapsed, unable to continue. "I can't get up, Ben," she said to her distraught husband. Attempting to reassure her, Ben told her of seeing plenty of game and hurried off to hunt. He and others were successful in killing many deer that very day, which certainly saved their lives. They reached John Marsh's ranch on November 4th.

AFTER RESTING a few days, they and others were arrested and detained in San Jose as illegal immigrants before finally obtaining Mexican passports from General Vallejo. Later the Kelseys were rowed up the Sacramento River by Indians to Sutter's Fort, arriving on Christmas day. Among others they met there was Mrs. Joel Walker, who had crossed into California from Oregon with her family about three weeks earlier. While Mary Walker was apparently the first white woman to come overland into California, Nancy Kelsey was the first to cross the Sierra Nevada.

At Sutter's Fort, Nancy gave birth to a son, who died about a week later. This means she was expecting during her entire journey. In all, she and Ben had ten children. The Kelseys left Sutter's Fort in April 1842, visiting Sonoma and exploring the Napa Valley, where they settled and built a cabin near present-day Calistoga. Expert hunters, Ben and his brother, Andrew, made a living by hunting deer and elk, which they rendered for tallow and hides. By 1843 they had accumulated a hundred head of cattle, and along with some others who had cattle of their own, they drove them north through Oregon to Fort Vancouver. Hostile Indians plagued them along the way, but they got most of the cattle through and sold them for high prices. After visiting with other members of the Kelsey family in Oregon, Nancy gave birth to another daughter.

They returned to California in 1844 and again settled at the cabin in Napa Valley. Apparently two other Kelsey brothers, Samuel and David, with their families, came with them from Oregon, because in June 1846 all the brothers took part in the Bear Flag Rebellion at Sonoma. Nancy and her children—including a new son, Andrew—joined her husband there, where she worked as a seamstress and cook for John C. Fremont's volunteers (see Fremont). Nancy states in her memoirs that she and two other women furnished cloth and sewed the first Bear Flag.

Apparently Ben had a falling out with Fremont during this period over the killing of Jose Berryessa and two companions. Fremont allegedly ordered Ben to execute them as spies, and when he refused Fremont authorized Kit Carson and others to carry out the onerous chore.

Shortly after the Mexican War ended, Andrew Kelsey settled on a ranch near Clear Lake, where he later founded Kelseyville, the first town in Lake County. Meanwhile Ben Kelsey had been operating a sawmill on Sonoma Creek with Mariano Vallejo, where Nancy cooked for the workmen.

After James Marshall's gold discovery became known in the spring of 1848, Benjamin Kelsey went to the mines, possibly with his brother Andrew. They made a gold strike in what became Kelsey's Diggings, now Kelsey in El Dorado County, a few miles east of the gold discovery site at Coloma. James Marshall eventually moved from Coloma to Kelsey, where he died in 1885 (see Marshall).

With money he had made from his gold, Ben bought a herd of sheep in Sonoma and sold it for a high profit in the goldfields. Then the two Kelsey brothers and Charles Stone bought livestock from Mariano Vallejo's brother, Salvador, and drove it to the Clear Lake ranch. The Kelseys had made life miserable for local Pomo and Wappo Indians by forcing them to work for them on their ranch and in the goldfields as virtual slaves. Ben left the ranch before the fall of 1849, when vengeful Indians attacked and killed Andrew Kelsey and Charles Stone. When word of the killings reached Benicia, Samuel Kelsey joined Army Captain Nathaniel Lyons and a large party of volunteers to locate and punish the Indians. Upon reaching Clear Lake, Capt. Lyon's forces attacked a band of local Indians, who sought refuge on an island. With the use of two field pieces and superior fire power, about 100 Indian men, women and children were massacred during the "Battle of Bloody Island." It is doubtful whether these were the guilty Indians.

NANCY KELSEY and her husband apparently had "itchy feet," for they never stayed very long at one place. By 1850 they were in Humboldt County, where they allegedly helped establish the towns of Eureka and Arcata. They did not do well there financially, and were back at their crude Napa County cabin a year later, where Nancy gave birth to their seventh child, another girl.

In 1856 they were living in Kern County, where Ben built a toll bridge across the Kern River. Three years later they sold out and headed for Mexico and the Southwest, ostensibly for Benjamin's health. His health must have been fairly good, for Nancy had two more children during this period. They were in Texas in 1861, where the family's camp was attacked by Comanche Indians while Ben Kelsey and other men from the area were out hunting. The tragic story is recounted in Nancy's memoirs: [4]

The oldest two girls ran and hid in the brush and the sixteen-year-

Benjamin Kelsey
Courtesy Phyllis Gernes and Cailfornia State Library

old boy looked out for himself by hiding alone. We [Nancy and a neighbor woman] and the smaller children hid ourselves in a cave in the side of a ravine. I could hear the Indians above, but they did not discover us....After they...pillaged the camp and started off, they found the girls. They succeeded in catching one of the girls [Mary Ellen Kelsey] and the other said she could hear the blows as they struck her down. Poor girl, she was only 13 years old, and even now I can hear the screams that she made when they caught her.... We returned to the camp and heard the girl's [Margaret's] story, but could not find the captured one. She had recovered sufficiently to wander around in search of help. Oh, the anxiety of that night! We found her the next day and my anguish was horrible when I discovered she had been scalped [and probably raped]. My husband and 17 men followed them [the Indians] for 200 miles, but failed to overtake them. The poor girl died in Fresno when she was 18 years old, from the injuries she had received six years before.

IN THE MID 1860s the Kelseys were living in Fresno County, where Mary Ellen died. After brief sojourns in Inyo County and Lompoc, they moved to Puente, a suburb of Los Angeles, and then to Los Angeles proper. Benjamin died there February 17, 1889 at the age of 75; he was buried in Rosedale Cemetery.

Nancy, then 65, again migrated; this time to a lonely place called Cottonwood Canyon near Cuyama Valley, about 60 miles east of Santa Maria. This was apparently after her first child, Martha Ann, married Cuyama rancher Jessie B. Lewis. Her relatives helped her build a small cabin on land she intended to homestead but apparently never did. She lived by raising chickens and practicing herbal medicine.

By 1893 Nancy was suffering from cancer and faced her inevitable death bravely, asking only for a real coffin instead of "something scraped up with old boards." Friends and relatives took up a collection to buy her a "store-bought" coffin, which was kept stored at a neighbor's house until her death on August 10, 1896, just short of her seventy-third birthday.

Nancy Kelsey's only other wish—to be buried next to Benjamin in Los Angeles—could not be honored because of the distance and expenses involved. Instead, she was buried near her cabin. Today her gravesite is located on private property and is not accessible. As reported in the *Grizzly Bear* magazine in 1915:

> She [Nancy] is buried in this beautiful, but wild lonely place at the foot of Cottonwood Canyon, with a grandchild, who died at birth, buried on one side of her, and a neighbor's child on the other. [5]

This secluded spot seems an appropriate resting place for such an intrepid pioneer, the first to prove that a family could, indeed, cross the mighty Sierra Nevada into California and survive. To Nancy Kelsey goes the honor of being the first woman emigrant to achieve this terribly difficult task. Near her old cabin site, a section of the Sierra Madre mountains carries her name. Besides the towns of Kelsey (El Dorado Co.) and Kelseyville (Lake Co.), state historical markers identify the Kelsey cabin-site at Calistoga and the Kelsey-Stone gravesite at Kelseyville.

BIBLIOGRAPHY

—Ault, Philip. "Pioneer Nancy Kelsey," *Californians* Magazine, March/April, 1992. [2 & 3].

—Bancroft, Hubert H. *History of California*, Vol. I-IV. History Co., San Francisco, CA, 1886. Reprint, Wallace Hebberd, Santa Barbara, Ca, 1966.

—Bidwell, John. "Echoes of the Past," *Century Illustrated Monthly Magazine,* 1890-91. Reprint, State of Calif., 1974.

—Hunt, Rockwell. *John Bidwell, Prince of Pioneers.* Caxton Printers, Caldwell, ID, 1942.

—Gernes, Phyllis. *Hidden In the Chaparral.* Garden Valley, El Dorado County, CA, 1979. [5]

—Karshner, Gayle. "Nancy Kelsey," *The Humboldt Historian.* Humboldt Co. Historical Society, Eureka, CA, Nov-Dec., 1991. [4]

—Malsbary, George. "Clear Lake's 'Bloody Island'," *Golden West* Magazine, July 1971.

—McCubrey, Joanne. "The First Pioneer Woman to Cross the Sierra," *Sierra Heritage* Magazine, Auburn, CA, Jan-Feb., 1992.

—National Geographic Society. *Trails West.* Washington, D.C., 1979.

—Stewart, George. *The California Trail.* McGraw-Hill Book Co., New York, 1962. [1]

NOTES

Thomas Oliver Larkin
Courtesy California Department of Parks & Recreation

– 26 –

THOMAS OLIVER LARKIN

1802 – 1858

LTHOUGH Thomas O. Larkin is not as well known as some California pioneers, his many contributions place him high in the historical hierarchy. He was of English stock, his mother, Ann Rogers, being from Alderney in the Channel Islands. The daughter of sea captain William Rogers, she was born in 1771.True to the family's seafaring traditions, her first marriage was to English sea captain Thomas Cooper. They had one son, John Rogers Cooper, born in 1791. In 1823 Their son became a prominent trader in California. Capt. Thomas Cooper was lost at sea a few years after the birth of his son. His widow, Ann Rogers Cooper, then emigrated to Boston with her young son to live with her sister.

In 1801 she married 32-year-old Thomas O. Larkin, a native of Massachusetts, and moved to Charlestown, Mass. Their first child, a son named after his father, was born September 16, 1802. Four other children followed; two of them died in infancy. Another son died in his mid-teens, leaving only Thomas O., Jr., and his sister, Ann Rogers Larkin, later married to Otis Wright. Thomas O. Larkin, Jr. never used the "Junior" because his father died when he was six.

Widowed a second time, Ann R. Cooper Larkin moved her family to Lynn, Massachusetts in 1813, where she married Amariah Childs, a widower with ten children. They had one child of their own; a son, George E. Childs. To complicate matters, Childs' first wife, Ruth Larkin, was a sister of Thomas O. Larkin, Sr. Childs was a banker and leather maker and treated young Thomas Oliver like his own son.

Though Thomas O. Larkin had some formal education, he did not continue it for long and remained rather unpolished and a poor speller and writer all his life. Nevertheless, he loved books and was constantly reading. At age fifteen he moved to Boston to learn the bookbinder's trade. A short time later (1818) his mother died at age forty-seven.

Larkin's stint as a bookbinder lasted about a year. He then bounced from job to job in New England before moving to Wilmington, North

Carolina. By age twenty he was a successful storekeeper, and three years later he owned a small plantation and was appointed justice of the peace for Duplin County. He also became postmaster when the post office was moved into his store. During this period he began accumulating wealth and developed a reputation as a womanizer. He also contracted an unidentified chronic illness that plagued him for many years.

By 1830 he had sold his store and acquired a sawmill. This business proved a failure, and by the following year he had lost everything. Broke and ill, he returned to Boston. While casting around for a new opportunity, he learned that his half-brother, Captain John the Baptist Rogers Cooper, known as John B. R. Cooper, needed help in running his California trading business.

IN SEPTEMBER 1831 Larkin bought trading goods and sailed for California aboard the trading vessel *Newcastle*. At that time he was twenty-nine and described as about five-feet-eight inches tall with a dark complexion and dark hair and eyes. Though he apparently recovered from his long-standing illness, his health was said to be "delicate." It couldn't have been too delicate, because aboard the ship was an attractive young woman named Mrs. Rachel Hobson Holmes. Though she was on her way to California to join her seafaring husband, Captain A. C. Holmes, she and Larkin became intimate friends.

The *Newcastle* reached Honolulu (Hawaii) the following year, where Larkin sold his goods for a small profit. After a short stop at Yerba Buena (now San Francisco), the ship dropped anchor off Monterey in mid-April. Mrs. Holmes' husband was at sea, and because there were no hotels, both Larkin and she stayed with John B. R. Cooper and his family. Larkin immediately went to work for Cooper as his bookkeeper-clerk.

A short time later Larkin was shocked to learn that Rachel Holmes was expecting a child and named him the father. She then left for Santa Barbara, and by the end of January 1833 had given birth to a daughter christened Isabel Ann. At about this time Larkin left Cooper's employ and went into business as a middleman, trading in hides and tallow.

Fearing to face her husband with the news, Rachel Holmes learned belatedly that he had been lost at sea a year earlier. She then had to wonder whether Larkin would want to marry her. For one reason or another the nuptials did not take place until June, when Larkin traveled to Santa Barbara. He married Rachel aboard the trading vessel *Volunteer*, captained by John Coffin Jones, U. S. Consul for the Sandwich Islands (Hawaii). U.S. Consul Jones performed the ceremony, with his young step-son, William Heath Davis, as a witness (see Davis chapter). Years later the Larkins learned that Jones had no legal right to marry them, and they had to be remarried.

Rachel Holmes-Larkin, nee Hobson, daughter of Daniel and Eliza Hobson, was born in Ipswich, Mass. in 1807. She had married Captain Holmes, a native of Denmark, in 1827. Five years later she became the first American woman to settle in California. After their marriage, the couple stayed in Santa Barbara until fall, when they returned to Monterey and settled on a nearby ranch belonging to John B. R. Cooper. To their dismay they had lost baby Isabel Ann a month after their wedding. While living on Cooper's ranch, Larkin was engaged in trading. Within a year the Larkins moved to Monterey, opened a store and built a gristmill.

Larkin's enterprises prospered, and he expanded into the lumber business. A series of letters written by Larkin at that time reflect his feelings and tells of his growing redwood lumber trade from a sawmill in Santa Cruz. Most of these letters were written to Abel Stearns, a successful entrepreneur from Los Angeles. Larkin's grammar and spelling leave much to be desired:

> Monterey July 22d 1834...Our townsman Mr Hall J. Kelly is yet here. He says you treated him like a brute. (N.B. you did not flatter him & give him a few dolls, I expect). He is now living with me, expects to start next week. 10 sailors agreed to go with him, but all backout. Capt Young has now promised to go. If he [Kelly] should ever be king of the Oregon, I think he may be call'd King of Beggers. I sett him down as the greatest Bore I ever knew. I shall be happy to see him start ...[Hall Kelly was an ardent promoter of the Pacific Northwest, especially Oregon.]
>
> Monterey Aug 10 1834...Owing to such a stirr among the Sawyers to go with Kelly, there has been but little work. Among them they owe me several ml. & have run off owing me 5 m. I have much Lumber at Santa Cruz. When it can be shipt dont know. Will send joice & Lumber every chance. Mr Spear [trader Nathan Spear] ships plenty of flour by the Don Q...[the ship, *Don Quixote*].

Meanwhile Larkin was building a fine house for his bride. He did it in style, constructing the first two-story building in Monterey. It was a New England design, with a hipped, wood-shaked roof, but had wide Spanish-type verandas to provide shade. The walls were of thick adobe blocks for natural insulation. This house became famous throughout the territory for offering generous hospitality. It stands today as a California State Historical Landmark.

In April 1834 Rachel gave birth to a son, named after his father. Over the years they had four more children. Rather than seek Mexican citizenship, as many Yankee settlers did to obtain land grants, Larkin obtained annual *cartas,* similar to visas. Though he played no active role in politics, he quietly supported Juan Alvarado's movement to overthrow

Governor Gutiérrez in 1836. When Alvarado became governor two years later, Larkin had a well placed friend indeed.

In 1840 the Mexican Government arrested a large group of dissident American settlers for treason in the notorious Isaac Graham affair. Larkin did what he could to help them, but because he chose not to join actively with Graham he was subject to much criticism from the Americans (see Graham). Larkin also worked to attract ships to the Port of Monterey for business purposes. In this he was successful, and whalers used a scenic cove at Point Lobos to render their whale carcasses. Larkin went on to build the first wharf for ships and was given a contract to rebuild the Monterey Custom House, which doubled as a community hall. It stands today as an important historical landmark.

When U.S. Naval Commodore Thomas ap Catesby Jones erroneously ordered his men to storm and capture Monterey in 1842, Larkin helped smooth over the explosive political situation with diplomatic skills seldom found in a man of his limited education and political experience. Jones was convinced that the U.S. and Mexico were at war, and it took the efforts of Larkin and William Hartnell to convince him otherwise (see Hartnell) After offering apologies to Mexican officials and to the new Governor, Manuel Micheltorena, Jones took his men and departed. Fortunately there were no lasting repercussions.

This same year Larkin opened another lumber business in Santa Cruz, placing it under the management of Josiah Belden (see Belden). A disastrous fire in 1843 burned $6,000 worth of lumber, causing it to close down. Early the following year came news of Larkin's appointment as United States Consul in Monterey. This resulted in his turning over most of his business responsibilities to Talbot Green, a trusted clerk who later became a full partner. Larkin was now free to devote his time to diplomatic responsibilities and to submit numerous written reports to the State Department. He also became a tireless advocate for California, urging influential settlers like Dr. John Marsh to write letters to the East Coast extolling it (see Marsh).

IN EARLY 1844 Larkin made a business voyage to Mexico. Upon his return to Monterey, he learned to his dismay that he had apparently brought smallpox with him. Both he and his children contracted it but all eventually recovered. Though Larkin had loaned large sums of money to Governor Micheltorena, he tried hard to remain neutral when rebel factions—led by former Governor Juan Alvarado, General José Castro and Pio Pico—overthrew Micheltorena in 1844-45. He took his losses philosophically when Micheltorena was banished to Mexico, and did his best to cultivate the new administration, now located in Los Angeles under Governor Pio Pico. His feelings are clearly reflected in a letter dated March 4, 1845 to Abel Stearns, who had warned him not to lend money to Micheltorena:

You may think I have large sums against the General [Micheltorena]. I have. He even owes me for near 2000 silver dollars lent him in 1843. My Mazatlan debts where 12,000$ besides the funds I carried there. All these goods and [sic] gone, and I owe near 3000$ in Cash & bearing interest in Monterey, by reason of my selling so much and lending so much Cash to the General during 43 & 44...I am very sorry a single Foreigner took up arms in the late affair. Sutter, [Captain John A. Sutter] to do away the ideom [odium?] on him and his Neighbors, as thro' on him in Mexico, will do away much disconfidence there. So far so good. Otherwise, it was bad.Those who took up arms against the established Gov't done worse in my opinion. They and their property, foran age, may suffer for it, by some iron handed Mexican Gen....

In addition to his losses from the former governor, what Larkin seems to be saying is that Sutter, and others who joined to defend Micheltorena against the rebels, did wrong and could suffer from it at the hands of heavy-handed Mexican generals. Actually Sutter was forgiven by the new administration, and all his rights and powers were restored. He did, however, suffer heavy financial losses from the escapade; furthermore, a huge land grant to Sutter from Micheltorena was later revoked (see Sutter).

By the fall of 1845, Larkin was a secret agent for the United States, but he didn't receive word of it until much later. He, along with most others, knew that war with Mexico was inevitable unless California could be acquired by other means. Personally, Larkin favored outright purchase from Mexico. If not, then he hoped the Californians would declare independence and seek protection from the U. S. He feared England would act first.

THE TINY PUEBLO at Yerba Buena was growing, so Larkin appointed trader William A. Leidesdorff his vice-consul there (See Leidesdorff). Trouble resulted when the British vice-consul, James Forbes, refused to recognize Leidesdorff's appointment. Larkin advised Leidesdorff to ignore Forbes' stubborn refusal to accept him and to continue with his duties as instructed.

Larkin found time for business affairs; he convinced Pío Pico to confer title of the 45,000-acre "Children's Ranch," located in present-day Colusa County and granted to his children by former Governor Micheltorena. Larkin was ineligible because of his United States citizenship, which he would not renounce, but his children were native-born Californians, and he thought they were eligible to acquire the land. He also bought Rancho Jimeno, an adjacent parcel to the south of his Children's ranch. His combined holdings stretched along the west side of the Sacramento River for many miles.

Captain John C. Fremont's name appears in a letter from Larkin dated February 8, 1846, addressed to Vice-consul Leidesdorff:

> The U.S. have five ships of war in Mazatlan & three times that number in Vera Cruz. By the conveyance of this letter, I send one to Mr Weber for Capt. Fremont...

This is slight reference to the man who was to upset Larkin's carefully developed plans for annexing California through peaceful means. It began in March 1846, when Fremont took exception to General José Castro's orders to clear out of the territory. In defiance of that order, Fremont led his men to the top of Gavilan peak, a few miles east of Mission San Juan Bautista. After building temporary fortifications there, the American flag was raised and Fremont awaited Castro's reaction. This bold but foolhardy gesture severely damaged Larkin's chances for a peaceful solution.

Castro bluffed an attack, but finally withdrew without a shot being fired. Apparently Fremont thought he had made his point, so he evacuated the camp and headed north to Oregon Territory to await further orders. Though Larkin was upset by Fremont's actions, he was not disheartened by it. Marine Lieutenant Archibald Gillespie then arrived with a secret dispatch for Larkin from the Secretary of State. Gillespie continued on to Sutter's Fort, then headed north toward Oregon with other dispatches for Captain Fremont.

Larkin's dispatch was dated in October 1845, but it had taken six months to arrive. Fortunately, he had already anticipated much of what it contained and was well prepared. Both he and Captain John Montgomery, with the U.S. warship *Portsmouth* anchored in San Francisco Bay, were busy collecting information regarding Castro's threats to drive out foreign settlers, including many Americans. Things were rapidly coming to a head as reflected by correspondence from Larkin to Vice-Consul Leidesdorff in April 1846:

> Our minister has been refused in Mexico. By the message of President Polk that I forwarded to you by W.H. Davis you find his recommendation to do nothing with M. [Mexico] until the reception of our Mexican Minister was known. That is now known. And in all likelihood the states have declared War against M. to bring her to peace in proper time, in which case the com. may be weekly expected here ...There is every appearance of war with Mexico, none with Eng...it appears over 1000 Mormons are coming...If you are selling any Real Estate, hold on a time, and see if it may not bring more in '47...I am inclined to think some of the great ones here are preparing for the coming change. If so I hope the[y] will not allow their followers to be entirely in the dark. And after all, these reports may prove but squalls. Yet the pear is ripe for falling...

In late April Larkin wrote Stearns that President James Polk "has taken a high stand respecting Oregon from which he will not descend. Mr. Tyler had before said the Oregon is ours, and we shall people it." It was clear now that the administration was committed to Oregon as well as Texas. This left only California in a precarious state of limbo, which Larkin and his friendly confidant, John A. Sutter, knew could not last long.

In May, Larkin appointed his trusted friend, Abel Stearns as his confidential agent for Southern California (see Stearns). He also wrote Secretary of State Buchanan, offering to undertake a secret diplomatic mission to Mexico to seek a peaceable solution to the political stalemate he thought existed between the two countries. He probably received no reply to this magnanimous gesture, because by then war had been declared.

THE BEAR FLAG REVOLT on June 14 caught Larkin by surprise and upset all his plans. He had been working with General Mariano Vallejo—who was pro-American—to wrest California from Mexican control by peaceful means. When he learned that Vallejo and his closest advisors had been taken prisoners and incarcerated at Sutter's Fort, he was shocked and dismayed (see Vallejo).

Furthermore, he was upset that he had learned the news first from a letter dated June 16 from U.S. Navy Commander John Montgomery, whose ship *Portsmouth* was still anchored off Yerba Buena. He thought Vice Consul Leidesdorff should have notified him immediately, and hoped Fremont and Lieutenant Gillespie were not the instigators of the revolt. But after Fremont replaced William Ide as military commander at Sonoma, Larkin began to wonder (see Ide). A letter dated June 18 to William Leidesdorff reflects his feelings at the time:

> ...I am supprised that you did not informed me at the moment respecting the taking of Sonoma, and carrying off Messrs Prudon, Leese & the two Vallejo [s] by Foreigners. I can hardly believe it and do not understand the affair, altho' in the Pueblo and in M. [Monterey] I am supposed to be well acqainted with the whole. Do not hereafter let such important news passed unnoticed....

Though Larkin must have been furious at not being informed sooner, he did nothing but issue this warning. The mild reprimand probably crossed Leidesdorff's letter dated June 19, in which the vice consul gave Larkin full particulars of the affair. As Leidesdorff explained later, he did not pass the news until he had verified it; hence the slight delay.

There were rumors that Larkin, himself, might be taken prisoner in exchange for Vallejo, but he made no attempt to escape, and nothing came of it. Later he was able to arrange the release of Vallejo and his aides. Rumors of war with Mexico ran rampant; American warships were in the area, but this was not considered unusual. Furthermore, Stearns had written that British warships were also cruising in California waters.

In another letter to Leidesdorff on July 5, Larkin states: "Certainly the Bear goes ahead beyond all animals in these parts. Should not be surprised to see him here in 15 or 20 days. If he does come, I suppose he will enter, as people do not seem enclined to prevent him." Two days later U.S. Commodore Sloat sent his men ashore to take Monterey and raise the Stars and Stripes over the customs house. This came as a surprise to Larkin but this time he could not blame Leidesdorff for delaying the news.

His feelings were certainly ambivalent about the military occupation and official word that war had been declared as far back as May. All his efforts to secure the country without war appeared dashed, and he feared that many of his friends on both sides would die. Even so, he helped Sloat draft a proclamation announcing the occupation of California and ultimately profited greatly from it. When Fremont and his men arrived in Monterey a few days later, Sloat and Larkin received him coldly. Fremont's volunteers were not formally accepted as part of the United States armed forces until Sloat was replaced by Commodore Robert Stockton on July 15. Ironically, this was just before the surprise arrival of a British warship.

Larkin wanted to sail directly to the East Coast and report to the Secretary of State for further orders. Instead, Stockton took Larkin with him when his invasion force sailed south to occupy Southern California. Before the occupation took place, Larkin contacted Abel Stearns in a final attempt to avoid bloodshed. He (Stearns) was to convince Pío Pico and General José Castro to submit to the U.S. forces without resistance.

Though Larkin's efforts failed to obtain official approval, the occupation took place on August 13 without the bloodshed he feared, while both Castro and Pico fled to Mexico. Stockton then appointed Larkin a naval agent to supply the U.S. fleet with food and other necessary supplies. Assuming Southern California was safely secured, Stockton left Fremont and Gillespie with a small occupation force in Los Angeles and sailed north with Larkin. Upon reaching Monterey, Larkin worked with William H. Davis in supplying the navy and acquiring land for himself in Yerba Buena (San Francisco); See Davis. Fremont was then ordered north by Stockton.

In early October came unbelievable news that a rebellion had taken place in Los Angeles; Lt. A. Gillespie's occupation forces had been driven to seek safety aboard a ship anchored off San Pedro. When Stockton hurriedly took his ships back south to reinforce them, California was in turmoil, and Larkin faced real danger for the first time during the war. After moving his family to Yerba Buena for safety, he was captured by hostile Californians near there on his way to visit his sick daughter, Sophia Adeline, who died a short time later. After witnessing the Battle of La Natividad with his captors, he was taken on a grueling four-day horseback ride to Santa Barbara. Besides being chronically deaf, Larkin was ill, and his captives allowed him to rest at the ranch of Irish settler, Nicholas Den (see Den). Larkin was later imprisoned in Los Angeles. For awhile he was threatened with execution, but cooler heads won out and he was treated well by his captors.

B Y FEBRUARY 1847 the fighting was over, and Larkin sailed to Monterey, where he and his remaining family were re-united. By then Larkin had business interests in Yerba Buena, renamed San Francisco, which was beginning to grow. Unfortunately, he and Leidesdorff had a falling out over business matters and never had much to do with each other after that. Leidesdorff died less than a year later.

After James Marshall's gold discovery in January 1848, Larkin moved permanently to San Francisco and was there when the town began to boom. Meanwhile, an altercation between John C. Fremont and General Stephen Kearny had resulted in Fremont's being returned to Washington D.C. to face a Court Martial for insubordination and worse. Before leaving, Fremont enlisted Larkin and Ned Beale as his agents to purchase for him a suitable ranch near San Jose.

When Fremont's Court Martial failed to exonerate him, he resigned his army commission and headed back to California in mid-1848. After his arrival, he reportedly felt betrayed by Larkin's choice of a ranch for him. Instead of finding land near San Jose, Larkin had purchased from ex-governor Alvarado a huge parcel called Las Mariposas, in an eastern portion of the San Joaquin Valley. To Fremont and his aristocratic wife, Jessie Benton, it seemed a wild, primitive place indeed; certainly not a place where civilized people would choose to live.

But when gold was found there in large quantities, all was forgiven, and Fremont went on to take a vast fortune from his mines. Larkin also prospered; not from gold, per se, but from business opportunities and land speculations that sprang up after the Mexican War, especially during the Gold Rush. He invested heavily with Josiah Belden in San Francisco real estate and was closely associated with Samuel Brannan and William H. Davis in various enterprises there. He also bought property in Sacramento and in Benicia, which he helped to develop with M. G. Vallejo and Robert Semple (see separate chapters).

After serving as a delegate to the Constitutional Convention during the fall of 1849, Larkin and family boarded a ship bound for Panama

City in early 1850. After crossing the Isthmus, they reached New York in April. Larkin spent time in Washington, petitioning Congress for large sums allegedly due him for supplies delivered to the navy during the war, for constructing the wharf in Monterey and all the work he had done on the customs house. He received little or no payment for any of these claims.

Apparently it was Larkin's intention at the time to settle in New York, but business interests in California required him to travel back and forth until 1853, when he and his family returned to California for good. Larkin hadn't felt comfortable in New York, and now he built an opulent mansion in San Francisco. The next few years were largely devoted to land speculations throughout Northern California as Larkin bought and sold many large parcels. At one time he owned or controlled about 250,000 acres, yet he never felt really comfortable with his new life, as evidenced by a letter to Abel Stearns dated April 24, 1856:

> ...I begin to yearn after the times prior to July 1846 and all their honest pleasures and the flesh pots of those days. Halcyon days they were. We shall not enjoy the like again.

Thomas O. Larkin spent his final years in compiling a comprehensive list of around 300 names of U.S. citizens and British subjects who had lived in Alta California prior to 1840. This list has been invaluable to historians.(See *First and Last Consul* in the bibliography). Larkin died in 1858 at the age of 56 from typhoid fever, a tragic and premature end to such a full and fruitful life. He is buried in Colma, a suburb of San Francisco.

Larkin's role was crucial in building good will and commerce during his early residence in Monterey and his service as U.S. Consul from 1844 until July 1846, when U.S. forces occupied the territory. It is possible that, if left to his own pursuits, he could have brought California into the Union without war. Historian Richard Dillon, in his book *Fool's Gold*, says Larkin "...was second only to Sutter in importance in the transformation of Alta California into an American state." It is fitting that Larkin served as a delegate with John A. Sutter during the Constitutional Convention held in Monterey in the fall of 1849. Larkin Street in San Francisco was named in honor of the old pioneer; his home in Monterey stands as a historical attraction, as does the old Custom house he built.

BIBLIOGRAPHY

–Bancroft, Hubert H. *History of California*, vol. I-VI. History Co., San Francisco, 1886. Repub., Wallace Hebberd, Santa. Barbara, CA, 1966.

–Bryant, Edwin. *What I Saw In California.* University of Nebraska Press, Lincoln, 1985.

–Clyman, James. *Journal of a Mountain Man.* Mt. Press Publ. Co. Missoula, MT, 1984.

–Davis, William Heath. *Seventy-Five Years in California.* John Howell Books, San Francisco, 1967.

–DeVoto, Bernard. *The Year of Decision-1846.* Houghton Mifflin Co., Boston, 1942

–Dillon, Richard. *Fool's Gold, a Biography of John A. Sutter.* Coward-McCann, Inc., New York, 1967.

–Egan, Ferol. *Fremont, Explorer for a Restless Nation.* University of Nevada Press, Reno, 1977.

–Gay, Theressa. *James Marshall.* Talisman Press, Georgetown, CA, 1967.

–Harlow, Neal. *California Conquered.* University California Press, Berkeley, 1982.

–Hague, Harlan & Landgum, David J. *Thomas O. Larkin, A Life of Patriotism and Profit in Old California.* University of Oklahoma Press, Norman, 1990.

–Hawgood, John A. (editor). *First and Last Consul: Thomas Oliver Larkin and the Americanization of California..* (A selection of letters written by T. O. Larkin.) Huntington Library, San Marino, CA, 1962. Excerpts of letters included in the text are quoted from this publication.

–Lewis, Oscar. *Sutter's Fort, Gateway to Gold Fields.* Prentice-Hall, Englewood Cliffs, NJ, 1966.

–Lyman, George D. *John Marsh, Pioneer.* Chas. Scribner's Sons, New York, 1933.

–Underhill, Reuben L. *From Cowhides To Golden Fleece.* Stanford University Press, Palo Alto, CA, 1939 & 1946.

–Wilcox, Del. *Voyagers To California.* Sea Rock Press, Elk, CA, 1991.

Peter Lassen
Courtesy California State Library

PETER LASSEN (DON PEDRO)

1800 – 1859

THE SECOND SON of Joanne Sophie Westergaard and Lars Nielsen, Peter Lassen was born in Farum, Denmark, October 31, 1800. According to Danish custom, Peter's surname would have been Larsen (Lar's son), but later Peter changed it to Peter Larsen Farum. It wasn't until he emigrated to the United States in 1830 that he again changed his name to Peter Lassen.

As a farm laborer, work was sporadic for Lars Nielsen, and he moved his family around the country seeking work. During this period Lars sired two other children, who died in infancy. When Peter was around nine, the family moved to Hillerod. At least three more children were born to the family after their arrival there; however, the oldest boy, Johan, died in 1811. After getting a basic grade school education, Peter left home as a teen-ager and moved in with his Uncle Christen Nielsen in Kalundborg to learn the blacksmith trade.

At age 23 young Lassen moved to Copenhagen, where he practiced his trade. Peter was described as having blue eyes and brown hair and was a short man, standing a bit over five-foot-two. Military service was required to become a master blacksmith, but because of his short stature Peter could only be admitted into the service as a member of the guard's reinforcement battalion. To overcome this obstacle, Peter petitioned the King in 1827 for permission to join the Civic Guard in Copenhagen. Permission was granted, and Peter went on to become a master blacksmith.

Despite his newly won qualifications, Peter found he couldn't make a decent living in Copenhagen. In 1830 he petitioned the King for permission to emigrate to America. Permission was granted that same year, whereupon Peter sold his shop and sailed for the United States. He arrived in Boston around the first of the new year and promptly changed his name to Lassen. A short time later Lassen got caught up in the western migration and moved to Charlton County, Missouri. He practiced his trade there for several years, during which he met John A.

Sutter and others who were talking about the new promised land of California. He also became a member of a Masonic Lodge: Warren Lodge No. 74, Keytesville.

BY 1839 Lassen had given in to an urge to go farther west, as John Sutter had done the preceding year, and he was on the overland trail to Oregon with a small emigrant party of eleven men and two women. The Oregon Trail was then in its infancy, so the journey must have been a difficult one indeed. Upon reaching Fort Hall, the two exhausted women stayed there to rest while 27 trappers joined Lassen's small group of men for the final leg to Oregon. Upon reaching The Dalles on the Columbia River, they apparently left their livestock there and continued downriver to Fort Vancouver by boat or raft. Finally Lassen arrived safely in the Willamette Valley, where he spent the long, wet winter.

During early summer 1840 Lassen boarded the ship *Lausanne* on the Columbia River. With him were six others, including William Wiggins, a native of New York who had accompanied Lassen on his overland journey, Pablo Gutiérrez, Sebastian Keyser and Niklaus Allgeier, who had traveled overland to Oregon with John A. Sutter a year earlier.

Sailing south along the dangerous, rugged coast–where they nearly lost the ship–they landed at Bodega Bay, Alta California, in late July. Though Mexican authorities tried to arrest them, Russian Governor Rotcheff from Fort Ross intervened in their behalf. He then escorted the grateful emigrants to nearby Fort Ross for a visit, while they appealed to Mariano Vallejo for permission to remain (see Vallejo).

After a pleasant ten-day stay at Fort Ross, Lassen, Wiggins and the others then acquired horses to make their way southeast to John A. Sutter's New Helvetia settlement at the confluence of the Sacramento and American rivers. Sutter welcomed them warmly (as described by Wiggins) with "all the hospitality that famished men could desire."

Ten days later Lassen and Wiggins were on Sutter's launch on their way down the Sacramento River to Yerba Buena and then south to the pueblo of San Jose. Finally they received official permission from Mexican authorities to stay and were issued passports. Lassen spent the winter of 1840-41 in San Jose plying his blacksmith's trade. That spring he and some partners built a sawmill on Rancho Zayante, near Santa Cruz and Mt. Herman. Later the mill was sold to Isaac Graham and Henry Naile. This was said to be the first water-powered sawmill in California (see Graham).

Lassen took 100 mules in payment, which he drove to the Cosumnes River. There he established a small ranch and did some blacksmithing. He also did considerable work for John Sutter and helped Charles Weber establish his settlement that eventually became the City of Stockton (see Weber). In 1843 Lassen, John Bidwell and other Sutter employees rode north to recover stolen horses. After chasing the thieves north to present-day Red Bluff, they recovered the horses and drove them back to Sutter's Fort (see Sutter).

This was Lassen's first journey to what became Tehama County, and he found the area very appealing. Later he had a falling out with Wiggins over a horse Wiggins claimed Lassen stole from him. That same year Lassen became a naturalized Mexican citizen with the name Don Pedro Lassen. He then applied to Governor Micheltorena for a 22,000-acre land grant called Rancho Bosquejo, well located on Deer Creek near its confluence with the Sacramento River in present-day Tehama County. There, on wild land inhabited mostly by Indians, he established a cattle ranch and raised wheat and grapes. Like many other settlers, he used Indian labor.

In early January 1845 Lassen rode toward Monterey with John A. Sutter and his tiny army of volunteers to assist Gov. Micheltorena against a band of Mexican rebels led by General José Castro and ex-Governor Juan B. Alvarado. With them were such well-known settlers as John Bidwell, Isaac Graham, Caleb Greenwood and two of his sons, and Ezekial Merritt (see Bidwell & Greenwood).

Other volunteers feared Micheltorena's defeat would mean expulsion from their properties; while some were Indians who simply loved a fight. Ill conceived from the start, the expedition was doomed to early defeat. After Micheltorena capitulated to the rebels near Los Angeles, he and his hated *cholos* sailed back to Mexico and oblivion. Meanwhile, Peter Lassen and the others who had joined Sutter made their way back home as best they could, arriving in the spring of 1845.

Later that year, Lassen, Merritt and William Moon quarried grind-stones from Stony Creek, brought them down the Sacramento River and peddled them to anyone who needed them. Two of those stones were still in existence in the early 1980s at the town of Milford, near Honey Lake.

That same year Josiah Belden acquired the 21,000-acre Rancho Barranca Colorado (Red Bluff), not far from Lassen's Ranch. That fall a newly arrived migrant, William Ide, arrived at Sutter's Fort with a large circular saw and some mill irons (see Ide and Belden). When Lassen learned of this, he offered to house Ide and his family at his ranch and provide Ide a place to build a water-powered sawmill. Ide took him up on the offer and moved his family to Lassen's Ranch before Lassen returned.

When Lassen did return, he allegedly brought with him another emigrant family to live in the same small quarters where Ide's family was staying. Ide took exception, and moved his family to a nearby ranch belonging to R. H. Thomes, where they spent the winter. Later Josiah Belden sold his Rancho Barranca Colorado to Ide.

Early in the spring of 1846, Lassen was paid an extended visit by Capt. John C. Fremont and his brigade of U.S. Army "topographers" (see Fremont). A quotation from Fremont's memoirs dated March 30 reads:

> In the afternoon, about half a mile above its mouth, we encamped on Deer Creek, another of those beautiful tributaries to the Sacramento...Mr. Lassen...has established a rancho here, which he has stocked, and is gradually bringing into cultivation. Wheat, as generally throughout the country, gives large return; cotton planted in the way of experiment, was not injured by frost, and succeeded well; and he has lately planted a vineyard, for which Sacramento is considered to be singularly well adapted....

By the time Fremont headed farther north to Upper Klamath Lake in April, he and Lassen were good friends. A few days later, U.S. Marine Lt. Archibald Gillespie arrived at Lassen's Ranch with letters for Fremont from his wife and a secret message from the government. Lassen and two others then escorted Gillespie north toward Fremont's camp. They camped for the night on the Klamath River, sending riders ahead to inform Fremont.

Fremont appeared the next day with an escort to accept the message and letters from the relieved and exhausted Gillespie. That night they suffered a sneak attack by Klamath Indians, during which several of Fremont's men were killed. With Lassen's help, Fremont launched an attack of his own, during which many of the Indians were killed.

War between the United States and Mexico had been threatening for some time, and Lassen knew the message to Fremont must involve that possibility. His suspicions were reinforced when Fremont abruptly moved his men south toward Sutter's Fort. It is not certain whether Lassen took part in the Bear Flag Rebellion that followed.

In mid-June 1846 Ezekial Merritt invaded Sonoma with a small band of around 20 "Bear Flaggers" and took General Mariano Vallejo and three aides prisoner. The next day they were taken to Sutter's Fort and locked in the *calabozo*. Meanwhile, Merritt's men raised a crude bear flag and declared California an independent republic. Fremont reacted by raising a small army of volunteers and led them to Sonoma to reinforce the Bear Flaggers.

By then William Ide had been elected "president" of the new republic. As a naturalized citizen of Mexico, Lassen may have avoided taking sides during Mexican War as some other settlers did; there appears to be no record of his serving with Fremont's California Volunteers. It was probably during this period that Lassen began selling off parcels of his land in an attempt to establish a settlement he named Benton City. Apparently he also built a store and water-powered gristmill there.

In the spring of 1847 Lassen accompanied Commodore Robert Stockton's party on his overland journey to Missouri with John Fremont, Kit Carson and Archibald Gillespie. Piloted by Joseph Chiles and Caleb Greenwood and sons, the 46-man party traveled east via the Old Spanish Trail to the Santa Fe Trail. They reached Independence in early November (see Chiles).

Before Lassen left, he had deeded part of his ranch to his ranch manager, Daniel Sill. This was probably payment for Sill's agreement to oversee Lassen's ranch during his lengthy absence. Apparently the gristmill had been constructed on that property, because Lassen retained ownership of the "running gear and stones of the mill." [1]

Lassen spent much of his time in Missouri organizing a small emigrant party, which he would lead over a new trail to his ranch. By the time Lassen's 12-wagon emigrant party left Missouri in May 1848, gold had been discovered in California by James W. Marshall at Sutter's Sawmill in Coloma. But of course no one on the overland trail had heard of it. Like others before them, these emigrants sought good farmland and Lassen had convinced them to buy land from him at Benton City, named in honor of Fremont's father-in-law, the powerful U.S. Senator Thomas Hart Benton.

By then the Applegate Trail had been blazed from the Humboldt River into Northern California and Oregon, via Goose Lake. Lassen would follow it to Goose Lake, where he would turn southwest to blaze a new trail heading into the upper Sacramento Valley to his ranch. Unfortunately he had not thought about the difficulty of getting wagons through such wild, mountainous terrain. He failed to learn from Lansford Hasting's tragic mistake with the Donner Party two years earlier.

By September 1st they were at Lassen's Meadows, where the Applegate Trail began. Two hard days later they had crossed the desert to Rabbit Hole Springs. Another long day of desert travel brought them to Black Rock, where they camped beside a large spring of hot but potable water. Though Lassen's Ranch lay directly west from there, they continued north on the Applegate Trail, seeking a more promising route across the mountains. (Three years later Lassen helped William Noble blaze a much shorter trail, leading almost directly west of Black Rock Springs via Honey Lake).

Somewhere along the Applegate Trail, as the story goes, Lassen ran short of rifle-balls and lead. Apparently he found some kind of metal, which he managed to melt into rifle-balls. Later, someone discovered these balls were nearly pure silver. Though many have searched for the alleged lost mine, it has never been located.

By mid-September Lassen's Party reached Goose Lake and the Pit River. Here Lassen broke away from the Applegate Trail to head south-west. Proudly he led his party along the Pit River through beautiful wooded country until they reached the end of a box canyon. By then they were running short on food and growing uneasy. The box canyon forced them to detour south and finally to a complete dead end. By the time they backtracked to find another route, they knew they were lost and were killing off their livestock for food.

Finding the terrain too steep and rugged for wagons, they took time out to cut some of their wagons in half to make two-wheeled carts. Starvation was becoming a reality as they groped their way around end-less volcanic peaks. By October they were actually losing ground and had lost patience with Lassen. Some wanted to hang him. Finally five men strapped their vital belongings on the backs of oxen and left the others struggling with their five remaining carts.

Then, like a miracle, relief came from an unexpected source. A large emigrant party led by Peter Burnett had journeyed into California from Oregon on the Applegate Trail (see Burnett). Having learned of Marshall's discovery of gold, they were on the way to get their share before it was gone. When they reached the Pit River, they saw where another party (Lassen) had followed it southwest. Assuming this party knew the way, they followed their tracks until they caught up with the beleaguered Lassen train—a classic case of the blind leading the blind.

But at least Burnett's party had ample food to share, and probably saved Lassen's group from starvation; otherwise, they could have suffered a disaster similar to the earlier Donner Party's. With renewed vigor, the combined party managed to blaze a new trail through to Lassen's Ranch, which they reached by the end of October. Because of the new gold rush, the disappointed Lassen found the Benton City site virtually deserted.

ONE MEMBER of Lassen's party, Presbyterian minister Sachel Woods, brought the first charter for a Masonic lodge in California. Because Lassen was a Mason and had led the party, Western Star Lodge no. 98 chartered in the town of Benton, is sometimes referred to as the "Lassen Charter." Later it was moved to the booming gold town of Shasta and changed to Western Star Lodge Chapter 2.

Despite the horrific hardships they had endured, Lassen began pub-licizing his new route. It was a shorter, easier route to the northern mines, he claimed. Although it was used heavily during the 1849 Gold Rush, it soon lost favor and fell into disuse. One of those who traveled Lassen's Trail in 1849 was J. Goldsborough Bruff, who nearly perished and didn't reach Lassen's Ranch until the following spring. He then led Lassen back to where Bruff's party had abandoned some wagons and other useful equipment the year before. They salvaged what they could, and brought it back to Lassen's. They also made some shingles and prospected for gold along the way.

Upon learning that Bruff was an engineer, Lassen prevailed on him to formally lay out Benton City. Bruff agreed, and his description of this experience follows:

> I procured an old surveyor's compass, and 2 defective chains of Col. Davis, on credit, for $50. Commenced today drawing a guide plan of the town. My tent is under a large oak, 60 yards in front of the house, in this I sleep, on the ground. In it I have fixed the tail-board of a wagon for a table, and a trunk answers for a seat.

Both Lassen and Bruff were stubborn, headstrong men. When Lassen–who thought he knew something about surveying–kept interfering with the survey, Bruff gave it up, and the job was never completed. Nevertheless, Lassen had opened a store there and the Masonic lodge was chartered in 1849. The following year Lassen hired Bruff to run his store while he went prospecting. Though he prospected areas that were later proved rich—for example, Rich Bar—Lassen was never known to have made a big strike.

THE FAILURE of Lassen's Trail and Benton City resulted in heavy financial losses. He also lost heavily in a steamboat venture when he acquired a steam-powered paddle wheeler named the Lady Washington. The boat was to be used for trading along the Sacramento river between Sacramento and Benton City, but it apparently sank on its maiden voyage. After this catastrophe, Lassen reportedly sold a large portion of his ranch to Gen. John Wilson and Joel Palmer. Payment was to be made in installments and Lassen received little cash. In 1850 Lassen led a prospecting party, including Bruff, who wrote:

> Old Pete [Lassen] expressed a strange desire, to return at this sea-son, to one of the Feather River valleys we passed through, to prospect, and pass the winter. This morning we went, with a cou-ple of comrades, to examine the adjacent hills...Late in the after-noon, Jones & Co. returned without finding the mules; and Lassen & Co. without discovering gold....

Bruff further stated that the main objective of this party was to dis-cover the fabled "Gold Lake," whose shores were supposed to be lined with huge nuggets. After spending several miserable, fruitless months in rugged terrain, the disappointed party disbanded. One thing discovered was Honey Lake Valley, which Lassen found to his liking. By 1851 he had lost control of his ranch and moved to Indian Valley near present-day Greenville, in Plumas County. There he operated a trading post with former trail companion Isadore Meyrowitz and another man named Burton. They were successful in growing produce and livestock for sale to other prospectors.

In 1852 Lassen pledged the remainder of his ranch to Henry Gerke for a $25,000 loan and filed papers to validate his Mexican land grant. It is doubtful that this loan was ever repaid, and Gerke probably foreclosed. Three years later Lassen and Meyrowitz moved to a parcel in Elysian Valley near Honey Lake, not far from present-day Susanville. They built a cabin there, planted a garden, and mowed wild hay for their stock.

The area was originally settled by Isaac Roop, who had come a year earlier and built a small fortress-like log building called Roop's Fort. Later it became part of Lassen County and the City of Susanville. In 1856 Roop, Lassen and about 22 other settlers agreed to a resolution to secede from California and establish an independent territory named Nataqua with Lassen as its president. They were so cut off from California they saw no benefits in that direction and no advantage for annexing themselves to Utah Territory (now Nevada).

SHORTLY THEREAFTER Congress cut Utah Territory down to its present Utah-Nevada state line and established the Territory of Nevada. The capital was established in Genoa, and Isaac Roop became one of the early governors. Honey Lake Valley was assumed to be in Nevada Territory; however, it was later declared to be part of California. This ultimately led to the "Sagebrush War", in which resulted in several men were shot and wounded. By then the grandiose Nataqua idea had faded into oblivion.

Even before then Lassen had been known as "Uncle Peter" or "Old Peter" by his many friends, including those local Indians who liked and trusted him. Though he was pushing 60 years of age, he never gave up his interest in prospecting for valuable minerals. In 1859 he joined a party of prospectors and returned to the Black Rock area, possibly seeking the lost silver mine.

The party separated later, and Lassen and two companions— Edward Clapper and Lem Wyatt—camped for the night. They were sound asleep at dawn's light when a rifle shot rang out. Wyatt leaped out of his bedroll in alarm, but when he tried to rouse the others he found Clapper dead from a ball through his head. Wyatt began running, shouting at Lassen to do the same. Instead, Lassen grabbed his rifle and stood, trying to find where the shot had come from while shading his eyes from the early-morning sun. Suddenly he clutched his chest as another shot boomed out.

The horrified Wyatt saw him fall, but soon lost sight of him as he ran after their stampeding horses. After catching one, he rode bareback for four days without food to make his escape. Upon reaching Honey Lake Valley, he reported both Lassen and Clapper dead. A relief party was immediately dispatched to the scene of the killing. After locating the decomposing bodies a few days later, they buried them on the spot.

No trace of the attackers was ever found. Finally the killing was labeled the work of hostile Indians, especially after Wyatt reported that Indians had been at their camp earlier. Others thought it was the work of another miner attempting to steal a map Lassen may have had, showing where a rich silver mine might be located. Apparently a suspected miner left the area shortly after the killing and was never heard from again. At any rate, the killers were never identified or apprehended. Indian tradition says the Northern Maidu "didn't think much" of Lassen–that he was a squaw chaser. Maidu traditional lore says that their people "got rid of him" somewhere in the mountains when he ran off with a man's wife. [2]

In November 1859 a three-man party was sent to bring back Lassen's body for burial beneath a "magnificent pine tree five miles southeast of Susanville." He was laid to rest there with full Masonic honors beside a monument inscribed, "In memory of Peter Lassen, the pioneer, who was killed by the Indians, April 26,1859." Nothing was said about whether Clapper's body was also brought back for proper burial.

In July 1990, the Sacramento Bee published a story about an old human skeleton being found by rock hounds in the Black Rock area, where Lassen and his companion were originally killed and buried. Because murders are not covered by the statute of limitations, it was treated as an unsolved case, and a homicide investigation was underway as of that date. Some thought the remains could be those of Lassen's companion, Clapper, or even Lassen himself. In May 1992 another article in the Bee stated that after a full investigation the remains are "very likely Clapper's." They were moved to Susanville and buried alongside Lassen's remains.

WHILE SOME of Lassen's contemporaries failed to regard him as a "history maker" and did not think he deserved to have a mountain or county named after him, others venerated him as "the Cecil Rhodes of Upper California." There is little doubt that his ranch on Deer Creek was second only to Sutter's Fort and possibly equal to Johnson's Ranch (Wheatland) as the best known settlement in California during the late 1840s.

Except for his treatment of some Indians, Lassen was said to be a kindly man, industrious, generous and honest. As a personal friend of Chief Winnemucca and a sub-Indian Agent, he helped keep peace with the Paiutes for many years. After Lassen's death, trouble flared again. Lassen made his share of mistakes, one of them being high praise for the trail he established into the Upper Sacramento Valley. Some called it the "greenhorn" or "Cape Horn" route because of its long detour to the north and difficult terrain. It is estimated that about a third of the argonauts who came overland to California in the 49er gold rush used this trail. It fell into disuse in 1852, replaced by a shorter, more direct "Nobles' Road," blazed by William H. Nobles. Besides a National Park, a county and a mountain named in Lassen's honor, several state historical markers identify Lassen's trail and grave.

BIBLIOGRAPHY

–Bancroft, Hubert H. California *Pioneer Register and Index.* Regional Publishing Co., Baltimore, MD, 1964.

–*Calhoon, F. D. & Eaton, James.* The Lassen Trail. CAL-CON Press, Sacramento, CA, 1987.

–Davis, W. N., Jr. *Sagebrush Corner, the Opening of California's Northeast.* Garland Publishing, Inc. New York, 1974.

–Dillon, Richard. *Fool's Gold.* Coward McCann, Inc. New York, 1967.

–Dozier, Dr. Dave Sr. "Peter Lassen Was An Outstanding California Pioneer," *Sacramento Bee,* May 31, 1981.

–Lassen, Rene Weybye. *Uncle Peter, the Story of Peter Lassen and the Lassen Trail.* Ox Shoe Publications, Paradise, CA, 1990. [1]

–Little, Jane Braxton. Two Lassen articles, *Sacramento Bee,* 1990 & 1992.

–Potts, Marie. *The Northern Maidu.* Naturegraph Publishers, Inc., Happy Camp, CA, 1977. [2]

–Stewart, George R. *The California Trail.* University of Nebraska Press, Lincoln, 1962.

–Swartzlow, Ruby Johnson. *Peter Lassen, His Life and Legacy.* Loomis Museum Ass'n., Lassen Volcanic National Park, Mineral, CA, 1982. All quotations except [1 & 2] taken from this publication.

–Taylor, Bayard. *El Dorado.* University of Nebraska Press, Lincoln, 1988.

–Unruh, John D. Jr. *The Plains Across.* University of Illinois Press, Chicago, 1982.

NOTES

William Alexander Leidesdorff
Courtesy California State Library

– 28 –

WILLIAM A. LEIDESDORFF

(Don Guillermo) 1812 – 1848

WHEN THE SCHOONER *Julia Ann* left New York Harbor outbound for the west coast of California in January 1841, Captain William A. Leidesdorff had decided to avoid dreaded Cape Horn by cutting through the Straits of Magellan. The ship was owned by John Coffin Jones, former United States Consul at Honolulu, and carried trade goods for the Pacific Coast. Jones was to cross the Isthmus of Panama and join his ship at Panama City. He would then sail with Captain Leidesdorff to Monterey.

Though the voyage around the Horn was fraught with perils from killer seas, the voyage through the Straits was not without hazards of its own. Narrow passages snaked past steep, rocky cliffs and winds were often fluky. Stiff head winds, blinding fogs and flooding tides brought the vessel to a standstill at times. This is when canoe-loads of hostile natives sometimes circled the ship to harass them. The natives were said to be cannibals, and a constant watch was kept to head off any chance of a surprise attack.

After waiting two months for his ship to arrive in Panama City, Jones feared she had been lost. He was ready to find passage on another ship when the *Julia Ann* finally appeared to pick up her impatient owner. They reached Monterey in June after nearly six months at sea. After unloading cargo there, they continued to San Francisco Bay and anchored off the tiny pueblo of Yerba Buena about a week later.

Captain Leidesdorff–a native of the Danish island of St. Croix in the West Indies–was the son of a Danish sailor and Anna Marie Spark, an unmarried mulatto woman with five other children. William was raised by an English plantation owner who provided the boy with a good education and an English accent. He developed into an intelligent, rather good-looking lad who enjoyed dressing well. He was honest and industrious, and he spoke several languages by the time he was sent to New Orleans to learn the cotton business. His worst faults were a quick temper and a quarrelsome attitude at times.

Nevertheless, he did well in New Orleans under sponsorship of a successful cotton planter. One has to wonder how he carried it off in a land where sharp-eyed slave owners could usually spot a person of mixed blood. It wasn't long before Leidesdorff fell in love with a lovely French girl from a prominent New Orleans family. Her strict father would not allow her to become engaged until her eager swain learned the cotton business and proved his ability to support her in style.

The cotton planter apparently had no family and had taken a liking to Leidesdorff. When the planter suddenly died, he willed his fortune to the surprised young Dane. Suddenly the girl's father had no objection to his daughter marrying Leidesdorff, and they became engaged. But when he confessed to her that he was the son of an unmarried mulatto woman, she was devastated. Fearing terrible repercussions from her father, she broke off the engagement. Though it reads like fiction, the story is that the crushed young man ran off to sea like his father before him. Apparently the girl died soon after from a broken heart. [1]

Upon landing in the crude hamlet of Yerba Buena in 1841, Leidesdorff somehow recognized its potential and decided to enter the cowhide and tallow trade. He must have been good at it, for within three years he had bought waterfront property, built the largest, most impressive residence in town (at what became California and Montgomery Streets) and constructed a spacious adobe warehouse in which to store his trade goods at the foot of what became Pine Street.

IN HIS MEMOIRS, trader William Heath Davis describes how he and the other traders, including Leidesdorff, would smuggle in trade goods, such as coffee, to avoid high duties (see Davis). Whaleships would unload large casks, which supposedly contained "Boston Pilot Bread," a form of ship's biscuits. Actually, the bread was packed about 18 inches thick at each end of the barrels. But in the center were packed the valuable trade goods. If a Mexican official should happen to inspect them, he saw only bread.

In 1844 English trader Henry Dalton bought the vessel *Julia Ann* from John C. Jones and a partner (see Dalton). He kept William Leidesdorff on as captain until the following year, when the Dane retired from the sea and agreed to be Dalton's agent in Yerba Buena. Leidesdorff then became a Mexican citizen–which required him to be a Catholic–and acquired a 35,000-acre land grant, Rancho de los Americanos, fronting the southeast bank of the American River from the eastern edge of present Sacramento to the present city of Folsom.

He also purchased another large parcel where lies the city of Lafayette. That same year United States Consul Thomas O. Larkin–a prominent Monterey trader–trusted him enough to name him Vice Consul. Even before then the wily Dane had enlisted the aid of his friend, John A. Sutter, to keep him informed about events in and around Sutter's Fort (see Larkin & Sutter). Sutter and Leidesdorff did considerable trading throughout the years and became good friends. An 1845 letter from Sutter to Leidesdorff reads:

> I will send two Indian girls, of which you will take the best. The other is for Mr. Ridley, whom I promised one longer than two years ago. As this shall never be considered as an article of trade, I make you a present with this girl. [2]

This may not have been as bad as it appears, for Sutter sometimes "adopted" orphaned Indian children, whom he often distributed to friends for use as servants. While this undoubtedly was a form of slavery or serfdom, at least the children weren't left to starve or to be killed by hostile tribes. In any event, Sutter owed Leidesdorff a good deal of money and hoped his generosity would buy him more credit. Sutter ordered striped cloth a short time later to make clothes for his Indian workers, who had nothing to wear. "When strangers come here, it looks very bad," he told Leidesdorff. "After having received this favor of you, I will no more trouble you until I have made a good remittance." [2]

IN MID-JANUARY 1846 Leidesdorff and Yerba Buena's Port Captain, William S. Hinckley, paid a visit to Sutter's Fort. They were on their way to inspect the Dane's huge Rancho de los Americanos, where a hired man was planting wheat. Sutter decided to accompany them. A mile or so above Sutter's Fort on the American River, they were surprised to meet Kit Carson and U.S. Army Captain John C. Fremont, who had brought a party of soldiers on a "surveying expedition."

Always a grand host, Sutter invited the officers to dine with him, Leidesdorff and Hinckley that evening. Rumors of possible war with Mexico had been running rampant, but Fremont denied knowing anything. Even if he did know something, he was not about to reveal it to people who had become Mexican citizens. He considered them disloyal; however, they were actually opportunists. Fremont misjudged many others during his stay in California, including General Vallejo, who was pro-American (see Vallejo).

Sutter's launch left for Yerba Buena January 19. On board were Fremont and eight of his men plus Leidesdorff, Hinckley and William B. Ide, a newly arrived immigrant (see Ide). While in Yerba Buena Fremont described a visit with Leidesdorff, who lived in the finest house in Yerba Buena:

> His wife, a handsome, girl-like woman, Russian from Sitka, gave the element of home which had long been missing to my experience. [Leidesdorff] was a cheerful-natured man, and his garden and his wife spoke pleasantly for him. [3]

Fremont enjoyed their garden and "bungalow sort of adobe house" with a long piazza facing the Bay for the sunny mornings. Although Leidesdorff never married, it appears that he did not deprive himself of intimate companionship.

On January 24 Leidesdorff accompanied Fremont to Monterey to meet Consul Larkin; Fremont was much impressed with Leidesdorff's knowledge of the terrain and the vegetation along the way. By the time he returned home, the Vice Consul had received authorization from Larkin to issue proper credentials to any U.S. citizens who needed them. This became necessary after the Mexican Government issued orders barring further immigration by unauthorized foreigners, especially Americans. Foreigners already there were threatened with expulsion when their permits expired. The Mexicans were taking precautions in the event of war. Correspondence from Sutter was hot and heavy as the Swiss-Mexican kept the Mexican-Dane informed of events near Sutter's Fort.

In late April 1846, U.S. Marine Lieutenant Archibald Gillespie arrived in Yerba Buena with a letter from Consul Larkin, requesting Leidesdorff to provide the lieutenant with his best room and accommodations. Gillespie was no stranger to the Dane, who had met him in 1844 when he visited Yerba Buena on a U.S. naval vessel. Gillespie left Yerba Buena the following day on a whale-boat bound up the Sacramento River for Sutter's Fort. Leidesdorff guessed that Gillespie was carrying important news to John C. Fremont about war being imminent; he wrote to Consul Larkin: "It will be glorious news for Capt Freemont. I thinck I se him smile." [4]

When Gillespie left Sutter's Fort on April 29th, Sutter wrote to Leidesdorff: "He wanted that nobody shall know that he was an officer." [5] In his capacity as a "loyal" Mexican citizen, Sutter also wrote to Gen. José Castro to warn him of Gillespie's journey to find Fremont.

ON JUNE 14 the startling Bear Flag Rebellion took place in Sonoma, during which William B. Ide played an important role. Consul Larkin did not learn about it from Leidesdorff until June 17th or 18th, not as promptly as he thought he should have; he got the news from a rider from San Jose. U.S. Navy Captain John Montgomery wrote Larkin from Leidesdorff's house that same date, and the next day the Dane said it was "very strange" that the Bear Flaggers had taken Jacob Leese prisoner in Sonoma. He had been known as an American and a friend. "I suppose there is something going on that we know nothing of," he added. [6] That was surely the understatement of the year.

The three prisoners taken at Sonoma by the Bear Flaggers were General Mariano G. Vallejo, his secretary, Victor Prudon, Vallejo's brother Salvador, and his brother-in-law, Jacob Leese. They were all incarcerated at Sutter's Fort under Captain Fremont's jurisdiction. Soon Sutter wrote the Vice Consul requesting a demijohn of brandy, some sugar and tumblers for the prisoners. To Fremont's annoyance, Sutter treated them more as guests than prisoners.

When Leidesdorff's hired men bungled the wheat harvest at his American River ranch, Sutter took over the chore with a crew of his Indian workers. They also rounded up over a hundred of the Dane's horses, probably for Fremont's forces. In early July came the hoped-for news about an invasion of Monterey, led by U.S. Navy Commodore John Sloat. Within days the Stars and Stripes were flying all over Northern California. It was about then that Leidesdorff had an altercation with his employer, Henry Dalton, and broke off relations.

A week later Sloat was replaced by Commodore Robert Stockton, who enlisted the aid of John C. Fremont and his "California Volunteers" to invade Southern California. From the very beginning there was little resistance anywhere. Stockton was confident that the entire territory had been secured, and he sent Kit Carson east with the news. Leidesdorff began construction of the City Hotel in San Francisco, and in September he was visited by Edwin Bryant, who described his visit in his book, *What I Saw in California:*

> The house in which he [Leidesdorff] resides, now under the process of completion, is the largest private building in town...The servants waiting upon the table were an Indian Muchachito and Muchachita, about ten or twelve years of age [These must have been sent by Sutter per his previous letter]. They had not been long from their wild rancherias and knew but little of civilized life. Our host...scolded them with great vivacity, sometimes in their own tongue...It seems to me that the little fat Indians were more confused than enlightened by his emphatic instructions...At the table, besides ourselves and host, was Lieutenant W.A. Bartlett, of the U.S. sloop-of-war Portsmouth, now acting as alcalde of the town and district of San Francisco [7]. [It was still Yerba Buena then].

Bryant was also present in early October when Commodore Robert Stockton was feted by local dignitaries and entertained at Leidesdorff's home with a reception and grand ball. By then Stockton had received word of the renewed fighting in Los Angeles; he had sent reinforcements, but it seems a bit strange that he would remain behind to be formally entertained. The *Californian* dated October 24, 1846, described the momentous event when Stockton arrived:

> Agreeable to public notice, a large number of the citizens of San Francisco and vicinity, assembled in Portsmouth Square for the purpose of meeting His Excellency Robert F. Stockton, to welcome

his arrival, and offer him the hospitalities of the city. At ten o'clock, a procession was formed, led by two aids, followed by an excellent band of music–a military escort...When the Commander-in-Chief [Stockton] had closed his reply, the procession moved through the principal streets, and halted in front of Capt. Leidesdorff's residence, where the Governor and Suite entered....

The day after Stockton's reception, Edwin Bryant and the Vice Consul [Leidesdorff] went with Stockton to lunch on a Russian ship anchored in the bay. Stockton then sailed south, and Major Fremont led reinforcements overland toward Southern California, where they knew fighting had broken out with reinvigorated Mexican troops. The fighting finally ended in January 1847, but the formal Treaty of Guadalupe Hidalgo was not signed until a year later.

Leidesdorff must have sold his house toward the end of the year, as evidenced by a short article in the *Californian* dated Dec. 5th: "Mr. Brown has taken the large and commodious house formerly occupied by Capt. Leidesdorff...."

In November 1847 Leidesdorff bought a two-year-old house from Robert Ridley and surprised the residents of Yerba Buena with the purchase of a 37-foot steam-powered side-wheeler called the Sitka. She had been built by the Russians in Sitka, Alaska, as a pleasure vessel, and was fitted out as a steamer at their post in Bodega Bay. She was used for trading along the Sacramento River until the machinery proved defective and was removed. As a sailing vessel in 1848, she sank in the Sacramento River on the way to Yerba Buena with a load of John Sutter's precious wheat.

MEANWHILE, Leidesdorff had been purchasing city lots and taking part in local politics and civic affairs. He served as treasurer of Yerba Buena and as a member of the newly established City Council and School Board. The town's name was changed from Yerba Buena to San Francisco in early 1847. Two important events affected Leidesdorff a year later in March. The first involved betting on a horse race. Leidesdorff is credited with organizing the first formal horse racing in the area, and apparently he and a man named McDougal got into an altercation serious enough to warrant their arrest by Alcalde George Hyde. Leidesdorff took it personally and used his considerable influence with Governor Mason to force Hyde to resign his position as alcalde. Later Hyde was reinstated by General Kearny.

The other matter involved the astounding discovery of gold by James W. Marshall at John Sutter's sawmill. Though the discovery had been made in late January, Leidesdorff did not learn of it until the end of March, when he received a letter from John A. Sutter as follows:

...My sawmill in the Mountains is now completed. She cuts 2000 feet of planks in 12 hour's. The Grist mill is advancing. We intend to form a company for working the Gold mines, which prove to be very rich. Would you not take a share in it? So soon as if it would not pay well, we could stop it at any time [8].

Another letter to Leidesdorff came in late April from Pierson Reading, a close associate of Sutter's:

Some more recent discoveries on the upper part of your ranch prove that the gold washing could be pursued with much profit. Tomorrow I shall leave for the upper part of the valley. On my return will write you the news [9].

This was followed by another letter from Reading a few days later:

..After Searching for two days in the hills, I found the Mormon Camp, which I believe to be about 16 miles from your house [Apparently Leidesdorff had built a ranch house by then]. They are washing on the South fork of the American Fork [river], about 1 1/2 miles from the junction of the North and South forks [Mormon Island]. As you did not inform me how far your lines run East from you[r] house, I did not feel at liberty to...order them off...I was obliged to take Mr James W. Marshall with me in exploring your land, for which I agreed as your agent to pay him Twenty five Dollars. He was with me three days, leaving the Saw Mill and two Placero's [placer mines] which he is working. I could not get him for less. This is the only expense attending my trip, and I am happy to have had it in my power to render you my services...[10].

WE WILL never know what Leidesdorff's reaction to all this would have been. Instead, we have the following invoice from Benjamin Buckelew:

Estate of Wm. A. Leidesdorff, May 18th
To Furnishing Sheet Silver for Coffin plate for deceased: $2.00
To preparing & Engraving the same: $6.00
Amt. Rec'd 18th July $8.00
  —B R Buckelew [11]

On May 18, 1848, Leidesdorff had become suddenly ill and died at the age of 36. He had never married nor had children, and he left no will. As a result, his sizeable estate became embroiled in lengthy litigation. George Howard was named administrator of the estate, whereupon he moved into Leidesdorff's house. The estate was in debt $60,000 when Howard took charge of it, but there were vast land holdings worth much more than that.

Lt. Joseph L. Folsom, a young U.S. Army quartermaster, was quick to recognize a golden opportunity. He slipped away from San Francisco and traveled to the island of St. Croix, where he looked up Leidesdorff's mother, Ann Marie Spark. Apparently she was the sole heir, and somehow Folsom had raised enough money to purchase the rights to her son's estate. He talked her into selling these rights for $75,000 cash, plus a later payment of around $20,000 [12].

When Folsom returned to San Francisco with a signed bill of sale, the property was turned over to him. In the end it turned out to be worth hundreds of thousands of dollars. Litigation over his ploy dragged on for years, but in the end Folsom got legal title to the property and had a town named after him.

ALTHOUGH Leidesdorff had spent only the last seven years of his short life in California—most of it in San Francisco—he accomplished a great deal. He was one of San Francisco's charter members, having settled there in 1841 when it was nothing more than a drab hamlet. He quickly became a successful trader and constructed several substantial buildings over the years, including the finest home and the first hotel in the infant city.

Many other foreign immigrants, in order to achieve Mexican citizenship and thus be eligible for a land grant, not only adopted the Catholic faith, but also married a lovely senorita; Leidesdorff never married, and yet his house seems to have been the center of a lively social life.

All that remains of Leidesdorff today is a tiny alley named in his honor in San Francisco, his grave at Mission Dolores, and a street named for him in the city of Folsom.

BIBLIOGRAPHY
–Bancroft, Hubert H. *California Pioneer Register and Index.* Regional Publishing Co., Baltimore, MD, 1964.
–Block, Eugene. B. *The Immortal San Franciscans.* Chronicle Books, San Francisco, 1971. [1]
–Bangert, Ethel. "The Dane Who Helped Build San Francisco." *True West,* March, 1983. [1]
–Bryant, Edwin. *What I Saw In California.* Ross & Haines, Inc., Minneapolis, 1967 [7].
–*Californian* newspaper. Facsimile edn., Vol. 1, Aug. 5, 1846-May 6, 1847. John Howell Books, 1971.
–Davis, William Heath. *Seventy-Five Years In California.* John Howell Books. San Francisco, 1967 [12].
–Dillon, Richard. *Fool's Gold,* A Biography of John Sutter. Coward-McCann, Inc. New York, 1967 [2].

–Egan, Ferol. *Fremont, Explorer for a Restless Nation.* University of Nevada Press, Reno, 1977, 1985.

–Gay, Theressa. *James W. Marshall.* Talisman Press, Georgetown, CA, 1967.

–Hague, Harlan & David J. Langum. *Thomas O. Larkin, A Life of Patriotism and Profit in Old California.* University of Oklahoma Press, Norman, 1990.

–Harlow, Neal. *California Conquered.* University of California Press, Berkeley, 1982 [3-6].

–Hawgood, John A., Editor. *First and Last Consul.* Huntington Library, San Marino, CA, 1962 [8-11].

–Jackson, Sheldon G. *A British Ranchero In Old California, The Life and Times of Henry Dalton and the Rancho Azusa.* Arthur H. Clark Co., Glendale, CA, 1987.

–Muscatine, Doris. *Old San Francisco.* G. P. Putnam's Sons, New York, 1975.

–Wilcox, Del. *Voyagers To California.* Sea Rock Press, Elk, CA, 1991.

Dr. John Marsh & Family
Courtesy California Department of Parks & Recreation

– 29 –

JOHN MARSH (DON JUAN)

1799 – 1855

DESCENDED FROM an old New England family, John Marsh was born June 5, 1799, and grew up in his grandfather's pre-revolutionary house near Boston. The eldest of seven children, he was raised to become a Protestant clergyman. At the age of fifteen he was sent off to boarding school at Andover. Marsh didn't last long there; he was expelled because of a prank involving cannon balls being tossed out of the upper story of a building.

But his experience there proved to him the value of higher education. He hated the farm work he was forced to do at home, and wanted to earn money to continue his schooling. Though he was not quite seventeen, he landed a teaching job in an elementary school. Some of the pupils were his same age; in fact, one was slightly older. It was a sink-or-swim situation, and Marsh learned at an early age how to gain respect from his students.

Somehow he saved enough money to attend an early day prep school to prepare for the tough entrance exams to Harvard University. He returned home at the age of eighteen to undergo private tutoring, and attended Phillips school in Andover for strict religious training. After graduating in 1819, he entered Harvard and majored in Greek and Latin. He was expelled the following year for becoming involved in student demonstrations.

Marsh returned home in disgrace; understandably, his irate father refused further funds for his education. Disillusioned and morose, Marsh decided to end his pursuit of the ministry. Instead, he would earn what money he could and return to Harvard to study medicine. A year later he was readmitted. A bachelor's degree was required before he could study medicine, but he did manage to complete an anatomy course, and he studied directly under a practicing physician.

Marsh obtained his bachelor's degree in 1823. Needing money for medical school, he accepted a tutoring position in the upper Mississippi wilderness, near Prairie du Chien, in Southwest Wisconsin. He was to teach classes there for Colonel Snelling, commander of nearby Fort Anthony. Pupils included the Colonel's children, along with those of other personnel at the fort.

NEVER ONE to waste time, Marsh arranged to study medicine there under the post surgeon. A large concentration of Sioux Indians lived in the area, and Marsh became fascinated with them. He spent what free time he had in their village, learning their language and befriending many of them. He enjoyed the life of frontiersman and once carried important mail 600 miles on foot through the wilderness.

Because of his intense interest in Indian affairs, Marsh was soon named an acting Indian agent. In 1824 the head agent left temporarily, leaving the agency in charge of his brother, who had been assisting him. A serious dispute arose between him and Marsh, during which Marsh beat his adversary mercilessly with a cane. As a result, Marsh was discharged from the agency.

After appealing to Col. Snelling, Marsh was re-hired as sub-agent and placed in charge during the agent's absence. A short time later, Marsh fell in love with a lovely half-French/half-Sioux Indian girl, Marguerite Decauteaux. He taught her English, and together they began writing a Sioux language dictionary. After an altercation with the head Indian Agent over back wages, Marsh took Marguerite to Prairie du Chien on his way to appeal to the territorial governor. He needed money to continue his medical education and was determined to get it. At this point Miss Decauteaux confessed she was expecting their baby.

Marsh was torn by his love for the girl and the disgrace he would endure if word of his affair reached his parents. Finally he left her there with friends, explaining that he would return shortly. He was adamant about seeing the governor about his money. By chance, Marsh met Governor Cass at Green Bay. The governor was sympathetic to Marsh's plight. Not only did he agree to help, he appointed Marsh as Sub-Indian Agent in Prairie du Chien. Marsh was then directed to appear in Washington, D.C. for confirmation of his appointment.

He met President John Quincy Adams in Washington when his commission was approved in January 1826. After spending the rest of that winter with his parents near Boston, he started back to Prairie du Chien to take on his new duties and reunite with Marguerite. He had expected to return before the baby was born, but became ill along the way and didn't arrive until after the baby arrived in February.

Marguerite Decauteaux had suffered a hard, cruel winter and had almost given up on her lover, especially when he hadn't returned in time for his son's birth. But Marsh was so wan and wasted from his long illness that she immediately forgave him and proudly placed her infant son in his father's arms. Marsh was thrilled to have a healthy son, who seemed perfect except for webbed toes on his right foot. They named the boy Charles and settled down to a reasonably normal life. Of course Marsh wrote nothing to his parents about the child.

Prairie du Chien was the main fur depot for the upper Mississippi, and many Indians lived nearby and traded there, most of them Winnebagos. Marsh's main duties involved their welfare. Before long Governor Cass appointed him a Justice of the Peace for Crawford County, which gave him more pay and responsibility. Later he was partly responsible for quelling a brief Indian war involving the Winnebagos, under Chief Red Bird, and another tribe, probably the Sioux.

Marsh and Marguerite Decauteaux completed their dictionary of the Sioux Indian language in 1827. Despite his duties as agent for the Winnebagos, Marsh's sympathies had always been with their arch enemies, the Sioux. By 1830, another Indian uprising developed between the Sioux and the Foxes and Sauks. Somehow Marsh learned that the Foxes and Sauks had arranged a council meeting to determine future strategy, and he tipped off his friends, the Sioux. They then set up a deadly ambush for their enemies, resulting in the massacre of all but one of the eighteen Fox-Sauk council members. This was followed by a horrendous orgy of mutilation and a parade through town, where human parts were displayed like trophies. Many believed this was what triggered the subsequent Black Hawk War, and they blamed Marsh.

Marsh must have entertained the same thoughts himself. At any rate, he knew it was time he took his part-Sioux family away from that area for good. Paddling downriver in a canoe, the family fled to New Salem, Illinois. There, Marsh's son was befriended by a gangly frontiersman named Abe Lincoln. Meanwhile, Marsh got well acquainted with a half-trained mystic and herbalist named "Uncle Jimmie" Pantier, who practiced medicine without a license.

THOUGH PANTIER was a bit eccentric, Marsh trusted him and his wife enough to leave Marguerite and Charles with them while he returned to Prairie du Chien to resume his duties. Marguerite was miserably unhappy in Illinois, especially when she learned she was pregnant again. Finally she could stand it no longer and ran off to rejoin her lover. The boy was left with the Pantiers.

Somehow the distraught girl made her way back to Prairie du Chien on foot, but was terribly weakened by the journey. Marsh watched helplessly while she drew on reserve strength to give birth to a stillborn girl. Weakened past the point of no return, Marguerite Decauteux died in her lover's arms shortly thereafter. Marsh was devastated, and could only find solace in recalling the good years they had spent together.

Marsh returned to New Salem and made arrangements to leave six-year old Charles there with the Pantiers. He also left money for the boy's education, intending to move farther west to seek a new life. But fate dealt him a different hand, and he ended up involved in the bloody Black Hawk War–the very war many blamed on him. Among other things, Black Hawk–a powerful chief of the Sauks–was still seeking revenge against the Sioux for the treacherous Fox-Sauk massacre.

The infamous Black Hawk War of 1832 is a story in itself and will not be repeated here. To summarize, Marsh was commissioned to recruit Sioux and other Indians who would be willing to join the white settlers and fight against Black Hawk's Fox-Sauk hostiles. Many casualties resulted on both sides before Black Hawk's forces were badly mauled and finally defeated. The result was the loss of a huge tract of valuable land to the white men.

Even before then, Marsh had become morose and depressed about his lot in life. The loss of Marguerite and abandonment of his son preyed on his mind, as did the constant fighting among the various Indian factions within his jurisdiction. In addition, a devastating epidemic of cholera had wiped out many of his friends–whites and Indians alike. He resigned his position as Justice of the Peace, sold his store, his trading business and his house in preparation for leaving the country.

Unfortunately, he left under a cloud of controversy. It appears that greed had replaced love in his heart, and he was accused of selling illegal rifles and ammunition to the Indians. A warrant for his arrest was issued in 1832, but Marsh fled before it was enforced. He then headed for the Missouri frontier at St. Louis, where he joined a fur-trading expedition leaving for the Rocky Mountains.

Riding a cantankerous Missouri mule, he and his companions followed the fledgling Oregon Trail to the Sweetwater River, finally ending up at the annual fur trapper's rendezvous on the Green River. There they freely caroused with the trappers and traded their foofaraw and trade goods for valuable beaver pelts. Rather than returning to St. Louis, Marsh stopped at Independence, where he established himself as a general merchant and bar owner.

There he met well-known settlers, such as John A. Sutter, Col. John Bartleson and L.W. Boggs, a former governor of Missouri. He also continued his Rocky Mountain fur trading and began accumulating the wealth he coveted. Finally he felt secure enough to risk arrest by returning to New Salem, Illinois, to visit his son. The Pantiers were doing a good job raising the boy, and Marsh was pleased with the results.

The year 1835 saw a sharp turndown in the economy of Independence, and Marsh lost nearly everything he had worked so hard to accumulate. He also got word that the authorities had located him. It was time to leave, and this time he headed down the Santa Fe Trail. His assets included a fine horse, a pack mule loaded with supplies and his beloved collection of books.

Marsh was 36 years old by then, a fine figure of a man who stood well over six feet tall. Somewhere along the way he became separated from his companions and was captured by hostile Comanches. His life was spared when he was successful in removing an arrowhead from the arm of the tribal chief. The chief insisted that he stay, and "married off" his favorite grand-daughter to the Yankee miracle worker. Marsh finally escaped when his well-bred horse was able to outrun the Comanche mustangs.

Finally Marsh reached Santa Fe, where he began hearing intriguing stories about California. He had planned to head for South America but soon changed his mind and decided on California instead. After spending several months in Santa Fe, where he learned to speak Spanish, he joined a an exploration party and left for Alta California. Jedediah Smith had blazed a trail there a decade earlier, but Marsh's party went farther south into Mexico before heading west. They finally reached Los Angeles in February 1836.

L OS ANGELES was the capital at the time, presided over by Governor Nicolás Gutiérrez. A short time after Marsh's arrival, Gutiérrez was overthrown and Juan B. Alvarado became governor. The capital was then moved to Monterey. Los Angeles wasn't much more than a scattering of crude adobe buildings at the time, and Marsh wanted to leave there for "greener pastures" in the north. But he was out of funds and needed work to replenish them.

After learning that the pueblo was in need of a doctor, he presented his Harvard diploma to Mexican officials, leading them to believe it was a degree in medicine. It was written in Latin; as no one could translate it, he was accepted at face value. He rented a crude adobe *casa*, obtained a few drugs and instruments and set up practice. His practice was not limited to Mexicans, as many Yankees passed through from ships that stopped in San Pedro for hide trading. And of course there were many births among the Mexican and Indian women.

Marsh was forced to take many of his fees in hides and tallow, which were the main media of exchange at the time. In 1838 he was able to sell his practice to another physician and left to locate a ranch for sale in the more desirable north. But before he could own land, he was told he would have to convert to Catholicism and swear allegiance to Mexico. This was a bitter pill for a hard-nosed Yankee Calvinist like Marsh to swallow, and he postponed it until 1844. Meanwhile he did not intend to let this technicality stop him from purchasing land; he traveled throughout Northern California and the Pacific Northwest before making a decision on where to settle. While exploring the great San Joaquin Valley, he and some companions came across a river, near which they discovered large mounds of human skulls and bones. Assuming it was a burial ground or the site of a huge Indian battle, they named the river, "Calaveras," the Spanish word for skulls. It retains that name today.

During the spring of 1837, Marsh agreed to buy Rancho Los Meganos on the eastern slope of Mt. Diablo in the upper San Joaquin Valley. Many warned him it was too far removed from civilization and too close to hostile Indians who frequented the area. The threat of Indians did not frighten Marsh. He wished to hide away from civilization, hoping U.S. authorities would never find him. The property extended to the San Joaquin River, nine miles away. It took time to transfer title and he moved onto it a year later.

He lived in a four-room adobe building with a thatched roof, and he immediately began to befriend local Indians, hoping they would agree to work for him. He would need much labor for tending the livestock, fields, vineyards and orchards he envisioned. Meanwhile, he became acquainted with his closest neighbors, including Robert Livermore, who owned a rancho about thirty miles away, near San Jose. By the autumn of 1839, he had a new "neighbor" when his old acquaintance from Missouri, John A. Sutter, established his New Helvetia at the confluence of the Sacramento and American Rivers, about fifty miles northeast of Marsh's ranch (see Sutter).

Marsh's other neighbors were Mexican ranchers such as Martinez, Pacheco and Sunol, with whom he rarely associated. In the fall, trappers from the Hudson's Bay Company came to trap the vast delta waters for furs. Marsh seized the opportunity by trading fiery home-made brandy for beaver pelts. Finally he and Sutter convinced Governor Alvarado to place high duties on Hudson's Bay Company operations, to the point where they eventually discontinued their operations there.

Marsh was quick to acquire an attractive Indian mistress, whom he promptly installed in his newly built adobe *hacienda*. Though he had never married, he did not lack for feminine companionship. He had a weakness for Indian women—a "squaw man," he was called behind his back. While the *Californio rancheros* were hospitable to a fault, Marsh preferred to be alone and became widely known as a tight-fisted recluse. He did cater to the local Indians, however, and won their loyalty and trust by treating the sick among them. Soon he had a sizable cadre of workers to help on the ranch. They worked mostly for trade goods and food.

He trained two of them as *majordomos* to supervise the others and had them sleep in the loft of his casa at night to act as personal body guards. The purchase of the ranch had depleted Marsh's resources, and he needed money badly to buy breeding stock. He again fell back on his medical background and set up a professional practice. One of his rooms was converted to a crude clinic-hospital, where he treated the sick. He also began traveling to visit patients who were too ill to travel the rough trails to his Rancho Los Meganos.

For this he extracted high fees, mostly in livestock to build up his herds. He had no competition, so the sick were at his mercy and paid dearly for services rendered. In the fall of 1838, Marsh was in San Jose when his hacienda was sacked and looted by thieves. They also drove off most of his horses. The loss of priceless personal effects such as his Harvard diploma, deeds to his ranch and license to practice medicine infuriated Marsh, and he put together a posse to track down the thieves.

Riding east toward the Sierra, they found a band of Indians encamped. When they found Marsh's horses mixed with a large herd of stolen horses, they attacked the Indians and killed eleven of them. Altogether, around 500 horses were recovered, many of them stolen from Mexican *ranchos*; however, Marsh's valuable papers were lost. Pleased by recovery of the horses, General Vallejo advised Governor Alvarado, who made a public announcement to show his appreciation.

SINCE ARRIVING in California, Marsh had seen the need for a strong government to protect its citizens from outlaws and its shores from potential invaders such as the Russians, the British and the French. The distant, indifferent government in Mexico City seemed virtually impotent to accomplish this, and Marsh was determined to assist the United States in taking over California. If it couldn't be done any other way, perhaps he could encourage enough settlers to come and overwhelm the Mexicans.

He began a letter writing campaign to friends and acquaintances in the U.S., pointing out the many attractions in California. Word of this did not escape the Mexicans; in 1840 he was summarily arrested, taken to Monterey and thrown into jail. He wasn't alone there; many others suspected of trying to overthrow the government were also taken prisoner, including Isaac Graham, who had helped overthrow the previous governor to install Alvarado (see Graham). All of them faced immediate deportation.

Marsh finally talked himself out of the awful jail and watched helplessly as Graham and the others were herded aboard a ship that set sail for San Blas, Mexico. Though these men were later released and returned to Monterey, Marsh never forgot nor forgave the Mexican government for the harsh treatment meted out to him and the other prisoners. He was more determined than ever to lure settlers into the troubled land. Both he and Captain Sutter agreed on this; unfortunately, they agreed on little else.

Marsh's letters had an effect on many in the U.S., especially along the Missouri River, where a party of emigrants formed in the spring of 1841 to make the risky overland journey to the promised land. Marsh's old friend, John Bartleson was elected captain, and a 21-year-old school teacher, John Bidwell, was named secretary. Their epic journey is a story in itself (see Bartleson-Bidwell Party). After enduring horrendous hardships, they finally arrived at Marsh's ranch in early November. Theirs was the first emigrant party to come overland to California.

Instead of the fine accommodations they expected, they found a small adobe house set in the midst of barren, brown hills and parched fields. The rains were just beginning after the usual long, torrid summer. Marsh put them up as best he could and "killed the fatted calves " (actually hogs because they craved fat, and the cattle were too lean). Most of the emigrants were shocked to find an Indian squaw acting as hostess. The warm welcome didn't last long before Marsh reverted to his usual surly ways.

As required by law, he sent a list of the immigrants to the Mexican authorities. Some then left for San Jose to obtain the required passports, but were intercepted and arrested. Marsh had to go there to speak for them, but had a hard time explaining his part in their journey. General Vallejo interceded, stating that the immigrants would be released and issued passports if Marsh would post bond guaranteeing their good conduct. Marsh objected strenuously, but finally relented and did so. Though the passports had cost nothing, he demanded payment of $5.00 from each immigrant. Most had no money and had to give Marsh personal notes for it. Thus the bitter-sweet meeting with Marsh drew to a conclusion, and the disillusioned immigrants went on their way. Some, including Bidwell, went east to New Helvetia, where Sutter offered employment and far better hospitality.

THE NEXT few years brought more and more immigrants. In 1844, John C. Fremont and Kit Carson made a call on Marsh. They had visited Captain Sutter earlier, and after a short rest they left. By then the Mexicans were concerned enough about the influx of settlers to depose Governor Alvarado and replace him with Manuel Micheltorena. The new governor brought with him a small army of malcontent troops and was under orders to expel unauthorized immigrants and squatters from their lands.

Naturally this alarmed the settlers, including John Marsh, who then took Mexican citizenship. Governor Micheltorena proved a reasonable, affable man, but he couldn't keep his ex-convict troops in line for long. Soon the *Californios* turned against him; they wanted him and his men out of the country. A revolt was organized by ex-Governor Alvarado and José Castro. Micheltorena decided to fight back and requested assistance from Captain John Sutter.

Sutter recruited a small army of Indians and settlers to assist him. He had the power to conscript Mexican citizens and did so with Marsh.

The two had been feuding off and on for years; instead of appointing Marsh an officer, Sutter forced him to become an ordinary soldier. When Marsh refused to accept the humiliation, Sutter threatened to arrest and imprison him as he had done with others. Marsh swallowed his resentment, deciding to comply and sabotage the effort any way possible. Soon he was attacking troop morale by constantly criticizing Sutter, Micheltorena and those who supported them against Alvarado and Castro.

When Sutter and his men joined Micheltorena and his forces to pursue the rebels into Southern California, Marsh's efforts proved successful when many of Sutter's recruits deserted along the way. The government forces were so weakened they could do no better than reach a "Mexican standoff" near Los Angeles, when Micheltorena capitulated to the rebels.

Marsh returned home in March 1845, and got together with Charles Weber to recruit men and organize an effort to establish an independent republic, including both California and Oregon Territory (see Weber). They were fed up with political infighting among the Mexicans; if the United States wasn't willing to move, they would. Perhaps Marsh would end up as governor, or even president of the new republic. John Sutter had the same idea in mind, but the conspirators had not reckoned with newly elected U.S. President, James Polk, who was determined to annex California into the Union (see Polk).

Thomas O. Larkin, a Monterey merchant, had been appointed U.S. Consul by President Polk in 1844, and Larkin later contacted Marsh to enlist his support in annexing California by purchasing it from Mexico (see Larkin). Marsh took to the idea with an enthusiasm he seldom exhibited. He wrote to his old friend, ex-governor Lewis Cass, who was now an important national figure, and enlisted his support. Cass helped reinforce President Polk's determination to move on with the conquest. Shortly thereafter, John C. Fremont returned to the area with a party of U.S. Army "topographers" (see Fremont).

Though it seemed obvious to Marsh that Fremont's appearance was not a coincidence, he was worried that the impetuous soldier might do something rash and upset Larkin's plans to annex the country peaceably. When Fremont tried to enlist his help, Marsh refused. Before he realized what was happening, a band of hot-headed settlers had captured Sonoma, taken General Vallejo prisoner, and raised a crude bear flag containing the words, "California Republic."

Concerned that this meant war with Mexico, Marsh went to Sutter's Fort to try to hold Fremont back from further attacks, which he considered foolhardy and unnecessary. Given a little more time, he was convinced that Larkin could negotiate a treaty and accomplish the same end without war. But things were moving too fast. Before he knew it, Commodore Sloat had taken Monterey, Captain Montgomery had invaded Yerba Buena (San Francisco), and the Stars and Stripes had been raised over Sutter's Fort. President Polk had declared war and that was that.

The war in California did not last long; almost the only violent opposition came from Southern California. Fighting there resulted in moderate casualties, but by the following year it was all over. Marsh was relieved at the outcome and that none of his friends had been killed. Now it was time to settle down and attend to business. Things were beginning to come together in the spring of 1848, when an excited messenger arrived with news of James Marshall's discovery of gold in Cullomah Valley (now Coloma). The precious flakes had first been found in the tailrace of Sutter's sawmill in late January, but the discovery was kept quiet until early spring.

MARSH QUICKLY outfitted himself with supplies and equipment and headed for the foothills of the Sierra, where gold was being found almost everywhere. He ended up about fifteen miles north of what is now Marysville, on the Yuba River. There he struck it rich, at a place that was first named Marsh's Diggings and then Park's Bar. He was one of the first to bring trade goods along, which he used to buy gold from the Indians. Soon he had a good many of them digging out the heavy yellow metal. In their eyes, the whites were crazy to covet it so much that they would trade colored beads, blankets, even clothing for it.

Marsh nearly worked himself to death and left for home only after becoming seriously ill. He had accumulated about $40,000 worth of gold within a few months. Not trusting banks—or anyone else for that matter—he buried it somewhere near his *casa*. Unlike Sutter, who lost everything because of the Gold Rush, Marsh benefited enormously. Somehow he kept his Indian workers on the job and was able to supply the gold camps with wheat, fruits, beef and pork, at a great profit to himself. During 1850 he was on his way to becoming one of the wealthiest, most influential men in the West.

He was past fifty by then and had come to realize he had no heir to take over his ranch or inherit his great fortune. He began looking for a wife, but the pickings for attractive, well educated women in the Far West were slim indeed. Then he met a young school teacher named Abigail Smith Tuck, nick-named Abby. A devout Baptist from Massachusetts, she had come West for her health after developing a chronic cough in the East. She and Marsh made a good match, and they were married in June 1851.

Abby Marsh took to ranch life with a will and proved a good companion and an astute businesswoman. Marsh began enjoying life for the first time in many years. He was overjoyed when his wife became pregnant. A daughter, Alice, was born in March 1852. Marsh was so elated that he began planning a new house. It was to be the largest, most elaborate house in California, and the family devoted much time to it.

The baby's birth had weakened Abby Marsh, and her cough returned with a vengeance. The oppressive heat of summer made her worse, and she began making final arrangements. Finally she requested a family named Thompson to adopt baby Alice. Abby Marsh died peaceably, and the Thompsons took the baby to be raised as their own. Marsh was left to grieve alone; it seemed that everything he loved had once again been taken from him. The fairy-tale house remained unfinished, and he lost interest in it.

The Gold Rush had brought tens of thousands of young gold seekers into the area; many were becoming desperate as the gold began to play out. They resented the large land owners and began squatting wherever it suited them. They also appropriated livestock when needed, especially cattle. Marsh found himself embroiled in a constant battle to drive them off his land and keep his herds intact. When the fledgling courts failed to help, he resorted to force and hanged a few until he was arrested and charged with conspiracy. He was forced to take the case to the U.S. Supreme Court before the charges were dropped.

CALIFORNIA had become a state in September 1850, but thieves ran rampant. The notorious Joaquin Murrietta was said to have mugged and robbed Marsh in his own home about then. Marsh was wary of strangers, when a bedraggled-looking young man showed up at his door seeking food and shelter. At first he refused to admit the stranger, but finally relented. Upon questioning the man, he learned that his name was Marsh and he had come to California from Illinois seeking his long-lost father. Marsh's eyes widened with disbelief. Was it possible this man was his son? He had been told long ago that his son, Charles, had died. The man did look like him, but there was one sure way to find out:

"Would you mind removing your right sock and shoe?" he asked the man. One can imagine Marsh's reaction when the young man complied and displayed his strange webbed toes. Satisfied that the stranger was really his son, a tearful reunion took place. Once again Marsh had something to live for, and he took his son around the area, proudly introducing him to his surprised friends and neighbors.

In 1855 Marsh hired a Mexican *vaquero*, Jose Olivas, to break some horses. He had used him before and offered to pay him the usual fee. But Olivas was not satisfied and demanded more money. Marsh refused to pay it, and Olivas left seething with fury. He knew Marsh was a wealthy man and could not understand his tight-fisted policy. On September 24th Marsh left in his buggy to attend to business affairs in

Martinez. He had nearly reached there when he was accosted by Olivas and two surly companions. Olivas demanded his money, but Marsh ignored him and drove on.

The infuriated trio then attacked Marsh, dragged him out of the buggy and stabbed him nearly to death. He was still alive when one of them cut his throat to finish him off. Charles Marsh had been reunited with his father only a few months when he lost him for good. Broken hearted and filled with hate for the murderers, he devoted himself to running them down. Finally he was successful in seeing the worst of them jailed.

Alice Marsh married W. W. Cameron and lived to inherit part of Marsh's huge estate. Charles Marsh moved to Antioch, where he became a justice of the peace. Rancho Los Meganos was sold, but Marsh's buried treasure was never found. The great, empty house stands today, a dreary reminder of Marsh's failed visions of grandeur. A bronze plaque on the highway fronting the mansion marks the spot. Another state historical plaque marks the site of Marsh's murder, and is located on Hwy. 21, west of Martinez.

BIBLIOGRAPHY

–Bancroft, Hubert H. *History of California,* Vol. I-VI. History Co., San Francisco, 1886. Reprinted, Wallace Hebberd, Santa Barbara, CA, 1966.

–Davis, Harold R. "John Marsh, The Magnificent Fraud," *Old West,* Spring, 1984.

–Davis, William Heath. *Seventy-Five Years in California.* John Howell Books, San Francisco, 1967.

–Dillon, Richard. *Fool's Gold.* Coward McCann, Inc., New York, 1967.

–Gay, Theressa. *James Marshall.* Talisman Press, Georgetown, CA, 1967.

–Hague, Harlan and Langum, David J. *Thomas O. Larkin.* University of Oklahoma Press, Norman, 1990.

–Harlow, Neal. *California Conquered.* University of California Press, Berkeley, 1982.

–Lewis, Oscar. *Sutter's Fort, Gateway to the Gold Fields.* Prentice-Hall, Inc., Englewood Cliffs, NJ, 1966.

–Lyman, George D. *John Marsh, Pioneer.* Charles Scribner's Sons, New York, 1933.

–Wilcox, Del. *Voyagers to California.* Sea Rock Press, Elk, CA, 1991.

NOTES

James Wilson Marshall
Courtesy California Department of Parks & Recreation

30

JAMES WILSON MARSHALL

1810 – 1885

T HERE ARE THOSE who hold that James Marshall does not deserve a place in California history equal to such illustrious men as John A. Sutter, John Bidwell or John C. Fremont. He was nothing more than a hard-drinking, eccentric millwright who happened to be at the right place at the right time, they claim; the fact that he was first to discover gold at Sutter's sawmill was just a lucky accident that could have happened to anyone. Others had discovered gold in California before him; why lionize Marshall for that?

But there is much more to this complex, misunderstood man than his discovery of gold. If the truth were known, he probably rued the day he made that earth-shaking discovery. It did bring him fame, but certainly not fortune. The fact is it brought both him and his sawmill partner, John Sutter, to the brink of financial ruin.

Born October 8, 1810, James Wilson Marshall was the first child and only son of wagon-maker Philip Marshall and his wife, the former Sarah Wilson. Sarah Wilson was of English stock, while Philip Marshall was English and German. Both were natives of New Jersey and lived in the old Marshall farmhouse at Round Mountain, Hunterdon County. Three years later Sarah Marshall gave birth to her first daughter, Abigail.

When James Marshall was six, the family moved to nearby Lambertville, where his father built a sturdy two-story brick house that stands today. Three more girls were born there: Rebecca, Mary and Sarah. As there were no public schools, young Marshall attended private schools and did well in the sciences, such as geology and astronomy. He also served an apprenticeship as a wagon-maker under the stern tutelage of his father. Over the years he became a skilled woodworker and mechanic, gaining experience in lumber and sawmill businesses that proliferated the area.

Though there was no Baptist Church there at the time, the Marshalls were strict Baptists. In 1825 a Baptist Church was built across the street from the family home, which made it difficult for young

Marshall to miss Sunday services. Then came an incident that estranged him from his father forever. Philip Marshall held that Sunday was literally a day of rest and no work of any kind should be done. Before church services began one Sunday, his son decided to shine his shabby shoes to look more presentable. As the story goes, his father caught him at it and administered the mature teen-ager a sound thrashing. Young Marshall resented what he considered unjust treatment and left home. He never returned until after his father's untimely death in 1834.

MEANWHILE, James Marshall had drifted around the area working at various sawmills and lumber companies, where he learned the millwright's trade. When his father died insolvent, he returned home to help his mother and younger sisters. Soon he fell in love with a local girl, who apparently didn't return his feelings. At any rate she jilted him for another man. This blow, coupled with his family responsibilities, must have been too much for Marshall. He left home again and headed west, wandering from town to town, taking odd jobs until he reached Western Missouri at a place called the "Platte Purchase." It was an area of rich river-bottom land recently acquired from local Indians and was being opened for homesteading. Marshall quickly joined the landrush, and by 1837 had built a cabin and was putting in crops. He probably knew John Bidwell, who moved there around 1839 and left for California two years later.

A year later Marshall contracted feverish ague, a form of malaria, and was forced to rent out his cabin and move into the town of Platte City. There he lived in a boarding house run by a family named Green. For the second time in his life Marshall fell in love, this time with the comely daughter of the proprietors, a girl aptly named Missouri Green. About the time he thought he had a chance with her, she married a prominent local physician, Frederick Marshall. This ironic coincidence apparently soured James Marshall on women forever, for he never married.

Once he regained his health Marshall returned to his farm, doing carpentry work on the side. By 1843 he probably knew Peter Burnett, who lived in the same area (see Burnett). When Burnett left for California that spring, it may have encouraged Marshall to do the same a year later. For six years he had fought the chills and fevers of the accursed ague, often moving to higher ground to be free from it. The more he heard, the better California sounded. Heeding a doctor's warning, he decided to sell out and head for the Far West on the newly established Oregon Trail. From there he could go on to California.

The sale of his farm netted him enough to outfit himself for the long journey ahead. In the spring of 1844 he joined a party of emigrants led by General Cornelius Gilliam on the western side of the Missouri River. About 80 covered wagons, hundreds of livestock and more than

300 people left in early May. By mid-July Gilliam had been ousted as captain, and Marshall was traveling with a small party of seventeen wagons under a different captain. Marshall was named sergeant.

James Clyman, another member of the party, wrote in his diary on July 20: "our entire company makes 96 teams wagons & occupies with loose stock & all more than two miles of tolerable close collumn" (see Chiles). When they reached Fort Hall in mid-September, they found a letter left by Peter Burnett the year before, advising that if they were short of food they should send a few men ahead to Fort Vancouver to buy food and bring it back. It was good that they followed this advice, for when the advance party returned to meet the party near The Dalles six weeks later, they found them in dire need.

By year's end they reached the Willamette Valley in Oregon, where Marshall spent a long, wet winter doing carpentry work. He must have found time to thank Peter Burnett, who had settled there a year earlier after leaving such good advice at Fort Hall about sending ahead for food. Meanwhile, Marshall agreed to join a party of emigrants heading south into Alta California with its warmer, drier climate. Led by mountain-men Green McMahon and James Clyman, they left in early June 1845. A month later they reached Gordon's Ranch on Cache Creek in the Sacramento Valley. Local settlers there informed them about the recent civil war, during which Mexican Governor Micheltorena had been deposed and replaced by Pío Pico.

By mid-July the party had split, with some going to San Francisco Bay while others scattered throughout the great valley. Marshall and a few companions went on to Sutter's fort, where Captain John A. Sutter had built a high-walled, adobe fort. Sutter was always in need of skilled craftsmen who were willing to work cheap or take their pay in livestock, land or trade goods. Often he provided meals and lodging as well. Marshall arrived in mid-July 1845, seeking employment. When Sutter learned of his many mechanical and woodworking skills he was quick to hire him.

Marshall was amazed by what Sutter had accomplished since his arrival there six years before. The fort seemed huge; almost impregnable, with cannon barrels poking ominously through slots in the corner bastions. Inside, the walls were lined with living quarters, shops of all kinds and storage facilities. A large two-story barracks building stood in the center, and many smaller buildings were clustered outside the walls. Sutter had thousands of cattle, horses, sheep and hogs under the care of well-trained vaqueros, and hundreds of acres under cultivation, mostly wheat. There were vineyards, fruit trees, a liquor distillery and hundreds of Indian field-hands to look after it all. In addition, Sutter had a contingent of Indian guards wearing Russian uniforms obtained with his purchase of Fort Ross.

Marshall was put to work making tools, furniture, spinning wheels, looms, virtually anything made of wood around the bustling community. In time he acquired enough livestock to need a place of his own. Finally he bought two sections farther north on Butte Creek, where he established his ranch. He then divided his time between his ranch, Sutter's Fort and Sutter's "Hock Farm," located farther north on the Feather River.

B Y SPRING 1846, rumors were prevalent among the settlers about a new Mexican policy that threatened their very existence. Alarmed by the influx of foreign immigrants invading the country, the Mexicans were allegedly preparing to expel those who had not become Mexican citizens. This included James Marshall and many others like him, who were not about to leave without a fight. It was said that General Jose Castro was inflaming local Indians against the settlers. Whatever the reason, the Indians began burning crops and raiding ranches for livestock.

Captain Sutter immediately recruited a band of volunteers to chase down the renegades and punish them. Although Marshall had been harassed by hostile Indians during his journey to California, he had never taken part in an actual battle until he joined Sutter's volunteers. He barely escaped being hit by an arrow which struck his nearby companion in the head. After a brief engagement, the Indians were defeated and Sutter's men returned to the fort for a victory celebration.

The Indian threat was only one of a series of incidents that eventually led to rebellion by the settlers. Captain John C. Fremont was in the area with a sizable group of soldiers and topographers on a mapping and exploring expedition. Most of the settlers assumed he was there for other reasons, but nothing was done until June, when the Bear Flag Rebellion took place in Sonoma. When Fremont took over Sutter's Fort and began recruiting volunteers to hold off an expected Mexican attack against Sonoma. Marshall was one of the first to volunteer. He and the other volunteers then followed Fremont to Sonoma to reinforce the "Bear Flaggers".

U.S. Navy Captain Montgomery was anchored off Yerba Buena in the warship *Portsmouth*, so Fremont sent Marshall and a few others there to try and get badly needed ammunition. Alarmed by the news about the Bear Flag Rebellion, Montgomery refused to aid Marshall and his companions; however, he did happen to have a few kegs of black powder laid out to dry. While he and his men were conveniently absent, Marshall and his companions hurriedly carried it off. A few badly aimed shots from friendly sentries were far off their mark as they left the scene with the precious powder. Satisfied that they had done their duty, the sentries let them go.

War with Mexico appeared inevitable, and Marshall soon found himself drilling and training with other raw recruits like himself. On July 7, 1846, U.S. Navy Commodore John Sloat landed men at Monterey and took it without a shot being fired. Montgomery did the same at Yerba Buena, and soon the Stars and Stripes fluttered over the entire northern area, including Sutter's Fort.

When Commodore Robert Stockton relieved Sloat, Fremont and his volunteers rode to Monterey and were sworn into the U.S. Navy so they could be paid and draw stores. On July 25, Stockton loaded them on a navy ship sailing for San Diego. Fremont was then ordered north, leaving Marshall's company under command of Lieutenant Archibald Gillespie in San Diego.

After Los Angeles was taken without a fight, Stockton went back to sea, leaving Fremont in charge as Military Governor. Lt. Gillespie was ordered north to take charge as Military Commandant over Los Angeles. James Marshall was part of the group that accompanied him. He was appointed chief carpenter, and kept busy remodeling buildings for use by the military.

Because his work brought him into contact with many of the people there, Marshall knew they were growing discontented with Gillespie's harsh military rule. He was soon convinced that the Mexicans were planning a revolt, but when he warned Lt. Gillespie about it, he was ignored. Despite the rebuff, Marshall remained alert; as predicted, the Mexicans staged an all-out attack on the city at the end of September. By then Fremont had left for the north, and Gillespie and his men were driven to San Pedro, where they sought sanctuary aboard a ship; Marshall among them. Reinforcements were needed in San Diego, so Lieutenant Gillespie and some of his men, including Marshall, boarded a ship and sailed south.

Constant harassment by Mexican forces in the area kept Marshall and the others confined to the immediate area. Other than a raid south to acquire badly needed livestock led by Lt. Edward Beale, Marshall saw little action. After the arrival of General Stephen Kearny from Santa Fe with about a hundred battered dragoons, they joined with Commodore Stockton's men to march north toward Los Angeles. When Mexican forces met them at the San Gabriel River in early January 1847, Marshall helped man one of the artillery pieces with decisive results. A running battle then took place until the Mexicans broke off, allowing U.S. forces to recapture Los Angeles. The Mexicans soon surrendered, and Marshall and most of the other volunteers were relieved from active duty. After receiving their discharges at the San Gabriel Mission in early March, they began making their way back north.

When Marshall returned to his Butte Creek ranch during the spring of 1847, he was dismayed to find it plundered and his livestock gone. There was nothing to do but return to Sutter's Fort and look for employment. During Marshall's nine-month absence, Sutter had decided to build two water-powered mills. The first was a gristmill, to be built a few miles upstream from the fort on the American River; the other a sawmill in the nearby mountains.

Marshall was a natural choice to build them, so Sutter sent him to choose a site for the sawmill. Several potential sites had been located, but Marshall was to decide on the best one. He and Sutter finally agreed on Cullomah Valley, about forty-five miles east of the fort. Located on the South Fork of the American River, the elevation was below the snowline, and the site was heavily timbered with usable pine.

But before construction could start, Sutter directed Marshall to get the gristmill under way. He spent the summer grading and digging a long millrace and installing a foundation for the gristmill. After it was well under way, Marshall took a small crew of workers to Cullomah to get the sawmill site established.

With him was the Peter Wimmer family, consisting of several children and Peter's wife, Jenny, who was to cook for the workmen. It was nearly September by then, and Marshall knew they would have to hurry to avoid winter flooding. First they built a double cabin for the Wimmers and the workers to share. Then they built another, smaller one for Marshall.

A SHORT TIME LATER, a large number of men from the Mormon Battalion made their way through Sutter's Fort after being discharged from the army. They were on their way to join Brigham Young at Salt Lake, but some of them agreed to work for John Sutter on his mills. A few were sent to Cullomah to assist Marshall. Local Indians were also recruited for unskilled labor, such as building a low rock and log dam to raise the water level, and to dig the millrace. Other workers felled trees, cut off the branches and skidded them to the millsite with teams of oxen. Skilled men used adzes to square them up for foundation timbers.

By early January 1848, the mill was beginning to take shape; the irons and water-wheel had been installed and it was ready to test. When water was released into the millrace, the wheel began to turn, and Marshall led the crew in a loud cheer. Their joy was soon replaced by dismay when the wheel did not turn fast enough to saw logs efficiently. After inspecting the entire system, Marshall located the problem in the tailrace—the ditch that returned water to the river.

Clearly the tailrace had to be deepened so water would flow through faster. Some of the men set to work with picks and shovels, while others used gunpowder to blast chunks of bed-rock from the bottom. It was late January by the time Marshall was satisfied with the results. On Sunday, the 23rd, the Mormon workers moved into a new cabin they had built, while Marshall inspected the tailrace. He returned to the Mormon cabin that evening with some strange-looking rock he called quartz and reportedly told them, "Where there's quartz there could be gold." No one took Marshall very seriously, as he was known to tell tales about spiritual visions or strange voices he claimed to have seen or heard. As usual that night, he directed that the watergate be opened to flush debris out of the tailrace.

On Monday morning, the 24th, Marshall arose early and closed the watergate, insisting that it be packed with leaves and moss to make it water-tight. After waiting for the water to drain out through the tailrace, he waded through what little water was left to inspect the bottom. It was a crisp, clear morning and the sun shown through the transparent water, magnifying debris trapped in crevices along the bottom.

Suddenly Marshall stopped and leaned over to see better. Some kind of metal was shining in the sunlight, and Marshall reached into the shallows to pick it up. He sucked in his breath and stared in disbelief. The small particle looked like pure gold! Peering back into the water, his eyes widened with surprise when he saw other particles shining in the sun. They varied in size from tiny shavings to small nuggets the size of peas. Quickly he placed one of the nuggets on a flat rock and pounded it with another round rock.

He knew from school that real gold was soft and malleable and should not shatter, as would Fool's gold—iron pyrite or mica. Though he pounded the nugget hard, it did not shatter; instead, it spread out and thinned. Marshall's heart was pounding with excitement when he placed some samples in the crown of his hat and ran back to the sawmill, where the others were working. "Boys, boys!" he cried, running up to them. "By God, I think I've found a gold mine!"

The men crowded around, biting the metal and passing it around to the others. None had seen gold in its raw form and were skeptical to say the least. Other tests were then made; the blacksmith pounded a small nugget into a thin wafer on his anvil. Jenny Wimmer was making lye soap by boiling a caustic mixture of animal fat and ashes in a large, black pot over an open fire, creating a strong lye solution. She tossed in a small nugget to see what would happen. When it was retrieved later, the only change was a brighter hue. Soon even skeptics became believers, and Marshall knew he would have to take samples to show John Sutter. A quotation from millworker Henry Bigler's diary recorded this event for posterity: "Monday 24th this day some kind of mettle was found in the tail race that looks like goald."

It was raining hard and nearly dark when Marshall reached Sutter's Fort a few days after the discovery. He found Sutter in his office, surprised and concerned by the unexpected arrival of his chilled millwright.

Sutter was even more surprised when Marshall asked for his apothecary scale and two small bowls of water. When Sutter returned with the requested equipment, Marshall unfolded a dirty bandanna and placed it wide open on Sutter's cluttered desk. He grinned and stood back to enjoy the expected reaction.

Sutter stared for a moment, then picked up a few of the gleaming mineral samples to examine them more closely. "What is it– where did you get it?" he gasped. Before Marshall could explain, the office door flew open and one of Sutter's clerks entered.

Marshall snatched up the bandana to hide the contents from view. "This man must leave," he snapped. After Sutter shooed the flustered clerk out, Marshall insisted that the door be locked. After he calmed himself, he placed the scale between the two bowls of water so the balancing trays were directly over the bowls. He then poured the contents of the bandana into one tray and balanced the scale with silver coins in the other.

When the two trays were immersed in the water, the one containing the gold dropped, while the one with the silver rose. Marshall's eyes gleamed. The simple test seemed to prove the metal in the lower tray was gold because of its greater specific gravity in water. Though Sutter was half convinced, he was not satisfied until he had consulted an encyclopedia about the strange metal and made some other tests. Finally he faced Marshall and said, "I believe this is the finest kind of gold."

Marshall was ecstatic. He and Sutter were equal partners in the sawmill venture, and he assumed he would have half interest in whatever gold was found there. "We'll be rich!" he cried, dancing a jig. "It's all along the tailrace."

Sutter held up his hand to restrain Marshall's enthusiasm. He had been doing some fast thinking, and cautioned Marshall to keep it quiet, explaining that if word leaked out before the mills were finished the workers would desert to look for gold. Seeing the logic in Sutter's statement, Marshall agreed to say nothing about it outside the millsite; but what about the sawmill workers who already knew? It was finally agreed that he would tell them the truth and plead with them to stay on the job long enough to finish the mill. Perhaps they would go along with the idea if they were allowed to keep gold they found during their time off. Sutter concluded by agreeing to travel up to Cullomah (Coloma) within a few days to talk to them. A quotation from Sutter's diary dated January 28th shows: "Mr. Marshall arrived from the Mountains on very important business." This may have been the greatest understatement of the century.

After spending the night at the fort, Marshall left for the sawmill with Sutter's message for the workers. Sutter had judged them correctly;

they agreed to his terms and stayed on the job until the sawmill was completed and began sawing logs in mid-March. By then some other Mormons had made a rich gold strike at a place they named Mormon Island on the lower river, closer to Sutter's Fort. But the word was beginning to spread, and Samuel Brannan and others came up from Yerba Buena (San Francisco) and Sutter's Fort to see if the rumors were true (see Brannan).

WHEN BRANNAN announced the gold discovery, first orally, and then in his *California Star* newspaper in mid-May, the rush began. Soon all the coastal towns were being deserted, as gold-crazed argonauts grabbed up what supplies they could (most of them from Samuel Brannan's stores) and hurried to the mountains. New strikes were being made along all the rivers and tributaries in the Sierra foothills. Though Marshall did his best to hold off the prospectors, or at least collect a percentage of gold found near the sawmill, it became an impossible and dangerous chore.

Instead of joining in the Gold Rush wholeheartedly, Marshall entered into a few mining ventures but stayed mostly at the sawmill. He worked it until spring flooding shut it down. It was clear plenty of money would be made if only the mill could be kept operating. Meanwhile he prospected for gold with everyone else. He found his share of the precious metal but never made a big strike. By mid-summer 1848, Cullomah—shortened to Coloma—was becoming a frontier town complete with tent stores, saloons and gambling dens.

Unable to attract competent help, Marshall did not operate the sawmill the rest of the year. By December, John Sutter was hard pressed for money and sold his interest in the sawmill to two others. Marshall retained a one-third interest. As Sutter had predicted, the Gold Rush nearly wiped him out. His field workers and *vaqueros* left him to seek gold, leaving crops and livestock untended. It wasn't long before squatters moved onto his vast holdings, his livestock was killed off for food and his crops withered and died. Like Marshall, he seemed unable to profit from the gold; he was basically an agriculturist and Marshall a mechanic.

With new capital available for the sawmill, the three partners installed a more efficient water-wheel and put it back into operation. By the summer of 1849, the Gold Rush was on in earnest, and demand for lumber increased accordingly. The mill was running around the clock, and the partners waxed fat. Marshall owned several pieces of real estate and was doing very well, when he became involved in a series of altercations with hot-headed miners who were killing and abusing local Indians.

He and Sutter had always got along with the Indians and had hired some of them to work on the sawmill. Unfortunately, most of the miners had no use for them and wanted them exterminated or driven off. When Marshall remonstrated with them, he was threatened and virtually run out of town by a few toughs. During his absence, some aggressive miners moved in on the sawmill property. Marshall returned and attempted to establish a pre-emption claim to the entire premises surrounding the millsite. This and other problems with miners drove him out of town again.

Marshall returned to Coloma in 1850 to find many lawsuits filed by the sawmill partners to collect overdue accounts and by dissatisfied customers and creditors against the partners. Lawyers had arrived with a vengeance. Statehood came on September 9, 1850, and El Dorado County was chartered shortly thereafter, with Coloma as the County Seat. The new courthouse got a thorough workout with all the lawsuits and litigations eager lawyers could dream up. Marshall was caught up in some of these, especially after the sawmill shut down in the fall. Newer, more efficient sawmills had been built in the area, and the old sawmill finally closed down for good.

MARSHALL'S FORTUNES had been declining even before then; he had to sell his Butte County ranch to pay creditors. His other real estate holdings went the same way; there was nothing left for him to do but go prospecting again. There were those who believed in his claims of spiritual powers; some followed wherever he went, hoping his alleged skill in finding gold would rub off on them. A few of these hopeful argonauts became abusive when Marshall couldn't produce results.

By 1853 it had reached the point where Marshall packed a few supplies on his back and took off for the hills to hide out. A quotation from his memoirs reflects his plight at the time:

> I was soon forced to again leave Coloma for want of food. My property (that could be reached by a course of false litigation) was swept from me, and no one would give me employment. I have had to carry my pack of thirty or forty pounds over the mountains, living on China rice alone. If I sought employment, I was refused on the reasoning that I had discovered the gold-mines, and should be the one to employ them; they did not wish the man that made the discovery under their control...Thus I wandered for more than four years.

This wandering found Marshall mostly in the Georgetown Divide area, where he built a cabin near present day Camp Virner. He also spent time around Iowa Hill. He never struck it rich, barely eking out an existence like so many other hopeful prospectors. Finally he gave it up and returned to Coloma in 1857. By then, most of the easily found placer gold had been taken out of the immediate area, and the argonauts had moved on to richer diggings to the north or south.

Disillusioned with mining, Marshall bought about fifteen acres of poor hillside land for $15.00, with the idea of planting a vineyard. Others were making good money growing fruit and making wine—why not he? He then constructed a small cabin adjacent to the Catholic church. A man named "Doc" Hutchins moved in with him, and with the help of some Chinese laborers, they cleared off chaparral, terraced the hillside and planted grape cuttings.

An irrigation system tapped into a nearby miner's ditch, and a hydraulic ram pump was used to move water up the hill. While he and Hutchins waited for the vines to mature, they scratched out a living making furniture and wooden mining equipment such as long-toms and rockers. They also made coffins for the local undertaker. By 1860 the vineyard began producing fruit, and Marshall was successful in growing many different varieties of grapes. Some won prizes at local and state fairs. Meanwhile the County seat had been moved to Placerville, and Coloma became a tiny out-of-the-way agricultural community.

A cave was dug into the hillside and Marshall began making wine. Soon he was selling it throughout the area and doing fairly well with it. Tragedy struck in late 1862, when his cabin caught fire and burned to the ground with everything in it. Marshall always thought the fire was deliberately set by his enemies. Whatever the cause, friends came to his aid, and the cabin was rebuilt. Unfortunately, all his valuable papers, memoirs, and possibly a diary, were gone. In 1864 he applied for a bounty land warrant for his services during the Mexican War. This entitled him to a quarter section of land in public domain, but he never used it.

Marshall's business was seasonal, so he began hanging out at various saloons and developed the reputation of a hard-drinking "man about town." Perhaps he was imbibing too heavily in his own wines. As a result, his appearance became shabby and unkempt, and his cabin was filthy. He was a tobacco chewer, and the juice often dribbled down his beard and shirt. Embittered by his ill fortune, he was often cranky and obnoxious. At other times he was friendly and industrious, depending on the amount he drank.

In the late sixties, the market for fruits and wines was saturated by larger growers, and Marshall could no longer compete. He lost interest in agriculture and invested what money he had saved in the Grey Eagle quartz mine in Kelsey, a few miles east of Coloma. He moved there and began working the mine himself. Hard pressed for money as usual, he started a lecture tour organized by an ex-partner named William Burke. The first lecture was held in April 1870, at Grass Valley, followed by one in Nevada City.

Marshall was not a good speaker, but people were interested in his story about the gold discovery. He augmented his income by selling his autograph on special cards for 50 cents, and with the sale of a book, *The Life and Adventures of James W. Marshall, the Discoverer of Gold in California*. Financed in part by William Burke, the publication's accuracy was doubtful. Marshall made other appearances in San Francisco, Sacramento and Reno, where it was decided to begin a national tour on the new Central Pacific Railroad. The next stop was in Salt Lake City, where Marshall enjoyed a reunion with some of the Mormons who had helped him build the Coloma sawmill.

UNFORTUNATELY Marshall's tour was not profitable, and by the winter of 1871 he was stranded in Kansas City without funds to pay his hotel bill. Instead, he signed over his veteran's land bounty to settle it. After railroad magnate, Leland Stanford, provided a railroad pass, Marshall left Kansas City at age 61, and went home to Lambertville, New Jersey, for the first time since he'd left there as a young man. His aging mother was still alive, as were his sisters, who had families of their own. He spent time with them all, but his crude frontier manners were not appreciated.

Again using his railroad pass, Marshall returned to El Dorado County in the spring of the following year and moved into the tiny Union Hotel in Kelsey. By then action was under way to get a bill through the state legislature to pay him a small pension in appreciation for the gold discovery. After a long debate, a bill paying Marshall $200 a month for two years was passed in February 1872. He used most of the money to purchase tools and equipment to open a blacksmith shop in Kelsey. Marshall Hubbard, his partner in the quartz mine, helped him build the shop.

Another story was that he treated his friends and cronies to drinks every time he received a check. There is no doubt that he used, and often abused, alcohol. One reason was his chronic rheumatism, a form of arthritis. He was constantly in pain and treated it with an odorous mixture of creosote and turpentine and a galvanic battery machine that produced mild shocks. Perhaps alcohol also helped.

Part of the pension money went into developing the Grey Eagle mine, which never paid off. When the two years were up, another bill was initiated to extend the pension; however, this time it was cut to $100 per month. When this one ran out, no further extensions were granted, and Marshall was once again on his own. He then returned to prospecting, doing odd jobs in his shop and working the quartz mine. During really hard times, he lived off the charity of friends and neighbors.

In 1884 Marshall was invited to attend a gala celebration with other old pioneers, including Jenny Wimmer, in San Francisco. It was sponsored by The Society of El Dorado County Pioneers, who paid Marshall's expenses. Later in the year he was invited to appear in Sacramento for an Admission Day celebration, sponsored by The Native Sons of the Golden West, who were to pay Marshall's expenses. He took with him two dear friends from Kelsey, Margaret Kelly and Mathilde Siesenop, young daughters of his close neighbors.

Marshall had a high old time in Sacramento, enjoying the festivities and the generous hospitality of the Native Sons. Unfortunately, the trip home didn't go so well. Through some mistake, no return railroad tickets had been provided; Marshall and the girls had to board the train without them. Furthermore, when they reached Auburn, no transportation had been provided to Kelsey. The matter was finally resolved, but Marshall never forgave the Native Sons for what he considered outrageous treatment.

Marshall spent his last days eking out a meager living in his blacksmith shop. On Monday morning, August 10, 1885, friends found him lying dead on his bed. He was fully clothed with his hat over his face as if taking a nap. As he had no relatives in California, a close friend took charge of the final arrangements. He died intestate, and a public sale of his meager assets barely covered his funeral expenses. Then came a dispute over where he should be buried. Even in death, controversy followed him.

Some said he had grown to hate Coloma and should be buried in Kelsey, while others insisted that he had always intended to be buried on a hilltop overlooking his old vineyard and the gold discovery site. Meanwhile, his body was packed with ice to preserve it from the torrid August heat. Finally the Coloma contingency won out, and Marshall's body was transported to the Sierra Nevada Hotel, where it was laid out for final viewing. Later, Rev. Charles Peirce officiated over funeral services in the Emmanuel Methodist-Episcopal Church.

There was no road to the burial site on the hill, so a group of burly pallbearers had to carry the heavy redwood coffin to the top. Marshall was laid to rest there on August 12th. About a month later, Placerville Parlor no. 9, Native Sons of the Golden West, passed a series of resolutions on Marshall's behalf. One of them read, "We pledge our utmost endeavors to perpetuate his memory...by erection of a suitable monument over the site where gold was discovered."

Later, Placerville Parlor no. 9 drew up a memorial plan and contacted other parlors throughout the state to enlist their support. A petition was submitted to the state, and a bill passed to appropriate $5,000 for a suitable monument. A committee was then appointed to implement a plan to design, build and erect the monument. A short time later a lien was discovered on the land title. The Native Sons of the Golden West took up a collection to pay it off, and work finally began. It is hoped Marshall's hard feelings toward the Native Sons had softened by then.

IT TOOK ANOTHER $4,000 to complete it, but finally a handsome metal statue of Marshall was erected on a high concrete pedestal overlooking the gold discovery site, just as he had requested. The monument was officially dedicated on May 3, 1890, with an elaborate program attended by thousands. Legend has it that the statue was not positioned exactly right, and over the years it has shifted slightly, so Marshall now points to the exact spot where he found the first flakes of gold.

Marshall Gold Discovery State Historic Park in Coloma commemorates the gold discovery and contains artifacts and memorabilia involving the man himself. An authentic replica of the sawmill still operates and a few old gold rush buildings remain intact. As of 1993, the author of this book plays the role of James Marshall in living history programs and demonstrates the sawmill on special occasions. There is also a historical marker and ruins of Marshall's blacksmith shop in Kelsey. Despite his many flaws, Marshall accomplished a great deal indeed.

BIBLIOGRAPHY

–Bancroft, Hubert H. *History of California*, Vol. I-VI. History Co., San Francisco, CA, 1886. Republished, Wallace Hebberd, Santa Barbara, 1966.

–Dillon, Richard. *Fool's Gold*. Coward McCann, Inc. New York, 1967.

–Gay, Theressa. *James Marshall, a Biography*. Talisman Press, Georgetown, CA, 1967. Unless otherwise indicated, quotations are from this publication.

–Gudde, Erwin G. *Bigler's Chronicle of the West*. University of California Press, Berkeley, 1962.

–Harlow, Neal. *California Conquered*. University of California Press, Berkeley, 1982.

–Holliday, J.S. *The World Rushed In*. Simon and Schuster, New York, 1981.

–Jackson, Donald Dale. *Gold Dust*. Alfred Knopf, New York, 1980

–Lee, W. Storrs. *California*. Funk & Wagnalls, New York, 1968.

–Lewis, Oscar. *Sutter's Fort, Gateway to the Gold Fields*. Prentice-Hall, Inc., Englewood Cliffs, NJ, 1966.

–Paul, Rodman W. *The California Gold Discovery*. Talisman Press, Georgetown, CA, 1967.

–Smith, Azariah. *The Gold Discovery Journal*. Ed. by David L. Bigler, University of Utah Press, Salt Lake City, 1990.

Notes

Martin Murphy
Courtesy Archives, San Francisco Public Library

31

MARTIN MURPHY, SR. 1785 – 1865

The 1844 Stevens–Murphy Emigration Party

THE STEVENS-MURPHY PARTY, also known as the Stevens (Stephens)-Murphy-Townsend Party, and even the Miller-Murphy Party, has been credited with being the first emigration company to bring wagons across the formidable Sierra Nevada into California. There was an interruption during the fall of 1844, when the wagons were temporarily abandoned. They were recovered the following summer and brought down into the Sacramento Valley.

Not one of this stalwart group was lost along the way; indeed, the number was increased by the birth of at least two children. The first, born at Independence Rock, (now Wyoming) was aptly named Ellen Independence Miller, daughter of Mrs. James Miller. The second, born along the Yuba River, was named Elizabeth Yuba Murphy, daughter of Mrs. Martin Murphy Jr.

A native of Wexford County, Ireland, Martin Murphy Sr. was born November 12, 1785. He had limited education and grew up to become an intelligent, industrious man who took his Catholic upbringing seriously. After marrying Mary Foley in the early 1800s, he became the father of several children over the next few years, during which he grew more and more dissatisfied with his life in Ireland. By 1820 he had become disillusioned to the point of emigrating to Canada. All the Murphy children except the two oldest, Martin Jr. and Margaret, accompanied their parents. Their close friends, the Miller family, also agreed to go. They bought land and built houses in Frampton township, near Quebec. The two older Murphy children joined them later.

Martin Murphy Jr. married Mary Bulgar in 1831 and settled near his parents. Another son, James, married Ann Martin whose family lived nearby. In 1837 twenty-four-year-old James Miller married Mary Murphy, third daughter of Martin Sr. Now the long friendship between the Murphys and Millers was bonded through marriage.

By 1840 Martin Sr. was again growing dissatisfied, and eyed the promising land to the south. In that year he again moved his family—except for Martin Jr. and James—to Holt County, Missouri, part of the recent Platte Purchase. The James Miller family accompanied them. Other friends and neighbors from Canada followed, and a settlement named Irish Grove was established. By then Martin Jr. and James Murphy had joined their father with their respective families. The Missouri River bottomland in the area proved rich, and the settlement prospered until, one by one, the settlers fell ill with the violent chills and fever of the "ague", which was prevalent in the area.

Actually it was a form of deadly malaria. Nearly everyone suffered from it; some died, including Martin Sr.'s wife, Mary, and Martin Jr.'s infant daughter. While mourning their losses, the Murphy family was consoled by Father Hoeckens, a Catholic missionary from Holland who had learned of opportunities for Catholic families in the Far West.

FATHER HOEKENS extolled the wonders of the new promised land in California, although he probably had never been there. But after hearing of its virtues and learning that the Mexican Government had close ties with the Catholic Church, Martin Sr., who was nearly 59, decided to emigrate there during the spring of 1844. Not only did his entire family agree to accompany him, many others did the same. Among them were Patrick Martin, his wife's father, and two of her brothers, as well as the James Miller family.

After selling their property and outfitting themselves with sturdy wagons, supplies and livestock, the Murphy Party journeyed to Council Bluffs (now Iowa), on the Missouri River north of its confluence with the Platte River. They were joined there by middle-aged Elisha Stevens, an ex-trapper and blacksmith, who was traveling alone. Also joining them was Dr. John Townsend, with his wife and her teen-aged brother, Moses Schallenberger. Another valued member was Allen Montgomery, a young gunsmith, with his wife, Sarah.

There were others, including their pilot, "Old" Caleb Greenwood, with his two half-Indian sons, and sixty-four-year-old Isaac Hitchcock, who claimed to have journeyed to California with the 1833 Joseph R. Walker Party. Finally there were around 67 people with forty wagons. Most of the wagons were heading for Oregon, and frontiersman Elisha Stevens was elected captain. Only eleven of the wagons with about 50 people—a good portion of them from the Martin Murphy family—were bound for California.

It was mid-May when the wagon train assembled and made ready to cross the Missouri River. Their first real test was crossing the Missouri River, which was accomplished by using a small flat-bottomed boat to ferry the wagons and supplies across. The livestock was forced to swim, though with great difficulty. They then made their way toward the north side of the Platte River, which later became known as the Mormon route.

Another river crossing at the flooding Elkhorn River was accomplished by water-proofing a wagon with cowhides and using it to ferry the disassembled wagons, people and supplies across–a tedious and dangerous task indeed. Though they had feared problems with Indians along the Platte, they experienced none. They enjoyed exciting buffalo hunts as they neared Fort Laramie and crossed to the south side of the Platte. The sight of several thousand Sioux Indians camping outside the fort unnerved them until Old Greenwood explained that when Indians were with their families they posed no threat (see Greenwood).

The trail-weary travelers spent a few days resting and trading for moccasins and horses before moving on. Finally they reached Independence Rock, where Mrs. James Miller gave birth to Ellen Independence. They stayed nearly a week, hunting buffalo and curing the meat. Independence Day was celebrated with a fine buffalo feast before they headed up the Sweetwater River to cross the wide, gentle grade of South Pass.

While camped west of there on the Big Sandy River, Isaac Hitchcock offered a plan for a shortcut to the Green River, which he claimed would save them nearly a hundred miles and several days of travel. He thought they could make it in one day and water should be no problem. But instead of the twenty-five miles he estimated, it turned out closer to fifty miles, and the party had to make one overnight stop without water. The livestock suffered greatly; many of them ran off in search of water. Valuable time was lost in retrieving them, and Hitchcock lost much of his credibility. He regained it in later years when the shortcut was widely used (to the dismay of Bridger and Vasquez at Fort Bridger) and became known as Greenwood's Cutoff; later, Sublette's Cutoff.

Upon reaching the Bear River in rugged country, where they met mountain man "Peg-leg" Smith, the party made their way north to Fort Hall, arriving around August 10th without undue hardship. Some of the party were short of food, and bought flour there for a dollar a pound. Then the party bound for Oregon chose to split off from the others and celebrated a fond adieu. Eleven wagons and more than forty people remained, while their leaders tried to gain information on the trail to California.

Though Joseph Chiles and Joseph R. Walker had traveled the route the year before, no one there knew the outcome of their trip and had little to offer in the way of instruction. The Greenwoods hadn't traveled past Fort Hall, so they were no help. Neither was "Old" Hitchcock. Captain Stevens chose to follow Walker's tracks from the previous year, and headed southwest along the Snake River (See Chiles & Walker).

When they reached the Raft River, the party turned south, probably through what became the City of Rocks, and into present-day Nevada, searching for the elusive Mary's River (now the Humboldt). This seems a likely place to list the travelers in alphabetical order by wagon number:

1. Isaac Hitchcock, his daughter, Isabella Patterson and her children (estimated at four to six, including some teenagers).
2. Patrick Martin (James Murphy's father-in-law) and grown sons, Patrick and Dennis.
3. James Miller, his wife, Mary Murphy Miller, and four children, including William and ten-week-old Ellen Independence.
4. Allen Montgomery and wife, Sarah. (See Sarah M. Wallis).
5. James Murphy (son of Martin Murphy Sr.) and family, including his wife, Ann Martin Murphy, and daughter, Mary.
6. Martin Murphy Sr. and four children, Daniel, Bernard, Ellen and John.
7. Martin Murphy Jr. and wife, Mary Bulgar Murphy, and four boys, James, Martin, Patrick and Bernard.
8. Elisha Stevens and one or two hired men (names unknown).
9. John Sullivan, his sister, Mary, and young brothers, Michael and Robert.
10. Dr. John Townsend, his wife, Elizabeth Schallenberger Townsend, her eighteen-year-old brother, Moses, and a hired man named Deland.
11. Wagon owner unknown, perhaps Joseph Foster, or may have belonged to Hitchcock.

THERE WERE also five single men, Edmund Bray, Vincent Calvin, John Flomboy, Matthew Harbin and Oliver Megnent. Old Greenwood and his two sons, John and "Brit" (Britton), were along but no longer piloting. Thus it appears there was a total of about 50 men, women and children in the party, but with all the duplicate names, especially within the Murphy family, one can't be absolutely certain. [1]

The travelers left only sparse information about the journey from Fort Hall to the infamous Humboldt River sink, limited mostly to their bad impression of the Indians who frequented the area. They apparently reached the sink in reasonably good condition and stared apprehensively at the vast shimmering desert lying before them. Which direction should they take? A mistake could prove fatal.

Fortunately they met an intelligent Indian they called Truckee, with whom Old Greenwood managed to communicate their need for directions to the nearest water. Taking Truckee as a guide, Captain Stevens, Dr. Townsend and Joseph Foster went ahead to scout out the trail. They returned three days later and confirmed a fine stream of water about forty miles to the southwest. This area was later known as the "forty-mile Desert," and the welcome stream was named the Truckee River.

Carrying all the water possible, they made their way to some hot springs, where they rested two hours before continuing. On they pushed through the arid land, through a day and a half of almost continuous travel, before reaching the river barely in time to save their vital live-stock. The going upriver proved pleasant at first, but became difficult when they had to cross and re-cross the river as it snaked its way through a rather narrow canyon. The continuous plodding through water softened the animal's hooves until they became badly stone-bruised and lame from abrasive rocks and gravel. Then came snow, which covered up what fodder there was and caused the stock to weaken even more. By doubling and tripling yokes of oxen to each wagon, they made it to a fork in the river at present-day Truckee. By then the snow had melted enough so the stock could feed.

It was finally decided that the wagons would continue up the tribu-tary to the west, while a small party would follow the main stream south. If they found a decent-looking pass to the west, they would try it. Those who left the main party were Mrs. Townsend and her servant, Francis; John and Daniel Murphy, Miss Ellen Murphy and Oliver Magnent. Each of the six rode a good horse and took two pack animals loaded with food and supplies.

The ride up the meandering river was probably pleasant; one can imagine their awe when they first sighted the magnificent body of water that fed the stream. Though Captain John C. Fremont had seen the azure splendor of the huge lake nine months earlier, this was the first non-Indian party to arrive on the shore of what became Lake Bigler and finally Lake Tahoe (pronounced by some old timers as Lake Tayhoe).

Seeking a crossing over the high mountains that hugged the lake to the west, the intrepid riders followed the west shore to a pass and head-ed up to where it crested near the headwaters of the Rubicon River. Forced to cross it many times, they followed it into the Sacramento Valley and finally to the ranch of John Sinclair, across the American River from John A. Sutter's New Helvetia settlement (Sutter's Fort). It had taken them about three weeks.

The wagon train had worse luck. Following the smaller stream, they struggled up a rise to the headwaters where they, too, found a large sparkling lake, which they named after their savior, Truckee. After the Donner Party tragedy took place there two years later, it was changed to Donner Lake in their honor. The snow was about two feet deep when the Murphy Party arrived, and after spending several days scouting out a trail over the sheer granite precipices blocking their way to the summit, they decided to leave half the wagons behind and return for them later.

Young Moses Schallenberger, Allen Montgomery and Joseph Foster agreed to stay behind to guard them and their valuable contents from being plundered by Indians. Two weakened cows were left for a food supply, and the men wasted little time building a small log cabin with a fireplace for protection against the expected fierce winter weather. It was completed before three feet of snow fell, virtually snowing them in.

But before then, the others were fighting to get their wagons over the summit. This required the Herculean effort of unloading them and carrying their contents, including small children, to the top. Using rock ledges like a ladder, they managed to push, pull and wrestle five wagons to the summit. It was around Thanksgiving time, and they surely gave thanks when they reached the top without serious injury to anyone.

A drive of about twenty miles brought them to the headwaters of the Yuba River, which they followed westerly for three days before camping, because of a threatening storm, at what became known as Big Bend. There Martin Murphy Jr's. wife gave birth to Elizabeth Yuba Murphy. It was decided that most of the men would leave on horseback for the Sacramento Valley and Sutter's Fort to seek help. The others, mostly women and children, would remain with the wagons. Two men, James Miller and Patrick Martin, were to stay with them. Several feet of snow covered the ground, and they built a small, crude cabin to provide shelter. Most of the remaining cattle were then slaughtered and butchered to provide a frozen meat supply until food could be brought back from Sutter's.

A WEEK AFTER their arrival at Big Bend, seventeen men left, driving the few remaining cattle before them as a food supply for themselves. They arrived safely at Sutter's Fort in mid-December, finding that the other party of six who had traveled on horseback, via present-day Lake Tahoe, had arrived shortly before them. The next logical step would have been for at least some of the men to get supplies from Sutter and return for their people left behind in the mountains. But this was not to be. Sutter had agreed to form a military force to help Mexican Governor Manuel Micheltorena fight against forces led by ex-Governor Juan Alvarado and Gen. José Castro, who were trying to overthrow him.

The arrival of twenty-one able-bodied Americans must have seemed like a Godsend to Sutter, and he wasn't about to let them leave. Somehow he managed to convince them that no rescue attempt could be made to evacuate their people until spring when the snows melted; he thought the food they had would see them through until then. By using a combination of money, promises and threats, he enlisted all the men in his rag-tag army. With them were many local settlers and Indians Sutter had recruited. They were to leave on New Year's Day 1845, heading toward San Jose.

Meanwhile at Big Bend, the cold and hungry group there were surprised in mid-December by the arrival of Joseph Foster and Allen

Montgomery, who had hiked over the summit from Truckee Lake on crude snowshoes. Sarah Montgomery must have wept with relief at the sight of her husband. Moses Schallenberger had been left behind alone because he was too weak to reach the summit, but his two ex-companions thought he would be safe until help could be sent back later. After spending a few days at Big Bend, the two men took a few supplies and headed for Sutter's Fort, arriving shortly before Sutter's "army" left. Foster and Montgomery apparently went with them.

When Castro's rebels retreated south toward Los Angeles, Sutter joined forces with Micheltorena and pursued them. They had been on the trail only a short time before some of the men grew disillusioned and began to desert. Some returned to Sutter's Fort. Among them was Dennis Martin, son of Patrick Martin, who had been left at Big Bend. Thinking it was high time someone did something to help the stranded party, he decided to mount a one-man rescue mission. Before he left on February 20, Mrs. Townsend begged him to check on her brother, Moses Schallenberger, who had been left at Truckee Lake.

As he made his way up the mountain, Martin met James Miller and his son, William, walking out. He reached the camp a few days later, appalled to find his father and others existing on boiled cowhides. Snows were light in February, and Martin told the people to make ready to leave while he went over the summit to see about Schallenberger. To his surprise, he found the young man not only alive, but reasonably fit and able to travel.

Fashioning makeshift snowshoes for Moses, Dennis Martin led off and brought him safely back to Big Bend (Schallenberger's lone ordeal at Truckee Lake is a story in itself and will not be repeated here). Meanwhile, others from Sutter's Fort—possibly including Allen Montgomery whose wife was still at Big Bend—had arrived and began taking the refugees out. By March 1st they were all safely at Sutter's Fort, glad to be alive. Some of them returned for the wagons that summer and brought them out. Only the wagons at Truckee Lake had been pillaged by Indians.

Following a short rest at Sutter's Fort, the close-knit group said their emotional farewells and went their separate ways. Martin Murphy Sr., with his six unmarried children, made their way to Santa Clara County, where Murphy purchased the Rancho Ojo de Agua de la Coche, located on Monterey Road, south of San Jose, near what became the Twenty-one Mile House. He remained there most of his life as a prosperous and successful rancher, acquiring several other ranches in the area.

To express his gratitude to God for a safe deliverance of his family to California, Murphy constructed on his ranch a chapel, which he named San Martin in honor of his patron saint. Because his ranch and spacious home were located on one of the most well-traveled roads in the area, near what became Morgan Hill, visitors were frequent and Murphy's hospitality became legendary. He and his large, civic-minded family were instrumental in helping to develop Santa Clara Valley.

Long a widower, Martin Murphy Sr. never remarried. After retiring from active ranching he spent the last three years of his life in San Francisco. He was visiting his daughter, Margaret Kell, near San Jose when he died on March 16, 1865 at the age of eighty. Many mourned his passing; courts adjourned and businesses closed in his honor. Hundreds came to pay their respects to the famous old pioneer. What better epitaph could one have?

NO ATTEMPT will be made to account for what happened to all fifty members in the Stevens-Murphy Party; however, information on some of them follows: Martin Murphy Jr., with his wife and seven children, bought four leagues of land on the Cosumnes River in what became Sacramento County. There was no school in the area, so Murphy started one of his own by hiring a teacher and using a building on his ranch. This became the first school in Sacramento County. Murphy's Ranch became the staging area for the Bear Flag Rebellion in early June 1846, when Ezekial Merritt and others "confiscated" a herd of horses near there belonging to Gen. José Castro's Mexican Army. Two additional Murphy children were born there.

In 1850 Murphy Jr. moved his family to San Jose while building a house on another large ranch he purchased nearby. Named Rancho Pastoria de las Borregas, it was adjacent to present-day Mountain View and Sunnyvale (which Murphy founded). Later called Bay View Ranch, it became the permanent home of the family, which increased with the birth of another son. Murphy Jr. became a prosperous, successful rancher and eventually acquired property throughout the state. He was first to make large grain shipments throughout the world.

Murphy financed the first Santa Clara County Courthouse in 1851 and was largely responsible for the establishment of the College of Notre Dame in Belmont. He also funded the Jesuits' Santa Clara College, now the University of Santa Clara. In 1881, he and his wife celebrated their golden wedding anniversary at the ranch with a huge party and thousands of guests from all parts of the state. Shortly after, Murphy's health began to fail, and he died in San Jose October 10, 1884 at the age of 78. His wife followed him in 1892. A historical plaque honoring Murphy is located on the old ranch property, now a Sunnyvale City park, located at the corner of No. Sunnyvale and California Avenues.

James Murphy, second son of Martin Murphy Sr., moved with his wife and two children to what became Marin County, where he engaged in the timber and lumber business. He furnished the timbers for

Leidesdorff Wharf, the first such facility constructed in Yerba Buena (San Francisco). When James Marshall's gold discovery became known in May 1848, James Murphy left his lumber business for the gold fields.

After prospecting around Cullomah (Coloma) and Dry Diggings (Placerville), probably with Charles Weber and his brothers, John and Daniel, he retired from gold mining. He must have done well, for he and Daniel bought Rancho de las Llagas, near Gilroy's Ranch. James moved to San Jose in 1849, where he bought several 500-acre parcels north of San Jose. He built a grand mansion there in 1872 and planted one of the first olive groves in the area. He lived there until his death in January 1878, leaving his wife and nine children. His home at "Ringwood Farm" is today a Santa Clara County landmark.

Bernard Murphy, another son of Martin Sr., lived at his father's home before and after his marriage to Catherine O'Toole. They had one son, Martin J. C. Murphy, who died at a young age. Bernard died tragically in an explosion on the steamer *Jennie Lind* in 1853.

John M. Murphy, another son of Martin Sr., went to work in a store operated by Charles M. Weber in San Jose. As a lieutenant in Fremont's California volunteers, he helped Weber to recruit men in late June 1846 for the "Battle of Santa Clara" against Mexican forces. As stated previously, the gold rush saw John, Daniel and James Murphy prospecting with Charles Weber in the area of Dry Diggings (Placerville), where they found gold on a tributary of the South Fork of the American River. Later it was named Weber Creek. Weber and the Murphy brothers then recruited a band of Indians, paying them in trade goods for the gold they mined.

WHEN GOLD in the area played out after a few months, all but James moved south. The gold town of Murphy's Camp (now Murphys) was named after John and Daniel Murphy during this halcyon period, and they became wealthy from their efforts. Henry Walsh wrote: "John Murphy took $2,000,000 in gold from Murphys Diggings in about a year's time" [This is 10% of the estimated total of gold taken from the area]. It was said by some that "he [John] probably had more gold than any other man in California." [2] See historical marker at Main Street and Jones in Murphys.

After returning to San Jose, John became the first treasurer of Santa Clara County. He went on to be elected County Recorder and sheriff. During this period he married Virginia F. Reed, adopted daughter of James F. Reed of San Jose and survivor of the Donner Party (see Reed). They had eight children. In later years he operated a mercantile business until ill health forced his retirement. He died in 1892 at the age of 67.

Daniel Murphy, yet another son of Martin Sr., lived with his father until he served in Fremont's California Battalion during the Mexican

War. As explained above, he later joined his brother, John, and made a fortune in the gold fields. He and another brother, Bernard, then bought land throughout the area while managing their father's ranches. Daniel married Mary Fisher and eventually sired five children. He went on to acquire even more land in California, Nevada and Mexico. His ranch in Durango, Mexico, was said to total a million and-a-half acres, including a mountain of iron made famous by the German explorer, Alex Von Humboldt. At the time of his death in Halleck, Nevada, in October 1882, Murphy's cattle numbered in the thousands.

Ellen Murphy, daughter of Martin Sr., married Charles M. Weber of San Jose in 1850. He later founded the City of Stockton and became an extremely wealthy and powerful man (see Weber chapter, where Ellen is called Helen). Weber died in 1881, leaving Helen and three children. She continued to live in their mansion until her death in 1895.

James Miller and family settled in what became Marin County, where he purchased part of Timoteo (Timothy) Murphy's Los Gallinas Rancho. (Timothy was not related to Martin Murphy). The two Irish immigrants had much in common and became fast friends. Perhaps they were not quite so friendly with their neighbor, English immigrant William Richardson (see Richardson).

During the gold rush, Miller drove cattle to the Placerville area and sold it at high prices. He soon become a successful rancher-businessman and acquired other property. He built Miller Hall, in what became the heart of Marinwood, and carried on a prosperous dairy business in San Francisco. He and his wife raised ten children and devoted much of their lives to civic and cultural affairs in Marin County. Miller died in San Rafael November 27, 1890 at the age of 76.

Dr. John Townsend moved to Yerba Buena (San Francisco) after the Mexican War, where he became one of the first alcaldes under the U. S. Flag. He moved to San Jose in 1849, settling on 195 acres in an adobe house on Milpitas Road. There he intended to retire and live the quiet life of a rancher. Unfortunately, his and his wife's lives were cut short when they died of cholera in 1850. They left one son, John H. M. Townsend, who was raised by none other than Mrs. Townsend's younger brother, Moses Schallenberger.

Moses Schallenberger settled in Monterey, where he worked for traders Thomas O. Larkin and Talbot Green until the end of the Mexican War. Later he operated a trading venture of his own until the death of his brother-in-law, Dr. John Townsend in 1850. He then moved to San Jose to settle the Townsend estate and to care for his orphaned nephew.

Schallenberger married Fannie Everitt in 1854 and settled temporarily at Dr. Townsend's ranch in San Jose. Later they moved to a place of their own on 115 acres. Their house burned down in 1870; however, they immediately built a new and larger home to replace it. They prospered there over the years, and had five children. Moses lived a long, fulfilling life and died at home January 30, 1909 at the age of 83.

ELISHA STEVENS, born in Georgia in 1804, appears to have been a rather solitary person, even a bit eccentric at times. Possibly this was because of his beaver trapping experiences on the Upper Missouri River during his earlier years. He was also an experienced blacksmith, and served in Fremont's volunteers as an ordnance mechanic during the Mexican War. After the war he returned to trapping in the mountains of Santa Clara County for a number of years. He then made his way south to what became Bakersfield in Kern County. As one of its earliest settlers, he bought 38 acres, where he lived the life of a hermit raising chickens and tending bees.

Stevens became embittered in his old age, resenting the fact that the trail he helped blaze, via Truckee Pass, was renamed Donner Pass. The Central Pacific Railroad used the same route when it crossed the Sierra Nevada in 1869, yet Stevens never received credit. He died in 1887 at the age of 83, and was buried in the Union Cemetery. Stevens Creek and Stevens Creek Road in Santa Clara County carry his name, as does a historical marker at the northwest corner of West Columbus and Isla Verde in Bakersfield. At least Stevens wasn't totally forgotten. So ends the rich saga of one of the most significant immigrations in California history.

BIBLIOGRAPHY

–Bancroft, Hubert H. *Register of Pioneer Inhabitants of California, 1542-1848.* Dawson's Book Shop, Los Angeles, 1964.

–Crosby, Alexander L. *Old Greenwood, Pathfinder of the West.* Talisman Press, Georgetown, CA, 1967.

–Foote, H. S. *Pen Pictures from the Garden of the World, Santa Clara.* Lewis Publishing Co., Chicago, 1888. Republished, Pacific Press, Oakland, CA.

–Miller, William J. "The Miller-Murphy Immigration Party-1844." In *Old Marin With Love*, Marin County American Revolution Bicentennial Commission, San Rafael, 1976.

–Schmidt, Earl F. *Who Were The Murphys, California's Irish First Family.* Mooney Flat Ventures, Murphys, CA, 1989. [2]

–Stewart, George R. *The California Trail.* University of Nebraska Press, Lincoln 1962. [1]

–Taylor, Bayard. *El Dorado.* University of Nebraska Press, Lincoln, 1949.

NOTES

– 32 –

FRANCISCO P. PACHECO

(Don Francisco Perez)   1790 – 1860

TWENTY-NINE-YEAR-OLD Francisco Pacheco was serving in the Spanish Army when he arrived in Monterey, the picturesque capital of Alta California, in 1820. This was shortly before Mexico declared itself independent from Spanish rule and began replacing Spanish viceroys with Mexican governors. Born in Guadalajara in 1790, Pacheco was a carriage maker turned soldier at the time. He brought with him a wife–the former Feliciana Gonzales y Torres–and two children. As a Mexican-born artisan, Pacheco was socially a step below the haughty native-born *Californios*.

Feliciana Pacheco gave birth to a son in mid-May 1820, possibly aboard the Mexican frigate *Cleopatra* which reached Monterey in early May. It is thought the Pachecos arrived on this ship; however, they always said they came to California the year before. The confusion probably arose because they reached Baja California in 1819, thinking it and Alta California were all one country. They probably did not reach Monterey before 1820.

Pacheco's carriage-making skills were put to good use on gun carriages in the Army Artillery Corps. Few, if any, civilians used carriages in California. Horseback riding and crude ox-drawn carretas with solid wooden wheels provided the principle modes of transportation. After the Mexican takeover, the missions at Santa Barbara, Santa Ines and La Purisima faced uprisings by disgruntled mission Indians. Indian attacks were beaten off at Santa Barbara and Santa Ines, but they succeeded in capturing La Purisma. When word of this reached Monterey, Governor Luis Argüello called out his small army to quell the uprising.

Pacheco rode out with a company of soldiers, which was successful in defeating the Indians and recapturing La Purisima. After distinguishing himself in battle, Pacheco was promoted to Brevet Alferez, a temporary junior officer. He was also granted a town lot in Monterey by the governor. The lowly officer knew the rocky road to prosperity lay with land ownership, and he petitioned the governor for another lot with a better source of water.

In 1826 Pacheco had some livestock and petitioned for still a larger parcel between Missions San Carlos and Soledad. The new governor—Jose Echeandia—denied this request because of violent opposition by the mission padre in charge (the mission governor), who claimed it was mission land. Nevertheless, Pacheco managed to work his way into a position of power by being selected a member of the junta of electors, a kind of legislator.

By 1829 he was commandante of custom house guards and had seven children. The following decade found Pacheco serving in several responsible positions, including commandante of the home guard, a rural judge, treasurer of Monterey, and alderman. This era was a tumultuous one insofar as governors were concerned. Echeandia was replaced by Manuel Victoria, who was deposed by Augustin Zamorano, who attempted to enlist Pacheco's loyalty by getting him to sign the "Zamarano Manifesto" to preserve the legitimate Mexican government.

This earned Pacheco the everlasting hatred of young extremist *Californios* like Juan B. Alvarado, José Castro and Pío Pico, who preferred independence from Mexican rule. In 1835 José Carillo backed a decree to move the capital from Monterey to Los Angeles. Pacheco and English settler William Hartnell were appointed to prepare a formal protest in which they were to emphasize the superiority of Monterey. One of its statements read: "Here women, plants and animals are very productive" (see Hartnell).

M EANWHILE, Pacheco had been trying to acquire more land on which to graze his increasing herds of livestock. While still in power, Governor Echeandia called for secularization of the missions and their valuable lands, which were to be distributed to citizens. In 1833 Governor José Figueroa granted Pacheco two leagues of land belonging to Mission San Juan Bautista, called Rancho Ausaymus y San Felipe, lying east of present-day Gilroy. This was sparse grazing land, and Pacheco needed more to sustain his growing herds. He petitioned for additional land adjoining his ranch, and three years later Gov. Nicolas Gutierrez granted him two more leagues of mission land.

But Pacheco was not satisfied, and he continued to acquire land in the area until he owned 35,505 acres. This land included an alkaline lake with heavy shoreline deposits of "salts" that were used for making soap. Naturally the place was known as Soap Lake, and Pacheco made good use of it by making soap, which he sold to traders such as Thomas O. Larkin (see Larkin).

When Juan B. Alvarado became governor in 1836—with the help of American settlers led by Isaac Graham—he authorized General Mariano Vallejo to arrest Pacheco and other Mexican-born rancheros as possible "plotters" against Alvarado's administration. Apparently Alvarado could prove nothing against Pacheco, and he was released. To make up for Pacheco's false arrest, the governor granted him additional mission lands totaling 6,800 acres, called Bolsa de Felipe. Pacheco allowed Indians living there to stay. His headquarters, consisting of a large adobe house, corrals and twelve cabins for Indian workers, was established seven miles north of present-day Hollister. In 1838 Pacheco suffered a serious setback when hostile Indians raided and sacked his ranch.

By 1843 Pacheco's son, Juan, had reached the age when he could claim land of his own. Along with a partner, he was granted eleven leagues of land called Rancho San Luis Gonzaga, adjacent to his father's ranch. Later Juan Pacheco's partner deeded his half to Juan, who became its sole owner. Within a year Francisco Pacheco bought yet another large parcel from Gen. José Castro. Containing 33,690 acres, it was called Rancho San Justo.

A strategic pass on Pacheco's ranch led west from the San Joaquin Valley over the coastal range into the Salinas Valley. This pass became known as Pacheco Pass and is still in use today. When Manuel Micheltorena was sent from Mexico to become governor in 1844, Pacheco served as Captain of Defenses and Commandante at Mission San Juan Bautista. Somehow he managed to steer clear of the 1844-45 rebellion that swept Gov. Manuel Micheltorena from power. The last Mexican-born governor to serve, Micheltorena was replaced by Pío Pico and the capital moved to Los Angeles.

William Heath Davis in his book, Seventy-Five Years in California, includes Pacheco in his "list of solid men" and states:

> Ranchos San Felipe and San Luis Gonzaga, about 40,000 acres of land; 20,000 cattle, 500 horses and mares, and 15,000 sheep. That rich hacendado was a large buyer of merchandise and I sold many goods to him in 1844-45. [1]

IN EARLY 1846 Pacheco was serving the church as district tithe collector. War with the United States seemed imminent, and U.S. Consul Thomas O. Larkin wrote of Pacheco, "...not having any hope of protection from the president [of Mexico], nor affection for the government of California [he] would have his interests and views advanced by admission to the Union."

Larkin's assessment of Pacheco's lack of loyalty to Mexico is borne out by an incident involving Capt. John C. Fremont shortly after word came that war had been declared against Mexico. In late July Fremont and his volunteers appeared on Pacheco Pass seeking General José Castro and his army. Pacheco rode out and told Fremont he thought Castro could be found at San Juan Bautista.

Fremont hurried there to engage the Mexicans, only to learn that they had retreated south toward Los Angeles. Fremont then went south by sea, and returned that fall as Military Governor. In early December 1846 the Monterey newspaper *Californian* wrote that Fremont was giving horses to some *rancheros* to carry on their business:

> To Don Francisco Pacheco, a Mexican gentleman, who had done everything in his power to forward the American cause, he sent upward ninety horses. . . . Two or three days after Colonel Fremont had left these horses . . . the Indians from the Tulares . . . came down and swept off every horse they could find...."

William Garner also wrote about this raid:

> This gentleman [Pacheco] is owner of about thirteen or fourteen thousand head of cattle, and is now left without one horse to gather them with. What an immense loss he will have to suffer if the war continues six months longer!

After the war Pacheco recovered his losses. His ranch house is described by Chester Gillespie, who lived in it during the 1890s:

> ...two stories [high], long and narrow, and containing twenty-two rooms. Broad verandas extended the full length of the house, both front and rear. The building had a large attic for storage, and the roof was shingled in redwood cut in the Santa Cruz Mountains....

SHORTLY AFTER the Treaty of Guadalupe Hidalgo officially ended the war in early January 1848, James W. Marshall made his earth-shaking gold discovery at Sutter's Sawmill in Cullomah (Coloma). By spring word had spread, and by the following year thousands of wild-eyed gold seekers swarmed into the Sierra Nevada foothills. Suddenly, cattle which had been slaughtered for their hides at $2 a head, were worth about $50 a head delivered to the gold fields.

Enterprising *rancheros* who drove their herds to this lucrative market accumulated sudden wealth beyond their wildest dreams. Francisco Pacheco was one of these, and it was fortunate that he did. Newcomers to California envied, resented and hated the comparatively few Mexican land barons who owned most of the livestock. After all, they had lost the war. Why should they wax fat at the expense of victorious American settlers?

Aggressive squatters virtually took over portions of some *ranchos* and dared the *rancheros* to try and evict them. When California was admitted to the Union in September 1850, a land commission was established to examine old Spanish and Mexican land grants for legalities. This usually required land owners—who were now citizens of the United States—to hire expensive lawyers to defend their rights. Those who were "land poor" and short of cash often lost their land.

Fortunately, Pacheco had enough cash reserves to prove his land claims and managed to gain legal title; however, the court battles dragged on for many years. Meanwhile, in 1851 he suffered a costly robbery. Jules B. Lombard, Vice Consul to France at the time, wrote:

> Two months ago, fifteen to twenty Americans presented themselves at his [Pacheco's] home in broad daylight and demanded to drink. The good man hastened to satisfy their desires, but they had hardly entered than these bandits grabbed him and his family (women without defense), bound them, locked them up and, pistol on throat, ordered the old man under penalty of death to hand over his money. It was only common sense to submit to such a formulated request. In an instant trunks, chests, boxes, everything was looted, broken into and the band disappeared, taking with them a sum evaluated at more than fourteen thousand piastres (seventy thousand francs)....

As a result of this raid, Pacheco built a large, new home in Monterey and moved his family there that year. This home is described by Amelie Elkinton as follows: "This Pacheco house was probably the most elaborately furnished in Monterey..." A two-story adobe house of twenty-five rooms, it still stands. Shortly after moving there, Pacheco began selling some of his vast land holdings. In 1855 he sold Rancho San Justo to Flint and Bixly, who sold half of it to W.W. Hollister.

This decade brought much sorrow to Pacheco, whose health was beginning to fail. In January 1855 his son, Juan, died. Two years later he lost his wife, Feliciana. He was the wealthiest man in Monterey County and one of the most miserable. Lawsuits and court battles over land disputes continued to plague him; even his wife's will was contested by family members. Despite his troubles, Pacheco bore most of the heavy expense in renovating and enlarging the Royal Presidio Chapel (now San Carlos Cathedral) at Monterey in 1858. When the work was finished, in January 1859, Pacheco was praised for his generous donation of $10,000.

B Y THE END of the decade Pacheco sensed his end was near and began making final arrangements. His devoted thirty-year-old daughter, Isadora–known as Lola–had remained unmarried and still lived at home at the time. Pacheco was determined to see her married before he died and devoted himself to finding her a proper husband. Finally he chose Mariano Malerin, son of a prominent Monterey family, who had attended William Hartnell's school until it closed in 1836. He then attended school at his father's homeland in Lima, Peru, where he graduated from law school and taught at the university there. Mariano Malerin and Isadora Pacheco were married at San Carlos Cathedral in October 1859.

With his last desire fully met, Pacheco wasted away and died in

March 1860 at the age of seventy. It is fitting that he was buried in the family crypt at San Carlos Cathedral, under the floor just outside the sanctuary. It is inscribed "Pacheco Family—1858."

DESPITE the fact that Francisco Pacheco was one of the largest and wealthiest land owners in California, his best known legacy to the state is Pacheco Pass. As the only pass through the coastal range for 100 miles to the north or the south, connecting the San Joaquin Valley with the geographic area around Monterey, it was used by most of the early California pioneers. Apparently Pacheco never denied its use to anyone except hostile Indians, who used it to raid coastal ranches. During the Gold Rush, it was used by *hacendados* to drive cattle to the gold fields. A toll road crossed it in 1856-57, and a year later it became the route of the Butterfield Transcontinental Stage Line. A telegraph line followed in 1861, and there was talk of a railroad that never materialized. Today busy State Highway 152 crosses Pacheco Pass and serves as a memorial to the pioneer family.

BIBLIOGRAPHY
–Bancroft, Hubert H. *Register and Index of Pioneer Inhabitants of California, 1542 to 1848*. Dawson's Book Shop, Los Angeles, 1964.
–Davis, William Heath. *Seventy-Five Years in California.* John Howell–Books, San Francisco, CA, 1967. [1]
–Shumate, Dr. Albert. *Francisco Pacheco of Pacheco Pass.* University of Pacific Press, Stockton, CA, 1977. All quotes except [1] were taken from this publication.

Notes

Pío Pico
Courtesy California Department of Parks & Recreation

PÍO PICO (DON PÍO)

1801 – 1894

P ÍO PICO was the second son of José María Pico, a lowly non-commissioned officer in the Mexican Army. Though he was a corporal at the San Diego garrison, José María Pico took his wife–the former María Eustaquia Gutiérrez–to San Gabriel for the birth of their second son. Pío Pico was born at the San Gabriel Mission on May 5, 1801. Shortly after his birth, the family returned to their modest home in San Diego.

Young Pico was taught to read by a family friend before attending small informal classes taught by his older brother-in-law, José Carrillo. Under Carrillo's guidance he learned to write and do simple arithmetic. Pío Pico had seven sisters and two brothers; Andres was nine years younger, while José was seven years older. By the time Pío Pico was sixteen his brother, José, was in the military, and the family had moved to San Gabriel where his father–probably in his late fifties–hoped to retire.

Instead of retirement, José María Pico was transferred back to San Diego in 1818 to help defend the pueblo from a possible attack by the notorious pirate, Hippolyte de Bouchard, who had been raiding along the coast. Young Pío Pico was left in charge of the fifteen-man guard at San Gabriel until his father returned. A year later, while awaiting the retirement he coveted, José María Pico died, and the family returned to San Diego.

As the oldest boy still at home, Pío Pico became a surrogate father to his younger siblings and was very close to his widowed mother. They were very poor until Pío Pico opened a small store and began trading along the coast. Despite being unofficial head of the family, the enterprising young man was closely supervised by his strict mother and was not allowed to stay out past eight o'clock until he was in his mid-twenties. Like many young men of that era, he developed a love for gambling and would gamble anything of value. Fortunately, he seems to have won as much as he lost.

In 1827 he was named secretary to Captain Don Pablo de la Portillo, the Attorney General of San Diego. Before long he became involved in politics, and by the following year he was elected to a legislative body called the Territorial Chamber of Deputies. These deputies were invited by then Governor Echeandia to represent their various communities in government affairs. When Echeandia was replaced by Governor Victoria, things began to unravel.

Pico described Victoria as a "tall, dark, rather hunch-backed despot" who did not recognize the deputies. When Pico, Juan Bandini, José Carrillo and others protested the governor's high-handed methods, Victoria had Pío Pico's younger brother, Andres, arrested. Not satisfied with that, he threatened to bring troops from Monterey to hang Pío Pico and Don Juan Bandini. As a result, Pico got together with Bandini and his brother-in-law, José Carrillo, to plot the overthrow of Victoria. They also enlisted the aid of Don Abel Stearns, a powerful Yankee trader who had become a naturalized Mexican citizen and lived in Los Angeles (see Stearns & Bandini).

Revolutions were a way of life with the early *Californios*, and governors were purged on a regular basis. Pico was quick to seize the initiative; in 1831, he led his first revolution against the hated Victoria, who was bringing troops to Los Angeles from Monterey. Former Governor Echeandia was named president of the *junta*, fifty men were enlisted and they marched to Los Angeles to meet Victoria.

Instead of crushing the rebellion and hanging Pico and Bandini as he had intended, Victoria and his troops were defeated, and the rebels took over the government. At the tender age of thirty, Pío Pico was sworn in as unofficial governor by General Mariano Vallejo, who had come from the north with Juan B. Alvarado (see Vallejo). Meanwhile Echeandia went north to Monterey to combat a counter revolution led by Agustín Zamorano. When Echeandia returned to Los Angeles and found Pico the new governor, he refused to recognize him as such.

What followed was a period of political chaos (see Introduction). Zamorano—a military officer stationed in Monterey—refused to accept results of the revolt against Victoria, and named himself Commanding General of the North, the equivalent of governor. Then Lt. Juan M. Iberra came to Los Angeles from Monterey with a troop of soldiers in support of Zamorano against both Pico and ex-governor Echeandia.

Echeandia chose to leave Pico in Los Angeles, while he retreated to San Diego. Pico followed soon thereafter. While there, Echeandia decided to recognize Pico as governor to lead a campaign against Iberra. Pico made ready to attack and was joined at the San Gabriel River by a group of soldiers and a large band of Indians. Echeandia met him there the next day with 100 men and a cannon hauled in a wagon. Together they marched toward Los Angeles. Unable to face the threat of so many men, Iberra fled back north.

Echeandia then returned to San Diego, where he tried to govern the South while Zamorano governed the North. Affairs continued in this confused manner until 1833, when Mexico sent General José Figueroa as governor and military commander. He began to set things right by pardoning political prisoners and sending officials to contact the elected deputies with a message seeking stability. After a year of anarchy, Figueroa was firmly in charge, and the shaky government was coming together.

THIS BLISSFUL STATE didn't last. Military officers from Mexico arrived with Bandini, J. M. Padres and over 200 emigrants to help colonize the Sonoma Valley as a buffer against the Russians at Fort Ross. One of the officers, José M. Hijar, was commissioned to take over as governor and Director of Colonization. Governor Figueroa refused to comply with Hijar's commission; instead, he called Pico and the other deputies together for a conference in Monterey. The deputies recommended that Figueroa stay on as governor and that Hijar be recognized as Director of Colonization only. After a series of meetings between Figueroa and Hijar, this was done.

Another attempt to overthrow Figueroa in 1835 was put down with little or no bloodshed. Meanwhile, in 1834, Pío Pico married María Ignacia Amador, with Governor Figueroa acting as best man. A month later Pico accompanied Figueroa to Santa Barbara to celebrate the governor's birthday with a high mass, bull fighting, musketry salutes and a grand ball. Bull fighting was a sport Pico really enjoyed. According to his own account, he stated that many times he made the journey from Los Angeles to San Diego in one day to take part in bull fights, requiring six or more changes of horses along the way.

Even before 1835 the missions were being secularized; in April Figueroa named Pico Administrator of Mission San Luis Rey, a position he held for several years. Figueroa's health had been failing for some time, and he died that fall in Monterey. His death was felt keenly throughout the land. A series of governors succeeded him, beginning with José Castro, who took over temporarily after José Estudillo begged off by feigning illness. Within a short time, Castro turned over the reins of government to Col. Nicholás Gutiérrez (see Introduction).

Then came Mariano Chico in 1836, succeeded again by Col. Gutierrez. This comic opera chain of events continued when José Castro, Juan B. Alvarado and Mariano Vallejo overthrew Gutiérrez and replaced him with Alvarado. Southern California refused to recognize Alvarado as governor, so a delegation made up of soldiers led by Alvarado and Castro went to see Pico in Los Angeles. With them was settler Isaac Graham and a band of frontier riflemen (see Graham). Finally Pico agreed to accept Alvarado as governor.

But the agreement didn't last. In the North, Alvarado and his followers quickly declared California a free and sovereign state, while Southern California remained loyal to Mexican rule. Again Alvarado and Castro returned to the Los Angeles with their supporters. Fighting was avoided when Don José Sepulveda intervened. Southern California leaders then named Carlos Carrillo as governor. He immediately declared Los Angeles the capital, but naturally the North refused to recognize it.

Over a period of many months the two groups skirmished up and down the Southern California coast with little harm to anyone; however, Pico was arrested and jailed at one time. One has to remember that most of these families were related by blood or marriage, and politics became a kind of sport, where one group tried to outwit the other. Occasionally blood was spilled, but it was rare and usually regretted. Finally, by 1840, Alvarado was more or less accepted as governor. One of his first acts was to relieve Pico as Administrator of Mission San Luis Rey. Though Pico was embittered by his replacement, he wrote the following in his memoirs:

> At least I had the satisfaction of turning over the buildings in perfect condition, whitewashed inside and out; a shoemaker's shop which I myself established; two blacksmiths' and one carpenter's shop with all their tools; a soap manufactory completely furnished; a loom with forty carders, ten weavers, ninety to one hundred girls occupied at the spinning wheels, working with pleasure as they sang all day; twenty-five thousand sheep; one hundred and twenty-five mules—of these, forty fully equipped....All of the debts incurred during my administration were liquidated. I left no debts pending and I canceled much that was owed by a few poor farm workers. ...I succeeded in securing approval from the government of Senor Alvarado that each of the Indians who founded the pueblo of Las Flores be given a yoke of oxen or a mule, besides two hundred and fifty head of cattle for the community. But it is a deplorable fact that when General Micheltorena came in 1842, these Indians no longer had any of these goods, nor anything to eat, and the majority of them had gone to the mountains. I took advantage of this circumstance to buy from the remainder their equity in the town, with the approval of the superior authorities.

Pico eventually ended up with the 133,000 acre Rancho Santa Margarita y Las Flores and thousands of head of livestock. He apparently did a good job of administering the mission property, but it also allowed him to feather his own nest. From the time he left the mission in 1840 to the arrival of yet another new governor in 1842, Pico remained politically inactive. But upon the arrival of Manuel Micheltorena from Mexico to replace Alvarado, Pico returned to his duties as a voting member of the Assembly.

At the express invitation of Governor Micheltorena, Pío Pico and his brother, Andres, visited him at Monterey in 1844. During the visit, they became suspicious that the governor was plotting with John A. Sutter to make California independent from Mexico. Sutter, a Swiss immigrant, had arrived in 1839 and established a settlement named New Helvetia (New Switzerland) inland on the Sacramento River. He had become a naturalized Mexican citizen and been granted nearly 50,000 acres by ex-Governor Alvarado (see Sutter).

Later, both Pico brothers were commissioned to sell mission property to raise money to outfit civilian squadrons and strengthen the presidios in San Diego and Los Angeles. There was considerable resistance from townspeople, but they were finally reconciled to it. While he was in San Juan Capistrano trying to sell mission property there, Pío Pico was summoned to Los Angeles by José Castro, who had brought soldiers south from Monterey and attacked military barracks that were under command of Andres Pico.

Several casualties had resulted, and Castro told Pío Pico he had come south after rioting had taken place in Monterey over the depravations of Micheltorena's band of undisciplined, ex-convict troops. As a result, the governor had agreed to remove them from California. Instead, he had allied himself with John Sutter to form a small army made up of well-armed settlers and savage Indians. This motley force was moving south to threaten Los Angeles with pillage and rape. Due to superior manpower, it had driven Castro and his men south from Monterey.

Castro went on to offer Pío Pico the governorship if he would join to help defeat the combined forces of Micheltorena and Sutter. Pico did not agree to this but did offer to take it up with the Assembly. This was done, and a delegation was sent to meet with Micheltorena at Santa Barbara. Apparently the governor greeted them with contempt and refused to bargain. He was determined to force his will and make himself respected by hostile factions in the South.

The Assembly then refused to acknowledge Micheltorena as governor and swore in Pío Pico as the new governor. He appointed captains to organize a defense and ordered Castro north to San Buenaventura to hold the line there. After a skirmish with Sutter's men, Castro was forced to retreat to Rancho Cahuenga. By then Pico had recruited several hundred volunteers and reinforced Castro with men and two artillery pieces. His old friend, Juan A. Alvarado, was also on hand to fight by his side.

When Micheltorena's men approached, Alvarado fired the first cannon shot and the long-range "battle" was on. The exchange of cannon fire proved noisy and somewhat entertaining, as citizens from surrounding areas came to watch from the hillsides. The thundering barrage resulted in one casualty—a horse was killed; one man had his hat blown off by grapeshot. Whether by design or accident, not one man was even wounded.

The next day General Castro sent word that Micheltorena wanted to see Pico to discuss the possibility of surrender. When Pico met with the beleaguered governor, he was surprised when Micheltorena warned him not to trust Castro and that war with the United States appeared inevitable. Moreover, Pico was advised to join Mariano Vallejo to plan strategy against the U.S., and was told that Vallejo should replace Castro as Military Commander.

Curtly, Pico informed the governor that Castro was in charge of the operation. With that, Pío Pico returned to Los Angeles. A short time later, he learned that Micheltorena had surrendered to Castro, and that the governor and his men had been taken to San Pedro for a few days while a ship was made ready to transport them back to Mexico. John Sutter had been captured before the surrender and was given a hearing for possible treason. After convincing the tribunal that he had been acting on the governor's orders, he and his remaining men were released.

Micheltorena's ship sailed first to Monterey to pick up his wife and a few officers and men who had been left there on garrison duty. It then sailed south to Mexico, and California was at last free of the hated *cholo* troops that had accompanied Micheltorena from Mexico three years earlier. By early 1845 Pico was recognized throughout the country as the governor and Castro as Military Commander, even though Pico believed Vallejo was a better choice for Commander.

PICO APPOINTED Alvarado as Administrator of Customs in Monterey and moved the capital to Los Angeles. Along with one other, Andres Pico was appointed a commissioner to visit all the missions and inventory their remaining properties. Pico's aim was to abolish the mission regime once and for all and replace the missions with pueblos. The chapels were left for religious services, while other usable buildings were turned into schools or offices, or were sold outright for whatever they would bring.

Pico was tired of being governor by the end of 1845, and was disillusioned by the lack of support from Mexico City. He had no resources to defend the country from potential invaders. He therefore instructed his secretary, Juan Bandini, to contact any British ships in Mexican ports, and to tell their commanders that in the event Mexico wasn't interested in defending California, Pico would welcome their protection.

Many *Californios* preferred occupation by the United States or France, and virtually all of them were calling for independence from Mexico. Pico opposed that, unless the North agreed, and Castro refused to come south to discuss it; he apparently feared arrest and imprisonment by Pico. When Bandini approached Castro in mid-July 1846 about the proposal to seek protection from the British, Castro told him that a British admiral had already sailed to Monterey, only to find the U.S. flag flying over the settlement.

U.S. Commodore John Sloat had beaten the British by a matter of days, and had seized Monterey July 7th. Bandini's belated report to Pico was the first word the governor had received of the U.S. invasion, and he was so disturbed by this news—plus other matters involving Castro—that he put together a force of 150 men and headed north to confront his errant military commander. As he neared San Luis Obispo, he received a message from Castro that U.S. forces had captured the entire North and were on their way by ship to invade the South.

Castro's credibility with Pico was so low that the governor wanted more evidence before he accepted the message as fact. Continuing north, he was confronted by Alvarado and Manuel Castro, who confirmed the news and informed him that General Castro was a short distance behind with what forces he could muster. When Castro arrived, Pico met with him to reconcile their differences, and they united to plan strategy against their common foe, the United States of America.

Together they returned to Los Angeles and made plans to defend the South against the expected invasion. Though united by a common effort, they continued to feud over real or imagined differences. Upon receiving word that John C. Fremont had landed forces at San Diego, Castro sent a small force of men under Juan Alvarado to repel them. They soon returned to Los Angeles, and Pico received word that Fremont's men were marching north from San Diego. He immediately informed Castro, who agreed to go south to intercept Fremont's forces.

That evening Pico got a written communication from Castro, stating that he did not have sufficient resources to counter Fremont and was leaving the country. He was going to Mexico to seek help and advised Pico to do the same. The alarmed governor immediately called a meeting of deputies to discuss the matter. It was decided in a late-night meeting that Pico should dismiss all department officials to prevent any meaningful negotiations with the enemy, and that he, Pico, should leave the country for the same reason.

Andres Pico saw things differently. When Castro and Pico pulled out in mid-August, he took over to defend Los Angeles. But when Fremont and Commodore Stockton's men took Los Angeles, Andres Pico was captured and paroled. Shortly thereafter, he broke his parole to assist José Flores in driving the Americans out of Los Angeles to San Pedro, where they boarded a ship to escape the victorious Mexicans. Later, Andres Pico went to the San Diego area, where he served with distinction at the Battle of San Pasqual. There he led about one hundred

Mexican cavalrymen to a decisive victory over newly arrived troops under command of General Stephen Kearny.

Meanwhile, Pío Pico had left Los Angeles for Sonora, using back roads and hiding out along the way to avoid detection. He passed through Mulege and Guaymas, where he stayed in the private home of a friend. While in Sonora, he did all he could to obtain assistance from the Mexican government to oust the invaders, but without success. When the armistice was finally signed in Mexico City, he returned to his Rancho Santa Margarita in California. After a short rest, he went on to Los Angeles and surrendered himself to American authorities there. The local officials allowed him to return to his ranch while the Military Governor, Colonel Richard Mason, decided his fate. Later he was ordered back to Los Angeles and placed under arrest. He was not jailed, however, and was released three weeks later when the Treaty of Guadalupe Hidalgo was approved by both countries in May 1848.

PICO RETURNED to his ranch for a while, but by February 1849, he was back in Los Angeles, where he bought Rancho Los Coyotes. After the American occupation, Pico changed from a revolutionary to an opportunist, and built considerable wealth. Fortunately for California, he used his wealth and influence to good advantage, both for himself and for the state. (See the summary at the end of this chapter.)

Pico sold Rancho Santa Margarita in 1864 and bought Rancho Paso de Bartolo, on which he constructed the Pico "mansion." Located near the banks of the San Gabriel River near present-day Pico Rivera, this lovely rancho became his home for nearly the rest of his life. It was near there, at present-day Montebello, where the last battle of the Mexican War was fought between Fremont's forces and the remaining Mexican patriots. In 1883, when Pico was an eighty-two-year-old widower, he found himself temporarily short of cash. Unable to speak or understand English, he relied on a trusted friend to negotiate a loan of $62,000.

As collateral, Pico pledged his ranch, which was valued at around $200,000. When he went to repay the loan a few months later, he was astounded and dismayed to learn that the "loan" had actually been an outright sale of the property. Naturally Pico didn't recognize it as a sale, and the case dragged through the court system for seven long years before it was decided in favor of the lender-purchaser. By then the property was worth much more, but Pico had no legal rights to it. It appears he had been fleeced by experts. Pico died in poverty on September 11, 1894, at his Los Angeles home. He fathered no children.

What were Pío Picos' contributions to California? Prior to American occupation, he had served twice as governor and was largely responsible for the orderly disposal of many mission properties. Whether this was an achievement or a disaster is left for others to decide; in any case, he was acting on orders from Mexico and had little choice. After occupation by the United States, he became a solid American citizen and was prominent in civic and business affairs.

He served on the Los Angeles City Council, helped establish a public school system and a banking system, built the impressive Pico House on Main Street and developed various towns in the area. Pico also pioneered California's first oil venture, which eventually became the gigantic Standard Oil Company of Southern California. He expanded Rancho Paso de Bartolo, part of which is now a state historical park honoring Pico, and built the famous "Pico Mansion," which still stands.

After living a long, full life, he died in poverty, as did so many of the early California "Dons" who were exploited by ruthless, land-hungry swindlers who took advantage of their naive trust and ignorance of the English language and American law. While the *Californios* had their faults, they did not deserve to be cheated or forced to endure the discrimination that plagues their many descendents even today. These injustices place a stain on our "Manifest Destiny" that may never be removed.

Bibliography

–Bancroft, Hubert H. *History of California,* Vol. I-IV. History Co., San Francisco, 1886. Repub., Wallace Hebberd, Santa Barbara, 1966.

–Botello, Arthur P. (translator). *Don Pío Pico's Historical Narrative.* Ed. with intro. by Martin Cole and Henry Welcome. Arthur H. Clark Co., Glendale, CA, 1973. Quotations come from this publication.

–California State Department of Parks and Recreation. *Pío Pico,* State Park brochure.

–Dakin, Susanna Bryant. *A Scotch Paisano, Hugo Reid's Life in California, 1832-1852.* University of California Press, Berkeley, 1939.

–Davis, William Heath. *Seventy-Five Years in California.* Ed. by Harold A. Small. John Howell Books, San Francisco, 1967.

–DeVoto, Bernard. *The Year of Decision, 1846.* Houghton Mifflin Co., Boston, 1942

–Dillon, Richard. *Fool's Gold.* Coward McCann, Inc., New York , 1967

–Egan, Ferol. *Fremont, Explorer for a Restless Nation.* University of Nevada Press, Reno, 1977.

–Gay, Theressa. *James Marshall.* Talisman Press, Georgetown, CA, 1967.

–Hague, Harlan and Langum, David J. *Thomas O. Larkin.* University of Oklahoma Press, Norman, 1990.

–Harlow, Neal. *California Conquered.* University of California Press, Berkeley, 1982.

–Taylor, Bayard. *El Dorado.* University of Nebraska Press, Lincoln, 1949.

James Knox Polk
Courtesy California Department of Parks & Recreation

– 34 –

JAMES KNOX POLK

1795 – 1849

THOUGH JAMES POLK never set foot in California, he served as President of the United States from 1845 to early 1849, probably the most important four-year period in California history. These four years saw the beginning and successful conclusion of the Mexican War, the annexation of Alta California into the Union, the startling discovery of gold, and the beginnings of the greatest migration of people in the history of the world. It also saw also annexation of Texas into the Union and the establishment of a permanent border in the Pacific Northwest between Oregon Country and territory held by Great Britain (now the Canadian border).

Despite these remarkable achievements, Polk became almost a forgotten president; no serious effort was made to write his biography until 80 years after his death. Perhaps this was because he served only one term in office and had alienated powerful members of the Whig Party throughout his political career as a Jeffersonian-Jacksonian Democrat. Further, he never accomplished much in the private sector, having been a professional politician most of his adult life.

Polk's grandfathers on both sides were American patriots, who served honorably in the Revolutionary War. His father, Samuel Polk, was of Scottish ancestry, the name having been changed from Pollock long before his birth. He married Jane Knox in 1794, and James was born a year later on the family farm in Mecklenburg, North Carolina. Young Polk was a rather frail lad who loved books far more than farming, and soon became a devotee of Thomas Jefferson.

In 1806 the family moved to the Tennessee wilderness to take up land near Samuel Polk's parents. There Samuel Polk founded the town of Columbia. James Polk had some schooling, but was not a brilliant student. His studies were interrupted during his mid-teens by a serious attack of gallstones. The only qualified surgeon was located in Kentucky, so young Polk was forced to ride horseback some 200 miles to see him. His survival of the ride and the surgery was miraculous in itself.

Andrew Jackson was a family friend who became Polk's mentor at an early age. After the Battle of New Orleans during the War of 1812, Jackson became his hero. At the age of eighteen Polk was admitted to a small church-sponsored academy to continue his education. What he lacked in natural ability, he made up with perseverance and hard work, becoming a top student and an above-average public speaker. He went from there to Bradley Academy to prepare for college.

After graduating with honors in 1815, Polk enrolled at the University of North Carolina, where he honed his public speaking and debating skills and won recognition as a top student. By the time he graduated in 1818, he had become interested in politics and decided to study law. This required a move to Nashville, where he went to work as a law clerk for a prominent lawyer, Felix Grundy.

Following the financial crash of 1819, Grundy ran for the State Legislature on a liberal platform designed to aid suffering debtors. Upon being elected, he helped Polk get an appointment as a clerk in the State Senate. Polk promptly moved to Murfreesboro to take the job and continued to study law on the side. After being admitted to the State Bar in 1820, he hung out his shingle to practice law but kept his job as a Senate Clerk. Within three years he had fallen in love with Sarah Childress and moved to Nashville to run for a seat in the Tennessee Legislature.

POLK SELDOM SAW Sarah Childress during the campaign, which he won in a close race with the incumbent. By then his former mentor, Felix Grundy, had switched from liberal to conservative. This put him at odds with Polk, who worked closely with Davey Crockett to defeat Grundy over a number of issues, including divorce laws, property rights and tax reforms. When Andrew Jackson announced for the presidency, Polk backed him as an independent.

James Polk and Sarah Childress were married in 1824 and settled in Columbia. By then Polk was preparing to run for the U.S. Congress and supported Jackson for president. When Jackson lost to John Quincy Adams in a bitter struggle within the Electoral College, many thought Jackson had been cheated, including Polk who spoke out strongly about it. This did not endear him to Adams, and they became arch rivals. Polk won a seat in Congress by a narrow margin after a long and tiring campaign. Within a year he and his wife were living in Washington, D.C.

With Polk's help Jackson was elected president in 1828, and the president elect never forgot it. After he was re-elected four years later, Polk became Jackson's unofficial spokesman in the House of Representatives. Together they forced bank reforms that alienated them from powerful banking interests. Polk had become what we now call a workaholic, or perhaps he had always been one. At any rate his health began to deteriorate, and he was forced to take time off from his grueling schedule.

After recovering, he was elected official Speaker of the House in 1835. Four years later he and Mrs. Polk moved back to Nashville, where he ran for governor of the state. He won the contest by a very narrow margin. Polk had inherited land after his father's death, but was cash poor and in failing health when he ran for re-election and was defeated by a colorful character named "Lean Jimmy" Jones. This defeat turned out to be fortunate, as it forced Polk to rest and plan his strategy to become Vice President under Martin Van Buren.

By then Polk was determined to see Texas re-annexed to the Union and to settle the border dispute in the Pacific Northwest between the United States and Great Britain. He called Texas a re-annexation because he held that it was included in the previous Louisiana Purchase. A quotation in his own words expressed his beliefs very well:

> Let Texas be re-annexed and the authority and laws of the United States be established and maintained within her limits, and also the Oregon Territory, and let the fixed policy of our government be not to permit Great Britain or any other foreign power to plant a colony or hold dominion over any portion of the people or territory of either.

At about that time Van Buren came out with a letter opposing annexation of Texas. This split the Democrats so severely that Van Buren could not gain a clear majority to win the nomination. As a result, Polk was finally nominated as a "dark horse" candidate for president to run against the Whig candidate, Henry Clay, and an abolitionist, James Birney.

The Whigs went all out to defeat Polk, accusing him of mistreating slaves, being "wholly unworthy of trust in every point of view", and with "no talent to command respect." Because of his close ties with "Old Hickory" Andy Jackson, Polk relished his own nick-name, "Young Hickory." The final election results were so close that the Whigs declared Clay the victor (shades of Harry Truman in 1948). Actually Polk had won, but people in his home town of Columbia weren't aware of it for twenty-four hours; many offered their condolences, thinking he had lost.

He and Sarah left for Washington in late January 1845, stopping off to visit "Old Hickory" in Nashville along the way. After settling in the White House in mid-February, he named Senator James Buchanan Secretary of State, a move he later regretted. George Bancroft was appointed Secretary of the Navy.

Other than problems he inherited regarding annexation of Texas and the border dispute in the Pacific Northwest, Polk's worst problems dealt with congressmen and cabinet members (including Buchanan), who wanted friends and relatives appointed to government jobs. Quotations from his own writings tell the story eloquently:

> The passion for office among members of Congress is very great, if not absolutely disreputable, and greatly embarrasses the operations of the Government. They create offices by their own votes and then seek to fill them themselves. I shall refuse to appoint them, though it be at the utmost certain hazard of incurring their displeasure...

P RESIDENT POLK believed in free trade and considered passage of a low tariff act the most important of his domestic bills. Thanks to efforts by his predecessor, John Tyler, and his own relentless work, Texas was finally admitted to the Union as the 28th state at the end of Polk's first year in office. Next came the Oregon Country border dispute, during which the Democratic Party had previously demanded, "54-40 or fight." This referred to the 54-40 parallel of longitude, which would have placed the northern border far above its present location.

This, of course, was entirely unacceptable to the British. President Tyler had offered a compromise at the 49th parallel, with Britain to keep Vancouver Island even though it extended south of there. Now it was up to Polk to resolve it once and for all. When the offer was again abruptly refused, Polk withdrew it and reverted to the original 54-40 claim. Congress backed him, and preparations were made for war, should it come to that. Polk gambled that it wouldn't.

He turned out to be right, and Great Britain finally agreed to the 49th parallel offer. The Senate approved, and in June 1846 a parcel that subsequently became Oregon, Washington, Idaho and parts of Wyoming and Montana was added to the expanding Union. Unfortunately, when Texas had been annexed the year before, the actual boundary had been left open for negotiation with Mexico. This became a sore spot with Mexico, who threatened to re-take the new state. Polk then made it clear that any aggression by Mexico meant war.

H e hoped that a firm stand would result in peace and make possible the purchase of New Mexico and California. When Mexico refused to consider such an offer, the dispute along the border began to heat up. It finally came to a head in May 1846, when Mexican troops engaged American dragoons commanded by General Zachary Taylor on the American side of the Rio Grande River. Taylor sent word to Polk:

> I regret to report that a party of dragoons, sent out by me to watch the course of the river...became engaged with a very large force of the enemy, and after a short affair, in which some sixteen were killed or wounded, appear to have been surrounded and compelled to surrender. ...Hostilities may now be considered as commenced.

WITHIN twenty-four hours, Congress declared war against Mexico. Even before that, Polk had agents working in California (John C. Fremont and U.S. Consul Thomas O. Larkin, among others), who were prepared to move. The official message still had not reached Commodore Sloat in late June; even so, he invaded Monterey July 7th. There was little or no opposition from native Californians in the north, and the Stars and Stripes flew over the main settlements by the end of the month (see Fremont & Larkin).

President Polk became Commander-in-Chief in fact as well as in title, and personally directed much of the war strategy himself. Unfortunately for Polk, two of his key generals were Whigs, who did their best to embarrass him at every opportunity. One of them was General Zachary Taylor. By late September, General Taylor's troops occupied Monterrey, Mexico. The next goal was Mexico City. A landing was made at Vera Cruz in March 1847, and six months later Mexico City fell to the victorious Americans.

The vigorous campaign left Polk with his health again deteriorating, forcing him to work flat on his back at times. While the war in California seemed to be won in mid-1846, the Mexicans in Southern California had rallied and fighting there continued into late summer. It ended with the Treaty of Cahuenga in January 1847; however, peace negotiations with Mexico over Texas and New Mexico dragged on until the Treaty of Guadalupe Hidalgo was signed by Mexico in early February 1848.

The U.S. Congress made some changes in the treaty and re-submitted it to Mexico for ratification in March. Mexico approved the changes and the treaty was finalized in May 1848. Gold had been discovered in California on January 24th, but word had not yet reached the East Coast or Mexico City. One can't help wondering what might have happened if Mexico had learned of it before the treaty was signed by them.

President Polk's last year in office was not a pleasant one. He had no intention of running for a second term and had so stated. To his dismay, the Democrats split their votes between abolitionist Martin Van Buren and Lewis Cass. The Whigs tried to discredit the Democrats by attacking everything Polk had accomplished during his term of office. Some claimed he had deliberately provoked war with Mexico to create slave states in newly acquired territory.

On the other hand, Democrats accused him of not using his office to promote slavery. Polk did own slaves but had never promoted the practice and had always been moderate in his beliefs about the vexing problem. As a Southern Democrat, there was no way he could oppose slavery and exist politically. The constant whipsawing and the splitting of the party allowed Whig candidate Zachary Taylor to win the election.

Polk had little use for Taylor, especially when the new president-elect told him that California was too remote to become a state and should form an independent government of its own. Fortunately for California, Taylor changed his mind after he took office. The following quotation from Polk's diary reflects his thoughts about Taylor:

> Gen'l Taylor is, I have no doubt, a well meaning old man. He is, however, uneducated, exceedingly ignorant of public affairs, and, I should judge, of very limited capacity.

With all the abuse that had been heaped upon him, plus the loss to the hated Whigs, Polk's health failed more than ever before. Although he had accomplished a great deal indeed, he left office a broken man. The long journey home was a trial because of the many public functions he was required to attend along the way. When he finally reached his home in Nashville, he wrote:

> My journey is now over and I am again at my home, in themidst of the friends of my youth and of my riper years. My political career has been run and is now closed. I have been much honored by my countrymen and am deeply grateful to them....Though fatigued and feeble....

He continued to weaken after that, and died quietly on June 15, 1849, three months and a few days after leaving office. James Polk was a true patriot who literally gave his life for his country. Although he was initially buried in the Nashville city cemetery, his body was moved to a vault next to his home and finally to the grounds of the State Capitol. Sarah Polk joined him there forty-two years later.

JAMES POLK brought about the successful conclusion of the Mexican War and the annexation of California into the Union. It vexed him that California's admittance was being delayed because Southern Congressmen wanted it to be a slave state. Although Polk was a loyal southerner, he pushed hard for admittance in early 1849 with the understanding that the new state could then decide the slavery issue for itself.

This proposal had been submitted to Congress as the "Douglas Bill," and Polk stayed up all night on his last day in office hoping it would be approved in time for him to sign it. Sadly, he did not live to see it happen; California was not admitted until September 9, 1850.

BIBLIOGRAPHY

–DeVoto, Barnard. *The Year of Decision-1846.* Houghton Mifflin Co., Boston, 1942

–Egan, Ferol. *Fremont, Explorer for a Restless Nation.* University of Nevada Press, Reno, 1985.

–Gay, Theressa. *James W. Marshall, a Biography.* Talisman Press, Georgetown, CA, 1967.

–Harlow, Neal. *California Conquered..* University of California Press, Berkeley, 1982.

–Lorant, Stefan. *The Presidency.* The Macmillan Co., New York, 1951.

–Severn, Bill. *Frontier President.* Ives Washburn, Inc., New York, 1965. Quotations are from this publication.

––Thompson, Gerald. *Edward F. Beale & The American West.* University of New Mexico Press, Albuquerque, 1983.

–Unruh, John D. Jr. *The Plains Across.* University of Illinois Press, Chicago, 1982.

*Margaret and
James Reed*
*Courtesy California
Department of
Parks & Recreation*

JAMES F. REED   *1800 – 1874*

His Role in the Donner Party Disaster

THE 1846 OVERLAND EMIGRATION to Oregon and California was the largest ever to attempt the hazardous journey prior to the Gold Rush. It involved around 2,000 men, women and children, traveling in hundreds of wagons. They sought land, not gold. Mexico ruled California and war seemed probable. This caused some anxiety among the emigrants; however, other Americans like John Marsh and John A. Sutter had written letters from California to the East encouraging emigrants to come (see Marsh & Sutter).

Among those who decided to make the journey were the James Frazier Reed family from Springfield, Illinois. At the age of 45, Reed had been a successful furniture manufacturer who saw the economy around Springfield beginning to falter. He had heard about the wonderful climate in California and hoped it would benefit his 32 year-old, semi-invalid wife, Margaret.

Though he had been born in Ireland, Reed was descended from a line of Polish exiles named Reedowsky, and was a Protestant. At the time of his birth, November 14, 1800, his Polish blood had been diluted by his Scotch-Irish mother, a descendent of Clan Frazier in Scotland. As a youngster, Reed had emigrated with his mother to the United States, where they settled in Philadelphia. James got a few years of schooling there before leaving at age eight or nine to live with his maternal uncle in Virginia. At age 20 he went to work at lead mines in Illinois, and by 1831 he was living in Springfield, where he became a prosperous furniture maker.

By then he was known as a man of action who made fast decisions. He was described as proud, intelligent, loyal and energetic—some called him headstrong. In 1832 he served in the Black Hawk War with Abraham Lincoln, James Clyman and possibly John Marsh. He was also a Master Mason in the Springfield Masonic lodge (see Clyman).

In the mid-1830s Reed married Margaret Backenstoe, a widow with one child, Virginia E., and they had three children of their own. When they left for Independence, Missouri, in April 1846, Virginia was thirteen, Martha J. (a.k.a. Mattie or Patty) was eight; James Jr. was five and Thomas K., three. Margaret Reed's elderly mother, Sarah Keyes, had also agreed to accompany them.

Two Donner brothers from Springfield were as eager to emigrate to California as Reed. At age sixty-two, George Donner was a prosperous farmer. He and his third wife, Tamsen, had three children of their own and were raising two teen-aged girls from Donner's previous marriage (see Tamsen Donner). Donner had many grown children and some grandchildren who would be left behind. Why would a man of his age and substance pull up his deep roots to head for California?

Even more surprising was the decision of his older brother to accompany him. Jacob Donner was three years older than George, and his health was failing. His large family consisted of his 45-year old wife, Elizabeth; her two sons from a former marriage, and five young children of their own. The saving grace was their financial security. They and the Reeds were able to outfit themselves handsomely and take along hired men to do the heavy work.

THE REED FAMILY loaded three fine wagons with all the supplies and equipment needed for a semi-luxurious journey; one of the wagons was nearly two stories high, with a built-in stove and all the amenities possible. This was to ease the hardships for Margaret Reed and her elderly mother. They also had four hired hands and a hired girl to help Mrs. Reed. The Donners had six more wagons, all overloaded with people and goods. There was also a herd of beef cattle, milk cows, extra oxen and riding horses. Seldom was a party of emigrants better equipped.

Their overland journey from Springfield to the Missouri River meant crossing the Mississippi River, which was probably done on a ferry boat, and became a mild test for what was to come. After joining with others at Independence, they pulled out in early May. A few miles above the Arkansas River, the Donner-Reed party of nine wagons joined a much larger group led by Col. W. H. "Owl" Russell. Shortly after the Reeds joined Russell's party, Margaret Reed's mother, Sarah Keyes, died and was buried on the banks of the Little Blue River.

Some of the emigrants were following *The Emigrant's Guide to Oregon and California,* written by Lansford Hastings, an opportunistic lawyer-adventurer from Ohio (see Hastings). In that publication Hastings outlined a proposed short-cut leading around the south end of the Great Salt Lake. He claimed it would save several hundred miles over the more traditional Fort Hall Route. This was true for horseback riders, but no one, including Hastings himself, had taken wagons there before. Nevertheless he was sure it could be done and had offered to meet at Fort Bridger any party who dared try it.

Among those who agreed to try it was James Reed. It was like Reed to choose the closest route and to ride the finest saddle horse in the group. At Fort Laramie the emigrants were camped for the night when they were joined by frontiersman James Clyman, who had served with James Reed in the Black Hawk War and had just returned with Hastings over the new trail from California. After a pleasant visit, he warned them not to try the new route with wagons and went on his way.

IT WAS ALREADY the end of June and Reed continued to argue for the new route to make up valuable time. After crossing South Pass and reaching Little Sandy Creek on July 19th, part of the company split off for Fort Hall, while Reed and the Donners took the trail to Fort Bridger. Another group, including the Irish-Catholic Patrick Breen family, joined them; altogether there were over eighty people with many wagons in the party. Although George Donner was elected captain, James Reed's imposing demeanor and decisiveness made him a natural leader.

Despite envious gossip from some of the less affluent members, Reed exercised his power and pushed hard for the new short-cut. Margaret Reed's health was still not the best, but she was managing. Her hired girl, Eliza Williams, had proved a Godsend, even though she was hard of hearing. Eliza's older brother, Bayless, was one of Reed's drovers. They were both in their mid-twenties and anticipating a new life in California. Reed's other three hired men, also in their twenties, were Milton Elliott, Walter Herron and James Smith. Like the Donner's hired men, they were working their way to California any way they could. It can be assumed that Eliza Williams had no lack of suitors along the way.

Arriving at Fort Bridger in late July, Reed and the others were shocked to learn that Lansford Hastings was already gone, but he had left a message: He was piloting another large party; if late comers could catch up, he would guide them as promised. But they would have to hurry, as every day was crucial if they were to cross the Sierra Nevada before heavy snow blocked the passes. An alleged note, left by one of Reed's friends, warned him not to use the Hastings route. It was never delivered.

Feeling betrayed and guilty about his decision, Reed joined Charles Stanton and William McCutchen to ride after Hastings with the hope that he would wait for the others to catch up. Nearly killing their horses, Reed and his companions finally caught up with Hastings and the Harlan-Young Party on the Salt Lake flats. They had paused to rest there after a torturous journey across the Wasatch range through Weber Creek Canyon. Hastings apologized for leaving the Donner Party in the lurch, but he justified it by pointing out his responsibilities to the large group with him. Every day counted, and he simply could not wait a week or more for the Donners to catch up. Instead, he accompanied Reed part of the way back to point out another possible route, explaining that it offered a better chance for wagons.

With their horses worn down, Stanton and McCutchen remained with Hastings, while Reed borrowed a fresh horse to explore the proposed new route. He followed it part way, blazing trees along the way to guide them later. Within a week he had rejoined the Donners, bringing the Donner Party to crisis. Should they gamble with the new untried route, or return to the safer Fort Hall Trail? Finally the decision was made to try the new shorter route. It was simply too late for Fort Hall, they decided.

IT WAS EARLY August; Stanton and McCutchen rejoined the Donner Party and they finally got moving again. After three weeks of back-breaking work, hacking out a semblance of a trail, they had covered only 36 miserable miles to flatter terrain near the lake. At this point their first man died. He was buried on the trail with Masonic rituals spoken by Reed. After a few days of relatively easy travel, the party was confronted by what seemed an endless desert. They found tattered note: "Two days travel without water ahead. Carry water and fodder with you."

By then it was nearly September and blazing hot. Instead of two days, it was three, and still no sign of water. Livestock began dropping in their tracks until they had lost about a quarter of their vital oxen. It had taken six days to cross a desert they estimated was 80 miles wide. Some wagons, including two of Reed's, had to be abandoned on the spot. Margaret Reed and the children cried bitterly when many of their prized possessions lay buried in the drifting sand. God, how they hated Hastings by now! Reed had to endure plenty of abuse himself for having gone along with Hasting's scheme.

They reached the main trail on the Humboldt River at the end of September, the last wagon train to arrive there that season. As feared, the new route had proved no shorter and actually took longer than the Fort Hall route. Meanwhile, McCutchen and Stanton had been sent ahead on horseback to obtain food at Sutter's Fort. Reed and the Donners were running short and knew their supplies would never last.

Seemingly endless days of travel along the Humboldt River frayed everyone's nerves and finally erupted into violence between Reed and a young German drover, John Snyder. One version states that Snyder had been beating a yoke of oxen unmercifully with his bullwhip. When Reed remonstrated with him about it, the enraged Snyder allegedly struck Reed on the head with the butt of his whip. The blow stunned Reed, who fell to his knees and drew his hunting knife. When Snyder continued the attack, Reed struck out with his knife and stabbed the maddened German in the chest. Snyder collapsed with blood gushing from the wound.

Another version states that Snyder was attempting to pass Reed's big wagon on a sandbank. Words passed between them, and when Snyder threatened to strike Reed with his whip, Reed leaped across the tongue of the wagon and stabbed Snyder. During the melee, Snyder lashed Reed's head with his whip. [1] However it happened, when Patrick Breen rushed to Snyder's aid, the young man gasped, "Uncle Patrick, I am dead." Within moments his dramatic prophesy came true.

Reed, sobbing with anguish, threw his knife into the river. There were cries among some to hang Reed as a murderer. Enough of them disliked Reed to carry out the threat; in fact, it was alleged that another German, Lewis Keseberg, went so far as to raise a wagon tongue in the air to be used as a gallows. But there were others, including Reed's close friend, William Eddy, who thought Reed had killed in self defense. They refused to go along with the lynching; instead, they reluctantly recommended banishment.

This decision prevailed, and Eddy promised to look after Reed's family. Reed may have been given a horse and sent on his way alone and without a gun or provisions, virtually a death sentence. In her memoirs, written many years later, Patty Reed states that her father was denied a horse, and that she and Milt Elliott later took him a horse, a rifle and supplies. [2] Reed's hired man, Walter Herron, then ran off to join him. There is little doubt that Herron took some provisions and a gun with him. Reed himself always insisted that he had merely gone ahead to obtain provisions.

B Y NOW the party was completely disorganized. To add to their misery, they came across a note left by Reed to watch out for hostile Indians ahead. As predicted, their stock was killed and wounded with arrows day after day. More wagons were abandoned, including Reed's "Palace on wheels." Margaret Reed had to discard everything except a few clothes, and she and her children were left to the mercy of William Eddy and his family. Before long Eddy also abandoned his wagon and transferred some of his supplies to one of Breen's wagons.

Most of them had been walking and were running out of provisions when they reached the blessed Truckee River. By then a man named Wolfinger had disappeared, and they were down to fourteen wagons. Then, like a savior reincarnated, Charles Stanton arrived from Sutter's fort with two Indians and several pack-horses loaded with food. William McCutchen, whose young wife and child were with the group, had stayed behind. Stanton, who had no family, attached himself to James Reed's distraught family. He also brought news that Reed and Herron were alive and nearing Sutter's fort. Then William Pike died from an accidental shooting, and his wife and children were left at the mercy of others in the group.

It was early November and snowing when the strongest of the scattered Donner Party made an attempt to cross the summit above Truckee Lake (now Donner Lake). The attempt failed, and they brought back the disheartening news that it was already impassable. When it became certain that they would have to spend the winter where they were, the Breen family occupied the Schallenberger cabin built two years earlier by members of the Stevens-Murphy Party. Others built shelter of their own. Some, including the Donners, had not even made it to the lake; they were isolated about six miles northeast, on Alder Creek. Bad luck and poor decisions began taking a terrible toll.

MEANWHILE, Reed and Herron stumbled into Sutter's Fort on October 28, only to learn that the Mexican War was underway and manpower was too scarce to mount a rescue attempt. Furthermore, John C. Fremont had taken over Sutter's Fort and was recruiting volunteers to fight the Mexicans (see Fremont & Sutter). The place was now known as Fort Sacramento. Reed enlisted in Fremont's California Volunteers, but begged permission to lead a search party to rescue his family, whom he correctly assumed were trapped by heavy snow. Sutter provided pack mules and provisions, and Reed and William McCutchen left for Johnson's Ranch (now Wheatland) and the high mountains beyond it (see Johnson).

After a valiant struggle, they came within twelve miles of the summit before being forced back down by a vicious storm. Heartbroken, Reed and McCutchen returned with two stragglers from the Harlan-Young Party. Sutter apparently convinced Reed that it would be impossible to reach his family before spring and tried to ease their fears by stating that the trapped people could survive by eating their remaining livestock. He further advised the two men to head for Yerba Buena (San Francisco) to solicit funds and manpower to launch a major rescue effort the following spring. Reed could also see about his previous enlistment in Fremont's Volunteers and get his orders.

In mid-January 1847 two men and five women staggered out of the mountains to Johnson's Ranch on crudely made snowshoes. The trek from the lake camp had taken them 33 days. Then came shocking news: The survivors had made it through only by eating the flesh of those who had perished along the way. Among the survivors was William Eddy, who said that most those at the lake camp, including his own wife and two children, were stranded and starving.

James Reed had gone to Mission San Jose in early December 1846. While there he was made guardian of property at Mission San Jose and petitioned American authorities for land grants for himself and his family. He also solicited funds for the Donner rescue party and joined Charles Weber's forces to fight against the Mexicans (see Weber).

Reed made his way to Yerba Buena in late December, and by New Year's Day 1847 he had joined with others to defeat Mexican forces at the "Battle of Santa Clara." In February Reed solicited funds in Yerba Buena to purchase supplies and pay the expenses of volunteers needed for an all-out rescue attempt. He was successful there and recruited old Caleb Greenwood, a crusty mountain man who knew the country well (see Greenwood). McCutchen joined Reed, and they left the great bay by launch on February 7 with manpower and money enough to make the rescue effort. They planned to recruit men along the way and to start the search from Johnson's Ranch on the Bear River.

On February 4th, frontiersman A. Glover left Johnson's Ranch with a small rescue party. By then William Eddy had recovered enough to accompany Glover as a guide. There were fourteen riders, plus a string of pack mules loaded with food. When the horses could go no farther, seven men managed to reach the lake camp on foot with back-packs of jerked meat and coarse flour.

There they found horror compounded by more horror. Partially eaten naked bodies were strewn about, and the emaciated, half-crazed survivors lived in unspeakable filth. They judged 23 of them fit to travel, while 17 were left behind. Among those taken out were three men, four women—including Margaret Reed—and 17 children. Two of the Breen children and the four Reed children were included; however, Patty and Tommy Reed could not keep up and had to be returned to the Breen cabin, where the Reed family had been living. Imagine the guilt suffered by Margaret Reed at this decision. She apparently consented to it only with Glover's solemn promise as a true Mason to return later for the other two children.

Several days later, when it appeared all of them would perish, a man ran back to them. "Is Mrs. Reed here?" he called out. "Tell her Mr. Reed's coming for her!" The messenger had gone ahead to seek food, and after running into Reed's large search party, he had rushed back with the news. The greeting between James, his wife and two children on the trail must have been an overwhelming emotional experience. Their joy was marred by the absence of Patty and Tommy, but Reed vowed he would get them out alive.

REED'S PARTY left food for the survivors and set off for the lake camp to bring out the others. By March 4th, Mrs. Reed, Virginia and Jimmy had made it to Sutter's Fort and were housed at Alcalde Sinclair's ranch across the American River. Reed and his rescuers pressed on to find both his remaining children still alive. The survivors were in desperate condition, so Reed and McCutchen fed and cleansed them as best they could, including bed-ridden Lewis Keseberg, who had allegedly wanted to hang Reed on the trail. Later, Reed was horror-stricken to find the partially eaten body of his former drover, Milton Elliott, and to verify the loss of William Eddy's wife and children.

Continuing on to the Donner camp on Alder Creek, Reed and his men again found abysmal conditions awaiting them. Many were dead or dying, and evidence of cannibalism was rampant. George Donner still clung to life, but his valiant wife, Tamsen, refused to leave him. Both Jacob Donner and his wife, Elizabeth, were dead. Reed left there with three children, leaving Charles Cady and Charles Stone behind to care for the remainder, who were too weak to travel. Returning to the lake camp, Reed's party made ready to take out 17 survivors, 14 of them children, including Tommy and Patty Reed and the Breens. Some children had to be carried, and they left for Johnson's Ranch on March 3rd.

The survivors were so weak it took three days to scale the summit, where three able-bodied men were sent ahead to bring back badly needed food. Camped as they were near the exposed summit, they were vulnerable to the weather. That very afternoon, a severe snowstorm ravaged them. Reed, weakened by exhaustion and lack of food, went temporarily blind and became helpless. McCutchen was able to keep a fire going so they didn't freeze, but it was a close call for them all.

FINALLY the cruel storm abated enough so they could proceed, but two families refused to go on. The Breen and Graves families were reluctantly left behind at a place that became known as "Starved Camp." Mary Donner had to return after a short distance, but somehow Reed and the others kept going, including Reed's two small children. Together, the group continued to make slow progress, taking turns carrying the children. Despite frozen feet and toes, the Reed Party made their way down to Bear Valley. Somewhere near there they met William Eddy and another rescue party coming up. This party brought out those left behind at starved camp and everyone else left alive except Keseberg, who said he couldn't walk.

Soon Reed and his two youngsters were reunited with Margaret and the other children at Sinclair's Ranch, near Sutter's fort. Through some miracle they and the Patrick Breens were the only families to escape the disaster intact. It was the end of April before the last survivor, Lewis Keseberg, was finally brought to Sutter's Fort. There a member of the last rescue party accused him of murdering and eating Tamsen Donner after her husband died and probably killing Mr. Wolfinger earlier. Keseberg sued him for defamation of character, and although Keseberg won his case, he never lived down his unsavory reputation.

Reed took his family to the ranch of George Yount in Napa Valley to recuperate. In June 1847 he was appointed sheriff of the District of Sonoma. Later he moved to San Jose, where he leased a vineyard from Thomas O. Larkin and again became custodian of property at Mission

San Jose. After acquiring land of his own, he went into fruit ranching. By then he and his wife had adopted Mary Donner, the orphaned daughter of Jacob and Elizabeth Donner. Margaret Reed, having recovered her health, gave birth to a son, Charles C., in February 1848. Shortly after James Marshall's gold discovery in Cullomah (Coloma), Reed headed for the gold fields. He did well enough to buy a large parcel of land in San Jose and soon found himself a land developer.

In accordance with the Constitutional Convention held in 1849— and in anticipation of full statehood—the State Capital was to be moved from Monterey. Largely through the efforts of James Reed, it was moved to San Jose. Though he spent over $30,000 of his own money to keep it there, it was moved to Vallejo in 1851. In June 1850, Virginia Backenstoe Reed married John M. Murphy, son of Martin Murphy Sr. of the 1844 Stevens-Murphy Party (see Murphy). Reed was upset because she married a Catholic, but he got over it when he met his first grandchild. By then he was on his way to becoming a wealthy man and served in several public offices in San Jose. About 1850 he fathered another son, William (actually Williamoski) Yount Reed, who died at an early age.

In the 1850s Reed helped build the Methodist Seminary in San Jose. Later it became the College of the Pacific, and much later the University of the Pacific in Stockton. Margaret Reed died in 1861, and James followed her in July 1874 at the age of 73.

THE REED CHILDREN recovered from their 1846 ordeal and lived full lives; for example, Patty Reed married Frank Lewis of Santa Cruz in 1856 and had eight children; Virginia Reed, who had converted to Catholicism while living in the Breen cabin, had at least four children with her husband, John Murphy. Several streets in San Jose are named after the family; namely, Reed, Margaret, Virginia, Martha and Keyes Streets. The old Reed home stood for many years at the corner of Third and Margaret Streets. Donner State Historical Park just west of Truckee commemorates the Donner disaster, as does the Alder Creek historical site on Highway 89, about six miles north of Truckee.

BIBLIOGRAPHY

–Bancroft, Hubert H. *History of California,* Vol. I-VI. History Co., San Francisco, CA, 1886. Repub., Wallace Hebberd, Santa Barbara, 1966.

–Bryant, Edwin. *What I Saw In California.* University of Nebraska Press, Lincoln, 1985.

–Crosby, Alexander L. *Old Greenwood, Pathfinder of the West.* Talisman Press, Georgetown, CA, 1967.

–DeVoto, Bernard. *The Year of Decision-1846.* Houghton Mifflin Co.,
   Boston, 1942
–Dillon, Richard. *Fool's Gold.* Coward-McCann, Inc. New York, 1967.
–King, Joseph A. *Winter of Entrapment.* P. D. Meany Publishers,
   Toronto, 1992. [1 & 2]
–Lewis, Oscar. *Sutter's Fort.* Prentice-Hall, Englewood Cliffs, NJ, 1966.
–McGlashan, C.F. *History of the Donner Party.* Truckee, CA, 1879.
   (Several subsequent editions)
–Several publications from Santa Clara County Historical &
   Genealogical Society; namely, *Coast Counties* by Guinn; *Signposts* by
   Patricia Loomis; *Historic Names, Persons & Places in Santa Clara
   County* by Clyde Arbuckle.
–Stewart, George R. *Ordeal By Hunger.* Houghton Mifflin Co., Boston,
   1936. Repub., Pocket Books, New York, 1960. Except for [1 & 2],
   all quotations taken from this edition.
–Stewart, George R. *The California Trail.* University of Nebraska Press,
   Lincoln, 1962.

– 36 –

HUGO REID (DON PERFECTO)

1810 – 1852

A NATIVE OF Renfrew County, Scotland, Hugo Reid was born in 1810 to Charles Reid and his wife, the former Essex Milchin. Young Hugo was well educated in his homeland, completing two years at Cambridge University. He also gained practical experience in merchandising and accounting practices by working in his father's store.

Reid was around eighteen when he was employed by Henry Dalton's Trading Company in Lima, Peru. After learning that Hermosillo, Mexico, was in the midst of a gold rush, Reid saw an opportunity to prosper. A partnership arrangement was set up between him and his employer, whereby Reid became the company representative in Hermosillo dealing in miner's supplies. The business was quick to prosper, and Reid soon became well known there. His best friend was a young American physician, Dr. William Keith. In 1832, Reid accepted an invitation from Captain John Wilson, a fellow Scotsman, to sail north and visit San Pedro and Los Angeles. Captain Wilson commanded a speedy merchant vessel, which traded for hides and tallow along the California coast.

The ship's officers were Scottish, English and American, but the crew consisted mostly of *Kanakas* from the Sandwich Islands (Hawaii). Reid was the only passenger. He put his business acumen to good use by assisting the supercargo, James Scott, in his complex duties. A rather handsome man with sandy hair and keen blue eyes, Reid had a lively, adventurous personality and an above average singing voice. The long voyage to San Pedro offered plenty of opportunities for good fellowship with the ship's officers.

Though San Pedro offered little protection from high winds, especially from the southwest, its huge and numerous cattle ranchos provided abundant trade in hides, horns and tallow, making the risk worth it. Ships had to anchor well off the shallow beach and transport people and cargo ashore in launches. When the surf was running high, these short trips became treacherous indeed; the launches could not reach dry land.

When they reached the shallows, the passengers were required to wade ashore over slippery rocks and clinging kelp. Loading and unloading cargo required crewmen to hazard these conditions time after time, as they balanced heavy loads on their heads, backs or shoulders. On shore, the only facility was a crude adobe building used as temporary storage for trade goods.

Supercargo Scott knew the nearest Mexican official lived a few miles away and must be notified of the ship's arrival. Fortunately, near the dilapidated warehouse, a few bony horses were grazing, lassos dangling from their scrawny necks. They had been left for the convenience of visitors. Scott caught one of the horses and rode off, while Reid and Captain Wilson stayed behind.

THE FOLLOWING MORNING, Mexican *carretas* (crude ox-carts) began squealing their way toward the landing, loaded with stiff, smelly cowhides, horns and tallow. More hides came, haphazardly loaded on plodding mules. Captain Wilson ordered that trade goods be brought ashore, and trading commenced. The ship was to stay a week, so Reid caught one of the horses for the estimated 20-mile ride to the pueblo of Los Angeles.

He spoke some Spanish and was able to exchange a few words with hacendados (property owners), who were transporting hides along the rough dirt road leading down to the landing. It was apparent that supercargo Scott was doing his job of spreading the word. When Reid reached Los Angeles, he saw few people about. There were supposed to be around 1,500 residents, but they weren't in evidence. He correctly assumed it was because of the afternoon *siesta*; the weather was warm and everyone was resting.

Reid thought the *pueblo* (town) was not "prepossessing in appearance, being mud-colored and built without plan." The pueblo had been founded in 1781 as "*Reina de los Angeles*" (Queen of the Angels). The early Mexican settlers built their tiny adobe casas wherever they pleased. Finally Reid saw a man sitting outside an adobe shop. By chance he turned out to be an American named Nathaniel Pryor, an ex-trapper, silversmith and clockmaker from Kentucky. He reportedly came to California in 1828 with the James Ohio Pattie trapping party.

With Pryor was Abel Stearns, a traveling representative of Captain John B. R. Cooper, a trader from Monterey (see Stearns). Pryor offered Reid overnight accommodations, which the young Scotsman could hardly refuse, as there was no other boarding house. Another guest was an American nicknamed "Handsome Dick" Laughlin, another ex-member of the Pattie party. By the time they had shared a bottle of aguardiente (fiery Mexican brandy) and a late-night card game, the four adventurous young men had become fast friends.

When Reid mentioned his friend, Dr. William Keith in Hermosillo, his companions begged him to bring him to Los Angeles, which had no doctor and desperately needed one. A few days later Reid's new friends invited him to accompany them to a supper hosted by Father José Sanchez, the pastor at Mission San Gabriel. During the 15-mile ride to San Gabriel, Pryor told Reid about the arrival of Jedediah Smith's party a few years earlier and the subsequent arrival of American settlers such as William Wolfskill and J. J. Warner (see Wolfskill). The site where Father Sanchez held his supper party was described by Reid as follows:

> The water, which now composes the lagoon of the mill (one mile and a half distant from the mission), being free, like everything else, to wander and meander where it pleased, came down into the hollow nearest the mission, on the Angeles road. This hollow was a complete thicket, formed by sycamores, cottonwood...besides brambles, nettles...and wild grapevines [which] lent a hand to make it impassible, except where footpaths had rendered entrance to its barriers...This hollow, cleared of all encumbrance, served to raise the first crops ever produced at the mission....

Reid went on to describe Fr. José Sanchez: "He was of a cheerful dis-position, frank and generous in his nature, although at times he lost his temper with the strange, unruly set around him." Because the supper party continued into evening, Fr. Sanchez insisted that his guests stay overnight at the mission. Reid's companions jumped at the chance, but he had learned that his ship was ready to sail and had to decline. He took his leave, frustrated that he had not had more time to learn about the fascinating mission. He could see opportunities in the area, and hoped to convince his friend, Dr. Keith, to migrate to Los Angeles with him.

Upon his return to Hermosillo, Reid was so busy with the flourish-ing trade there he had little time to think about leaving. But as the gold rush waned and business slowed, he finally talked Dr. Keith into visiting Los Angeles with him. They arrived in mid-summer 1834. The moment Dr. Keith hung out his "shingle," he had more patients than time to care for them. Reid formed a trading partnership with Keith and Jacob P. Leese. A native of Ohio, Leese had experience as a Santa Fe Trail trader and had arrived in Los Angeles a few months earlier. Their adobe build-ing contained a store and a small warehouse, where they stored the hides and tallow taken in trade for manufactured goods imported from over the world. The business did well from the start. Author Richard Henry Dana, Jr. reported: "One found everything from Chinese fireworks to English cartwheels" in the interesting store.

That fall the store was visited by Señora Eulalia Pérez y de Mariné, an older, genteel Mexican woman from San Gabriel. When Reid helped carry Doña Eulalia's purchases to her cart, he was surprised to see an attractive young woman waiting patiently. Her face combined the bronze complexion of an Indian with the handsome, fine features of Spanish aristocracy. She wore a lacy, white mantilla over her raven-black hair and was dressed in style. He learned that she lived with Doña Eulalia and was called Victoria. Reid was pleasantly surprised when Doña Eulalia invited him to tea at her San Gabriel home. Seldom had a woman made such an immediate impression on him as did Doña Victoria, and he stared longingly after the cart as it rumbled up the dusty road.

A WEEK PASSED before he was able to leave for San Gabriel to look for Señora Eulalia Peréz's house, which he learned was on the edge of the extensive mission gardens. As he neared the mission, he was shocked to see piles of bleaching cattle bones and a sense of quiet desolation surrounding the mission itself. He found the Peréz place located on three-and-a-half leagues of land called Rancho San Pascual. He was greeted by Doña Victoria herself, who unlocked massive wooden gates to admit him into a spacious central patio.

Reid had learned from friends that the attractive young woman was pure Indian, the daughter of a well-respected chief and the ward and companion of elderly Doña Eulalia. It was said she lived there with several children from a former marriage, but Reid wasn't certain about her current marital status. She was fairly tall and well-formed, unlike most local Indian women, who tended to be short and dumpy. She carried herself proudly and spoke impeccable Castilian Spanish. From the very start they felt a magnetic attraction toward one another.

Victoria explained that her patroness was taking her siesta and could not be disturbed until later. Reid boldly told her that he was glad because he really had come to see her. He learned that Doña Eulalia had long served the mission padres as housemother and had been married to a Spanish military officer. For his services to the King, he had been awarded Rancho San Pascual. After his death the property had gone to Doña Eulalia and her second husband, Juan de Marine. She had outlived her second husband and now owned the property outright.

She had taken in Victoria as a young girl and treated her like a daughter. When Reid asked about the mission, she explained that Fr. José Sanchez had died the year before (January 1833) and everything had gone wrong since then. The Mission Secularization Act had been passed shortly thereafter, and the mission was being systematically looted of its livestock and personal property. Even some buildings were torn down, and most of its land had been taken by others. Both Victoria and Doña Eulalia were devastated by the wanton destruction and helpless to do anything about it.

It was late afternoon when Reid left, but he made the journey to San Gabriel often after that. It wasn't long before his relationship with Victoria became a scandal in the area; he was accused of being a "squaw man" and was cut off from many Los Angeles social events. His close friend, Dr. Keith, told him it was a mistake, and that Victoria had an Indian husband who had fathered her three children. But nothing could dissuade Reid. He was in love with Victoria, and nothing else mattered.

In 1835 things started going wrong for Reid. Several "foreigners", including Reid and Dr. Keith, were accosted by revolutionaries and relieved of arms and provisions. Later, the government accused them of aiding the rebels and arrested them for being traitors and for complicity in a plot they knew little about. Fortunately, they were later pardoned by Governor Figueroa. If that weren't enough, Reid's partnership began to crumble. Jacob Leese had become so difficult to deal with that the business had to be liquidated. Reid had hoped to earn enough to buy land, but he could not do so.

THE YEAR 1836 found the disappointed Reid working in San Pedro, where he was assisting Abel Stearns in Stearns' latest enterprise there. Later in the year Dr. Keith convinced Reid to accompany him back to Hermosillo for a visit. Keith was hoping Reid's absence from Victoria would cool his ardor. Reid taught school in Hermosillo for over a year, trying to wash away the bad taste of his California experiences. But then came news that changed everything: Victoria had given birth to another child, and her husband had died of smallpox.

Though Reid was in no position to support a wife and four children, he had never gotten over Victoria. He sailed north to Los Angeles, hoping to marry her. Later, Dr. Keith received a letter from Reid requesting that he catch the first ship to Los Angeles and stand up for him at his wedding. Still hoping to bring Reid to his senses, Keith left for San Pedro a few days later.

Reid had to convert to Catholicism before any marriage could be performed, and he also became a naturalized citizen of Mexico. He then petitioned Governor Alvarado for permission to marry under his new name, "Perfecto" Hugo Reid (it was traditional for naturalized citizens to take a Mexican name). He then became known as Don Perfecto. Next he had to request permission from the clergy as shown in the following petition:

> Perfecto Hugo Reid, native of Great Britain, legitimate son of Charles Reid and Essex Milchin, natives of Scotland in the County of Renfrew, resident of Our Lady of the Angels, before your Reverence, hereby makes known his intention to marry [Victoria] Bartolomea Comicrabit, a neophyte of this mission [Reid may have given her the name "Victoria"]. I entreat your Reverence to order

that the customary steps be taken to carry this out. I swear and promise, et cetera.

—Mission of San Gabriel.
—Perfecto Hugo Reid. July 30, 1837.

VICTORIA'S AGE was given as 29, and her parents' names as Bartolome and Petra of the Comicrabit *rancheria*, adjacent to the pueblo. She was described as the widow of the Indian Pablo Maria "de Yutucubit, Partida 512," by whom she had four children. The marriage petition was approved by Padre Narciso Durán. The wedding was held at the mission in September and was well attended by foreign settlers and the local Mexican community. A festive and colorful fiesta followed at Doña Eulalia's spacious home, and merrymaking continued for a week.

Don Perfecto moved in with the gracious old lady and began building a house for him and his new family on a few acres he acquired near the mission. The land may have been a wedding gift or dowry given by Doña Eulalia. Furthermore, Victoria obtained a land grant from the government, including two ranchos: Santa Anita, totaling three square leagues of land, and a smaller one of 123 acres.

Victoria was one of the few Indians to acquire a land grant, and it was probably due to Doña Eulalia's influence. Through his marriage to Victoria, Reid had at last acquired land and was now a hacendado. It wasn't until they moved into their new two-story house that Reid learned about his wife's fear of earthquakes. She flatly refused to set foot upstairs, so a downstairs living room had to be converted into a bedroom. The children and guests would use bedrooms on the second floor. Victoria's oldest child, a boy named Felipe, was fifteen. He was followed by José, thirteen; Maria, nine, and the baby, Carlitos. Reid agreed to adopt them all. There were several servants in the household who worked only for board and room, plus others who lived outside the house and worked for food and bare necessities.

Before long Reid's house became known for its pleasant hospitality. Visitors such as "Kanaka Bill" Davis and fellow Scotsman James McKinley—a representative of Thomas O. Larkin in Monterey—enjoyed many visits there. Where there had formerly been many snide remarks about Reid's "Indian squaw," Victoria's charm and grace soon dispelled them. Because there were no schools in the area, the older children were sent to a mission school in Honolulu. They had problems there, so Reid took it upon himself to educate his new family. He also taught his illiterate wife to read and write.

During this period it appears that Reid and his family were living off income from rents and share-cropping from their two ranchos. A letter to Abel Stearns, in October 1838, shows Reid's humorous side:

Ink, paper, and health are scarce commodities at the Uva Espina [gooseberry, a name he chose for the house] por ahora [for now]. The ink was taken from the mill pond fresh this morning, being composed of three parts of water, two of mud, and one of tadpoles well ground...Let me know what knews [sic] and what satisfaction the northern gents gave you.

During the fall of 1838 his friend Juan Bandini moved to San Gabriel from Rancho Tecate, near San Diego, where he had been burnt out by hostile Indians. Bandini became Administrator of Mission San Gabriel and later acquired Rancho Jurupa, which straddled present San Bernardino and Riverside County lines (See Bandini). He built a new home there, where he established a large cattle ranch. A short time later his old bachelor friend Abel Stearns moved in with him. Reid was very close to both Stearns and Bandini. Reid was elected to the ayuntamiento (Los Angeles City Council) the following year.

There had been problems gaining clear title to Rancho Santa Anita because of Victoria's Indian heritage; however, it was finally resolved in the Reid's favor in 1841 after Don Perfecto petitioned Governor Alvarado and one of his influential assistants, William E. P. Hartnell. By then Reid was eager to develop the property and to build a second home there.

The year 1841 proved a significant one for Reid. Having gained clear title to Rancho Santa Anita, he began building a new home located on a small lake complete with a boat landing. He stocked his ranch with livestock and planted orchards, vineyards and wheat. The family liked it so well they moved there from San Gabriel. Reid's middle-aged friend Abel Stearns then married Arcadia Bandini, the flirtatious and fun-loving daughter of his friend, Don Juan Bandini. Arcadia was fourteen at the time. Now a wealthy man, Stearns installed his bride and her younger sister in a fine mansion he built in Los Angeles.

Apparently tiring of his many duties as rancher, father, teacher and city council member, Reid purchased a small trading vessel. A note to Abel Stearns in October 1842 tells his state of mind: "I shall be very glad to leave—go with me. The gentlemen say that the boat will be ready to sail on the twentieth...."

Don Abel did not accompany him on his first voyage; however, his old friend Dr. Keith came from Hermosillo and acted as supercargo for Reid. The voyage took six months. When Reid unloaded cargo from Honolulu at Monterey in the fall of 1842, the duties proved higher than the value of the cargo. He returned home to a forgiving family, poorer but wiser.

This was shortly after the abortive invasion of Monterey by U.S. Navy Commodore Thomas ap Catesby Jones. Jones thought war had been declared against Mexico and had sent troops ashore to secure the town. After Thomas O. Larkin finally convinced him there was no war, Jones apologized to Mexican officials, struck the American Flag and left. He then sailed to San Pedro, made his way to Los Angeles and apologized directly to the new governor, Manuel Micheltorena. His apology was accepted, after which a gala supper party was arranged, which was attended by all the prominent people, including the Reids. The event was hosted by Abel Stearns and his teen-aged wife in their new mansion.

SOON REID became restless again. He had a large quantity of wine and brandy to sell, but the local market was soft. He decided to take it aboard his trading vessel and sell it up and down the coast. This he did with some success, but the voyage ended with accusations that he had engaged in illegal smuggling. After his experience the year before with exorbitant duties, he may have succumbed to the temptation of smuggling as other traders did from time to time.

Finally the charges were dropped, and in 1843 Reid left on a trading voyage to the Orient. During his absence his old friend Henry Dalton came to Los Angeles seeking business opportunities (see Dalton). Reid apparently overlooked the possible ruination his long absence would have on his laborious ranching activities. Furthermore, his trading efforts proved unsuccessful. He wrote to Abel Stearns in the spring of 1844:

> As you are one of the few persons with whom I can consult, or ask advice from, I shall at once go ahead. In debt as I am at present, I find it necessary to dispose of either the rancho [Santa Anita] or the vineyard; in fact, even were I not in debt, I would have to do one or the other.

When Reid returned from his failed trading trip, he found Pio Pico had taken over as governor and moved the capital from Monterey to Los Angeles (see Pico). Henry Dalton then requested Reid's help in acquiring land from Mission San Gabriel adjoining his Rancho Azusa. Dalton also purchased Rancho Santa Anita from Reid for $2,700. Despite his financial woes, Reid was elected *juez de paz*, justice of the peace.

Before long he became an Indian rights advocate, and tried to right some of the many wrongs that had befallen the natives, who had become rebellious. But by then it was too late. They began attacking outlying ranchos and running off livestock until several ranchero families were forced to seek sanctuary at the mission. In his new role as a magistrate and Administrator of Mission Affairs, Reid requested help from the Mexican Army, Henry Dalton and Don Benito Wilson to help keep the peace (see Wilson).

In June 1846 the remaining mission property was sold by order of Governor Pio Pico to Hugo Reid and William Workman. They were to pay $7,000, assume all the debts and pay the padre. But before this took place, U.S. forces under Commodore John Sloat invaded Monterey, and war between the United States and Mexico commenced. Within a month Comm. Robert Stockton and John C. Fremont landed troops in Southern California and raised the Stars and Stripes over the plaza in Los Angeles.

Reid had his hands full dealing with hostile Indians and sent Don Benito Wilson off with a small force to quell the hostiles. When the war started, Wilson enlisted in the U.S. Army and was captured by Mexican forces. Reid side-stepped the war with civil responsibilities. After the United States won the war, federal troops under Colonel Jonathon Stevenson were dispatched to San Gabriel to help keep order among the Indians.

In July 1847 Pío Pico returned to San Gabriel and sought refuge at Reid's home there. Somehow he had the impression that he might regain power, and he asked Reid to help him. His letter to Reid follows:

> Don Perfecto, you go to Colonel Stevenson. Remind him that Pio Pico is a gentleman and has given his word to be a private citizen now. But, Don Perfecto, you must also tell him that it would be for the glory of the Americanos and for the happiness of the Californians to restore Pio Pico to his rightful rank.

Reid dutifully delivered Pico's naive request to Stevenson, who told the former governor, in effect, that if he promised to stay on his ranch and not meddle in American government affairs, he could live in peace on his Rancho Santa Margarita.

Reid remained neutral during the war but received a bitter blow when the new government invalidated Picos' hasty mission land grants, including the one Reid and Workman had received. With the sale of Rancho Santa Anita to Dalton, the only properties left to Reid were the few acres in San Gabriel and the small rancho his wife still owned. His financial condition was growing desperate when he learned of James W. Marshall's gold discovery at Sutter's sawmill in January 1848. Hugo Reid arrived at Cullomah (Coloma) in early 1849 but quickly became disillusioned, as evidenced by a letter he wrote to Abel Stearns in April:

> Don't go to the mines on any account. They are full of goods, and a rush of cattle streaming likewise to every digging. The mines are, moreover, loaded to the muzzle with vagabonds from every quarter of the globe, scoundrels from nowhere, rascals from Oregon, pickpockets from New york, accomplished gentlemen from Europe, interlopers from Lima and Chile, Mexican thieves, gamblers of no particular spot, and assassins manufactured in Hell....

Later, Reid got word that his step-daughter, Maria, was dying from smallpox. He reached San Gabriel too late for the funeral, and had to endure his wife's bitter tirades until he left again for the North. It seemed Victoria blamed him for Maria's death because he insisted on educating her, thus tiring her and weakening her resistance to disease. By then Reid had entered into a trading business with his friend, James McKinley in Monterey, and was glad for an excuse to leave home. It wasn't until Victoria took in an Indian girl as a substitute for her deceased daughter that she regained her perspective and forgave her perplexed husband.

THE GOLD RUSH in Northern California shifted world attention away from the Los Angeles area, leaving its agrarian society to provide food for the North. San Francisco and Sacramento mushroomed into the largest and most important centers in California. In April 1849, Bennet Riley replaced Richard Mason as Military Governor, and he issued a proclamation as follows:

> As Congress has failed to organize a new territorial government, it becomes our imperative duty to take some active measures to provide for the existing wants of the country.

Effective September 1, Riley organized a Constitutional Convention in Monterey. Its goals included formulation of a State Constitution, setting up a judicial system and electing representatives to serve in the United States Congress once California was admitted into the Union.

That same year Hugo Reid's Los Angeles friends elected him a delegate to the convention, whereupon he was appointed to two committees; one to establish state boundaries, the other to take a census of the current population— formidable tasks indeed. He also seized the opportunity to make his case for the downtrodden Indians; he helped get them some constitutional rights, but failed to get them the right to vote.

Reid's three-month absence during the convention played havoc with the firm of McKinley, Reid and Company. Never an astute manager, James McKinley allowed the business to slip past the point of no return. It closed at the end of 1850, leaving Reid without adequate assets. Again he had to return home a broken man. He had long suffered from tuberculosis; this, combined with financial worries, made him look much older than his years, and he became known as "Old Reid."

Reid's weakened condition prevented him from engaging in active farming, which might have helped his finances. Instead, he began writing letters about the history, religion and customs of California Indians. Victoria became a valued source, and they traveled the area interviewing the few older Indians who still lived there. Shortly after this, Reid disappeared for several months. His only explanation after returning was that "he needed to get away to complete his writings and get them ready for publication."

The *Los Angeles Star* newspaper published his writings in 1852, paying him a fair amount for the rights. The letters attracted national attention when they served as a basis for a lengthy report submitted to Washington, D.C. by Indian Agent, Don Benito Wilson. This success led Reid to begin another ambitious project, where he compiled an Indian vocabulary and Indian-English language manual.

Unfortunately he never lived to finish it. He died December 12, 1852 at the age of 42. After a well-attended funeral paid for by Henry Dalton, he was laid to rest in the old Catholic cemetery. Victoria continued to live in the lovely two-story house Reid had built after their marriage. The Daltons looked after her, but three years later her worst fears were realized when the house was ruined by a devastating earthquake.

VICTORIA LIVED an austere life until December 1868, when she died of the dreaded smallpox. Ironically, it had swept away her first husband and all her children before then. She was buried on the grounds of her beloved San Gabriel Mission. Reid never fathered any children, so there was no family legacy left to carry on. Reid's old Rancho Santa Anita adobe is located on the grounds of the Los Angeles County Arboretum in Arcadia. His extensive writings on local Indians can be found in Susanna Bryant Dakin's biography of Reid, listed below.

BIBLIOGRAPHY

–Bancroft, Hubert H. *History of California,* Vol. I-VI. History Co., San Francisco, 1886. Repub., Wallace Hebberd, Santa Barbara, 1966.

–Dakin, Susanna Bryant. *A Scotch Paisano in Old Los Angeles.* University of California Press, Berkeley, 1939. All quotations taken from this volume.

–Davis, William Heath. *Seventy-Five Years in California.* John Howell Books, San Francisco, 1967.

–Jackson, Sheldon G. *A British Ranchero In Old California.* The Life and Times of Henry Dalton and the Rancho Azusa. Arthur H. Clark Co., Glendale, CA, 1987.

–Wright, Doris Marion. *A Yankee In Mexican California: Abel Stearns, 1798-1848.* Wallace Hebberd, Santa Barbara, CA, 1977.

William A. Richardson
Courtesy California State Library

WILLIAM A. RICHARDSON

(Don Guillermo Antonio) 1795 – 1856

NO BOOK ABOUT California history would be complete without including William A. Richardson, the first Anglo-Saxon to settle at Yerba Buena Cove, now San Francisco. He first stepped ashore there in 1822, about the time Mexico gained independence from Spain. Though he lived in California for the next seven years, he did not settle on the cove until 1835. He did so at the urging of Governor Jose Figueroa, who appointed him Captain of the fledgling port at the munificent salary of $60 per month.

His duties were to pilot trading vessels into Yerba Buena Cove, inspect their cargos, collect custom duties and guide them across the bay to *Ensenada del Carmelita* (cove of the Carmelites, now Sausalito), where they could obtain fresh water. Neither water nor firewood was available in large quantities at Yerba Buena, but it was plentiful on the north side, which became known as Whaler's Harbor.

Richardson was born in London, England August 27, 1795. He went to sea at the age of twelve and apparently learned both seamanship and the carpentry trade. When his whaleship *L'Orient* (or *Orion*) made her way into San Francisco Bay in 1822, he either jumped ship or was put ashore after a dispute with the captain. At that time the only inhabitants lived at Mission San Francisco de Asis (Mission Dolores), or at the military presidio overlooking what would be called the "Golden Gate."

In October 1822, Richardson petitioned Pablo Vicente Sola, the last Spanish governor, for permission to remain in California. The governor granted Richardson's request, providing that he agreed to teach carpentry to Indians at the mission. This he did, and with their help he built a launch with which he earned a living for the next few years hauling provisions to the presidio from missions at San Jose and Santa Clara.

During his early days living at the presidio, Richardson fell in love with Maria Antonia Martinez, young daughter of the *commandante* of the Presidio, Lt. Ygnacio Martinez. In order to marry her, he was required to become a Catholic and a naturalized citizen of Mexico, which he did in 1823. His name was changed to Guillermo Antonio Richardson, and he married Maria Martinez in May 1825. A daughter, Mariana, was born the following year at the Presidio.

In 1829 the Richardson family moved to Mission San Gabriel, while Captain Richardson engaged in coastal trading with two small schooners, the Josephine and Maria Antonia, that he had built with mission facilities. A few years later, the Josephine was lost off Catalina Island and replaced by the Crusader. In 1835 Governor José Figueroa decided that another official port of entry should be established at Yerba Buena. Until then, Monterey had been the only official port along the upper California coast, and many traders found it too inconvenient.

WHEN FIGUEROA offered Richardson the position of Port Captain at Yerba Buena, including a parcel of land, Richardson accepted and the family moved back to San Francisco Bay. By then, two sons, Stephen and Francisco, had been added to the family in San Gabriel. Upon their arrival at the bleak, deserted cove at Yerba Buena, Richardson selected a parcel of land where he erected a tent-like shelter at what was later to become the northwest corner of Clay Street and Grant Avenue. At Figueroa's request, Richardson assisted *Alcalde* Francisco de Haro in surveying and laying out a small town. Lots along the waterfront were reserved for future commercial use, and others were staked out for residential use. Lots measured 100 varas, or 275 feet square.

After Figueroa's death in August 1835, Governor José Castro took over and authorized completion of the plans for the town of Yerba Buena. Richardson then paid the sum of $25 for a grant to his lot. A few months later, the canvas structure on his lot had been replaced by one made of wood. Within a year the wooden building had given way to a roomy adobe building Richardson called *"La Casa Grande."* This became the heart of the town's early growth.

About a year after Richardson's arrival at Yerba Buena, business competitors Jacob Leese, Nathan Spear and William Hinckley set up shop next to him. Not only were they in the trading business, Spear went on to install a wind-powered gristmill on his property to grind grain into coarse flour. Hinckley married Susana Martinez and became Richardson's brother-in-law.

Jacob Leese married Mariano Vallejo's sister in 1837, while Spear was married to Jane Holmes, a half-Hawaiian from Honolulu. Later Spear was joined by William "Kanaka Bill" Davis, his nephew by marriage from Honolulu. They all built houses in the area, and after the partnership split up in 1838, they operated trading ventures of their own (see Davis).

That same year Richardson acquired a 20,000-acre grant west and north of Whaler's Harbor, covering all the land to the ocean and north to the foot of Mt. Tamalpais. It was named Rancho Saucelito for the willows that grew around springs in the area. There Richardson built an adobe house, which eventually became the northeast corner of Bonita and Pine streets in Sausalito. Apparently his family remained in Yerba Buena during this transition.

Before long he had hired Indian workers to tend his growing herds of livestock and to cut firewood for sale to ships that called for water and wood. He also fitted out a barge-like ship named *Water Nixie* with a large water tank and began delivering potable water directly to the ships for a modest price. In 1841 Richardson sold his Casa Grande at Yerba Buena and moved his family across the straits to the Saucelito adobe that became his home for the rest of his life.

DESPITE HIS VARIOUS business ventures, cash was always short and Richardson did a bit of smuggling on the side–as did virtually all the traders–to avoid the excessive custom duties. When discrepancies were found in the collection of these duties, he was dismissed from his position as Port Captain in 1844. By then his other enterprises were paying off well enough, so he scarcely missed the $60 a month salary.

Richardson continued to pilot ships into San Francisco Bay, and some were by-passing Yerba Buena and anchoring at Whaler's Harbor, now called Richardson's Bay. There they could get water, wood, fresh produce and meats delivered to their ships by Captain Richardson himself. When ships arrived offshore, they would fire two cannon shots to alert Richardson, who then rang a bell to summon his Indian crew. They made their way out to sea in a small boat, probably a pinnace, where Richardson would board the waiting vessel and pilot it inside the bay. His Indian crew returned in the pinnace.

By early 1846 rumors of possible war between the U. S. and Mexico were rampant. There was also talk that the *Californios* might declare upper California independent from Mexico and become a protectorate of Great Britain. As an Anglo-Saxon himself, Richardson and other British settlers had nothing to lose if this took place. Because of this, they did not take part in the Bear Flag Rebellion or the subsequent Mexican War on the side of John C. Fremont and invading U. S. naval forces (see Fremont).

It was, in fact, Richardson's launch that evacuated Mexican Army Captain de la Torre and his men from Saucelito when he was being hotly pursued by Fremont and his volunteers after the Bear Flag incident. The wanton killing of unarmed José Berryessa and the young de Haro twins by Kit Carson and his men at Mission San Rafael infuriated Richardson and his friends.

One reason was personal: Francisco "Chico" de Haro was reportedly engaged to marry Richardson's daughter, Mariana. (Two years later, she married Manuel Torres, a Peruvian business associate of her father). Frightened by Fremont's aggressive actions, many Mexicans fled Yerba Buena to seek sanctuary with Richardson at Rancho Saucelito. When

Fremont demanded food and requisitioned 30 of Richardson's best horses for his volunteers, it exacerbated hard feelings between the two. Naturally, Richardson's loyalty was to the people who had accepted him as a fellow citizen for 24 years, but there was little he could do to resist the American invasion.

Commodore Robert Stockton recognized Richardson's skill as a harbor pilot and used him to pilot the U.S.S. Congress. He also named him Port Captain once again, but his tenure was short lived; he was replaced by Capt. Joseph L. Folsom in 1847. During that same year U. S. Navy Lt. Washington Bartlett became alcalde at Yerba Buena and renamed the village San Francisco.

The town limits were expanded to accommodate the fast-growing population caused by the war and the surprise arrival of Samuel Brannan and over two hundred Mormon immigrants from New York (see Brannan). In 1848 Richardson became a citizen of the United States under the treaty of Guadalupe Hidalgo, which officially ended the war with Mexico. Then came the electrifying news of James W. Marshall's discovery of gold at Sutter's Sawmill in Cullomah (Coloma).

WITHIN A YEAR San Francisco's entire character changed from a sleepy Mexican trading port to an exploding boomtown. Ships arrived by the hundreds, bringing thousands of excited argonauts from all points of the globe. Richardson profited from it at the beginning, but like Capt. John A. Sutter to the east, he was eventually ruined. His ranch was deluged by squatters and other lawless people, who destroyed his enterprises.

Within three years he was forced to begin selling off his property to survive. In 1850 he entered into a business venture with "Kanaka Bill" Davis to develop New San Diego. After losing a virtual fortune in the failed venture, Richardson had to mortgage his holdings to the maximum; he sold the portion of his ranch known as Old Town Sausalito.

In 1851 Richardson contracted to build a sawmill in Mendocino County on land he acquired from the Albion grant authorized by former Gov. Manuel Micheltorena. Unfortunately, he was unable to satisfy the newly established land commission of his ownership and lost title to the valuable timberland. This blow was followed by another when Richardson became involved with a fraudulent land scheme dreamed up by José Yves Limantour, a larcenous Frenchman from Mexico. When it was over, Limantour was arrested and jailed. Released on $30,000 bail, he managed to sell hundreds of thousands of dollars worth of San Francisco property he did not own, skipped town and escaped to Mexico. Richardson, a victim of the smooth-talking Frenchman, was left holding an empty bag with nothing but losses to show for his efforts.

Things got even worse for Richardson in 1855 when all three of his trading vessels were lost in shipwrecks. By then he had lost virtually everything but 640 acres surrounding his home, which he had wisely deeded to his wife. When his water distribution system was taken over by the Saucelito Water Co. in 1856, his mortgage holder agreed to sell off Richardson's remaining assets; one-fifth went to Richardson.

Unfortunately he never lived to collect anything; he died April 20, 1856, from an overdose of mercury tablets prescribed for his rheumatism. Flags all over the area flew at half mast after his death, and he was buried in Wildwood Glen on April 22. After his bereaved widow received payment of $10,000 for her 640 acres, she apparently went to live with her children.

Two years after his burial Richardson's remains were removed for a subdivision and re-buried at Mt. Olivet Catholic Cemetery near Mission San Rafael. After this second burial, his simple wooden marker was later destroyed by fire. As a result, his final resting place is unknown. His eulogy read: "Captain Richardson, during his life in California, was highly esteemed by all who were acquainted with him and he was known to be a man of honor and integrity." Richardson Bay and the bridge crossing it are two legacies left by this grand old pioneer.

(A state historical marker, showing a "Richardson Adobe" site, is located on Highway 101 about a mile south of Soledad. Though this historical adobe was apparently owned by a William Richardson, married to Maria Josefa Soberanes, the name is coincidental; this is not the man we honor herein.)

BIBLIOGRAPHY

–Bancroft, Hubert H. *Register of Pioneer Inhabitants of California, 1542-1848*. Dawson's Book Shop, Los Angeles, 1964.

–Block, Eugene B. *The Immortal San Franciscans*. Chronicle Books, San Francisco, 1971.

–Davis, William Heath. *Seventy-five Years in California*. John Howell Books, San Francisco, 1967.

–Egan, Ferol. *Fremont, Explorer for a Restless Nation*. University of Nevada Press, Reno, 1985.

–Holmes, Kenneth L. *Ewing Young, Master Trapper*. Binfords & Mort, Portland, OR, 1967.

–Muscatine, Doris. *Old San Francisco, The Biography of a City*. G. P. Putnam's Sons, New York, 1975.

–Phelps, William Dane. (Ed. by Busch, Briton C.) *Alta California 1840-1842*. Arthur H. Clark Co., Glendale, CA, 1983.

–Trudell, Clyde F. Chapter entitled "Captain William Anthony Richardson," from *Old Marin With Love*. Marin Co. American Revolution Bicentennial Commission, 1976. Quotations taken from this publication.

–Wilcox, Del. *Voyagers To California*. Seal Rock Press, Elk, CA, 1991.

Robert Baylor Semple
Courtesy California State Library

— 38 —

ROBERT BAYLOR SEMPLE

1806 – 1854

A<small>LTHOUGH</small> R<small>OBERT</small> S<small>EMPLE</small> lived less than a full decade in California, his many contributions far outweigh his tenure. His story begins in Kentucky, where he was born in 1806. By the time he finished formal schooling he stood over six and one-half feet tall. After serving an apprenticeship as a printer, he somehow learned enough about dentistry to serve in that capacity. Perhaps he moved to Illinois during that period, for his brother was an Illinois Congressman. He also had a wife, who died, and a young son he left in the East.

By 1845 Semple was at Independence, Missouri, where he joined Lansford Hastings and nine other men for an overland journey to California (see Hastings). Theirs was the last emigrant party to leave Independence that year and did not hit the Oregon Trail until mid-August. This was far too late for a cumbersome wagon train to leave, but these men were traveling fast in a pack train. Hastings had recently published a book entitled *The Emigrant's Guide to Oregon and California.* In it he outlined a new route to California, which he claimed would save weeks of travel by skirting the south end of the Great Salt Lake. He was hoping to pilot these nine adventurous men over the new route on this trip.

They made good time to Fort Laramie, but Indian problems forced them to detour to the north, and then south to Fort Bridger. By then their food supply was not sufficient to attempt the new route, and they headed for Fort Hall, hoping to replenish their supplies. It was late autumn by then, and by rights they should have stayed at Fort Hall for the winter. But Hastings was not noted for caution. Neither were the men with him, including 39-year-old Robert Semple

After reprovisioning, they started out along the fledgling California Trail via the Raft River, City of Rocks and Thousand Springs. This brought them to the reliable Humboldt River, near present-day Wells, Nevada. Their greatest fear after reaching Truckee Pass was heavy snow, which would make it impassable. Fortunately their luck held; there were no serious storms, and they crossed the difficult pass in early December. They were camped at William Johnson's newly established ranch on the Bear River just before Christmas, and they reached Sutter's Fort by Christmas Day.

WHILE SEMPLE was at Johnson's Ranch, he may have agreed to return and work for Johnson and his partner, Sebastian Keyser. Whatever the reason, he was employed there during the early part of 1846. He must have been at Johnson's when Hastings returned that spring on his way east. Hastings was joined there by James Clyman—who had arrived from Oregon the year before—and Old Caleb Greenwood with two of his sons (see separate chapters). They were escorting a small group of eastern-bound emigrants and intended to return that fall with emigrants coming west. Semple also met John C. Fremont and his U.S. Army "topographers" when they camped there on their way north to Oregon that spring (see Fremont). All who met "Doctor" Semple, as he was often called, were impressed by his imposing demeanor. He stood six-foot-eight-inches tall and was described as "lean, lank and good natured."

In early June, John A. Sutter chose Semple to accompany his assistant, John Bidwell, to explore the Feather River as a possible site for a sawmill he intended to build (see Sutter & Bidwell). Bidwell and Semple agreed that the area had potential for a sawmill, but they disagreed about the feasibility of floating milled boards down the river. Semple thought it could be done at high water, but Bidwell did not. Apparently Semple was a bit put out by Bidwell's stubbornness and decided not to return to Sutter's Fort. Instead, he headed for present-day Sutter Buttes, where he had heard Fremont was camped on his way south from Oregon. On June 10th he rode with Ezekial Merritt and a small band of seven settlers who had heard rumors that Mexican General José Castro was planning to expel all foreign settlers.

Undoubtedly they discussed the matter with Captain Fremont beforehand. When Fremont stated he could not help them because no formal declaration of war existed between the United States and Mexico, they decided to take matters into their own hands. They learned that a large herd of horses belonging to the Mexican Army could be found at Murphy's Ranch on the Cosumnes River (see Murphy). They were being driven south by a small party of *vaqueros* under Lt. Francisco Arce, and had stopped at Murphy's for the night.

Waiting until dawn on June 10th, the seven determined Americans charged and rounded up the horses to drive them off, while Arce and his surprised men were still waking up. They offered no resistance, and the triumphant Americans drove the herd north to Fremont's camp for his use. Flushed with success, and probably prodded by Fremont, Merritt and Semple attracted a few more settlers to the cause, including William Ide (see Ide). On June 14th, a force of 21 rode throughout the night to Sonoma and overran the settlement just before daybreak. General Mariano Vallejo, his brother, Salvador, and two aides were captured without bloodshed, which proved fortunate for everyone involved (see Vallejo).

Semple and William Ide were able to exert a stabilizing influence over hot-heads in the group, which probably prevented gross depredations against General Vallejo and other Mexicans by zealots in the party. William Ide was left in charge of Sonoma with a few of the men, while Merritt, Semple and the others escorted Vallejo and his aides to Sutter's Fort for incarceration. The next day Ides men raised a home-made flag bearing a crude bear, a star and the words, "California Republic" over Sonoma; they then declared California an independent republic.

Then Fremont decided he could wait no longer; he declared war of his own against the Mexicans. (Actually war against Mexico had been declared by President Polk in mid-May, but no one in California was aware of it). Fremont immediately occupied Sutter's Fort and began recruiting a small army of "California Volunteers," which included Merritt, Semple and other Bear Flaggers there. Then Fremont led them to Sonoma to reinforce Ide and his men, who had been left to garrison the presidio.

ALTHOUGH IDE had been elected president of the new republic, Fremont disliked him and accused him of being a Mormon. In less than a day, Ide found himself reduced from president to a private in Fremont's volunteers. Fremont wasted little time initiating an offense against General Castro and his Mexican forces. In early July he led Semple and the rest of his men to Mission San Rafael in upper San Francisco Bay. Although the enemy was sighted, they failed to attack and escaped across San Francisco Bay on a boat furnished by William Richardson (see Richardson).

Fremont then convinced Capt. William Phelps of the ship Moscow to ferry him and his men across the bay in the ship's launch. They landed near the Yerba Buena presidio and spiked the old bronze cannons that were placed there to protect the bay from attack by sea. It was during this action that Fremont named the entrance to the bay the "Golden Gate." The next day Semple and ten men entered Yerba Buena unmolested and captured the port captain, English-born Robert Ridley. He was eventually taken to Sutter's Fort to be imprisoned with Vallejo and other Mexican leaders. About a week later, on July 7, U.S. Navy Commodore John Sloat raised the Stars and Stripes over Monterey. Within days the American Flag was raised over all of Northern California.

By then Semple was in Monterey serving in Fauntleroy's Dragoons.

There he met U.S. Navy chaplain Walter Colton. The two of them res-
urrected an old Mexican printing press, after which they obtained permission from the Navy to publish a newspaper they named *The
Monterey Californian*. The first issue, dated August 15, was printed on
coarse tobacco paper they had found on a trading vessel. The sheets
measured 11 ¾ by 10 ¼ inches, and Colton wrote of it as follows:

> The press was old enough to be preserved as a curiosity; the mice
> had burrowed in the "balls," there were no rules, no lead, and the
> types were rusty and all in pi; it was only by scouring that the let-
> ters could be made to show their faces;...Luckily, we found with
> the press the greater part of a keg of ink; and now came the great
> scratch for paper. None could be found except what is used to
> envelop the tobacco smoked by the natives.... [1]

This turned out to be the first newspaper published in California,
although it was closely followed by the *California Star* at Yerba Buena
(San Francisco). The latter was published by Samuel Brannan, a Mormon
Elder who had arrived by ship with more than 200 Mormon emigrants a
short time before (see Brannan). With him came Edward Kemble, a
young non-Mormon with writing and printing experience. Brannan eventually hired Kemble as his editor and right-hand man. With two newspapers in fairly close proximity, and a sparse English-reading population,
keen competition could be expected. Just how keen it was is demonstrat-
ed by the following editorials. First came one from the *Californian* in
early 1847:

> We have received the first two numbers of a new paper just com-
> menced at Yerba Buena. It is issued upon a small but very neat
> sheet, at six dollars per annum. It is published and owned by S.
> Brannan, the leader of the Mormons, who was brought up by Joe
> Smith himself, and is consequently well qualified to unfold and
> impress the tenets of his sect. [2]

Later the *Star* wrote:

> It [the *Star*] is the only independent paper, and the only paper of a
> respectable size and typographical appearance now published on
> the whole coast of the Pacific, from the northern boundary of
> Mexico to the frozen regions of the north. We have the only office
> in all California in which a decent looking paper can be published,
> and we intend to add to it as the country grows. [3]

Then came a much sharper follow up:

> We [the *Star*] have received two late numbers of the *Californian*, a
> dim, dirty little paper printed at Monterey, on the worn out mater-
> ial of one of the old California war presses. It is published and edit-
> ed by Walter Colton and Robt. Semple, the one a lying sycophant
> and the other an overgrown lickspittle.... [4]

Pretty harsh words even then; duels were sometimes fought over less. In April 1847 Colton's name was dropped from the Californian's masthead. It was probably then that English trader William E. P. Hartnell–who was fluent in Spanish–was hired as editor (see Hartnell). By early May Semple loaded his press and other supplies and equipment on a ship and moved to Yerba Buena to be closer to Benicia, a new settlement he was promoting.

Benicia was located on the north side of Carquinez Straits, and the land had been acquired from Mariano Vallejo. Semple was convinced it had great potential. So did Monterey trader Thomas O. Larkin and of course, Vallejo, whose wife's name the new town carried (see Larkin & Vallejo). Semple also became active in local politics and gave a rousing 4th of July speech in San Francisco (recently changed from Yerba Buena).

The *Californian* was running editorials about the need for a school, and to show good faith Semple donated a lot he owned in San Francisco for the new school. As a widower who had remained unmarried for several years, Semple married Frances Cooper, daughter of Stephen Cooper. The marriage proved a good one, and soon they had a daughter, whom they aptly named Mary Benicia.

THEN CAME NEWS about a gold discovery made by James W. Marshall at John Sutter's new sawmill (see Marshall & Sutter). Neither of the papers got very excited about it. Apparently other such rumors had come to nothing, and they were not about to be taken in again. The first report was published by the *Californian* on March 15, 1848:

> GOLD MINE FOUND.–In the newly made raceway of the Saw Mill recently erected by Captain Sutter, on the American Fork, gold has been found in considerable quantities. One person brought thirty dollars worth to New Helvetia, gathered there in a short time. California, no doubt, is rich in mineral wealth; great chances here for scientific capitalists. Gold has been found in almost every part of the country. [5]

Three days later the following appeared in the *Star*:

> We were informed a few days since, that a very valuable silver mine was situated in the vicinity of this place, and again, that its locality was known. Mines of quicksilver are being found all over the country. Gold has been discovered in the Northern Sacramento Districts, about forty miles above Sutter's Fort. Rich mines of copper are said to exist north of these bays. [6]

Yet another report dated March 25th in the *Star* read:

> So great is the quantity of gold taken from the mine recently found at New Helvetia, that it has become an article of traffic in that vicinity.... [7]

Still no one got excited, which suited Samuel Brannan's purposes very well. Through fellow Mormons, who had worked on Sutter's sawmill, he had learned just how rich the gold strike really was. Not even his trusted editor Edward Kemble was told. As a true entrepreneur, Brannan was not about to let the opportunity to acquire riches slip by him.

SEMPLE PROBABLY went to the gold fields himself, because after everyone left town in early summer there was virtually no one left to read his newspaper. Soon it closed down, along with Brannan's *Star*; the wily Brannan had other fish to fry. Fortunately Semple had begun operating a profitable ferry across Carquinez Straits to Benicia. It was in great demand, and he waxed fat from that astute enterprise. Semple sold the *Californian* to B. R. Buckland in mid-July.

In 1849, John Semple–Robert's son from his first marriage–came to California to live with his father. Things were going well for Semple that fall. In September he was named a delegate to the newly formed Constitutional Convention and was elected its president by his esteemed peers. Though he was ill at the time, he managed to see the convention through to a successful conclusion, and knew that California was well along the rocky road to statehood.

While the city of Benicia never lived up to his expectations, Semple made a good deal of money from his ferry during the period 1848-1850. Some joked that he was so tall he could wade across the straits towing the ferry behind him. During this period he acquired the Colus Rancho in present-day Colusa County. Having shed his business interests in the Bay Area, he moved there to begin a new life as a rancher. He and his brother, Colonel Charles Semple, are credited with founding the town of Colusa. Tragedy struck in 1850 with the death of Semple's son, John.

In 1854 Semple fell off a horse and was seriously injured. He died from his injuries during the prime of his life at age 48. His wife, Frances, married a man named Van Winkle a year later. A historical marker in the city of Williams cemetery honors Semple as the founder of Colusa and the president of the Constitutional Convention.

BIBLIOGRAPHY

–Bancroft, Hubert H. *Register of Pioneer Inhabitants of California, 1542 to 1848.* Dawson's Book Shop, Los Angeles, 1964.

–Dillon, Richard. *Fool's Gold.* Coward-McCann, Inc. New York, 1967.

–Egan, Ferol. *Fremont, Explorer for a Restless Nation.* University of Nevada Press, Reno, 1977.

–Gay, Theressa. *James W. Marshall, a Biography.* Talisman Press, Georgetown, CA, 1967. [5-6]

–Hague, Harlan & Langum, David J. *Thomas O. Larkin.* University of Oklahoma Press, Norman, 1990.

–Harlow, Neal. *California Conquered.* University of California Press, Berkeley, 1982.

–Kemble, Edward C. (Ed. and foreword by Helen H. Bretnor.) *A History of California Newspapers, 1846-1858.* Talisman Press, Los Gatos, CA, 1962. [1-4,7]

–Stewart, George R. *The California Trail.* University of Nebraska Press, Lincoln, 1962.

–Taylor, Bayard. *El Dorado.* University of Nebraska Press, Lincoln, 1949.

–Scott, Reva. *Samuel Brannan And The Golden Fleece.* Macmillan Co., New York, 1944.

Louis Sloss
Courtesy Bancroft Library

– 39 –

LOUIS SLOSS

1823 – 1902

THIS BOOK largely includes pioneers who came to California before the Gold Rush. But limiting the book only to those early pioneers virtually eliminates some minority groups who did not appear on the scene until after the 1848 gold discovery. Surely a few slipped in before then, but there is precious little information available. Among these minority groups were Jewish pioneers such as Louis Sloss and his subsequent business partner and lifelong friend, Lewis Gerstle, who arrived in 1849, and Adolph Sutro, who came a year later.

Much has been written about Adolph Sutro, one of the more prominent figures of the 19th century in the Far West, who divided his time between San Francisco and Virginia City, Nevada. Many people have never heard of Louis Sloss, whose importance to California history is major. Since his life is inseparable from that of his closest friend, Louis Gerstle, this chapter sketches the lives of both men.

Few Jewish pioneers chose the overland trails to reach California; most traveled by sea, usually via the Isthmus of Panama, as did Lewis Gerstle and Adolph Sutro. Louis Sloss was an exception to the rule, which is one reason for his inclusion here. Somehow it seems more pioneer-like to have suffered the earthy extremes of overland travel.

Lazarus and Laura Sloss were one of the two Jewish families in the Bavarian village of Untereisenheim, where Louis was born in 1823. The tiny village was surrounded by farmlands and vineyards, yet the Slosses and other Jews were prevented by law from cultivating the vines. Young Louis was ten when his father died, and he lost his mother two years later. His formal education ended with the death of his father; he was apprenticed at age fourteen to the owner of a general store in the Grand Duchy of Baden, not far from John A. Sutter's birthplace (see Sutter).

Though he did well in learning business practices, Sloss saw no future for himself in Bavaria. His older brother, Abraham, had emigrated to Louisville, Kentucky, a few years earlier, and before long Louis began making plans to join him; he made the move in the mid-1840's.

At age twenty-one he was described as being "five feet seven inches, stockily built, in vigorous health, [with] a pleasant, outgoing disposition."

Sloss soon found that opportunities in Louisville were too limited for an ambitious young man like himself, and he began looking beyond. When he learned about the California gold discovery in late 1848, he decided to head west, as so many others were doing. In Mackville, Kentucky, he met a promising young physician, Dr. Richard McDonald (probably R. H.) and his friend, Dr. Herman Swift (probably Charles H.). Jointly infected with "gold fever," they decided to travel overland to California.

They were in St. Joseph, Missouri, by early spring and joined the Turner and Allen Pioneer Line for the journey. They paid $200 each, which was supposed to cover all expenses. They did get food, two mules, and a wagon for six; however, they did their own driving and cooking. It was fortunate that the party had at least two doctors with them, for within a matter of weeks they were plagued by the dreaded cholera. By the time they reached Fort Laramie they had lost 42 out of 165 people in the party.

Disgusted, the remaining travelers threatened mutiny, and many left. Sloss and the two doctors acquired horses and pack animals enough to leave the wagon train, and they struck out on their own. Their first attempt to cross the North Fork of the Platte River nearly ended in disaster, until they found a crude temporary bridge built by a previous party. Their difficult journey across the Rockies and along the Humboldt River was made a bit easier as they helped themselves to food, such as flour, coffee and bacon left along the trail by desperate emigrants trying to lighten their overloaded wagons.

Following the Truckee River route, they must have felt a chill when they passed the Donner encampments, where they knew so many had perished two years earlier. Once over the difficult summit above Donner Lake, they followed a newly established trail into Steep Hollow near present-day Nevada City, arriving there on July 18, 1849. From there they headed toward the American River near Sacramento. After camping at Norris's ranch, they hired a small wagon to finish the trip, apparently to make a better appearance when arriving in the bustling new city of Sacramento.

S LOSS AND his companions camped within the city and began making decisions regarding their future. By pooling their capital, they had enough to start a business of buying up livestock, wagons and harness from newly arrived argonauts. These were then resold to others in need of such things. Business was conducted from a small space between two tents, which became the sides of their makeshift "store." A canvas roof provided shelter, and the tailboard of a wagon served as a counter.

Soon they bought a 60-foot-long vacant lot at the rear of their tent to store hay and feed for their stock, which was also corralled there. The trio of fledgling entrepreneurs shared living space with their animals. The madness of the gold-crazed town proved infectious, and as more and more prospectors poured in, the partners found themselves buying and selling thousands of dollars worth of stock and equipment daily. Their mark-up averaged about a hundred percent on every deal, and within seven weeks they split profits of $17,000. Apparently they had contained their own gold fever, concentrating on their business instead.

Business slowed during the winter months, and they boarded their livestock at a nearby ranch for $1.00 per head per month. With the animals building up strength and fat during the winter months, they looked forward to a profitable spring. But they hadn't anticipated the spring floods, which inundated the entire area for weeks on end. Their animals drowned, their supplies and equipment were ruined, and they faced financial disaster.

The partnership broke up; Dr. Swift moved to a boarding house, and Dr. McDonald began practicing medicine in a tent, where he and Sloss spent the winter of 1850-51. Meanwhile Sloss continued in the same business. McDonald went on to become a bank president in San Francisco, while Swift became a judge and the mayor of Sacramento. Before then Louis Sloss had met German immigrant Simon Greenewald, and they opened a small general store in Sacramento.

THEN GERMAN IMMIGRANT Lewis Gerstle arrived on the scene. Having reached California via the Panama Isthmus in 1850, Gerstle had spent a fruitless year in search of the elusive gold that lured him there. He and Sloss had known each other in Louisville and soon renewed their friendship. Recognizing Gerstle's keen and steady business acumen, Sloss and Greenewald agreed to take him in as a partner in their thriving general store.

Among other prosperous Sacramento merchants were clothiers Jacob and Herman Greenebaum. Jacob, a widower, had left his two daughters, Hannah and Sarah, in the care of close, childless friends in Philadelphia when he came to California. These friends, the Marcus Cauffmans, raised the girls as their own, though no legal adoption took place. In 1855, when Louis Sloss made a buying trip to Philadelphia, he looked up the Cauffmans, apparently to check on the two girls for their father, Jacob Greenebaum.

By then Sarah Greenebaum was a blooming nineteen years of age, and Sloss fell in love with her almost immediately. They were married in Philadelphia July 25, 1855, and sailed for California in early August, via Nicaragua. Sarah fell ill there, probably from cholera, which was prevalent in the area. Fortunately, she recovered and was able to continue overland by stagecoach to San Juan del Sur on the Pacific Ocean side. There they boarded a steamer heading north to San Francisco.

Before his departure to the East, Sloss had purchased a comfortable brick house in Sacramento, where he now installed his exhausted bride. For an eastern city girl, Sarah adjusted well to her new environment, and the happy couple wasted little time starting their family. First came Hannah Isobell, nicknamed Bella, then Leon, followed by Louis Jr.

DURING THIS period, Lewis Gerstle, a bachelor, lived with the Sloss family. Learning that Sarah's sister, Hannah, was still single and living in Philadelphia, Gerstle went east on a buying trip and ended up marrying Hannah Greenebaum in May 1858. After bringing her to Sacramento, they moved into their own home on M Street, very close to the Slosses. Soon they had two children of their own. Sometime during this period, both Sloss and Gerstle became naturalized citizens of the United States.

Even before then, Sacramento had a thriving Jewish community with its own synagogue, a benevolent society and burying ground. But as happens so often within religions, conflicts sprang up between different groups, namely the Polish and German factions. Finally the German Jews split from B'nai Israel and formed B'nai Hashalom. Louis Sloss and Jacob Greenebaum took turns serving as president.

Though business was good and the partners worked well together into the early 1860's, a series of disasters including floods, squatter's riots, cholera and fires finally drove them to sell out. The flood of 1862 was the worst, requiring evacuation by boat of both the Slosses and Gerstles. As a result, they sold their interests in Sacramento and moved to San Francisco. The Greenewalds and Greenebaums soon followed.

Though they moved during the Civil War, they saw few signs of strife in San Francisco. The city had become a unique meld of cosmopolitan sophistication and gold town crudity, with some attempts at culture. Half the city remained barren sandy hills, while grandiose mansions of the nouveau riche began lining the streets of Nob Hill. The business district was being built up with multi-level brick buildings, whose owners hoped to avoid disastrous fires that had virtually leveled the city several times.

Eventually the Slosses bought a substantial residence at 1500 Van Ness street, and the Gerstles bought a large house across the street. Two more sons, Joseph and Marcus C., nicknamed Max or Dick, were born to the Slosses there. The Gerstles also had six more children. By the mid-1860's, Louis Sloss and Company—still made up of the original three partners from Sacramento—was a brokerage house dealing principally in risky mining stocks.

The firm did well enough to expand operations into leather and wool, and the partners operated their own tannery. After the United States purchased Alaska from the Russians in 1867, American entrepreneurs like Louis Sloss and Company began looking for opportunities there. The primary trade involved seal-skins from the Pribilof Islands. Sloss and Company invested heavily with others in a trading company to exploit the sealskin trade. Eventually the firm became the Alaska Commercial Company, with Louis Sloss serving as president.

By 1870 the company had obtained exclusive rights to the lucrative fur trade from two of the richest islands, St. Paul and St. George, with annual seal-kill rates limited to around 100,000. This was thought to be the number that could be safely harvested without decimating the specie. Good housing, medical care and schools were provided for their Aleut employees on both islands, and the arrangement worked well for both the employer and employees.

Skins were salted by the Aleuts before being shipped to San Francisco in company-owned steamers. They were then shipped to London for further processing before being auctioned off. They brought an average of $15.00 each, sometimes more, depending on the market. The company made immense profits and declared dividends of around 50%, or one million dollars per year, for twenty years on stock that sold originally for $100 per share. Taxes paid to the U S. Government by the company for the same twenty-year period totaled $10.5 million; the U.S. had paid only $7.2 million for Alaska in 1867 to begin with. Not a bad investment for "Seward's Folly."

THE OFFICES of Louis Sloss and the Alaska Commercial Company were moved to 310 Sansome Street in 1871. When that building was destroyed in the 1906 earthquake and fire, it was replaced by a fine 12-story building on the same site. This one stood until 1974, when it was razed for new construction. Salmon canneries were added by the company in the early 1870's, and some of the partners' children were getting old enough to work in the thriving business.

By then the partners had gained great wealth and were rubbing elbows with the likes of sugar king Claus Spreckels, pants maker Levi Strauss, coal magnate John Rosen, and David Starr Jordan, who became president of Stanford University. These, along with bankers, politicians and other successful men, made up the elite of San Francisco society. Soon the partners had bought handsome summer estates in San Rafael, where they spent many pleasant seasons.

Sarah Sloss and her sister, Hannah Gerstle, served as volunteers with the Pacific Hebrew Orphan Asylum, where their husbands served on the Board of Directors. Sarah was an intimate of Phoebe Hearst, wife of mining millionaire George Hearst and mother of William Randolph Hearst. Though she had little formal education, Sarah Sloss became an acknowledged "grande dame" in San Francisco society.

Jews had played a vital role in laying the foundation for the area's economic growth, and there was little or no discrimination among San Francisco's "upper crust." These included the "Big Four" railroad magnates, Leland Stanford, Collis Huntington, Charles Crocker and Mark Hopkins, whom Sloss and Gerstle had known since their days as Sacramento merchants. The biggest mistake either of them acknowledged was not investing in the Central Pacific Railroad in the mid-1860s when urged to do so by the Big Four.

In 1879 San Francisco's Elite Directory featured a lengthy Jewish listing, a situation unequalled by other cities in the nation. In May 1876 Louis and Sarah Sloss's only daughter, Bella, married liquor distributor Ernest R. Lilienthal. His company went on to become the successful Crown Distilleries. They eventually had five children and built a handsome home next door to the Slosses on Van Ness. In 1887, Leon Sloss married Bertha Greenewald, daughter of Simon and Louisa Greenewald. Marcus "Max" Sloss married Hattie Lima Hecht in 1898 and went on to become a State Supreme Court Justice in 1906.

Family ties went deep, as did close ties of the partners and their extended families. They all had free run of any of their magnificent homes in San Francisco and San Rafael. In 1930 the Gerstle heirs donated their San Rafael estate to the city as a public park, known today as Gerstle Memorial Park.

During the spring of 1902 Louis Sloss suffered a series of heart attacks and retired to his San Rafael estate, where he died on May 27 at the age of 79. His death shook the entire clan, who gathered in San Rafael for the funeral. They accompanied the elaborate casket on a special train to the San Francisco ferry and on to its final resting place at Emanu-El's Home of Peace Cemetery in Colma. Among the pallbearers were old friends Levi Strauss and Philip Lilienthal, along with members of the Society of California Pioneers.

Flags throughout San Francisco flew at half mast and eulogies poured in from everywhere, hailing Sloss as a "self-made, charitable man—a pioneer whose money was acquired honestly," and "a genuinely Good Man." His generosity was legend, and he loved helping to set up friends and relatives in business. Money was no object, and he paid the debts of some who had hit streaks of bad luck.

He left large bequests to the Pacific Hebrew Orphan Asylum, and to Roman Catholic and Protestant orphan asylums as well. His old friend and partner Lewis Gerstle was devastated by Sloss's death; they had lived like brothers for over a half-century. Shortly after his partner's death, Lewis suffered a slight stroke. A few months later he had a severe stroke and died in his Van Ness home November 2, 1902 at the age of 78. He had outlived his inseparable partner by a mere six months.

L IKE HIS FRIEND before him, he was also eulogized as an "honorable man, one of the grand men", who immeasurably influenced early California. Leadership of the Alaska Commercial Co. passed to Sarah Sloss and Hannah Gerstle and then to Sophie Gerstle Lilienthal, who carried on the dynasty.

Louis Sloss's contributions to his adopted state were largely economic, extending on into Alaska. Assisting worthy people to get started in the business world and the proper care of orphans seem to have been his main philanthropies. Subsequently, his prominent family went on to make their own marks throughout the Bay Area.

BIBLIOGRAPHY

–Muscatine, Doris. *Old San Francisco, The Biography of a City from Early Days to the Earthquake.* G.P. Putnam's Sons, New York, 1975.

–Narell, Irena. *Our City, The Jews of San Francisco.* Howell North Publishers, Inc., 1981. Most information and quotations were taken from this publication.

–Severson, Thor. *Sacramento, An Illustrated History: 1839 to 1874.* California Historical Society, 1973.

–Stewart, George R. *The California Trail.* University of Nebraska Press, Lincoln, 1962.

Jedediah Strong Smith
(an artist's rendition)
Courtesy California Department of Parks & Recreation

– 40 –

JEDEDIAH STRONG SMITH

1799 – 1831

ALTHOUGH JEDEDIAH SMITH never settled in California, he is included herein because of his extraordinary exploits there and elsewhere in the country. He was the first "American" to travel overland from the United States to California, the first to cross the Sierra Nevada and first to cross overland from California to the Columbia River. Furthermore his short life is filled with more adventures and narrow escapes than most others who lived to ripe old ages. The State of California obviously values Smith's contributions, because his name is remembered with what borders on historical reverence.

When Jedediah Smith was born January 6, 1799, his parents, Jedediah and Sally Strong Smith, were operating an unprofitable trading post in Susquehanna Valley, Chenango County, New York. Named after his father, a native of New England, Jedediah S. Smith was the sixth of a family that grew to fourteen children. In 1811 the burgeoning family moved to Erie County, Pennsylvania. By then only half the children were still living with the family; the others had grown up enough to make their own way.

Conditions weren't much better in Erie, so six years later the family packed their goods in a covered wagon and left for the wilderness of Northeast Ohio for a fresh start. After reaching Pittsburgh, they felled trees and built a passable flatboat to float their wagon, themselves and all their worldly goods down the Ohio River. Jedediah Smith was twelve by then and old for his age—especially after he helped to defend his family when they were attacked by Indians on the river. They reached Cincinnati safely, and after selling the flatboat, they continued the journey overland to Ashtabula, Ohio, near the shore of Lake Erie.

Young Jed Smith stayed about a year to help build a log cabin and clear land for crops, but his heart was set on becoming a Great Lakes seaman. He left home at the age of thirteen and walked to Detroit to seek employment on a merchant ship. Fortunately he had enough education to qualify as a clerk and quickly landed a job. The ship carried a few passengers and traded staple goods for furs from the Hudson's Bay Company. Among the passengers were colorful, rugged fur trappers who filled young Smith's head with tall tales about Indian fights and attacks by massive grizzlies. From them Smith caught a chronic case of itchy feet, relieved only by constant travel, hunting and trapping. He had seen for himself how well trapping paid if one was skillful enough.

The War of 1812 ended his Great Lakes career, as the merchant ships were needed elsewhere. He returned home and mixed fur trapping with farm work until the war ended in 1814. By then he was a mature fifteen years of age and ready to strike out on his own as a free trapper. He thoroughly enjoyed his new profession as he explored the wilderness country of Ohio and Illinois. After a few successful years, he learned that a new fur company was recruiting enterprising hunters and trappers to travel up the Missouri River and trap beaver for good wages.

In 1821 he walked all the way to St. Louis to interview for a job. There he was interviewed and hired by General William H. Ashley himself. Ashley and his partner Andrew Henry both had reputations as honest, knowledgeable fur traders and businessmen. Ashley's keelboat, the *Enterprise*, left St. Louis in May 1822, destination the Yellowstone River. Andrew Henry was to establish a company trading post there, and Smith went along to help.

SMITH WAS NOT the usual roughshod, hard drinking trapper; instead, he was a bible-toting Methodist who neither smoked nor drank and seldom used profanity. Furthermore, it was said that no squaw ever shared his bedroll. He has been described as slightly over six feet tall, with a hard, lean build. His face was long, his nose aquiline, his bright-blue eyes intelligent and shrewd. He seems to have been a born leader. Unfortunately, he never had a legitimate portrait painted; the one often seen (a trapper on horseback) is not considered authentic by some historians.

Poling, hauling and sailing the heavy keelboat up the Missouri River in June 1822 proved an exhausting task, and the company was glad for a chance to stop at an Arickara Indian village to trade for horses. Smith gained valuable experience there, dealing and trading with these shrewd Indians, who were called Rees for short. He also learned invaluable skills in handling horses. Continuing upriver, trappers were sent out to trap, while Smith and Thomas Fitzpatrick hunted game for the insatiable cooking pots.

By the time winter set in they had reached the mouth of the Yellowstone River, where they established a trading post. There Smith used his spare time to write his daily experiences in a journal. When most of their horses were stolen during a Sioux Indian raid that spring, Smith volunteered to return to St. Louis for replacements. Along the way he met General Ashley and some of his men bringing supplies upriver in keelboats. Shocked by the news about the loss of the horses, Ashley decided to stop at the Ree village to trade for replacements. They were surprised to find the Rees entrenched behind a sturdy log stockade. The wily Rees were willing to trade their horses, but insisted on getting lead and gun powder, rather than the usual trade goods.

Against advice from his men, Ashley approved the deal. Smith, James Clyman and others were then assigned the duty of holding the horses ashore overnight, while Ashley and the rest of the men stayed aboard their keelboats (see Clyman). The treacherous Rees attacked at dawn, shooting down men and horses alike. Ashley sent skiffs ashore to evacuate the wounded, but they were driven off. Smith and the others fought fiercely, before he and other survivors swam to the keelboats. In all, thirteen of Ashley's men were lost, as were the horses.

ALL BUT 30 of the 68 survivors refused to go on and wanted to return to St. Louis immediately. As a result, one keelboat returned, while Ashley and the remaining 30 men moved downriver to establish a camp. Smith and another trapper volunteered to seek help from Henry at the Yellowstone trading post. After reaching there, Smith led Henry and his men back to where Ashley waited at the mouth of the Cheyenne River. They brought a good load of furs with them, and Ashley then sent Smith with one of the keelboats back to St. Louis to deliver the furs, buy horses and seek help from the army.

After hearing the story of the Ree attack, many frontiersmen volunteered to join in an expedition to punish them. The army agreed to send men under Colonel Leavenworth, and several hundred Sioux Indians also were recruited. They hated the Rees worse than the whites, and were eager to help. The army provided 125 men in three keelboats, while the frontiersmen filled two others. The Sioux rode horseback, but insisted on boat rides when they got the chance. The Indians proved an unruly, troublesome lot, but the whites put up with them, realizing how badly they were needed.

Finally the tiny armada reached Ashley and his men, where they split into two companies. Smith was named captain of one, while Ashley took the other. Smith had several other officers under his command with colorful names like Edward "Cut-nose" Rose, Thomas "Broken Hand" Fitzpatrick, and William "Cut-face" Sublette. The impatient Sioux attacked the Ree fortress first, and while they did some damage, they retired before the army's "Missouri Legion" could mount an attack of their own.

When they did attack, they found themselves unable to penetrate the solid Ree fortress. They did, however, cause the Rees to parley for a cease fire. The parley went on for some time before it broke down, and the Indians retired. Later, when Ashley's men checked on them, they found they had slipped out the back and made their escape. Disgusted and discouraged, the army group pulled out. They were followed by the wily Sioux, who stole some of Ashley's remaining horses on the way.

Though the unofficial war had been lost, Ashley and most of his men were able to move up to the Yellowstone trading post safely. Competition for beaver was getting fierce, so Ashley decided to send a group of men under Smith and Thomas Fitzpatrick down the Missouri River to explore Crow Indian country for fresh sources of beaver. In all there were sixteen in the party, including William Sublette, Edward Rose and James Clyman. Smith's spirits were high as he saw boyhood dreams coming true–dreams he'd had for years about exploring new country and pitting his wits against wild animals and wary Indians.

Heading west, they skirted the Black Hills of the Dakotas and found themselves traveling through the rough country of the Bad Lands. It was fall when they reached the Powder River Valley in southeast Montana, and high time to begin trapping prime beaver. Soon the men were finding them by the hundreds, and the bundles of valuable pelts began to multiply. Then Smith's luck ran out. He had been setting a line of traps in a promising-looking creek when he suddenly came face to face with a nightmare grizzly.

He ran for his rifle, but it was too late; the grizzly was upon him, and with one swipe of its long claws and a glancing bite from its immense fangs, it laid open the side of Jed's head, virtually tearing off an ear. Fortunately, Smith's screams brought help from his nearby companions, and they shot and killed the mighty bear before it did even more damage. Though Smith was in shock and suffering great pain. he remained conscious and directed James Clyman to sew his ear back on and cleanse the deep head cuts. Worst of all, his hip had been injured badly enough to disable him completely. It was ten days before he was able to travel. He was still weak and woozy, but there were beaver to trap and new lands to explore. He grew his hair longer after that to hide the awful scars.

AFTER A GOOD season of trapping, Smith's group ended up in Wind River country (Wyoming). "Cut Nose" Rose had close ties with some Crow Indians, so when the party reached the main Crow encampment, they were warmly received. The hard freeze of winter had arrived, and they were more than grateful to spend it with the hospitable Crows.

In early spring 1824, they said farewell to the Crows and started up the Sweetwater River, searching for fresh hunting grounds. The Indians had told them about an easy pass that crossed through the formidable Wind River mountain range. Following the Sweetwater, they traveled west for days but couldn't believe they had found the pass until Smith noticed water in a creek flowing west instead of east. It took a while before he realized he stood on the Continental Divide and had made an important discovery–actually a rediscovery–that became South Pass and opened up the country west of the Rocky Mountain barrier.

Later that summer they recrossed it on their way to meet Ashley and Henry for the trapper's rendezvous on the Sweetwater River. There Andrew Henry offered to sell Smith his half interest in the fur trading company. Smith jumped at the offer. Still in his twenties, he became a partner in the Rocky Mountain Fur Company, one of the most active in the country.

Smith had mentioned his desire to explore the country to the northwest for new areas to trap, but had been warned it was controlled by the British-held Hudson's Bay Company, who did not take kindly to American competition. Nevertheless, Smith left with six experienced men. Along the way Smith's party came across a small band of horseless starving Indians, who had been robbed by Snake Indians and were trying to reach Alexander Ross of the Hudson's Bay Company to trade furs they had managed to hide from the Snakes.

In exchange for their furs, Smith offered to take the Indians along with them to search for Ross. A few days later they found Ross, who had been looking for the missing Indians. Instead of gratitude for having helped the destitute Indians, Ross greeted Smith and his party with accusations that they had taken the furs by illegal fur trading in what he considered to be exclusive HBC territory.

Smith argued that the territory was open to all. Finally he was able to reason with Ross, who led the party to Flathead House, a trading post in Flathead Indian country. There Smith had a chance to study company operations, and was impressed with their efficiency. After spending the winter of 1824-25 there, Smith and his party accompanied Peter Skene Ogden's trapping party south for awhile, before leaving him and making their way east until they reached a plain of strange salt crystals. Finally they came to the shore of a great salt sea-like lake, where Smith stopped long enough to update his diary and draw maps of the country he had explored.

After meeting Ashley at the 1825 rendezvous on Henry's Fork of the Green River, Smith accompanied him back to St. Louis with a huge load of furs. They arrived in early October, and within days Smith was ready to head west on what became the Oregon Trail on another expedition with James Beckwourth (see Beckwourth).

The 1826 fur trapper's rendezvous was held in Cache Valley, near present-day Logan, Utah, where Smith and his men met Ashley's group. A surprise greeted him when Ashley offered to sell him his remaining interest in the business for $30,000. Smith did not have the money, so he offered partnerships to William Sublette and David Jackson. When the deal was confirmed, Ashley suggested that Sublette and Jackson trap north, while Smith returned to the Great Salt Lake. He could then travel southwest to locate an ice-free route to the Pacific Ocean. They could return by heading north to the Columbia River, which they would follow to Fort Colville and east to Flathead Lake, before following the Bitteroot Range South to Pierre's Hole.

Earlier, James Bridger had explored a portion of the Great Salt Lake, as it was known, but because of its heavy salt content he believed it was part of the Pacific Ocean. Smith decided to lay this belief to rest once and for all. He returned to the Salt Lake area in mid-August, where he established a camp. After exploring it, he then chose sixteen trusted men to accompany him and made ready to leave for the Southwest. Among the men was Harrison Rogers, an educated man who acted as company clerk and kept a running journal. Smith's partners were to continue trapping and look after things until his return.

SMITH LED HIS MEN south until late August, when they encountered a Ute Indian camp near Utah Lake. The Utes proved friendly enough, so he arranged a treaty between them and their arch enemies, the Snakes, which allowed white men to travel through the area and trap beaver. A few days later they reached a river, which Smith named for Ashley (Later the name was changed to the Sevier). Then came desert country, and Smith learned the hard way that people hadn't been lying about the mean deserts of the Southwest. But at least he was able to map the area with some degree of accuracy for those who might follow.

Things went from bad to worse as they continued. There was little if any water or forage for the horses, and they began dropping and dying. Smith dubbed the area, "a Country of Starvation." Soon everyone was walking, and horsemeat became the order of the day. Some wanted to give up and turn back, but Smith convinced them they had reached the point of no return—they had to go on or perish. Reaching a small river they named the Virgin River (southwest Utah), they traded with Indians for food and continued on.

Finally they reached a great, muddy river they thought was the lower Green. Actually it was the Colorado, and it saved them. They followed it south to a Mojave Indian village (near present day Needles), where they were able to trade for food and horses. The horses were obtained from mission Indians who had escaped. Two of them offered to guide Smith to Mission San Gabriel, and they left a few days later.

Following an elusive river that kept disappearing into the sand, they called it the "Inconstant." Later it was named the Mojave after the Indians. Their goal was a distant mountain range on the far side of the Mojave Desert. It took days to reach it, but finally they crossed over the lofty mountains to Rancho San Bernardino. A quotation from Jedediah Smith's journal, written in mid-November, describes it (it had taken three months to get that far):

> The next day following the valley of a creek alternately sinking and rising and passing through a range of Mt for 8 miles where I was obliged to travel in the bed of the creek as the hills on both sides which were thick covered with cedar came in close and rugged to the creek. About ten miles from camp I came out into a large valley having no timber except what was on the creeks coming from the Mountains. Here we found a plenty of grass and what was still more pleasing we began to see track of Horses and Cattle and shortly after saw some fine herds of Cattle in many directions. As those sure evidences of Civilization passed in sight they awakened many emotions in my mind and some of them not the most pleasant. It would perhaps be supposed that after numerous hardships endured in a savage and inhospitable desert I should hail the herds that were passing before me in the valley as harbingers of better times. But they reminded me that I was approaching a country inhabited by Spaniards....

Actually the Mexicans had overthrown the Spanish in 1821. Smith saw the Spanish/Mexicans as religiously bigoted against Protestants. He expected the worst, assuming they might think him a spy for the United States. But at any rate, he and his companions had finally reached the environs of the Pacific Coast—the first white men to make the journey overland from the Midwest on a southerly, ice-free route. The first thing they did was kill a cow for badly needed fresh meat. They kept the hide, knowing the brand could be identified, so they could pay the owner later. One thing they did not need was to be arrested for stealing cows.

They kept heading west to a pueblo called La Puente, where they rested overnight. Leaving his men there the next morning, Smith took Harrison Rogers and followed the two Indian guides to the impressive San Gabriel Mission. There they met Father José Sanchez, who confiscated their firearms and immediately clapped their two guides in the *calabozo*. Smith and Rogers were provided with a small guest-room. Father Sanchez proved to be a hospitable host, but warned Smith that he must obtain passports from Governor José Echeandia before he or his men could leave.

It turned out that the horses Smith had acquired from the Indians had been stolen from the mission; this was the reason for the swift imprisonment of his hapless guides. Furthermore, Father Sanchez told him that anyone coming overland from the east was automatically suspected of being up to no good. He also insisted that the rest of Smith's men be brought to the mission. This was done the next day, after which a messenger was sent to Governor Echeandia in San Diego. There was nothing to do then but wait.

Their stay was made as pleasant as possible at the mission, which Smith and his men found fascinating. It was one of the most successful missions, with hundreds of Indian converts and thousands of fat livestock. It had outlying farms at La Puente and San Bernardino, and the entire operation was virtually self sustaining. But as time dragged on, Smith and his men were anxious to leave. Meanwhile, Smith had made a friend of William Cunningham, captain of an American ship anchored in San Diego.

Finally the messenger returned, stating that Smith was required to go to San Diego to see the governor in person. Cunningham was also returning there, so they made the trip together on horseback in three days. After Smith explained his reason for entering Mexican Territory uninvited, he was told the governor would have to consult with Mexico City. It seemed he didn't believe that Smith's journey was motivated only by his dire need for supplies. Finally the procrastinating governor told Smith he would have to make the long journey to Mexico City to plead his case personally. Smith was outraged, knowing it could take months.

When the benevolent Cunningham learned of Smith's plight, he gained the confidence of several other American seamen and together they convinced the governor to issue the required passports. Captain Cunningham even offered to take Smith back to San Pedro in his ship. From there he could borrow a horse for the one-day ride to the San Gabriel Mission. Smith jumped at the opportunity. On the way they stopped to visit Santa Catalina Island.

IT WAS MID-JANUARY 1827 before Smith accumulated the supplies and horses needed to resume his journey. Part of the agreement Smith made was that he would head east and get out of Mexican Territory as soon as possible. He kept his word in a way; that is, he returned to the Mojave Desert via San Bernardino and Cajon Pass. But instead of continuing east, he turned north, making his way over the Tehachapi Mountains into the great San Joaquin Valley. He was still determined to reach the Columbia River.

There were beaver aplenty as they headed up the valley, trapping along the way. There were plenty of Indians too, but they caused little trouble until they reached the upper reaches of the South Fork of the American River. Near a ravine, at a place which later became Placerville, they were attacked by Indians called Diggers, who were armed with crude bows and arrows. Though they caused little damage, the attack hastened Smith's departure into the high country, where he and his men hoped to find a pass leading over the looming Sierra Nevada.

Their hopes were dashed by insurmountable terrain, and they had to retreat to the San Joaquin Valley, via the Cosumnes River. Rather than head farther north, they turned south and retraced their trail until for some distance. Finally they decided that the Upper Stanislaus River offered the best possibility for a route over the mountains. It was May by then, and Smith knew he had to hurry if he was to reach the Great Salt Lake in time to rendezvous with his partners that summer. He had to travel light, so he chose Arthur Black and Silas Gobel to accompany him. The other men were placed under the supervision of Harrison Rogers to guard the camp and continue trapping. Smith and his two companions left on May 20th.

Though they were forced to travel through deep spring snow, they made it across the Sierra in eight days, via present day Ebbett's Pass. Instead of the wooded country they had hoped for, they soon found themselves in the desert again. Game, fodder and water were scarce, and the familiar suffering of desert travel soon set in. They saw scattered Paiute Indians, but they were too destitute to share even their meager fare of grasshoppers and scorpions. Finally they found themselves again eating horsemeat. Somehow they toughed it out and found strength to reach Sublette and Jackson's campsite at Bear Lake on the third of July.

Smith spent much of his time there updating his maps and journals and writing letters to the government to explain the situation in California. He also made plans and accumulated supplies for the return trip to bring out the rest of his men and the pelts that had been left behind. Though he dreaded another journey through the unforgiving Mojave Desert, he decided it was a better option than another Sierra mountain crossing. Besides, this time he knew what to expect. He left in mid-July with eighteen men, including Black and Gobel, and two Indian squaws. Food, water and other supplies to last two years were packed on a long string of pack animals.

In mid-August they arrived at the Mojave Indian village, near the Needles, without undue hardship. After resting there for a few days, they left on the 18th. But this time the Indians proved treacherous and attacked the party as they were crossing the Colorado River on makeshift rafts. Taken by surprise, half of the party—including Gobel—were killed immediately, while Smith and the others managed to fight off the Indians to escape. The two Indian squaws in their party were captured, two of the survivors were wounded, and they lost all their horses and most of their supplies. Carrying what they could on their backs, the grim survivors set off into the desert on foot.

Despite severe shortages of food and water, the intrepid men crossed the Mojave desert and over Cajon Pass to Rancho San Bernardino. While resting there they traded for badly needed horses. Leaving their wounded behind, they re-crossed Cajon Pass, then headed north across the Tehachapi Mountains to the San Joaquin Valley near present day Bakersfield.

On September 18 they reached the rest of Smith's men at their encampment on the Stanislaus River. Two days later Smith made his way alone to Mission San Jose, hoping his reception there would be better than he could expect at San Gabriel. He had hoped to avoid the Mexicans altogether but had to get supplies and horses before he and his men could leave.

But when Smith reached Mission San Jose, Father Narciso Durán proved to be the opposite of hospitable Father Sanchez in San Gabriel, and ordered him arrested and jailed. Smith was allowed to write one letter, which he directed to Governor Echeandia, then in Monterey. Weeks later he was summoned by the governor to Monterey, where he was again jailed for twenty-four hours. After a lengthy interrogation, Smith was given his freedom in Monterey but was kept waiting there while the governor procrastinated about his fate.

THIS TIME Smith was befriended by another sea-captain and trader named John B. R. Cooper. Nevertheless, the entire episode became a repetition of Smith's miserable experience in San Gabriel. When the obstinate governor repeated his threat that Smith would have to travel to Mexico City—at his own expense—to plead his case, Captain Cooper came to his aid. He enlisted the sympathy of other Yankee seamen in Monterey, who agreed to post bond for Smith's character and good conduct.

Meanwhile, his men had been taken to San Francisco Bay, and Smith was allowed to sail there to join them. The furs had been sold to a Yankee trader, so at least Smith had money to buy the supplies, horses and mules needed for the return trip to the Great Salt Lake. At last he was given permission to leave by acting Governor Don Luis Argüello. But instead of going east, Smith chose to head north into Oregon Territory. Even though the British controlled the area, he saw it vulnerable to American occupation and intended to prove it. His party left December 30, 1827 with nineteen men and 300 horses.

The journey went slowly, as they explored and trapped along the Sacramento River and its many tributaries on the way. Reaching the Trinity Alps, they faced hostile Indians who took a toll on their horses by shooting arrows into them. Other horses were lost to falls, drowning and other accidents. It was mid-July 1828 when they reached the Umpqua River and made camp near a Kelawatset Indian village. The Indians seemed friendly enough, so they stayed several days to rest.

There had been an unpleasant incident when an Indian stole an axe from the camp, but everyone thought the matter had been settled. But suddenly, without warning, the Indians attacked. Smith and a companion were away at the time, and one of the men escaped to warn them. When it appeared the others had been killed and their supplies and livestock stolen, Smith and the other two men escaped on foot. They were especially saddened by the death of Harrison Rogers. Though they were without anything but the clothes on their backs, they made it through to Fort Vancouver at the confluence of the Columbia and Willamette Rivers. Despite the threat of Indian attacks, traveling through the cool forests of Oregon proved easier than crossing the desert.

Safe at Fort Vancouver, Smith and his companions learned that Arthur Black had also escaped and made his way to the fort before them. He had received invaluable help from the Chief Factor, John McLaughlin, who was about to send out a search party to look for Smith. Smith found it embarrassing to accept aid from the Hudson's Bay Company, but differences were quickly forgotten as McLoughlin and George Simpson—the Chief Hudson's Bay Co. area manager—did what they could to help.

IN EARLY September Smith and his companions accompanied a search party of Hudson's Bay men back to the scene of the bloody massacre. Upon arriving there, the H.B.C. men were able to coerce or persuade the Indians to return part of Smith's supplies and livestock. Even some valuable furs were recovered. After returning to the fort in mid-December, Smith sold his furs and horses to the company for $2,370. He and his companions then spent a relatively comfortable winter of 1828-29 there.

Smith and Black left Fort Vancouver in March 1829, heading east for the Snake River, where they hoped to find Sublette and Jackson. The other two men from the original party stayed behind. By then Smith's partners had set off to look for him and had separated to widen the search. Jackson was first to make contact with Smith and Black, and he immediately sent word to Sublette so they could rendezvous later. It was the second time they had nearly given up hope of seeing Smith alive; by then they must have thought him virtually invincible.

Now that the partners were together again, they made the best use of the year by taking a record catch of beaver. When it was time for their winter "hibernation," Smith suggested they sell out the company and move elsewhere. He suggested the Santa Fe Trail area, where they could use wagons to haul their goods in place of vulnerable and expensive pack animals. The agreement made, Sublette left on snowshoes for St. Louis to obtain supplies and trade goods, which he intended to bring back in wagons.

True to his word, he returned to the Wind River rendezvous in July 1830. This was the first time wagons had traveled the difficult route, which soon became part of the Oregon Trail. When they offered their company for sale, it was bought by a consortium of trappers for over $15,000 and renamed the Rocky Mountain Fur Company. Furs valued at $80,000 were then loaded in the wagons for the long journey back to St. Louis.

A LONG THE WAY Smith, who was only 31, told his partners he was thinking of retiring from the strenuous life and would like to have his younger brothers take over for him. His partners wouldn't hear of it, and after resting in St. Louis, Smith decided on one more trip to help scout out the best place for their new operation. It would be somewhere along the Santa Fe Trail, but where? Their furs were sold at good prices, and the partners were now well to do; nevertheless, they were not ready to retire.

They left St. Louis in the spring of 1831 with a caravan of 74 men and 22 wagons loaded with trade goods. The year had been a dry one, and after reaching the desert they found reliable water holes dried up. With so many men and animals to water, this soon became a serious problem. Smith had always been successful in finding water, so on the morning of May 27 he rode off alone to scout it out. No one knows for certain what happened after that; however, the tragic event has been reconstructed by knowledgeable historians:

After riding to the ridge of a hill, Smith was encouraged by the sight of a partially hidden streambed below. Sliding his horse down the steep embankment, he reached it only to find it dry. He knew water often could be found by digging a few feet into dry stream-beds, so he dismounted and started digging with a shovel he had brought along. Sure enough, a bit of water began percolating through the sand and he accumulated enough for himself and his suffering horse. Then he noticed a band of Comanche Indians watching him from the rim of the arroyo.

Smith knew from experience that his only chance lay in befriending the Indians, which he tried to do by riding his horse up the hill toward them with his empty arms outstretched. The stoic Indians watched him approach, then attacked without warning. Though shot in the shoulder, Smith managed to return the fire, killing the chief. He had no chance after that and was killed before he knew where he had gone wrong. He was 32 years old.

So ended the life of a truly remarkable pioneer, a man whose many accomplishments fill numerous books. He is another of those men whose lives seem destined, like meteors, to burn bright and hot for a short time, then burn out or bury themselves deeply within the earth. Jedediah Smith Redwoods State Park, just north of Crescent City, is dedicated to this great pioneer, and the Smith River is also named for him. A historical marker identifies the site of the 1828 Indian massacre on the Umpqua River in western Oregon. Also there is a Jedediah Smith Society, headquartered at the University of the Pacific in Stockton, California.

BIBLIOGRAPHY

–Brooks, George R. *The Southwest Expedition of Jedediah Smith; His Account of the Journey to California, 1826-27.* Arthur H. Clark Co., Glendale, CA, 1977. Quotations are from this volume.

–Cleland, Robert Glass. *This Reckless Breed of Men.* A. Knopf, Inc. New York, 1950.

–Dillon, Richard. *Humbugs and Heroes.* Yosemite-DiMaggio, Oakland, CA, 1983.

–Hafen, LeRoy R., editor. *Mountain Men and Fur Traders of the Far West.* Selected and intro. by Harvey L. Carter. University of Nebraska Press Lincoln, 1982

–Smith, Alson J. *Men Against the Mountains.* John Day Co., New York, 1965.

–Weston, May Forth. *The Great Pathfinder.* Robert McBride & Co., New York, 1944.

Abel Stearns
Courtesy California State Library

– 41 –

ABEL STEARNS (DON ABEL)

1798 – 1871

L IKE THOMAS O. LARKIN in Monterey, Abel Stearns was the leading
merchant in Los Angeles and San Pedro during the 1830s and
1840s. While he was not the first settler to inhabit San Pedro, he
was first to colonize it by establishing a trading post in 1834. His store
and warehouse became a convenient port for trading vessels that plied
the coast. They brought tempting manufactured goods to *Californio
rancheros* in exchange for cattle products, such as cowhides, horns and
tallow.

Abel Stearns' early experience on worldwide trading vessels served
him well in his land-based trading venture, and he went on to become
the wealthiest man in Los Angeles. A descendent of an old-line New
England family, Stearns was born February 9, 1798, in Lunenburg,
Massachusetts, one of eight children of Levi and Elizabeth Goodrich
Stearns.

Orphaned by the age of twelve, young Stearns went to sea, presumably as a cabin boy. Facts about his early life are scant, but he had a fairly
good education as evidenced from his business acumen and his volumi-
nous correspondence. A marriage before the age of twenty resulted in
two children, one of whom died in infancy. The fate of his wife and the
other child is unknown.

By 1820 he was the master of a trading schooner and a member of
the Masonic Lodge in Roxbury, Massachusetts. A few years later he had
settled in Mexico, as evidenced by the following letter written by him to
a Mexican official:

> On the 16th of May, 1826, I arrived at the port of Vera Cruz,
> where, after having shown the necessary documents, I obtained
> permission to reside in the Mexican Republic. Consequently I con-
> tinued on my journey as far as the capital, which I reached on the
> 2nd of June of that year, and in which city and its environs I
> remained about three years.

By 1828 he had become a naturalized citizen of Mexico and had applied for a land grant in Upper California. The following year, he arrived by ship in Monterey to seek a suitable site for his expected grant. For this he petitioned Governor José Echeandia, who was based in San Diego. Thus began a prolonged and frustrating waiting period while Stearns explored the area, seeking a good place to settle. After he and a partner located suitable land bordering the Sacramento River, they requested action on Stearns' petition.

MEANWHILE, Stearns worked for trader John B. R. Cooper in the San Francisco Bay area, visiting various missions along the coast to trade for cattle products, otter pelts and salt. After a delay of over a year, the governor approved a sizable land grant for Stearns; however, it was on the San Joaquin River rather than the Sacramento River as requested. Even this had to be approved by territorial deputies and Mexico City before it was official. So began another prolonged wait.

To complicate matters, Gov. Echeandia was replaced by Manuel Victoria, a military professional who came to office determined to set things straight in a land of seeming laxity. He had been in office only a few weeks in 1831, when Stearns approached him about his long-delayed land grant. Stearns was put off with assurances that it would be taken up shortly, but when nothing happened he continued to request action, to no avail.

For one thing, Victoria did not like Stearns, placing him in the same category as other so-called "subversives" like Juan B. Alvarado, Mariano Vallejo, the Pico brothers—Pio and Andres—José Carrillo and Juan Bandini (see Vallejo & Bandini). Finally Victoria ordered Stearns to go Mexico City to take up his quest for the land grant. Stearns did leave Monterey by ship as ordered, but he debarked at San Diego, determined not to leave Alta California.

In San Diego, Stearns met with other dissidents who were disgusted with Victoria's high-handed methods. Together, they prepared a petition to replace Victoria as governor. It was signed by Pío Pico, Juan Bandini and José Carrillo (see Pico). Stearns did not sign it, even though he was recognized as one of its organizers. Echeandia was requested to act as temporary governor, and the dissidents took up arms to depose the hated Victoria.

During the altercation that followed, Victoria was wounded and Stearns helped raise money to send him back to Mexico in January 1832. But Victoria's deportation did not help Stearns' quest for a land grant. Giving up his dream of a cattle empire, Stearns decided to become a trader and merchant in the Los Angeles area, in association with Juan Bandini, who remained in San Diego.

Then he met Scotsman Hugo Reid, a trader from Peru, who decided to settle in Los Angeles in 1834 (see Reid). Stearns spent two years acquiring a stock of merchandise from trading vessels, which he paid for with hides and tallow accumulated from local rancheros and missions. He also worked as a debt collector and commissioned salesman for others. Furthermore, he learned how to survey land, and hired himself out for this purpose.

By 1834 income from these enterprises allowed Stearns to acquire two parcels of land in Los Angeles. One he used as a residence and the other as a trading store, which he operated in partnership with Bandini. For the sake of convenience, he decided also to purchase and expand a San Pedro warehouse established ten years earlier by William E. P. Hartnell and a partner (see Hartnell). Trade goods and cargo could be stored there, while lighters from ships anchored offshore were being loaded and unloaded on the beach.

That same year Stearns built a pipeline to bring water to San Pedro from a nearby spring, and added a new structure to provide room for a store and living quarters for the manager and a few guests. He also built a corral to provide horses for guests to ride to Los Angeles and back. To assist in this venture, Stearns hired ex-fur trapper Nathaniel Pryor. Drawbacks to the place were twofold: At low tide, goods from ships had to be carried about a quarter mile over slippery stones to shore, and there was no protection for ships from hazardous southwesterlies that sometimes lashed the landing site.

Nevertheless, it was the closest port to Los Angeles; convenience alone made it worthwhile. The venture was successful from the beginning, as was the other store in Los Angeles. Within a short time Stearns was forced to defend himself from smuggling charges. Smuggling was common in those early days. In trying to finance its struggling government in California, Mexico levied high tariffs on everything imported from foreign ships. These tariffs were often two or three times the value of such cargos, causing most traders to look for ways of circumventing them.

One method was to offload a good portion of the cargo on another ship at sea, or at an isolated area like Santa Catalina Island. The ship carrying the remaining cargo would then sail to an authorized port such as Monterey, pay duties on its cargo and get a receipt showing duties paid in full. It would then return to the isolated area, recover the rest of its cargo and freely trade up and down the coast. If the captain was challenged by Mexican authorities, the receipt offered evidence that duties had been paid.

It can be assumed that Stearns played the game and occasionally brought contraband ashore at night to be stored in his warehouse. One incident, involving illegal trading of cowhides, resulted in a petition to the Governor signed by several prominent citizens to investigate Stearns' business activities. While the subsequent investigation resulted in no charges being filed against the wily merchant, it did not clear him of suspicion. Other such incidents resulted in a reprimand and warning from Governor Juan B. Alvarado in 1840. Then came a formal warning to Stearns from Mexican official José Z. Fernandez:

> His excellency the Governor orders me to say to you: that in the port of San Pedro there is a house with warehouses belonging to Don Abel Stearns, and since quantities of hides go out from there to be loaded on the vessels that trade on the coast, and since the jueces [certain government officials] of Los Angeles have confiscated some of them that had been wrongfully acquired,...in order to provide a corrective measure to prevent this evil and the continual theft of cattle, His Excellency has thought it necessary to order you to notify the aforementioned jueces that from the moment they receive this order, they will indicate to said Abel Stearns that on no account will he ship any hides without previous permission of some of the jueces....

Upon receipt of this directive, Stearns immediately ordered his San Pedro manager, John Forster, to comply. It is assumed that the matter was finally resolved to everyone's satisfaction.

IN THE MID-1830's came a sorry affair that resulted in Stearns receiving the nickname, "horseface." It happened after a local liquor dealer bought a barrel of inferior wine from Stearns. Stearns had warned him earlier that the wine was tainted, but the dealer agreed to accept it as is.

The liquor dealer returned in a day or two demanding a full refund because "the wine was unfit to drink." There was an altercation, after which the dealer left. He returned later, apparently under the influence of drink, and attacked Stearns with a knife. Stearns received serious wounds in the hand and shoulder, but his most severe injury was a slashing cut on his face that almost severed his tongue. He nearly died from the wounds, and for over a month was unable to talk. Only the skill of a local doctor saved him, but he was left with terrible scars and a permanent speech impediment.

Adding to his misery was the arrival of a new governor, Mariano Chico, another zealot like Governor Victoria, who "wanted to put the country to rights." Chico immediately requested Stearns to report to him in Monterey, which he finally did. After a rather innocent beginning, Chico began chastising Stearns as a foreign criminal who had attacked and wounded former governor Victoria. He even went so far as to threaten the astonished trader with a public hanging.

By morning the bombastic governor had cooled off. Chico ordered Stearns to return to Los Angeles, promising to follow up and conclude the matter at a later date. He also ordered Stearns to wind up his personal and business affairs in preparation for banishment to Mexico. Stearns immediately petitioned the governor for clemency, to no avail. Like Victoria, Chico was convinced that Stearns, along with other outspoken dissidents like Juan Bandini, Victor Prudon, Father Narciso Durán and José Carrillo, were plotting against him.

He wanted all of them banished, and went so far as to charter a ship to take them to Mexico. Ironically, it was he who left on the ship after a delegation of prominent *Californios* demanded that he leave the country. During the three months he had served as governor he had alienated not only the *rancheros,* but the clergy as well. The day before he left, he appointed Nicholás Gutiérrez as acting governor and ordered him to carry out his instructions to oust the dissidents, especially Stearns and Fra Durán, from the country. Gutiérrez had no means of enforcing the order and it was soon forgotten.

In 1836 Stearns hired Hugo Reid to help out in San Pedro. That same year José Castro and Isaac Graham, a Yankee sawmill and distillery operator, helped lead a revolt against Gutiérrez by Juan B. Alvarado, who took over as governor (see Graham). His appointment was not recognized by Mexico City or loyalists in Southern California, so Carlos Carrillo was appointed governor. Northern California leaders would not accept Carrillo and he was deposed after a short mini-revolution. Finally, in 1838, with strong support from Abel Stearns and others, Alvarado received sanction from Mexico City and became the official governor.

A
T ABOUT THAT TIME Juan Bandini moved from San Diego to San Gabriel, where he became Mission Administrator. Soon he acquired Rancho Jurupa, adjoining present Riverside and San Bernardino Counties, where he began building a house for his rather large family. Because he was a close friend and lonely bachelor, Abel Stearns moved there to live with the Bandinis after the house was completed.

By then Stearns was a wealthy man and looking for a wife. Though he was forty-two years old, he pursued Arcadia Bandini, the attractive fourteen-year-old daughter of Juan Bandini and his wife, the former Dolores Estudillo. By April he had announced his intentions and received her father's blessing. They were married at Mission San Gabriel by Fr. Durán on June 22, 1841.

They moved to a spacious adobe hacienda, *El Palacio de Don Abel* (the palace of Don Abel) at what is now the corner of Main and Arcadia Streets in Los Angeles. Arcadia, who had apparently never done any work on her own, turned the running of her house over to her more capable younger sister, Isadora. Imagine the incongruity of two semi-literate teen-agers running the finest household in the pueblo of Los

Angeles. Despite their youth, Arcadia Stearns and Isadora Bandini quickly earned reputations as great hostesses for innumerable social events held at Don Abel's *El Palacio*

The year 1843 saw the arrival of English-born trader Henry Dalton from Peru (see Dalton). He was a former business associate of Hugo Reid, seeking opportunities in Los Angeles. Stearns and Bandini greeted him in the absence of Reid and rented him space to start a small store there. Soon he became a business associate and close friend of theirs, along with Reid.

By 1845 business at the San Pedro store had fallen off to the point where Stearns decided to sell out. After the sale was consummated, he began investing in the large parcels of land he had always coveted. His first substantial purchase was Rancho Los Alamitos, which bordered the Pacific Ocean south of present-day Long Beach.

He next bought Rancho Los Vallecitos in Lower California, south of San Diego. He augmented this purchase with a land grant from Pío Pico in early 1846. He added even more holdings in Lower California with the purchase of Rancho Valle de San Rafael. Thus, Abel Stearns finally achieved his dream of becoming a cattle baron.

DURING THE 1840s Stearns also acquired other smaller parcels of land, one adjacent to Mission Dolores on San Francisco Bay. In 1842 came the debacle when U.S. Navy Commander Thomas ap Catesby Jones's forces erroneously invaded Monterey. Jones had acted on information that war between the U.S. and Mexico had been declared, only to learn too late that the information was faulty.

After offering his abject apologies to Mexican officials in Monterey, Jones withdrew his forces and sailed to San Pedro to mend fences there with Governor Manuel Micheltorena, who had taken over from Alvarado. Because Stearns had the only guest accommodations in San Pedro, he took responsibility for providing Jones with hospitality and transportation to Los Angeles.

With the finest house there, Stearns and his wife had Jones as a house guest and gave a ball which everyone of social prominence attended. The only unpleasantness involved a bill for $15,000, which Micheltorena presented to Jones for expenses and damages caused by his invasion of Monterey. Jones chose to ignore it as a crude extortion attempt.

One thing was made apparent by Commander Jones' rash action: Stearns and other prominent citizens of Mexico recognized how vulnerable California was to foreign invasion. As a result, Stearns decided to become more active in local politics in an attempt to rectify the situation. He and the others feared a similar but more permanent takeover by England or France if something wasn't done.

Micheltorena proved an amiable, fairly effective governor, but he had brought with him from Mexico several hundred soldiers who had been plucked from prisons and drafted into the army. Underpaid, underfed and generally undisciplined, these troops—called *cholos* by the locals—committed depredations enough to earn the hatred of nearly everyone with whom they came in contact. Many *Californios* banded together to demand that Micheltorena be deposed and returned to Mexico with his men.

Some of the Mexicans, including Micheltorena, supported a proposal to make Upper California a protectorate under Great Britain. What they didn't know was that Great Britain had declared a policy of non-interference in California. Meanwhile, others, such as Stearns and Thomas O. Larkin, began promoting the United States as a protector (see Larkin). Larkin was officially made U.S. Consul in Monterey in 1844, which eventually gave him more credibility in dealing with the Mexican Government. For some time he had been trying to negotiate a purchase of California by the United States; now he redoubled his efforts and enlisted the help of Abel Stearns in his cause.

Faced with an armed insurrection in late 1844 from Mexican rebels led by José Castro and Juan B. Alvarado, Micheltorena turned to John A. Sutter for help (see Sutter). Sutter, a Swiss immigrant who had become a Mexican citizen and established an important settlement on the Sacramento River, quickly raised a small army of Indians and American settlers. After a short mini-revolution, during which no casualties resulted, Micheltorena was defeated at Cahuenga Pass near Los Angeles.

In early 1845 he and his hated *cholos* were shipped back to Mexico, and Pío Pico was named governor by the rebels in Los Angeles. Having been captured and jailed by General Castro's forces, John Sutter was tried and released by the merciful rebels. To his credit, Stearns managed to skirt this rather bizarre affair. By then he had become a confidant of Thomas O. Larkin and was aiding him in his plan to annex California to the United States. Correspondence between the two was thick and heavy during succeeding years; much of it is available for historical research. (see bibliography). It shows that Stearns tried to help Larkin in collecting heavy debts Micheltorena had incurred while governor.

Mexico had not yet recognized Pico as governor and sent José Hijar to make peace with the rebels. In a letter to Larkin dated June, 1845, Stearns wrote:

> We have here Sor. Dn. José M. Hijar a commissioner sent by the Mexican Govt. to inquire into the State of affairs in California, re[c]omend the organizing the affairs of the govt., Aduana & tribunals of justice &c I learn is the principal object of his visit...

From the Character of this gentleman I have no doubt his visit will
be of much service to California if her sons give him proper information and let him know her wants.

Whatever his intent, Hijar did not live to carry it out. In December,
he died while staying as a house guest in the Stearns home.

Throughout 1845 the old rivalry between Southern and Northern
California intensified to the point where they were governed separately
by Pico in Los Angeles and Castro in Monterey. The following year saw
Captain John C. Fremont's second arrival in Northern California, his
short, provocative encounter with General Castro at Gavilan Peak and
his apparent retreat to Oregon.

All this was revealed to Stearns in letters from Larkin, who saw
Fremont's aggressive acts as a threat to his attempts to acquire California
peacefully. Then came U.S Marine Lieutenant Archibald Gillespie with
an appointment for Larkin from President John Polk as a "Confidential
Agent" for California (see Polk). He also carried secret messages for
Capt. John C. Fremont, which he finally delivered at Fremont's camp
near the Oregon border (see Fremont).

Larkin wrote Stearns, apprising him of the situation and requesting
his help in feeling out the political leanings of people in Los Angeles.
Stearns was slow to reply, but at last he agreed to help Larkin bring
California into the Union peaceably. In June 1846 came the startling
news about the Bear Flag Revolt in Sonoma, and the fact that Fremont
occupied Sutter's Fort and had imprisoned General Mariano Vallejo
there.

WORD OF THE Declaration of War against Mexico had not yet
reached California, and both Larkin and Stearns were shocked by
Fremont's actions. They recognized that all their efforts for a peaceful
transition had been in vain and girded themselves for the battle that was
sure to come, especially in Southern California. A month later came
official notice of the war and Commodore Sloat's successful invasion of
Monterey. Within days the Stars and Stripes were flying over Northern
California and Fremont was recruiting volunteers to fight with him and
Commodore Robert Stockton (who had replaced Sloat) in Southern
California.

In a last ditch effort to avoid the spilling of blood, Larkin immediately wrote Stearns to inform him about the pending invasion of San
Diego. He also urged him to get together with appropriate Mexican officials and meet with Commodore Stockton at San Pedro for a peace conference. This proposed conference never took place. Within a few days
both Pico and Castro had fled to Mexico and Stockton's forces occupied
Los Angeles without serious opposition or casualties.

Stearns kept a low profile during the occupation, but shortly there-after was appointed to a commission to investigate claims for damages allegedly suffered by citizens from U.S. military operations. He was asked also to consult with acting Governor Fremont regarding appoint-ments to vacated public offices. After Fremont was ousted as governor by General Stephen Kearny and was replaced by General Richard Mason, Stearns acted as an advisor to help keep the civil government operational.

The Treaty of Guadalupe Hidalgo was signed February 2, 1848, rat-ified in Washington on March 10 and approved in Mexico City May 30. The Mexican War was officially over, and Stearns was once again a U. S. citizen, free to choose his own destiny. On January 24 James Marshall discovered gold at Sutter's Mill in Cullomah (Coloma). Fortunately for the United States, word of it did not leak until after the treaty was signed. Imagine the repercussions this might have had on treaty negotiations if the gold discovery had been made public by John Sutter or Marshall beforehand.

The gold discovery indirectly affected Stearns and his associate, Henry Dalton, when they benefited from demand for beef during the Gold Rush. Beef on the hoof proved much more lucrative than mere hides and tallow. Over the next decade Stearns devoted his time and considerable energy to acquiring more land and adding to his herds. In late 1849 he was appointed a delegate to the California Constitutional Convention in Monterey.

A year later California was admitted to the Union. Within a decade Stearns was recognized as the greatest land owner in Southern California. But these halcyon days ended in the early sixties when the land was stricken by a severe drought. As a result, Stearns lost thousands of cattle and faced bankruptcy. Finally he was forced to sell some of his land, including his beloved Rancho Los Alamitos.

Finally Stearns placed the remainder of his land in a trust company to be subdivided into smaller parcels. Led by Alfred Robinson, Samuel Brannan and others, the trustees split the land into small farms of 20 to 160 acres (see Brannan). Thus Stearns became one of the first large sub-dividers in the Southern part of the state. The parcels sold well and helped change the area from a monopolistic, pastoral economy to a small farm economy.

BY MID-SUMMER 1871 Stearns was well on his way to recouping his lost fortune when he died suddenly in San Francisco at the age of 73. He and his wife, Arcadia, had no children, and he left her an estate that eventually made her a person of great wealth. Ironically, much of Stearns' land had been acquired from his wife's family, the Bandinis.

Upon his death, it reverted back to them. Arcadia Stearns later married Robert S. Baker; she lived in Los Angeles until her death in 1912.

For a man nicknamed "Horseface" because of his homely appearance—a man who started out with nothing in a strange and rather primitive land—Abel Stearns accomplished a great deal indeed.

BIBLIOGRAPHY

—Bancroft, Hubert H. *History of California*, Vol. I-VI. History Co., San Francisco, 1886. Repub., Wallace Hebberd, Santa Barbara, CA, 1966.

—Dakin, Susanna Bryant. *A Scotch Paisano in Old Los Angeles*. University of California Press, Berkeley, 1939.

—Davis, William Heath. *Seventy-Five Years in California*. John Howell Books; San Francisco, 1967.

—Dillon, Richard. *Fool's Gold*. Coward-McCann, Inc., New York, 1967.

—Hague, Harlan and Langum, David J. *Thomas O. Larkin.*. University of Oklahoma Press, Norman, 1990.

—Hawgood, John A. (editor). *First and Last Consul: Thomas Oliver Larkin and the Americanization of California*. A selection of letters written by Thos. O. Larkin and others. Huntington Library, San Marino, CA, 1962.

—Jackson, Sheldon G. *A British Ranchero In Old California. The Life and Times of Henry Dalton and the Rancho Azusa.*. Arthur H. Clark Co, Glendale, CA, 1987.

—Phelps, William Dane. *Alta California, 1840-1842*. Ed. by Briton C. Busch, Arthur H. Clark Co., Glendale, CA, 1983.

—Rolle, Andrew F. *An American in California*. Henry E. Huntington Library, San Marino, CA, 1956.

—Wright, Doris Marion. *A Yankee In Mexican California: Abel Stearns, 1798-1848*. Wallace Hebberd, Santa Barbara, CA, 1977. Excerpts of letters and other quotations are taken from this publication.

NOTES

John A. Sutter
Courtesy California Department of Parks & Recreation

– 42 –

JOHN A. SUTTER (DON JUAN AUGUSTO)

1803 – 1880

ALTHOUGH HE WAS of Swiss parentage, Johann August Sutter (a.k.a. Johann Augustus Suter and John A. Sutter) was born in Kandern, Germany, in 1803. Young Sutter left school in his mid-teens and moved to Basel, Switzerland, where he had been apprenticed to a printing firm. After serving out his apprenticeship, he moved to Aarburg, Switzerland, to work as a clerk in a draper's shop—a far cry from printing and publishing. Apparently printing was a trade he did not relish.

In Aarburg he met Annette Dubeld, whose widowed mother ran a bakery and was considered fairly well off. Sutter and Annette fell in love, and he followed her home to Burgdorf, where they were married in 1826. A son, Johann August Jr., was reportedly born there the very next day. Having become a bridegroom and a father within a matter of twenty-four hours, Sutter apparently toed the line for awhile and became a clerk in a grocery shop. Shortly thereafter his new mother-in-law apparently set him up in a dry goods business. In 1828 he joined a Swiss Army guard unit; within three years he was promoted to lieutenant.

Unfortunately he did not do so well as a businessman. After four years of struggling to keep his business going, it finally failed, leaving Sutter with crushing debts. Now 31, Sutter found himself with a wife and five children to support and no job or good prospects. He faced two unpleasant choices: Risk debtor's prison or leave the country to seek opportunities elsewhere. Salvaging what cash he could by liquidating his business, he scraped together enough to leave for Le Havre, France, where he boarded a ship bound for New York, leaving his substantial family under the benevolent care of his long-suffering mother-in-law. His youngest child, Carl, died at the age of six—at about the time his adventurous father reached the West Coast of Alta California.

Sutter arrived at New York in 1834 and immediately joined other German emigrants, who were heading west to the Missouri River. By then there were several German-speaking colonies in the upper

Mississippi Valley. Sutter tried several ventures there, including farming and merchandising, before going into trading on the Santa Fe Trail.

He did fairly well for a few years, but just when he was anticipating a windfall profit from a caravan of trade goods, the bottom fell out of the market and Sutter was left virtually destitute. Badly in need of another new start, he went to Westport, Missouri, with plans to head for the Far West. He had long dreamed of going to the Pacific Coast, where he planned to establish a settlement called New Helvetia (New Switzerland).

Alta California was under Mexican control, but Sutter thought he could gain permission from the government to establish his settlement there. He had heard that most of the small population was scattered along the coast, and thought the Mexican government would approve his plan to open the interior for settlement. By the spring of 1838 he had managed to raise enough funds to outfit himself and was ready to leave on the largely uncharted trail to Oregon.

THOUGH SUTTER was not a tall man, he had an imposing demeanor with a military bearing and a flair for attracting people to him. He was generous to a fault, but often used borrowed money to accomplish this generosity. It was on the Santa Fe Trail that he began using the title, "Captain Sutter," which sounded more impressive than his proper title of lieutenant in the Swiss Guard. From his Santa Fe Trail days he had acquired an able and loyal mule-skinner, Pablo Gutiérrez, who was to accompany him to Oregon.

Together they joined an American Fur Company caravan led by frontiersman Andrew Drips, destined for the Wind River Mountains in present-day Wyoming. The annual fur-trapper's rendezvous was scheduled there in early July. They left Westport in late April 1838 and were soon joined by a small party of missionaries bound for the Walla Walla mission of Dr. Marcus Whitman and his wife, Narcissa. Worthy of note was Sutter's interest in the strategic location of Fort William (later Fort Laramie), which he hoped to duplicate at New Helvetia.

The long journey to the trapper's rendezvous was an arduous one, and Sutter celebrated Independence Day there in grand style. He thoroughly enjoyed the wild abandon of mountain men and Indians alike. Meanwhile, a Hudson's Bay Company trapper, Francis Ermatinger, had come from Fort Hall (Idaho) to guide the missionary party there. Sutter and a few others were fortunate to join them for that leg of the journey.

After pausing a short time at Fort Hall, Sutter and Gutiérrez left the missionaries near Walla Walla and made their way to The Dalles on the Columbia River. From there it was another tough, mountainous trek over the Cascades to the Willamette Valley mission run by Rev. Jason Lee at present-day Salem, Oregon.

After trading their worn horses and mules for log canoes, they drifted down the Willamette River to Fort Vancouver. Located at the confluence of the mighty Columbia, this Hudson's Bay Company outpost was the only significant settlement in the territory. By then Sutter had attracted several other footloose men, who had agreed to follow him to California.

James Douglas was in charge of Fort Vancouver at the time, and he hastened to make the Sutter entourage welcome. Though it was mid-October, Sutter wanted to leave, hoping to reach California before heavy snows closed the pass over the Siskiyou Mountains. Somehow Douglas convinced him it was already too late. Rather than wait for spring to make the overland journey, Sutter left most of his men and boarded the trading vessel *Columbia*, which was sailing for the Sandwich Islands (Hawaii). There he hoped to gain passage on another ship heading for California.

But this was not to be. Sutter spent five long months in Honolulu waiting for a ship. Finally he talked a local trader into chartering the ship *Clementine*, with himself as supercargo, to deliver cargo to San Francisco Bay. The trader agreed, but only if Sutter would first deliver some cargo to the Russian outpost at Sitka, Alaska.

Desperate to leave, Sutter agreed. He had not wasted his time in Honolulu, managing to recruit a small band of *kanakas* (native Hawaiian men) and two *wahines* (Hawaiian women) to accompany him. Further, he had acquired many of the supplies and some equipment he would need in California, including three small brass cannons and an English bull-dog. All this he accomplished with virtually no cash; somehow, he always managed to finagle credit when he needed it.

Sutter enjoyed his stay at Sitka, but the voyage south to San Francisco Bay proved a rough one. He was especially vexed when, after their leaking ship finally sailed into the great bay in July 1839, he was refused permanent admittance by Mexican officials at Yerba Buena, the only settlement there. After making emergency repairs, they sailed to Monterey, the official port of entry for Alta California.

This may have proven a blessing in disguise, because Sutter visited with Gov. Juan B. Alvarado and gained permission to proceed with his rather grandiose scheme for New Helvetia. Once the settlement was established, he was to return and apply for Mexican citizenship. When this was accomplished he would qualify for a substantial land grant at a place of his choosing. He also met other prominent people in Monterey, including Yankee trader Thomas O. Larkin, from whom he hoped to get credit (see Larkin).

The ship's company sailed the *Clementine* back to Yerba Buena a few days later in good spirits. This time they were greeted more warmly and wasted little time unloading the ship to take on new cargo. Meanwhile Sutter visited with Gen. Mariano Vallejo in Sonoma and Russian Governor Alexander G. Rotcheff at Fort Ross (see Vallejo). This fort, established to provide food for the Russian settlement at Sitka, also supplied thousands of valuable otter and seal pelts for the fur trade.

SUTTER RETURNED in time to see the *Clementine* off on its return voyage to Honolulu, after which he chartered two small sailing vessels to transport his people and equipment up the Sacramento River. He wanted to establish New Helvetia on the river, far enough inland to avoid surveillance by General Vallejo's men. He also bought—on credit, of course—a pinnace which could be rowed or sailed. It would be used to scout out safe channels in the river before the larger ships followed.

Two experienced captains and some seamen were engaged to handle the ships. The *Isobel* was captained by young Kanaka Bill Davis, who was part Polynesian, while the smaller *Nicholas* was commanded by an Irishman, Jack Rainsford. After a gala party at Yerba Buena, the heavily-laden ships left for the unknown on August 9, 1839 (see Davis).

Sutter had one more stop to make after they passed through the narrows of Carquinez Straits and reached Suisun Bay. He went ashore there to visit *ranchero* Ygnacio Martinez, whom he had been told might sell him (on credit) seed, breeding stock and leather goods he needed. His charisma worked again, when Martinez promised to have his *vaqueros* deliver the needed stock and supplies once Sutter was settled upriver.

Sutter spent the next two days trying to locate the elusive mouth of the Sacramento River in the maze of sloughs and tributaries that made up the vast San Joaquin River delta. Finally he found it, and they headed northeast through a virtually unexplored wilderness. Other than one or two explorers and Hudson's Bay Company trappers, no white men had been there before. Apparently Sutter had obtained some knowledge of the area from Governor Alvarado, who learned about it from these few explorers.

Though they experienced at least one touchy confrontation with potentially hostile Indians, the trip went fairly well, and they camped at the confluence of the *Rio Americano* (American River) on August 13. The area looked promising, but Sutter wanted to ensure that he found the best possible site for New Helvetia, and he continued up the Sacramento River the next morning.

Upon reaching the confluence of the Feather River, he used a ship's boat to follow it upstream to the Bear River before turning back. Then, under pressure from disgruntled seamen on his ships, he returned down the Sacramento River to the confluence of the American. Heading up the American River, they sailed easterly for two miles before anchoring below an oak-wooded knoll to the south. It was high enough to escape seasonal flooding, there was a good water supply, and game abounded. It was there Sutter decided to settle.

A temporary camp was set up, and the ships were unloaded in a hurry. The seamen, eager to trade the oppressive heat and voracious mosquitos of the Sacramento Valley for the cooler climes of San Francisco Bay, left the next morning, amidst a salute fired by Sutter's three brass cannon. The cannon's frightening roar may have helped subdue the local Indians, for Sutter had little trouble befriending them and coaxing them into working for him.

They made adobe blocks by the thousands for the buildings Sutter's men began erecting. They also collected pole rafters and armloads of tules for the roofs. The loyal *kanakas* proved to be the backbone of the enterprise; without them, Sutter's enterprise would have been much more difficult or virtually impossible. Though fish and game abounded, Sutter's designated hunters were hard-pressed to feed the ever growing crew of workmen, including increasing numbers of Indians.

SUTTER DESPERATELY needed the livestock, seed and other supplies promised by Ygnacio Martinez. When it finally did show up, Sutter complained of the quality and was quick to chastise Martinez, alienating him forever. He did the same with Antonio Suñol; even Mariano Vallejo, who saw Sutter as a threat to his great power and long-standing dominance. A copy of a letter Sutter wrote to Antonio Suñol on October 7, 1840, reflects his dependence on the *ranchero* before their relationship soured:

> Sir: I take pleasure in notifying you that I have received the cattle you sent by Mr. Sinclair [An American neighbor, John Sinclair]. I have credited you with the $295, which sum I will pay, in the agreed upon, in beaver skins. Will you kindly get a small cargo of corn, beans, peas etc. for my launch? I would like to send for these provisions in three or four weeks.We have really begun to make brandy from wild grapes, and in a short time we shall know the result of this enterprise. Grapes are plentiful, and the Indians bring us sufficient quantities. In the meantime, I am most respectfully
> —Your faithful servant, J. A. Sutter
> P.S. Dr. J. Marsh sent me a cow and calf, and a young cow, that bear the mark of your brother-in-law, Mr. Bernal. I wrote to the gentleman [Marsh] that I could not accept them, as they were the property of another. Kindly buy these from your brother-in-law [the legal owner], and I shall credit you with 9 more. Mr. Robert Livermore made the discovery [These men were nearby ranchers].

This would seem to indicate that "Dr." Marsh was trying to sell Sutter stolen animals, though they may have been some he took in exchange for medical care (See Marsh).

A rough road was graded to the Sacramento River, where a landing was prepared for larger ships. Having heard of Sutter's fledgling settlement, skilled tradesmen who traveled there were added to supply metal parts, clothing and leather goods needed by Sutter and for sale or trade to others. Fields were cleared and sown with grain, livestock thrived in lush, irrigated meadows, and a vineyard and orchard were planted.

Most of the work was done by domesticated Indians, who were paid with crude metal chits, which could be exchanged for trade goods at Sutter's new store. While some accused Sutter of enslaving Indians, others accepted the system as normal. After all, Mexican *rancheros* had been using it for years, and Franciscan missionaries for decades before them.

THE FIRST YEAR at New Helvetia passed quickly for Sutter, and he could scarcely wait to report his progress to Governor Alvarado in Monterey. While there, he finalized his Mexican citizenship and reaffirmed his coveted land grant, which was approved a year later. It encompassed nearly 50,000 acres, stretching along the Sacramento River from New Helvetia to the Feather River and present-day Marysville. Sutter was also appointed alcalde, which made him a magistrate and chief law enforcement officer. As such, he virtually had powers of life or death over his "subjects" and was fast becoming the powerful "potentate" he had envisioned for so many years.

In 1840 he began construction of his fort, which he thought necessary to protect his interests from hostile Indians and unpredictable Mexican authorities alike. The following year he bought all the buildings and livestock at Fort Ross from the Russians for $30,000—mostly on credit, of course. They had offered it to General Vallejo first; Sutter's successful bid did nothing to improve his stormy relationship with the haughty Vallejo.

As luck would have it, a few members of the Bartleson-Bidwell immigration party arrived in New Helvetia at the end of 1841. Among them was John Bidwell, whom Sutter hired to take charge of dismantling the buildings at Fort Ross (see Bidwell & Bartleson-Bidwell Party). The lumber, supplies and other equipment were then transported to New Helvetia on the Russian-built schooner that went with the deal. Sutter also acquired military equipment, such as cannon, muskets and uniforms, for the Indian guard unit he was forming to maintain order in his large domain.

To pay his debts, the enterprising Swiss hired what artisans he could recruit to manufacture all manner of goods. In addition to growing wheat and many other farm products, Sutter sent a brigade of trappers into the beaver-rich delta to gather pelts. He used fishermen to catch the plentiful salmon, which were cured and stored in wooden barrels made by his cooper. He also distilled a potent brandy called *aguardiente* and operated leather-tanning vats.

A NOTHER PARTY of overland immigrants, led by Joseph B. Chiles and Joseph R. Walker, arrived in 1843 (see separate chapters). With this party was Pierson Reading, whom Sutter hired as one of his main associates. Whatever his faults, Sutter had a good eye for talent, as evidenced by the cadre of skilled, trustworthy people he recruited over the years.

In early March 1844, John C. Fremont's bedraggled, starving band of "trail blazers" arrived, needing nearly everything. The troop of U. S. Army topographers had run out of provisions on the east side of the Sierra Nevada and were forced to make a winter crossing to seek help. Assisted by Christopher "Kit" Carson and Thomas "Broken hand" Fitzpatrick, Fremont was first to cross over what is now Carson Pass. Sutter managed to feed the men and re-outfit them so they could continue their explorations (see Fremont).

By the time Sutter's Fort was completed in 1844, Governor Alvarado had been replaced by Mexican Gen. Manuel Micheltorena. Unfortunately, the new governor brought with him a small army of rag-tag, ex-convict soldiers, who soon raised the ire of *Californios* in the area. Finally a group of dissidents, led by ex-Governor Alvarado, the Pico brothers—Andres and Pío—and the Castro brothers—José and Manuel—raised a small army of rebels to overthrow Micheltorena. The beleaguered governor turned to John Sutter for help, promising him another huge land grant if he helped defeat the rebels (this 1844 "Rancho Sobrante" land grant was later invalidated).

Perhaps Sutter viewed himself as a loyal Mexican protecting the legal government; it's more likely that he was lured by the promise of more land. In any event, he quickly raised a motley army of "volunteers," consisting of Indians, white settlers and newly arrived immigrants from the Stevens-Townsend-Murphy Party (see Murphy). Apparently Sutter convinced them that the rebels would evict them from the country if Micheltorena was deposed. Besides, Sutter had the power to conscript. One of his reluctant conscripts was Dr. John Marsh, who did all he could to incite mutiny amongst the others.

Upon joining forces with Micheltorena near San Jose, Sutter and the governor led their forces south with little opposition. After a quick victory outside Mission San Buenaventura, they continued south to Rancho Cahuenga, near Los Angeles, where the rebels waited in force. An artillery barrage resulted in no casualties; however, Sutter and his adjutant, John Bidwell, were captured by rebel forces under Gen. José Castro. Finally Micheltorena capitulated, and he and his men were escorted to San Pedro, where they were herded aboard a ship bound for Mexico.

Pío Pico took over as governor, and the capital was moved from Monterey to Los Angeles. Sutter's men were pardoned; most of them left the area, while Sutter remained to be tried by the rebels. Some wished him executed; however, cooler heads, such as Juan Bandini's, prevailed, and he was released after swearing allegiance to the new government (see Bandini). Fortunately for Sutter the new governor left his lands intact and allowed him to retain his powers and privileges. After scrounging for horses for himself and some of his men, Sutter returned to his fort, a chastened and wiser man.

Though the fort had been left in the capable hands of Pierson Reading, Indian problems had surfaced, and Sutter found things in disarray. A group of fighting men was recruited to punish the hostiles, and peace soon reigned. It was time to expand; more immigrants were arriving every month, and Sutter needed their business. His strategic location became the Mecca where trail-weary emigrants could obtain needed supplies, replace worn livestock and renew sagging spirits.

In July 1845 a group of immigrants straggled in from the Willamette Valley in Oregon. Among them was an erstwhile millwright who would change the history of California and the world. His name was James Wilson Marshall. Sutter hired him immediately as a handyman-carpenter (see Marshall). By November the Mexicans were becoming alarmed by the numbers of immigrants Sutter was attracting. Rather than trying to oust him, they offered to buy him out. He would have realized enough to pay off his debts with some left over, but for reasons of his own he refused the offer and dared them to try and force him out.

Late in December Capt. John C. Fremont and Kit Carson showed up with another contingency of army topographers, reportedly on a charting expedition. Sutter was away at the time, and though John Bidwell did his best to satisfy Fremont's seemingly insatiable needs, Fremont left with hard feelings.

After exploring the area around Monterey, and provoking the ire of Gen. José Castro at Gavilan Peak, Fremont returned to Sutter's Fort and camped outside the walls. By then tensions between the settlers and Mexican authorities had reached the breaking point, and most knew that war with Mexico was inevitable. Many believed this was the main reason why Fremont and his men had reappeared on the scene.

By spring Fremont had moved his men north, via Peter Lassen's ranch, to the Klamath Lakes (see Lassen). Events began moving fast after a military messenger arrived at Sutter's Fort and went on to Fremont's camp, accompanied by Lassen. Fremont then moved south to Sutter Buttes until after the Bear Flag Rebellion in mid-June, when he again returned to Sutter's Fort (see Ide, Semple & Fremont for details re the Bear Flag Rebellion).

General Vallejo and three of his assistants were captured at Sonoma during the rebellion and brought to Sutter's Fort. They were imprisoned there by Fremont, who had just arrived. Fremont then rode off to Sonoma with volunteers he had recruited to fight the Mexicans. Not until July 7th, when U. S. Navy Commodore John Sloat invaded Monterey, did anyone knew war had been declared against Mexico. Within days the Stars and Stripes flew over the entire area, including Sutter's Fort. At last Sutter could shed his loyalty to Mexico and embrace his U. S. citizenship.

Fremont soon occupied the fort, renaming it Fort Sacramento. Sutter was appointed a Second Lieutenant by Fremont, but First Lt. Edward Kern was placed in charge during Fremont's absence in the Mexican War. Most of Sutter's key men joined Fremont's California Battalion of Volunteers, leaving Sutter a guest in his own fort. At least he could see that Vallejo and his men were treated properly.

THE MEXICAN WAR is described in other chapters of this book and will not be repeated here (see Fremont and Beale). When the fighting ended in early 1847, Fremont's volunteers were discharged in San Gabriel and Sutter's cadre began the 400-mile journey back to the fort. They arrived that spring, resuming their various duties with enthusiasm under the cherished flag of the United States. The only thing that marred their enthusiasm was the Donner Party disaster, which was virtually over by the time most of them returned in early 1847 (see Donner & Reed).

By mid-1847 Sutter knew he needed water-powered mills to cut logs into lumber and to grind grain into flour. The crude methods currently then is use were far too slow and cumbersome. James Marshall was quickly recruited to build the two mills on a partnership basis. The gristmill was to be built a few miles upstream from the fort on the American River; however, a suitable location for the sawmill had to be found before construction could begin.

In a small, well-timbered valley called Cullomah (now Coloma), about forty-five miles east on the South Fork of the American River, Marshall approved the site for the sawmill. By late August he had the gristmill well under way. Leaving it for others to finish, he took the Peter Wimmer family and some other workers to Cullomah to begin work on the sawmill.

Sutter was to furnish all the supplies, equipment and manpower, while Marshall designed and supervised construction of the sawmill. For this he was to receive a half interest. The mill was still unfinished on January 24, 1848, when Marshall discovered gold in the newly dug tailrace. Swearing the workmen to secrecy, he took a few samples and rode to the fort to show Sutter.

Sutter made some tests to make certain it really was gold, then sat back in awe. He knew it was an important discovery and that it had to be kept quiet; otherwise, his workers would desert to go prospecting. He also needed assurance that his rights in Cullomah Valley would be protected. He told Marshall to return to the millsite and convince the mill workers to continue their work, at least until the mill was completed. Meanwhile they could look for gold during their time off. He also agreed to visit Cullomah within a few days and talk to them himself. An excerpt from his diary follows:

> February 1st. Left for the sawmill attended by a Baquero [an Indian named Olympio]. Was absent 2d, 3d, 4th, & 5th. I examined myself everything and picked up a few specimens of gold myself in the tail race of the Sawmill; this gold and others which Marshall and some of the other laborers gave to me (it was found while in my employ and Wages). I told them I would a Ring got made of it so soon as a Goldsmith would be there. I told them that as they do know now that this metal is Gold, I wished that they would do me the great favor and keep it a secret only 6 weeks, because my large Flour Mill at Brighton would have been in Operation in such a time....

Fortunately for Sutter, the mill workers—many of them Mormons recently discharged from the Mormon Battalion of the U. S. Army—stayed on the job. By mid-March the sawmill began sawing timber into rough boards, and the workers were free to leave. By then rumors about the gold had leaked out, and men were coming to see if it was true.

ONE OF THESE curious men was Samuel Brannan, an opportunistic Mormon newspaper publisher from San Francisco. He got some gold and wasted no time in lining up all the prospector's supplies he could find. He then made arrangements to open stores in strategic locations and publicized the gold discovery widely in his newspaper. He went on to become the richest man in California (see Brannan).

Meanwhile Sutter had tried and failed to obtain legal property rights in Cullomah Valley. Though he had contracted with local Indians for these rights, the military governor refused to honor the agreement. This was at a time when California was in a state of governmental limbo; that is, it was neither a state nor an official territory of the United States. The Mexican alcalde system had been left in place under jurisdiction of the U. S. Army.

By mid-year 1848 a full-blown gold rush was under way, and Sutter's worst fears were realized when he could not keep his workers on the job. Who wanted to work for small wages when gold was available for the taking? He was unable to complete the gristmill, starving prospectors slaughtered his livestock, and he could not harvest his crops. In short, he faced financial ruin.

An inevitable question is, why didn't Sutter give up his various enterprises and seek gold for himself? The answer seems to be that he knew nothing about prospecting for gold and wanted to stick with what he did know. He did finance several parties of prospectors on shares but never realized anything from it. He invested in a Cullomah store but received little in the way of profits. Finally he was reduced to renting out buildings in and around the fort. Another excerpt from his diary:

> March 7th. The first party of Mormons, employed by me left for washing and digging Gold and very soon all followed, and left me only the sick and the lame behind. And at this time, I could say that every body left me from the Clerk to the Cook. What for great Damages I had to suffer in my tannery which was just doing a profitable and extensive business, and the vatts [sic] was left filled and a quantity of half finished leather was spoiled, likewise a large quantity of raw hides collected by the farmers and of my own killing. The same thing was in every branch of business which I carried on at thetime. I began to harvest my wheat, while others was digging and washing gold, but even the Indians could not be keeped [sic] longer to Work....

By the end of that fateful year Sutter had sold his half interest in the sawmill, leaving Marshall with two new partners to operate it. He also sold the fort. By then Sutter knew he was in trouble and sent for his oldest son, John A. Jr., to help him. He also contracted with attorney Peter H. Burnett to assist in selling off real estate to keep himself financially afloat (see Burnett). When Sutter's son, whom he called August, took over real estate sales with Burnett, Sutter retired to his other farm on the Feather River—a place he called the "Hock farm."

For awhile the arrangement seemed to be working well. The 1849 gold rush was in full swing, and real estate prices climbed accordingly, especially in the area adjacent to the Sacramento embarcadero. August and Burnett were selling enough real estate to pay off most of Sutter's debts, and a town named Sacramento sprang up. But this "honeymoon" period didn't last long when Sutter found out they had been subdividing property in the embarcadero area, where the city was finally established. He had authorized sales only in Sutterville, a development he was promoting on higher ground about two miles downriver. Feeling betrayed, Sutter fired both his son and Burnett. August later emigrated to Mexico.

By then Sutter had brought the rest of his family from Europe to the Hock farm. After a sixteen-year separation, they were finally reunited. Sutter had been drinking quite heavily for some time as his fortunes continued their downward slide. Former friends and acquaintances cheated him out of much valuable real estate in Sacramento, and still his creditors plagued him.

Despite all his problems, Sutter and his family lived fairly well for a number of years and were reasonably happy. He served as a delegate to the State Constitutional Convention during the fall of 1849 and lost a heated race for governor, where he was defeated by his former attorney, Peter Burnett. After statehood was approved in September 1850, Sutter was appointed a general in the State Militia and received a small pension from the state government. Unfortunately this good fortune did not continue, as is shown in a letter written in 1853:

> Hock Farm July 1th 1853
> John Halliday Esqre
> Dear Sir:
> I received your letter, and allways [sic] thought that I should be able to pay you, but I could not get money. I have a large quantity of cord wood cut and ready for market, but the steamers give to the squatters the preference which surrounds me, and therefore I cannot realize the large amount of money invested in this wood, the only source to me for the present, untill [sic] the land Commissioners decid [sic] one, and then immediately I could sell some land. I will satisfy you so soon as possible, but for the present I have to borrow, the most necessary amount to live. I am sorry that I am not able at present to settle this small amt.
>
> I remain very respectfully,
> Your Obediant Servant
> J. A. Sutter

REAL TRAGEDY struck in 1865 when Sutter's beloved Hock farmhouse was destroyed by fire. Some, including Sutter, thought it was arson. This blow seemed to devastate him more than any other misfortune he had endured. As a result he and his long-suffering wife moved to Lititz, Pennsylvania.

Sutter then spent much of his time petitioning Congress for money allegedly due him for the loss of his fort to Fremont during the Mexican War and later to squatters, who virtually stripped him of his property during the Gold Rush. He was unsuccessful in these quests; the final blow came in June 1880, while he was staying in a Washington hotel anticipating approval of long standing legislation to reimburse him for his losses. When Congress abruptly adjourned on June 16th without taking action on his reimbursement bill, Sutter took to his bed and refused to be comforted. He died in despair June 18, 1880 at the age of 77. His body was taken back to Lititz, Pennsylvania, where on June 22th he was buried in the community's Moravian cemetery. Among those attending the services was John C. Fremont, who read the eulogy.

Anna Dubeld Sutter survived her husband by less than a year. She was buried beside him, and the joint grave was covered by a marble slab engraved as follows:

General John A. Sutter
Born Feb. 28, 1803,
At Kandern, Baden
Died, June 18, 1880,

Anna Sutter (nee Dubeld)
Born Sept. 15, 1805
Died January 19, 1881
At Lititz

Requiescat in Pace

SOME CONSIDER John A. Sutter to be the "Father of California." He was certainly the father of Sacramento. Historical plaques at the Hock Farm site in Sutter County and Sutter's Fort State Historical Park in Sacramento attest to this. Unique jagged buttes in Sutter County are named after him, as are streets, schools and buildings throughout California. Though he and his wife were buried in Pennsylvania, Sutter's son, John A. Sutter Jr., is buried in Sacramento's pioneer cemetery on Broadway.

BIBLIOGRAPHY

–Bancroft, Hubert H. *History of California*, Vol. I-VI, History Co., San Francisco, 1886. Republished, Wallace Hebberd, Santa Barbara, 1966.

–Bidwell, John. "Echoes of the Past." *Century Illustrated Monthly* Magazine, 1890-91; republished, State of California, 1974.

–Bryant, Edwin. *What I Saw in California.* University of Nebraska Press, Lincoln, 1985.

–Dillon, Richard. *Fool's Gold.* Coward McCann, Inc., New York, 1967.

–Dillon, Richard. *Humbugs and Heroes.* Yosemite-DiMaggio, Oakland, Ca, 1983.

–Egan, Ferol. *Fremont, Explorer for a Restless Nation.* University of Nevada Press, Reno, 1985.

–Gay, Theressa. *James Marshall, a Biography.* Talisman Press, Georgetown, CA, 1967.

–Gudde, Erwin G. *Sutter's Own Story.* G.P. Putnam, New York, 1936.

–Harlow, Neal. *California Conquered.* University of California Press, Berkeley, 1982.

–Lewis, Donovan. *The Sawmill of Destiny.* Donella Enterprises, Placerville, CA, 1982.

–Lewis, Oscar. *Sutter's Fort: Gateway to the Gold Fields.* Prentice-Hall, Englewood Cliffs, NJ, 1966. [1]

–Stewart, George R. *The California Trail.* University of Nebraska Press, Lincoln, 1962.

–Stewart, George R. *Ordeal by Hunger.* University of Nebraska Press, 1936-1960.

–Sutter, John A., et al. *New Helvetia Diary; 1840s.* Grabhorn Press, San Francisco, 1939. Excerpts in text are taken from this publication.

–Watson, Douglas S. *The Life of Johann August Sutter.* (Includes his diary from 1845 to 1848.) Grabhorn Press, San Francisco, 1932.

Mariano Guadalupe Vallejo
Courtesy California Department of Parks & Recreation

- 43 -

MARIANO GUADALUPE VALLEJO

(Don Guadalupe)   1807 - 1890

MARIANO GUADALUPE VALLEJO was the eighth child and the fourth boy of thirteen children born to Don Ignacio Vallejo, whose family ties stretched back 200 years in Jalisco, Mexico. Mariano's mother, the former Maria Antonia Lugo, was a native of San Luis Obispo, Alta California. Descended from a long line of Spanish aristocrats, Mariano was born in Monterey, July 4, 1807; his story reflects the history of California from the time Mexico overthrew Spanish rule to eventual statehood and beyond.

Don Ignacio Vallejo's claim to fame resulted from his long service in Father Junipero Serra's military guard during the mission era. During that period he learned not only military procedures and tactics, but agriculture and Franciscan religious practices. Much of this valuable knowledge was passed along to his five sons. Despite his many abilities and his Castilian heritage, a stubborn streak of non-conformity hurt Don Ignacio's military career, and he never advanced beyond sergeant. A devout Catholic, his son, Mariano, was always proud that his father had carried the sword so that Father Serra could "plant the cross."

Mariano Guadalupe (his family called him by his middle name) and his brothers were subjected to strict discipline by their father and brought up to honor old world customs and traditions. Like most boys of that era, "Guadalupe" Vallejo learned to ride and rope at an early age. Formal schooling, which was largely religious, began at seven under the harsh discipline of a transplanted army corporal who made generous use of the whip. Finally it led to Vallejo leading a formal protest, with his fellow students José Castro and Juan B. Alvarado, against the tyranny of the schoolmaster. This protest was a forerunner of many to follow by these ardent, dynamic *Californios*.

A year or two after Spanish Governor Pablo V. Sola arrived in 1815, he took young Vallejo under his wing to educate him further. Sola must have been an inspiration to the boy, who never lost his zeal for learning. When he learned to read and write well enough, the governor let him do secretarial work, where he learned the intricacies of complex state documents.

IN 1818 came an event Vallejo never forgot: Monterey was sacked and burned by the notorious French pirate, Hippolyte de Bouchard. Vallejo's mother fled with him and the other children to Rancho del Rey (Salinas), while her husband and eldest son, José de Jesus, stayed to fight. The Vallejo family remained at the *rancho* several weeks, until the pirates had had their fill of looting and left Monterey. That tense period helped Vallejo's decision to become a soldier like his father and older brother.

English trader William E. P. Hartnell came to Monterey during the overthrow of Spain in 1822 and set up a trading store (see Hartnell). Soon fourteen-year-old Mariano Vallejo was working as a clerk for him and other traders, David Spence and Nathan Spear, from whom he quickly learned simple arithmetic, bookkeeping and English. He also learned some French and Latin from expert linguist Hartnell.

Occupational choices for promising young men were limited to the clergy, the military, politics or ranching, if they had land. Vallejo chose the military, hoping it would lead to politics and possibly ranching, which it certainly did. At age sixteen in 1824 Vallejo became a military cadet at the Monterey Presidio and was appointed secretary to Governor Luis Argüello. While there he helped draw up articles of capitulation for the transfer of the government from Spain to Mexico. Thus began the downfall of the Spanish missions, an era of political, revolutionary unrest, and a burgeoning of the lucrative hide and tallow trade.

By 1826, at the age of nineteen, Vallejo had won his sergeant's stripes and became known as a strict disciplinarian in his own right. After a year as sergeant, Vallejo became an *Alferez* (a Jr. officer comparable to ensign) in the army, outranking his far more experienced father. Even before then, Vallejo had been a substitute member of the Territorial Legislature, along with José Castro and Juan Alvarado. Despite their youth, they became members of the Provisional Assembly in 1827; their close association remained intact for much of their lives.

About a year later Vallejo led an expedition of 35 men against some of Chief Estanislao's hostile Indians in the Tulares of the San Joaquin Valley, where around forty hostiles were killed without Vallejo losing a man. Estanislao escaped, and charges of unwarranted cruelty from that action were surfacing when, in 1829, Vallejo was ordered to lead a hundred soldiers against an even larger band of hostiles led by Estanislao.

This action proved more difficult. Formerly a mission Indian, Estanislao was an effective leader; he held off Vallejo's men until the Mexican troops ran short of ammunition and had to disengage. Unfortunately, several old Indian women were killed. When news of this came out, Vallejo again faced charges of brutality and using unnecessary force. He was subsequently cleared of all charges; however, one of his men was found guilty and was jailed for five years for killing a helpless old woman. Estanislao survived to have the Stanislaus River and a county named after him in an abortive misspelling of his name. Also in 1829 Vallejo was sent with some men to map and identify geographic points to the north and east of San Francisco Bay.

During a mutiny by disgruntled soldiers later that year, Vallejo, Alvarado and Castro were captured and imprisoned. Later, Vallejo was shipped by the rebels to San Diego. By the time the mini-revolution ended in 1830, he had fallen in love with a 14-year-old, petite Señorita with the formidable name of Francisca Felipe Benicia Carrillo, daughter of a distinguished San Diego family.

Shortly after Vallejo returned to Monterey, he was transferred to the San Francisco Presidio. He was also elected to the Territorial Legislature, a step up from the Provisional Assembly, but he couldn't forget the lovely Francisca Carrillo. When he returned to San Diego a few months later, he was determined to win her heart and her parents' permission to marry. Though he won both, military regulations required permission from Mexico City. During the long, frustrating wait, he continued his duties at the presidio on San Francisco Bay.

To FURTHER his education, Vallejo became an avid reader. Many books, considered too worldly by the strict California clergy, were banned. Hungry for information, Vallejo bought several crates of books from the captain of a trading vessel to stock his personal library. Word of this purchase leaked, and he was placed under a "ban of excommunication" by the Church. Later it was lifted.

By 1831, at the age of 24, Vallejo had been promoted to *Commandante* at Presidio San Francisco, replacing Ygnacio Martinez, who was retiring to his Rancho Pinole beside the Carquinez Straits. By then Manuel Victoria had been sent by the government in Mexico to replace José Echeandia as governor. A confirmed autocrat, Victoria soon alienated his subjects with harsh edicts and arrogant disregard for any democratic process, such as refusing to call the Territorial Legislature into session.

Vallejo was approached by Alvarado and Castro to lead a revolution to depose Victoria, but chose to support Echeandia's "San Diego plan," which would have reinstated Echeandia as governor and apparently moved the capital to San Diego. When Victoria was shoved aside, Pío Pico was elected Civil Chief in lieu of an official governor (see Pico). When Echeandia refused to recognize Pico, Vallejo turned against the former governor. Vallejo and Alvarado then swore Pico into office anyway, on the sly (see Introduction).

Meanwhile the North had been taken over by Agustín Zamorano, who resisted moving the capital from Monterey. Pico then withdrew from the picture, leaving Zamorano ruling the North and Echeandia ruling the South. Then, while Vallejo was serving a stint at Mission San Juan Capistrano, word finally arrived from the military that he was free to marry. It had taken seventeen months, but Vallejo made up for lost time by marrying Francisca a few days later, on March 6, 1832. The reception and fiesta were held at the *casa grande* of his godfather, Don José Bandini, father of Juan Bandini (see Bandini).

That same year José Figueroa was sent from Mexico as the new governor. He and Vallejo hit it off from the very start. Even so, Vallejo was relieved of his duties as a member of the legislature, because military personnel were ruled ineligible. He had returned to Presidio San Francisco by then and waited impatiently for his wife's arrival. Finally he sent his brother, Salvador—also an army officer—with a military escort to bring her there. By 1833 they had a baby boy, who died in infancy.

Governor Figueroa was worried about the Russians, who had settled at Fort Ross in 1812 after "buying" land from the Indians with foofaraw and other gifts. He assigned Vallejo to deal with them and ordered him to lead a group of soldiers to Fort Ross for a peaceful visit and to determine the Russian's intentions. Vallejo was also instructed to purchase arms and supplies from the Russians, if possible, and to obtain their recognition of Mexico's sovereignty over the territory. Vallejo was amazed by the size and efficiency of the settlement at Fort Ross. Not only was it nearly self sufficient, it provided food for the Russian settlement in Alaska. More important, Vallejo learned that humane treatment of Indians often resulted in their loyalty and willingness to labor in the fields and mills.

VALLEJO WAS successful in buying books, saddles, guns and cutlasses from the Russians; in his subsequent reports to Governor Figueroa, he pointed out differences between Russia's treatment of Indians and the far harsher methods used by many mission padres. Furthermore, the padres did little to supply the Mexican soldiers with food and supplies they required. Instead, the clergy and those who were supposed to be protecting them had become adversaries. The soldiers were often underpaid (if paid at all), underfed and overworked. More often than not, Vallejo was forced to feed and equip them at his own expense; this situation continued for years.

Both Vallejo and Figueroa agreed that settlement by Mexican nationals north of San Francisco Bay should be encouraged to counter the Russian presence. Figueroa then commissioned Vallejo to establish a pueblo to be called Sonoma, adjacent to the San Francisco Solano Mission founded some eleven years earlier. Vallejo was also named administrator to secularize the mission. Vallejo had a new son when he left Yerba Buena for Solano (Sonoma) in June 1834 with 80 cavalrymen. There he found his encampment surrounded by thousands of curious Indians. A quote from Vallejo's report follows:

> After breakfast I mounted my troops and took them to a spot near the springs known by the name of Chiucuyen and now as Lachryma Montis. After eight days of feasting and dancing I finally was freed of so many dancers and proceeded to outline and lay out the new town. First I outlined a plaza, 212 varas square. I left the small building which had been constructed as a church to the east of the plaza. I built a barracks about 100 varas west of the church and after that I outlined the streets and divided the lots as prescribed by law. In this task I was ably assisted by Captain [William] Richardson, the same, who, a year later built the first house in San Francisco [then Yerba Buena]. [1]

Vallejo had been so impressed by the country north of the great bay that he also tried to establish small settlements at Petaluma and Santa Rosa. And though hostile mission padres attempted to block him, he acquired a sizable land grant from Figueroa for Rancho Petaluma. Finally, problems with hostile Indians caused both settlements to be temporarily abandoned. Another area Vallejo explored and fell in love with was a valley north of Sonoma, a place the Indians called the "Valley of the Moon."

After settling a rebellion among his overworked, underfed men in 1834, Vallejo was promoted to lieutenant. His 30-man cavalry company and their families from the presidio of San Francisco were moved to Sonoma in December 1834, and in July the following year he moved his pregnant wife and infant son, Andronico, there to occupy empty rooms at the mission. He and his wife then inventoried all church property on the premises for the record. Vallejo also brought his brother, Salvador, to Sonoma to assist him.

Soon after his arrival Vallejo was confronted by José Hijar and José Padres, who were bringing a good number of settlers from Mexico. They presented documents signed by the former president of Mexico naming Hijar as governor and Padres as Military Commandant. Fortunately Figueroa had been tipped off by the new *Presidente*, General Santa Ana, that this was no longer true and that he (Figueroa) was still in office.

Vallejo was aware of this, and when he refused to honor the outdated orders, Padres threatened to use his troops to enforce them. Instead, Vallejo arrested the two frustrated officials, and they were sent back to Mexico. He then had to provide food and shelter for the new settlers until they could survive on their own.

Because Governor Figueroa's many duties included secularization of the missions, he was to dispose of mission properties gradually, granting half the land and livestock to the mission Indians. Vallejo, as administrator over Mission San Francisco Solano in Sonoma, was ordered to apportion the property there. The youngest of the missions, it had been active only a little more than ten years before being disbanded.

Most of the Indians wanted to leave, and some asked Vallejo to care for their livestock on shares. Though there was no precedent for this, Vallejo went along with it. After ending up with much of the land and livestock in his own name, he was accused by some of plundering the mission for his own benefit. If so, it wasn't unusual, because the results of secularization became a scandal throughout the entire territory. A noticeable trait of the Spaniards was *Viva yo*, an expression meaning "long live me," or "me first." Vallejo was apparently one who practiced this philosophy; however, a more palatable explanation is that he purchased Indian property at bargain prices. Many wanted to return to the freedom of their own tribes, and they disposed of their holdings any way they could. In any case, ownership of land was a concept entirely foreign to them.

INDIAN PROBLEMS were still plaguing the settlers, especially a tribe known as the Satiyomis. Vallejo then befriended Chief Sem-Yeto, of the Suisuns, who were constantly warring with the troublesome Satiyomis. Chief Sem-Yeto was an imposing-looking giant of a man, standing six-and-a-half feet tall. He adopted the Christian faith and was baptized with the name Solano. Though Chief Solano had been accused of slave trading among the Indians, he and Vallejo formed a long-standing alliance, which eventually was successful in subduing the Satiyomis and other hostiles in the region.

Meanwhile, Governor Figueroa had been seriously ill. Tired of the machinations of self-serving assistants, he named Vallejo "Military Commander and Director of Colonization of the Northern Frontier." Governor Figueroa died in the fall of 1835, leaving Vallejo grief-stricken and, at age 28, without a mentor. But by then he was well enough established to continue on his own; in fact, he later described this period as one of "youth, strength and riches."

Vallejo fathered a daughter that year. Sonoma was growing slowly; his cattle had multiplied to the point where he needed more room. He then transported men, materials and livestock to Petaluma, where he owned much more land. The former settlement was re-established, and a huge fortress-like hacienda was built, mostly by Indian laborers, to protect its inhabitants from possible hostile attack. A two-story casa grande, with a three-story observation tower, was also constructed for Vallejo's use in Sonoma. He had now become the autocrat of both Sonoma and Petaluma.

With Figueroa gone, several men in succession took over the reins of government, including José Castro, Mariano Chico and Nicolás Gutiérrez. The *Californios* were fed up with a series of Mexican governors who offered little financial help or stability. Juan Alvarado and José Castro tried to enlist Vallejo's help in overthrowing Gutiérrez, but he declined, stating that he and his troops had their hands full with hostile Indians.

Alvarado then enlisted Isaac Graham and a group of frontier riflemen to help him overthrow Gutiérrez in 1836, and Alvarado was named governor—the first native Californian to hold that office (see Graham). Despite Vallejo's lack of support during the affair, Alvarado named him Commander-in-chief of the Mexican Army in California. Not quite 30 years of age yet, Vallejo was promoted to Colonel and made the provisional governor.

Meanwhile, William A. Richardson and Jacob Leese had been authorized by Figueroa to open trading businesses near Presidio San Francisco and establish a tiny settlement called Yerba Buena. Leese then married one of Vallejo's sisters. Richardson was named alcalde (see Richardson). Another of Vallejo's sisters married an English sea captain, John B. R. Cooper in Monterey.

By 1837 Vallejo had another daughter. Though he was charged with keeping foreigners at bay, he obviously had trouble doing so within his own family. He later granted land to George Yount, a Yankee trapper who shingled his house and eventually founded the town of Yountville (see Yount).

WHILE ALVARADO was recognized as governor in the north, Southern California saw it differently—especially Pío Pico and Juan Bandini, who led a rebellion in Los Angeles. In an attempt to unite the *Californios,* Alvarado traveled to Los Angeles with Isaac Graham and his riflemen, hoping to solidify his position. He wasn't entirely successful, but he did manage to put down the rebellion temporarily. He had previously petitioned Mexico City, asking authorities to approve him as governor; instead, they appointed Carlos Carrillo. The first thing Carrillo did was move the precarious capital to Los Angeles.

The San Diegans didn't like that and rebelled. Continued political unrest finally brought a reaction from Mexico City: Carrillo was deposed and Alvarado appointed. Much of this political intrigue involved family members and friends, who were constantly maneuvering for power. The struggle reached the point of absurdity before it was resolved by Alvarado's final appointment in 1838. Finally it seemed that he and Vallejo were firmly entrenched. That same year Dr. John Marsh arrived to settle on a ranch he purchased between the eastern base of Mt. Diablo and the San Joaquin River (see Marsh).

The next three years saw Vallejo's fortunes building; he had two more children, his cattle numbered in the tens of thousands, his fields produced tons of grain. He had become known as the "Autocrat of the North" and was described as "haughty, aristocratic and strict." The Petaluma *casa grande* was open to visitors from far and wide; however, local citizens were required to doff their hats when they passed his hacienda.

Horse-thieving Indians continued to plague local ranchers; in an effort to control them, Vallejo granted his brother-in-law, Jacob Leese, rights to trade on the Sacramento, Feather and San Joaquin Rivers. In 1838 the entire area was swept by a swift and deadly epidemic of small-pox. Whites and Indians alike came down with the dreaded disease. After it ran its murderous course, an estimated 60,000 to 75,000 Indians had died.

THE YEAR 1839 saw the arrival of John A. Sutter, a Swiss immigrant who hoped to establish his New Helvetia somewhere in the interior (see Sutter). Vallejo hoped to keep the wily Swiss adventurer close at hand to control him, but that proved impossible. Sutter, after a short visit to Fort Ross and then Yerba Buena, led his tiny flotilla of three boats—manned mostly by island *kanakas*—up the Sacramento River to its confluence with the American River, where he settled.

Later that year Vallejo was officially promoted to Colonel and finally received overdue compensation for his ongoing financial support of the Sonoma garrison.But by then, he and Governor Alvarado had fallen out over lack of funding for Vallejo's troops and problems with secularizing the missions. Vallejo hired away Alvarado's able secretary, Victor Prudon, who soon became Vallejo's right-hand man. Vallejo contended that many of the missions were being systematically looted by those responsible for making fair distribution of their assets. Perhaps it took one to know one.

Alvarado then assigned William Hartnell, Vallejo's old employer in Monterey, the unenviable task of visiting the missions and reporting on the progress of secularization. As might be expected, some of his reforms angered those in charge, including Vallejo, who felt his authority was being undermined. After an angry confrontation with the vulnerable inspector, Hartnell left Vallejo's domain a humbler and wiser man. In an attempt to ease tensions with Alvarado, Vallejo made a trip to Monterey in the spring of 1840, but he returned with many problems still unresolved.

Alarmed by reports of treasonous acts, Alvarado then ordered Vallejo and José Castro to round up and arrest Dr. John Marsh and Isaac Graham and his followers. In all, 47 foreign settlers were arrested. After being tossed in the Monterey *calabozo* briefly, they were herded aboard a ship heading for Mexico. Dr. Marsh was released before the ship left, and within a year all of them had been released and allowed to return. At about this time Vallejo's younger brother, Salvador, married Maria De La Luz Carrillo, one of Francisca Vallejo's sisters, in San Diego. Thanks to a generous land grant from Don Guadalupe, they moved to Sonoma and became close neighbors. Vallejo now had two sons and three daughters of his own, and he was far from through.

Vallejo had known for some time that the Russians were growing dissatisfied with their settlement at Fort Ross. By July 1841 they were negotiating with him and John Sutter to sell the place, lock, stock and gun barrel. Both wanted the livestock only, but the Russians insisted on selling everything—the buildings, their schooner, farming equipment and several cannon in the fort. Sutter and Vallejo had become rivals over the past two years, and Sutter was eager to put one over on the haughty *Californio* aristocrat.

Though he was already heavily in debt, Sutter offered the Russians $30,000 for all their interests, and it was accepted. He paid some money down and promised to pay the balance with wheat over a period of years. This move infuriated Alvarado and Vallejo, who felt they had been betrayed. The building of sturdy Sutter's Fort added to the apprehension of the Mexicans. Vallejo was not certain what Sutter's motives really were. Sutter was a Mexican citizen and had been appointed an alcalde, yet he encouraged immigration from the United States—a clear violation of Mexican policy. What Vallejo may not have realized was that the sale left Sutter precariously indebted.

While the Russians were pulling out of California, the British-held Hudson's Bay Company got permission to open a trading store at Yerba Buena. Against the wishes of John Sutter and John Marsh, they were also given permission to continue their annual fur trapping throughout the fruitful San Joaquin delta. Jacob Leese then sold his store and land in Yerba Buena to the Hudson's Bay Company and moved to Sonoma, where he built a house facing the plaza.

ANOTHER SON, Platon, was born to Vallejo in 1841, but two-year-old Platarco died. Two boys were left and two others, José Altimira (later changed to José Mariano Vallejo), and Enrique Licaldo (later changed to Vallejo), both of Indian blood, were adopted by the Vallejos. Prior to his marriage, Vallejo was involved with at least two Indian *novias* (girl friends). José was probably born to one of these women, as he was about ten in 1840 when he was taken in by the Vallejos. Enrique came to the Vallejos as a baby shortly after the death of their son, Platarco, and was considered by Francisca as a "gift from heaven."

By then other countries had been showing interest in Alta

California. In 1841 France was ably represented by M. Eugene Duflot de Mofras, who was apparently spying out the area for possible "protection" by France or even annexation [2]. The United States was well represented by navy Lt. Commander Cadwalder Ringgold of Commander Charles Wilkes' expedition. This was the first U.S. expedition to officially chart the waters of the Pacific coast. Both groups spent time exploring and charting the Sacramento River past New Helvetia to the northeast and then south to the San Joaquin River.

ALSO IN 1841 came the first party of destitute overland immigrants from Missouri. They appeared at Dr. John Marsh's ranch at the foot of Mt. Diablo in November. Known as the Bartleson-Bidwell Party, it consisted of 31 people, including one young mother with a baby (see Bartleson & Bidwell). Marsh's letters extolling the virtues of California had attracted them, yet he did not welcome them with open arms. Many of them were jailed by Mexican authorities in San José until Vallejo reluctantly came to their aid by approving their passports. A few headed for Sutter's Fort, while others scattered throughout the territory.

Later that year Vallejo received a visit from George Simpson, chief of the Hudson's Bay Company in the Pacific Northwest. Vallejo provided his best hospitality, and Simpson reacted by offering to make Alta California a British protectorate. He was determined to drive stubborn Americans out of the fur trade any way he could. To this unofficial offer, Vallejo made no commitment. Nevertheless, there were those who claimed he courted the British. Because of fierce Yankee competition, the Hudson's Bay Company store in Yerba Buena never did well. A few years later the manager committed suicide and the company pulled out.

Meanwhile, General Santa Ana was sending a new governor, Manuel Micheltorena, to replace Alvarado. The new governor proved able enough, but had brought with him a rag-tag army of ex-convicts who soon alienated nearly everyone. The new governor appointed Vallejo military commander of the territory north of Santa Barbara, a formidable task indeed.

Then came the erroneous "invasion" of Monterey by U. S. Navy Commodore Thomas ap Catesby Jones, who thought war between the U.S. and Mexico had been declared. Before Vallejo reacted, he received a message stating that the invasion had been a terrible mistake. Fortunately, Thomas O. Larkin—later the U.S. Consul in Monterey—managed to convince Jones that no war had been declared (see Larkin). The red-faced commodore had no choice but to haul down the Stars and Stripes and withdraw his men after making formal apologies to all concerned. No real harm had been done except to Jones' pride and his future naval career. Vallejo's eighth child, another boy, was born in 1843.

Because Vallejo had been subsidizing the army for years and had lent Governor Micheltorena large sums of money, the governor awarded him additional land grants: the 80,000-acre Soscal Rancho, fronting the north side of Carquinez Straits, and an additional 35,000 acres adjacent to his Rancho Petaluma. Vallejo had also purchased from Chief Solano, at bargain rates, the four-league Rancho Suisun. Though he now owned an estimated 175,000 acres, it was hardly worth it; Vallejo had found himself in the untenable position of being held responsible for the governor's unruly *cholo* troops. Micheltorena had promised to return them to Mexico, but it never happened. Instead, the governor turned to Mexico City for help that never came. Finally, in November 1844, Vallejo disbanded his inadequate Sonoma garrison, unwilling to support it any longer or to deal with the wild *cholos.*

Not long after, he learned that John Sutter was building up a band of volunteers to assist the governor against a rebel force that threatened to overthrow him. The rebels were led by ex-governor Alvarado and José Castro, who had joined with the Pico brothers and others in Southern California. Once again revolution was brewing in the troubled land, and once again Vallejo managed to skirt it by remaining neutral. When Micheltorena capitulated just outside of Los Angeles (Cahuenga Pass) in February 1845, Pío Pico took over as governor and the capital was moved to Los Angeles.

To Vallejo's chagrin, Sutter was released and returned to New Helvetia with his powers and land grants intact. Soon Vallejo and others became so anxious over Sutter's mounting power that the government offered to buy him out. Though Sutter was tempted, he refused the rather generous offer. By late 1846 Sutter's various enterprises were becoming profitable, and he was on his way to acquiring the wealth and power he coveted.

VALLEJO WAS doing the same; his large family kept increasing and he held the honorary title of "General", while Sutter was still known as "Captain." By then overland immigrants were pouring into Sutter's Fort by the hundreds, and Vallejo was greatly concerned. A letter he wrote in early 1846 to the Mexican Minister of War reflects that concern:

> If the invasion which is taking place from all sides is carried out, all that I can guarantee is that California will die. I cannot dare to assure that California will be saved.

Despite his apprehension, Vallejo had begun to change his attitude toward the new immigrants; he was beginning to admire their industry and tenacity. He and his brother, Salvador, even helped some of them when they arrived destitute and starving. By early 1846 he had become so disillusioned with ineffective leadership from Mexico City that he began hoping that the United States would take over the country and make something out of it. In fact he spoke out in favor of U.S. occupation at a junta conference held at Consul Larkin's home in Monterey. His change of heart is shown clearly in a letter written after the conference by U. S. Consul Thomas O. Larkin to his superiors in Washington.

> [Vallejo] has been formal, stiff, pompous and exacting toward his countrymen and foreigners of the lower or middle class. Within a year, he has become pleasant and condescending, anxious for popularity, and the good will of others.

LATER EVIDENCe of his rather hurried conversion is his treatment of former Missouri Governor Lilburn W. Boggs and his family, who arrived in Sonoma in early January 1847. Vallejo put them up at his Petaluma *hacienda* for several months, during which a grandchild was born to the ex-governor. The child was named Guadalupe Vallejo Boggs and was said to be the first Anglo child born in California under the U.S. flag.

But before then, events had been moving swiftly toward American annexation. Captain John C. Fremont arrived at Sutter's Fort for the second time in slightly over a year with a party of U.S. Army "topographers "(see Fremont). After tangling with General José Castro in the spring of 1846, he led his men north through the Sacramento Valley and camped at Upper Klamath Lake. By June the settlers feared they would be driven out by Castro and his Mexican forces, who were becoming increasingly aggressive against foreigners. Castro was especially suspicious of Fremont's intentions, and with good reason.

Some of the hot-headed settlers decided to go on the offensive and stole a herd of horses belonging to the Mexican government. After reporting to Captain Fremont, they recruited more men for a sneak attack on Sonoma. Taken by surprise in the early morning hours of June 14, 1846, Vallejo and his men were captured without a shot being fired. The next day a crude flag featuring a bear, a star and the words "California Republic" replaced the Mexican flag in Sonoma plaza. Thus the "Bear Flag Rebellion" spawned a new independent republic.

Mariano Vallejo and his brother, Don Salvador, along with Jacob Leese and Victor Prudon, were taken to Sutter's Fort under armed guard and imprisoned on the order of Captain Fremont, who had returned there during the fracas. Sutter remained there, but the fort was clearly under Fremont's control. Fremont then began recruiting volunteers to fight in the war, which by now was certain. When official word came from the U. S. Government he would be ready to move. He was often away during the recruitment period, and Sutter took the opportunity to make prison life better for the captives. Lt. Edward Kern had been left in charge, but Sutter managed to circumvent him.

Though they had been bitter rivals, Sutter treated Vallejo and his men more like guests than prisoners until Fremont returned and put a stop to it. Sutter found himself torn by loyalty to Mexico and his admiration for the United States. It was obvious that Vallejo suffered the same ambivalence; in fact, he had previously argued with other loyalists that he would prefer U. S. occupation to that of England or France. It seemed inevitable that one of the three countries would prevail. Most native *Californios* apparently agreed, for there was very little resistance to U. S. occupation in the North.

Fifteen days after the Bear Flag Rebellion, U.S. Navy Commodore John Sloat's men invaded Monterey. Finally it was official—the United States had declared war against Mexico. Details about the war are covered in other chapters and will not be repeated here (see Fremont and Beale). Within weeks the Stars and Stripes were flying over all of California, and Castro and Pico had fled to Mexico. Even before then, Stockton had arranged for General Vallejo and his men to be freed on parole. Vallejo and the others left for home in early August.

After weeks of confinement, Vallejo was weakened by an attack of ague. He claimed to have been "stolen blind" during his absence, primarily a heavy loss of livestock. But he was not one to nurse grievances against Fremont or other U. S. officials. Instead, he got rid of his Mexican military uniforms and equipment and devoted his energies to agricultural pursuits. After the war was over in 1847 he deeded five square miles of land to Robert Semple, one of the Bear Flaggers who had captured him at Sonoma. Vallejo wanted Semple to establish a settlement on his Rancho Soscol land. He wanted to call it Francisca after his wife, but because Yerba Buena had been changed to San Francisco by then, Vallejo decided to call the new town Benicia, his wife's other name. Thomas O. Larkin, also an investor, was to assist Semple in attracting settlers and selling lots.

Besides having lost much livestock and a large wheat crop during his incarceration, Vallejo had provided livestock and supplies for the U.S. Armed Forces. For this he was finally reimbursed nearly $50,000 in late 1847. His brother Salvador and Jacob Leese received lesser amounts. Once Vallejo had recovered his health, the ranch began to run smoothly again. His personal life suffered another blow with the death of another son, three-year-old Guadalupe. This was partially offset by the arrival of his adopted son, José, who had been away at college in Valparaiso, Chili. During this same period in 1847, Vallejo was named Sub Indian Agent for the areas adjacent to Sonoma and Petaluma.

Then came news that shook the entire countryside. In February 1848 an exhausted messenger arrived with news from John Sutter. Millwright James Marshall had been overseeing construction of a sawmill for Sutter in a remote valley called Cullomah (Coloma). While deepening the tailrace, he had discovered quantities of pure gold. Before long Vallejo and ex-governor Boggs—who became an alcalde at Sonoma—made a trip there to see for themselves.

As the news spread, more and more men went to the mountains to see if the wild rumors about rich gold strikes were true. Soon the slow trickle of hopeful argonauts swelled to a raging torrent of wild gold seekers, all determined to make their fortunes before the precious metal played out. Rather than mine gold from the ground, Vallejo got his share selling beef and wheat to the miners, who paid higher and higher prices for everything they needed. He also invested in several stores carrying miner's supplies.

BY 1849 it had become evident that a formal government was required to provide law enforcement, a court system, and general stability in a land gone berserk. In September 1849 Military Governor Richard B. Mason called for a Constitutional Convention in Monterey for that purpose. Both Vallejo and Sutter were appointed official delegates. After a proper constitution was drafted, the delegates celebrated with an elaborate Mexican fiesta. Vallejo returned to Sonoma feeling good about his part in launching the fledgling state. The constitution was ratified in November, and by December, Vallejo had been elected to the State Senate.

He then offered land and money to construct a new capitol in the East Bay area, at the mouth of the Napa River not far from where he had established Benicia. He wanted the new capital named Eureka, but friends insisted that it be named Vallejo. California was admitted to the Union on September 9, 1850, and the legislature met in San Jose. They tried moving to Vallejo in 1851, but the buildings were so incomplete and inadequate that they went on to Sacramento instead. The flood of 1852 drove them back to Vallejo and finally to Benicia in 1853-54.

For reasons of their own, other legislators fought for the capital, which was permanently located in Sacramento in 1855. Naturally Vallejo was disappointed that his generous gesture for a permanent location for the capital in Vallejo had been refused, but he swallowed his pride and continued playing the role of a lavish host to everyone of importance who visited the area. This was especially true after the U. S. Army moved their headquarters to Sonoma. Vallejo's *casa grande* there became almost an extension of the Officer's Club.

Before then Vallejo had decided he needed a larger, more opulent house in which to entertain his many guests. He wanted to build it by a nearby spring, and though he owned tens of thousands of acres nearby, he had to buy the property from profit-minded Anglo settlers. In 1852 he spared little expense building a lovely Victorian house he called *Lachryma Montis*, meaning "Tear of the Mountain," for the clear, cool spring on the property. Though the house was built of wood, Vallejo astutely had adobe bricks laid inside the outer walls for insulation. With plenty of water for irrigation, lavish landscaping was planted, including a large variety of fruit trees—citrus and tropical fruits for example—and ample gardens for flowers and vegetables. Before long Vallejo became a successful vintner.

Before the family left the casa grande, Vallejo's daughter Epifania, called "Fanny," married U. S. Army Capt. John Frisbie. In 1853 Vallejo built a unique prefabricated chalet adjacent to the house, and by the mid-1850's, another daughter, Adelayda—called Adela—had married Captain Frisbie's younger brother, Levi. All told, the petite, powerful Francisca Vallejo bore fourteen children, of whom eight survived to adulthood. The last two girls were born in 1856 and 1857. Because they had been born under the United States flag, they were known as the "Little Yanks." Counting two adopted boys, José and Enrique, the Vallejos had at least sixteen children and raised most of them to maturity.

THROUGHOUT the entire Gold Rush, Don Mariano and Don Salvador had helped innumerable prospectors and settlers when they were down on their luck. And many people took advantage of them. Ruthless squatters moved on to many choice lands and refused to leave. To complicate matters, a land commission was formed to establish legal ownership of land throughout California. The *Californios* had to prove their titles to their vast land grants, often resulting in huge legal fees that many could not afford. It was during this period that Vallejo became a successful vintner and was elected Mayor of Sonoma.

Land boundaries were often unmarked and many holdings remained legally unregistered. Newcomers were constantly looking for land, and they coveted the choice parcels belonging to the *Californios*. Soon unscrupulous lawyers were contesting many of the titles for technical omissions. As a result, land that had been handed down from one generation to the next was confiscated and taken over by strangers. Old families were evicted without compensation and left to shift for themselves. To his dismay, Vallejo lost much of his land to these legal sharks.

Despite having spent a fortune fighting them in the courts, he finally lost Rancho Soscol. In 1865, just before the Civil War ended, he and John Frisbie made a voyage East to Washington, D. C. in an attempt to salvage his Petaluma property. In this he was finally successful and was able to sell the property later. Vallejo and Frisbie were in New York when President Lincoln was assassinated and glumly watched the funeral procession pass through.

Largely because of the expensive fight to save his property, Vallejo's fortunes declined after the Civil War. Unable to repay money borrowed on his home, Lachryma Montis, it was taken by foreclosure. Fortunately the sympathetic creditor allowed the Vallejos to remain there as renters until the loan was paid off by John Frisbie five years later. Frisbie then deeded it over to Francisca.

MEANWHILE VALLEJO had been writing his memoirs, and though a fire destroyed many of his important papers, he persevered. He was a sought-after speaker and became a member of the Society of California Pioneers and the Native Sons of the Golden West. He also donated his historically rich collection of documents to the Bancroft Library. In 1869 Vallejo, again accompanied by John Frisbie, traveled east on the newly completed Central Pacific Railroad. The following year Francisca took the same trip to visit her daughter, Fanny, and her grandchildren in the East.

In 1876 Vallejo mourned the death of his brother Don Salvador, who had died penniless after bank failures in San Francisco had wiped him out. Vallejo made the long trip to Mexico City about two years later with some New York financiers, hoping to interest the Mexican Government in building a railroad from the capital to Acapulco.

The year 1882 saw the death of Vallejo's older brother, José Jesus, and his nephew, Juan Alvarado. It was also the year of Mariano and Francisca's golden wedding anniversary. Unfortunately, their later years were plagued by financial problems, to the point where a state pension was proposed, similar to those awarded to John Sutter and James Marshall. Nothing came of the proposal, and the Vallejos eked out a living, largely by growing and selling fruits and vegetables.

In 1889 Vallejo was unable to attend the 12th annual Native Sons of the Golden West grand convention because of ill health. He must have had a premonition of death, for in June that year he wrote his will. All that was left was the house and 228 acres of land, plus one cow and two aging horses. He died January 18, 1890, at the age of 82, holding Francisca's hand. Ill herself, and unable to bear life without her beloved husband, Francisca followed him a year later. They lie side by side at Mountain Cemetery, overlooking Sonoma Valley. A massive granite tomb erected by the family marks the place.

Because of Vallejo's many contributions to California, the city of Vallejo carries his name, as do state historic parks near Petaluma and in Sonoma; the Petaluma Adobe is the largest surviving adobe in the state. In 1965 a Polaris class submarine was named in his honor, and many streets names and historic markers throughout California pay homage to him; is it any wonder that people doffed their hats in respect when they passed his home? His lovely old house and the barracks building in Sonoma remain open to the public.

Bibliography

–Bancroft, Hubert H. *History of California,* Vol. I-VI. History Co., San Francisco, 1886. Republished, Wallace Hebberd, Santa Barbara, 1966.

–Botello, Arthur P. (translator). *Don Pío Pico's Historical Narrative.* Ed. by M. Cole & H. Welcome. Arthur H. Clark Co., Glendale, CA, 1973.

–Davis, William Heath. *Seventy-Five Years in California.* John Howell Books, San Francisco, 1967.

–Bryant, Edwin. *What I Saw in California.* University of Nebraska Press, Lincoln, 1985.

–DeVoto, Bernard. *The Year of Decision-1846.* Houghton Mifflin Co., Boston, 1942

–Dillon, Richard. *Fool's Gold.* Coward McCann, New York, 1967. [2]

–Dillon, Richard. *Humbugs and Heroes.* Yosemite-DiMaggio, Oakland, CA, 1983.

–Egan, Ferol. *Fremont, Explorer for a Restless Nation.* University of Nevada Press, Reno, 1977.

–Emparan, Madie Brown. *The Vallejos of California.* Gleeson Library Assoc., University of San Francisco, 1968. [1]

–Gay, Theressa. *James Marshall.* Talisman Press, Georgetown, CA, 1967.

–Harlow, Neal. *California Conquered.* University of California Press, Berkeley, 1982.

–Hawgood, John A. (editor). *First and Last Consul. A selection of letters written by Thos. O. Larkin.* Huntington Library, San Marino, CA, 1962.

–Hunter, Alexander. Vallejo, *A California Legend.* Sonoma State Park Ass'n., Inc. Sonoma, CA, 1992.

–Lee, W. Storrs. *California.* Funk & Wagnalls, New York, 1968.

–McKittrick, Myrtle M. *Vallejo, Son of California.* Binfords & Mort, Portland, OR, 1944. Except for T. O. Larkin and [1 & 2], quotations came from this book.

–Taylor, Bayard. *El Dorado.* University of Nebraska Press, Lincoln, 1949.

–Wilcox, Del. *Voyagers To California.* Sea Rock Press, Elk, CA, 1991.

Captain Joseph Rutherford Walker
Courtesy California State Library

- 44 -

JOSEPH RUTHERFORD WALKER

1798 – 1876

ALTHOUGH JOSEPH R. WALKER spent only the last part of his life here, no history of early California would be complete without a section devoted to this remarkable frontiersman. Like Jedediah Smith before him, he was driven to explore new lands with the hope that fur trapping or horse trading would support his extensive expeditions. Perhaps a blood-strain for adventurous travel was carried in Walker's Scotch-Irish family genes, because several of his kin became prominent Californians after exploring far corners of the West.

Walker's father, also named Joseph, married Susan Willis in 1787. Though they resided in Goochland County, Virginia, at the time, Joseph emigrated to what became Roane County, Tennessee, to acquire land. While establishing a farm there, he traveled back and forth to visit his wife. Two daughters, Lucy and Jane, and a son named Joel were born in Virginia before the family moved to Tennessee in 1798. It was there, on December 13th, that Joseph R. was born.

Here we can correct a misconception regarding Joseph R. Walker's middle name, which appears to be Rutherford, rather than Reddeford, as commonly believed. The correct name is documented by Bil Gilbert in his fine biography of Joseph R. Walker, *Westering Man*. Gilbert believes that Rutherford was an old family name that was misspelled in Walker's 1876 obituary. Subsequently the misspelling was carried on in virtually everything written about him.

At least three more children were born to the Walkers in Tennessee, including two sons, John and Samuel, and Susan, named after her mother. Along with numerous cousins, aunts and uncles, there was a sizeable clan of Walkers in the area. Raised in the wilderness of Tennessee, the children received some schooling and got an extensive education in farming, hunting and trapping.

In 1814, when Joseph Walker was a maturing six-foot teen-ager, he and his older bother, Joel, took part in the Creek Indian War under Andrew Jackson. During the Battle of Horseshoe Bend, about 800 out of 1,000 Creeks were killed, while Jackson's men suffered casualties of around 50 killed and 150 wounded. One of the wounded was Joel Walker, who made a fast recovery.

After serving in several more Indian campaigns in Tennessee, Alabama and Mississippi, Joseph and Joel returned to Roane County in early 1819. By then Joseph Walker was a handsome figure of a man, standing well over six feet tall and was an experienced Indian fighter and frontiersman. Later most of the Walker clan emigrated to Missouri. After a long trek through the wilderness by wagon train, they reached St. Louis in the fall of 1819.

MOVING FARTHER WEST, they finally settled near Fort Osage, about thirty miles east of present-day Kansas City. Osage was a fort in name only, serving primarily as an Indian trading post under George Sibley. Once the Walkers had built a house and planted crops to feed the family, Joseph, Joel and John gave in to their adventurous heritage and left to explore farther west. By 1820 Joseph Walker had joined a trapping party heading into the Rocky Mountains and New Mexico. After arriving in the Santa Fe area without permission from Spanish authorities, Walker and others were arrested and imprisoned.

As the story goes, the Spanish needed assistance to punish hostile Indians. When Walker's group agreed to help, they were released from jail and granted trade concessions. Another version states they were merely released with a promise to leave the territory. Later, on their way to Missouri, they met a destitute trapping party heading up the Arkansas River. In it was Joseph Walker's older brother, Joel, who at first mistook Joe for an Indian. Theirs was a welcome reunion.

By the time the Mexicans overthrew the Spanish in 1821, Joseph Walker was apparently a member of a shadowy group known as "The Taos Trappers." Based in Taos, they made their living by trapping, smuggling and trading in contraband goods. While in Taos he met veteran trader William Becknell and trappers William Wolfskill and Ewing Young (see Wolfskill).

By 1825 Walker was back at Fort Osage, and traffic on the Santa Fe Trail had increased enough to warrant attention from the Federal Government. A commission headed by George Sibley was formed to survey the best route and enforce treaties with Indians to protect traders from harassment. Among those hired by the commission to carry out their edicts were Joe R. Walker, his brothers Joel and "Big John," and experienced frontiersman Bill Williams. Williams was ten years older than Joseph, a violent, profane man—especially when he drank. Eventually he became known as "Crazy Bill."

After the survey was completed in 1827, Joseph Walker returned home. By then part of the family had abandoned Fort Osage and the settlement moved fifteen miles west to present-day Independence. Largely through the efforts of his influential brother-in-law, Abraham McClellan, Joseph Walker was appointed sheriff of newly formed Jackson County. After serving a year, he ran for election in 1828 and won by a large margin. Though he served with distinction, Walker became bored with the job within a year and refused to run for re-election. Instead, he went back to livestock trading—especially horses—and drove a sizeable herd to Fort Gibson on the upper Arkansas River. While there Walker agreed to join U.S. Army Captain Benjamin Bonneville and St. Louis trader Michael Cerré for an expedition into the Rocky Mountains. Bonneville—on detached duty from the army—was forming a large party and hoped to pay their way by fur trapping.

By 1832 Bonneville was dealing with investors in New York, while Cerré acquired supplies in St. Louis. Walker returned to Fort Osage, where he recruited men for the long journey ahead. Made up of trappers, teamsters and Delaware Indians, the 110-man party opted for 20 wagons in lieu of pack animals to haul their extensive supplies and equipment. Walker was made a lieutenant—possibly a partner—and they left Fort Osage in May 1832. This was the largest and one of the earliest wagon trains to make its way along the North Fork of the Platte River to the Sweetwater and over South Pass to the Green River. Later this route became the main emigrant trail to Oregon.

A crude fort was established on the Green River at its confluence with Horse Creek. Before winter, the camp was moved to the Salmon River. Walker then led a party of trappers to surrounding areas to trap throughout the winter months. When Walker and the rest of Bonneville's group attended the 1833 trapper's rendezvous on the Green River later that summer, they had only 23 packs of beaver plews—not nearly enough to pay expenses for such a large operation.

It was then Bonneville divided his party into two sections. Walker was named captain of a group heading for California, ostensibly to seek out the elusive beaver. With him went Joe and Stephen Meek, Bill Williams, George Nidever and Zenas Leonard, who kept written accounts of the journey. Later, Leonard wrote:

> I was anxious to go to the coast of the Pacific, and for that purpose hired with Mr. Walker as a clerk for a certain sum per year. [1]...Mr. Walker was a man well calculated to undertake a business of this kind. He was well hardened to the hardships of the wilderness—understood the character of the Indian very well—was kind and affable to his men, but at the same time at liberty to command without giving offense—and to explore unknown regions was his chief delight. [2]

By then Walker was described as "a bearded bear of a man who wenched with abandon and turned hellion come rendezvous time." Another states he was "a bit of a dandy for a mountain man." Could he have been both?

Captain Walker and his party left the rendezvous in late July 1833 with about 40 of Bonneville's men and up to 20 free trappers, including Nidever and Leonard. They took no wagons, and like the Bartleson-Bidwell Party which followed in 1841, Walker probably traveled the Bear River south to where it flowed into the Great Salt Lake. He then struck west above the north shore of the lake, crossing torrid, blinding salt flats and arid desert country to Mary's River (the Humboldt). This he followed to what became the Humboldt Sink, well within sight of the formidable Sierra Nevada Range.

They suffered much thieving along the way from Paiute Indians, who seemed to melt in and out of the harsh landscape. In violation of Walker's strict rules, Bill Williams and others killed some of the Indians. Perhaps because of this killing, more hostile Indians gathered at the sink. Finally Walker authorized a full-scale attack against them, during which many Indians were killed. It appears that Walker never forgave Williams for what he considered an avoidable encounter that terminated with needless slaughter.

Later, Walker passed by two lakes in present western Nevada. The first, southeast of present-day Fallon, was later named after Kit Carson; the other, near present-day Hawthorne, was eventually named after Walker. He followed the river that drained into that lake along the eastern base of the Sierra Nevada range until he spied a gap in the towering peaks where a crossing might be made. The party crossed the mountains somewhere between the Merced and Tuolumne River watersheds on the Western side. It proved extremely difficult; there were places where frantic horses and pack mules had to be eased down impossible precipices with ropes wound around trees or rocks. By then the entire party was existing on horse and mule meat.

Though Walker's men eventually reached a state of near rebellion, he convinced them to continue on. Finally they reached a granite outcropping where the creek they followed dropped over the edge, forming a mighty waterfall. Awed by the wondrous sight of what became Yosemite Valley and the adjoining sequoia forest, Leonard described the trees as follows:

> In the last two days traveling we have found some trees of the redwood species; incredibly large—some of which would measure from sixteen to eighteen fathoms around the trunk at the height of a man's head from the ground. [3]

Before long they sighted the vast San Joaquin Valley below. After a short rest in the valley to replenish themselves with nourishing venison, they made their way down the San Joaquin River, to where it disappeared into the sprawling Sacramento River Delta. Passing through the pueblo of San Jose a few days later, they crossed over the Coastal Range for their first thrilling view of the Pacific Ocean.

AFTER ENJOYING the sights in Monterey and Santa Cruz, Walker led his men over the Coastal Range to Gilroy's ranch and on to Mission San Juan Bautista, where he made arrangements to spend the winter of 1833-34. But first Walker went to Monterey and obtained permission from Governor Figueroa to stay. He then returned to San Juan, where he and his men enjoyed the relatively easy lifestyle of the *Californio rancheros* with their fandangos, fiestas and afternoon siestas. Six of the party, including Nidever, liked what they saw in California; when Walker moved his camp into the San Joaquin Valley in January 1834, the six men elected to stay behind.

After setting up a hunting camp, Walker began acquiring horses for the return trip to rejoin Bonneville on the Green River. Finally, with 52 men, over 300 horses and a small herd of beef cattle, Walker's party headed south to the present-day Kern River. Local Indians guided them easterly up the South Fork of the river and over the ice-free pass that bears Walker's name to this day. Leonard described the eastern side:

> We here made our pilots presents of a horse, some tobacco and many trifling trinkets captivating to the eye of an Indian, when they left us to return to their friends...The country on this side is much inferior to that on the opposite side—the soil being thin and rather sandy. [4]

About a dozen of the men, probably including Bill Williams, Joe and Stephen Meek, left Walker there to return east via a southern trail to Santa Fe. Walker took the remainder of his men north through present-day Owens Valley and turned east, hoping to find a more direct route to the Great Salt Lake. Instead, he led them into a wasteland that cost them dearly in lost time and livestock. After backtracking to their original trail, they retraced their earlier route via present-day Walker River and across the desert to what is now the Humboldt Sink.

Again they were severely harassed by aggressive Paiute Indians to the point where Walker ordered another attack. After 14 Indians were killed, they withdrew, leaving a few of Walker's men slightly wounded. The party then continued easterly along Mary's River. It was later named the Humboldt by John C. Fremont (see Fremont).

Finally they reached the Bear River and made their way back to rendezvous with Bonneville on the Green River. Though Walker returned with crude charts and tall tales of his epic journey, he brought few furs to the disappointed Captain Bonneville, who had done no better. For the second year in a row, fur trapping had proved a bust. When

Bonneville took his remaining men to the upper Columbia River, Walker led his party to explore and trap the Bighorn, Yellowstone and upper Missouri rivers.

Walker and his trapping party spent an eventful winter among friendly Crow Indians, during which Zenas Leonard recorded valuable ethnological studies which were later published. When Walker met Bonneville at the 1835 rendezvous, he turned over his furs and resigned his position. He then joined the American Fur Company, where he was made a brigade leader for a short time. More often he worked as a free trapper throughout the Green and Bear River country.

WALKER LIVED with Snake Indians (eastern Shoshones) during this period and "married" an attractive Snake woman, with whom he apparently had several children over the years. At the 1837 rendezvous, Walker met artist Alfred J. Miller, who painted his portrait. Miller also painted a picture of Walker and his Indian wife sitting on their horses. This one was entitled, "Bourgeois Walker and his squaw."

Walker was reportedly in Arizona the following year, where he claimed to have found gold. He acquired a herd of horses there, which he brought to the 1838 rendezvous for trade or sale. An interesting event took place the next year when Walker was at Fort Davey Crockett in Colorado territory, and a trapping party had their horses stolen by a band of marauding Sioux. Unable to recover their horses, the trappers made their way to a peaceful Snake encampment and stole around forty of the tribe's horses.

The wronged Snake Indians appeared later at Fort Davey Crockett to complain about the theft of their horses, and Walker led a force of men, including Kit Carson and Joe Meek, to recover the horses and return them to their rightful owners. This did nothing to endear Walker to the horse thieves, but he certainly cemented his friendship with the Snake Indians. He also befriended the well-known Utah Indian chief, Wakara, who sometimes borrowed Joseph Walker's name when dealing with whites. Chief Walkara was widely known as an accomplished horse thief, which caused some confusion about their respective identities and occupations.

By 1840 the fur trade was drying up, and Walker at age 42, looked around for something more profitable. Trade along the Santa Fe Trail had intensified, and horses were being stolen in California to be delivered for good prices in Santa Fe. But rather than steal, Walker entered the trade on a legitimate basis by gaining permission from the Mexican government. He and Henry Fraeb then took a load of beaver pelts overland via the Virgin River and Colorado River route into Southern California.

In Los Angeles they sold 417 pounds of pelts to trader Abel Stearns for $1,147, which they used to purchase a herd of horses and mules (see Stearns). By coincidence, perhaps, Joel Walker was taking his wife and four children overland to Oregon about the same time. They were met at the Green River by Joe Meek and a few companions, who accompanied them on to Oregon. In late 1841 the Joel Walker family paid a visit to Sutter's Fort.

Meanwhile, Joseph Walker, Fraeb and some hired men were driving a large herd of horses to Santa Fe, where they were sold at a good profit. By the end of 1841 Fraeb had been killed by Indians, the Bartleson-Bidwell Party had blazed a trail to California, and Walker had taken his Indian wife home to Missouri for a visit. By 1843 he was trapping with Louis Vasquez in what became Southwest Wyoming. Later, Vasquez and James Bridger established Fort Bridger on Black's Fork.

BY THEN emigrant travel to Oregon was beginning to boom, and Walker was being described as "a fine old mountaineer—hale and stout-built and eagle-eyed with gray hair." Early that summer he and Vasquez were heading east along the Sweetwater River toward Fort Laramie with a load of pelts, when they met an emigrant train heading for California. With this group was Joseph Chiles, a neighbor of Walker's from Jackson County, Missouri. Chiles had made the trip to California two years earlier with the Bartleson-Bidwell Party and was on his way back (see Chiles).

No one had been successful in getting wagons across the Sierra Nevada, but Chiles was determined to try and had recruited about 50 emigrants to accompany him. His wagons carried mill-irons needed to build a gristmill on property he owned in Napa Valley. Learning of Walker's new route across the southern end of the Sierra Nevada, he hired Walker for $300 to pilot the wagons. Though Walker wasn't sure about getting wagons across, he agreed to try.

By the time they reached Fort Hall on the Snake River, they were running out of food. Frustrated by his inability to buy food at the fort, Chiles decided to split the party. Walker was to pilot the wagon train along the Mary's River (the Humboldt) and across his new pass, taking a few men and the women and children. Chiles was to lead the rest of the men on horseback to Fort Boise and Sutter's Fort to buy food. They were to meet later at the Humboldt Sink or in the San Joaquin Valley, depending on circumstances.

This was all right by Walker, but he refused to leave until Chiles bought a few head of expensive beef cattle to supply the wagon train with fresh meat. This Chiles managed to do, and the two groups went their separate ways. Later, Walker sent two men back to Fort Hall to coerce the chief factor into selling them some vitally needed food supplies. As it turned out, this brash act may have saved their lives.

To make a long story shorter, Chiles was able to buy only a little food at Fort Boise. As a result, he and his half-starved men blazed a new trail to Sutter's Fort, via the Malheur River and into the northeast corner of California. After passing snow-capped Mt. Shasta, they continued south through the upper Sacramento Valley to John Sutter's newly built fort on the American River. They arrived there in early November 1843, exhausted and half starved. Chiles knew it was far too late to meet Walker at the Humboldt Sink. Instead, he obtained food supplies and horses from Sutter and traveled south to search the San Joaquin Valley for Walker's party.

Meanwhile, Walker had guided his people safely along the Mary's River and past the sink, probably following his 1833 route part of the way. But this time he continued farther south into present-day Owens Valley. There the livestock gave out and all wagons were abandoned. Chiles' associate, William Baldridge, had stayed with the wagons to help escort the women and children and to look after Chiles' precious mill-irons. He then faced the unpleasant task of burying the irons in the alkaline sands.

Once everyone had abandoned all but absolute necessities, those absolutes were packed on the remaining livestock and Walker guided the footsore emigrants over his pass into the comparative safety of the San Joaquin Valley. Finding no sign of Chiles, he led the group across the valley to the Salinas River near Mission Soledad. There they found plenty of game. The climate proved mild enough despite it being mid-December. After spending Christmas together, the party split into smaller groups and made their way north. Some ended up at Sutter's Fort, where Chiles reappeared after being unable to find them. Although the long journey had proven a fiasco, all the travelers had survived, and many went on to personal greatness.

As FOR Joseph Walker, he went to Monterey for a Mexican passport and then headed south toward Los Angeles. In 1844 he acquired a herd of horses and drove them east over the Old Spanish Trail. Upon reaching the Mountain Meadows in present-day Utah, he caught up with John C. Fremont, who was returning east from his first trip to California (see Fremont). Although Fremont had frontiersmen Kit Carson, Thomas Fitzpatrick and Alex Godey with him, he chose Walker to guide them to Bent's Fort on the Arkansas River. These men respected Walker's knowledge and reputation as a trailblazer, and apparently there was no resentment.

Walker left Fremont at Bent's Fort and returned to Fort Laramie on the Platte River. Somewhere along the way he sold off his horses. From Fort Laramie he guided a party of emigrants captained by Cornelius Gillium to Fort Bridger, where he spent the winter of 1844-45 with his wife. The following spring found Walker, his wife and Bill Williams with Fremont's party exploring the Great Salt Lake. There Walker and Williams had a dispute, and Williams left. Pushing across present-day Nevada, Fremont decided to split his party. He placed Lieutenant Edward Kern in charge of one group, with Walker acting as his pilot. Apparently Walker's wife left him there to return to Fort Bridger with some other Indians.

LATER WALKER and Fremont met at the southernmost lake Walker had discovered a decade earlier in present-day Nevada. Fremont named the lake, and the river feeding it, after Walker. Walker then led one group south and across his Sierra Nevada pass, which was also named in his honor. Fremont took the remainder over Carson Pass, and they met near San Jose in February 1846. After traveling to Monterey, Fremont received permission from Gen. José Castro to explore the area.

Apparently Castro had second thoughts about this decision, or was ordered to revoke it. When Castro informed Captain Fremont that he must leave the territory, the haughty captain took offense and moved his men to the heights of Gavilan Peak overlooking San Juan Bautista. There he established a strong defensive position and dared Castro to dislodge him. Although Castro bluffed an attack, he finally backed off.

After a few days of Castro's blustering, Fremont tired of the dangerous game and began evacuating his position. By then Walker had grown disgusted with the game-playing and decided to leave. When Fremont led his men north toward the Oregon border via Sutter's Fort, Walker left to visit his friend, John Gilroy, at his ranch near Monterey. From then on Walker had no use for Fremont, stating that "he [Fremont] was timid as a woman if it were not casting an unmerited reproach on the sex." [5]

Walker then headed south to Southern California, where he again acquired a herd of horses. He and some drovers, including Solomon Sublette, drove the herd over Cajon Pass and north to Fort Hall via the newly established California Trail. Walker continued on to Fort Bridger, presumably to rejoin his wife and family. By then the Mexican War had begun, and Fremont returned to California from Oregon to play an important role in the subsequent conquest of California.

Walker sold most of his horses to emigrants at Fort Bridger before driving the remainder to Bent's Fort that fall. He apparently remained there until his horses were sold to the U.S. Army. Walker seems to have disappeared for about six months before reappearing in the Santa Fe area in March 1847 with Solomon Sublette. He then headed east to Missouri to deliver letters from west-bound emigrants and visit old friends and relatives. He sat out the rest of the Mexican War in Independence.

There has been speculation as to why Walker avoided the war rather than take part in it. Perhaps it was because of his disillusionment with Fremont, or possibly he had lost his wife and was in mourning. There is no record of her after late 1846. At any rate, Walker decided to return to California, which now belonged to the U. S., during the autumn of 1847, taking along two nephews, Frank McClellan and James Walker, nicknamed Jeems.

By the time frigid weather set in, they had reached Henry's Fork on the Green River, where they spent a long, miserable winter. In May 1848, the two younger men went on to Fort Laramie, where they joined a wagon train heading for California. Walker remained behind for a few months before going to California on his own. By coincidence, Fremont and a party guided by Bill Williams left to cross the Rockies a short time later. They sought a railroad route, but the expedition met with disaster when many were lost by starvation and freezing. Among those lost was Bill Williams, who was killed by Indians while attempting to recover lost equipment. Fremont barely escaped alive and ultimately made his way into California, where he had purchased a ranch sight unseen.

WALKER ARRIVED in California during the fall of 1848. His timing couldn't have been better, for he was there at the beginning of the mad-paced Gold Rush. Apparently attracted by the gold, Joel Walker brought his family from Oregon about the same time. They had visited California in late 1841, but this time they settled in the Napa Valley, where Joel bought a ranch. About a year later he served as a delegate to the Constitutional Convention in Monterey.

Meanwhile, Joseph Walker acquired property in the vicinity of present-day Gilroy, where he collected and fattened livestock for sale. Rather than dig for gold, he scoured the land for cattle, which his four nephews drove to the gold fields and sold for huge profits. But even the excitement of the gold rush could not hold the aging Walker in one place for very long.

By early 1851 he was leading an expedition with his nephew Jeemes on the upper Virgin River. After exploring fascinating Zuni and Hopi villages, they returned to California the following year with tales of confrontations with hostile Navajo and Apache Indians. The *Los Angeles Star* noted in its news column of December 13, 1851:

> Captain Joe Walker, the renowned mountaineer, has arrived from New Mexico with a company of twelve men...Capt. W. had a slight skirmish with the Apaches, but saving that, had no trouble with Indians. [6]

For a few years Walker acquired and fattened cattle in the vicinity of present-day Gilroy, but by 1855 he was leading a prospecting expedition to explore the area around Mono Lake. Though they found gold ore there, Walker left before the rich gold towns of Bodie and Esmeralda were established. Meanwhile, Jeemes Walker brought part of the Walker clan from Missouri to a ranch he acquired on the western slope of Mt. Diablo near present-day Martinez. He soon married and bought more land to add to his "Manzanita Ranch" property.

AFTER RETURNING to California, Joseph Walker sold his interests in Gilroy and used the Manzanita Ranch (today's Concord) as his base of operations. In 1858 he and William Goodyear were piloting army troops to the Colorado River in a campaign against hostile Mojave Indians. When he returned to California a year later, he claimed to have found gold near the muddy Colorado River. He then piloted a party of gold seekers over his pass, across the Mojave Desert to the Colorado River, and then across the Rockies to the vicinity of Denver.

Unable to reach his previous gold discovery site because of hostile Indians in what became Arizona, Walker continued on into New Mexico. By 1862 the Civil War had reached New Mexico and Confederates were fighting Union forces in the area. Because Walker and some of his men were Southerners, they were accused of being rebel spies. Though there was no truth to it, it did cause trouble for them for a short time. But this was nothing compared to the trouble the Apaches caused when a large band led by Mangus Coloradas began pursuing Walker and his men.

Only Walker's skill as a frontiersman saved them from disaster, for he evaded the determined hostiles and led his grateful followers to safety in the heart of the Arizona wilderness near present-day Prescott. There Walker established a camp and the men spread out to prospect the area for gold. When a substantial strike was made on Lynx Creek, the camp was moved there and Walker built himself a cabin. Later Fort Whipple was established and Prescott, located in the midst of Walker's Diggings, was named capital of the territory.

By 1867 Walker was nearly seventy years of age; with his eyesight failing, he moved back to California to live with Jeemes Walker on his Manzanita ranch. In time he became a local celebrity when journalists came to interview him about his many adventurous exploits. As his robust health began to fail, he made the simple request that his gravestone should be inscribed, "Camped at Yosemite November 13, 1833." Despite Walker's many accomplishments, this single discovery apparently stood out in his mind as his most important. He died on the ranch October 27, 1876, just short of his 78th birthday. He was buried at the Alhambra Cemetery in Martinez, where Jeemes Walker erected a monument with the following inscription:

Born In Roan County, Tenn—Dec 13, 1798
Emigrated to MO—1819
To New Mexico—1820
Rocky Mountains—1832
California—1833
Camped At Yosemite—Nov. 13, 1833 [7]

ALTHOUGH Joseph R. Walker was not politically active in California and had little to do with it becoming a state, his trail-blazing contributions throughout the West certainly qualify him for a place on any honor-roll of early pioneers. Perhaps the best summation of Walker's unique and colorful life was penned by Historian Hubert H. Bancroft:

Capt. Joe Walker was one of the bravest and most skilful of the mountain men; none was better acquainted than he with the geography or the native tribes of the great basin; and he was withal less boastful and pretentious than most of his class. In his old age he was moved by the absurd praise accorded to a "pathfinder" [Fremont] who had merely followed the tracks of himself and his trapper associates....[8]

In addition to Walker's name being carried by a river originating in California, and the Nevada lake it feeds, it carries over to a small town south of the Nevada border on Highway 395 and the mountain pass on Highway178, leading from the Owens Valley into Bakersfield.

BIBLIOGRAPHY

–Bancroft, Hubert H. *History of California.* History Co., San Francisco, 1885-86. [8]

–Chaitin, Peter M., et al. *Story of the Great American West.* Reader's Digest Ass'n., Inc. Pleasantville, New York, 1977.

–Cleland, Robert Glass. *This Reckless Breed of Men.* Alfred A. Knopf, New York, 1950.

–De Voto, Bernard. *The Year of Decision-1846.* Houghton Mifflin Co., Boston, 1942.

–Egan, Ferol. *Fremont, Explorer for a Restless Nation.* University of Nevada Press, Reno, 1985.

–Fisher, Ron, et al. *Into The Wilderness.* National Geographic Society, Washington, DC, 1978. [2]

–Giffen, Helen S. *Trail-Blazing Pioneer, Colonel Joseph Ballinger Chiles.* John Howell Books, San Francisco, 1969.

–Gilbert, Bil. *Westering Man.* Atheneum, New York, 1983. [5, 6, 7]

–Hafen, LeRoy R., ed. *Mountain Men and Fur Traders of the Far West.* University of Nebraska Press, Lincoln, 1982. [1, 3, 4]

–Stewart, George R. *The California Trail.* University of Nebraska Press, Lincoln, 1962.

– 45 –

SARAH MONTGOMERY WALLIS

1825 – 1905

THOUGH PASSABLE ROUTES had been blazed to California by Joseph R. Walker in 1833 and the Bartleson-Bidwell Party in 1841, one would not have known it by the time the Stevens-Murphy Party traveled it three years later (see Bartleson-Bidwell, Walker & Murphy). It was August 1844, at the confluence of the Raft and Snake rivers in present southern Idaho, when the Stevens-Murphy Party split off from the main party, which was heading for Oregon. That same month Sarah Montgomery celebrated her 19th birthday.

Born into a Ohio farm family named Armstrong in 1825, Sarah was around nine when her family moved to Indiana. Five years later the Armstrongs were living in St. Joseph County, Missouri. In 1843 Sarah married an erstwhile gunsmith, Allen Montgomery. By the following year she and her husband had joined the Stevens-Murphy Party, heading west from Council Bluffs. They were piloted by Caleb "Old" Greenwood, who was said to be 80 years old, and two of his half-Indian sons. Though Greenwood had capably led them to Fort Hall, he had never been west of there and would be of little help beyond.

After splitting off from the main party west of Fort Hall, Elisha Stevens led the apprehensive group of about 40 emigrants (sixteen of whom were children) southwest into present Nevada. They roughly followed a route blazed by frontiersman Joseph R. Walker, which ran north of the one used by the Bartleson-Bidwell Party. There was grass and water enough along the way, and they reached Marys River (the Humboldt) in fairly good condition. The trail from there followed the river westerly to the sink, where it disappeared into the alkaline sands of the desert. After crossing what became known as the "forty-mile desert," they reached the life-giving waters of the Truckee River, where they turned directly west into the dreaded Sierra Nevada range.

When they reached the place where the river veered south toward its source (present Lake Tahoe), a few riders took that route, while the main party with the wagons continued west to Truckee Lake (now

Donner lake). It was fall by then; already two feet of snow blanketed the ground, making it difficult for the stock to feed. Glancing up the precipitous granite walls looming over them, the exhausted emigrants knew they'd never make it with all ten wagons. Reluctantly they agreed to leave half of them there under the care of three volunteers. The others would go ahead and return later with fresh livestock and provisions.

ONE WHO AGREED to stay behind was Allen Montgomery, along with Moses Schallenberger, who was still a teen-ager, and Joseph Foster. They immediately set to work building a log cabin, while the others began the horrendous task of lifting five wagons up the almost sheer granite walls to the summit. Looking at those forbidding precipices today, one can only wonder how they did it. The wagons had to be emptied and disassembled, then hauled up by teams of oxen placed strategically on the few wide ledges that existed. Watching her husband waving goodbye from far below, Sarah Montgomery was weeping when she climbed out of sight over the summit. Certainly she wondered whether she would ever see him again.

One would think that once the wagons were over the summit, the rest of the journey into the Sacramento Valley would have been relatively easy. This was not the case; a heavy snowstorm closed in before they eached the lower elevations. They were further delayed when Mrs. Martin Murphy gave birth to a daughter along the way, on the Yuba River. Named Elizabeth Yuba Murphy, she was probably the first Anglo child born in what later became Nevada County.

With four feet of snow on the ground and the livestock starving, the emigrants decided that the last of the wagons would have to be left behind at a place called Big Bend, near the head of the Yuba River. They threw up a crude log cabin and slaughtered livestock to provide a frozen food supply for the women and children and the two men who were delegated to stay with them. The others left on horseback to seek help.

They hoped to reach Sutter's Fort and bring back provisions and fresh oxen to recover their wagons. Imagine Sarah Montgomery's surprise when her husband and Joseph Foster showed up in mid-December. They had made their way from Truckee Lake on crude, homemade snow-shoes. Nearly out of food, they had been forced to leave Moses Schallenberger behind when he was unable to climb the summit. They felt confident he would be all right at the cabin until help could be sent back.

A few days later, Sarah's husband and Joseph Foster left for Sutter's Fort to find the men who had gone ahead. They arrived there shortly before Christmas 1844. Incredible as it seems, John A. Sutter managed to coerce these men into joining his rag-tag volunteers to fight in the mini-revolution between Mexican Governor Micheltorena and a band of dissidents working to overthrow him. Sutter had pledged to help the governor and was recruiting men wherever he could. Somehow he convinced the new arrivals that the snow was too deep to return to the mountains, and that their families would be safe until spring. Sutter and his makeshift army left for San Jose on New Year's Day 1845. Later some of the men deserted.

One of them was Dennis Martin, whose father was stranded at Big Bend. Dennis returned to Sutter's Fort to outfit himself for a rescue attempt and left on February 20th. It had been a relatively mild winter and Martin reached the camp in about a week. He was shocked to find women and children existing on boiled ox-hides; their food had run out long before. When other rescuers arrived a short time later, arrangements were made to evacuate the camp. Allen Montgomery was probably in this last group.

Meanwhile, Martin had snowshoed over the summit to Truckee Lake to check on Moses Schallenberger. Surprisingly, he found him not only alive but able to travel. He had been subsisting mostly on foxes he had trapped. By March 1, 1845, the last of the stranded party was brought safely to Sutter's Fort. Though their wagons had been abandoned temporarily, this was the first emigrant party to bring wagons across the Sierra.

SHORTLY AFTER Sutter's return to his fort that spring, he sent Allen and Sarah Montgomery to the "Pine Woods", a few miles up Sutter Creek in present-day Amador County, where timber was being whipsawed by hand into badly needed lumber. Later the Montgomerys built a cabin somewhere in the area. Sutter noted in his diary on January 29, 1846, "All the people attended a quilting party at Mrs. Montgomery's."

This had to be the first such affair in the area. Considering the distances involved, a surprising number of women attended. According to some records, there could have been twenty people there, mostly women, of course. Allen Montgomery participated in the Bear Flag Rebellion in June 1846, when he joined Ezekial Merritt, James Gregson and other disgruntled settlers to steal a herd of horses from the Mexican Army at John Murphy's Ranch. When John C. Fremont arrived to take over Sutter's Fort and assist the Bear Flaggers, Montgomery and Gregson joined his California Volunteers (see Fremont & Gregson).

During their absence, both wives shared quarters at Sutter's Fort with Mrs. Leahy and her two girls. Mrs. Leahy's husband, Daniel, also had joined Fremont. Sarah Montgomery, who had little education, attended classes in reading and writing taught by Mrs. Gregson. Sarah remained there until the spring of 1847, when her husband returned from the war.

Historian Hubert H. Bancroft says in his book, *History of California,* "[A. Montgomery] went to Honolulu on the Julia in '47, and I find no further record of him." He apparently deserted his wife and later may have died; she and Montgomery never had children. Sarah married Talbot Green in October 1849. Green, a former member of the 1841 Bartleson-Bidwell Party, had become a prominent, wealthy merchant in San Francisco.

Talbot Green had come to California posing as a physician, carrying with him a heavy bag of metal he claimed was lead for rifle-balls. He was running for mayor of San Francisco in 1851 when he was denounced as being Paul Geddes, a fugitive bank clerk from Pennsylvania who had deserted his wife and children a decade earlier. Presumably the bag of "lead" was gold stolen from the Pennsylvania bank. Of course Green denied it all and left his pregnant wife to sail for the East Coast to "clear his name." He later wrote his business partner Thomas O. Larkin and admitted his guilt.

Sarah Montgomery Green apparently had her illegal marriage annulled or divorced Green shortly thereafter, and took in boarders for a time. In July 1854, at age 29 and with a young son to raise, she married Joseph S. Wallis, a prominent attorney and politician from Santa Clara County. Wallis later became a judge and a State Senator. Bancroft states (Vol. IV, p. 743): "In 1885 Mrs. Wallis was living in Mayfield (now Palo Alto) 'taking part sometimes in public meetings of progressive and strong minded females.'"

IN 1856 Sarah acquired Mayfield Farm from Elisha Crosby in her own name, an unusual event in those days. The Wallises built a large home there, surrounded by orchards and gardens. Sarah became deeply involved in community affairs and championed several causes, including bringing the railroad station to Mayfield and starting the first women's club. In addition she lobbied the State Legislature in Sacramento for women's right issues: Bills allowing property rights for women, access to state colleges for women and allowing women to practice law. [1]

Sarah became president of the California Women's Suffrage Association in 1870, and entertained Susan B. Anthony at Mayfield Farm. After the Wallises suffered financial losses in 1878, they sold Mayfield Farm and moved to a smaller place nearby. [2] Judge Joseph Wallis died in 1898, and Sarah moved to Los Gatos, where she died January 11, 1905. Both she and her husband were buried at Union Cemetery in Redwood City. Today, on La Selva near the site of Sarah's house in Palo Alto, is a state historic plaque honoring her. The house burned down in 1936.

Sarah Wallis mothered five children, of whom a son was fathered by T. H. Green a short time after their marriage. This boy, Talbot H. Green

Wallis, later became the California State Librarian in Sacramento. Another son, Joseph B. Wallis, was a lawyer in Sacramento when he died at the age of twenty-three. There were two girls, Eva Wallis Hess and Josephine Wallis Ingalls; both had previous marriages. Another son, William A. Wallis, lived in Oakland.

Sarah Wallis, after having survived the harrowing trip across the Sierras in winter, was apparently the first to tame the wilderness with a quilting bee. Unfortunately she died six years before women won the right to vote in California.

BIBLIOGRAPHY

–Foote, H. S. *Pen Pictures from the Garden of the World, Santa Clara.* The Lewis Publishing Co., Chicago, 1888. Republished, Pacific Press, Oakland, CA.

–Garoutte, Sally. *California's first Quilting Party.* Mill Valley, CA, 1982.

–Gregson, James and Eliza. *The Gregson Memoirs.* Reprinted from California History Quarterly, 1940.

–Gullard, Pamela & Nancy Lund. *History of Palo Alto: The Early Years.* Scottwall Associates, 1989. [1 & 2 partially quoted from this publication.]

–Kelly & Morgan. *Old Greenwood.* Talisman Press, Georgetown, CA, 1965.

–Stewart, George R. *The Opening of the California Trail.* (Memoirs of M. Schallenberger). Truckee, CA, 1953.

–Sutter, John A., et al. *New Helvetia Diary.* Sacramento, CA, 1845-48. Grabhorn Press, San Francisco, 1932.

Charles D. Weber
Courtesy California State Library

- 46 -

CHARLES D. WEBER
(Don Carlos Maria) *1814 – 1881*

A MONG OTHER European emigrants settling in what became known as the "Wild West" was Charles Weber. Like John Sutter, he was from Germany. But unlike Sutter, Weber sprang from a conservative religious background of Protestant ministers, and he was trained to continue the long family tradition. Instead, he came to America and became an intrepid frontiersman, soldier, Indian fighter, gold miner and all around successful entrepreneur.

Weber, a native of Steinwenden in the Homburg district in Germany, entered the world February 17, 1814, as Carl D. Weber. His father, Carl Gottfried Weber, was a minister of the Reformed Protestant Church in Steinwenden, as were his father and grandfather before him. Carl's mother was the former Henriette Geul, daughter of Protestant minister Johann David Geul.

Carl was determined that his son should follow in his footsteps as a minister, and his religious education began early. Over the next decade four more sons and a daughter followed: Johann C., Juliana P., Philipp, Ludwig and Carl L., a.k.a. Adolph. Young Carl D. attended school in Homburg until he was twelve, at which time he entered a preparatory school in Zweibrucken. He did well there until King Ludwig I of Bavaria changed the curriculum, and required that all students be of the Catholic faith.

His Protestant family found this intolerable; Carl left the school, and continued his education with private tutors. When he was nearly eighteen, and ready to enter the university, he suffered "loss of Memory"–said to be from overwork–and could not continue formal study. Instead, he found he had a flair for merchandising and went into business for himself, apparently starting at his uncle's gristmill.

Political foment gripped the country at the time, and in 1836 Carl obtained permission from his father to visit an uncle, who had emigrated to Illinois in the U.S.A. a year earlier. He set off, accompanied by a cousin, Theodore Engelmann; by September they were in Paris. This was a thrilling, worldly experience for twenty-two year-old Carl, who had led a closely supervised and religious life until then. He was described as being "five feet, ten inches tall, with dark hair and brows. His complexion was healthy, his nose and mouth average, and his chin round." [1]

By late September the cousins were in Le Havre waiting for their ship, which sailed in early October. Because they intended to reach Carl's uncle in Illinois via the Mississippi River, they landed in New Orleans at the end of November. Learning that the river was already blocked by ice, Weber elected to stay in New Orleans, while Engelmann went overland to Illinois. It was probably then that Carl changed his name to Charles.

In New Orleans, Charles Weber became involved in several business ventures, until he was felled by a bout with the dreaded yellow fever. Upon his recovery he apparently decided to risk severing relations with his family–at least for awhile. Perhaps his visit to Paris had unleashed a passion for adventure; at any rate, he traveled to Texas. There he joined Sam Houston's forces in the fight for Texas independence from Mexico.

WEBER WAS BACK in New Orleans by 1840, where he failed in a restaurant business. After suffering a recurrence of his illness, Weber was warned to seek a cooler climate. Then his father wrote, instructing him to come home. His passport, which authorized a visit only, had long expired, and his family wanted him back in Germany. But Weber recognized his chances for independence in America and did not mean to leave, even if it meant alienating his family.

Seeking cooler weather, Weber borrowed $500 and took a steamboat up the Mississippi with the intent of finally visiting his uncle in Illinois. It was early spring when he reached St. Louis, Missouri, a bustling frontier community that had long been a staging area for the fabulous fur trade. It was there he learned of opportunities in the Far West.

Before long Weber was in Independence, Missouri, where he read letters published in newspapers telling about the wonders of California. Weber may also have attended lectures by frontiersmen Antoine Robidoux, who also extolled advantages of the new promised land. It was probably then that he befriended Henry Huber, another young German emigrant who was interested in California.

In early spring 1841 Weber and Huber joined the Western Emigration Society, which left Sapling Grove in early May with around 60 men, women and children. Most used two-wheeled carts and canvas-covered farm wagons pulled by oxen, although mules and horses were used by some. Within a matter of days others had joined until membership totaled around 77, about half of whom were bound for Oregon.

Experienced frontiersman Thomas Fitzpatrick had been hired to pilot a party of Catholic missionaries led by Father P. J. DeSmet. This turned out fortunate for them all (see Bartleson-Bidwell).

Weber and Huber attached themselves to a "mess," a small group who shared cooking chores, with John Bartleson—who was elected captain of the entire party—Joseph Chiles, Talbot Green and two other German emigrants, Charles Hopper and Robert Rickman. The journey to Oregon followed the fledgling Oregon Trail, but no emigrant train had ever attempted to enter California.

Details of this fascinating adventure are covered in other sections of this book and will not be repeated here. After abandoning their wagons northwest of the Great Salt Lake, they managed to cross the treacherous Sierra Nevada range and reached the safety of John Marsh's ranch by late fall. Marsh's ranch, located on the eastern slope of distinctive Mt. Diablo, was one of the few non-Mexican settlements west of John Sutter's New Helvetia (see Marsh).

Along with others from the party, Weber went to the pueblo of San Jose to apply for a passport from Mexican authorities. Despite the fact that most of them were temporarily jailed in the San Jose *calabozo* for entering the country without permission, Weber liked what he saw. But first he spent the winter at John A. Sutter's New Helvetia settlement on the Sacramento River. He moved to San Jose the following spring, and before long he entered into a partnership with William Gulnac to open a store, blacksmith shop, flour mill and bakery.

WEBER ALSO opened the "Weber House," a small hotel and saloon, operated a salt works, made tallow soap and candles, and started a leather tannery from which he made boots and shoes. In short, he did anything he could to make money. Within two years Weber acquired a half interest in the 48,000-acre *Rancho El Campo de los Franceses* (French Camp) owned by William Gulnac. Because he needed to become a Mexican citizen to acquire land, he was baptized a Catholic—a big step for a confirmed Protestant. Later Gov. Manuel Micheltorena approved his Mexican citizenship, after which Weber bought out Gulnac's interest in the ranch and purchased another smaller ranch southeast of San Jose. Soon he was known as Carlos Maria Weber, and was doing so well he thought himself to be "Lord of the Country."

In late 1844, Mexican *Commandante* José Castro had asked Weber to help recruit foreign settlers to help unseat Governor Micheltorena because of his unruly and despised *cholo* troops. Weber agreed, and by November he was parading a small force in San Jose.

Having learned of the planned rebellion in late November, Gov. Micheltorena marched his troops from Monterey toward San Jose to confront Castro. Castro then retreated from San Jose to Mission Santa

Clara, leaving San Jose undefended. To protect the thriving town, Weber contacted the governor—who was camped at Laguna Seca—and pleaded with him to bypass San Jose. He feared many depredations would take place if the governor's undisciplined troops were allowed to enter.

When the governor refused his plea, Weber immediately raised volunteers to defend the town from the looters they expected. Castro then joined with Weber, and with combined forces of about 220 men, they confronted Micheltorena in the hills of Rancho Santa Teresa. Following several days of negotiations, the governor signed the Treaty of Laguna Seca or Santa Teresa, binding him to expel the worst of his officers and men from his service. Later he reneged on his promise, thus exacerbating the rebellelion.

John Sutter, another naturalized Mexican citizen, saw things differently (see Sutter). He accused Weber of treason against the governor and jailed him and two henchmen at Sutter's Fort during the subsequent uprising. Shortly after New Years Day 1845, Sutter led a motley band of volunteers to reinforce Micheltorena's *cholos*. After marching south to Los Angeles, he and the governor were defeated by Castro and his rebels at Cahuenga Pass in a virtually bloodless artillery duel.

Sutter was arrested but finally released by the rebels and was fortunate to retain his previous land grants, rights and privileges. When Pío Pico was named the new governor, he moved the capital from Monterey to Los Angeles. After Weber was freed from Sutter's jail, General Castro named him a captain in the Mexican army. Despite this gesture, the wily Weber was conspiring with Marsh and others to unite foreign settlers to overthrow the weak new government and declare the territory independent from Mexican rule.

NATURALLY WEBER saw himself as a leader of the new country, possibly even president. John Marsh probably wished the same for himself, but their fantasies were interrupted by the arrival of Capt. John C. Fremont and his party of U.S. Army "topographers" (see Fremont). Fremont had traveled overland to California during the winter of 1845-46 and had run afoul of General Castro. Weber was elated when he learned in March that Fremont had fortified his troops on Gavilan Peak and defied General Castro in a "Mexican standoff." Weber wasted no time trying to exploit this event, in the following letter he wrote to Marsh:

> I will form the Electric chain of Facts, more terrible than Thunder and Lightning, hurrican, vulcanic Eruptions! Hear! Hear! Great News! War! War! Capt. Fremont...with 60 or more riflemen has fortified himself on the hights between San Juan [Bautista] & De Juaquin Gomeres Ranch the Stars and Stripes fleying over their

Camps. José Castro and 2 or 300 hundred Californians with Artillery are beseiging his position...I think I will see the repitition of the Texas History in this Country. [2]

This rather garbled message clearly points out Weber's excitement at the possibility of war, and may explain why he took part in the battle for Texas. But before Marsh received this message, Fremont had withdrawn his forces and led them north toward Oregon to await further developments. After learning of the Bear Flag Rebellion in mid-June, Weber wavered between loyalty to General Castro and to the United States. When Castro ordered him to help put down the rebellion, he replied:

[I am] compelled to decline said appointment because the various forms of circumstance, and my business engagements prohibit me from accepting said appointment. I beg of you take this into consideration and excuse me of said command. I hereby also explain that I am ready to execute any service under your authority. [3]

Castro excused Weber, ordering him to return any arms and ammunition in his possession. Weber then made his way to Yerba Buena (San Francisco) to find Fremont. He and some friends found him at San Rafael, and when they offered to oppose the Mexicans if the Americans would furnish them with arms, they were apparently rebuffed. Despite Fremont's refusal, he may have approved a plan to allow Weber and his companions to recruit a secret defense force for San Jose; this they did.

But when loyal Mexicans in the San Jose area learned of Weber's alleged treachery, he was arrested and forced to seek refuge in General Castro's army to protect himself. Possibly taken as a prisoner, he was with them in July when they retreated south toward Los Angeles, following U.S. Navy Commodore John Sloat's successful invasion of Monterey.

THERE WAS LITTLE hostility toward the Americans in Northern California at the time. Conditions were fairly stable when Fremont's California Volunteers sailed south from Monterey to help secure Southern California. By then Comm. John Sloat had been replaced by Commodore Robert Stockton, who worked closely with Fremont. When Mexican forces in Los Angeles learned that Stockton and Fremont were on their way with strong naval forces, most gave up and the army was disbanded.

General Castro and Pío Pico then fled to Mexico, leaving General Andres Pico in charge of what forces remained. Charles Weber was apparently placed on parole by the occupying forces, as were other Mexican soldiers. Fremont was named Military Commandant by Stockton and ordered north to set up a government, leaving Captain Gillespie in charge of southern forces. Weber returned overland with one of Fremont's companies, arriving in Monterey the first week in September. Unfortunately Gillespie proved too much of a military martinet for the formerly peaceful Mexicans in Los Angeles. At the end of September an outbreak took place, and Gillespie and his men were driven to San Pedro to seek sanctuary aboard a merchant vessel there. A rider was sent north to inform Stockton about the rebellion and to seek reinforcements.

While Stockton was reorganizing his forces to sail back to Southern California, he named Weber a sergeant in charge of the militia in San Jose under command of U.S. Navy Captain John Montgomery. The navy captain's orders to Weber read: "Endeavor to the extent of your means, to secure all in the enjoyment of their [the *Californios*] rights and property and to maintain good order within the bounds of your command." [4]

At last Weber had the command he sought, and he was eager to exploit it to the fullest. He recruited 65 men rather than the 10 authorized, which he promptly and dramatically named "Weber's Rangers," from his Texas days. Montgomery then ordered Weber to keep the Stars and stripes flying in San Jose and "to take charge of all arms found in the possession of Californians residing in the towns of San Jose and Santa Clara and their vicinities." [5]

Rather than seizing only arms, Weber directed his men to seize livestock, mainly horses for Fremont. This resulted in loud protests from *rancheros* to U.S. officials demanding Weber's removal, but he continued in power, with the blessing of Montgomery. Apparently acting on orders from Fremont to gather horses, saddles and supplies for his volunteers, Weber redoubled his efforts. He and his men became even more ruthless as they ranged over the countryside, stripping helpless *rancheros* of horses and tack they desperately needed to operate their own ranches.

Montgomery expected an uprising because of the revolt in Southern California and placed Lt. Lansford Hastings in command of the militia in San Jose during Weber's absence (see Hastings). This freed Weber for even more depredations. He was authorized to offer scrip in payment of what was confiscated, but record-keeping was sporadic at best and many frustrated *rancheros* received neither scrip nor payment.

One of the worst blows came when Weber's men raided Rancho Buri-Buri, the ranch of José de la Cruz Sanchez, a brother of Francisco Sanchez, the former *commandante* of Mexican forces in Yerba Buena. Francisco Sanchez had surrendered to U.S. occupation forces early in the invasion after being persuaded that Mexicans in the area would not be molested. But now that this agreement had been violated, the furious commandante began recruiting armed followers to fight back. Depredations against the *rancheros* ended when Fremont led his forces south toward Los Angeles in late November, but the Mexicans were not through yet. The heated caldron came to a boil when U.S. Navy forces arrested Manuel Sanchez, brother of Francisco and José Sanchez. The furious Sanchez brothers immediately mobilized their armed *ranchero* volunteers and moved against a small U.S. occupation force under Navy Lt. Washington Bartlett, alcalde at Yerba Buena.

MEANWHILE, increasing numbers of immigrants from the East had been arriving overland from Missouri. Arriving at Sutter's Fort in the fall of 1846, they found the place a virtual mad-house. Fremont had taken over the fort from John Sutter and used it as a staging area for recruiting and training exercises for his California Volunteers. Many newly arrived men were recruited. The remainder, including older men, women and children, were directed to seek sanctuary from possible hostile Mexican troops at Mission Santa Clara (see Hecox).

After the aggressive Mexicans captured Bartlett and some of his men, U.S. Navy Capt. William Mervine ordered a force of about 100 men sent out to locate and free them. This force was made up of naval seamen, marines and mounted volunteers, including Charles Weber and most of his rangers. With them they had a 6-pound field-piece hauled on a crude cart by plodding oxen. Marine Captain Ward Marston was named commander.

Meanwhile Sanchez's volunteers had moved their captives outside Mission Santa Clara, where they made camp. On New Year's Day, 1847, their scouts reported sighting U.S. forces hauling their small cannon along the crest of the coastal range. Later, scouts from Weber's Rangers sighted the Mexicans' encampment and preparations were made to attack them the next morning.

Though the cannon became bogged down in mud along the way, Captain Marston's men and Weber's Rangers managed to free it. Finally it was put into place facing Mexican forces, who were maneuvering on horseback within sight of the mission. Staying out of musket range, the Mexican horsemen feigned an attack which brought a quick response from the field-piece loaded with grapeshot. After the big gun fired several noisy but relatively ineffective salvos, the Mexicans retreated. Casualties were slight, consisting of a dead horse and one or two slightly wounded men on both sides.

When a grim-faced messenger arrived under a white flag, negotiations commenced for a cease-fire. A treaty was negotiated on January 7th and the short-lived "Battle of Santa Clara" was over. About a month later, Weber was thanked for his services and discharged from military duty. After disbanding his rangers, he left San Jose for his huge, undeveloped French Camp Ranch. The move to his wilderness ranch on the San Joaquin River was risky, because hostile Indians frequented the area.

Probably the main reason Gulnac sold out his interest to Weber was his previous unsuccessful attempts to settle the land. Weber had one telling advantage; he had previously befriended the powerful Indian chief, José Jesus, who had taken over after the death of Chief Estanislao.

Weber wasted little time in negotiating a peace treaty with the chief, who helped him tame local Indians. He also began wooing newly arrived emigrants to assist him with promises of land. Though the ranch had been called French Camp and the adjacent settlement Tuleberg (Tuleburgh), Weber named it Stockton in honor of Commodore Robert Stockton. For many years people called it Weber's Embarcadero.

Weber had learned to deal with Indians during his early days with Sutter, using a combination of reward and punishment. The punishment part was severely tested in early January 1848, when a large band of Indians from outside the area raided the ranches of Robert Livermore, Martinez and Pacheco, stealing many of their horses. At the urging of the ranchers, Weber organized a band of 200—mostly friendly Indians—and pursued the hostiles into the foothills.

Because of recent rains the going was slow and muddy, and by the time they reached the snowline where the Indian *rancherias* were located, they had evacuated the area. Weber recovered a few horses, but most had been killed and eaten before then. Weber and Sutter vowed to join forces in the spring to punish these marauding tribes, mostly made up of well-armed Polos and Chowchillas. Their plans were negated by news of James W. Marshall's exciting gold discovery a short time later (see Marshall)

Once the gold discovery became known, during the spring of 1848, Weber joined other eager argonauts to seek gold for himself. Quickly he engaged a band of local Indians to pan gold in exchange for trinkets, blankets and food. They struck gold on the Mokulumne River and worked their way north toward present Coloma, stopping on a creek west of Dry Diggings (Placerville), where they made a rich strike. The creek, which was named after Weber, was a heavy producer and Weber took a small fortune from it. Its richness was later described in a report written by U.S. Army Colonel Richard Mason:

> A small gutter not more than a hundred yards long, by four feet wide and two feet deep, was pointed out to me as one where two men—Wm. Daly [Daylor] and Perry McCoon—had, a short time before, obtained seventeen thousand dollars worth of gold. Captain Weber informed me that he knew these two men had employed four white men and about a hundred Indians, and that, at the end of one week's work, they paid off their party and had left ten thousand dollars [worth] of this gold. [6]

The gold town of Weberville was established on Weber Creek, just south of Dry Diggins, later named Hangtown and finally Placerville.

Nothing remains of Weberville today. Later, Weber led his mining party to the southern mines near the present-day town of Murphys, named after the Martin Murphy family who had come overland in 1844 (see Murphy). By then Weber was providing supplies to the miners, and he formed the Stockton Mining [and trading] Company to handle the commerce. Stockton swiftly became the major supply center for the southern mines. Land values soared, and Weber quickly became rich.

NOW THAT he was a wealthy man and an extensive land owner, Weber decided to take himself a bride. In November 1850, at the age of 36, he married Helen Murphy, daughter of Martin and Mary (Foley) Murphy. Helen was one of a small splinter group of the 1844 Stevens-Murphy Party who were first to cross the summit from the west side of present Lake Tahoe. While the City of Stockton was coming into its own, three children were born to the Webers: Charles Jr., Thomas J. and Julia H.

Weber went on to construct the finest mansion in the area, devoting many pleasant years to landscaping it, installing a complex irrigation system and making it a true showplace, admired by all. He was a generous man, well known for his philanthropic work and warm hospitality. Unfortunately, Weber's mental health apparently deteriorated during his later years. Hubert H. Bancroft described him as "eccentric to the verge of insanity, morbidly sensitive, avoiding his fellow men". [7] This may have been an exaggeration, but there is little doubt that he did became morose and withdrawn.

Weber died unexpectedly on May 4, 1881 at the age of 67, leaving his wife and three children. The funeral, held at St. Mary's Church, was elaborate; thousands of mourners passed by his casket to pay their respects. His good deeds were magnanimous; for example, newspapers mentioned that every schoolhouse but one was built on land that he donated. Helen Murphy Weber lived in the mansion until three years before her death on April 11, 1895.

Weber's shift in loyalties between Mexico and the United States, and between his Protestant upbringing and later Catholic conversion, picture him as an arch opportunist, which many of the foreign settlers were. And though his methods of acquiring livestock and supplies during the Mexican War may seem harsh and heartless today, we must weigh them against the adverse consequences to Fremont, and the final conquest of California, if he had failed.

When one considers Weber's background in Germany before his arrival in the U. S., his achievements seem astonishing, indeed. It's no wonder people living in Germany and other parts of Europe remain fascinated to this day about the "Wild West" adventures experienced by their pioneer countrymen. A large monument marks the site of Weber's lovely old home in Stockton; an entire wing in the San Joaquin County Museum (located off Highway 99 at Micke Grove Park near Lodi) replicates the interior of the mansion. A monument also marks French Camp, the site of Weber's ranch, which later was displaced by the city of Stockton.

BIBLIOGRAPHY

–Bancroft, Hubert H. *Pioneer Register and Index.* Dawson's Book Shop, Los Angeles, CA, 1964. [7]

–Dillon, Richard. *Fool's Gold.* Coward-McCann, Inc. New York, 1967.

–Gay, Theressa. *James W. Marshall, A Biography.* Talisman Press, Georgetown, CA, 1967.

–Hammond, George P. *The Weber Era in Stockton History.* The Friends of the Bancroft Library, University of California, Berkeley, 1982. [1 & 6]

–Harlow, Neal. *California Conquered.* University of California Press, Berkeley, 1982.

–Hartmann, Ilka S. *The Youth of Charles M. Weber, Founder of Stockton.* University of Pacific Press, Stockton, 1979.

–Regnery, Dorothy F. *The Battle of Santa Clara.* Smith & McKay Printing Co. San Jose, CA, 1978. [2, 3, 4, 5]

NOTES

Benjamin D. Wilson
Courtesy California State Library

– 47 –

BENJAMIN D. WILSON

(Don Benito)   1811 – 1878

IN 1845 BENJAMIN WILSON was a 34-year-old Tennessee trapper turned California ranchero. Horse-thieving Mojave Indians had been plaguing ranches in the Los Angeles area, and Wilson was leading a large force of potential Indian fighters to punish them. After climbing the mountains above San Bernardino, Wilson's party camped by a lake where the forest was infested with bears. Quite naturally they named the place Bear Lake. A dam later raised the water level, enlarging it to present-day Big Bear Lake.

Four days later they rode down the east side of the mountains into the Mojave Desert, where they found four of the thieving Indians they sought. Wilson's diary describes it as follows:

> My object was not to kill them, but to take them prisoners that they might give me information on the points I desired...The leading man of the four happened to be the very man of all others I was seeking for, viz., the famous marauder Joaquin who had been raised as a page of the church, in San Gabriel Mission, and for his depredations and outlawing, bore on his person the mark of the mission, that is, one of his ears cropped off and the iron brand on his lip. This is the only instance I ever saw or heard of this kind. That marking had not been done at the mission, but at one of its ranchos..Immediately that he [Joaquin] discovered the true state of things, he whipped from his quiver an arrow, strung it on his bow, and left nothing for me to do but shoot him in self defense; we both discharged our weapons at the same time. I had no chance to raise the gun to my shoulder, but fired it from my hand. His shot took effect in my right shoulder, and mine in his heart.
> The shock of his arrow in my shoulder caused me involuntarily to let my gun drop. My shot knocked him down disabled, but he discharged at me a tirade of abuse in the Spanish language such as I never heard surpassed...Those three men [Indians] actually fought eighty men in open plain till they were put to death [1].

Though the arrow that had wounded Wilson was said to be poisoned and caused him much pain and discomfort, it's obvious from his remarks that he admired the courage of Native Americans, possibly as a result of his experiences with Indians as a Santa Fe fur trapper in his younger years.

A NATIVE OF TENNESSEE, Benjamin Wilson was born in 1811. At the age of eight he was orphaned and apparently raised by relatives, who gave him a decent education. Little is known of his youth, except that he moved to Mississippi in his early teens, after which he joined a party of Santa Fe fur trappers. After a series of narrow escapes from hostile Apaches in the Southwest, he accompanied the Workman-Rowland wagon party on a journey into Southern California in 1841 on the Old Spanish Trail. This was the first wagon train to make this difficult trek.

Though Wilson had his heart set on the China trade, he was unable to make the right connections and gave it up to settle in Los Angeles. There he made many new friends, among them colorful figures such as Hugo Reid, Abel Stearns, Juan Bandini, Pio Pico and William Wolfskill, who he probably knew from his Santa Fe trapping days. (see separate chapters). By 1843 he had acquired enough money to purchase Rancho Jurapa, straddling present-day Riverside and San Bernardino Counties, from Juan Bandini. A year later he married 16-year-old Ramona Yorba, daughter of Don Bernardo Yorba of Rancho Santa Ana. As a welcome wedding gift, Yorba gave Wilson part of his vast rancho, which Wilson stocked with sheep and cattle. He was just getting a good start as a hacendado (ranch owner) in late 1844, when he sided in with rebel forces led by the Pico brothers and José Castro to overthrow Gov. Manuel Micheltorena. Early the next year Pio Pico was named the new governor; by then Wilson was known as Don Benito.

When U.S. forces under Commodore Robert Stockton and John C. Fremont invaded Los Angeles during the summer of 1846, Governor Pico and General Castro headed for Mexico (see Fremont & Pico). Stockton was greeted in Los Angeles by Wilson and John Rowland, who rode out with the news of Pico and Castro's departure. Though Wilson had strong ties to the Californios, his loyalty lay with the United States, and he joined the U.S. Army as a breveted captain.

Once the pueblo was secured, with no casualties on either side, Fremont and Stockton left the area, putting Marine Captain Archibald Gillespie in charge. The zealous marine enforced such harsh military discipline that the citizens rebelled. Don Benito thus reported:

> ...that, having established very obnoxious regulations, Gillespie upon frivolous pretexts had the most respectable men in the community brought before him for no other purpose than to humiliate them, as they thought. [2]

This eventually caused such resentment that paroled Mexican Captain José M. Flores enlisted a company of dissidents and attacked the outnumbered Americans. After a stalemate, Flores demanded Gillespie's surrender. Finally Flores led his men in an attack that forced an American retreat to San Pedro, where the frustrated Gillespie sought refuge for his men on a merchant ship.

Captain Benjamin Wilson's duties included guarding Cajon Pass near San Bernardino to prevent Mexican reinforcements from entering California. When he and about twenty men learned about Gillespie's difficulties in September, they rode to the Chino Rancho seeking William Workman. There they were attacked by a superior force of Mexicans, led by Serbulo Varela, including some of Wilson's own men who had switched sides. There were several casualties on both sides before Varela convinced Wilson and his men to surrender.

"You know I am your friend," he told Wilson, "neither you or any of your friends shall be injured." [3] On those terms, Don Benito and his remaining men surrendered. But none of them had reckoned with Antonio M. Lugo, who had five sons in the attacking force. The Lugos demanded that the Americanos be put to death, and only Varela's stubborn refusal to allow it saved the lives of Wilson and his men. They were then escorted to the Los Angeles area to be imprisoned. Not surprisingly, Don Benito never forgave Lugo.

Another man Wilson never forgave was English settler Henry Dalton, who owned Rancho Azusa and operated a store in Los Angeles (see Dalton). When José Flores' campaign against Stockton's forces threatened to collapse from lack of supplies, Flores prevailed on Dalton, who was to become his brother-in-law, to sell him supplies to be paid for later by the Mexican Government. There were also rumors that American settlers were to be arrested and deported. Wilson thought this tantamount to treason, even through Dalton remained a British subject. Later Wilson wrote of Dalton:

> In a few days we heard of the hellish plot concocted by Flores and Henry Dalton (whose wives were sisters) to send us as prisoners and trophies to Mexico, having its conception in Dalton selling the remains of an old store to Flores as commander in Chief, for the pretended purpose of clothing the soldiers, and Flores giving to Dalton drafts for large amounts against the Mexican treasury. [4]

Actually Dalton did not marry until almost a year later, and there is no evidence that he had anything to do with a plot to deport Americans. What everyone expected came to pass very quickly. Fremont was bringing men from the north, and after Stockton was reinforced in San Diego by General Stephen Kearny's troops from Santa Fe, they marched together and recaptured Southern California. Wilson and his men were released from prison even before Fremont stopped the Mexicans at Cahuenga Pass, where he negotiated a cease fire treaty With General Andres Pico. The fighting in California was over; all that remained was a formal treaty between Mexico City and the United States. Stockton was having problems with Kearny trying to usurp his authority; then came Lt. Col. John Fremont, who had taken it upon himself to execute a treaty with the enemy and alienate Kearny even more.

Later, when Benjamin Wilson escorted Andres Pico to see Stockton, the Commodore told Pico that neither he nor Fremont had any legal right to execute such a treaty. When Wilson told Stockton that Fremont did not intend to recognize him or General Kearny as commander, the Commodore is said to have snapped, "What does the damned fool [Fremont] mean?" [5]

Kearny was prepared to form a government, which Stockton opposed. Finally, after Kearny wrote President Polk about the impasse and threatened to take his men and leave the country, Stockton backed off. "I must go away," he told Wilson, "and let Kearny settle the matter with Fremont." [5] Kearny, fearing Fremont's large force of undisciplined men, asked Wilson to stand by and keep him posted.

Wilson then escorted Kearny and his staff from Los Angeles toward San Diego. There the general hoped to meet Col. Philip St. George Cooke's Mormon troops, who were on their way from Santa Fe to reinforce his tenuous strategic and political position. Meanwhile, Stockton had set up a government, with himself as governor until he appointed Fremont governor on January 19, 1847. He then journeyed to San Diego to settle the matter with Kearny, arriving there a few days later. To his chagrin, Stockton learned that he had been relieved of his naval command by Commodore William B. Shubrick.

WHEN Lt. William Tecumseh Sherman arrived in San Francisco and learned of the stalemate between the commanders, he asked, "Just who the hell is in command here?" [6] With so much infighting between American commanders, it's a wonder the United States won the War. The victory was probably due to even worse problems within the Mexican high command. Once the Treaty of Guadalupe Hidalgo was approved by both governments in early February 1848, the war officially ended. Within a matter of weeks came rumors of James Marshall's discovery of gold at John Sutter's sawmill in present-day Coloma (see Marshall).

Rather than get caught up in the Gold Rush as did many of his friends, Wilson stayed behind to tend to his ranching responsibilities. Like many other rancheros, he profited greatly from the Gold Rush by shipping beef, fruit and wine to the gold fields. Such commodities were in demand at extremely high prices. In fact, much more money was made by the providers of goods than by most of the men who toiled in the mines, enduring appalling hardships and privations.

By the time California was admitted to the Union, September 9, 1850, Wilson was serving as alcalde (justice of the peace) in Los Angeles. He also served as honorary mayor and as the first County Clerk. Just before the death of his friend, Hugo Reid in December 1852, Don Benito bought his 128-acre "Lake Vineyard" ranch from poverty-stricken Victoria Reid. This encompassed present-day San Marino and part of Pasadena.

MEANWHILE, the Secretary of Interior had ordered U.S. Navy Lt. Edward Beale to leave Washington D.C. and travel overland from Missouri to California (see Beale). He was to locate possible sites for Indian reservations along the way. After an arduous journey along the Old Spanish Trail, Beale's party crossed through Cajon Pass and entered the valley of San Bernardino, a welcome sight indeed. Upon reaching Los Angeles, they enjoyed the hospitality of "Mr. Wilson, Indian Agent, and his accomplished lady." [7]

When Beale was appointed Superintendent of Indian Affairs for California in March 1852, Wilson was named Indian Sub-agent for Southern California–an area about the size of New England. His duties were manifold; maintaining discipline among the Indians, providing subsistence and assisting Beale in his attempts to relocate them to appropriate reservations. In February 1853 Dona Ramona Wilson became ill and died, leaving Wilson with two children to raise. On September 5, 1853, the San Francisco *Daily Herald* noted:

> Beale left Los Angeles on an expedition through the San Joaquin Valley to have a talk with the various Indian tribes, and to look out lands for reservations, accompanied by Don Benito Wilson, Indian Agent for that section of the country, and several members of the expedition [8].

Upon Wilson's request, he was dismissed by Beale as Sub-Indian Agent in November that same year. Apparently Wilson threw himself into democratic politics after that, and was elected to the Los Angeles County Board of Supervisors. Wilson then built a beautiful house for his family at Lake Vineyard. He sold his former home in Los Angeles, which stood on land later used for the impressive Union Pacific Railroad depot.

After Beale's removal for political purposes in June 1854, an era of corruption took place, causing Wilson to later agree with writer J. Ross Browne that "Indians need protection from the whites, not vice versa." Also that reservations were places "where a very large amount of money was annually expended in feeding white men and starving the Indians." [9]

Shortly after finishing the Lake Vineyard house, he was married to Margaret Hereford, widow of Dr. T.A. Hereford, by whom she had one son. Later, their own daughter, Anne Wilson, married George Patton II, a U.S. District Attorney; their son was General George Patton, Jr. Reid had improved the Lake Vineyard ranch extensively, but Wilson did even more. It was obvious that he loved this property, as evidenced by a letter he wrote to his older brother in Mississippi:

I am so comfortable here and enjoy such fine health with all my family in fact, no Country can be more healthy than this...there is on the farm growing Grapes pears Oranges apricots Amonds peaches apples English walnuts cherries figs Olives Quinces plumbs & other fruits of the smaler kinds two numerous to mention...the above perchase I made is one of the most beautiful places that heart could desire fine water and land and about 30 acres in fruits of the kinds just mentioned above this place lies about seven miles from this town [Los Angeles] [9].

IN 1855 WILSON was elected to the California State Senate. He served through 1860 and was re-elected to the Los Angeles Board of Supervisors. In 1869, he was re-elected to the State Senate. He sponsored two bills which had great implications: One required livestock owners to build fences around their property, thus obviating the vexing need for others to fence their lands to keep the stock out. The other bill involved a bond issue to subsidize building the Southern Pacific Railroad to Los Angeles and beyond. Both passed, and the railroad arrived in the 1870's. To no one's surprise, it passed through Wilson's ranch.

By the end of the 1850s, Don Benito had purchased even more land adjacent to Lake Vineyard. He acquired Rancho San Pascual from Don Manuel Garfias, which included present-day North Alhambra and South Pasadena. In the early 1860's, he bought Rancho San Pedro with Phineas Banning, and purchased an interest in Rancho Buenos Ayres, site of present-day Westwood. At one time Wilson was said to have owned half the land (every other section) between Los Angeles and Riverside.

Throughout these halcyon years, Don Benito was arranging livestock drives to Northern California, seeking funds from the U.S. Congress to improve the harbor at Wilmington, experimenting with sugar cane and exporting fine wines and brandy. He also invested in the fledgling Pioneer Oil Company, which was a bit ahead of its time. As a native of Tennessee, Wilson's sympathies were with the South during the Civil War; in fact, this almost led to his leaving the area for Mexico.

Wilson's son, John, had died at the age of 24. His daughter, Maria, married James De Barth Shorb. Shorb named their home "San Marino", and the property was eventually incorporated into the city of San Marino. By the end of the 1860s, Wilson and Banning were promoting the Los Angeles and San Pedro Railroad, which provided efficient shipping from the San Gabriel Valley to Banning's new Port at Wilmington. By the following decade, Shorb was running Lake Vineyard, and production of fruits, wine and brandy increased dramatically.

This left Wilson more time to devote to his new real estate enterprises. Water had always been in short supply in Southern California. Don Benito solved that problem on his San Gabriel Valley land by piping water from the mountains. Later he built a storage reservoir and began subdividing irrigated parcels into small ranch homesites, selling thousands of acres through his "Lake Vineyard Land and Water Association."

IN 1871, A CONTINGENT of Wilson's relatives arrived from Mississippi to see if his stories about "paradise on earth" were really true. Among them were James C. and Mattie Wallace, who built the first house in what became the City of Alhambra. Caught up in the romance of Washington Irving's book, Tales of the Alhambra, they named the area The Alhambra Tract and gave many of the streets old Spanish names.

Proper schools had been a problem in the area since the days of Mexican rule. Now that settlers with children were arriving, something had to be done. Don Benito was an early member of the school board and donated land for a new school in The Alhambra Tract. He never lived to see the fine new school built, as he died March 11, 1878, at the age of 67.

Wilson built a gigantic agricultural empire, pioneered the first aqueduct to bring water from the mountains and subdivided thousands of irrigated acres into permanent homesites and cities such as San Marino and Alhambra. Mt. Wilson, which looms dramatically to the east of the lovely valley, provides a magnificent monument to Don Benito. He deserves a lofty location on the honor roll of early California pioneers.

BIBLIOGRAPHY
–Bancroft, Hubert H. *California Pioneer Register and Index*. Regional Publishing Co., Baltimore, 1964.
–Briggs, Carl and Clyde Francis Trudell. *Quarterdeck & Saddlehorn: The Story of Edward F. Beale*. Arthur H. Clark Co., Glendale, CA, 1983 [5,6,7].
–Caughey, John W. (Interpreter) (Ed. by Morris Hundley, Jr.and John A. Schutz.) *The American West, Frontier & Region*. Richie Press, Los Angeles, 1969. [8]
–Churchill, Charles B. "Benjamin Wilson, Man in the Middle." *The Californians*, Vol. 10, No. 3, 1993.

–Dakin, Susanna. *A Scotch Paisano in Old Los Angeles.* University of California Press, Berkeley,1939 [1].

–Dillon, Richard. *Humbugs and Heroes.* Yosemite-DiMaggio, Oakland, CA, 1983. [9]

–Harlow, Neal. *California Conquered.* University of California Press, Berkeley, 1982 [2,3,4].

–Jackson, Sheldon G. *A British Ranchero In Old California.* Arthur H. Clark Co., Glendale, CA, 1987.

–Rybicki, Euphemia Ratkowski. *A Century To Achievement. The History of the Alhambra Elementary School District.* Alhambra, CA, 1986.

–Thompson, Gerald. *Edward F. Beale & The American West.* University of New Mexico Press, Albuquerque, 1983.

William Wolfskill
Courtesy California State Library

– 48 –

WILLIAM WOLFSKILL
(Don Guillermo)   1798 –1866

HOUGH WILLIAM WOLFSKILL is a relatively obscure pioneer, his contributions to the birth and growth of California were considerable. His German father, Joseph Wolfskill, Jr., married a Scotch-Irish lass named Sarah Reid in 1797. William was born in Boonesborough, Kentucky March 20, 1798, the first of twelve children. In 1809 the Wolfskill family moved to Boone's Lick, a tiny hamlet in Missouri Indian territory, named after a nearby salt lick and settled by Daniel Boone a few years earlier.

Colonel Benjamin Cooper, a former neighbor, who had settled in Boone's Lick earlier, persuaded the Wolfskills to join him. Two years later the Lindsay Carson family moved to the area with several boys, including young Christopher, who was nick-named "Kit". The growing community eventually became part of Howard County. Life wasn't easy on the Missouri frontier, where families had to live off the land until successful farming saved them from virtual starvation.

Indians became a threat during the War of 1812, causing the settlers to build small community forts. The Wolfskills moved into Fort Cooper with the Cooper family, where they stayed until the war was over. George Yount, with two of Daniel Boone's sons, fought Indians there during the war, and stayed on afterwards (see Yount). The settlers provided a primitive school for their children, but William Wolfskill and two of his sisters were sent to Kentucky for more advanced studies. Wolfskill was sixteen when he returned to Boone's Lick, where he lived for eight more years.

By then he had gained enough knowledge and experience as a skilled frontiersman to pursue his own destiny. Captain William Becknell was organizing a trading expedition to Santa Fe, New Mexico, so young Wolfskill and some of his friends from the Cooper and Carson families agreed to go along. Ewing Young and a friend, probably George Yount, also accompanied them. The heavily laden wagons, hauled by sturdy Missouri mules, left on the fledgling Santa Fe Trail in May 1822.

Becknell is credited as the first to haul his goods in wagons. Until then, trade goods had been hauled in two-wheeled carts or packed on mules. As a result he became known as "The Father of the Santa Fe Trail." After many hardships, and near death from lack of water, the party reached Santa Fe in mid-summer. By fall, Wolfskill and Ewing Young had formed a partnership and left on a fur trapping expedition.

WOLFSKILL JOINED with a Mexican partner the following year to trap along the Rio Grande River. They were camped on the snowy shore of the river one freezing winter night, when Wolfskill was shocked awake by a thunderous explosion and choking gunsmoke. It was accompanied by intense pain in his hands and chest and spatters of blood. Acting from trained reflexes, he reached for his rifle, finding it gone. When he called out to his partner, there was no answer. He knew he had been shot but thought he had a chance of making it—if his assailants had left and he didn't bleed to death.

It was Wolfskill's custom to sleep on his back with his arms crossed over his chest. The ball had been partially spent by his blankets, but had torn through his right arm and left hand before lodging in his breast-bone; otherwise, he would surely have been killed. Wolfskill assumed he had been shot by marauding Indians and that his partner had run off or been killed. Apparently the Indians had left as well. There was nothing to do but try to walk the twenty-five miles to the nearest town to seek help.

Somehow he made it to the tiny village of Valverde, where he was cared for by the local alcalde. Later, the astute alcalde told him that his partner had showed up, claiming that Indians had attacked, killing Wolfskill. His story had aroused the alcalde's suspicions to the point where he insisted on being taken to the scene of the alleged killing. When the partner "discovered" Wolfskill's rifle where the partner had apparently hidden it, the alcalde's suspicions were aroused even more. Then, after finding only two sets of footprints in the snow, he accused the Mexican trapper of trying to murder Wolfskill.Once the ball had been removed from Wolfskill's breast-bone, he rested in Santa Fe, where he made a rapid recovery. Despite the evidence, the would-be killer served only a short sentence before being released from custody. [1]

By the winter of 1824, Wolfskill had joined Ewing Young in Taos to trap along the headwaters of the San Juan River and other tributaries of the mighty Colorado. They returned to Taos in June with $10,000 worth of furs. With plenty of money in his pocket, Wolfskill returned home to Boone's Lick the following year to visit his family.

After a good rest and a successful mule trading venture, he joined Young in 1825 for a trapping expedition into Mexico. When Young became ill, Wolfskill took over and led the eighteen-man group himself.

Among others, the party included well-known trappers Milton Sublette and George Yount. In an attack by Apaches, Sublette was wounded, and the disgusted group returned to Santa Fe, where they disbanded.

IN 1828 WOLFSKILL returned to Missouri, where he loaded a wagon with trade goods for his third trip over the Santa Fe Trail. In Santa Fe, he sold his goods to his former partner, Ewing Young. They then joined forces to start another trapping trip from Taos. After returning from their successful expedition the following year, Wolfskill stayed behind while Young took out another group, including Wolfskill's young friend and neighbor, Kit Carson.

Young had made up his mind to scour the Far West for beaver, and he didn't stop until 1830 when he reached California. Young's party went as far north as Mission San Rafael before turning back. When they returned to Taos later in the year, Young found that Wolfskill had left to lead a trapping party to California to see the new promised land for himself.

Because he knew he would be trapping mostly in Mexican territory, Wolfskill had previously applied for Mexican citizenship. First he had to file a petition showing he had been baptized a Roman Catholic and would renounce all foreign governments, including the United States. His application had been approved a decade earlier, but his permit to trap was not received until 1830.

By September Wolfskill had recruited about twenty men and collected the supplies and livestock needed for the long trek to California. Shortly after leaving the Taos area, his group joined smaller party led by George Yount, and the combined party partially followed the old Spanish Trail through present-say Durango (Colorado), before turning westerly. Wolfskill never did run into Young; he had taken a different route and returned to Santa Fe in 1832.

The Wolfskill-Yount party reached the Sevier River before encountering a sizable encampment of Utah Indians, whom they befriended with gifts before being allowed to proceed. After becoming lost and suffering from extreme cold, Wolfskill gave up his attempt to cross the Mountains on a northerly route; instead, he turned southwest and followed the Virgin River to the Colorado River, joining it near present day Lake Mead.

They followed the river south to a series of potentially hostile Mojave Indian villages, but perhaps the sight of a small artillery piece mounted on a pack saddle intimidated them. Reaching a village near present Needles, California, they traded for food. Heading west across the Mojave Desert and Cajon Pass, they reached Antonio Lugos's ranch near San Gabriel in Feb. 1831.

Then Wolfskill and Yount went to San Gabriel Mission to confer with padre Jose Sanchez. The hospitable father invited them to bring the rest of their men from Lugos's ranch, which they did. When Wolfskill later visited Los Angeles, the pueblo had a population of about two hundred Spanish and Mexican families, plus a sprinkling of Yankee seamen, trappers and traders. Later, Wolfskill learned that his newly blazed trail from Taos had become the most commonly used route into Southern California. It remained so for the next decade.

HAVING LEARNED that good money could be made hunting sea otters, Wolfskill decided to keep Yount and a few others with him to hunt them; the rest of the men were sent back to Taos. Once he obtained his trapping permit, Wolfskill needed a ship capable of coastal sailing to hunt the wary otters. He had learned the carpentry trade as a young man in Missouri, and with true Yankee ingenuity he and some friends agreed to build a ship. There was a lack of proper lumber but Wolfskill didn't let that stop him.

He took some men into the surrounding mountains, felled trees, whip-sawed them into lumber and hauled it to the San Gabriel Mission. There Father Sanchez kindly lent him enough tools and Indian man-power to construct a 75-foot schooner. If the ship was constructed there as one version alleges, it had to be partially dismantled so it could be hauled to San Pedro in freight wagons; it's probable that at least part of the ship was constructed in San Pedro. The schooner was launched in 1832 and otter hunting commenced that spring. [2]

Wolfskill's first voyage up and down the coast was his last, as the trip proved unprofitable. He sold the ship and bought a small vineyard in Los Angeles. Then he entered into a common-law marriage with one Maria "Luz" Valencia and settled down for the first time since leaving home. A daughter, Maria Susana, was born in 1834. A son named Timoteo followed a year later.

Wolfskill fell back on carpentry to support his new family, while he developed his vineyard. Secularization of the missions had made land available, and the early 1830's brought an influx of people to the area. By 1836, the population of Los Angeles had swelled to 1,675 non-Indians, of which about 50 were foreigners. They included such well known people as trader Abel Stearns, Dr. John Marsh–the only doctor in the area–and ranchers Hugo Reid and Jean Luis Vignes (see separate chapters on Stearns, Marsh, and Reid).

Census rolls in 1836 showed Wolfskill as "Esten Guillmo Wolfskil" age 38, a property owner and laborer, married, and a native of the United States." His name was followed by "Luz Valencia, 30...Juan Je [Timoteo] Wolfskil, 1, and Suzanne Wolfskil, 2." Wolfskill knew he must have more land if his vineyard was to amount to anything. He petitioned for unoccupied land surrounding his small parcel, which was finally granted after influential friends, especially Abel Stearns, assisted him. With his holdings increased, he provided a better house for his family.

Soon Wolfskill was operating a saloon and a billiard parlor in addition to his agricultural interests. The vineyard was expanded and he planted a citrus orchard. He must have been spending too much time at work in 1837, for Luz ran off to Mexico with the local silversmith, leaving Wolfskill with two small children to raise. The following year he was surprised by a visit from his younger brother, John, who had come west seeking opportunity. Wolfskill traded his small vineyard for a hundred-acre parcel already planted with several thousand grape vines, between what is now San Pedro and Alameda Streets, bounded roughly by Third and Ninth Streets in present Los Angeles.

WITH HIS brother's help, he began working on a large adobe house. Within a year they had constructed a house that eventually became known throughout the area as the "old adobe." Soon Wolfskill's finances improved enough to allow purchase of expensive furnishings for his new house. His children and the ranch were thriving; all he needed now was a loving wife to share it with. He found her in 1840: the lovely niece of his old friend, Antonio Lugo. Magdalena Lugo was visiting her Uncle Antonio's rancho when she met Wolfskill at a social gathering there. They were married in mid-January 1841.

Their first child, a daughter named Juana Josefa, was born in late November; however she died in infancy. Four more children followed: two sons, Jose and Luis, and two daughters, Maria Francisca and Maria Magdalena. Eventually they all married, became prominent citizens and had large families of their own. The same held true for the two older children from Luz, Timoteo and Susana.

In 1842 Captain William Phelps described Wolfskill's ranch as "Under excellent cultivation and abundance of fruit trees, kitchen vegetable, &c. His vineyard contains 11,000 vines, mostly of his own planting and now in full bearing...." [3]

After Wolfskill's marriage, his brother, John, began thirsting for land of his own. There were no suitable large parcels left in the Los Angeles area, so John Wolfskill journeyed to Northern California to seek land there. One parcel he'd heard about lay in a protected valley along Putah Creek, about thirty miles west of John Sutter's New Helvetia (now Sacramento). But when he inquired about it from General Vallejo, he was told it was not available to him because he was not a Mexican citizen.

When John Wolfskill returned to Los Angeles with his tale of woe, William sent him back to try again. William needed more land of his own to raise cattle, so a partnership arrangement was worked out between him and his brother. William Wolfskill was a Mexican citizen, so the land grant would be deeded to him; however, his brother was to run the ranch and share the profits. The grant for four square leagues (over 17,700 acres) was approved by Governor Juan B. Alvarado in 1842:

> Whereas, William Wolfskill, a naturalized Mexican, for his benefit and that of his family, has made application for a tract of land bounded on the East by the Bullrush Swamp and on the West by the hills and located on the banks of the River called Los Putos... by virtue of the powers conferred upon me in the name of the Mexican Nation, I have granted him the above mentioned land declaring him the owner of it by these present letters, subject to....

Wolfskill named his new acquisition Rancho Rio de los Putos, and his brother drove a herd of mixed livestock north from Los Angeles to stock the new ranch. Arriving at a Mission Dolores outpost on San Francisco Bay, he left his herd there and crossed the great bay to visit George Yount, who had acquired ranch property in Napa Valley from Mariano Vallejo, and had built a house, a gristmill, and later a sawmill (see Vallejo).

JOHN WOLFSKILL spent several months with Yount before returning to gather his livestock for the drive to the Wolfskill ranch. He arrived there in 1842 and built a crude temporary house made of tule, willow-branches and mud. By the following year he had planted fruit trees, barley, corn and beans. He also started a vineyard. In mid-1844 the Wolfskills were shocked to find themselves involved in a property dispute with Manuel Vaca and Juan Pena, who claimed Governor Micheltorena had granted them land adjacent to—even overlapping—Wolfskill's grant.

Through tricky political maneuvering, Vaca succeeded in evicting John Wolfskill from his ranch, forcing him to move in with a neighbor. The case dragged through the Mexican court system until 1846, when the Mexican War began. John Wolfskill had possession of the land by then but had left to join John C. Fremont's California Volunteers to fight against the Mexicans. Apparently he had gained title to the property, because he sold a portion of it to a well-known mountain man, Green McMahan.

It wasn't until 1849 that the Wolfskill brothers divided the remaining property between them. By then the Gold Rush had brought three more of their brothers to the Sacramento Valley to seek their fortunes. Shortly after, John Wolfskill married Susan Cooper, daughter of their old family friend, Colonel Stephen Cooper of Missouri. The Cooper family had come to California on the Overland Trail during the 1846 migration, the same year as the tragic Donner Party.

John and Susan Wolfskill had three children over the years and founded the town of Winters on their ranch property. After their daughter, Frances Taylor Wolfskill, inherited the property, she bequeathed a good portion of it to the University of California at Davis for use as an experimental farm. Family members have been prominent ranchers in the area for many years.

Meanwhile, William Wolfskill had actively been pursuing wine growing in Los Angeles and was beginning to produce large quantities of wine and brandy. He specialized in sangria, a potent mixture of wine, brandy and fruit juice. He also was experimenting with tropical fruits and various types of citrus trees. Water has always been a problem in Southern California. In 1844 Wolfskill served both on the Water Commission and the City Council. He continued to serve on the Council in 1846 after the American occupation.

By 1850 he was operating the first successful orange shipping business. Others quickly saw the possibilities and orange groves sprouted throughout the Los Angeles area. In 1855 Wolfskill purchased the La Puente Rancho, bordering the San Gabriel River, and planted it with several thousand orange and lemon trees. Within a few years he had the largest citrus orchard in the United States. He also grew peaches, pears and apples with good success.

IN 1856 WOLFSKILL was awarded a certificate for the best vineyard by the California Agricultural Society. By then the wine growing industry in the North—particularly in Napa Valley—was offering serious competition with its fine wines. The Rancho Rio de los Putos was producing well, so Wolfskill had the best of two worlds; he was producing wines in both Northern and Southern California. Always interested in education, Wolfskill operated a private school at his "old adobe" for his own children and those of his neighbors. When the first public school opened in Los Angeles, he subsidized it from his own funds to get it started.

In 1860 Wolfskill bought Rancho Lomas de Santiago from Teodosio Yorba. It was bounded on the north by the Santa Ana River, east by the mountains, south by Rancho Aliso and west by Rancho San Joaquin. He built a house there and used the ranch to raise cattle for six years before selling it. His wife, Magdalena, died there in 1862. A year earlier he may have acquired part of Henry Dalton's Rancho Azusa by foreclosure. He also bought Rancho Santa Anita, formerly owned by Hugo Reid and Henry Dalton (see separate chapters).

During this period Wolfskill experimented with the first eucalyptus trees, raising them from seeds sent from Australia. During droughts the annual Santa Ana winds brought destructive dust storms. Rows of tall trees tended to break the wind, and the fast-growing eucalyptus trees quickly grew in favor. In September, 1865, Wolfskill was elected Public Administrator for Los Angeles County. Shortly after, he bought a block of commercial property on Main Street and began construction of a large dry goods store.

But fate had other plans for Wolfskill; he suffered a slight heart attack in mid-September, 1866. Edema swelled his feet to the point where he was unable to walk, a cruel fate for a physically active frontiersman like William Wolfskill. Though he improved considerably over the next few days, he must have had a premonition, for he drew up his last will and testament and arranged for a photographer to take a portrait—the only one he ever had. Six days later he was dead. A few years later his son, Luis, married a daughter of Henry Dalton. Historian Hubert H. Bancroft wrote:

> [Wolfskill] died in '66 at the age of 68, leaving an enviable reputation as an honest, enterprising, generous, unassuming, intelligent man. He and Louis Vignes may be regarded as the pioneers of California's greatest industry, the production of wine and fruit....

Major Horace Bell, one of the early rangers in California, wrote of him as follows:

> The first few days after my arrival in Los Angeles, I visited the then famous vineyard of William Wolfskill, the best then in California. Mr. Wolfskill was a very remarkable man; in fact, he was a hero—not the kind of a hero poets like to sing about, but still a hero. A man of indomitable will, industry and self denial; an American pioneer hero; one who succeeds in all he undertakes, and is always to be trusted, of the kind of men who enrich the country in which they live....

Enough said.

BIBLIOGRAPHY

—Bancroft, Hubert H. *History of California*, Vol. I-VI, History Co., San Francisco, 1886. Repub., Wallace Hebberd, Santa Barbara, CA, 1966.

—Cleland, Robert Glass. *This Reckless Breed of Men*. Alfred A. Knopf, New York, 1950. [1]

—Dakin, Susanna Bryant. *A Scotch Paisano. Hugo Reid's Life in California, 1832-1852*. University of California Press, Berkeley, 1939.

—Holmes, Kenneth L. *Ewing Young, Master Trapper*. Binfords & Mort, Portland, OR, 1967.

—Jackson, Sheldon G. *A British Ranchero In Old California, The Life and Times of Henry Dalton and the Rancho Azusa*. The Arthur H. Clark Co., Glendale, CA, 1987.

—Phelps, William. (Ed. by Briton C.Busch). *Alta California, 1840-1842*. Arthur H. Clark Co., Glendale, CA, 1883. [3]

—Wilson, Iris Higbie. *William Wolfskill, Frontier Trapper to California Ranchero*. Arthur H. Clark Co., Glendale, CA, 1965. Quotations, except [1 & 3], are from this publication.

- 49 -

YEE FUNG CHEUNG

1825 - 1907

C HINESE PEOPLE BEGAN COMING to the American continent much earlier than many people realize. There is ample evidence that fairly large numbers of Chinese men migrated to mainland Mexico during the era of the Spanish galleons. These galleons followed the trade winds and currents between Acapulco and the Philippine Islands, where Chinese had been migrating for years. Some historians contend that Chinese and Japanese mariners sailed across the Pacific to the North American coast in junks, long before the arrival of Spanish explorers.

As other foreigners had done before them, many Chinese in Mexico converted to Catholicism, took Spanish names, became Spanish citizens and married local women. During the era of expansionism in the 18th century, some of these people, many of mixed blood, emigrated to Alta California. Thus, the Chinese were well represented there much earlier than supposed. Because Monterey had been named the capital of Alta California by the Spanish, most of these early immigrants settled there. The first documented Chinese in Monterey was Amman (Ah Nam?), baptized Antonio Maria de Jesus, who was Gov. Pablo V. Sola's cook in 1815. "Amman" died two years later. [1]

But it wasn't until after the 1849 Gold Rush that they began coming to Gum Shan, the Golden Mountain, in large numbers. Most of them emigrated from Kwangtung Province (Canton); many sailed directly to California in small junks. Despite the fact that large numbers of these pioneers played important roles in California during that period, they are not well represented in our annals of early history. Undoubtedly this is largely due to lack of documentation; many were illiterate, and those who kept diaries or written accounts of their experiences wrote in their native languages, which varied greatly, depending on which province in China they were from. And of course, American historians rarely read Chinese.

As a result, most historical information about Chinese pioneers during the Gold Rush comes to us second hand from translators. Often these were family members and historians who pieced together information from whatever facts were available. Like most gold seekers, the Chinese sought wealth–at least enough to return home to a brighter future. The amount needed varied greatly, depending on the expenses incurred in gathering this wealth and the amount required to start a new life in their homeland–and, of course, inevitable greed.

Some met their goals and returned home to new lives, but most did not. Instead, they became stranded in a strange, often inhospitable land and had to make do as best they could. Most argonauts from foreign lands did not reach the gold fields until 1850 or later. By then the most productive areas had been claimed by others. Many miners were barely eking out a living and naturally resented competition, especially from foreigners with strange customs who neither spoke nor understood English.

The Chinese, with their sing-song language, strange-looking clothes and pig-tails, were ridiculed mercilessly and often abused physically. They were usually relegated to sifting through old mine tailings found unproductive by others. If, through hard work and innovative methods, they were able to make their mines pay well, they were sometimes driven off by ruthless claim jumpers. Foreign miners were also subjected to discriminatory "miner's taxes", collected by rough-shod law officials. The overwhelming majority of Chinese led lives of quiet desperation, with little compensation. This could be said of most miners, but foreigners suffered even more. Many Chinese, disillusioned with mining, returned to previous occupations such as farmwork, fishing and gathering shell-fish, especially the highly prized abalone.

YEE FUNG CHEUNG (Cheung denotes the generation) was descended from Yee Fung Shen, an eminent counselor in the Soong Dynasty a thousand years before gold was discovered in California. Many Yee descendants still reside in and around present-day Toishan near what was Canton, China. Yee Fung, his wife and four children lived in Sing Tong village (Kee Sui District), a suburb of Toishan in Guangdong province.

After learning about the gold discovery in California, 25-year-old Yee Fung left his wife and children in 1850 and emigrated to San Francisco. Like most gold seekers, he came up the Sacramento River to John Sutter's embarcadero, probably on one of the new steam-powered paddle-wheelers. Apparently Sacramento didn't appeal to Yee, for he went overland to a newly settled Chinese camp in Fiddletown, now a small village on the northern edge of Amador County.

Yee Fung probably prospected for gold before giving it up to practice what he knew best–herbal medicine. There was much sickness in the gold towns, but in the beginning Yee's practice was probably limited to the growing Chinese population. But as he became known, he certainly must have treated Caucasians as well. Miners visited Dr. Yee's office, not only for his herbal concoctions, but because he was known as a good natured man. Some said "it was only a dose of his smile they needed" [2].

FEW CHINESE entered the medical field prior to the turn of the century, and eventually Yee did well enough to hire a man to help run his Fiddletown shop. In 1859 a rich gold strike was made in what became Virginia City, Nevada, a strike which later led to the fabulous Comstock silver lode. Until then nearly all overland traffic had been heading west into California. But after that, thousands began heading east from California. Many Chinese were among them. Yee was quick to seize the opportunity he saw in Virginia City and opened an herbal medical practice and store there.

A few years later he recognized a different kind of golden opportunity: the Central Pacific Railroad was under construction from Sacramento. It was to cross the mighty Sierra Nevada over Truckee Pass, a trail blazed by early California-bound emigrants in the 1840's. To build it required thousands of laborers capable of enduring the hardships of extreme weather and horrendous terrain.

What better people to do it than the hardy Chinese? Their mettle had been tested time and time again during the Gold Rush, and later after the gold played out, when they were forced to perform the hardest kind of labor for bare subsistence. Endless miles of Chinese-built rock fences, rock buildings and hard-rock mine tunnels remain in use today. Because many of them had returned to China, many more had to be imported to build the railroad. With thousands of Chinese in the vicinity, Yee prospered from an herb store he opened in Sacramento.

Sometime during this period, Yee sent for his two sons, still living in China. The eldest, Yee Lun Wo, decided to remain at home, where he farmed and managed the only grocery store in the district. The younger son, Yee Lock Sam, responded to his father's call and sailed for California with his wife, her young "hand maiden" and several children. Soon Yee Lock Sam had become a practicing herbalist like his father. Later his wife died and he married the hand maiden, with whom he had many more children.

By 1870 one out of seven Sacramento citizens was Chinese, of which ninety percent were single young men. The few Chinese women were brought as slaves, and most ended up in prostitution [3]. The men took any kind of menial work they could get, while they saved money for their return trip home. Seldom owning land, these transient "Celestials" lived in mean rented quarters along "I" Street between Second and Sixth.Many Chinese who died in California were buried for up to ten years before being exhumed. Their bones were then carefully cleaned and packed in air-tight containers to be shipped back to their homes in China.

Discrimination continued to plague the Chinese far into the 20th century; its remnants still cling today. One story illustrates it very well: In 1862, when Leland Stanford was being inaugurated as Governor of California, he made a speech in which he reportedly said the Chinese were "the dregs of Asia" and should be banished from the country.

Later, when Stanford's wife lay dying from a pulmonary disorder, their Chinese cook went looking for herbalist Yee Fung. He was finally located playing majong at his favorite "men's club," the Wah Hing grocery store at Fifth and I street. Upon learning about Mrs. Stanford's plight, Yee Fung hurried to his herb store and concocted a medication that ultimately saved her.

The primary herb was later identified as "majaung," a natural source of ephedrine, a drug commonly prescribed for pulmonary disease (note the similarity between the game "majong," and the drug "majaung"). The governor's staff—not knowing Yee's real name—called him Dr. Wah Hing, after the name of the store he frequented. Ironically, twenty years after Stanford's fiery 1862 speech—in which he denounced the Chinese—enough support was gained in Congress to pass the infamous Chinese Exclusionary Act, banning further immigration (with some exceptions). This law remained in effect until 1943.

YEE FUNG'S SON, herbalist Yee Lock Sam, then decided to adopt the name, Dr. T. Wah Hing, for himself. In 1901 he ran the following ad in the Sacramento Bee: "Dr. T. Wah Hing, Physician and Surgeon. Eye, ear, nose and throat. 707 J Street, Sacramento". In 1906, shortly after his father had returned to China, Hing sent for his promising nine-year-old nephew, Henry Yee, the son of Yee Lun Wo, who had remained in China as manager of the grocery store during the California Gold Rush. T. Wah Hing lived in Sacramento until his death in 1935.

Apparently the Baptists in Sacramento were the first Protestants to convert some Chinese to Christianity. By 1854 they had a chapel at sixth and H streets, and two years later they ordained a Chinese Baptist clergyman. The Methodists were not far behind. In 1860 they had a Chinese Methodist Church at 915 Fifth Street. This may have been when the Yees converted to Christianity. In 1925 the church moved to Sixth and N, where it remained until 1960 when a new one was opened on 28th Avenue. This church is still in existence, conducting services in both English and Cantonese. By 1880 there was a Chinese Y.M.C.A. in Sacramento.

By 1904 Yee Fung was getting old and decided he had accumulated enough wealth to return home to China. He apparently sold his "mother store" in Fiddletown to an employee named Chew Kee, who operated it for nine years until he left for China himself. Meanwhile, a young Chinese boy named Fong Chow Yow (Jimmy Chow) had been raised by Yee Fung. When he left for China, Chew Kee "adopted" the teen-ager. When Chew Kee left for China in 1913, he deeded the property to Jimmy Chow.

Chow was not a herbalist, so the old "Chew Kee" store was closed. Chow lived in separate quarters on the premises and worked elsewhere to make a living. Nothing in the store was ever removed; in fact, Chow added to it over the years. He was an avid junk collector, and when he died in 1965, the place was locked up as is.

Residents in the area kept an eye on it to prevent vandalism until it was fully restored in 1987-88. The restoration was accomplished through the combined efforts of the State of California, Yee Fung's great-grandson, Dr. Herbert K. Yee, and the Fiddletown Preservation Society. It is the only fully equipped store of its kind left in the gold country and is open to the public as an authentic museum.

DR. T. WAH HING'S young nephew, Henry Yee, stayed in Sacramento long enough to graduate from Sacramento High School and get a university education. He returned home to China in 1915 to marry. A short time later he left his pregnant wife and returned to the U.S. to continue his education. After acquiring an M.S. in Civil Engineering from the University of Michigan in 1923, he returned to China and met his seven-year-old son, Paul, for the first time. Henry Yee worked in China building roads and railroads until he returned to Sacramento in 1928 with his oldest son, Paul. Unable to find engineering work during the great depression in the 1930's, he studied to become a chiropractor and herbalist. In 1930, he sent his son, Paul, back to China to bring his wife and other children to Sacramento. Among them was five-year-old Yee Kik Ming, later Dr. Herbert Yee, prominent citizen of Sacramento.

Dr. Herbert Yee is the only Asian member in the Sacramento Pioneer Association., whose criteria state that the family arrived in Sacramento before 1850. At present (1992) he is also president of the 30,000 member Yee Family Association of America. Dr. Yee's great-grandfather, Yee Fung, certainly deserves an honored place on the roll of California pioneers.

State parks and historical landmarks honor Chinese pioneers as follows: China Camp State Park, Marin County; Chinese Camp, Tuolumne County; Temple of Kaus (Joss House), Mendocino County; Chinese Taoist Temple, city of Hanford; Chinese Temple and Garden, city of Oroville; Weaverville Joss House, Trinity County; Bok Kai Temple (Joss House), city of Marysville.

BIBLIOGRAPHY

–Costello, Julia G. (photography by Daniel D'Agostini). "An Archive of Artifacts: The Chew Kee Store". *Pacific Discovery Magazine.* Spring, 1989.

–Kingston, Maxine Hong. *China Men.* Alfred Knopf, New York, 1976.

–Lyndon, Sandy. *Chinese Gold.* Capitola Book Co., Capitola, CA, 1985. [1]

–Mote, Sue. "Open for business: Chinese History." *The Sacramento Union,* March 31, 1988.

–Thompson, Willard and Ruth. "Roots: The Saga of a Chinese Family Here." *The Sacramento Bee,* Sept. 18, 1988.

–Weston, Oleto. *Mother Lode Album.* Stanford University Press, 1948 [2].

–Yee, Dr. Herbert K. Personal interview by the author, and many newspaper and magazine articles collected by Dr. Yee over the years.

–Yung, Judy. *Chinese Women Of America, A Pictoral History.* University of Washington Press, Seattle & London, 1986 [3].

NOTES

George C. Yount
Courtesy California State Library

GEORGE C. YOUNT

(Don Jorge Concepcion) 1794 – 1865

ANATIVE OF BURKE COUNTY, North Carolina, George Yount was
born May 5, 1794, the sixth of eleven children born to Jacob
Yount and his German-born wife, the former Matilda Killiam.
Jacob Yount (formerly spelled Jundt) had served in the Revolutionary
army; after the war he built and operated a grist mill on Drownden
Creek.

When George was ten the family moved to a farm at Cape
Girardeau, Southern Missouri. The Yount family were among the first
whites to settle there amidst large groups of Indians. Although young
George had no schooling, he honed his frontier skills to a fine edge and
became a skilled hunter. He never learned to read or write; he depended
on his woodsman's skills to survive in later years. He learned also to
respect deserving Indians and how to deal forcefully with those not so
deserving.

In May 1812 George Yount and two of his older brothers joined the
army to fight against the British during the War of 1812. They were
sent to St. Louis and did their fighting against Indians who had been
recruited by the British. After being mustered out about a year later,
George Yount was recalled in 1814 to fight the enemy, supposedly holed
up at the Miami Bottoms Indian Fort. When the fort was charged, the
attackers were chagrined to find it deserted.

Before long Yount was promoted to lieutenant and sent off to fight
hostile Indians under two of Daniel Boone's sons, Col. Nathan Boone
and Major Daniel M. Boone. After engaging the enemy at Boone's Lick
and Cooper's Fort, Yount was discharged at St. Louis. He then returned
to Boone's Lick, where he rented a farm to raise corn. The next two
years he farmed, hunted, fought Indians and fraternized with the likes of
young Kit Carson, William Wolfskill and Ewing Young (see Wolfskill).

Yount augmented his sparse income by driving a cattleherd about
two hundred miles up the Missouri River, after which he hunted bears
for their hides. In 1818 Yount married 15-year-old Eliza Wilds in

Howard County. Later, when he went to retrieve his hard-earned savings from a trusted friend, he found most of his money stolen. He was a long time recovering from this setback. Two children later–in 1826–he sold everything, gave most of the proceeds to his wife, and left to seek his fortune elsewhere.

His first job was driving a supply wagon to Santa Fe, probably with William Becknell. Jobs there were scarce, so Yount joined a party of trappers to learn that trade, working with William Wolfskill, Ewing Young and Thomas "Peg leg" Smith. "Peg-leg" had lost a leg some years before, but it never seemed to hinder him as a trapper or Indian fighter. He was renowned for his piercing war cries and for lifting Indian scalps.

DESPITE MANY CONFLICTS with hostile Indians along the way, the trappers did well on Hog Creek, a tributary of the Gila River. Having been forewarned that a large band of Pimos and Maricopas had massacred Michel Robidoux's party of trappers a short time before, Yount's party was well prepared for another such attack. When it came, they inflicted many Indian casualties with no losses to themselves. This decisive defeat caused the Indians to sign a long-lasting peace treaty with the trappers.

The journey back toward Santa Fe was fraught with hazards and privations. When the party ran out of food, they began killing their livestock, even their dogs, to avoid starvation. What livestock remained was so weak they could travel only a few hours a day, carrying the precious beaver pelts. Eventually the emaciated men and animals stumbled into a Zuni Indian camp. The kindly Indians fed and nursed men and animals alike until all but four of the men recovered.

When Yount's rejuvenated party reached Santa Fe, a new Mexican governor confiscated their precious pelts, stating that they had been obtained illegally. Completely destitute, Yount found work at William Workman's liquor still in Taos, making potent "white lightning." By the autumn of 1827 he had recouped enough to outfit another trapping party with James Ohio Pattie and his father. There were 24 in all when they headed for the Gila River country (southwest Arizona). Somewhere above the mouth of the Gila River, the Patties and some others made canoes out of cottonwood logs and broke away from Yount to drift down the Colorado River, ending up in Southern California. Yount and his remaining men continued their trapping along the river on horseback.

After spending some time with friendly Hopi and Zuni Indians along the way, the Yount party traveled northeasterly and cached a rich catch of hard-won beaver pelts outside of Taos before entering the town, to avoid having them confiscated again. Their precautions paid off, and by 1828 Yount was entertaining thoughts of returning to his family in Missouri. He had accumulated some money for once, but decided to wait and try to double it with one more successful trapping season.

A party of 30 men was outfitted the following year, and Yount led them northwest, this time to the Green River. They trapped the area around Utah Lake before moving to the Bear River Valley, where they became snowbound. In the spring of 1830 they headed farther west. Within days they met members of the trapping company of Jed Smith, David Jackson and Milton Sublette. With them was Arthur Black, who had recently returned from California with Smith (see Smith).

These men spoke about a land of "sun, milk and honey." There was even talk from Arthur Black about a gold discovery. By the time the two parties separated, Yount was planning a California expedition as he led his party back to Taos with a rich catch of beaver pelts. He was especially eager to see California when he learned that his friend, Ewing Young, had gone there.

ALTHOUGH YOUNT had not accumulated the wealth he expected, he had enough to outfit a small party that fall, when he headed west toward the Pacific Coast. Shortly after leaving Taos in September 1830, they were joined by a larger party led by Ewing Young's partner, William Wolfskill, who was also eager to see the new "promised land" (see Wolfskill). Roughly following the Old Spanish Trail to Durango (present Colorado), they turned off on a more westerly course and crossed the Green River before being halted by extreme cold in the mountains. Wolfskill then led the party south along the Sevier River and finally the Virgin River. Reaching the Colorado River near present Lake Mead, they followed it to the main encampment of the potentially hostile Mojave Indians.

One husky mule carried a small artillery piece mounted to a swivel on a pack saddle, possibly one used previously by Col. Stephen Kearny. This gun, plus the 16 well-armed men in their party, held the Mojaves at bay and probably prevented another massacre like the one perpetrated by them against Jedediah Smith's party a few years earlier. Continuing down the Colorado, they reached a large encampment of friendly Indians near present-day Needles. They stopped there long enough to renew their food supply, before heading west across the desert to Cajon Pass, and on into the Valley of San Bernardino.

An outpost of Mission San Gabriel, the rich valley teemed with cattle. Another day brought them to the mission itself, where they were warmly met by Father Jose Sanchez in early February 1831. To say Yount and Wolfskill were impressed would be an understatement. On the mission grounds they found herds of livestock, fertile gardens, orchards and vineyards. Father Sanchez proved a hospitable host, providing the best food, wine and accommodations available.

It was late February before Yount left to explore the surrounding area. He had heard that sea otters possessed waterproof coats that were extraordinarily soft and warm. Though the animals were hard to catch, the pelts were much more valuable than beaver skins. Yount first tried hunting otters with Wolfskill in the latter's home-made sailing vessel, with such poor results that Wolfskill sold the ship and took up farming in Los Angeles.

YOUNT THEN hunted with experts until he mastered the technique, which was to shoot the otter in the head and send an Indian or Kanaka (Hawaiian) diver to retrieve the carcass before it sank too far below the surface. Only then did he try it on his own, with two divers in a light-weight "bull boat" of his own design, constructed of saplings held together with rawhide thongs and covered with the thick, tough hide of sea elephants. Aleut hunters from Fort Ross had been using similar boats with good results, and yount's boat proved as good, if not better.

Though Yount managed to obtain a permit from the Mexican Government to hunt otters legally, other hunters weren't so particular and poached them wherever they could. Before long Yount had a small fleet of these cheaply-built boats, manned mostly by Kanakas, with one sharp-eyed hunter in each boat. Yount then hunted north to the Channel Islands, off Santa Barbara, and south into Baja California.

In 1833 a storm drove Yount into Santa Barbara just in time to attend the wedding of Monterey trader Thomas O. Larkin to Rachel Holmes. Yount and Larkin became good friends, and Larkin invited him to Monterey to discuss a business proposition (see Larkin). The wedding party traveled overland, via El Camino Real, stopping off at missions along the way. While in Monterey Yount did some repair work for Larkin on his buildings. The frontiersman had learned the rudiments of carpentry and shingle making as a youth, trades greatly in demand there.

While there Yount built another bull-boat for otter hunting, but he and his Kanaka divers found otter hunting in the Monterey area marginal; by then the Russians at Bodega Bay and Fort Ross had pretty well cleaned them out. Finally Yount had his bull-boat transported on a Russian ship to San Francisco Bay, where he had heard otter were plentiful. Along with George Nidever and a small crew of Kanakas, Yount explored the great bay before continuing through the Carquinez Straits and into the vast delta at the confluence of the Sacramento and San Joaquin rivers. While there they were horrified to find cholera widespread. It had taken a devastating toll, especially among the native Indians.

Wherever they went they found deserted villages and smoking funeral pyres consuming countless bodies. One evening, while setting up their camp near a deserted village, they heard the faint cries of a baby. At first they ignored it, assuming at least one parent was caring for it. But when it persisted, Nidever went to investigate. He returned with news that a girl about three years of age was alone in the village.

When Yount accompanied Nidever to the village the next day, they found the filthy naked child very weak from starvation. Unwilling to leave her, Yount took her back to their camp. There he bathed the emaciated girl, wrapped her in a blanket and fed her. Later, when they met a party of Indians, Yount was unsuccessful in getting them to accept her. When it became obvious that he would have to desert her or accept her, he kept her.

Yount found the north arm of San Pablo Bay bordering Rancho Petaluma a rich hunting ground for otter, and he made a permanent camp on Petaluma Creek. Before long he met Father Jose Quijas, padre of Mission San Rafael and Mission San Francisco De Solano at Sonoma. From the Padre Yount learned that most of the land in the area was owned by General Mariano G. Vallejo of Sonoma (see Vallejo).

When the padre learned that Yount possessed carpentry skills, he persuaded him to go Sonoma and do some badly needed repair work on mission buildings. This he did, while Nidever and the Kanakas continued hunting otters. Yount then divided his time between his Petaluma camp and Sonoma. When Father Quijas had to leave Sonoma for a month, he left Yount in charge of the mission as caretaker. This responsible position gave Yount a chance to get acquainted with Vallejo, who hired him to split and install wood shingles on his *casa grande*.

Yount had his foundling to care for, and the relative comforts at Sonoma lured him to stay on into 1835. While there he became a naturalized Mexican citizen and was baptized a Catholic under the name Jorge Concepcion. In gratitude for Yount's work on his buildings (and to provide a buffer from hostile Indians), General Vallejo granted him over two leagues of land (about 12,000 acres) in Napa Valley. Named Rancho Caymus, it was located about 20 miles north of Sonoma and became Yount's property in 1836.

WITH ONE HIRED MAN and his five-year-old foundling, Yount took possession and began construction of a two-story "blockhouse" residence. Built like a fort with rifle slots throughout, the house was stocked with enough water and provisions to withstand expected attacks from hostile Indians that frequented the area. While Yount was technically under the protection of General Vallejo and his troops, Sonoma was too far to offer immediate assistance, and he was largely on his own.

Grizzly bears abounded, and Yount killed many of them to protect his small herd of cattle. Gifts of bear meat and foofaraw to the local Caymus Indians helped ease the transition, and he gradually built up trust and good will among some of them. His past experience dealing with Indians was invaluable. Nevertheless he sometimes had to call on

Vallejo for assistance to punish hostile Indians; at other times Vallejo asked him for help in subduing hostiles in other areas of his vast domain.

Shortly after settling on his ranch in 1836, one battle in particular involved Yount, Mariano Vallejo, and his brother, Salvador. Together with a small army of Mexican soldiers, volunteers and friendly Indians, they faced hundreds of Satoyomi Indians on the Russian River. Vallejo wisely split his forces to encircle the Indians. What followed was described by Yount's friend, Rev. Orange Clark:

> The action was severe and bravely & perseveringly fought. Many, very many Braves fell and 'bit the dust'–They recoiled at the onset, for it was fierce–But it was in vain nay; it was worse. Salvadore Vallejo was upon them–He was just the man to execute such an order–Between two fires they fell like the leaves of Autumn–Endeavoring to escape upon the flank they were met by Yount & his scout, which, although few in number, had the effect to lead them erroniously to suppose that they were out flanked by a third division & they retreated to the other flank, between two galling fires–Thus frantic with fear, they ran wildly in every direction, or secreted themselves in the chapparel...

AFTER SUCH A VICTORY, Vallejo's mission Indians would not be restrained. They burned their enemies' villages, stacked the dead in hideous piles, and burned them. Prisoners were carried to Sonoma, where they were confined to the mission to be taught "Christianity, agriculture and the arts". Even after this Indian disaster, other hostiles in the north continued to raid Vallejo's ranchos and steal livestock belonging to him and Yount.

In December 1837 Yount thought he had 170 head of cattle, plus horses and sheep. But when he rounded them up for an accurate count, he had half that number; Indians had stolen the rest. Again Vallejo authorized a force of soldiers and volunteers to help Yount find and punish the thieves. Among Vallejo's men was Chief Solano. When the large band of hostiles were located in Pope Valley, another battle occurred, during which many Indians were killed. Yount nearly lost his own life there.

After that he went back to shingle making for money to buy more breeding stock. But when Indian depredations continued, he was obliged to join Vallejo's men to help fight them. Finally, after the tribes were decimated by a devastating scourge of smallpox in 1838, the raiding eased but did not stop entirely. Both Vallejo and Yount were saddened by the dreadful toll the disease took among hostile tribes. They would rather have defeated their enemies in battle. Yount then employed some of the remaining Caymus Indians to help build a gristmill on Napa Creek, which bordered his land.

In 1841 Yount received the first news about his family from members of the Bartleson-Bidwell emigrant party, the first to cross the Sierra Nevada into California (see separate chapter). Among them were Charles Hopper and Joseph Chiles, who had been neighbors of the Younts in Missouri. From them he learned that he had not only two daughters, but a son born after Yount left home in 1826.

When Chiles and Hopper decided to return temporarily to Missouri the following year, Yount prevailed on them to bring his family when they returned to California. Upon leaving for Missouri in 1842, they took along some mules and supplies provided by Yount for that purpose. Chiles and Hopper reached Missouri that fall, but when Chiles called on Yount's wife, he found she had given up Yount for dead. After obtaining a divorce in 1830, she had remarried. She and her new husband had children of their own by then, and she chose to stay.

Yount's son wanted nothing to do with his father, but his teen-aged daughter, Elizabeth Ann, decided to accompany Chiles back to California the following year. Yount's older daughter, Frances, had married Bartlett Vines and had two children of her own. Together she and Vines decided to make the hazardous journey with Chiles and Elizabeth Ann. Apparently Yount's pioneer genes were passed along to his daughters.

THOUGH THE OVERLAND emigration to California in 1843 was fraught with hardships, including loss of all their wagons in present-day Owens Valley, the Yount girls and other emigrants were guided safely over Walker Pass into the San Joaquin Valley by Joseph R. Walker himself. Before the end of the year most of the Yount family was reunited at Caymus ranch for the first time in more than a decade. They were undoubtedly surprised to find themselves with an Indian girl as a foster sister.

Ironically Yount's son, Robert, died after the safe arrival of his sisters in California. Robert's wife and two children then made their way to Yount's Caymus ranch to became Californians themselves. Joseph Chiles liked what he saw in the Napa Valley, and he soon acquired land of his own near Yount's Caymus Ranch. Eventually he built a gristmill and became a friendly competitor.

Possibly because of loyalty to Vallejo, Yount did not involve himself in the Bear Flag Rebellion or the resulting Mexican War in 1846-47. Instead, he remained neutral, devoting his energies to building up his herds, growing wheat and increasing his milling activities, which had expanded to include a sawmill.

But the 1848-49 Gold Rush brought a new problem. Just as native Indians had once fought to keep their lands, Vallejo and Yount now had to battle immigrant squatters, who settled wherever they pleased on the huge ranchos owned by Mexican citizens. Many gold-crazed argonauts had became disillusioned when they failed to find enough of the precious metal to satisfy their needs. Naturally they sought other ways of making a living. Most had been farmers, and they coveted land, especially the good rich lands in Napa Valley. Why should men like Vallejo, Yount and Chiles own so much land, while they had none? Why not squat on their land and dare them to do something about it?

Now that Mexico had lost the war, immigrants assumed some Mexican land grants would be declared invalid by the United States Government. And if it came to intimidating the greasers or their turncoat Yankee friends, so be it. It wouldn't be the first time. These desperate squatters made life miserable for large land owners throughout California. Yount and others like him were forced to hire expensive lawyers to defend their rights and gain legal title to their rightful lands.

AFTER STATEHOOD was achieved on September 9, 1850, a federal land commission was established to investigate land titles. Many old titles were invalidated and huge ranchos were broken up with little or no compensation to their former owners. Squatters sometimes gained title to land they simply occupied and improved. Landholders who managed to prove their titles were subjected to heavy taxation; if they couldn't pay, they ended up losing their land anyway.

Yount managed to keep much of his land. He paid his taxes through hard work and perseverance. In 1855 he married Eliza Gashwiler, the widow of a Protestant minister. An educated woman, Eliza filled a void in Yount's life by taking over bookkeeping chores and other onerous paper work. The ranch prospered, as shown in the following report from Orange Clark:

> [Yount's] lands were cultivated with remarkable success—From Four to Eight Hundred acres of Wheat annually is the product of his farm—Two Hundred Hogs, seven Hundred Sheep. Five Hundred Horses & Two Thousand head of Horned Cattle, until the intrusions of squatters, have been the number of his flocks & herds...His vineyard yields him annually Two Hundred Gallons of Wine, & his Orchards & gardens are studded with fruit trees of every kind...His was the first flouring mill in California—That mill having grown old, & worn by long use & service, within the last year, he has rebuilt it upon an enlarged scale, & is now able to boast of the best & most productive mill in the state—It has four runs of stones, & he has spared neither toil nor expense to render it perfect as can be made in the country.

Yount had the satisfaction of seeing a small village established on his land. He donated the townsite and cemetery plot, and the town was appropriately named Yountville in his honor. After his death on October 5, 1865, at the age of 71, he was buried in the town cemetery. The

Indian girl he had adopted grew to adulthood; after rejecting several white suitors, she married an Indian. Ironically, after bearing him several children, he murdered her. [1]

A Caymus Indian graveyard adjoins the old cemetery, and Yount's grave is marked by a handsome tombstone, designed and erected by close friends. Since George Yount was a veteran of the War of 1812, it seems fitting that Yountville boasts one of the oldest veteran's homes in the country. The old Yount millsite and stockade are marked with a bronze plaque a mile or so from the pioneer cemetery.

BIBLIOGRAPHY

–Bancroft, Hubert H. *California Pioneer Register and Index.* Regional Publishing Co., Baltimore, 1964.

–Batman, Richard. *The Outer Coast.* Harcourt Brace Jovanovich, New York, 1985.

–Camp, Charles L., Editor, *George C. Yount and his Chronicles of the West, from the Orange Clark "Narrative" written in 1854-55.* Old West Publishing Co., Denver, 1966. All quotations are from this publication.

–Cleland, Robert Glass. *This Reckless Breed of Men.* Alfred a. Knopf, New York, 1950.

–Clyman, James. *Journal Of A Mountain Man.* Mt. Press Publishing Co., Missoula, MT, 1984.

–Dillon, Richard. *Siskiyou Trail.* McGraw-Hill Book Co., New York, 1975. [1]

INDEX

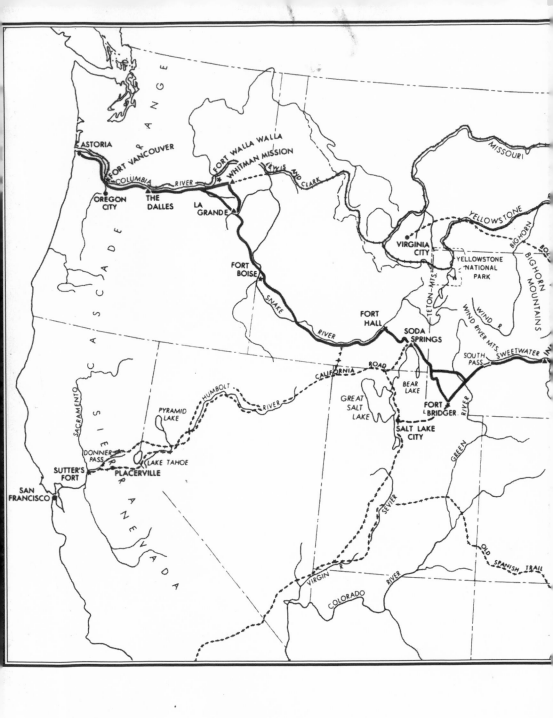